Blending first-hand accounts of grassroots politics with an original theory of social relations under communism, this book seeks to explain one of the seminal events of this century: the rebirth of politics in Russia amid the collapse of the USSR. The authors trace the process from the pre-political period of dissident activity, through perestroika and the appearance of political groups and publications, elections, the formation of political parties and mass movements, counter-revolution and *coup d'état*, the victory of democratic forces and the organization of a Russian state; to the struggle of power in the post-communist epoch, the violent end of the first republic and the contentious relations engulfing its successor. By focusing on the popular forces which accomplished Russia's political rebirth, rather than the reforms of the Soviet establishment, this book offers an original perspective on this critical period.

The rebirth of politics in Russia

The rebirth of politics in Russia

Michael Urban
University of California at Santa Cruz

with

Vyacheslav Igrunov
Institute for Humanities and Political Studies, Moscow

and

Sergei Mitrokhin
Institute for Humanities and Political Studies, Moscow

CAMBRIDGE
UNIVERSITY PRESS

Published by Press Syndicate of the University of Cambridge
The Pitt Building, Trumpington Street, Cambridge CB2 1RP
40 West 20th Street, New York, NY 10011–4211, USA
10 Stamford Road, Oakleigh, Melbourne 3166, Australia

First published 1997

Printed in Great Britain at the University Press, Cambridge

A catalogue record for this book is available from the British Library

Library of Congress cataloguing in publication data
Urban, Michael E., 1947–
The rebirth of politics in Russia / Michael Urban with Vyacheslav Igrunov and
Sergei Mitrokhin.
    p. cm.
ISBN 0 521 56248 1 – ISBN 0 521 56611 8 (pbk.)
1. Glasnost.   2. Political participation – Soviet Union.
3. Political culture – Soviet Union.
4. Political participation – Russia (Federation).
5. Political culture – Russia (Federation).
6. Soviet Union – Politics and government – 1985–1991.
7. Russia (Federation) – Politics and government – 1991– .
8. Post-communism – Russia (Federation).
I. Igrunov, V.   II. Mitrokhin, Sergei.   III. Title.
JN6581.U72   1997
320.947′09′048–dc20   96–43489   CIP

ISBN 0 521 56248 1 hardback
ISBN 0 521 56611 8 paperback

CE

For Mili and Brownie

Contents

Preface

This book got its start in Moscow during the ebullient spring of 1991. Still as fresh, hopeful and innocent as spring itself, political life had sprouted forth again in Russia, bringing to a close that seventy-year political ice-age, communism. In the face of that, it dawned on me and my colleagues – Vyacheslav Igrunov and Sergei Mitrokhin – that someone needed to write this story and that we might as well be the ones to attempt it. Ironically, however, the subject of our concern soon became the undoing of our collaboration as politics demanded more and more of the working lives of my Russian partners until autumn 1993 when, following their successful campaign for seats in the State Duma, it claimed them completely. Although the writing thus fell to me, they continued to participate in the project throughout: first, by composing segments for chapters 2, 4–6 and 8 that I have translated, reworked and blended into the text; and, second, by commenting on the draft chapters that I had produced, pointing out my errors, suggesting alternative perspectives on one or another question, sharing their knowledge and acumen with me. As such, the first-person plural pronoun has been used in this book to record that degree of collaboration that we managed to sustain.

Our study proceeds along two parallel lines. Along the first of these, we sketch Russia's political rebirth in broad strokes, offering an interpretation of that process that draws on structural, organizational and communicative perspectives to frame it in interactive terms. In our view, this topic can be neither exhausted nor explained by consulting the preferences, projects, calculations, actions and reactions of the individuals participating in it. However important these might be, we repeatedly detect another 'layer' of politics into which they would all dissolve or, alternatively, out of which they have all been constituted. This 'layer' is nothing more nor less than the interaction among the participants themselves that – perhaps counter-intuitively – begets those preferences, projects and so forth in the first instance, as well as in subsequent ones.

Along the other line, we provide relatively thick descriptions of a number of key episodes that reinforce our broad interpretative strokes with fine details. These situate the concept of interaction in the concrete, often disclosing quite unexpected moments in which the content of actions seems to have little, if anything, in common with actors' (original) intentions, but appears as something supplied by others in the web of their mutual relations. In this respect, we have occasion to explore a number of phenomena often regarded as 'givens' in the study of politics – among them, actors' identities and interests – and believe that these explorations shed critical light both on those phenomena themselves and on our accustomed ways of apprehending them. While conscious of the fact that we remain a long way from providing adequate answers to the questions attendant on the origins, formation and adaptation of identities and interests, excursions into the problem of politics *ex nihilo* chart unusual terrain, rich in implications for the ways in which we think about politics generally.

Unlike a great many studies of Soviet, and now Russian, politics that have focused on governing elites and, more recently, on mass opinions and attitudes, our attention is directed primarily toward a political society whose boundaries can loosely be drawn according to those alternative foci. Political society represents that interactive 'space' in which the affairs of state and the concerns of citizens are publicly mediated. Its ceaseless squabbles and solemn acts of solidarity infuse the political world with distinctions, purpose, intelligibility and meaning. The book's organization divides our topic into four parts, each prefaced by a brief introduction to the chapters included in it. The first and fourth parts serve as 'bookends' – one devoted to the pre-political period, the other to a consideration of the political order that has begun to take shape in Russia – while the two parts thus enclosed constitute the heart of our study, the rebirth of politics itself. Consequently, those readers whose interests pertain only to our central topic can read the book accordingly, skimming or skipping the theoretic elaborations set out particularly in chapters 1 and 12. With respect to terminology, readers will note that we have generally used the names assumed by the actors themselves. Hence, we employ terms such as 'democrats' or 'patriots' to refer to those respective political forces, leaving the issue of authenticity – Are these people *really* democratic or patriotic? – to the judgement of others.

Speaking for my partners, I would like to acknowledge some of the people and institutions whose assistance has made those book possible. In that regard we owe a special debt of gratitude to Andrei Berezkin and Aleksei Kuz'min who provided moral support, critical skills, helpful suggestions and – in Andrei's case – the data appearing in Table 6.2. Our thanks go, too, to another groups of scholars who actively participated in one or more of the three seminars conducted in Moscow and Berkeley at which our work in progress was presented and discussed. That list includes: George Breslauer, Marc Garcelon, Vladimir Gel'man, Gavin Helf, Il'ya Kudryavtsev, Galina Luchterhandt, Andrei Melville, Nikolai Petrov, Vera Pisareva, Marina Razorenova, Leonid Smirnyagin and Lucan Way. We are likewise grateful to colleagues who read and commented on portions of various drafts of this study: Victoria Bonnell, Valerie Bunce, Georgii Derluguian, Peter Euben, M. Steven Fish, Richard Gordon, Isebill Gruhn, Oleg Khar-khordin, Richard Sakwa, Rachel Walker, Stephen White and David Willer. Throughout its duration, my wife, Veronica, has contributed to this project with word-processing, editing, critical advice and, perhaps above all, by cheerfully enduring the monologues of someone preoccu-pied with Russian politics that she somehow would turn into conversa-tions. I acknowledge my debt to her in the knowledge that it cannot be repaid.

Financial support was essential to the execution of this project. In that respect, we wish to thank the National Endowment for the Humanities for a generous grant that sustained our work from 1992 to 1994. Likewise, we are grateful to the International Research and Exchanges Board for financing the seminar held at Berkeley in 1994; and to the Center for German and European Studies at the University of California at Berkeley, the Institute for Global Conflict and Cooperation at the University of California at San Diego and to the Division of Social Sciences of the University of California at Santa Cruz, all of whom supplied travel grants enabling me to work in Moscow and to confer with my partners there. Special thanks go to those at the Moscow Bureau of Information Exchange who patiently guided me through their extensive archives, sympathetically listened to my queries and requests and placed in my hands materials that have proven indispensable to this work.

Part I

The pre-political context

The two chapters in this part of the book provide a sketch of the context from which politics would reappear in Russia. Our aim, therefore, is to set out those aspects of the context most relevant to that reappearance and to develop certain concepts for analysing them. Accordingly, the first chapter begins with a model of 'politics' that articulates the concept across three spheres (state, political society and civil society) and along two dimensions (organization and communication). The discussion then turns to a consideration of the Soviet state that highlights from a structural perspective its relatively ineffective capacity for domination – despite certain appearances to the contrary, such as its arsenal of repressive practices. Our attention turns next to the ways in which this weak (yet repressive) state articulated with society. Its actions along the dimension of communication produced systematic distortions that had disrupted the formation of social identities and restricted their circulation to the narrow confines of face-to-face encounters. Thus, that singular exception to the Soviet state's weakness – its capacity physically to penetrate society – rendered society weak as well. This discussion then yields a number of problematics that serve as the book's principal themes.

These themes are first explored concretely in the second chapter. In contrast to the synchronic approach employed up to this point, the narrative in this chapter is organized diachronically in order to tackle the issue of how the structures of domination conditioned those of action. The time frame involved here is roughly bounded at one end by Stalin's death and, at the other, by the regime's inauguration of 'perestroika'. The focus of this chapter falls mainly on the development of the dissident movement which antedated, anticipated and contributed to the re-emergence of politics in Russia. As is the case with the first chapter, the second one introduces a number of concepts that we use throughout the book.

1   Politics and communism: figure and ground

The rebirth of politics in Russia is historically coextensive with the collapse of Soviet communism. More than mere contingency informs this temporal relationship. The key terms in it – politics and communism – define one another, like figure and ground, thesis and antithesis. On one hand, communism had represented a double-excision of politics: suppression of political activity, plus compulsory participation in ubiquitous pseudo-political rituals sponsored by the party-state. Here, we have in mind not only the repressive functions performed by the secret police, informers, prisons and labour camps, but also the appropriation of political forms for the purpose of preventing political practice, such as the empanelling of millions of individuals on soviets by means of single-candidate 'elections' who would represent their constituents by unanimously endorsing whatever measures the authorities had placed before them. On the other, the return of political life in Russia would witness a double-relationship to communism. Politics would be reborn as a struggle against the communist system that had denied it. It would reappear as heroic action, challenging, resisting and defying the communist system in the name of human dignity, national restoration, freedom and democracy. Measured against standards such as these, the prosaic aspects of political activity – ambition, advantage, influence and so on – would seem so many miscreants subverting this struggle from within. But the institutional inheritance bequeathed by communism to the new Russian polity would complicate the matter of rebirth in far more profound and ramified ways. It is not merely the case that individuals who had matured under the anti-political conditions of a communist system had developed certain dispositions, habits of mind and modes of action that would not readily supply that measure of civic virtue required for sustaining political life. While that may be true, of greater import would be the ensemble of structures peculiar to state socialism, a specific social formation that had existed in Russia for over seventy years, that the new Russian polity would inherit.

In order to develop the relationships between the categories of

Table 1.1 *Ideal–typical forms of political communication and organization*

Levels of system	Types of communication	Forms of organization
State	Authoritative	Hierarchical government bodies
Political society	Strategic	Parties and parliament
Civil society	Normative	Voluntary associations

communism and politics, we have recourse to a simple model that will serve to orient much of the discussion throughout this book. We might introduce it by specifying that which we include in our concept of politics.[1] In our view, politics – at least in so far as this term concerns questions related ultimately to the affairs of state in late twentieth-century societies – can be understood along two dimensions: communication and organization.[2] Both of these forms of action appear under different aspects in the relations depicted in Table 1.1. Along the top row, the domain marked off by 'state' refers to communication that appears as authoritative injunctions (laws, decrees, rulings and so forth) that are backed by coercive force.[3] Coercive action, as well as the other functions that the state might perform (say, post and communications, education, social security or data collection), transpires through hierarchically organized government bodies. Along the bottom row, 'civil society' encompasses that sphere of life in which communication is characterized as a normative discourse aimed at reaching understanding among socially differentiated participants. Individuals organize into 'voluntary associations' around certain 'interests' which they represent to others through normative claims, thus linking themselves to one another within these associations, producing social identities, and engaging others who may be linked in similar associations in various forms of dialogue which span a horizon including, at one end, overtures to undertake cooperative endeavours and, at the other, threats intended to secure some change of behaviour on the part of others.[4] The middle row is taken up by 'political society' whose premier organizations are political parties and parliaments. The principal mode of communication in this sphere is strategic, aimed at translating (or preventing the translation of) specific projects originating in civil society into policies adopted by the state and, conversely, producing either support for, or opposition to, state policies within the sphere of civil society.

This model, of course, is an ideal-type construct. Although its elements would be most closely approximated in contemporary democratic-capitalist systems, our intention in using it is not to idealize those same systems but to develop a concept of politics both broad enough and

sufficiently discriminate to facilitate our investigation of the reappearance of political life in Russia. In this respect, the model's utility consists
in the fact that, as a matrix, all of the elements in it are mutually related.
State communication appears as 'authoritative', for instance, because
state structures are connected to a normative discourse via the institutions of political society. The coercive force of the state therefore has the
capacity to appear as a 'legitimate' use of power. Its exercise can be
thematized in civil society, in principle producing a public consensus
that would accept, reject or modify the course of state policy. Equally,
the non-state sphere of civil society appears as something neither
removed nor isolated from the state, as – to take an extreme example –
laws or rulings on privacy and the inviolability of persons would remind
us.[5] The model thus helps us to bear in mind the fact that politics is
neither a thing nor a phenomenon reducible to an essentialist definition.
Rather, it represents a mode of human interaction whose varied forms
admit to specification along the lines of the types of communication and
organization that the model includes. In sum, 'politics' would be that
which occurs within the model's domain.

Besides framing that side of politics/communism that we take for
our 'figure', the model can also be used to sketch in its 'ground',
communism. In so doing, we avoid side-tracking our discussion
toward an empirical description of the communist past by maintaining
a focus on those analytic aspects of the communist system that are
indispensable to an understanding of our principal topic, the politics
that has been (re)born out of it. This discussion proceeds according
to the model's categories of 'organization' and 'communication'.
From the vantage of the former, our attention turns toward the
objectified side of social action. We concern ourselves here with those
forms and practices in the area of social organization that confront
individuals as ready-made – as existing independently of their will –
which condition, shape and direct the activity of individuals, even as
they might in turn attempt to reshape and redirect these organizational
forms and practices themselves. The mode of action corresponding to
these objectified forms of social interaction would be instrumental,
focused on securing or preventing some condition identified by the
parties to it as either desirable or undesirable. The second perspective,
that of communication, highlights the subjective side of the matter. Its
corresponding mode of action involves the meaning that those in
interaction derive from or impart to their activity. In this respect, our
concern is with subjects, especially political subjects, and how they
constitute themselves and their respective social worlds in the process
of communication.

Structure and the Soviet form of organization

By the end of the 1930s, the 'construction of socialism' in the USSR was officially acknowledged to have been completed. From the standpoint of organization, a brief outline of this accomplishment would include three main features. First, the Soviet state had taken on a 'total' character. Through application of historically unprecedented levels of force and violence, the state had abolished all hitherto existing institutions and replaced them with its own creations. All social intercourse, then, was confined to its agency.[6] Second, this transformation was abetted by massive personnel turnover among holders of state offices as hundreds of thousands of incumbents were removed from their positions through purge and terror while the roster of offices was further expanded by industrialization, the founding of new towns and cities, and so on.[7] Rapid upward mobility generated loyalty and obedience toward those officials who had engineered the respective promotions. Terror or the fear of its return reminded these same officials of the loyalty and obedience expected from them by the central authorities. Third, state and state-sponsored organizations tended to be designed along military lines, with centralized command structures that issued orders (tasks) which travelled down chains-of-command extending from Moscow to the far-flung reaches of the USSR.[8]

These features of Soviet state socialism – state violence and terror, rapid upward mobility generating loyalty and obedience, centralized, command-style administration of all aspects of life – masked the fact that the structural basis of this system was a weak one.[9] Following Stalin's death, however, this mask began to peel off. His successors ended the terror and drastically reduced the incidence of purging, thus jettisoning the principal mechanisms (mobility and fear) contributing to the system's integration in the context of its top-down organizational architecture.[10] They also unmasked enough of his deeds and his 'cult of the personality' to undermine the particular ideational complex whose symbolic structures had served to integrate individuals into the social order, a topic that we take up below. Here, our purpose is to sketch in more of the 'ground' of Russia's political rebirth by examining the communist order from the perspective of its structural basis.

Characteristics of structural strength

In order to develop this point, we need to say a few words about the concept 'structure'. We take this term 'structure' to indicate neither a thing nor a collection of things nor a mere ordering of things and/or people as suggested by the words 'hierarchy' or '(formal) organization' which often have functioned interchangeably with 'structure' in much that has been written on the Soviet order. Rather, we regard a given structure as that which determines the relations among the elements that comprise it and, in so doing, defines the content of the elements themselves. Following Jean Piaget, we understand the distinctive properties of structure to be 'wholeness' (or internal coherence), 'self-regulation' and 'transformation'.[11] The last of these connotes procedures internal to a given structure by which changes in its empirical state are effected.[12]

The concept of exchange is helpful in explicating the idea of structure as it pertains to social phenomena, particularly in so far as it enables us to overcome the nuance of 'static' which unfortunately often accompanies the notion of structure in everyday English usage.[13] Structures are the sites of movement, of interaction, of exchange. In those that we call economic, money might be exchanged for goods or services; in those labelled political, promises might be exchanged for votes; in those regarded as principally social, promises often exchange against promises, as do vows in a marriage contract. In each of these instances, the character of the exchange has been established by no one in particular. Whether we are concerned with buying and selling, the practices of candidates and voters in an election or the wedding ceremonies accompanying a marriage, we notice that individuals step into a particular institutional form independent of the particular parties participating in it. In this respect, the character of each can be taken as social as opposed to personal or individual. But in drawing attention to the institutional character that is stamped on each of these exchanges, we do not mean to imply that the individuals involved in them have somehow disappeared. Far from it. Our point is instead first, that the individuals have appeared as buyers, sellers, spouses and so forth within a structured relationship that has constituted them as such and, second, that the roles or positions that they occupy are more or less constrained, more or less determined, by the overall structure within which they find themselves. This second consideration concerns the relative strength of a structure, a characteristic conditioned by those exchange relations particular to it.

From this standpoint, we can define the strength or weakness of a structure according to two criteria: the degree to which the conditions of exchange are established independently of those participating in it (that is, the relative impersonality of the structure); and the degree to which the conditions of exchange produce rates that advantage one or some of the parties (that is, the structure's capacity to generate domination). To illustrate, let us take the example of a strong structure, an economic system based on private property in which exchange transpires through the medium of the market. Were a theoretically pure system of this type to obtain, social relations would appear only in the act of exchange itself. The frequent and ongoing repetition of these exchanges would provide them with a fixed, impersonal character. Accordingly, buyers and sellers would confront one another under specific terms – captured in the monetized aspect of the exchange relations, price – that are beyond their control. These terms have been fixed by the impersonal agency of the market. Exchanges under these conditions can be regarded as 'general'.[14] What is of value would emerge out of generalized exchange relations in the same way that value would govern the relation of the parties engaged in a particular exchange, setting the rates at which their media exchange one with another. Individual or collective will would neither constitute nor shape social relations of this type in a theoretically meaningful way. Rather, the activities of individuals would be set, shaped, constrained and disciplined by the market.[15] Along the lines of our first criterion, then, the impersonal character of exchange in a market would contribute to the strength of this structure.

Regarding our second criterion, the degree of inequality in exchange relations and its capacity to engender domination, the example of a system based on private property and market exchange will again illustrate structural strength. Here, we might begin by underscoring the obvious; namely, that private property refers solely to a relationship among people, not to a relationship between people and things. Above all, this relationship is structured by the condition of exclusion, such that the right of property entitles its holder to exclude all others from access to whatever, in a given instance, is governed by this right. Access for others, then, takes the form of exchange in which the property right of one party passes to a second in return for a simultaneous transfer of some consideration – typically another property right – from the second party to the first.[16] When we consider those cases in which so-called 'productive' property belongs to one class (owners) and access to it is sought by another (workers), it is apparent that the condition of exclusion structures exchanges between them. Denied access to the means of production, workers exchange their labour against wages. The rate of this exchange is, again, set impersonally by the (labour) market. Owners, *ceteris paribus*, occupy the dominant position inasmuch as no one of them can be excluded from this act of exchange while the reverse is true for any individual in the class of workers. Since any worker can be excluded from exchanging his or her labour for wages, and since the cost of not engaging in this exchange is for the worker particularly high, each worker finds himself or herself in an ongoing competition with other workers to participate in the exchange of labour for wages. The effect of this competition would then set a rate of exchange favourable to the class of owners. Private property, expressed in this instance as the exclusion of workers from the means of production, thus structures the exchange of labour for wages that results in the phenomenon of 'exploitation'. However, our concern here lies with another phenomenon, 'domination', so let us follow the parties involved in this type of exchange into an organizational structure in which domination occurs.

Max Weber has used the term 'domination' to characterize those relationships in which a command of the dominators is regarded by the dominated as if the latter 'had made the content of the command the maxim of their conduct for its own sake'.[17] In Weber's view, the ideal-type construct of domination displayed in this definition would be approximated in modern bureaucracy. Moreover, it is within modern bureaucracy that our criteria for assessing the strength of a structure – impersonality and domination – are fused. Two points might be made in this respect. The first concerns the fact that the surface characteristics of this form of organization – the location of authority in offices rather than in individuals, the organization and gradation of such authority according to written rules and so forth – are themselves rooted in the structural transformations that have accompanied the passing of traditional society. Foremost among these transformations has been the establishment of the 'commodity form', the impersonal exchanges between buyers and sellers in the market on which we have already commented in an abstract way.[18] It seems important to recall in this respect that the implanting of this form at the centre of the modern socio-economic order had involved an extended, thoroughgoing and often brutal uprooting of social relations[19] as well as a detailed refashioning of human subjects along the lines of the disciplines that restructure their inner worlds as described by Michel Foucault and others.[20] Modern bureaucracy would be one product of this transformation, representing a site of human interaction that is homologous to the commodity form of exchange relations in the market. Not only does bureaucratic interaction transpire through an impersonalized, rule-bound structure of authority, but the action of any individual within this mode of organization, just as any commodity in the market is measured by its price, always reduces to something outside the individuals themselves – the job description, the work schedule, the production target, the efficiency rating and so forth. It is precisely these thing-like relations among people that enable the higher layers of bureaucracy to think in characteristically bureaucratic fashion, calculating costs and benefits for the organization (rather than for the individuals who comprise it) and improving its performance (but not necessarily the performance of the individuals *qua* individuals within it) by means of an ongoing rationalization of the extant set of relations and routines that collectively constitute its capacity to perform.[21]

Second, bureaucratic domination coincides with bureaucratic performance. This coincidence springs from the relationship between superiors and subordinates in which the latter exchange obedience in return for any number of staples stored in bureaucracy's larder: employment, promotions, the promise of pension benefits on retirement and recommendations in the case of transfer to another organization. These incentives thus align individual motivations with organizational objectives such that the command of the superior (dominator) is received by the subordinates (dominated) along the lines of Weber's 'maxim of their conduct for its own sake'. Domination is enhanced by the impersonal bureaucratic structure through which it is exercised because the content of commands does not appear as the product of some subjective judgement – which, as such, would be open to scrutiny, criticism and resistance on the basis of other subjective judgements – but as something objective, something which is indistinguishable from the objectified relations (such as job description) that characterize bureaucracy in the first instance.[22] It is precisely these features of bureaucracy that have led a myriad of observers to see in it the quintessence of efficiency and effectiveness in human affairs.[23] Its objectified forms enable calculation to occur and rationalization to proceed (efficiency); its incentive structures that bring individual motivations into consonance with the commands of superiors enable it to marshal human energies and deploy them on specific targets (effectiveness). In sum, modern bureaucracy qualifies *par excellence* as a strong structure.[24]

Structural weakness of the Soviet order

On the basis of the argument outlined thus far, we would be compelled to conclude that the Soviet system's widespread reputation for being 'bureaucratic' had been rather richly undeserved. To be sure, until its final years, the party-state had methodically endeavoured to organize all forms of social activity along the lines of hierarchical administration, as well as to extinguish all attempts at pursuing organized social activity outside the ambit of the institutions that it maintained. Moreover, the organizations that it erected had many of the surface features of bureaucracy. After all, the USSR did produce an abundance of hierarchies, written regulations and formal instructions. Yet, were we to look through the outer shell of these organizations and beyond the mere appearance of these practices, we would notice that the internal structures and dynamics of Soviet organizations had little in common with the theoretical category 'bureaucracy'.

Comparisons with capitalist societies would again demonstrate the point here. In contrast to a system of private property anchored in the principle of exclusion, the system of state property that prevailed in the USSR was based on inclusion. Rather than denying workers access to the means of production, state property guaranteed it. As a consequence, there was no labour market in the proper sense of the term under Soviet state socialism. No 'industrial reserve army' existed either, and labour time could therefore not be measured by any objective standard that would facilitate calculation and rationalization.[25] Moreover, the exchange of labour for wages knew no denominator establishing standard rates of remuneration for performance.[26] The inclusive character of state property therefore provided no objective basis on which to quantify the media of exchange, whether labour, raw materials or finished goods.

What had been true of the *quantitative* side of exchange relations within the structure of Soviet state socialism also had characterized their *qualitative* side. Continuing our comparisons with capitalism, we remind ourselves that exchange in the market is governed by the 'impersonal' feature of commodity–money relations. What has been produced must be of value to someone else if exchange is to occur. Mindful of this, producers gear their actions to meet the standards of value established impersonally by the market. Particularly under conditions of mass production and mass consumption, the production of value takes on a general form. Articles that fail to meet the standard are not marketable, just as the labour that goes into the production of such articles ceases to find employment. However, within the command–administrative structures of state socialism, we notice an altogether different form of exchange that in many ways more resembles 'particular' than it does 'general'. That is, value is constituted not by the impersonal force of the market but by the individual parties to the exchange itself.

One of these parties would be superiors in the administrative hierarchy who would provide a plan instructing their corresponding units on what to do. And formally, at least, superiors could employ both positive and negative sanctions (promotions, bonuses, awards, reprimands and so on) to ensure compliance with their directives. But these mechanisms would represent no more than superficial analogues to the control–compliance apparatus built into modern bureaucracies, precisely because of the absence of objectified, quantifiable, calculable – in short, *impersonal* – relations among the elements of Soviet organization, as noted above. A simple question will illustrate the point: on what basis could superiors render judgements about the performance of the organizations that they superintended? Were, say, the steel, the potatoes, or the dramas that they produced of adequate quality? Without a structural relationship to relevant others – firms that might purchase their steel in preference to that produced by others, consumers who would select or not their produce from the grocers' shelves, a theatre-going public that would attend performances or go instead to the productions of other companies – the answer in each case would depend upon the relationship of the superiors to the particular steel, potatoes or dramas in question. Ultimately, superiors would be left with their personal judgements, more or less informed by a knowledge of metallurgy, agronomy or the arts, but personal all the same. In this respect the pseudo-objectifications of Soviet planning – 'norms', 'indicators' and so on – had tended to conceal the fact that planning represented one set of decisions taken in a personalized way 'above', while performance involved another set of negotiated micro-level decisions whose calculus would consistently run counter to the designs of superior authorities, resulting in padding, substitution, the hoarding of unused resources and so forth.[27] Thus, the abstracted production specifications appearing in the plan might be met without any guarantee that the actual product would be of much, if any, real utility.[28] Accordingly, should the production of shoddy goods appear as valuable to the firms producing them (because they have saved on materials or time) and to the outlets that sell them (because they have received an instruction from their superiors to accept and to offer for sale certain items), we could be sure that consumers would have shoddy goods from which to 'choose', just as the labour that went into their production would continue to be employed.[29] Along the lines of our first criterion (impersonality), then, we note the comparative weakness of state socialist structures.[30]

The weakness attending this dimension of state socialist structures has immediate implications for our second criterion, domination. The relative absence of impersonal forms of constraint on those occupying positions in a formal organizational hierarchy impedes domination in two ways. First, organization must be rather consciously superintended by the occupants of higher offices. Few, if any, of the objectified indicators prevalent in the capitalist context would be available to them for measuring, evaluating and (rationally) adjusting the performance of the organizations that they direct. This conscious and constant super-intending would seem to be fully congruent with our observation that the modal form of organization associated with the Soviet order had been the (pseudo-)military type. Brigades would be dispatched to one or another 'production front' to perform 'shock work' because – without the market and all that it would imply – the directors of this system could not expect anything to happen 'below' that would conform to their plans and expectations unless the actual activities of subalterns were enveloped in the thick presence of their authority. Moreover, the manifestation of this authority in unending streams of orders, directives and instructions would depend – for whatever real impact it might have – on additional armies of controllers and checkers, as well as the more or less immediate presence of various prefects and plenipotentiaries who would personally represent this authority on the ground.[31]

Second, the obverse of these authority relations had been the tendency among the occupants of organizational positions toward the personal appropriation of their offices.[32] This tendency might explain the non-bureaucratic, even anti-bureaucratic, orientations prevalent among Soviet officials which have led a number of scholars to portray the Soviet form of organization as a variant of Weber's (pre-modern) patrimonial bureaucracy.[33] In our view, the personal appropriation of office would refer to both condition – the relative absence of impersonal methods of bureaucratic control that would hold such a tendency in check – and motivation. The latter involves a reaction among subordinates not only to the opportunities available to them in the context of the weak structures that they inhabit but also to the form of authority regularly projected by superiors, namely, the 'impossible demand'. In either case, this tendency would militate against that coalescence of individual motivations and organizational objectives that we noted in our discussion of bureaucratic domination. Here, again, the personal element bulks large, for superiors could supplement the formal (and, as we have argued, rather weak) authority available to them by virtue of the positions that they might hold by generating dependencies on the part of those below. This would regularly involve an impossible demand, either in the form of issuing contradictory injunctions – for instance, fulfil the plan but do so by strictly obeying all laws and regulations! – or that of simply setting unattainable performance targets. Those below would, therefore, invariably fail. Failure would make them liable to some negative sanction. By then *withholding* the application of this sanction, the superior could extend his real domination over subordinates since they would be incurring a certain debt to him for protecting them against the punishment that would otherwise result.[34]

Within the matrix of these relations, subordinates, of course, would not adopt purely passive strategies toward superiors. Rather, they would forge ties among themselves – whether the 'communalism' described by Aleksandr Zinov'ev in the work group,[35] the inter-organizational protection networks formed in localities (*krugovaya poruka* or 'family circle'), or their vertically constructed counterpart within a given organizational hierarchy, 'departmentalism' – in order to act in concert, concealing failures and a host of other 'off the books' activities, from formal superiors or other outsiders.[36] Indeed, these methods of resistance from below in many ways would mesh with other authority-generating strategies pursued by those above. Superiors, in competition with others at a given level in the hierarchy, could extend their own influence by offering patronage to clients at lower levels (in the form of protection, promotion and so forth) in exchange for loyalty if not obedience.[37] Whether extending the protective hand of patronage or issuing impossible directives that would trap others in dependency relations, the implications for our second criterion of structural strength (domination) would be the same: namely, we find in these patterns the reflection of weak structures and, conversely, the presence of strong (personal) ties.[38] Accordingly, action takes on an arbitrary appearance. Relatively unconstrained by structures of impersonal domination, it tends largely to proceed on the basis of negotiations – including, of course, threats as well as promises – conducted by those directly participating in it.[39]

Structures and capacities

In order to conclude our discussion of the organizational 'ground' from which politics in Russia has re-emerged, we might pass our concept of structure through the prism of 'state capacities', as developed by Joel Migdal, thereby introducing a coarser grain into our picture of the Soviet state's performance in more or less discrete functional areas. In his work on Third World countries, Migdal has posited something of a zero-sum relationship obtaining between state and society with respect to how the actions of individuals and groups in the population are shaped and directed.[40] Simply put, the question here involves whether and to what degree formal state structures are able to introduce and sustain a system of power and authority that channels action toward established goals in the face of traditionally oriented social norms and institutions that constitute a counter-system of action resistant to these intrusions on the part of the state. In time and place, this relationship can be considerably more complicated, as in those instances in which the state might appropriate, refashion and utilize for its own purposes certain features of the normative order prevailing in society. There is ample evidence of such appropriation in the Soviet case, especially during the 1930s when the state-directed 'great transformation' had resembled in many ways a 'great retreat' to the institutions associated with the tsarist order.[41] Such complications notwithstanding, the problematic of 'strong societies' and 'weak states' that Migdal explores is particularly germane to our discussion of state socialist structures because of the way in which he untangles the various capabilities that together add up to the notion of state strength. A strong state, according to his schema, would be one evincing 'the capacities to *penetrate* society, *regulate* social relationships, *extract* resources and *appropriate* or use resources in determined ways'.[42]

When we consider the first of these capacities, penetration, in the context of Soviet state socialism, we immediately notice two important implications that follow for the other elements in Migdal's framework. First, since the Soviet state's penetration of society had been total, the zero-sum relationship between state and society that Migdal posits would no longer obtain. The weakness that characterized the structures of the state would, unlike Migdal's formulation, not imply a corresponding strength on the part of a society not only penetrated but thoroughly colonized by the apparatuses of the party-state. In the following section, we develop this point from the perspective of communication.

Second, and relatedly, this total penetration or colonization would radically alter the meaning that can be ascribed to Migdal's capacities for extraction, appropriation and regulation. Total penetration would mean total appropriation which, in turn, would imply for the state not extraction but self-extraction, not regulation but self-regulation. As we have seen, the relative weakness of state socialist structures along the dimensions of impersonality and domination would mean that these capacities of the Soviet state were quite limited. The fulcrum of extraction, for instance, would be the planning system assigning targets to performing units. Such assignments would not involve the setting of rationally formulated directives issued by superior authorities – who, even if they had had sufficient information on the physical capabilities of performing units, would lack the necessary medium, a rational price structure, to determine an efficient allocation of resources to achieve attainable goals – but the interplay of advantage-seeking, collusion and administrative influence on the part of planners and performing units alike. Consequently, an enterprise's administrative connections would determine the targets assigned to it and the resources for meeting them, thus measuring success or failure independently of actual performance, not to mention real potential.[43] In similar fashion, the capacity to appropriate that which had been extracted via the planning mechanism would be indistinguishable from a concomitant tendency toward waste, thus reducing the useful product to some fraction of the physical product, just as extraction capabilities had realized only a fraction of the potential product.[44] In those measures imposed by the central authorities intended to regulate and thus to improve the resource/waste ratio, the real weaknesses of the structures of domination would again become apparent. Subordinates would regularly reinterpret, ignore, or otherwise render harmless (for themselves) the salvos of laws, decrees, resolutions and instructions fired off by their nominal superiors.[45] And, returning to the matter of total penetration, a certain weakness appends itself to this notion as well. Not only did mass repression decimate the pool of talent available to the state – either by physically removing individuals from their professional spheres of activity or by erecting various orthodoxies inhibiting creative work[46] – but no firm line would appear to separate the repression of the regime's actual or would-be opponents from the use of power by subalterns simply for the purpose of settling personal scores or eliminating rivals along the avenue of career advancement and personal gain.[47]

Social communication and state penetration

Here, our focus shifts from the categories 'state' and 'organization' to those of 'civil society' and 'communication' as set out in our model (Table 1.1). From the perspective of organization, the Soviet state's total penetration of society would render 'civil society' a meaningless term. Society simply had had no forms, independent of those supplied by the state, within which its members might associate. From the vantage of communication, a similar story can be told. However, by examining the particular methods used by the state to extinguish social communication, we are able to shed light on some additional features of that ground that have important implications for the politics that has reappeared against it in Russia.

In order to capture in a simple way the significance of social communication in this respect, we have recourse to an ideal-typical construct developed by Jürgen Habermas who describes communicative action as 'the medium in which the intersubjectively shared life world is formed . . . [as one in which] every interaction unifies the multiple perspectives of perception and action of those present'.[48] As such, it is through the act of communication that identities are formed and recognized, meanings generated and collective action set in motion.[49] In a manner analogous to our earlier comments on structure as uniting the 'outer' and 'inner' worlds of the subject participating in it, communication might be thought of as a dialectic obtaining between the messages that the subject sends and those that he or she receives. The subject, then, appears not as some isolated or atomized self but as some composite of those messages, reproducing internally the entire spectrum of communication to which he or she has access and situating himself or herself as subject in the vortex of (familiar) others.

The Soviet state's capacity for social penetration can be formulated along these lines as the active prohibition of social communication. The adjective 'active', here, would signify both prevention in the normal sense of the term – censorship, surveillance, repression and, at times, selective or mass terror – and a kind of state-sponsored substitution. The two functioned in tandem. Not only did the state deny society a voice of its own, it proffered another, ready-made one and decreed that only this one shall be heard. This voice, of course, spoke the language of Marxism–Leninism, the official state ideology. It reverberated from party rostrums, through the lecture halls of academic institutions, at production conferences and voters' meetings, in newspapers and films, over television and radio and, iconographically, in the ubiquitous presence of propaganda billboards, wall posters and banners exhorting all to participate in its (literally) unquestionable 'truths'.

The particular content of Soviet Marxism–Leninism represented a rather peculiar admixture of ingredients that appeared as the outcome of a series of negotiations over time that were carried on between state and society. The first ingredient was, of course, Marxism, eviscerated of its critical capacities during the 1920s and conjoined with the approved corpus of Lenin's writings (suitably interpreted and reinterpreted by the authorities as circumstances might have required) that yielded a certain doctrinal dialect for the party-state.[50] Grafted onto this (by now, rather empty) doctrine were the various cults spawned by the leaders of the party-state, principally the cult of Lenin[51] and, until his official removal from atop the pantheon in the latter half of the 1950s, that of Stalin. These religious-like cults were no more congruent with the rational orientation of Marxism than was the third element of this amalgam – Soviet patriotism, whose categories and heroic figures closely overlapped those of Russian nationalism[52] – at home with doctrinal professions of internationalism. Although the make-up of this ideational complex was internally inconsistent, the party-state held it together in a negative sense by strictly policing all channels of public communication and preventing thereby the open expression of any views at variance with those propagated by the regime. In a positive sense, the very incoherence of this complex was indicative of the fact that elements added to it had a certain resonance in the larger population, reflecting archetypes, themes and modalities familiar to Russian culture and society.[53] These, in fact, it would consciously exploit.[54]

In this respect, the triad that we have identified – Marxism–Leninism, the cult of the leader (more or less derivative from the Lenin cult) and Soviet patriotism – would be homologous to tsarism's ideological complex as designated by its foremost scribe, S. S. Uvarov, who rendered it as 'orthodoxy, absolutism and nationality'.[55] In either construction, authority took on the characteristics of the sacred and functioned as a non-rational mechanism of social integration.[56] As the Soviet version of this sacral complex began to decompose in the wake of Stalin's death, its individual elements would supply the hub for one or another of the oppositionist and dissident tendencies that accompanied the breakdown of the Stalinist synthesis. We return to this question in the following chapter. Here, our purpose is to outline the implications of the complex itself for Soviet society.

From the perspective of communication, this complex can be regarded as a grossly disbalanced semantic structure whose mythic dimension had eclipsed its practical one.[57] It enabled a particular form of discourse whose capacity to make sense depended on the insulation of its categories from reports about the world.[58] Accordingly, Marxism–Leninism represented the Soviet state's great bulwark against communicative interaction that could engender social identities, social organization and social projects.[59] In place of these it imposed itself as a grand simulacrum, disorganizing society and driving identity formation out of the public sphere that it monopolized and toward that which has been aptly described as the micro-worlds of small groups whose members were as densely related one to another as they were severed from contact with their counterparts in other of these micro-worlds occupying, perhaps, the same geographic (but by no means the same social) space.[60] Soviet society, then, resembled what Jadwiga Staniszkis has referred to as 'indifferent variety'. Repressed communication prevented the circulation of individual and collective representations of identity; since none could name himself or herself openly, none could encounter the other as the other might wish to present himself or herself. Consequently, there was no interaction among subjects *qua* subjects, just the presence of manifest differences (variety) toward which each subject – in the absence of interaction – would remain 'indifferent'.[61]

Viewing Marxism–Leninism as an artificially constructed language of public communication maintained by the coercive force of the state need not imply that this language was either bereft of discursive potential or entirely static. First, as a number of scholars have argued, its diversity of elements and flexibility of forms could accommodate differing points of view. Second, its contents had been periodically updated by the addition of new terms – say, 'non-antagonistic contradictions', 'all-people's state', 'developed socialism' and so forth – that, at least ostensibly, would appear to adjust its semantics to changes occurring in the world.[62] But were we to focus on the content of these adjustments, it would be difficult to miss the element of sheer nonsense as evinced by terms such as 'non-antagonistic contradictions' or 'all-people's state'. Moreover, it would be shortsighted to dismiss this element of nonsense since it readily suggests something important about the status of the first claim regarding Marxism–Leninism's discursive potential. That is, as official state ideology, Marxism–Leninism had lacked the capacity to root itself in a community of speakers. Here, we remind ourselves of the fact that the ultimate arbiter in Soviet communication had never been the community itself, using as its standard what Habermas has called the force of 'the better argument'.[63] Rather, the arbiter had always been the party-state. The language that it had prescribed could be uttered publicly; the language that it had proscribed could not. To the same degree, then, that speakers had always been unable to refuse the discourse imposed by the party-state – or unable to challenge openly its preposterous assertions or question its nonsensical formulations – they had always in principle been unable to accept this discourse and to retain in so doing their own subjectivity.

From this perspective, the issue of whether anyone actually 'believed' in Marxism–Leninism would be largely beside the point. Surely, individuals believed. But the important questions for us would be: on what grounds? in what way? and to what effect? Inasmuch as imposition rather than persuasion guaranteed the dominance of this public discourse in the USSR, Marxism–Leninism remained unable to develop the capacity to subjectify itself, to colonize the internal world of the subject *qua* subject. Indeed, the party-state indirectly acknowledged this very fact by including 'subjectivism' on the list of official transgressions. When, in times of crisis, a subjective moment did appear *within* Marxist–Leninist discourse – for example, in the debates begun in Poland in the mid-fifties,[64] or, as we see, below, in the USSR during perestroika – this subjectivity would necessarily radicalize itself, as debate foregrounded the role of persuasion. When the element of subjectivity in this context reached a certain critical mass, it would necessarily reject as an irrational *object* the discourse of Marxism–Leninism itself.[65]

The general notion of Marxism–Leninism as a grand simulacrum for social identity can be extended to the specific organizations through which it had been mediated. Take the Communist Party of the Soviet

Union. In what respect would it have been accurate or meaningful to describe this organization as a political party? Equally, could we have described *Pravda* as a newspaper? Or a Soviet trade union as a trade union? In these and in countless other cases, we encountered a kind of fiction that maintained certain trappings associated with the institution in question while the content toward which these trappings would ordinarily point had gone largely or entirely missing. The Communist Party no more competed for power than did *Pravda* print the news or trade unions defend their members. In each case, their function was primarily a negative one inasmuch as whatever stability the Soviet system was capable of purchasing was bought at the expense of such institutions as political parties, newspapers and trade unions. Accordingly, the party-state occupied these and innumerable other spaces with its own ersatz institutions, employing negative sanctions against those who would as much as question their authenticity, let alone those who would endeavour to create the genuine article. For within the logic of the larger simulacrum, Marxism–Leninism, any attempt to construct or supply what was in fact missing – political parties, newspapers and so on – would simultaneously appear as action intended to dislodge the officially approved institutions from the spaces that they occupied. Such action would immediately assume the character of 'anti-Soviet agitation' or 'a slander against the party and people'. From the perspective of communication, then, the concept of simulacrum would represent the counterpart of weak structures. The meanings and identities purportedly associated with it in a given instance – the party, the press – were as ill-suited to eliciting inter-subjectively shared convictions free of compulsion as were the structures of the state with respect to shaping collective action.

Conclusions and implications

On the basis of the foregoing exploration of the Soviet system from the perspectives of organization and communication, it is possible to trace out four principal problematics attending the return of political life in Russia. Individually, each represents an identifiable cluster of factors shaping the contours of the field on which politics has re-emerged; taken together, they provide an index of the major themes running through the empirical analyses offered in this book. These four problematics concern state structures, social communication, interest formulation, and the construction of social and political identity. The four are inter-related, as any pairing of two of them – say, the first (total state structures) with the third (the formulation of particular interests) – would suggest.

Drawing out these inter-relations at one stage or another in the reappearance and development of politics in Russia is central to our methodology. However, for expository purposes, we treat them separately at this point.

The problem of state structures

Our discussion of the structural basis of the Soviet state and the particular focus brought to bear on this question by the concept 'capacities' has foregrounded a weakness with respect to the structural characteristics of internal coherence and self-regulation. This weakness has, in turn, been traced to the relative absence of impersonal forms of coordination and domination and the concomitant tendency to realize these functions by means of extended networks of (informal) personalized relations articulated through the (formal) organizational apparatus of the party-state. Over time, the consequent diminution of state capacities had engendered systemic crisis. Even leaving aside the fact that the USSR had been finding itself progressively less fit to continue its global competition with a much stronger system (capitalism), by the early 1980s (at the latest) its performance by any number of measures – economic, social, ecological – had degenerated to the point that its very reproduction had been thrown into question.[66] This crisis, then, would place in sharp relief the weakness of the Soviet order with respect to the third property of the concept of 'structure': transformation.

To illustrate this point, we might consider the role of law, that premier institution promoting coherence and regulation in the modern state. Law in the USSR had lived a double life, analogous to the articulation of personalized relations within the formal organizational apparatus of the state, noted above. On one hand, to have any effect whatsoever, a law would have to be translated into administrative rules – directives, regulations, orders and so on – which operationally *supplanted* the law in question. Inconsistencies between the content of the law and that of the administrative rules were resolved in practice by privileging the latter. On the other hand, these rules were themselves the products of the personalized authority relations in the party-state, providing interpretations of the law that modified, subverted or simply cancelled its formal text. Further aggravating the incoherence obtaining between law and rules were the facts that the rules were rarely if ever published, and that they were issued in such volume and variety as to ensure that some rules contradicted other ones as well as the law from which they were 'derived'.[67] This dominance of rules over law, of incoherence over coherence, was manifest in the failed attempt at transformation:

perestroika. Despite the official rhetoric of 'legality' and a 'law-governed state', the Gorbachev leadership did not introduce legal relations into the Soviet state and, accordingly, reorganized but never 'restructured' it.[68] Rather than transforming the structure of this system, then, perestroika simply hastened its collapse.[69]

The project of transformation has been inherited by the Russian polity along with the Soviet state's governmental apparatus that it annexed in the wake of the failed *coup* of August 1991. Since we have ample occasion to investigate this problem in later chapters, we confine our remarks here to one aspect of it that directly concerns the organization and communicative dimensions of our model of politics (Table 1.1). The effective absence of legal structures under communism would be coextensive with an absence of legal practices and a legal culture. Consequently, power relations within the Russian state would from the outset lack the mediating influence of these factors and resemble in many respects the personalized relations characteristic of the state socialist order that this state has replaced. As such, a replication of organizational forms and practices associated with the Soviet system would condition the initial development of the Russian state, influencing in turn the spheres of political and civil society, thus inhibiting the formation of coherent structures there as well. Under conditions of open political competition in both the late-Soviet and post-Soviet periods, law would function less as a regulator of conflict than as a weapon employed by state authorities against one another.

The problem of social communication

The combination of statized social relations and the proscription of social communication that were characteristic of state socialism sustained for generations an underdeveloped (or weak) society in the USSR. Here the concept 'underdeveloped' would have nothing to do with material progress *per se*, the connotation that typically has accompanied the usage of this term in the West. Rather, our point would be that society, *qua* society, was underdeveloped in the sense that social groups were little differentiated by either objective or subjective criteria. The total state in which all appeared as employees provided few markers that would distinguish one social group from another. Rather than a division of society along institutional lines – yielding economic classes and affiliated social groups such as managers, professionals and the like – the Soviet order might be thought of as a graded homogeneity in which every member was both tied to all others by means of employment for one and the same state and distinguished from others by virtue of his or her rank and sector. Moreover, the prohibition against social communication meant that subjective criteria would also have minimal influence on social differentiation. Those occupying similar positions in the social hierarchy suffered a deficit of means to communicate common concerns to one another by other than face-to-face methods. Within this society, then, the negotiation of social identities was severely restricted. Who were, say, the metal workers and what did they stand for, oppose and demand? Who were the teachers, the miners or the pensioners? In so far as they were prevented from communicating, from organizing and from telling us, we were unable to know and, by that measure, so were they. Civil and political society, in other words, simply did not exist.

As restrictions on social communication were eased during the course of perestroika, however, forms of association characteristic of civil and political society sprang to life. Literally thousands of clubs, societies, cooperatives, trade unions, political parties and so forth came into existence. While most disappeared in rather short order, those that have survived have been required to adapt the projects on which they had been founded to the conditions confronting them in late-communist and post-communist Russia. Moreover, these adaptations have usually not run in the direction reinforcing the organizational and communicative dimensions of political and civil society as specified in our model (Table 1.1), but toward those associated with the state. In subsequent chapters, we investigate the reasons for this. Here, we take note of an obvious but not unimportant consideration; namely, that the removal of restrictions on social communication is not at all equivalent to generating that same communication, particularly in forms approximating the ideal-type specifications employed in the model. This issue can be pursued further by outlining the problems of interest and identity in the context of Russia's transition from communism.

The problem of interest

Following directly on what we have argued thus far, the category 'interest' – understood as a social phenomenon mediated by communication rather than as advantage-seeking, preferences or concerns at the level of individuals – would not seem to pertain to the state socialist order. To avoid the fundamentally mistaken methodology of imputing interests (on the basis of *our* assumptions) to various social groups, we should exercise care in using this term. Therefore, following such theorists as Hannah Arendt, Alvin Goulder and Charles Lindblom, we regard interest as a particular confluence of objective and subjective factors such that those who occupy some position differentiated from others by social structure develop a shared consciousness of this fact and undertake in correspondence with it certain projects regarded by the group in question as beneficial. As such, interests always oppose other interests. They exist in argument rather than in fact.[70]

Were there not interests at play within the Soviet party-state? Did not various functional and sectoral groupings – say, professional associations or ministries and their allies in the party apparatus – compete against one another for resources, forming coalitions in the process of so doing; in short, engaging in politics? Western Sovietologists have tended to answer these questions in the affirmative, employing modified interest group or corporatist models of politics borrowed, respectively, from the fields of Western democratic and Third World political systems.[71] In our view, the problem with such an approach would be that it would depend in the first instance on that which was absent in Soviet state socialism, namely, a civil society in which interests could be formu-lated.[72] By bearing in mind this absence, our understanding of what was alleged to be present – interests – would be fundamentally altered. In the context of Soviet state socialism, interests could only assume the form licensed by the party-state. For the individual expressing an interest, this meant petitioning authority for something to which authority had granted the individual entitlement; say, so many cubic metres of housing space or a reinstatement of employment after having been improperly dismissed. For collectivities, interests could be expressed as a claim on resources by the recognized officials superintending on behalf of the party-state the collectivities themselves. In the poignant illustration offered by Ferenc Feher, Agnes Heller and Gyorgy Markus:

one can always be morally certain that the President of the Academy of Sciences (a middle-level member of the apparatus) will fight tooth and nail to get central funds committed to the founding of some new research institute, that he will constantly lament the insufficiencies of finances for the upkeep of resort houses, nurseries, etc. for the workers of the Academy – and that he will never raise a single question about the principle of censorship of scientific publications. The fact that the person in question may well be an elder scientist himself, one who in all probability personally considers the further proliferation of academic institutes to be mere folly, while deeply detesting the power which formal or informal censorship gives to the young and semi-educated headhunters in the cultural apparatus of the party over their scientific elders, will not change his behaviour one iota.[73]

Of course, individuals concerned with the question of free expression occluded in the example just given could also petition authority, as in the celebrated case of Aleksandr Tvardovskii, editor of *Novyi mir*, securing Nikita Khrushchev's permission to publish a story by Aleksandr Solzhenitsyn. But the personal decision to grant such a benefaction would scarcely sustain the notion of interest in either a socially or politically meaningful sense.

The problem of social and political identity

The obstacles presented by the Soviet order to the formulation of social interests also retarded the formation of social and political identities. The party-state's active prohibition against social communication – whereby it encouraged individuals to express themselves in the particular language, venues and organizations that it supplied while suppressing all forms of social expression occurring outside of these boundaries – left little if any possibility for the development of inter-subjective normative discourses through which individuals could identify themselves as social subjects bearing mutually recognized interests. But the implications of this regime were not altogether equivalent for the constitution of both interests and identities. Interest formulation, as we have seen, had been ruled out by the party-state's active prohibition against social communication. No potential interest could develop because each lacked the presence of other (opposing, intersecting, emerging) interests that it would require in order to mediate itself socially as an agent of needs satisfaction. Therefore, action oriented toward the satisfaction of needs would be channelled away from the public expression of interests and toward one or another restricted sphere of communication: either into some subdivision of the state or into the zone of illicit activities. However, with respect to identity formation, the party-state's active prohibition carried additional consequences. While almost exclusively confining the presentation and discovery of the self (and other) in communication unencumbered by repression to the face-to-face relations characteristic of the system's subterranean micro-worlds, the very ubiquity of the party-state also supplied that indispensable 'other' against which social and political identities might begin to acquire validity or authenticity.

Oddly, then, the total state both suppressed and contributed to identity formation. It negatively structured the sites in which this process occurred, appearing there as inverse and opposite. It was in the more or less secluded settings in which open expression was possible that the Soviet system was 'not'; not there to police communication and not there to impose its prefabricated identities. It was also in these settings that the system would often be thematized in a way that it, according to its authorized representations, was not. In endless jokes and anecdotes about it, in the interminable discussions and debates around (usually) the kitchen table that would (again, usually) extend into the small hours of the morning, this system and its all-embracing catalogue of identities would appear as 'other'. As such, those party to these interactions were in fact negotiating identities separate from and, in some measure, in opposition to the Soviet order. Moreover, individuals found ways to overcome the restrictions imposed on them by the party-state and to forge links – however tenuous and indirect – with a larger social world. These efforts were mediated in the main by underground and semi-underground literature and song that, with the advent of photocopying machinery and the tape recorder, could be reproduced and circulated on an expanding scale. A measure of the importance and prevalence of these practices can be taken from the status afforded to the figure of Vladimir Vysotskii. Especially after his death, this bard of the late-communist period – whose verse had circulated mainly in the form of bootleg tapes and carbon-copy manuscript – became a veritable icon of authenticity for a mass public.[74]

Given the systemic context, this act of identity formation outside the boundaries maintained by the party-state was ineluctably political. Even for those who consciously eschewed political activity themselves, the choice of an identity not appearing on the official inventory would contain some political moment. This aspect of choice would follow necessarily from those features of the Soviet order on which we have already remarked, namely its total character and, relatedly, its monopoly on public communication. Taken together, these amounted to the excision of politics from social life, to a declaration that politics was treason.[75] Within this context, the choice to pursue authenticity in the construction of identities would entail flirtation with the treasonous. For authenticity would involve, at a minimum, laying open to inspection, evaluation and either acceptance or rejection the ready-made identities confected by the regime. When the result was rejection, the choice of identity was simultaneously a political choice.

The differential consequences for interest and identity formation resulting from the party-state's active prohibition of social communication would help to account for the fact that Russian political life has reappeared to an exceptionally large degree in the form of identity-based politics. Once restrictions on social communication began to be eased by the policy of perestroika, the various tendencies, currents and groupings that began to express themselves were speaking, above all, the language of identity. This phenomenon might resemble in some respects those 'new social movements' – such as feminist, sexual orientation and cultural politics – that have been theorized in Western sociology.[76]

However, the Russian variant has been an especially radical one. Unlike their counterparts in the West who might endeavour to secure a place for new group identities by modifying the institutions of their respective societies, identity-based movements in Russia found themselves pitted against an already existing order that for generations had sustained itself at the ideational level by denying the permissibility of each and all of those conceptions of identity – religious, national, not to mention, political – that might rival its own constructs. Consequently, the politics of identity in Russia would follow another trajectory, one aimed less at modifying existing institutions than at replacing them.[77]

This form of identity politics, together with its radical edge which would be sharpened in one way or another by its (changing) context, is traceable to the ground of communism from which the figure of Russian politics has re-emerged. Moreover, even as more articulated forms of organization – such as political parties, parliamentary factions, duly incorporated public organizations, trade unions and business associations – have replaced more amorphous ones, identity rather than interest has remained at the centre of political discourse. This has been evident in the preoccupation with the past that some segments of the political spectrum regard as holding the key to recapturing authentic Russian institutions and modes of life, as well as in the decided proclivity among others to look to other societies for a model for constructing a 'new' Russia. In this context, not only does one identity confront another, they clash.[78] And from the fragments thrown off by these political collisions other identities are reassembled, decked out to continue the contest under new banners. While the number of permutations available in this identity politics seems limitless, the basic elements found in one or another compound derive ultimately from the ideological synthesis of the Soviet period: Marxism–Leninism, the cult of the leader and Soviet patriotism. Indeed, prior to the rebirth of politics in Russia, embryonic forms of these identities would be detectable in the various opposition movements that appeared in the USSR during the final decades of its existence.

2   Regime and opposition in the pre-political period

This chapter surveys a period that we call 'pre-political'. It can be likened to those intervals – pre-dawn or twilight – that separate night from day, intervals during which neither is quite present yet both seem to be there at once, incongruously, cancelling one another out at the same time. Pre-political suggests such an interval to us. It describes a period that is neither political in the sense of that term as we have used it, nor altogether anti-political as we have characterized communism. What defines the interval in this way would be the appearance and development of a small but none the less significant social movement that came to be known as 'the dissidents'. The presence of this novel element on the inhospitable terrain of state socialism represents a critical turning point for our subject, for it introduces a new and unique position into the field of cultural–political expression that reverberates as a series of reactions and permutations on the part of other actors. Moreover, the discursive practices associated with this movement would both anticipate a return of political life in Russia and contribute at least indirectly to that return itself.

Short exegeses of certain theoretic concepts, introduced to organize the discussion and to provide an inter-related set of categories for its principal elements, punctuate this chapter. One of these concepts – 'cultural–political field' – can be briefly introduced, here, by noting three aspects of its use pertinent to our discussion. First, the compound adjective is employed to connote politically related practices that have their origins in the sphere of cultural production. That is, we are concerned in this instance almost exclusively with individuals – poets, artists, writers, philosophers, historians – whose professional activities involve them directly in cultural discourses wherein the issues of meaning, values, subjectivity, interpretation and assessment bulk particularly large. Second, the thematization of these matters in discourses other than the one sponsored by the party-state established a field on which various discourses would contend over the questions of meaning, values and so forth. While the character of these conflicts would not constitute a form of political activity *per se* – any more than would, say, a dispute among participants in a seminar on classical philosophy or modern music – they necessarily challenged the party-state's active prohibition against social communication, thus engaging the pre-political issue of a right to expression rather than those substantive concerns mediated in political speech which would depend on the existence of that very right. Finally, 'cultural–political field' denotes a collection of sites on which a very small segment of the total population had been active during the time period encompassed by this chapter.[1] Nothing approaching a public possessed of beliefs in citizenship, a responsibility for the affairs of the nation and their own ability to participate in these affairs would be present until years later. In this respect, it is important at the outset to enter a certain caveat regarding the way in which the tenor of this chapter is distinguished from that of the preceding one. Since the present focus falls on small groups of individuals active on the margins of Soviet society, the description of their activities dominates the narrative, creating the impression, perhaps, of a robust political life *in statu nascendi*. Recalling the context and consequences of their actions, however, we are reminded that they fell considerably short of repealing communism's prohibition of politics.

This chapter is organized primarily along chronological lines, beginning with a brief consideration of the impact of the Second World War on Soviet society in the late-Stalinist epoch. Thereafter, the discussion turns to the emergence of various forms of opposition to the regime, each appearing around one or another element contained in the party-state's authority construct: first, in the form of small clandestine groups whose views derived from their interpretations of certain canonical texts; second, as small but open groups whose orientations toward the symbols of democracy and legality had been engendered by revisions of the canon undertaken by the regime itself; and, third, as those emphasizing other elements in the triad, primarily as a form of protest or pressure on the regime to correct its putative remissness regarding the respective aspects of the canon that they would valorize. We conclude the chapter by mapping the cultural–political field in the period preceding perestroika.

After the war

Despite the havoc wrought on the territory of the USSR by four years of war with Germany, Soviet society emerged from that experience united as never before. Two broad considerations might be cited in this respect. On one hand, the resurgence of the national–imperial idea in the regime's wartime propaganda – which placed the figure of Stalin in the succession of tsar-conquerors and illustrious generals from the past – along with the official restoration of the Orthodox Church created a profoundly effective patriotic ideology that struck deep roots in a people fighting for its very survival. On the other, the conditions of war had altered fundamentally the field of social action. Great numbers of people found themselves in situations in which central authority was either remote or effectively non-existent. Consequently, imperatives to act in the face of one or another exigency were commonly met by taking direct decisions 'below', in military units and partisan detachments fighting behind enemy lines, and in the towns, factories and farms on the home front. It may be no exaggeration to note that the combination of these factors – crowned, of course, by a spectacular victory purchased at the price of enormous national effort and bitter suffering – induced in society for the first time a genuine acceptance of, and identification with, the Soviet regime.

The experience of the 'Great Patriotic War', not unlike Russia's victory over Napoleon's armies more than a century earlier, also stimulated free thought and expression. Apparently, this was occasioned by a heightened sense of subjectivity (or autonomy) that accompanied the activities of masses of people together risking, sacrificing and, too often, dying in defence of *their* country and its state. A measure of this subjectivity can be taken from such things as Lev Kopelev's articles in the official press regarding the untoward behaviour of Soviet troops on conquered German soil, that led to his arrest; or from Aleksandr Solzhenitsyn's letter to a friend containing passages critical of Stalin that resulted in his arrest as well.[2] Solzhenitsyn even reported later that the person escorting him to his incarceration, a certain sergeant Korzhavin, figuratively remarked to him that 'he and I had gone through the same school'[3] and was not afraid to show Solzhenitsyn his own critical verse, seeing nothing seditious in it.[4] The readiness of some individuals at this time to express themselves more or less openly and critically contrasted sharply with conditions prevailing in the years immediately preceding the war.[5] Of course, the party-state's reinstatement of an active prohibition of social communication soon cut short such unauthorized expressions and swaddled society again with official Marxism–Leninism. But the elements comprising this unstable compound – Marxism, the cult of the leader and Soviet patriotism – would begin to undergo hypostatis, each suggesting quite different interpretations and evaluations of social reality, each colliding with the interpretations and evaluations associated with the others. The first element to separate itself out of the synthesis, proving a critical vantage on the others and on government and society in general, was Marxism.

Toward the close of the 1940s, an anti-Stalinist underground began to develop in Russia's larger cities which more and more regarded the practices of the Soviet state as a crude perversion of Marxist teachings.[6] In so far as we know, these groups were made up almost exclusively of young people, primarily students.[7] Some were children of repressed 'kulaks' and gentry whose families had been brought to the brink of starvation during the regime's war against the countryside in the 1930s. Others were scions of high party-state functionaries, raised under invidiously comfortable material conditions,[8] who more often than not were the initiators of these clandestine groups.[9] Theirs was an especially personal reaction to the hypocrisy surrounding them: privileges for the elite at the expense of working people, all in the name of Marxism. At school and in these underground circles, their acquaintance with the lives of others who had suffered the most severe deprivation only sharpened the dissonance that they experienced. But as children of the elite their associations also afforded them broader access to various types of literature, including illegal materials. Through reading and the exchange of ideas in these underground study groups, little knots of young men and women began to work out their own views independently of, and in opposition to, that Marxism–Leninism purveyed by the regime.[10] In some instances, this led them into revolutionary activity.[11]

In the early post-war years, Marxism thus served as the first basis for organized opposition to the Soviet regime. The very names adopted by these groups indicated their affinity with it: the Communist Party of Youth, the Circle of Marxist Thought, the Leninist Union of Students and others.[12] In general, they seemed to be rehearsing the romance of the country's revolutionary tradition as accentuated in Bolshevik mythology. Of principal importance in this respect was the devotion of one's life to the revolutionary transformation of the country, as Lenin had devoted his. By means of disciplined theoretical study and the ongoing preparation of the larger population through the distribution of revolutionary propaganda, somehow that Archimedean point could be found and employed to overthrow the Stalin regime.

In addition to this strain of youthful revolutionaries in the years following the war, other circles were formed which presaged the appearance of the dissident movement more than a decade later. One was the Brotherhood of Beggarly Sybarites, a group of talented, if eccentric, young people whose leader, Arkadii Belinkov, produced a novel in manuscript – 'Conspiracy of the Senses' – that used the Molotov–Ribbentrop pact to illustrate his thesis concerning the essential equivalence of Hitler's and Stalin's 'fascist' dictatorships.[13] Although this group was rather quickly apprehended by the authorities, another that formed around Ernst Neizvestnyi that devoted itself to discussing the works of such writers as George Orwell, Leon Trotsky and Nikolai Berdyaev carried on its activities from 1949 to 1960 when it was repressed on the baseless charge of constituting a 'youth terrorist organization'.[14] Similarly, the Moscow Logic Circle (later, the Moscow Methodological Circle) formed at Moscow State University in 1954 by Boris Grushin, Aleksandr Zinov'ev, Merab Mamardashvili and Georgii Shchedrovitskii has continued in one form or another to the present day.[15] It appeared as a philosophical alternative to the Marxist paradigm against the backdrop of a rudimentary free-speech movement at the university that spun off the circle led by the future dissident, Grigorii Pomerants.[16]

After Stalin

Stalin's death dramatically accelerated the decomposition of the Soviet authority structure, laying open to contention that element of its triad, cult of the leader, that for the overwhelming majority of the population had remained rock-solid while he was alive. Within the circles of the elite, his passing reinforced those fissiparous tendencies inherent in state socialism's weak structures: the formation of more or less stable patron–client relations, the personal appropriation of state offices (eventually apotheosized in Brezhnev's formula regarding 'stability' and 'trust in cadres') and the related phenomena of departmentalism and localism on which we commented in the preceding chapter. Here, our discussion will concern the effects of Stalin's death on the larger society.

The evidence recorded in memoirs about this period indicates that these effects had been of seismic proportions. For instance, K. M. Simonov recalls that 'something in us, in any case [something] in me, convulsed at this moment. Something in life had finished. Something else, yet unknown, had begun.'[17] Similarly, Vladimir Bukovskii remembers that 'the death of Stalin shook our life to its foundations . . . it was sensed that somehow there was no more authority [vlasti] . . . People were saying completely openly: "For whom will [people] now go forth to die? For Malenkov perhaps? No. Folk will not go forth to die for Malenkov."'[18] Moreover, it would seem that the road toward opposition to the Soviet order that many would traverse later actually started at the moment of Stalin's death. S. I. Osipov, a scientist arrested in 1956 for posting unauthorized leaflets, subsequently remarked with simplicity, 'I worked and studied with ardour, I believed in the final victory of socialism . . . After Stalin's death, my impressions changed.'[19] Moving in quite the opposite direction, Leonid Rendel' and Lev Krasnopevets, founders of one of the most sensational of the underground groups, drew from this same event the inference that it was time 'to seek their own course in party life'.[20]

Stalin's 'second' death, the partial exposure of his cult and crimes by Nikita Khrushchev at the Communist Party's historic Twentieth Congress, in many ways registered a more powerful jolt to Soviet society than had his 'first' mortality. N. Yanevich, for example, a researcher at the Institute of World Literature, later recalled that on hearing of Khrushchev's speech, 'many of us simply didn't believe it, grew livid and were filled with indignation . . . The majority of us, rank-and-file communists, were overcome by shame, shock . . . [and then] rejoicing over the end of the repression.'[21] Among the young and educated, the news of the speech carried an even greater impact, provoking not only reflection but often a public questioning of established 'truths'.[22] In institutions of higher education – for example, at Leningrad State University – discussions of the Party Congress sometimes voiced seditious ideas, such as calls to rehabilitate Nikolai Bukharin.[23] Gatherings to assess the results of the Congress at the Institute of Theoretical and Experimental Physics and at the Institute of Philosophy were witness to comparable speeches and remarks.[24]

The release of political prisoners that was begun shortly after Stalin's death – often on the initiative of the inmates themselves who staged spontaneous revolts in a number of labour camps[25] – was stepped up in the wake of the Twentieth Party Congress. While the return of millions from the camps had no immediate or direct impact on the formation of opposition currents in society, as a lingering sense of apprehension if not fear dissuaded those discharged from engaging in open political activity, the stories that they told of their experiences none the less exercised a strong influence on others who would soon begin to take part in illegal organizations.[26] Moreover, their return contributed its weight to that of other events unsettling for the social climate at the time: the Twentieth Congress and the discussions occurring in its wake, the revolts in Poland and Hungary that followed later in the year, and the defeat of the so-called antiparty group in the Soviet leadership that was engineered in summer of 1957. The impact of these occurrences, however, was by no means uniform.

In the history faculty at Moscow State University, the group gathered around Leonid Rendel' and Lev Krasnopevets became especially active in the cause of 'carrying through, defending and realizing with new, clean hands . . . the course of renewal' authorized by the Twentieth Congress.[27] However, this same group took umbrage at the way in which the 'antiparty' group was expelled from the leadership, regarding this episode as a violation of the norms of intra-party democracy. They enacted their protest by distributing leaflets with a summons 'to carry out the struggle for socialist renewal in the spirit of the Twentieth Congress'.[28] For others, however, these same events were a spur in the opposite direction, motivating them to rise not to the defence of democratic procedures but to that of Stalinism.[29] This tendency would remain dormant for some time, nurtured in incubation by the official renewal of sacrilegious assaults against the dictator and his legacy that began at the Twenty-Second Congress in 1962 and continued in its aftermath. Thereafter, neo-Stalinism began to surface in official publications sermonizing against the conveniently proximate objects of much popular wrath: philistine 'bureaucrats', intellectuals, Jews and other 'cosmopolitans' regarded as menace to its totem.[30]

Particularly jarring to many advocates of socialist renewal via the course of liberalization was the fate of the revolution in Hungary. As Vladimir Bukovskii has recalled,

After all the exposures, the censures and posthumous rehabilitations, after all the assurances about the impossibility of a return to the old [order of things], again [we saw] troops, tanks, violence and the lie . . . How exhausted we were from the quiet of Moscow, from the peaceful humdrum of life! It seemed that now the truck will pull up right in our yard . . . 'It's time', they'll say to us and they'll hand the brand-new sub-machine-guns over the side. Therefore, when [some] guys . . . guardedly began to initiate a conversation with me about some [unsanctioned] organization, I became so happy that I never even let them finish.[31]

Similarly, news of the Hungarian events arrived as 'welcome grounds' for the activities of the future Union of Communists organized by Viktor Trofimov among students at Leningrad State University.[32] The leaflets they distributed called on Soviet citizens to support the Hungarian insurrection. In November 1956, anti-Soviet shouts rang out at the Day of the Revolution parade in Leningrad, while in Yaroslavl a placard bearing the inscription 'We demand the withdrawal of Soviet forces from Hungary' passed before the rostrum of local party-state dignitaries.[33]

These outbursts of open political expression were short-lived. Until the mid-1960s, opposition existed almost exclusively in the form of underground groups.[34] Most of these professed the philosophy of Marx and Lenin,[35] counterpoising in particular the ideas that they found in State and Revolution and 'The Immediate Tasks of Soviet Power' to the realities around them so rudely at odds with the very principles enshrined in the official ideology.[36] In the context of this tension, the urge to express oneself, to communicate with others, would become irrepressible. In the capital, the catalyst was provided by the unveiling of a monument to the poet, Mayakovskii, in the summer of 1958 at which people soon began to congregate and to engage in spontaneous poetry readings and literary discussions. Gradually, as the talk turned more and more to political themes, a sort of miniature political society was convening at this 'Hyde Park' in Moscow. There, many of the luminaries of the future dissident movement struck up acquaintances that would grow fast in the years ahead.[37] But this island of free expression was repeatedly deluged by the police who broke up the meetings, arrested participants and, in a particularly violent attack in April 1961 on those assembled on the holiday honouring the cosmonaut, Yurii Gagarin, put an end to it once and for all.[38]

Yet out of these encounters another avenue of communication emerged that would become synonymous with the dissident movement – samizdat. Initially, its carbon-copied editions contained those works of renowned Russian poets – Osip Mendel'shtam, Mariya Tsvetaeva, Anna Akhmatova, Boris Pasternak and others – that had been refused publication in the USSR. Soon, a more political content was added in the form of articles penned by so-called 'revisionists' from foreign communist parties. But it was not long before samizdat became a vehicle for self-expression; initially, again, for literary works,[39] but soon for other tracts critical of the Soviet system.[40] In some instances, samizdat publication became hubs around which new groups formed; in others, existing groups were inspired by materials circulated in the underground to launch their own samizdat editions.[41]

In sum, the early post-Stalin years witnessed a social phenomenon both new to the Soviet Union and fundamentally at odds with its prevailing order. By taking it on themselves to discuss ideas and exchange information, individuals were violating a taboo. Simultaneously, they were opening that communicative space in which the first fragile shoots of civil and political society were sprouting: orally, in public gatherings such as those at Mayakovskii Square, in informal study groups and throughout the archipelago of Soviet kitchens whose freewheeling discussions would qualify them as state socialism's premier (pre-)political site; in written form, as rough samizdat copy, circulating through the archipelago, connecting those on its many islands (indeed, even some of those in prison camps) into a micro-society that had begun to take on its own identity in opposition to the official order. Stepping into this forbidden zone, many individuals had embarked on journeys that would lead them into new environments where world-views evolved at high speed. Most who had begun their unsanctioned activities as Marxists critical of the existing Soviet order would opt for other political orientations that, paradoxically, were less revolutionary in outward appearance but more destabilizing over the long haul for the triadic construct of Marxism–Leninism.[42]

Dissidents

In the act of debunking Stalin's cult, the leadership of the Communist Party simultaneously revived in a not insignificant way the category 'democracy' in Soviet society. Whether they did this consciously and sincerely would not be important for our purposes. Rather, the point would be that, by thematizing democracy and socialist legality as virtues to be recaptured in their proposed return to 'Leninist principles' they provided the official discourse with a counterpoint to the authoritarianism previously sanctioned by the cult of the leader. The introduction of these notions – however vague, limited or contradictory their content – transformed the communicative context. Whereas in the early postwar years internal opposition to the Soviet Union had formed around a critique of the regime on the basis of the same Marxist principles that it outwardly professed, after the Twentieth Party Congress opposition would increasingly congeal around another outward profession – 'democracy, legality' – that was also at odds with the leadership cult (Lenin's, as appropriated by his extant successor) still present in more attenuated form within the Marxist–Leninist triad. As such, the dyadic relation hitherto prevailing between (Marxist) regime and (Marxist) opposition was superseded by a triangular one that included in modified form the old (Marxist) regime–opposition couple and a new point from which would proceed a discourse oriented to the values of democracy and legality. A discursive field was thereby constructed.

This spatial metaphor 'field', for the ensemble of discursive practices existing in a given system, comes from the work of Pierre Bourdieu who has developed it in his investigation of cultural production.[43] In short, 'field' refers to a given mode of social activity or form of work – for instance, material production (class relations), cultural production, jurisprudence or, in the present instance, discursive practices relevant to politics – in which struggles internal to it generate a structure of positions that are occupied by actors pursuing 'strategies' in opposition to others doing the same from the positions that they have occupied. For present purposes, the utility of Bourdieu's conceptualization consists in its joining of the idea of structural relations within a field as determinate of the possible set of positions available to actors at a given moment with the dynamic notions of struggle, strategy and trajectory through which actors change the boundaries of fields, adding new positions and thus

altering the relations among those positions that continue to exist as well
as the content of the respective positions themselves.[44] In our view, it
would be mistaken to consider the dissident movement as something
apart from the field in which it had existed. To the contrary, we can
account for the positions taken by those involved and the permutation of
positions over time as defined by the structure of the field of cultural–
political discourse at one or another conjuncture, beginning with the
addition of the third point, democracy/legality, into the regime–Marxist/
oppositionist–Marxist dyad.

Since open political expression remained subject to immediate party-
state repression, position-taking relevant to politics occurred primarily
on the field of culture in the form of literary-publicist activities. In this
regard, the establishment journal of 'liberal' orientation, *Novyi mir*
(under the editorship of Aleksandr Tvardovskii) occupied a pivotal
position. Despite the party-state's close supervision and running battles
with the censors, *Novyi mir* managed to combine the respectability
attendant on its official status with a limited degree of criticism issuing
from a liberal point of view that earned it an enormous amount of
prestige within the country's intellectual elite. By remaining within the
ambit of the establishment, the journal exchanged editorial autonomy
for the possibility of exercising influence within the higher circles, never
openly opposing the official line but attempting to correct it by
introducing minor innovations and modifications which *Novyi mir*, as a
recognized organ of the party-state, was in a position to do. Although
restricted until 1970 (when its editorial board was purged) the journal
articulated a viewpoint that would be revived in the mid-1980s by the
Soviet regime itself. Perestroika's early outlines of a 'renewal of
socialism' mirrored much of what *Novyi mir* had managed to insert in its
pages under far less hospitable conditions.[45]

The powerful combination of elements comprising the position
occupied by *Novyi mir* – cultural prestige plus official respectability, a
liberal orientation combined with status in the world of the party-state –
exercised a profound influence on the structure of the cultural–political
field, determining a set of positions that others would occupy. These
positions can be divided into subsets of competitors and opponents,
each marked by its relative proximity to state power. Reserving
discussion of opponents for the following section, the focus here falls on
competitors. They consisted of individuals engaged in literary pursuits
who, for whatever motives, refused to submit themselves to the
restrictions imposed by the authorities in control of access to the
established hierarchy of posts in the field of culture. The positions that
they took would be characterized generally by an emphasis on values

associated with cultural production *per se*: competence, authenticity, creativity free of constraint and so forth. Those within them would tend to valorize central elements in the code of cultural production in an effort to accumulate what Bourdieu has referred to as 'symbolic' and 'cultural capital'.[46] Accordingly, these positions placed prestige within the field of culture over the respectability afforded by official organizations, and valued autonomy – the core of liberal ideology – over the rewards and recognition doled out by the party-state authorities.

Those assuming this set of positions entered from various directions. Some had already established careers in literature and in the academic world while others, having been expelled from institutions of higher education, could look forward to effectively no career prospects within their respective vocations. To some extent they shared a common discourse with those in the liberal establishment and were connected to it in various ways: through individuals occupying positions at the boundaries separating establishment from unofficial cultural actors (for instance, the poets Evgenii Evtushenko and Andrei Voznesenskii); via persons who had once held some rank in the establishment and retained contact with others still in it; and by means of works in manuscript or samizdat form, that criss-crossed the boundaries dividing these sets of positions. None the less, the refusal to acknowledge the intellectual authority of the party-state implied a measure of competition with those occupying official positions in the cultural field. In this competition, those outside the institutions maintained by the party-state would pursue a strategy that maximized the value of those resources that they commanded. Since they were not encumbered directly by the constraints of the party-state, their strategy for 'accumulating cultural capital' leaned heavily toward doing what they alone were free to do, namely, to innovate and thus to position themselves as a cultural avant-garde.[47]

Inasmuch as the authorities defined all unsanctioned innovations as hostile acts, those engaging in unsanctioned innovation within the context of the Soviet order were willy-nilly taking up a hostile position toward the authorities. This hostility was directly manifest in the priority assigned by dissidents to the individual, itself an assault on the collectivist ideology of the regime. In this respect, Andrei Amal'rik recalled in his memoirs that he 'had an intuitive enmity toward collective activities, that strongly developed individualism that warred with a Soviet upbringing'.[48] Similarly, Iosif Brodskii remarked in his Nobel Lecture in 1987 that 'if art teaches anything (and, above all, to the artist) it is the particularity of human existence. Being the most ancient . . . form of private entrepreneurship, voluntarily or not [art] stimulates in a person precisely his feeling of individuality, uniqueness, separateness, converting him from a social animal into a personality.'[49] This philosophical celebration of the individual – more or less characteristic of the dissident movement – required an innovation in the strategy and tactics of opposition if it were to acquire the capacity to answer the regime 'blow for blow' as individuals such as Amal'rik and Brodskii passionately insisted.[50] Discussions of these questions preoccupied dissident circles in the 1960s and early 1970s. One possible course of action, that of underground conspiratorial activity, remained a live option and was further radicalized by some in the form of armed struggle with terrorist objectives.[51] But the strategic and tactical innovation adopted, one that effectively inaugurated what came to be known as the dissident movement and characterized its thinking and actions throughout its existence, took precisely the opposite tack. Rather than conspiratorial secrecy and armed struggle, the movement would emphasize non-violence, publicity and open activity. Rather than opposition to the Soviet system, the movement would embrace and scrupulously observe the system's decorative self-representations as set down in Soviet law and the country's Constitution, demanding that the authorities do likewise. This strategy, then, would encase the philosophical emphasis on the individual in a social institution, law, thus establishing a pivot for collective action around the notions of respect for law and a defence of individual rights.

The author of this seminal innovation was the mathematician–philosopher, Aleksandr Esenin-Vol'pin, son of the famous poet, Sergei Esenin. A number of individuals in Moscow who had already participated in public actions, such as those on Mayakovskii Square, readily embraced his strategy, if for no other reason than the fact that their previous activities – followed by arrests, searches of their apartments and KGB surveillance – meant that the door to the underground was for them already closed. Esenin-Vol'pin overcame the skepticism of many others by patiently and relentlessly pointing out the obvious fact: 'our laws', he argued, 'exist only on paper for [purposes of] propaganda and are always turned against you'. They would mean nothing unless and until individuals began to think of themselves as citizens and demand that the laws be observed and enforced.[52]

In addition to this stroke of tactical genius that impudently turned the tables against the regime by speaking back to power its own words, Esenin-Vol'pin's innovation was of cardinal significance for the inception of political practice in Russia and elsewhere in the USSR. Because of its emphasis on legality, those in the movement would begin to acquaint themselves with law and legal procedure, acquiring thereby a sense of formal rights, learning how to conduct themselves under interrogation by the police and KGB, applying their knowledge of the rules against the authorities themselves (which sometimes succeeded in forcing open those closed courtrooms where their comrades stood on trial), and building over the course of these activities a rudimentary sense of citizenship.[53] At the same time, there were clear limits to the political import of this strategy, for it turned the face of the dissident movement ever toward the regime, never toward Russian society. When efforts to persuade the regime proved futile and dissidents turned to world opinion – or, practically speaking, to Western publics and governments – for leverage against the authorities, the socio-cultural divide between dissident elements and the larger society was deepened, as regime propaganda hastened to portray the movement as disloyal, opposed to the homeland and doing the work of foreign enemies. Perhaps these consequences were the unavoidable results of a project to mount public opposition to a regime that denied a public. But dissidents contributed to this same problem by directing their messages to the state, rather than to society.[54] Ironically, the movement did make an important impact in the sphere of the state but registered at most marginal gains in the sphere of its announced intentions: the creation of civic institutions and the development of citizenship in Russia.

The protests launched over the arrest of the writers Aleksandr Sinyavskii and Yulii Daniel in September 1965 have commonly been used to date the inception of the dissident movement.[55] As Peter Reddaway has suggested, these arrests appeared to signal a decision by the regime to return to the practice of jailing prominent figures in the cultural establishment for engaging in unsanctioned activities – in this instance, for publishing works of fiction in the West – a practice that had largely lapsed since Stalin's death.[56] But this observation should be placed in context. On one hand, repression of this type, while administered in considerably smaller doses, had by no means disappeared with the dictator's demise, as attested by the well-known cases of Boris Pasternak and Iosif Brodskii, the three-year internment (1962–5) of Mikhail Naritsa in a psychiatric hospital,[57] and the similar incarceration of Valerii Tarsis whose early release was prompted by the pressure of his sympathizers abroad.[58] On the other, various groups of intellectuals had already been organizing themselves in the summer of 1965 and thus were prepared to respond to these new arrests rather quickly,[59] indicating that the Sinyavskii–Daniel affair was more catalyst than cause of the sudden appearance of open dissent on a scale hitherto unprecedented in the USSR.

On 5 December 1965, the first demonstration for human rights was staged at Moscow's Pushkin Square, where Esenin-Vol'pin and others from the days of the Mayakovskii Square gatherings delivered speeches that raised the specific demand for glasnost (openness and full information) in the coming trial of Sinyavskii and Daniel, as well as the general slogan: 'Observe the Soviet Constitution!' This gathering was of seminal import in three respects. First, it inaugurated a new practice of public demonstration that would be repeated yearly on 5 December at Pushkin Square until the eclipse of the dissident movement at the close of the 1970s.[60] Moreover, it embedded at the foundation of the movement the principles associated with Esenin-Vol'pin's innovation: legality, glasnost and an explicit refusal to forsake the high ground of morality for the lowlands, as understood by the dissidents, of a more practically oriented politics.[61] Of course, this emphasis on morality was not without profound political ramifications in the context of the state socialist order. As Andrei Amal'rik observed, 'the dissidents ingeniously accomplished a simple thing – in an unfree country, they began to comport themselves as free people and by that alone [they began] to change the moral atmosphere and traditional methods for running the country'.[62] But the dissidents' proclivity to address the authorities rather than society as well as their abstemious attitude toward politics would show their painful effects in later years.

Second, the demonstration at Pushkin Square represented a Rubicon for all those participating in it. To undertake 'the walk out onto the square', as this rite of passage became known in dissident circles, was simultaneously to walk out of one world and into another. It marked a turning point from private non-conformity, easily camouflaged in the landscape of indifferent loyalty that characterized the Brezhnev years, to public opposition. For those participating in their first demonstration or, for the first time, affixing their signatures to petitions protesting the incarceration of other members of the movement,[63] the sense of moral choice in the face of potentially dreadful consequences – and, moreover, in the company of others who had made the same choice and were prepared to face those same consequences – was of inestimable moment in producing solidarity within the dissident community and raising its spiritual *élan*.

Finally, the demonstration at Pushkin Square and accompanying petition campaigns occurred as part of the first cycle in what would become a spiral of protest and reaction that characterized the relationship between the dissidents and the regime throughout the movement's existence.[64] In January 1967, a fresh batch of samizdat activists was arrested: first, Yurii Galanskov (editor of 'Feniks– 66') along with three colleagues; then, Aleksandr Ginzburg (who had edited 'Sintaksis').

Immediately, a demonstration in their defence was staged at Pushkin Square and almost as immediately broken up by the police.[65] The subsequent trials called forth new petition drives on behalf of those arrested, whose intention, like many similar petitions and open letters of this period, was simply to persuade the authorities that the observance of legality and human rights was in the interests of the entire social order, theirs included.[66] Tactically, at this point, the organizers pinned their hope on the possibility that the appearance on these petitions of a number of signatures from members of the scientific and literary establishments would encourage the regime to come to its senses.[67] But in vain.

The trials of Galanskov, Ginzburg and others that took place in January 1968 initiated a new round of position-taking on the cultural–political field, establishing patterns that would prevail for the duration of the epoch of dissent. Relations between the movement and the regime took a steep turn toward confrontation, thus altering those between the movement and the liberal establishment as well. Compiling a collection of materials on the trials that was then published abroad, Pavel Litvinov and Larisa Bogoraz for the first time turned from attempting to persuade the Soviet regime and 'toward world public opinion',[68] thus commencing a new epoch of appeals to the West and regular contact between dissidents and Western journalists stationed in Moscow. Concomitantly, many intellectuals on the apron of the dissident movement washed their hands of further association with it and retreated to the physical security of the establishment, whose liberal members were taking increasingly hostile positions toward their cultural–political competitors.[69] For the next two decades, 'dissident' would equate with 'pariah' for the Soviet establishment, many of whose liberal members participated in a new round of petition campaigns organized by the authorities to discredit various individuals in the movement and to drive them from their jobs.[70]

The year 1968 was also a critical turning point in other respects. It marked the appearance of Andrei Sakharov's *Thoughts on Progress, Peaceful Coexistence and Intellectual Freedom*, circulated first in samizdat form and then published abroad, a work that foreshadowed his entry into dissident activity.[71] In April, the *Chronicle of Current Events* made its first appearance. This unique journal, devoted to documenting human rights violations in the Soviet Union, represented a vital communications link among dissident groups scattered throughout the country, overcoming their mutual isolation and building a sense of the movement's presence on a nationwide scale. Carbon copies of its typewritten editions – coming out at first monthly and then, after a two year hiatus (1972–4) on a more irregular basis – were also smuggled out of the USSR, thus establishing a bridgehead to 'world opinion' that leaders in the movement, more and more despairing of the chances for persuading the Soviet regime, intensely sought to cultivate.[72] The year 1968 also witnessed the liberalization of the communist order in Czechoslovakia, the 'Prague Spring', toward which Russia's dissident movement, naturally, had a tremendous affinity. It was, indeed, during that same spring that the term 'democratic movement' first appeared in dissident circles as a replacement for their previous self-designation as a 'movement for human rights'. The attack launched on Czechoslovakia by members of the Warsaw Treaty Organization on 21 August was answered four days later by a small group of intellectuals and workers who staged a protest demonstration on Red Square which, however brief (the KGB pounced on the demonstrators immediately after they unveiled their placards), was noteworthy as a daring display of civic commitment.[73] Leaflets condemning the invasion appeared in Moscow and in a number of other Soviet cities, along with individual and small-group acts of protest.[74]

While prospects dimmed for persuading the regime or for exercising influence on it via liberal members of the cultural establishment, dissidents searched for other allies. By the end of the 1960s, the *Chronicle of Current Events* had expanded its focus on human rights to include those asserting the rights of national (such as Crimean Tatars, Volga Germans and Ukrainian nationalists) and religious minorities (principally Jews and the Lithuanian Catholic Committee for the Defence of the Rights of Believers). Similarly, the formation in November 1970 of the Committee for Human Rights in the USSR was undertaken primarily to increase the visibility of the movement abroad, to forge new links with national and international organizations outside the country and thus to lend the movement additional status and clout inside the USSR. In reply, the regime broadened its array of tactics, became more selective in the measures that it took against dissidents and succeeded in driving two important wedges into that internal solidarity so important for a movement constructing itself on the basis of moral criteria.

One wedge involved recruiting defectors and redeploying them on the side of the regime. The most successful use of this tactic involved Petr Yakir and Viktor Krasin, movement stalwarts who were pressured and/or persuaded by the authorities after their arrests in 1972 to repent of their actions (which they did in front of Soviet television cameras), to give testimony against others in the movement and to summon their former comrades-in-arms to follow their examples and make peace with the regime.[75] This episode dealt a heavy blow to a movement relying on individual commitment to the moral imperative of resisting the Soviet

Goliath. It shook its moral solidarity by rudely intruding the dark categories of ambition, personal advantage-seeking and betrayal into what had been a community defining itself solely in terms of pristine and selfless devotion to principles. Innocence lost would never be recovered.[76]

The second wedge was a relaxation of restrictions against emigration, coupled with a harshening of the consequences for engaging in dissident activities. This tactic had the double advantage of countering some of the dissidents' criticism of the Soviet regime by demonstrating with thousands of new exit visas the authorities' regard for certain liberal principles, while at the same time depleting the ranks of their opponents in the movement. Worn out by harassment, searches, blackmail and arrest, many dissidents emigrated. Having been removed from their professional or academic posts, here was an opportunity for them again to work in their chosen fields. Facing perhaps fewer prospects for achieving their announced goals than seemed present when they had taken their first 'walk onto the square', this was a chance for them to lay down their burdens in some country where human rights already seemed secure. Less perceptibly, perhaps, emigration eroded the moral solidarity of the movement in the same way as had defection and betrayal.

Despite a brief revival of activity in the mid-1970s – occasioned by the regime's campaigns against Andrei Sakharov and Aleksandr Solzhenitsyn that rallied many to their defence, as well as by the conclusion of the Final Act of the Helsinki Accords whose provisions on human rights, officially endorsed by the Soviet government, seemed to reopen possibilities for this struggle in the USSR[77] – the close of the decade roughly coincided with the collapse of the movement. Above all other factors, redoubled repression would account for this result, especially the step-level increase in dosage administered in the aftermath of the invasion of Afghanistan.[78] Yet repression alone cannot explain the fact that, when the regime relaxed its policy enormously a few years later under perestroika, there was no resurgence of activity among those active earlier in the dissident movement. Moreover, perestroika involved the regime's adoption of a number of the ideas previously espoused by the dissident movement, yet dissidents overwhelmingly stood aside from the challenge of implementing them. In order to address these apparent paradoxes, we turn to the content of those positions on the cultural–political field taken by members of the movement.

By the early 1970s, the general profile of the dissident movement had been established. The positions that it assumed, exploiting the cultural and symbolic capital available to effectively all its leading personages, was one of moral resistance to a regime that it correspondingly characterized as immoral. From this perspective, an orientation toward political activity would run the risk of depleting this same capital. Whereas it accumulated commensurately with acts of free expression, resistance and suffering in the name of ethical principles, the prosaic aspects of political activity – say, working out concrete solutions to one or another social problem, or seeking some form of compromise with the regime – would only cause it to dissipate. To be sure, prior to perestroika the Soviet regime sent no clear signals that it was prepared to seek any form of accommodation. If anything, it tended to reinforce the movement's overall posture of moral resistance by, on one hand, signing international conventions on human rights that (with the exception of easing restrictions on emigration in the mid-1970s) it would disregard while, on the other, singling out openly political activity as the target for its swiftest and hardest blows.[79] But if the position taken by the regime thus largely determined the pre-political 'moral space' on the cultural–political field occupied by the dissident movement, it would also be important to recall how the movement constructed its own identity in the process of filling it.

This construction, of course, was not free of disputes within the movement, but that viewpoint arguing against any dialogue with an immoral regime would appear to have held trumps in a game whose stakes concerned status within a community expressing itself in terms of moral categories.[80] Those members advocating a turn toward more practical activities had little impact[81] as energies flowed in other directions – defending luminaries such as Sakharov and Solzhenitsyn, monitoring human rights abuses for world opinion or publishing abroad the journal *Pamyat'* that recorded much of the history of independent social movements in the USSR – which, irrespective of the influence that they had on the course of events in the Soviet Union, did promise a higher return on the investment of symbolic capital. On this field, where material interests were marked negatively, the matter of identity was paramount. As such, the discourse developed by the dissident move-ment was rooted in the dyadic construct of dissident/regime whose derivative pairings – moral/immoral, legal/illegal, enlightened/doctri-naire, freedom/slavery, the West/the Soviet Union – tended to preclude a practical orientation toward surrounding social circumstances and some accommodation with the regime responsible for them. Since, prior to perestroika, the Soviet regime never seemed to waver in its resolve to perform up to these expectations, it helped to secure the particular identity adopted by the dissidents.

Yet, intermittently at least, reversals in the valence of the binary opposition – dissident/regime – occurred at micro-level. Here, it would be important to recall the apparently incongruous fact that ideas generated in dissident circles found their way into the highest echelons of the party-state and there contributed to the process of pursuing some alternative course that would renovate the Soviet system, a process under way by the early 1980s that led directly to the ascendance of Mikhail Gorbachev and his project of 'perestroika'. The principal conduit for these ideas was the KGB, an organization familiar with the content of dissident thought like no other. In addition to the copious collections of dissident writings obtained by conducting searches of their apartments and confiscating samizdat manuscripts, KGB officers led innumerable interrogations and 'conversations' with members of the movement that frequently probed the critical recommendations that not a few dissidents were prepared to offer. Inasmuch as one of us was involved directly with the KGB in this respect, we can say with some assurance that, by the late 1970s, certain officials in that organization were displaying a positive interest in what some dissidents had to say.[82]

Nationalists and Stalinists on the cultural–political field

Khrushchev's dismantling of the Stalinist triad – limited as it may have been and partially reversed by his successors as it was – contributed to the creation of two other sets of positions on the USSR's cultural–political field. Unlike the ideational core of the dissident movement whose identification with democracy and legality represented an inversion of one element in the triad (the cult of the leader) these positions were established by valorizing individually two of the elements themselves: nationalism and the leadership cult of Stalin. A number of derivative distinctions would then follow from the positions staked out on the basis of these elements dislodged from the Stalinist synthesis. First, whereas the dissidents' emphasis on human rights featured the individual as opposed to the collectivist doctrine of the regime, nationalists and Stalinists would distinguish themselves from that same regime and from others on the field by the particular collectivities that their ideologies celebrated – either the historical Russian nation or the Soviet people with that same nation marching at its head under the guidance of Stalin's teachings. Second, nationalists and Stalinists would take sharp issue with dissidents over Russia's relations with the West. Important in this respect was the affinity between the primary terms in the discourse of the dissidents and those accented in the dominant cultural–political system in the West. Since the dissidents shared a more or less common language with Western publics and governments, they monopolized these foreign sources of cultural and symbolic capital. Accordingly, nationalists and Stalinists would attempt to devalue that stock by reversing the valences apparent in the dissidents' discourse. For them the West would represent neither a model for Russia nor a (potential) ally against the Soviet regime but an aggressive 'other' whose corrosive influences on hallowed Russian or Soviet cultural values and institutions had to be arrested and undone. Third, nationalists and Stalinists cast their identities in large part against the secular–rational dimension of the dissidents' discourse. In opposition to its canonization of the individual in his or her capacity as a reasoning, conscientious being whose proper communitarian life reflected these values in social institutions based on law and consent, nationalists and Stalinists substituted – with varying degrees of obscurantism – mystical notions retrieved from a suitably idealized past that enfolded the matters of the individual, society and the structure of authority into visions of some millenarian community founded on righteous belief that they alleged to be clearly visible in their rear-view mirrors.

Schematically, Figure 2.1 sets out the structure of the basic positions taken by these groups on the Soviet cultural–political field. The organization of this chart derives from a semantic model, the 'semiotic square', developed by A. J. Greimas and F. Rastier to depict the set of relations implicit in any signifying act. The structure of the model is constituted by the rules of opposition and inversion, such that any unit of meaning calls forth an 'elementary structure of signification' composed of: a positive statement of the term (represented by A in Figure 2.1), which is distinguished by its opposite (-A), its inverse ($\bar{\text{A}}$), and the inverse of its opposite (-$\bar{\text{A}}$). The terms in the model stand in relations of 'mutual presupposition' whereby the positive one (A) necessarily conveys as integral to its meaning the other three terms in the square, in the manner that, say, the positive statement 'white' would derive its meaning by calling forth the corresponding terms in the elementary structure: 'black' (-A), 'non-white' ($\bar{\text{A}}$) and 'non-black' (-$\bar{\text{A}}$).[83]

Following the logic of this model, we can regard the structure of the Soviet cultural–political field in the post-Stalin period as consisting of the relations among the positive term, the triadic construct of Marxism–Leninism (in weakened condition due to the official discrediting of the Stalin cult), its opposite as represented in the discourse of the dissidents, its inverse thematizing the nationalist element torn from the Stalinist synthesis and rendered in non-Marxist–Leninist terms, and what appears as the inverse of its opposite, namely, the Stalinist position. For our purposes, the model has two obvious drawbacks. Since it is

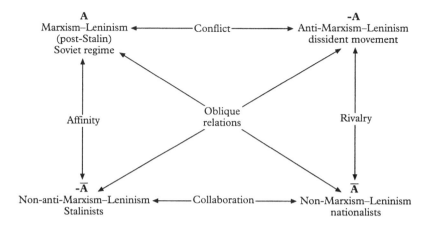

Figure 2.1   The structure of the Soviet cultural–political field (during two decades prior to perestroika)

synchronous and abstract, it neither captures the development of the positions appearing in it nor discriminates among the shades of difference empirically present at one or another moment within each of them. Moreover, translating its categories into those of our subject matter results in some abstruse terminology, particularly the rendering of the 'inverse of the opposite' as 'non-anti-Marxism–Leninism' (which is to say no more than that the Stalinist position, while opposed to the regime's version of Marxism–Leninism, was not constructed on opposition to Marxism–Leninism *per se*). In the face of these drawbacks, the model can claim two principal advantages: economy and elegance. The former refers to the fact that all of the basic positions on the cultural–political field are included in a simple formulation; the latter, to the symmetry that it discloses regarding the relations among them (conflict/collaboration and affinity/rivalry, as set out on the sides of the square). Below, we have occasion to refer to a few instances in which certain actors appear to behave in ways uncharacteristic of the positions that they occupy. These contrary cases, however, represent no obvious difficulties for our approach. Not only would they be consistent with Bourdieu's concepts of 'strategy' and 'trajectory' – according to which some probability obtains that actors will be disposed to produce new distinctions for themselves by taking risks that innovatively combine elements of one code with those of another – but these very cases constitute rare deviations from the patterns described by the model, amounting to exceptions that show the rule. Tellingly, none of them had succeeded in altering the structure in which it had appeared. Thus, the

model's utility consists in identifying the fundamental positions themselves and showing how these represent neither separate schools of
thought nor 'indifferent variety' but structured oppositions distinguishing by relations of 'mutual presupposition' that small section of the
overall population active on the cultural–political field in this period.

From this perspective, our attention is drawn to how the primary
constructs enacted in the discourse of each position define, and are
defined by, those of the others, resulting in the relations among them
that are specified on the four sides of the model as 'conflict' (between
A and -A), 'rivalry' (-A and $\bar{\text{A}}$), 'collaboration' (-$\bar{\text{A}}$ and $\bar{\text{A}}$) and 'affinity'
(A and -$\bar{\text{A}}$). These relations of attraction/repulsion would account for
the identities assumed by the various *positions*, irrespective of the
personal philosophies belonging to *individuals* who would take them.
So, for instance, the existence of a 'liberal' element within the
Communist Party, reported to have been furtively active in promoting a
radical reform agenda for the Soviet system,[84] would not count as a
distinction within this structure, since it would be defined against all
positions in the model except by that to which this element belonged,
namely, the Soviet regime. This liberal element would then be
distinguishable only *within* the position occupied by the regime.
Accordingly, in those specific situations characterized by an intensifica-
tion of conflict between positions A and -A, this distinction within
position A would readily come to nothing – as we have seen, above, in
the instance of hostilities between the liberal cultural establishment and
their competitors in the dissident movement. Similarly, individuals of
Marxist persuasion joined the ranks of the dissidents within which their
political–philosophic leanings would constitute a distinction that
neither added nor subtracted anything significant from the position
itself as defined by its relations with other positions in the structure.
Indeed, it would not be until the collapse of the dissident movement that
those articulating a Marxist discourse would be able to claim the
position left vacant by this collapse.[85]

If the dissident movement was pre-political – that is, as anticipating
rather than realizing a political practice in its fundamental constructs
regarding human rights, the rule of law and the desideratum of
democracy – then the other three positions depicted in Figure 2.1 were
anti-political. That aspect of the Soviet regime concerned us in the
preceding chapter; here we might add a word about nationalists and
Stalinists in order to complete our discussion of the USSR's cultural–
political field. The adjective 'anti-political' would refer to the content of
these positions as determined by their places in the overall structure of
the field. By valorizing one or another element split off from the Stalinist

triad, both positions consisted positively of certain fundamentalist 'truths' at odds with political life. This is more than a matter of abstract definition. Whereas the ideas espoused by dissidents, as well as the subsequent activities of a few members of the movement, contributed directly and importantly to the rebirth of politics in Russia, the same cannot be said for either the nationalists or the Stalinists. To be sure, nationalists and Stalinists would become players on the political field once it had been re-established. They would form parties, stage election campaigns, lead protest demonstrations and so on. But the trajectory of their political activities pointed toward closing down this field itself, in accordance with the mandate of their respective eschatologies. On the Soviet cultural–political field, Alexander Yanov's assessment seems to us a valid one. Despite surface differences between them or the planks in one or another formal programme, both positions 'share the project of constructing an economic and cultural model for Russia in which there would be no place for the intelligentsia sympathetic toward the West'.[86]

The right side of our model labels the relations between the dissidents and the nationalists as 'rivalry'. Above all, this rivalry concerned their struggle to define the grounds for opposing the Soviet regime, an issue that determined the relations between these positions. Nationalist opposition first appeared as the All-Russian Social-Christian Union for the Liberation of the People (VSKhSON in its Russian acronym), an underground organization formed in Leningrad in 1964 that consisted of some sixty members dedicated to staging an armed insurrection against the Soviet state and the subsequent establishment of an order based on traditional values and the Russian Orthodox religion.[87] The apprehension of this group by the authorities in 1967 brought an end to insurrectionary strategies in the nationalist camp. Thereafter, their activities mainly focused on disseminating their ideology via the written word, either in samizdat – an innovation that had been rather well developed by their dissident rivals – or in officially published periodicals and books.

Like those in the VSKhSON,[88] many adopting the nationalist position had previously been members of the radical Marxist underground. Following arrest and confinement in penal institutions where their views metamorphosed, they returned to society espousing one or another version of Russian nationalist ideology. Commenting on his own experience, Vladimir Osipov – who, for his Marxist writings in samizdat, had been sent to a strict-regime labour camp in 1961 – remarked that 'not without reason is a concentration camp officially called a corrective labour colony. They come in atheists and go out Christians. They have been *corrected*.'[89] Osipov's conversion led to his founding of the samizdat journal *Veche* (1968–74) whose brand of nationalism was distinguished from others by its relative moderation. While xenophobic, it was not rabidly so; nor was it overtly anti-Semitic. However, it also opened its pages to writers expounding such views and these proved immensely popular with the journal's readership.[90] Other manifestations of extremist nationalist ideology surfacing in the second half of the 1960s would include the manifesto 'Slovo Natsii' which was decidedly fascist in orientation[91] as were the views advanced by the circle around the economist, A. Fetisov,[92] or contained in the neo-Stalinist leaflet 'A Code of Morals' that issued clandestinely from the Moscow City Committee of the Komsomol.[93]

While at least one group in the nationalist camp, calling itself the Democratic Movement of the Soviet Union, explored the possibilities for joining forces with the dissidents,[94] the rivalry between these positions overcame any significant collaboration. The issue of the proper symbolic posture of resistance to the regime proved more important than the practical task of actually organizing a common effort against it. Moreover, the appearance of nationalist themes in Soviet publications,[95] the Great Russian chauvinist and Stalinist orientations assumed by official journals such as *Molodaya gvadiya*, *Ogonek* and *Oktyabr'*,[96] and the patronage afforded by the state to the All-Russian Society for the Preservation of Historical and Cultural Monuments within whose mass membership (numbering 7 million by the early 1970s) nationalists propounded their views and recruited new members to their groups,[97] indicated not only that nationalists could readily forge an alliance with Stalinists (which, by the beginning of the 1970s, they appeared to have done)[98] but that nationalists could expect a considerable measure of tolerance on the part of the regime. For this reason, as well as their common emphasis on patriotism – albeit with a somewhat different flourish in each case – regime–nationalist relations appear in Figure 2.1 as 'oblique'. Solzhenitsyn's famous *Letter to the Soviet Leaders*, in which the author advised the regime to keep its power but lose its Marxism, would qualify as a representative expression of this oblique relationship.

On the left-hand side of Figure 2.1, the relationship between regime and Stalinists is characterized by 'affinity' while the arrow running between Stalinists and dissidents is marked 'oblique'. In the latter instance, this connotes no more than the fact that although each of the ideologies advanced from these positions represented the inverse of the other, the relations between them were in each case mediated by the regime. Dissidents would sign appeals to the authorities arguing against the rehabilitation of Stalin,[99] just as official journals such as *Molodaya gvardiya* would fill their pages with Stalinist tracts denouncing the corrupting effect of 'foreign' influences in the country, influences associated domestically, of course, with the dissident movement. With respect to the affinity that we have noted in the relations between the regime and the Stalinists, we should underscore the fact that each of these positions, unlike the other two in the cultural–political field, shared a common Marxist–Leninist vocabulary which tended to muffle their quarrels, making them differences of interpretation more than differences of principle. In conclusion, we might rely on a couple of the exceptions that we have mentioned in order to show the rule here.

The exceptions concerned two incidents that occurred at the beginning of the 1970s in which official rebukes of Stalinist tracts were issued by top officials in the regime.[100] In one instance, the authoritative journal *Kommunist* overtly condemned *Molodaya gvardiya* for publishing a number of Stalinist articles and poems that contradicted the official ideology of the party-state prevailing at the time. However, contrary to standard Soviet procedures that required a reshuffling – if not a complete sacking – of the journal's editorial board in the wake of such a judgement, no jobs were lost and *Molodaya gvardiya*'s Stalinist orientation persisted thereafter. In the second case, Aleksandr Yakovlev, then acting head of the Propaganda Department of the Communist Party's Central Committee, published a long article in the November 1971 number of *Literaturnaya gazeta* in which he railed against the anti-Leninist positions taken by nationalists and Stalinists in a number of official publications. This episode resulted in the loss of one job, Yakovlev's, as the party-state's chief ideologist was packed off to Canada to serve as Soviet ambassador until Mikhail Gorbachev would fetch him home some thirteen years later to take up new duties as chief architect for perestroika.

Part II

Perestroika and the return of political life

This part of our study concerns a pivotal period in Russia's political rebirth, commencing with the 'beginning of the end' for the communist order and concluding with the 'end of the beginning' for the reappearance of political life. The four chapters in this section approach this double-sided process from two directions. Chapter 3 serves as a general introduction to those that follow. It surveys the party-state's grand attempt at reform, perestroika, from three different perspectives that characterize it, respectively, as: first, a reform designed to 'renew' the socialist system; second, a variant of the transnational process of transition from authoritarian to democratic government; and third, the initial stage of a systemic transformation that remains ongoing at this writing. Although each of these vantages proves useful, that provided by the concept 'transformation' seems most suitable to our purposes. It allows us to consider perestroika from the perspective of structural relations and thus to develop the relationship between civil society and property order that explains why the attempt at renewal had failed and why a transition of the Soviet system to democracy had been aborted. The remaining chapters make concrete the abstract discussion of these questions contained in Chapter 3. Each recalls our categories of 'strong' and 'weak' structures and illustrates in a specific instance how the weak structures associated with the Soviet form of organization proved incapable of transformation.

Chapter 4 focuses on the mass media under the impact of glasnost. From our perspective, this policy resembles an effort undertaken by the reform wing of the party-state to restructure the mass communications sector, thus generating more accurate, more reliable and more useful information for the authorities by altering the relations among those in this field. Instead of relying on the long-practised personalized forms of control over information – Communist Party directives and state censorship – glasnost would seek to introduce a measure of impersonal control whereby the regime would set general policy orientations that would be realized in practice via editorial self-policing periodically corrected by means of consultations with party-state authorities. This attempt to transform the structures of control would trigger new dynamics within the journalistic community, expressing themselves as a competition to push back restrictions on the permissible, correspondingly stimulating among glasnost's votaries a liberal ideology increasingly opposed to the extant order, and recasting the party-state's erstwhile engineers of reform as brakemen haplessly trying to halt a train of events in the publications sector driven by the new dynamics at play within it. In this instance, we see the first of the failed transformations examined in this part of the book. The attempt to reform the mechanisms of party-state control over the mass media would reveal the weak structural basis underlying the Soviet form of organization in this sector. Glasnost would mean that journalists would be less constrained by regime diktat but not at the same time subjected to other forms of discipline, such as those structures of domination characteristic of the mass media in capitalist systems, wherein owners, advertisers and executives occupy pivotal positions on the journalistic field that enable them to maintain boundaries with respect to that which is 'fit to print', ensuring that journalistic interpretations of the news do not transgress the bounds of capitalist ideology. The dynamics set in motion on this field by glasnost lead to a number of liberal publications developing an orientation inconsistent with the canon of the prevailing order and, with their hypertrophic circulation rates, stimulating the development of political subjects on a mass basis who would express themselves politically by decimating the representatives of this order at the polls in the national elections of 1989.

Chapter 5 investigates a comparable phenomenon, the emergence of informal organizations and their development into a political movement. Once again, an attempt to restructure the system along more impersonal lines of authority and control – in this case, establishing legal provision for forming voluntary associations independent of those sponsored by the party-state but under the general supervision of the authorities exercised via registration requirements and the granting of access to essential resources – would result in a breakdown of control mechanisms and the formation of an embryonic opposition to the communist regime. Like the preceding chapter, our concern in this one is primarily with the dynamics animating relations among actors on a particular field – in this instance, that of socio-political organization – which, through interaction, transform more or less individualized modes of thought and expression into recognizably social and political phenomena.

Chapter 6 is also about a failed effort to induce a measure of strength into the Soviet order. It concerns the introduction of limited competition into the electoral system that, by submitting a sizeable complement of officialdom to the voters' approval, would create a new relationship between regime and society. Those passing the test at the polls would enjoy the authority of a popular mandate while those failing it would have their careers resized by the impersonal instruments of the ballot which the leadership of the Communist Party could take into consideration in its own personnel decisions. Here, again, attempts to transform the structure of relations between regime and society and to create a mechanism promising to strengthen the party-state's actual capacity for government would lead to breakdown. Entrenched elites would violate the legal provisions of the electoral process with impunity, thus generating more popular contempt than legitimacy for the system, while the nuclei of opposition emerging from the informal movement would organize mass electoral actions against the authorities, initiating in the process a broad political front whose anti-communist orientation would imprint itself on Russia's political rebirth.

3 Perestroika: renewal, transition or transformation?

Standard nomenclature includes under the term 'perestroika' a number of initiatives advanced by the leadership of Mikhail Gorbachev that would change ('restructure') social, economic and political relations in the former USSR. As Mary McAuley, for instance, has described it, perestroika

> intended to produce major changes in the economic and political system. In the economy, the aim was to introduce elements of a market mechanism, and a variety of forms of ownership; in the political sphere, the vision was of a reformed Communist Party, still firmly in control, but a party whose officials . . . would, to some degree, be accountable to elected bodies.[1]

However, as soon as we descend a rung or two on the ladder of abstraction and attempt to characterize perestroika more concretely, we immediately find ourselves in a thicket of controversy. What prompted the adoption of this policy? What were the actual intentions lying behind it? Did it represent merely an attempt at liberalizing the Soviet regime or were its implications, if not design, more broad-reaching, thus heralding the introduction of democratic government? Has its ultimate failure shown that Soviet communism was, as many have maintained, un-reformable or, conversely, should failure here be ascribed to perestroika's partial, half-hearted and conservative thrust that proved inadequate to its announced task of reversing the decay of the Soviet system?

These questions in fact contain three distinct perspectives on perestroika captured in shorthand by the terms set out in the title of this chapter. The first two, which involve the perceptions and intentions of policy makers, refer to renewal. They direct our attention to leadership strategies, stated objectives and the calculations that may have gone into them. From this vantage, perestroika appears as a phenomenon amenable to investigation on the basis of the tools of policy analysis. Here the salient issues consist in how policy makers understood their environment, those aspects of it that they targeted for change, the specific measures that they implemented to reach these targets, the side-effects or unanticipated consequences of these measures, their subsequent reactions to these consequences and so forth.

The third question – liberalization or democracy? – shifts the focus of analysis beyond policy makers as a group directing a system, and toward a plurality of actors, mutually related in patterns of conflict and cooperation, whose interaction over time has the potential for affecting the 'rules of the game', thus generating a new political process altogether. This perspective has been featured in a host of studies documenting the transition from authoritarian regimes to democratic polities in Latin American and southern European states. Moreover, many of the conclusions drawn in this literature have been appropriated for the investigation of post-communist transitions, thus igniting a number of controversies in the field of comparative politics regarding the applicability of models formulated in certain areas or contexts to apparently similar phenomena occurring in others.

The last of our questions – was communism unreformable or simply insufficiently reformed? – enlarges the focus even more. Whichever side one might take in this controversy, one is forced to go beyond consideration of policy makers and strategic elite actors in order to formulate a reply that engages the question on the grounds that are implicit within it – the grounds of a communist system *qua* system. Rather than towards the rules of the (political) game, attention is here directed to the structures of a social formation. At this deeper level, the concepts of 'renewal' and 'transition' cannot adequately capture the object of investigation. Their immediate concern lies with the observable phenomena of politics, not with those structural conditions within which political activity occurs. To be sure, renewal can be interpreted to mean a policy aimed at accomplishing structural change, just as analyses based on the concept 'transition' might introduce certain structural factors bearing on the process of political change. But in both cases, structural issues are secondary. Analyses proceeding from an interest in renewal frame them as the targets or outcomes of renewal; those stemming from an interest in transition tend to regard them as intervening variables affecting the pace of transition, perhaps complicating the process in given instances. However, the perspective afforded by transformation would relativize the principal objects highlighted by renewal (the perceptions and intentions of the Soviet leadership) and transition (the dynamic interaction among strategic elites), and focus instead on those structural relations within which both leadership and elites are constituted and which themselves may undergo change as a consequence of the leadership's policy initiatives and/or the results of elite interaction. If it is an extant system that is susceptible to renewal and a rearrangement of relations among elites that counts for transition, then it is structures to which the term 'transformation' applies.

Our discussion of perestroika employs in turn each of these three orienting perspectives. Two advantages can be claimed for this approach. First, each perspective sheds light on certain aspects of our topic that would remain in the dim recesses of background when viewed from the vantages provided by the others. Thus, the separate perspectives contribute to a composite picture that emerges from the three employed together. Second, alternating the focus reminds us that what we see is contingent on the perspective from which we view it. This reminder helps to ensure that we avoid thinking about our topic in terms of some essentialist definition that would hypostatize perestroika and reify the human world in which it occurred.

Perestroika as renewal

The idea of renewal in one version or another can be found at the centre of both official Soviet statements on the scope and direction of perestroika as well as in the bulk of Western analyses of this topic. Whether, as in the latter instances, the notion of renewal has been encoded in terms such as 'reform' or 'opening up' – or, in the case of official Soviet pronouncements, rendered as 'a return to Leninist norms', ' a renewal of socialism' and so on – the common denominator here has generally been the idea that perestroika represented an attempt to introduce a number of changes in the Soviet order that would reverse its perceived decline by tapping certain sources of dynamism within it. In order to accomplish this, perestroika would restructure those forms of organization that had emerged in the Stalinist epoch which had either outlived their usefulness or had been inimical to the proper arrangement and functioning of a socialist society from the first. From this perspective, we could also apply the categories of 'weak' and 'strong' structures and arrive at the thesis that the Soviet leadership adopted perestroika in order to enhance their actual ability to direct and manage a system that had been spinning more and more out of (their) control. The thrust of their efforts, then, could be regarded as designed to repair the Soviet order by converting its weak structures into strong ones.

This thesis would be congruent with a wide array of commentary on perestroika which might seem on first inspection to be proceeding from different points of departure and arriving at altogether different destinations. To illustrate, consider the characterizations offered by perestroika's foremost champion, Mikhail Gorbachev, along with those viewing perestroika through more jaundiced eyes. Singling out perestroika's most radical aim, democratization, in his address to the Eighteenth Congress of Trades Unions of the USSR in 1987, Gorbachev remarked that:

Democracy is not the antithesis of order . . . On the contrary, it is a higher degree of order . . . Democracy is not the antithesis of discipline. On the contrary, it is conscious discipline . . . Democracy is not the antithesis of responsibility . . . On the contrary, it is society's [form of] self-control . . . the unity of rights and obligations.[2]

Given the personalized form of authority relations in the system inherited by Gorbachev, democratization recommended itself as an appropriate strategy for renewal.[3] It would reverse those systemic tendencies accounting for the stagnation that perestroika had been summoned to overcome: the personal appropriation of public office; the arbitrary and often corrupt exercise of authority; the ability of subalterns to close ranks against formal superiors, hiding information from them and, along with it, their own culpability for inaction, poor decisions and outright wrongdoing. Reversing Brezhnev's policy of 'stability in cadres', the Gorbachev leadership began with their renewal, launching the largest purge of officials witnessed in the USSR since the 1930s.[4] But altering the undesirable activities of party-state administrators turned out to require more than changing the nameplates on office doors.[5] And this democratization seemed to promise. For, in principle, it meant that authority would have to be earned; its holders would be *responsible* to wider electorates that had invested them with it. Additionally, it meant that authority would be delineated and graded according to an impersonal '(socialist) rule of law', thereby enforcing *discipline* on those entrusted with the responsibility of office. This was expected to strip away the dissimulations of officialdom, lay bare their machinations, recapture the system's lost dynamism and reclaim the future for socialism.[6]

Comparable analyses of these aspects of perestroika have been offered by Western observers.[7] Although they would substitute an ample dose of scepticism for that large increment of faith evident in Gorbachev's statements on the renewal of socialism, renewal would none the less serve as their yardstick to measure his progress.[8] The critical edge of this tendency would regard Gorbachev's perestroika as 'the last great myth' of the Soviet system whose pretensions 'toward social and political renewal' were rapidly outpaced by the forces that Gorbachev 'unleashed . . . [but] . . . could no longer control'.[9] Despite the glaring differences in evaluating both the Soviet system's potential for renewal and the utility of the policies intended to tap it, it seems that both accounts converge in depicting perestroika as a reform programme whose critical variable is the actual degree of control exercised by the top leadership. In one instance, the desire to achieve control sets policy in motion; in the other, the critic observes how this same policy leads to consequences quite the reverse of their intended outcomes, thus ending in a loss of control. This perspective coincides with unspoken assumptions that most of us entertain about modern governments; namely, that their characteristic mode of activity is purposive–rational and that, having selected certain objectives, governments implement policies that, in principle, have the capacity to achieve them. Within the ambit of these assumptions, the intentions of policy makers as well as the programmes designed to realize their goals would occupy the central place in the study of politics.[10] Since perestroika had been announced by the Soviet leadership as just such a policy, these assumptions would come into play. Irrespective of our assessments of perestroika, then, most of us tend to apprehend it in the language provided by its authors, that of renewal.

Approaching our topic from this direction, attention turns toward a particular set of questions: Who initiated this 'renewal'? Why did they do so? What were the consequences? Replying to each on the basis of the available evidence, we notice that some rather interesting aspects of perestroika come into focus which, paradoxically, tend to subvert the validity of that conceptual orientation, 'policy analysis', from which these questions spring. We begin with the first query: who?

Perhaps the principal source of ideas contributing to perestroika's intellectual thrust was the Soviet dissident movement. For anyone accustomed to the black-and-white categories generated by the Cold War – in either its Western or Eastern orthodoxies – this observation might be somewhat unsettling. Were not the dissidents the fervid opponents, if not the implacable enemies, of the communist order, the primary targets for its repressive practices? How could their ideas become official Soviet policy? To those considerations developed in the previous chapter regarding the specific relations that obtained between dissidents and the repressive apparatus of the Soviet state – particularly the way in which dissident ideas were channelled into the Soviet system via the medium of this apparatus[11] – we might add, here, an observation made by Vaclav Havel: where else would one expect to find serious and sustained thinking about the problems attending a state socialist system if not in those circles of intellectual dissent that had grown up within it?[12] Indeed, if we consult the text of the famous 'Letter to the Soviet Leaders', issued on 19 March 1970 by three of the leading figures in the USSR's dissident movement,[13] we find an analysis of the system's problems and a recipe of reforms for solving them which could easily be mistaken for a Gorbachev speech or a programme authored by the Communist Party's Central Committee appearing, say, seventeen or eighteen years later. Even the specific vocabulary featured in it – 'stagnation', the urgent need to accelerate 'scientific and technical progress', 'democratization' which should 'strengthen and maintain . . . the leading role of the party', the introduction of 'multi-candidate elections' and 'measures directed toward increasing public discussion in the work of governing bodies' – would become a prominent part of the regime's reform discourse in the perestroika period.

If the dissident movement contributed from without to that ensemble of ideas bearing the name 'perestroika', a second contribution was made from within by a stratum of intellectuals of more or less liberal persuasion who occupied important posts in the USSR's academic establishment. In general, their ideas represented revisions of particular elements of the official ideology of the Soviet state, revisions that appeared to owe something to the incorporation of certain concepts associated with Western scholarship. In the advent of Gorbachev's accession to power, leading Soviet journals published a number of articles challenging the correctness (from a 'socialist' point of view) of the prevailing relations among social groups and the institutional structures that constituted them. The condition of happy harmony prevailing in the Soviet social order, which had been one of the shibboleths of orthodox Marxism–Leninism, was contested by claims that antagonistic contradictions had appeared in society and that these, if unattended, could lead to explosive consequences.[14]

An extended analysis along the lines of this critical–revisionist perspective was submitted to the Central Committee of the Communist Party, among others, in April 1983.[15] This analysis argued essentially that the leadership of the party-state, due to the rigid and overly centralized forms of organization prevalent in the USSR, were more and more losing control of the society under their nominal direction. It spoke of a worsening contradiction between the developed 'forces of production' in the USSR and the country's 'outdated' system of planning and economic management that restricted the real possibilities inherent in the economy and accounted for the serious declines in its rate of growth. Finally, it outlined the 'objective necessity' for developing a new model of socialism that would account for opposing interests in society and secure their integration on the basis of a thoroughgoing restructuring of social and economic relations.

As radical a departure as these views were from the monotonic self-assurances regarding 'developed socialism' and its 'further perfection' that characterized the Brezhnev era, they were quite at home in the Politburo headed by former KGB chief, Yurii Andropov. Like many other top officials in the party-state,[16] Andropov had more than a passing familiarity with critical ideas worked out by individuals in the dissident movement.[17] Within weeks of assuming the post of Communist Party first secretary, Andropov tapped Mikhail Gorbachev and Nikolai Ryzhkov (who would serve later as chair of the Council of Ministers, 1986–90) to head a commission of the party's Central Committee tasked with preparing a programme to restructure an economy that in 1982, for the first time since the Second World War, had registered zero growth. Its initial recommendations were soon voiced by Andropov himself in his July 1983 report to the Central Committee, a report that outlined the kernel of what would be called 'perestroika' some two years later. Most importantly, it spoke of plans for instilling initiative among performing units by enlarging their autonomy while simultaneously imposing on them the putative discipline of those surrogate market mechanisms that in Soviet parlance went by the name *khozraschet* or 'cost-accounting'.[18] Along with this initiative toward supplementing the strength of state structures, Andropov launched another by explicitly signalling a campaign to expand and improve the sources of information available to the central leadership, especially those concerning the actual behaviour and motivations of individuals and groups in Soviet society.[19] Under Gorbachev's leadership, this campaign would blossom into glasnost and attention to 'the human factor' in organizational design.[20]

Perhaps as much as anything else, this term – the human factor – would betray the mentality standing behind the programme of perestroika and its emphasis on a 'renewal' of socialism. It suggested that not only had the leadership (recently) discovered that the order that they superintended was in fact composed of human beings, but that they were committed to taking this factor into account in their calculations for renewing it. As one of the principal actors in this enterprise, Nikolai Ryzhkov, has noted in his memoirs, the overriding impulse here was that of the engineer.[21] Accordingly, after decades of 'socialist construction', it appeared that flaws in the design were to be corrected by 'restructuring'. As another central actor, Aleksandr Yakovlev, has put it in his subsequent reflections on this period, the reformers laboured under 'the illusion that above all the entire matter [of improving things lay] in a sincere analysis of our life . . . [and in] . . . a self-evaluation of socialism, its "achievements" and potentials [a perspective which was freighted] by the inertia of technocratic thinking'.[22]

Alongside this engineering or technocratic element evident in the mentality of the reformers was another impulse that might be called 'moral'. Gorbachev has alluded to it by noting that the decision to launch perestroika stemmed in part from 'our troubled conscience'.[23] Vadim Bakatin (minister of the interior, 1988–90), as well as Yakovlev, have referred to simple human qualities offended by what had passed for public life in the USSR – described by both as a 'theatre of the absurd'[24] – and their increasing reluctance to act out their prescribed roles within it. Similarly, Oleg Bogomolov, one of the leading establishment intellectuals serving on perestroika's braintrust, has confessed his 'guilt' for scripting portions of the plays produced in this theatre, harbouring 'illusions' all the while that 'inserting into their [the pre-perestroika leaders'] speeches sensible ideas would make it possible to take even a single step away from dead dogmas'.[25]

The degree of influence exercised by this subjective, moral factor within the regime embarking on perestroika would, of course, be difficult, if not impossible, to determine. Indeed, whether one can speak of morality at all in this context is itself a point of contention. Many authors would seem to prefer more objective formulations – according to which reformers were simply responding to the erosion and collapse of the official ideology and were consequently searching for a refurbished regime identity[26] – that would dispense with any need to consider moral impulses. But the subjective notion of morality has a certain utility in accounting for perestroika as renewal. For once we admit a subjectivity into our analysis, it becomes possible to dissolve other objectified constructions and notice that, far from reacting to some alleged forces of history, the Gorbachev leadership was in fact making it. From this perspective, objective conditions such as economic stagnation cannot be counted as threatening the regime by themselves or forcing the leadership to embark on some course of reform, perhaps least of all the specific one that they selected. An explanation of perestroika preceding on the basis of the causality of objective economic conditions would certainly encounter difficulties in explaining either the violence visited on these same conditions by communist regimes in the past – say, the forced collectivization in the 1930s – or the longstanding neglect to deal with a deterioration of the economy as in the Brezhnevian epoch that perestroika propagandists execrated as 'stagnation'.[27] While Soviet reformers chose to present their plans in the language of 'objective conditions', this should disguise from us neither the fact that they chose this language nor that they had, as always, alternatives. To be sure, it would be equally mistaken to regard their language and action as pure subjectivity. They faced the constraints of objective conditions and they probably responded to their understanding of the incentive mix embedded in them. None the less, their decisions would remain just that: their decisions. And these seem to have been shaped by the general outlook under review here, an engineering mentality burdened with a 'troubled conscience'.

In this respect, subjectivity would appear in pre-political form, suspended somewhere between a technocratic consciousness expressed in the dialect of objective factors and a moral concern particular to individual actors. Perestroika appropriated this much from its own pre-history, the struggle between the regime and the dissident movement which was always a struggle of moral precepts, never one over practical social or political projects and the ways in which they might be realized.[28] As such, perestroika was from the start and would remain a philosophy without a corresponding social practice.[29] Yet out of the possibilities for action that perestroika opened up, and in apparent contravention of the intentions of its authors, a social practice, a politics, would emerge in the USSR; and it was precisely at this point that renewal began to resemble for the renewers that 'loss of control' mentioned above. Correspondingly, it is at this same point that an analysis of perestroika proceeding from the standpoint of renewal would give way to another oriented to the idea of transition.

Perestroika as transition

In contrast to the concept 'renewal', which would connote the continued existence of some (renovated) thing, that of 'transition' suggests 'movement from something toward something else'.[30] Since events have recorded the extinction, rather than the renewal, of the Soviet system, and since those forces directly responsible for its overthrow had waged their struggle explicitly under the banner of democracy, we might regard perestroika as a process of transition in which democratic politics and government would represent one possible outcome. Some observers have done just this, employing in their work that substantial body of scholarship concerned with transitions from authoritarian rule, thus defining transitions from communism as a 'sub-category . . . of a more generic phenomenon'.[31]

The vantage afforded by the literature on democratic transitions illuminates a number of issues important to our subject. First, it raises a critical question about the putative effects of socio-economic development ('modernization') on the province of government and politics, taking to task those arguments that implicitly or explicitly draw a causal arrow running from the former to the latter, thus suggesting that political change is an epiphenomenon attendant on the processes transpiring outside the political sphere.[32] In this respect, the transitions approach reminds us that, while such studies may contribute to an understanding of politics by alerting us to important factors conditioning political activity, they none the less remain vulnerable to criticism for neglecting political activity itself. As Giuseppe Di Palma has remarked, 'It is a dismal science of politics (or the science of dismal politics) that passively entrusts political change to exogenous and distant social transformations.'[33] Although analyses pitched around such transformations would have a bearing on perestroika considered from the perspective of renewal – conceiving reform as an attempt to catch up with those social changes that have outdistanced the capacity of the system's institutions to harness them – they would add much less to an understanding of democratic transition. At most, as Adam Przeworski has shown, arguments proceeding from the alleged role of those impersonal forces would be able to 'list all the possible states [outcomes of transition] in abstraction from any history'.[34] As the notion of 'movement' would imply, conceiving of perestroika as transition would mean grappling precisely with its particular history. Hence, a focus on macro-level phenomena – say, the incidence of higher education in the population or the percentage of the workforce in non-manual occupations – would have to be adjusted to micro-level in order to examine what the actors actually did.[35]

Of course, this examination would not proceed *ex nihilo*. Whatever is under investigation would be framed by the concepts applied to it by the investigator. In this respect, a second aspect of the transitions literature merits a word: its caveat against relying on the methodology of 'normal' social science in order to study the extraordinary conditions and processes intervening between the end of one regime and the beginning of another. By definition, transitions are 'underdetermined'. They witness 'insufficient structural and behavioural parameters' that cannot be counted on 'to guide and predict the outcome'.[36] They are packed with uncertainty, not only for the observer but, more importantly, for the actors themselves whose 'normal' orientations, perceptions of self-interest, and affiliations with social classes and so forth are often suspended or radically altered. The intentions of policy makers thus play a subordinate role in the transitions approach, for it conceives the process of political change as an interactive one, driven by multiple decisions arrived at by a variety of actors, each not only guessing at what others may be about to do, but often guessing incorrectly. Consequently, students of transitions underscore the broad range of possible and frequently unexpected actions that they have encountered, noting how these seem to be governed more by the interplay of subjective choices than by the conditions and shared expectations present under 'normal' circumstances.[37]

In view of state socialism's weak structures, these methodological concerns would go double for our topic. Not only would transition disrupt old patterns of behaviour but these have been rooted in structural relations of a type fundamentally different from those common to capitalistic systems, whether democratic or authoritarian. Consider, in this respect, the nexus between normal social science methodology and those societies in which it has appeared. From the vantage offered in the work of Michel Foucault,[38] it is clear that this methodology is not passive. Its constitution is consonant with the construction and deployment of certain forms of power, chief among which has been its capacity to 'normalize' the very object of its investigations, society. Normal social science, then, would be unthinkable outside of that ensemble of institutions and practices for whose existence it shares responsibility. These considerations would place the study of the Soviet system in transition at a double-remove from the direct utility of social science methodology, both for the reasons advanced in the literature on democratic transitions and because normal social science – and, correspondingly, that normalized society which it would imply – had scarcely existed in the USSR.[39]

Third, the transitions approach is inherently comparative, thereby engendering a knowledge that is not only cumulative but available for export and import. Even when – or, alternatively, especially when – certain phenomena accompanying some transitions fail to materialize in others, analyses informed by a comparative perspective would have an immediate advantage over ideographic approaches in isolating the phenomena (or their absence) in question, inquiring into the reasons that might account for, and the implications that may follow from, their want in the case at hand.[40] Of particular importance in this respect would be the sequential form characteristic of the literature on democratic transitions and, relatedly, its paleosymbolic subtext.[41] That is, beneath the social science concepts featured in this literature, it is possible to detect a storyline whose construction drives it forward from one situation to another. This subtext adds tremendously to the intelligibility of the theory's formal, sequential categories, giving them an intuitive plausibility over and above the data that might be marshalled to support them. In a nutshell, the plot residing within the formal constructs of this literature might be rendered as: a falling out has occurred among the elites who constitute an authoritarian regime over some issue that they have identified as critical but which cannot be resolved by consensus within their circle; thus divided, some or all sections of the elite reduce political repression generally in order to free up new sources of information and/or strengthen their respective positions in the inter-elite contest by acquiring new allies in society; once society begins to mobilize itself politically, new actors enter the stage, conflict and uncertainty mount and, eventually, a way out of the impasse is discovered in the form of an agreement (pact) among elites to transfer the issue in question out of the narrow arena of inter-elite competition wherein stalemate still prevails and into another wherein resolution appears possible (namely, a general election); and once democratic procedures have been introduced, they tend to become valued for their own sake (especially among the emergent political class that thrives on them) thus concluding the transition to democracy.[42]

Applying this scheme and its more formally elaborated categories to perestroika, we find both adherence to, and departures from, the overall sequence. As indicated in the preceding section, important elements in the Soviet elite had identified a critical issue (declining economic performance) on which no consensus had been reached for producing a solution. Thereafter, a policy of liberalization had followed in the form of glasnost and a broadened scope for the public expression of various viewpoints ('socialist pluralism'). But although there are grounds for arguing the conformity of the Soviet case to the sequence identified in the transitions literature up to this point, subsequent junctures provide reasons for arguing the reverse. Liberalization had expanded the amount of information that might have contributed to formulating practical solutions to the problems identified by the elite, just as it had strengthened the position of the liberalizers within the power bloc.[43] However, whereas a democratic transition is predicated on the continuation of a policy of liberalization required for a democratic outcome and for cementing the alliance between regime liberals and emerging political forces, at least until elections are called,[44] in the Soviet instance we find the reformers reining back their policy of liberalization once an election had been staged.[45] Perhaps of even greater moment, however, would be the fact that there is no evidence to suggest that conflict between the regime and those new forces that had mushroomed under liberalization was ever mediated by some pact that would provide minimal cohesion around temporary procedures culminating in a fair election.

The question of a pact has led to some basic disagreements among those viewing Gorbachev's 'democratization' through the lenses provided by the literature on democratic transitions.[46] To make matters more confusing, some of the principal crafters of these same lenses have claimed that while 'they can play an important role', inter-elite pacts are not 'necessary conditions of a successful transition'.[47] The problem, here, seems to result from reifying the notion of pact, and then viewing it as dispensable inasmuch as some 'successful transitions' have been completed in its absence. A more reasonable approach might regard the notion of pact as that which highlights a certain stage in the transitions sequence. The character of this stage, of course, would be defined by the sequence in which it appears, deriving its function from what comes before (liberalization and mounting political pressure on the regime) and after it (elections). Given the way in which the transitions model animates its actors – ignoring in principle the inner worlds of subjects and postulating a political universe in which the real players are taken to be self-interested elites engaged in strategic action[48] – pacts would function as one variant of that which this stage accomplishes in the larger transition; namely, the acceptance among elites of some set of rules that would resolve the stalemated and increasingly intolerable conflict in which they are struck by transferring it to the arena of a public election. Whether this acceptance takes the form of a pact or results from rules that have been imposed by a dominant faction or coalition would become, then, a matter of detail. The essential thing appears to be the function of this stage in the overall sequence, a function that mediates the transition from the phase of liberalization to that of democratization. Without it, the model would be completely unintelligible. Since the model's methodology includes only self-interested actors, the movement from liberalization to democratization would remain a mystery unless such actors identified the rules governing the latter as congruent with their interests. Otherwise, their willingness to participate in the elections that inaugurate a democratic outcome could not be explained, nor could their readiness to 'play by the rules' after these elections have been held. In short, we could not expect the self-interested to abandon self-interest. Whether various factions had reached a more or less specific agreement or had found acceptable the rules imposed by a dominant group, they would be participating in the democratic process because they had accepted its rules as not inimical to their own interests.

To what extent, then, might these considerations apply to the Soviet experience? Had the process of liberalization gone far enough to trigger a pact or its equivalent among contending elites that would pave the way for national elections heralding a transition to democracy? On the surface, at least, there would be indications of just this. At a January 1987 plenary session of the Communist Party's Central Committee, a compromise had apparently been struck between those forces, led by the party's general secretary, advocating the introduction of competitive elections, and conservatives who opposed such measures. The compromise contained two novel elements: a very limited experiment with multi-candidate elections at the local level set for June of that year;[49] and, subsequently, an extraordinary conference of the CPSU that would take up the question of democratization in full. The 'Theses' that issued from the conference in June 1988,[50] their subsequent translation by various 'working groups' assembled by the authorities into draft amendments to the Constitution and a new law on elections, the nationwide assessment of these documents that followed – involving both broad discussion in the mass media and numerous debates conducted by official organizations and informal citizens clubs – would resemble outwardly an agreement on the new set of political rules that the Supreme Soviet adopted in December 1988. Since the constitutional amendments and new electoral law could not be regarded instrumentally as legislation that created the possibility of competitive elections (there was neither anything in the previous legislation that prohibited such a thing nor anything in the new measures that required it), the entire process might resemble Soviet society making up its mind to change: on the one hand, a bargain struck among various factions in the regime; on the other, the public mediation of this bargain via the longstanding ritualized forms of party 'consultation' with the masses.[51] These events, then, seemed to present the visage of elite compromise and consensus on the question of introducing electoral democracy.

Although these features of Soviet democratization would recall the notion of pacting or its equivalent, other aspects of this same process would caution against accepting such a characterization. First, not only were political forces outside the regime completely absent at the bargaining tables at which the new arrangements were hammered out, but those that took part in the assessment of the new rules proposed by the regime rather uniformly rejected them.[52] At most, then, the regime succeeded in making a pact with itself. Not unexpectedly, the core of this pact involved not risk to, but assurance of, the regime's continued dominion. The elections that it foreshadowed could not unseat the communist authorities but instead promised to provide them with the appearance of unforced popular approval. Thus, the regime inscribed its own longevity into the new governmental institutions and the rules governing their composition. The 2,250 members of the new Congress of People's Deputies would be selected according to two methods: one-third by 'public organizations' authorized by the Communist Party (one of which was the Communist Party itself) and the remainder by voters in territorial districts. The two-thirds who actually had stood for popular election would have had to pass through what became popularly known as 'filters', a series of nominations meetings governed by procedures concocted and enforced by the apparatus of the Communist Party that kept the vast majority of their opponents off the ballot. Second, the elections that followed this would-be pact were not 'legitimate', even by the minimal standards of 'behavioural compliance' suggested by Di Palma.[53] Not only did the regime unilaterally impose a set of rules, it manipulated and violated them with impunity. In the face of this, other participants began to draw the appropriate conclusion; namely, that if democracy was indeed the objective, then not only must the rules be changed but their sponsor and principal beneficiary – the Soviet regime – would have to go, too. Rather than channelling and containing political conflict, then, the USSR's first competitive elections would aggravate and expand it.

At this point, the utility of the transitions model for analysing perestroika has been spent. Applying its sequential categories to the process of democratization has placed in sharp relief that critical stage at which the Soviet transition was aborted. Consensus on the rules was not achieved. Consequently, a 'founding election', leading to the institutionalization of a democratic order and to 'peaceful competition' among opponents, did not occur.[54] In order to carry the analysis forward we introduce a third perspective on perestroika, one that would situate it within the broader frame of the structures particular to state socialist systems. We begin this discussion by calling attention to the ways in which these structures foreclosed the possibility of a successful transition under perestroika by depriving Soviet society of the basic ingredients presupposed in the transitions scheme.

Perestroika as transformation

In the sequence identified in the literature on democratic transitions, the phase of popular mobilization represents that increment of energy necessary to advance the process toward a democratic outcome, much like a certain measure of heat might be required to change the physical state of water from liquid to steam. Although a considerable popular mobilization did attend the democratization process launched by perestroika, its content and character would be altogether different from that 'resurrection of civil society' referred to by students of transitions from (right-wing) authoritarian rule.[55]

This difference consisted in the fact that there was no civil society in the USSR to resurrect. To be sure, perestroika authorized some forms of autonomous private and public action, whether the 'space' provided for cooperative economic activity[56] or the licensing of social and, indeed, political groups. But the issue here would not so much involve the appearance or the number of autonomously organized groups as it would the structure underlying their internal constitution and their relationships with others, the state included. Although associations formed outside the province of the state anticipated a structural transformation in the direction of civil society – in fact, many taking part in these associations became instrumental in promoting it – they did not amount to civil society in and of themselves. From our perspective, those analyses that have conceptualized civil society simply as social and economic relations existing outside the sphere of the state[57] have identified a necessary, but by no means sufficient, condition to its existence.[58]

What, then, does 'civil society' connote? On the basis of his investigations of the concept's development in the West, John Keane has observed that it represents the outcome of a long process of historical transformation which, by the late eighteenth century, had been understood as one of 'taming and restraining the "natural" proclivities of human beings, their adjustment to politically regulated systems of commerce and manufacturing based on the private ownership of property'.[59] In this respect, we are reminded by Michel Foucault's research that the *negative* function of 'taming and restraining' has been inseparable from a *positive* one accomplished by the successive development, elaboration and extension of 'disciplines' into all spheres of modern society that over time have produced its normalized, 'civilized' individuals. The micro-level transformations effected by the methodical application of disciplinary knowledge have provided a sort of human base onto which have been erected the juridical forms of civilized intercourse, chief among which would be the institution of property.[60] Property is about socially recognized rights. Although these may assume a variety of forms – individual, communal or state-related – and remain mutable, their enduring characteristic would be that of a particular relationship among individuals that specifies the terms of their intercourse.[61] Over time, these relationships reflecting the possible modes of interaction contained within a given property system tend to be internalized by social actors, appearing to them as a kind of second nature. In a manner of speaking, a property system not only puts everything in its place but everyone in his or hers. It is precisely property relations that 'help a man form those expectations which he can reasonably hold in his dealings with others [and provide] the consent of fellowmen to allow him to act in particular ways'.[62] Civil society, then, cannot be specified as the mere *absence* of state control. It would also require the *presence* of a property order, articulated through juridical forms, that structures social intercourse, as well as disputes that arise within that intercourse, thus anchoring individuals in the matrix of its artificial or fictive forms in which they assume mutually recognized identities and interests.[63]

In the model developed from the experiences of democratic transitions from authoritarian regimes, it is these socially mediated identities and interests that spring to life during the period of liberalization, enfolding themselves in a mass democratic movement while civil society is 'resurrected', then rapidly demobilizing after 'founding elections' and the return of the 'normal': normal politics accessible to the methods of normal social science. The property order that structures civil society would not be appreciably disturbed by the transition to democracy. Indeed, within the model its inviolability counts as a condition for the success of the transition itself.[64] Methodologically, this would explain the privileged position occupied in this literature by individuals, interests, strategies and so forth. The social construction of the actors in the model requires no theoretic elaboration. It appears as ready-made because it has been accomplished by what the model presupposes: a civil society based in the institution of property. Accordingly, the sound and fury generated by a mass democratic movement signifies in this context merely a 'useful fiction during the first period of transition . . . unifying . . . the forces opposed to the current authoritarian regime'.[65] Soon enough, this fiction will be dispelled as the patterns of interest already inscribed in civil society by the property system will assert themselves and political activity will resume more 'normal', prosaic forms.

In state socialist systems – in which interaction outside the sphere of the state is neither regulated in a meaningful sense by property relations nor integrated socially by means of the institution of civil law – things are radically different. In place of socially recognized identities, we find what Jadwiga Staniszkis has called 'indifferent variety';[66] instead of socially mediated interests, we meet what Marc Garcelon has referred to as 'generalized unregulated particularism'.[67] With no civil society to resurrect, transitions from state socialism are necessarily deeper than those begun in authoritarian capitalist states. They involve a structural transformation. Accordingly, the creation of new modes of social interaction becomes in this context the project of a mass political movement aiming to transform the conditions of life. Although civil society and its immanent possibilities may function as a 'useful fiction' for this movement, the movement itself would represent considerably more than a useful fiction. It is the engine of that transformation itself. Moreover, the elements comprising it would share little with their politicized counterparts in authoritarian capitalist systems undergoing transitions to democracy. They have no ready-made organizations – professional associations, trade unions, benevolent societies and so on – to press into political service. Rather, they would emerge as informal citizens groups, not based on socio-economic interests but on various projected futures and, indeed, the projected identities of their participants.[68] As such, the categories of moral economy would be every bit as relevant to understanding this mass movement as would those of political economy. As Ken Jowitt has observed, the political discourse characteristic of state socialist transformations represents ethical imperatives 'moved from the purely personal realm to the public realm'.[69] And for good reason. This form of discourse had been available to individuals in the pre-political period. Not only had it been regularly practised in the intimacy of private conversation, but it had been fostered on the USSR's cultural–political field. As Igor' Kon has remarked, state socialism's mass media had operated under regime injunctions that encouraged moral critique of the shortcomings exhibited by individuals as part of the 'further perfection of (developed) socialism'.[70] Whether we consider the moral protest that formed the pivot of the dissident movement or the regime's 'troubled conscience' that contributed to its decision to strike out on the path that it hoped would lead to renewal, the moral–political dimension of the transformation that commenced with perestroika would be salient from the outset.

A methodology based on concepts such as the 'individual', the 'rational' calculation of socio-economic interests and attendant 'strategies' for pursuing them will not get us very far in investigating phenomena of this type. Therefore, our approach will focus on the dimensions of communication (glasnost) and organization (the 'informal' movement) that together set the stage for the appearance of political society in Russia during the elections of 1989. From the first, political society would be characterized by the relationship that it assumed with the Soviet state. In the absence of a civil society, forces on the political field would have little by way of established identities or ready-made interests to broker with holders of state power. Consequently, political society could express itself only in relation to state power directly, ultimately defining itself against the state. The development of this negative relationship is the theme running through the three chapters that follow. The one on glasnost concerns the forging of new identities on the cultural–political field while that on the informals treats the same subject from the point of view of autonomous social and political organization. The culmination of these developments occurs in the chapter on the elections of 1989 in which political society appears in the act of doing battle with its nemesis, the Soviet party-state.

4 Glasnost, mass media and the emergence of political society

During the late 1980s, the word 'glasnost' entered the international lexicon. The unprecedented openness and frankness that had begun to appear on the pages of newspapers and on television screens in the Soviet Union astonished the world. Perhaps inspired by what had been achieved in the USSR, perhaps unduly idealizing this achievement, citizens of this country or that began to employ the word 'glasnost' themselves, obliquely suggesting thereby that if such a thing could come to pass in, of all places, the Soviet Union, then surely they had a right to demand more information, more truth-telling, from their own governments.

What was this sensation, glasnost? Our answer to this question differs fundamentally from those accounts of this phenomena known to us. The difference, however, consists solely in the manner in which the question itself is framed. Drawing from our discussion of the various ways in which perestroika has been characterized, we notice that, from the perspective of renewal, glasnost appears as a more or less conscious and deliberate strategy of the communist leadership designed to attain certain ends. Accordingly, this view tends to focus on the intentions of the leadership, the means they employed to realize them and the results of their efforts. The transitions perspective shares some of these same emphases, viewing glasnost as a strategy of liberalizers within the regime who use the mass media to strengthen their own position, both by permitting into common circulation certain information and ideas that would discredit their rivals and by appealing to potential allies in society. Each of these approaches, then, frames the question by foregrounding the role of the leadership.

To illustrate, take the remarks of Aleksandr Yakovlev, widely purported to have been the architect of glasnost. In his view, glasnost appeared for no 'objective' reasons. Rather, it followed from the 'philosophy' of perestroika in two respects. First, the closed character of the Soviet system and its attendant dearth of available information was hardly conducive to the formulation of sound policy. Therefore, to set policy effectively and to pursue that renovation of the Soviet economy on which the Gorbachev leadership had fixed its sights, information flows had to be freed up and the accuracy of information improved. Second, Yakovlev has spoken, albeit vaguely, of some political moment with regard to the new policy, referring to the people generally, and to the technical intelligentsia in particular, as groups who would favour this new policy. In his view, these groups could be mobilized by the new leadership both to counter the conservatism of the entrenched party-state apparatus (expected to sandbag perestroika) and to contribute their energies and support to the leadership's new course.[1]

Western commentary on glasnost, while often introducing other considerations, has not fundamentally departed from the top-down perspective presented by Yakovlev. Some observers have focused on the second of his desiderata – building support among key groups in the population for the leadership's programme of economic reform[2] – while others have paid more attention to the first one, the leadership's intention of generating more information about the actual state of affairs in the country in order to enhance the effectiveness of its policies.[3] Related characterizations can be found in the Western literature as well. One is that glasnost represented an attempt to regain for the Soviet means of mass communication the credibility that had been seriously eroded by the increasing presence of foreign sources of information.[4] Another is that glasnost had been designed to enhance the longstanding function of mass socialization performed by the media in the USSR. In one version of this view, glasnost had involved an incremental change in the level of public discussion intended to increase the manipulative potential of regime-controlled messages aimed at the population.[5] In another, glasnost had represented 'a principal fulcrum in a massive effort at social engineering directed as much at reconstructing Soviet political culture as at reforming the structures of power'.[6] Irrespective of the specific intentions or purposes alleged to define glasnost as a policy, however, these characterizations all coincide with the perspective evident in Yakovlev's account.

Our view is different. While we by no means regard the top-down perspective as in itself mistaken, we do see it as not fully up to the task of explaining what this complex social phenomenon – glasnost – actually amounted to. Hence, we attempt an alternative interpretation that regards the Soviet mass media in this period as a politically contested site over which a number of opposing groups would struggle to define both the world and the words that could be said about it. At the top of the list was the word 'glasnost', itself. What did it mean? What were its limits? Could these be extended? And, finally, who should decide the question of what news was fit to print? It was in the vortex of these struggles that political subjects began to appear and develop in Russia. From our vantage, then, glasnost was not so much a top-down but an interactive process; and it was this very interaction that accounted for the particular ways in which political subjects formed their respective identities, making themselves over in opposition to either real or phantom others with whom they found themselves locked in a contest over the principal prize of any political fight: symbols.

Glasnost introduced

Let's begin at the top. Gorbachev's early encomia to glasnost – delivered in speeches to top editors and media professionals on 11 December 1984 and, on assuming the leading position in the Communist Party, to its Central Committee on 11 March 1985 and at the famous April Plenum that followed – represented in themselves no new departures for the party's general secretary. As Vera Tolz has observed, all of Gorbachev's predecessors had used the word 'glasnost' to describe their policy toward the means of mass communication.[7] Indeed, the word had appeared frequently in Soviet articles and monographs on government, party life and the mass media that were published in the pre-perestroika period.[8] What made glasnost, this time around, different? The bulk of the answer to this question will not lie with the intentions of the political leadership. Rather, it will involve the dynamics inherent within the practice of journalism during this period of Soviet history. We come to this topic shortly. But giving those at the top their due, we begin with the question: what did the Gorbachev leadership contribute to this 'different' glasnost that would serve as the clearest example of 'the changes' introduced by perestroika?

The initial strategy of the reformers in the Kremlin was to induce change in the Soviet system by changing those entrusted with managing it. Accordingly, under the aegis of Aleksandr Yakovlev – whom Gorbachev had sponsored to lead the Propaganda Department of the Central Committee of the Communist Party in mid-1985 and who shortly thereafter became a secretary of the Central Committee over-seeing the field of mass communications – some significant new appointments were made to the editorships of a number of newspapers and journals that would become flagship and fleet of glasnost in the months to come. *Moscow News*, that organ of Soviet communism hitherto published primarily for the foreign reader,[9] would emerge as the weekly embodiment of glasnost under the direction of Egor Yakovlev and other liberal colleagues of the 'sixties generation' such as Len

Karpinskii.[10] Similar personnel changes occurred among a number of journals and weekly newspapers, parachuting liberals into the leadership of their editorial boards: Vitalii Korotich was named editor of *Ogonek*, Georgii Baklanov took over at *Znamya*, Sergei Zalygin at *Novyi mir*, Boris Nikolskii at *Neva* and Vladislav Starkov at *Argumenty i fakty*.

The second contribution of the reformers to this different glasnost was a rather vague licensing of journalistic activities mandating the use of critical reporting in the cause of renewing the socialist system. In January 1986, the Central Committee of the CPSU passed a resolution, 'On crude administration and the suppression of criticism in the newspapers *Air Transport* and *Water Transport*', which took to task the trade unions respectively publishing these papers for scotching critical reporting from their pages in a manner 'not corresponding to the course [set by] the April (1985) Plenum of the Central Committee of the Communist Party for the open and upright assessment of social problems that are ripe [for discussion]'.[11] Within two weeks the official organ of the Communist Party, *Pravda*, would open the season on one such problem – 'the special dining facilities, special shops, special hospitals and so forth' enjoyed as unearned privileges by party-state officials – with an article that its editor, Viktor Afanas'ev, would later describe as 'the beginning of glasnost': namely, a cue that *Pravda* had provided to all newspapers and journals that this is what the Central Committee of the party has in mind under its new rules for the press.[12]

By June 1986, the setting of such new rules had gone a step further with a drastic reduction of the functions assigned to the organ of state censorship, Glavlit. Rather than the rigid and often arbitrary regulation of the means of mass communication as practised in the past, the Gorbachev leadership would rely on more flexible consultations between editors and party officials. The general secretary would himself often participate in meetings with leading writers and representatives of the mass media, sometimes encouraging them to tackle new themes[13] or to recover the country's past by filling in the many 'blank spaces' that remained in Soviet history.[14] Of perhaps even greater moment than the lengthening of the journalists' leash, however, was the decision to place its grip in the journalists' own hands. That is, on the basis of more or less regularized consultation with Communist Party authorities, editorial boards would be expected to police themselves.

The new mechanism for controlling the practice of journalism thus had two sides. One included editors, writers, party-state officials and eventually – as we see, below – a host of others. Over the period of glasnost, interaction among these actors drove forward the process of liberalization, sending it in directions scarcely anticipated by the actors themselves. The other side of self-policing, however, was intra-subjective. It involved what has been broadly known in the circles of Soviet and (now) Russian journalism as the 'internal censor' or 'self-editor'. It has been described by Vladislav Starkov, editor of *Argumenty i fakty*, with words uttered years later when glasnost was already giving way to full press freedom:

As editor, for example, just as before I have the same old problem: that internal self-editor who has been cultivated in [all] young journalists since the time of their professional training. Even now in the epoch of relative glasnost this [self-editor] does not give [journalists] the opportunity to show their real worth. I ask [him], 'What are you going to chop?' He says, 'I was afraid that you were about to chop it?' 'You know me,' I reply, 'you already have been able to understand that this time I'm going to keep it.' He goes silent.[15]

One of the quiet dramas of glasnost contributing to the recovery of political life in Russia was thus acted out in the interiors of the journalistic community. It entailed an often protracted effort to restructure, so to speak, their own professional selves from the inside out. But the process transpiring within individual journalists reflected, gave impetus to, and drew courage from, a corresponding struggle taking place between the authorities and the press that transformed the nature of public communication in the USSR.

Authority and the press

With the relaxation of censorship and vague commissions to expose the wrongdoing and furtive privileges of party-state functionaries and to 'study the new phenomena of life',[16] liberal publications set off by trial and error to explore the limits of the permissible. We would underscore in this respect the idea of exploration. On the one hand, it would be mistaken in our view to regard journalists, even the most liberal ones, as possessed of ready-made agendas for press freedom and open criticism which they brought to fruition one step at a time. Rather, in our understanding, journalists contributed to a collective process that swept them along as individuals, transforming their own conceptions of their craft and their roles as the process developed. On the other, the regime-imposed boundaries around press freedom proved to be not only elastic but chimerical.

Consider in this respect Gorbachev's remarks, delivered in January 1988 before an audience of leading figures from the field of mass communications: 'We are for glasnost without any reservations or limitations, but we are for glasnost in the interests of socialism.'[17] Who would object to this formulation? Indeed, the various slogans adopted to define the role of the press – 'a return to Leninist norms', 'the renewal of socialism' and so forth – were marvels of political ambiguity, enabling liberals and conservatives alike to share the same symbols and terms even while they might understand them in radically different ways. As conservative Politburo member, Egor Ligachev, would later recount, 'Leninist norms' for him have always meant that the role of the press is to shape public opinion according to the precepts and directives of the Communist Party. And then, to his horror, he had learnt at a meeting of the Politburo from Aleksandr Yakovlev, then supervising Soviet press, television and radio that 'the major task of the means of mass communications is to reflect that which is going on in life, in society. There is nothing astonishing in the fact that today [the mass media] are as they are.'[18] For Yakovlev *this* would clearly have been the essence of 'Leninist norms' and a 'renewal of socialism'.

To the notion that would-be discriminators such as 'socialism' represented no clear boundary between the permitted and the proscribed, we might add another element prominent in the profile cultivated by the Gorbachev leadership that helped to propel the press further along the path of opening new topics for public discussion. This was the aura of dynamic change that Gorbachev sought to promote for his leadership. In certain respects, Gorbachev fell victim to his own device. In May 1989 he chastized Egor Yakovlev of *Moscow News* by telephone for publishing an article implicating the Soviet army in the massacre of Polish officers at Katyn during the Second World War.[19] At a meeting with leading editors later that same year he threatened Vladislav Starkov with the sack for publishing both a letter from fifty construction workers criticizing the building of luxury residences for Communist Party officials and a readers' poll rating the popularity of members of the Congress of People's Deputies that placed members of the opposition – Andrei Sakharov, Gavriil Popov, Boris El'tsin and Yurii Afanas'ev – in the top four spots.[20] The following year, he thundered before the Central Committee about the media's 'abuse of glasnost for the purpose of incitement'.[21] In 1991 he mooted the idea of suspending the law on press freedom adopted only six months earlier.[22] These instances seem to reveal a Soviet leader either reluctant or simply helpless to rein in that one institution that would sustain his image as the author of change. The pressure from below and from around him in the ranks of party officialdom was enormous. Beginning with the Twenty-Seventh Congress of the Communist Party in February and March 1986, fusillades were fired at the 'destructive', 'anti-Soviet' liberal media by innumerable speakers at all party conclaves during Gorbachev's years as general secretary. Ligachev has claimed that criticisms of 'the destabilizing propaganda campaigns' conducted by sections of the Soviet press and television were spontaneously voiced at effectively every meeting of the Politburo (beginning, apparently, in 1987).[23] To no avail. To return to the episodes mentioned above: *Moscow News* went on to publish more on the Katyn massacre after Gorbachev's admonition; following Gorbachev's threats to Starkov for publishing a readers' poll on Soviet politicians, the next edition of *Argumenty i fakty* would carry the results of a survey that for the first time in history scored the popularity of the country's leader himself (Gorbachev garnered some 66 per cent approval in this poll);[24] and his threats delivered in 1990 and 1991 served only to warn others that Gorbachev may not be such a champion of glasnost after all.

Although it would be mistaken to infer from these accounts that restrictions on press freedom during the period of glasnost were mere paper tigers – the repression and, indeed, physical violence visited on journalists by the authorities, especially outside of Moscow, would dispel this image immediately[25] – it also seemed that these restrictions were woefully inadequate to the task of containing the dynamics at work within the world of journalism in this period. Relatively untethered from the straightjacket of supine conformity that had characterized the Soviet press before the advent of Gorbachev's glasnost, without a firm ideological embankment to contain and channel the flow of information and ideas, the directive impulses operating in the journalistic community were thus opened to a fundamental restructuring. Accordingly, the interest of readers and viewers as reflected in sales figures or the content and number of letters to the editor, the professional prestige accruing to those who crossed what seemed to have been the lines of the permissible and published on hitherto forbidden topics, came to replace the approval of the authorities as the principal ingredients in the amalgam of journalistic motivations. Indicatively, it was in the state structures of mass communications that perestroika began the process of transformation, and it was these structures that were the first to buckle and break.

In 1988, the USSR enrolled a new item on its list of deficit goods: newspapers. Although the volume of dailies had increased since 1985 by some 23 million copies per day,[26] supply now lagged painfully behind the burgeoning demands of the public whose appetite for news seemed to grow in proportion to its provision.[27] People queued at kiosks in anticipation of a delivery of the latest number of, say, *Moscow News* or *Argumenty i fakty*. When deliveries were made, they often sold out in minutes. If one of the goals of glasnost was to restore credibility to the Soviet mass media, then in this respect the policy scored a huge success. For example, once the jamming of foreign radio transmissions was terminated, the number of people tuning in to the BBC, Radio Liberty or other Western broadcasts rose to an estimated 67 million in the late 1980s, then fell just as precipitously – by as much as 50 per cent – at the end of the decade.[28] It would seem that the Soviet public had turned in massive numbers to the country's own sources of information. Journalists can be credited with this turnabout in public preferences by supplying what was of interest to readers and viewers. In the process, they were not only actively abetting the emergence of a citizenry interested in learning about their common affairs; through interaction with others on the field of journalism, they were reconstituting themselves.

A seminal article by the historian turned publicist, Yurii Afanas'ev, would illustrate this point. Under licence from one of the typically vague directives of the Central Committee of the CPSU 'to create favourable conditions for courageous scientific research [that would] overcome scholasticism, dogmatism and one-sided approaches [*nachetnichestva*]',[29] Afanas'ev took to task his own profession, arguing that Soviet historiography was 'stagnant and in the main lagged behind world standards'.[30] He then went on to argue that the 'Stalinist scheme . . . for the construction of socialism in the USSR' had remained intact. The response to this article was extraordinary. Formal replies were drawn up by established institutions and by well-known scholars.[31] The article was excised from copies of *Moscow News* that were held on library shelves, although it would be impossible to determine in a given instance whether this was due to spontaneous privatization on the part of patrons or to the ideological vigilance of certain librarians. A few weeks after its publication, Gorbachev told an assembly of leading figures in the mass media that 'there should not be any blank spaces in either our history or our literature', adding to his endorsement of glasnost the usual toothless qualification that 'criticism should always be from a party point of view'.[32] Although the general secretary's remarks have commonly been cited in Western accounts as the real beginning of glasnost, they would appear in this context as rather epiphenomenal, as an attempt to respond to a process that already had been assuming its own momentum. But the significance of this episode would lie less in the matter of who began the campaign to recover the country's history – whether the Central Committee of the Communist Party, Afanas'ev or Gorbachev – than in the interactive dynamics of the process itself. That is, the call to fill history's 'blank spaces' would be answered by a steady outpouring of fresh revelations that would not stop at Stalin's crimes but would dig deeper into the past with accounts that by 1989 were impugning the previously deified figure of Lenin himself.

The press and the public

There seems to be a certain intuitive logic governing the recovery of press freedom in Russia. In the face of injunctions from above to 'overcome dogmatism', fill the 'blank spaces' and so on, while simultaneously abiding by such empty qualifications as 'the interests of socialism' and the 'point of view of the party', it requires small imagination to understand how opening up one previously forbidden topic would but lead to the desire to open up others. Moreover, if we recall the unprecedented climate of public excitement generated during these years by the Soviet mass media, it may not be amiss to assume that there was pressure to be bolder, to explore new subjects, to increase the voltage of criticism coursing through the airwaves and coming off the presses. Just as journalists and editors had come to identify circulation rates as synonymous with professional success,[33] so they regarded the risky article as the key to it. Violating taboos drove circulation upward, while a supportive body of readers helped ensure their publications against official retribution.[34]

Although our focus in this chapter falls on the press, other forms of mass media had also contributed to the new climate. A number of films that previously had been deemed by the censor unsuitable for public viewing were taken from dusty shelves – in one instance, at least, due to the general secretary's personal imprimatur – and released to general audiences.[35] Some, such as *Repentance*, were personal glimpses of Stalin's terror that poignantly filled in a few of history's most painful blank spaces; other, such as *Little Vera* and *Intergirl* went far beyond previous restrictions in their portrayals of the sordid side of contemporary life.[36] As in the case of the cinema, previously banned works of literature began appearing in 'thick journals' such as *Novyi mir*, boosting its circulation by January 1988 to considerably over a million.[37] And television, the quintessential mass medium, took on a new profile as well. With unprecedented documentaries on the terror and repression of the past and corruption in the present, as well as public affairs programming featuring a critical perspective on events (sometimes supplied by interviews with former members of the dissident movement), the Soviet small screen played a large role in stimulating new forms of public consciousness.[38]

But there was more to this process than lightning raids on the fortresses of political orthodoxy and official truth. Indeed, the success of these raids owed something to a less spectacular trench warfare conducted by such establishment newspapers as *Izvestiya* that used its letters column as a means not only for relaying but for generating and shaping public opinion. An examination of letters to the editor appearing in this daily over a four month period in which the more radical exponents of glasnost were scoring their first major breakthroughs (February–May 1987) would disclose some of the changes that were taking place in the broader public. Certainly, there would be no reason to suppose either that the letters printed in *Izvestiya* constituted a representative sample of readers' opinions or that the contents of the letters actually published made up a cross-section of those that had been mailed in. Since the 1960s, the regime had supplemented its active prohibition against social communication with generous attention to 'work with letters', utilizing mass circulation dailies and weeklies as media for the expression of the concerns and complaints of ordinary Soviet citizens.[39] Published letters conformed to the prevailing standards of the active prohibition, to the point of relying on newspaper staff in some instances to confect the desired missives.[40] Although *Izvestiya*, during the four months of our survey, was likely continuing its 'work with letters' along much the same lines as it had in the past, selecting for its own didactive purposes which ones to publish and which to ignore, we can also observe some important changes in the manner in which it performed this work.[41]

Prior to the period in question, *Izvestiya* had already been receiving one of the largest volumes of readers' mail among all Soviet dailies, over 500,000 letters yearly.[42] To handle the sheer size of this correspondence the letters department had grown into the newspaper's largest division with a staff of over seventy members.[43] In May 1987, however, *Izvestiya* reported that 'in recent months, the volume of letters has doubled . . . [and] the character of the letters themselves has changed',[44] they have 'been suffused with a civic content, they have become more open. People believe what they have heard, that they don't have to hide their opinions.'[45] The particular forum in which this 'civic content' was expressed would lend it a special significance. Unlike either a sensational revelation accomplished by some champion of glasnost or Gorbachev's exhortations to the intellectual elite to engage in more critical analysis of social life, letters to the editor would involve a quite different frame for communication; one characterized by the familiarity associated with the words of readers not unlike oneself; one manifestly authentic, inasmuch as there appeared to be no motive for writing these letters other than the desire to express oneself, the desire to communicate. To illustrate, consider this simple sentence appearing in a letter that registered the writer's positive assessment of independent political initiative begun by certain 'informal' groups: 'All of us have been summoned to participate in perestroika.'[46] Were this same sentence uttered by Gorbachev or penned by even the most radical of Soviet journalists, then the phrase 'all of us have been summoned' could easily be converted in the reader's mind into 'we want you to do something'. Within the frame of a letter written by a fellow reader, however, 'all of us' remains intact. In this forum, *we* are communicating with one another, sharing *our* thoughts.[47]

In the letters column for this period, two particular themes assumed salience. The first concerned the existing system. Here, the tone of the letters ranged from angry to despondent. Consider these excerpts:

We must honestly recognize that there are many such people [self-seeking careerists, who] like scum have already come to the top of the wave of perestroika, they are again 'the leading ones' . . . Hoping to keep a warm place [for themselves] they cry with foaming mouths . . . calling on the working people to put their stomachs after perestroika.[48]

On the television and in the newspapers I see a revolutionary perestroika. But I don't live there, I live here. Here we don't hear the words 'perestroika' or '*uskorenie*' [acceleration], we hear 'hard times'.[49]

I am afraid that the decisions of the January Plenum [on democratization] will not be implemented in life. The opposition to a renewal of society is too great. Having sensed the danger, the bureaucrats have closed ranks and circled the wagons.[50]

The second theme represented an extension of the first. It concerned change. Here are a few examples:

though it is proceeding bloodlessly, perestroika is a revolutionary process in which someone loses and someone gains . . . Where and when have revolutionary processes transpired smoothly, without a hitch? Never and nowhere. We cannot retreat in the face of the first setbacks.[51]

the development of the initiative of the masses requires that competition be introduced into election campaigns, not only among those nominated [but among their] campaign programmes [so that] voters could evaluate more easily who among them fully merits their support.[52]

to confine democratization to the level of the economic enterprise would only make a game of democratization and nothing more.[53]

Taken together, these two themes in the letters – criticism of the prevailing order and calls for democratic change – signalled the emergence of a citizenry on the pages of one of the USSR's most widely circulated daily newspapers. The fact that the criticisms voiced in its letters column at this juncture were quite mild in comparison with what would become standard newspaper fare within a year or so would not be the issue here. Nor would the matter of introducing some kind of democracy into the process of government, although at the time this idea was still quite radical. Rather, the import of these letters to the editor is lodged on another plane – that of public communication by and for a public *in statu nascendi*. Accordingly, we should underscore the qualitative difference obtaining between these published letters and their counterparts in the preceding period. Whereas the Soviet press had long utilized the medium of readers' letters to air grievances and report on the malfeasance of local officials, the form of address taken by those letters invariably had situated the writer as a complainant/supplicant communicating with higher authority.[54] In our sample of letters, however, this form of address has obviously been replaced by another; the writer speaks not to power but to his fellow citizens. In this respect, newspapers such as *Izvestiya* were not only mediators of an emergent public consciousness but also its active purveyors.

The process of radicalization

Changes in public mood, as glimpsed through the prism of letters to the editor published in *Izvestiya*, would provide one substantive mooring for the increasing assertiveness evinced by a sector of the Soviet press during the era of glasnost. As subscription rates soared, as news copy and commentary became fresher, more candid and critical, the entire climate of professional journalism underwent deep changes. The influence exerted by the Communist Party's Propaganda Department – whose directives were now arriving only episodically and in vague if not contradictory form – diminished, while that of other factors commonly associated with the journalistic profession (readership and status within the professional community) correspondingly increased. These developments altered the contours of the cultural–political field on which journalists practised their craft, valorizing some elements of symbolic capital, such as the prestige accruing to those printing the hitherto unprintable, and introducing a stiffer and more open competition among those positioning themselves on this field.

Our principal concern in this section lies with the radicalization of the liberal wing of the Soviet journalistic establishment, a key phase in the reappearance of politics in Russia. In order to account for this radicalization, however, it is important to consider the liberals' relations with two other broad groupings active on the cultural–political field: 'competitors' and 'opponents'. The former consists of both old competitors – who had been members of the dissident movement – and new ones from the various 'informal' groups that had begun springing up in Russia toward the end of 1986. The latter includes the conservative wing of the Soviet press establishment and the liberals' longstanding opponents active within it: Stalinists and nationalists.[55]

Faced, on the one hand, by increasingly strident criticisms from their opponents directed against the defining characteristics of Soviet liberalism – glasnost and democratization – and, on the other, by competitors who would usually be a step or two ahead of them in defending and extending these same values, the liberal wing of the establishment press gravitated toward more radical interpretations of its liberal identity. We begin our description of this process with a word on the competitors.

In March 1987, *Moscow News* took the unprecedented step of publishing a letter written by eight prominent dissidents in emigration that took Gorbachev to task for promising so much while delivering so little. The unmistakable subtext of this letter warned against being hoodwinked by yet another communist 'reform'.[56] Western analysis of this episode has tended to focus on the sensation created by this letter: dissidents criticizing the general secretary of the Communist Party in an official Soviet publication! While this was, indeed, sensational,[57] Egor Yakovlev's accompanying reply to this letter's publication reasserted the division between dissidents and establishment liberals. Yakovlev expressed a certain bewilderment and irritation with these people 'still in the captivity of *sam0izdat*' who apparently have not realized that 'today one hardly has time to read what in the past was written in corners and now is published in periodicals and comes out in books'.[58]

Ironically, these words were penned on the eve of the largest resurgence of samizdat activity in Soviet history, borne primarily on the swelling wave of informal organizations. Publications such as *Glasnost* (edited by the former dissident, Sergei Grigoryants), *Ekspress khronika* (edited by Aleksandr Podrabinek), *Svobodnoe slovo* of the Democratic Union formed in May 1988, *Levyi povorot* (edited by Boris Kagarlitskii), *Otkrytaya zona* of Club Perestroika, *Merkurii* (edited by Elena Zelinskaya), *Khronograf* (put out by a number of informal activists in Moscow, including two of the present writers) and innumerable others were appearing openly, if irregularly and in limited editions, and thus challenging the liberal press's presumed monopoly on glasnost. Since the following chapter takes up the 'informals' and their publications, we shall not dwell on this topic here. But two aspects of the informal movement need to be recalled in the present context. First, the informals began their political activity as a kind of loyal opposition anxious to acquit themselves of any charges of anti-Sovietism. Accordingly, they also tended to regard the dissidents with suspicion if not hostility. As the group, Spasenie, stated:

All our activity is located in the channel of the course to perestroika chartered by the XXVII Congress of the Communist Party and by both party plena in 1987.

Neither we nor other associations are able to cooperate with that right wing of the human rights movement that speaks against socialism as it is. The position [taken by the journal] *Glasnost* is harmful and advantageous only to the bureaucracy.[59]

Yet even as a loyal opposition, the informals were not tethered to the authorities in the same way as was the official press. Consequently, they were freer to respond to events and would publish on subjects still too risky for even the most radical figures in the establishment's mass media. A good illustration of this difference between the liberal press and its informal counterparts involved Boris El'tsin's expulsion from the leadership of the Communist Party in October 1987. Accounts of this episode in the Soviet press ranged from the script composed by the CPSU's Control Commission – which basically convicted El'tsin of unfitness to serve in an important post – to attacks on El'tsin by the most liberal exponents of glasnost in the country's most liberal publications.[60] In the informal press, however, the shoe was entirely on the other foot. Here, protests against El'tsin's dismissal were published alongside demands that the Central Committee live up to its own declarations on perestroika and glasnost.[61] These informal newspapers, together with some equally informal activity on the margins of certain official organizations,[62] succeeded in running the information blockade thrown up by the regime around the country's most controversial public figure. In the wake of this episode, collaboration between establishment journalists and their informal counterparts increased markedly. Meetings were arranged, such as that at the Novosti press agency in July 1988, at which the participants exchanged views on the sundry matters of contemporary journalism in the USSR.[63] Informal publications circulated regularly through the journalistic establishment, some of whose editors would rely on informals for information and original copy. Subsequent forays by the liberal press into erstwhile forbidden zones can therefore be attributed in part to the influence exerted on them by their informal competitors.[64]

A second source of influence came from the opposite direction, from the right. Glasnost brought to a boil that feud between liberal and Stalinist–nationalist elements in the Soviet intelligentsia which had simmered since the 1960s when the liberal journal, *Novyi mir*, duelled with the conservative *Oktyabr'* over the place of Stalin and Stalinism in Soviet history. When *Ogonek* published the reminiscences of writer Yurii Trifonov concerning *Novyi mir*'s banner years of the 1960s, right-wing publications such as *Nash sovremennik*, *Molodaya gvardia* and *Moskva* counterattacked. As glasnost incensed Stalinists and nationalists by licensing public scrutiny and eventual demolition of their idols, the

contempt for the liberal press displayed by the right grew in proportion.[65] In its previous battle with the liberals, the Russian right had
developed its own ideology, an amalgam of xenophobia, celebrations of
national grandeur, anti-Semitism, and a number of other cock-eyed
conceptions connected with alleged 'conspiracies' and 'plots' not unlike
those with which the right wing has distinguished itself the world
around. Faced with opponents who claimed for themselves custody of
the nation and its traditions, liberals readily surrendered that ground
and migrated to ideological terrain marked out by 'the civilized world'
and 'universal hun.an values'.[66] Indeed, the 'renewal of socialism'
represented for liberal thought the suffusion of elements associated with
this 'civilized world' (read: the West) into the body of Leninist
principles. Like the process of petrification run at lightning speed, more
and more of these essentially foreign particles – market relations,
parliamentary democracy, a law-based state – lodged themselves in the
dead wood of the still official 'Leninist' ideology until they had taken it
over entirely.[67] By the end of the decade, the liberal programme had
been transformed from the renewal of socialism to the immediate
construction of unrestricted capitalism.[68]

The powerful impulse to distinguish themselves from their opponents
on the right would help to account for the many stereotypes dominating
liberal discourse. These, it seemed, were constructed more for the
purpose of shaming their opponents – the 'bureaucrats', the 'conservatives' – than for engaging in a practical manner the country's actual
problems. In symbolic jousts where verbal victories counted more than
concrete programmes, the whole issue appeared to turn on turning the
proper phrase, one that enshrined some incontestable principle so
validated in 'the civilized world' that liberals had come to accept it as a
simple matter of common sense. By implication, those not prepared to
accept it could be regarded as backward, ignorant or uncivilized
individuals whose arguments could be safely ignored. Among those
principles apparently requiring neither explanations nor further elaboration would be the stick-person of economic rationality. Pavel Bunich, for
example, would inform the Central Committee of the CPSU that
'financial incentives are the main thing for a society of working
people'.[69] Andrei Nuikin would tell his readers that replacing 'administrative pressure' with financial incentives would mean that 'we can and
should be rich. Besides, [this will happen] quite quickly . . . [had we
done so sooner] we actually would already have been living for a long
time as if in a fairy tale.'[70] Although Russia's eventual turn to market
prices in 1992 would be accompanied by the veritable collapse of its
scientific establishment, Gavriil Popov was convinced some five years

earlier that 'market prices will force the interests of enterprises in the direction of scientific and technical progress'.[71]

In one formulation rendered in folksy Russian, liberal ideology seemed to pivot on the proposition, 'If we have a market, we'll have a lot of pies.'[72] Indeed, the identification of market reform and democracy with high levels of material consumption was a hallmark of liberal thinking in this period, echoing the dashed dreams of communist abundance to be pursued now by other (capitalist) means. In a country so tortured by material deficits, it is perhaps not surprising to find social thought gravitating to subjects such as sausage. But the appearance of this figure in liberal discourse would also shed light on how that discourse was structured. In one respect, 'democracy' seemed connected with the great beyond: there, in the 'civilized world' where they have so much of everything. In another, it was also tied to Russia as a promise of those same things to come. Emblematically, Vladislav Starkov remarked, 'I am convinced, first – parliamentary chatter, then – sausage.'[73]

The sense of urgency and the dichotomous formulations so characteristic of liberal thinking in this period also evinced the influence of the right wing. To be sure, these characteristics were also derived from the semantic genealogy of perestroika that pitched its tent of Leninist revival on the common ground of revolutionary mythology. When Gorbachev called his perestroika a 'revolution',[74] publicists such as Afanas'ev would concur, arguing that 'the revolutionary energy of the people must not be locked in the freezer'.[75] Whom would this revolution oppose? Those, of course, who opposed perestroika: the bureaucrats and conservatives.[76] And then the notorious Stalinist manifesto of Nina Andreeva, 'I cannot forsake my principles', appeared in the daily, *Sovetskaya Rossiya*.[77] With its appearance official glasnost ground to a complete halt.[78] Until the authoritative chastisement was printed in *Pravda* some three weeks later,[79] public circles left and right came to the conclusion that this letter indicated that glasnost and perestroika had perished in a conservative coup.[80] Accordingly, party organizations and factory assemblies gathered throughout the country 'to study' the letter and propound a new, anti-perestroika line. In the Leningrad region, meetings in support of the Andreeva letter were even televised.[81] This episode seemed to focus all the fears of Thermidor that haunt revolutionaries. It now became clear that 'open and hidden enemies of perestroika . . . have bristled up and are able to deliver a blow to perestroika'.[82]

The sense of revolutionary urgency already present among those in perestroika's advanced guard was doubtlessly reinforced by the Andreeva episode. So, too, was the liberals' tendency toward dichotomous formulations. Though many fine words had been uttered about perestroika, precious few would supply it with anything resembling a substantive content. Instead of specific positive definitions, perestroika became fixed in social consciousness primarily as a panacea for the prevailing order, an order that perestroika's votaries dubbed with epithets such as 'stagnation' or the 'command-administrative system'. Perestroika, then, would acquire its significance not as a set of concrete practices but as an idea opposed to the extant and discredited state of affairs. This shadow significance was amplified and sharpened by portraying perestroika as the only alternative to the present situation. In approbatious reply to one of the stock phrases in Gorbachev's rhetorical arsenal – 'We simply don't have another way' – a chorus of confirmation issued from liberal publicists. For instance, Otto Latsis expressed his thoughts on the matter in an article entitled 'Another is not Needed',[83] while Egor Yakovlev added his under the heading, 'There is no Other Way'.[84] Indicatively, that sensation of mid-perestroika scholarship to which some thirty-four leading intellectuals – unencumbered by any form of censorship whatsoever – contributed political essays took for itself the title *Inogo ne dano* (literally: 'Another has not been given').[85]

The characteristics of liberal thinking thus far discussed – an orientation away from nation and tradition and toward what was thought to exist in 'the civilized countries', along with a revolutionary urgency for realizing a policy of perestroika, itself defined primarily as the putative negation of the prevailing order – would make it quite difficult to accept the common assumption that we are concerned here with reformers and reform. Rather, our examination of liberal ideology as it distinguished itself against its opponents suggests that thought was fashioned in and by struggle on the cultural–political field, and that the consummation of this thought was equated with victory in this struggle. The essential ingredient of a reformist orientation – a programme composed of practical measures designed to reshape existing institutions – had gone missing. Of course, perestroika eventually introduced political reforms. But when these occurred, most of perestroika's early proponents had been radicalized to the point that they quickly rejected them, announcing that the existing system was 'incapable of reform'.

In this context, 'reform' would thus be a slippery concept. Moreover, adjectives such as 'radical', 'liberal' and 'moderate' would be of little help for either sorting out varieties of reform proposals in a meaningful way or for assigning would-be reformers to various groups. On the surface, nearly all actors spoke the language of reform, but like so many other shibboleths of the period this word appeared to be little more than a common vehicle for advancing mutually hostile ideologies. Those occupying one position on the cultural–political field would debunk the reform posture of those occupying another – 'They speak of reform, but they are really conservatives who simply want to hold on to their power' – just as the latter would reciprocate in kind – 'They speak of reform but they are actually radicals who want to tear down everything.' Locating reform within this political milieu, then, suggests that its ordinary meaning had been largely, if not entirely, cancelled. There may be some social scientists who would like to repeat the Russian experiment with a different cast of characters in order to determine whether 'real reform' might have saved the system and whether 'reform communism' would represent a possibility in the universe of socio-political orders, just as a certain number of Marxists have long lamented the fact that socialism began in Russia, a country especially ill-suited to the realization of their project. The broad outlines of our discussion, however, would indicate that communism proved incapable of reform in the Russian instance because those forces that assumed political shape during the final years of its existence were not oriented in that direction, despite their superficial reformist rhetoric. At the core of the liberal world-view were concepts of opposition: at first, opposition to stagnation, to bureaucrats and conservatives; later, as perestroika proved disappointing, opposition to everything associated with the communist system, including perestroika and its chief proponent. Perhaps there was 'no other way'. At any event, the ascendancy of a radicalized liberal tendency in Russia ensured that there was not.

A note on the mass media and the formation of political subjects

A particularly concise indicator of the political orientations of the Russian population can be found in their reading habits. Rather than consulting, say, an individual's bank balance in order to predict how he or she might vote in an election, one would be much better informed by knowing which newspapers and journals the person in question happens to read. We make use of this indicator, below, in accounting for voting behaviour. Here, our intention is to identify the formation of the first contingent of political subjects that emerged in the USSR under the influence of the liberal press.

A survey conducted in early 1989 by the All-Union Centre for Public Opinion represents a particularly rich source of information on this question, especially inasmuch as the survey includes data on certain social characteristics, political orientation and activities gathered in a reader's poll conducted by the weekly *Literaturnaya gazeta* (*LG*) against which it compares a national sample of the overall population.[86] *LG* numbers among the more liberal publications of the glasnost period. Moreover, its readers would also be those who would tend to read other newspapers and journals associated with the liberal end of the spectrum and who are those more likely to read foreign publications and listen to foreign radio broadcasts.[87] In sociological terms, the sample of *LG* readers forms an identifiable group distinguished by higher education (60 per cent of respondents as compared to 16.4 per cent in the national sample) and professional employment (49.1 per cent are members of the technical or creative intelligentsia as opposed to 24.3 per cent of the national sample who had been so employed).[88] The survey documents a close correlation between those social characteristics and political orientations, observing that 'people with higher education gave responses on the majority of questions that were 1.5–2 times more critical and demanding than those given by people with middle-level education'.[89] Accordingly, respondents with higher education are those most likely to regard 'the domination of the bureaucracy' as the reason for most of the country's problems, blaming as well 'the dictatorship of the party' and 'the totalitarian state'.[90]

The comparison of the sample of *LG* readers against the sample of the general population recorded the fact that glasnost had promoted broad-scale political differentiation. To be sure, some differentiation had been present in an earlier period as such institutions as samizdat, informal discussion groups, semi-underground concerts and exhibitions would attest. But glasnost extended the process enormously, linking by means of mass communication the myriad of more or less isolated micro-worlds and engendering a process out of which mass ideologies would crystallize. This crystallization took time. Initially, individuals and groups emerging from isolation came forward with separate stores of information and ideas developed out of their immediate backgrounds. What they lacked, however, was a common discourse, a common code of communication, that would facilitate mutual understanding. By the end of 1987, especially in view of the burgeoning increases in the circulation of liberally oriented publications, this situation had begun to change dramatically. The common frame of reference that enclosed the country's first mass political community was the new discourse of liberalism, still working itself out on the pages of glasnost's standard bearers and buttressed by the credibility associated with publicists from the country's intellectual establishment.

This new discourse found a ready reception among an emergent mass public rooted in the intelligentsia, broadly defined. In comparison with the overall population, the sample of *LG* readers was much more favourably disposed toward liberal-populist ideas, agreeing that 'depriving the authorities of their privileges would be evidence of a positive change' (64 per cent among *LG* readers, 25.5 per cent in the larger population[91]). The names of leading liberal economists, such as Nikolai Shmelev and Vasilii Selyunin, evoked much more positive evaluation among the *LG* readers, who also distinguished themselves from the larger population by favouring in overwhelming majorities such measures as the right to private farming, reducing the size of the armed forces and military expenditures, the attraction of foreign investment on a broad scale and the legalization of private enterprise.[92] What is more, the data in these surveys would indicate that the sample of *LG* readers was far more politically active than was the general population; they were more inclined 'to address newspapers, soviet and party organs', 'to defend their own points of view at assemblies', 'to participate in the activities of new public movements, rallies and demonstrations' and 'to sign collective appeals, protests and proclamations'.[93] Beyond these forms of political action, the *LG* group – by a margin of 64.1 to 18.6 per cent – expressed dissatisfaction with their perceived ability to influence political events,[94] thus indicating a potential for political involvement that awaited a corresponding opportunity. That opportunity arrived with the national elections of 1989.

5   The informal movement: politics on the margins of the soviet order

The terms 'informals' (*neformaly*) and 'informal groups' (*neformal'nye gruppy*) would refer to those millions of Soviet citizens who took advantage of the relative liberalization introduced by perestroika to band together in associations independent of the party-state's direct sponsorship. By 1989, some 60,000 of these associations were functioning in the country, spanning a wide range of activities and interests: music, sports, literature, history, culture, religion, social service and politics.[1] The origins of the name for this amorphous mass movement have remained unclear. By the mid-1980s, 'informals' or 'informal groups' had entered the argot of Soviet journalism as a deprecatory descriptor for those people congregating outside of the 'respectable' world of the establishment, but a decade earlier it had also been used in Soviet sociology as a euphemism for teenage gangs.[2] However, the source of the name would not be as important for our purposes as would be an understanding of the significance that it came to hold for those to whom it was applied. It was precisely because the informal movement was rooted in one or another form of rebellion against the stifling restrictions of the Soviet order that informals would wear this veiled epithet as a badge of honour. The name became for them a vivid distinction separating their subculture – wherein authenticity, free expression and relevance were paramount – from the official world around them that they had come to regard as dominated by insincerity and pretension, one not only repressive but top-heavy with stupidity.[3]

Unofficial groups – from discussion clubs to insurrectionist organizations – had been to one degree or another a part of the Soviet social landscape throughout the post-war period. However, the party-state's readiness to issue limited licence for certain of these activities during perestroika represented one factor sharply distinguishing the informals, both quantitatively and qualitatively, from their predecessors. Already in 1985, as a response to the deepening disaffection displayed by widening circles of Russian youth,[4] the RSFSR's Ministry of Justice had begun promoting the revival of various clubs and the establishment of new ones in areas such as leisure activities, sports, education and health. During the summer of 1986, it advanced the process a giant step by issuing a new set of 'Regulations on amateur associations' that made it possible to form clubs and societies independently of party-state tutelage and to register these associations with local authorities, thus granting them access to the various resources required for their activities: premises, equipment, printing facilities and the like.[5] The ensuing flurry of youth organizing – occurring now outside, but enjoying none the less the imprimatur of, the party-state – launched the informal movement.

Although our focus in this chapter falls on that fraction of the movement distinguished by their direct involvement with politics,[6] we begin by situating them within the larger domain from which they emerged and whose overall characteristics would in many ways define their political practices. The first and most obvious characteristic of the informals would be their youthful profile. For instance, according to a study carried out in Moscow, some 90 per cent of those belonging to informal associations in 1987 had not reached the age of twenty-five.[7] For young people coming of age, informal associations provided a matchless venue for simply finding themselves, being themselves and expressing themselves in the absence of – and often enough *against* – authority. In the words of one member of the movement,

We've put on these leather jackets with studs and named ourselves with the loud word 'punks' in order to show everyone that we exist. Yes, we're filthy, ragged [and] strange, but we are your children. Yours by your own hypocrisy and lies. Yours by your own correctness in words and in slogans but not in real life. Society has given birth to us and now tries to blow us off [*otmakhnut'sya*].[8]

As even these petulant remarks might suggest, the desire to open up some new social space for oneself and one's peers was not tantamount to seeking complete detachment from society. On the contrary, the informals represented from the first a movement of social consciousness looking for outlets in concrete social action.[9] Since their attitudes toward established authority ranged from indifference to contempt, they sought these outlets outside of the official structures.[10]

A second and related characteristic of the informal movement was the phenomenon of 'initiativism' (*initsiativnost'*), an orientation toward addressing one or another specific social concern by means of pragmatic, remedial measures. Initiativism, then, was not directed against the Soviet system but toward various lacunae evident in its capacity to solve social problems, thus casting early informal organizations in the role of auxiliaries rather than opponents. It pertained mainly to three clusters of concerns: the socialization and development of young people; the defence of cultural and historic sites; and environmental protection. Perhaps the outstanding example of the first would be Moscow's Club of Social Innovators that was founded in February 1987.[11] This club brought together scores of young professionals working in the natural and social sciences and in pedagogy in order to develop 'scientifically-based programmes, projects, models and technologies' for promoting the harmonious development of the individual and society. 'Perestroika', the club's charter continued, 'above all [meant] new social technologies in the areas of labour, education, upbringing, creativity, leisure, sports and so forth.' These efforts were extended to the larger Moscow region – and to others such as Volgograd, Penza and the Urals – by the Fund of Social Initiatives (FSI), founded a few months later to support and coordinate local initiatives in these areas as well as to 'combat the appearance of anti-socialist views, dogmatism and conservatism in the social consciousness'.[12] As we see, below, this group would occupy a pivotal position in the multi-layered political relations that developed within the informal movement and between the informals and various sectors of the party-state apparatus in Moscow.

Examples of initiativism directed toward the preservation of cultural and historical sites and toward environmental protection were legion. Among the former, the most important would be the Moscow group Svoboda (Freedom) – which launched petition and letter campaigns and set up outdoor photo exhibits in 1986 to dramatize its concerns for protecting historic buildings in the Bauman district[13] – and its Leningrad counterpart Spasenie (Salvation) whose actions in 1986–7 to spare historical buildings the wrecker's ball (including a rally that drew some 3,000 people) quickly made it a force to be reckoned with in that city.[14] A large portion of Spasenie's efforts were channelled into the country's emerging ecological movement which, in the face of the party-state's appalling disregard for the natural environment and its willingness to subject the population to life-threatening levels of air and water pollution, grew rapidly into a vocal opposition to official policies and practices. In May 1987, the Movement for the Defense of Baikal was organized by scientific personnel in Irkutsk. In June its first protest rally brought out about 1,000 people; within a year its actions were drawing over 10,000.[15] In Volgograd the club Ecology was turning out as many as 5,000 people to its mass meetings, while the Ufa group For Clean Air and Water was attracting over 10,000 to its protests.[16] One of the more consequential of the environmental actions occurred in the Moscow sub-district of Brateevo, a high-rise, moonscaped housing estate constructed in the mid-1980s. Over 60,000 people – mainly working-class families and those of junior military officers – had been settled there when construction of heavy-industrial and high-pollution plants began across the road from the complex. In the words of one local organizer,

> We were simply thrown out there, like trash. We had no power, no rights. They knew that, and that was why they considered it perfectly fine to put up a petroleum refinery and other dirty industries right in our backyard . . . We had our children to think about, after all, and that was why even people like us decided 'enough', we have to organize against this, we have to stop this. Once we had done so, we were organized, self-reliant and we began to think about ways to use this to improve our lives.[17]

By 1988, these efforts had turned Brateevo into the USSR's first self-managed community whose residents and representatives would play an especially assertive role in local and municipal affairs.[18]

As these illustrations might indicate, the tendency for single-issue informal groups to gravitate toward more ramified political stances derived immediately from the structural features of the Soviet order. With neither property rights nor civil law to rely on, informal associations were directly dependent on the patronage of party-state authorities for those resources that they required to function. At the same time, however, their activities constituted a challenge to these same authorities: they breached the party-state monopoly on social communication; they undermined its ensemble of official organizations by representing a vital alternative to those ossified and sclerotic bodies as an outlet for social energies. This relationship between the authorities and the informals was therefore fraught with a powerful potential for politicization.

This potential would be actualized over the course of innumerable interactions transpiring along the intersecting axes of cooperation and conflict that characterized the relationship between the authorities and the informals. Along the lines of cooperation, it was the sufferance, if not encouragement, of officialdom that enabled informals to acquire standing. In addition to the Ministry of Justice's regulations, there was the symbolic protection afforded by Gorbachev's perestroika, especially its sanctioning of 'a socialist pluralism of opinions'.[19] Reciprocally, the vast majority of informal groups regularly reiterated their support for the 'progressive' elements in the CPSU leadership, signalled their allegiance to it by employing the word 'perestroika' in the names that they took for their clubs and saw their purpose as contributing directly to perestroika's fruition. Moreover, there was the patronage accorded informal organizations by a number of officials ones.[20] However, this patronage was by no means uniform, neither across officialdom generally nor among those officials not altogether ill-disposed toward the informals. It was amply complemented by varying degrees of hostility toward informal groups, ranging from refusals to register them or grant them premises for their gatherings, to attacks in the press and physical assaults by the police.[21] And there was more than mere ideological motive behind such actions, as the tensions that grew out of the relationship between informal organizations and their foremost competitor, the Komsomol, would illustrate. Founded under the auspices of the local Komsomol, small discussion clubs in places such as Novorossisk,[22] Naberezhnye Chelny[23] and Voronezh[24] became major irritants for their sponsors by utilizing their relative degree of freedom to take positions on a range of historical and contemporary issues that caused sensations among the steadily climbing numbers of young people who flocked to their public gatherings. These meetings were thus a vivid and, for some, unpleasant reminder of just how tedious, stiff and boring were those events put on by the Komsomol itself. As the authorities resorted to restrictions and pressure in order to rein in their competitors, so informal groups were increasingly politicized by their struggle against the agents of the party-state to realize that to which the party-state had entitled them.

Two questions related to those cultural–political forces surveyed in Chapter 2 should be addressed in this context. The first would concern right-wing extremist groups, among which Pamyat (and its many splinters) would be the foremost example. Pamyat issued from officially sponsored cultural organizations such as the Book Lovers' Society and the Historical–Literary Association, Pamyat, whence its name derived.[25] In terms of ideology, Pamyat resurrected the basic themes developed by Russia's ultra-nationalist movement nearly a century ago: the notion of the Russian people as chosen by God for an earthly mission of universal significance; the idea of evil forces taking the form of a Judeo-Masonic conspiracy seeking the destruction of God's chosen; and the necessity to combat this evil directly by restoring absolutist rule in Russia and recreating the nation as a community of the righteous that would realize its mission on earth.[26] To be sure, Pamyat was ostensibly among the first independent groups to put forth political demands; in May 1987, it organized the first demonstrations witnessed in Moscow during perestroika. However, like a number of analogous groups that concern us in subsequent chapters, Pamyat was above all an anti-political organization that functioned on the political field primarily as an objection to the fact that politics was becoming possible. In relation to the informal phenomenon, groups such as Pamyat constituted something of a parallel universe. Their activities – organizing discussion circles, staging rallies, leafleting in public places – outwardly resembled those of many informal groups. Yet the content of their discourse, to say nothing of the indulgence shown them by the authorities, set them worlds apart.[27] Consequently, we shall not include these organizations in our discussion of the informal movement.

The second question concerns the dissidents. We would distinguish our perspective from that evinced in a number of Western studies that have inferred a linkage between the informals and the dissidents, sometimes portraying the former as a resurfacing of the latter.[28] We have already adduced some general considerations on this matter: informals and dissidents represented two different generations, socialized under quite different circumstances (the Khrushchevian thaw in one instance, the Brezhnevian glaciation in the other); whereas dissidents engaged the Soviet regime as its bad conscience in the areas of constitutional and human rights, the informal movement began largely as a turn away from this same regime in an effort to establish niches wherein self-expression would be possible, subsequently initiating practices addressed to specific social problems which – rather than oppositionist activities – appeared in their self-understanding ('initiativism') as realizations of the regime's call for perestroika. Specific information available to us would amplify the distinctions between these two movements. Despite the fact that the mass release of dissidents from prison camps occurred simultaneously with the emergence of informal groups, effectively no contacts between the two were initiated until late 1987, a time at which many in the informal movement had already banked sharply toward political activity. Informals, having effectively no information on dissidents other than that provided by the official mass media, tended to regard them with varying mixtures of indifference, suspicion and fear. Perhaps for this reason the very few dissidents who entered informal circles at an early stage made it a point to conceal their pasts.[29] The first attempt to find some common ground between the two movements did not come until December 1987 when, through the Moscow grapevine, former dissident Lev Timofeev put out an open invitation to informals to attend a discussion on human rights at his apartment. Only two informals came, themselves both former dissidents.[30] A subsequent invitation from the peace and human rights group, Doverie (Trust) – in which many former dissidents were active – was declined by the Inter-Club Initiative Group (serving then as a general staff for the informal movement in Moscow) albeit with the proviso that members of informal groups could participate as private individuals. A few did so passively, and this led to contacts between a handful of former dissidents and the leading political groups spawned by the informal movement that had an impact on the movement's development and internal differentiation.[31] But that impact was from without.[32]

The politicization of the informal movement

The youthful impulse toward self-discovery and self-expression that motivated the formation of the first informal associations was clearly visible on Moscow's Arbat Street in autumn 1986. There, in scenes reminiscent of the gatherings at Mayakovskii and Pushkin squares decades earlier, young people began gathering for open-air poetry recitations which, true to previous patterns, quickly turned into free-for-all disputations on one or another philosophical problem exercising those assembled. At 10:00 p.m., the police would usually appear to close the discussions with the injunction, 'Comrades–philosophers, you are requested to disperse.'[33] The limitations of venues such as this thus underscored the simple fact that in order to communicate young people would have to secure premises in which to do so. This would require them to organize themselves into groups – clubs, societies or associations – that could petition potential sponsors for access to more commodious meeting places.

Once sponsors and premises had been found, another search began: a hunt for common language. To illustrate the communicative zero degree at which this process commenced, consider the short-lived Club of the Commonwealth of Sciences, a discussion group organized in May 1987 at Moscow's Polytechnic Museum.[34] A number of distinguished scholars from the Academy of Sciences arrived by invitation to address the meeting, just as a number of ordinary people, having heard of the event, trickled in from the street for the same purpose. At each of the club's two meetings, Babel ensued. Aside from the want to express themselves, the participants appeared to have nothing in common, neither common interests nor a common language. Each simply expounded on certain aspects dear to his or her vocation or avocation before an uncomprehending auditorium. Although dissonance, if not cacophony, marked both meetings of the club, its brief existence was by no means inconsequential. Drawn together by a mutual interest in self-expression, individuals began not only to encounter one another but to find one another. Here and at innumerable events of this type, people struck up new acquaintances 'informally' – in the vestibules of meeting halls and, often enough, by their entrances when admission to the hall had been denied them – exchanging telephone numbers, arranging future meetings, sometimes initiating new organizations on the spot.

In some respects, Hannah Arendt's concept of a 'web of human relationships' – in which individuals come to reveal and define themselves in communication with their fellows[35] – would capture this interaction among informals out of which various affinity groups crystallized, shattered and reformed. But in our view the connotations accompanying her usage of the term, which construe this web as something already existing prior to the appearance, self-revelation and self-apprehension of given individuals, would apply weakly, if at all, in this instance. Decades of the party-state's active prohibition against social communication meant that this web itself had to be rewoven, a process coextensive with the entry of individuals into an emerging public sphere wherein they would negotiate and renegotiate their own identities with and against one another.

Informal political groups emerged gradually in just this way, a feature of their inception and development that helps to account for a number of the movement's characteristics that close analyses have pointed out. First, only a small handful of groups achieved a membership in excess of a few score individuals. The modal informal political association was, then, a small, face-to-face micro-society constructed on the bonds of acquaintance or friendship. Even one of the largest groups – Democratic Union, the first self-proclaimed political party to appear during perestroika – was described by one of its leaders, A. Elinovich, as 'not an organization but a family'.[36] Second, the great majority of groups resembled clutches of acolytes braced around a leader who propounded one or another extensive philosophical–political world-view.[37] The status accruing to leaders as a result of their erudition, rhetorical skills or charisma bathed their respective groups in its light. As such, politics *within* the world of the informals developed largely according to its own logic quite apart from events in the larger world. The salience of various issues seemed directly proportionate to the opportunity that they presented to scribes and orators to battle one another at Olympian altitudes, each seeking to protect and extend his or her status within the circle of initiates via victories in the war of wits. Accordingly, like-minded groups tended to become the fiercest rivals, inasmuch as each represented a potential raid on the membership of the others, while groups espousing opposing philosophical-political world-views found common ground for cooperation rather easily.[38] Finally, the political discourse developed in the informal movement was conditioned by the ambiguous relationship that obtained between the movement and the authorities. On one hand, party-state officials displayed divergent attitudes toward informal groups. Although neglect and repression remained the predominant response to the youthful interlopers, various members of officialdom did render direct assistance to informal groups on a number of occasions.[39] On the other hand, the political orientations evinced by various groups, as well as the activities that they undertook, affected their eligibility for such assistance. In consequence, two competing considerations structured the movement as a whole, establishing niches for the respective groups within it: access to material resources, social visibility and a measure of respectable status; and accumulation of symbolic capital, principally by emphasizing one's independence from authority, one's refusal to bargain away moral-political principles, one's readiness to challenge and resist the party-state. For a political movement whose relationship to the regime's project of perestroika might be broadly described as supportive in principle yet critical with regard to innumerable particulars, the interplay of these opposing orientations constituted a powerful dynamic on the field of informal politics.

The first political groups

Although most observers have indicated that late 1987[40] or early 1988[41] marked the development of informal associations into a political movement, a number of individuals with their own political agendas had entered these circles prior to that period. A case in point would be the role played by former political prisoners Boris Kagarlitskii and Gleb Pavlovskii in founding the club, Nash Arbat, at the end of 1985 and quickly transforming[42] it from a discussion circle into an activist organization pursuing youth-oriented projects such as a computer club and theatre group.[43] Their inclination toward social action soon led these and other of their compatriots from the 'Young Socialist' group released from labour camps a few years earlier to begin attending meetings of the Club of Social Initiative (CSI), a group founded in early 1986 with a mixed and fluid membership, oriented generally toward social activity but unable to formulate any common goals or programme.[44] The experience and vision displayed by the newcomers immediately altered the character of the club, setting it on a path toward independent action aimed at bringing about socio-political change.[45] As a consequence of its new-found orientation, CSI began attracting a large membership, including that of entire clubs.[46] By spring 1987, it had been provided premises by the Communist Party organization in Moscow's Kropotkin district and had acquired sponsorship from the Soviet Sociological Association. A number of its leaders also took part in founding the club, Perestroika, which introduced an important new element into the informal movement.

The initial impetus that led to the creation of Perestroika actually belonged to certain members of Leningrad's liberal intelligentsia who, because of the heavy pall of political repression still hanging over their city, had been unable to realize their project of forming a group interested in working out concrete plans for furthering Gorbachev's reforms in the economy and society.[47] In Moscow they found kindred spirits among some young intellectuals, sympathetic ears in the Academy of Sciences and a more hospitable reception from the authorities. By February 1987, the club began meeting at the Central Econometrics Institute and was soon receiving favourable attention on Soviet television, a factor of immense importance not only for boosting the visibility of the club, but for easing restrictions against the founding of analogous organizations in other cities (among them, Leningrad).[48] At first, Perestroika was an elite intellectual club operating as a 'think tank' for the solution of social, economic and political problems. Its chairperson, Peruan Mitrov, was a member of the Academy of Sciences and thus able to include prestigious figures from the academic establishment in the club's proceedings,[49] a benefaction that undoubtedly reinforced the interest and enthusiasm of Perestroika's core of young scholars. Despite – or, perhaps because of – its respectable pedigree, however, Perestroika would soon be pulled into the maelstrom forming in the larger movement.

This whirlpool resulted from the confluence of hitherto separate currents flowing through the informal movement that first met in summer of 1987. Although the rivalry between them manifested itself as ideological struggle, it was above all a contest for the leadership of a movement that was beginning to assume national proportions. The initial bid for leadership came from Aleksandr Sukharev, a young scholar from Orenburg whose autumn 1986 letter to *Komsomol'skaya pravda* outlining his views on socio-economic reform had elicited a flood of readers' mail. The newspaper passed along many of these missives to Sukharev, who subsequently contacted the letter writers. On the basis of the list of people that he and his associates thus compiled, the All-Union Socio-Political Correspondence Club (A-US-PCC) was organized at a national conference in Moscow on 1–3 May 1987.[50] Since a number of the CSI's foremost figures had been entertaining their own ideas about a national movement that they would lead, the A-US-PCC's May conference, which ended by scheduling a return engagement for August, triggered an immediate reaction among them. To their good fortune, Boris El'tsin, then Communist Party boss in Moscow, delivered a speech in July to the CPSU's city committee in which he referred to the informals as 'the scum that has risen to the top of perestroika'.[51] El'tsin did not want for opponents in the city's party committee, as his subsequent sacking by that body when it next convened in November would indicate.[52] Accordingly, certain individuals working in the committee's propaganda department were especially receptive to overtures made to them by their acquaintances in the CSI and the FSI to organize a separate national conference of informal groups in Moscow that same August.[53] Thus a marriage of convenience was consummated between certain segments of the party apparatus in the capital and certain elements in the informal movement, inaugurating a pattern of patronage that would figure significantly into the differentiation of, and political contests within, the movement. On this occasion, the terms of the bargain were rather clear. The CSI–FSI conference deflected the A-US-PCC's bid for national leadership and consigned it to the periphery of events: its second conference was held in remote Taganrog, it failed to attract participants or supporters from established circles and it soon collapsed under the weight of internecine factional conflict.[54] This opened the way for the Muscovites to press their claim to national leadership. For their part, certain groups in the apparatus were able to play the informal card against El'tsin. Rather than 'scum', they could now demonstrate that the informals – or at least those whom they backed – were genuine participants in perestroika who were working for a renewal of socialism under the aegis of the Communist Party.

The divide-and-rule strategy deployed by the party apparatus had profound ramifications on the development of the informal movement. First, it ceded leadership in the national movement to the Muscovites. Unlike their rivals from the provinces, many informals in the capital had ties toRussia's liberal intellectual establishment, and these associations would figure significantly in the subsequent growth and direction of the democratic movement.[55] Second, the conference that the Moscow informals convened on August 20–3 could be counted a success in most respects. Encounters among the 300 or so delegates representing over fifty clubs from twelve of Russia's cities engendered a certain sensation that, far from being isolated activists condemned to face alone the obstacles and frustrations of their respective localities, a 'we' had come into being on a nationwide scale. Thus encouraged and energized, those from the provinces undertook a flurry of concerted organizing activities on returning home.[56] And the creation at the conference of a central information clearing-house for the movement – the Moscow Bureau of Information Exchange (M-BIO) – assisted their efforts considerably, both by symbolizing the nexus of a national network to which they now belonged and by serving as an information link for those in the movement, often putting in contact informal organizations that were located in the same city but which had been unaware of each other's existence. The conference also spawned a number of other initiatives, such as the creation of the Memorial society,[57] that would prove to be of critical importance in the months ahead. But the political division that emerged at the conference over the movement's proper objectives undid the designs of its organizers to unite those present under their direction and transformed the field of informal politics, altering the shape and direction of the movement itself.

The split was precipitated by Valeriya Novodvorskaya's address. Novodvorskaya, a former dissident, had recently begun leading a seminar at her apartment called 'Democracy and Humanism' whose discussions pivoted on a radical interpretation of liberal political philosophy. She stunned the August seminar by rejecting *in toto* the Soviet system and, for that matter, socialism in any variety whatsoever. Rather than working with the progressive elements in the Communist Party to promote reform, she advocated a fully independent political movement opposed to the party in every respect. Her summons to build a free society along the lines of the Western liberal-democratic model ignited both an enthusiastic endorsement from some quarters of the hall as well as catcalls, whistles and demands for her expulsion from others.[58] Latent differences among the delegates thus crystallized into clear distinctions as the conference concluded with a division of the assembled informals into two broad camps. The first, taking the name Federation of Socialist Clubs (FSOK), was composed of nine clubs leaning toward a Eurocommunist interpretation of socialism which were still prepared to work within the ambit of the Soviet order, explicitly recognizing the Communist Party's leading role in that respect.[59] The second group included those clubs disdaining identification with socialism. Although the alliance that they formed at the conference (the Circle of Social Initiative) proved to be stillborn, a number of these delegates and their respective clubs – such as the radical-liberal group, Civic Dignity, which formed during the conference itself – would go on to play a critical role in the movement, commanding attention by the boldness of their words and deeds, and injecting debate into informal circles over ideas that could scarcely have been entertained just a short time ago.[60]

The politics of differentiation

The August 1987 national conference represented a watershed in the evolution of the informals. In its wake, political activity would outshine other pursuits as a mark of prestige among groups, a development that resulted largely from the willingness of some clubs to violate existing taboos against political activity by staging demonstrations, leafleting in public places and putting out their own samizdat publications. For many in the non-conformist youth subculture from which the larger movement had emerged, this turn toward political activity was infectious. After all, here was the opportunity to enact publicly that very drive toward self-expression that had drawn them into that zone of activities neither fully sanctioned nor proscribed by officialdom. The qualitative side of politicization expressed itself through increasing differentiation. Fission within existing clubs, as well as the appearance of new groups, divided the movement into a variety of political tendencies and subdivided it further along the lines of esoteric distinctions confected within each. Those foregrounding the idea of democracy, for instance, fractured into 'liberal', 'constitutional', 'Christian' and 'social' democrats, just as those professing allegiance to socialism splintered into 'democratic', Euro-communist, Marxist–Leninist and anarchist varieties of that genus. From one point of view, then, ideas made the difference. It was under the banner of one or another idea that informals engaged their fellows in bitter polemics or confronted the authorities with slogans, placards and bodies. Moreover, many of the ideas nurtured in the hothouse of informal disputation would acquire practical significance on the field of mass politics. Beginning with the national elections of 1989, they represented a basis from which to criticize, to challenge and, eventually, to overthrow the communist system. But prior to the opening to mass political activity afforded by elections, ideas in the milieu of informal politics were primarily self-referential. Their role consisted far more in constructing identities for their purveyors than in framing practical projects or guiding action. Such was the arena in which they appeared.

After the August 1987 conference, those structural factors shaping the movement – access to material resources and the accumulation of symbolic capital – began to pull in opposite directions, altering the flow and content of communications within it. Both factors had been in more or less harmonious relation prior to August, but developments following the conference undid that congruence by valorizing certain elements within the complex of symbolic capital: independence, fidelity to principle and the readiness to resist the 'anti-perestroika' agents of the party-state. As a result, access to resources and social prestige became more visibly linked to a status whose respectability within the movement was open to challenge. Whereas patronage from the authorities had counted among the assets comprising a group's social capital in the earlier period, it now began to look like a liability.

This development stemmed largely from the divide-and-rule strategy pursued by a section of officialdom in Moscow which supported some informal organizations while repressing others regarded as more radical or dangerous. Democracy and Humanism, whose public demonstrations were rapidly and ruthlessly suppressed during this period, would count as a foremost example of the latter, but the CSI fell into this category as well. Following its investigations in autumn 1987 of a rash of police assaults on hippies in certain quarters the capital, the CSI lost its official sponsor, along with its registration and meeting hall.[61] Since many CIS leaders also belonged to Perestroika, they transferred their energies to that club while CSI meetings were mothballed. Others from their club also gravitated to Perestroika meetings, as did members of Democracy and Humanism and Civic Dignity who had a similar want of premises. As attendance increased at these sessions, so did the incidence and intensity of polemical exchanges. Soon discussions became pitched verbal battles, with veteran members accusing the new arrivals of 'extremism' for opposing the notion of socialist renewal under the auspices of the CPSU, while the latter responded by challenging not only the views but the integrity of their establishment counterparts. The polemical fireworks were doused at year's end by a decision of the Central Econometrics Institute (supported by Perestroika's coordinators) to bar the radicals from the premises. In January, a formal charter was drawn up for the club that codified the excision of the radical elements and, in so doing, provoked a split within the club itself. The larger wing, composed of established, if mainly younger, scholars backed the new rules; the smaller group – among whom were very few with advanced degrees and quite a number without either permanent residences or occupations – refused to go along and were themselves expelled.

The rump of Perestroika enjoyed the sponsorship of the intellectual establishment and the imprimatur of the district party committee. In its new incarnation as Democratic Perestroika, however, it gradually evolved in the direction of organizing an independent social-democratic party. The inspiration for this project had much to do with the activity of other groups, not least of which would be Democracy and Humanism whose members – prior to their expulsion from Perestroika's meetings – had argued tirelessly that any serious talk about democratization meant, at a minimum, breaking the Communist Party's monopoly on state power. Following their expulsion, these same individuals would join with others to do just this, proclaiming the creation of an independent political party, Democratic Union, in May 1988.

Others who left Perestroika as a consequence of the restrictive charter drawn up in January played a role in the politicization of their former comrades too. Taking for themselves the name Perestroika–88, the group searched in vain for some six months for an official sponsor. Meeting in a basement surreptitiously rented from a state agency, the group decided to compensate for the underprivileged status accorded it by officialdom by initiating public actions. On 6 March Perestroika–88 attempted to congregate at the massive monument to Lenin on October Square to stage an anti-Stalinist rally. They were immediately and brutally prevented from assembling on the square by a phalanx of police. A day later, Civic Dignity turned out about one hundred people to take their place. The police, acting with similar dispatch but employing less force, broke up that gathering too. Democracy and Humanism, along with other groups that would join in founding Democratic Union, took to the streets thereafter, and were greeted with even more violence than that which had been visited on Perestroika–88. However, during Ronald Reagan's visit to Moscow and with the Nineteenth Party Conference drawing near, the repression was relaxed. On 18 May Civic Dignity combined with Obshchina to lead a march that culminated in a successful rally at Pushkin Square. This action began an alliance between the two groups that involved them in a number of similar demonstrations in the days that followed. The example of these street actions – both their moral aspects, evinced by those prepared to face beatings and arrest in order to express themselves in public, as well as their success on the instrumental level, since the termination of violent repression seemed to indicate that the radicals had won the streets – had its effect on others in the movement. By the time that the CPSU began its extraordinary conference in late June upwards of 1,000 people were staging daily rallies on Pushkin Square.

The relative degree of political freedom that obtained in Moscow during this interval tended to advantage precisely those groups orphaned some months earlier by the authorities. The leadership that they exercised on the streets by force of example had three critical consequences. First, in clearing the way for unauthorized public expression, they altered fundamentally the context of informal political activity, sharply reducing the possibilities that groups such as Democratic Perestroika could content themselves with closed seminars on socialism while others were addressing many hundreds of activists and perhaps another thousand or so interested spectators in the open air at city centre. The more respectable groups therefore joined in, crossing the imaginary line separating those behaviours sanctioned by their party-state patrons from that representing the acme of the movement to which they belonged: free public expression. Second, when repression was renewed by the authorities in August, police batons fell not only on the heads of a few radicals from the margins of society whose fate could again be ignored by the liberal establishment. By now, among the thousands of peaceful demonstrators were the sons, daughters, relatives and acquaintances of many in that same establishment.[62] Consequently, something of a public outcry went up in certain sections of the press, and the voices of eminent writers and scientists added considerable weight to it. These events, then, reduced the social distance between the informal movement and establishment liberals, a result that would have profound implications for the election campaigns to come. Finally, the radicals' insistence on breaking their own path and, most importantly, on forming their own political party, accelerated the conversion of discussion clubs into organizations with explicitly political aims.

Organizing a party and a front

Since so many aspects of our general topic could be characterized by the word 'paradoxical', we have refrained from employing that term in the interest of avoiding overuse. However, in the case of Democratic Union[63] – the first self-proclaimed political party to appear in Russia since before the Revolution – a dispensation from that rule would be warranted. Plans to create an independent party were initially laid in autumn 1987 by members of Democracy and Humanism and Doverie led by Evgeniya Debryanskaya. These were publicized in January via Novodvorskaya's samizdat journal, *Poedinok*, and the informals' grapevine.[64] Thereafter, an organizing committee composed of members from those two groups – and from Perestroika–88, the Young Marxist society and others – announced a founding congress to be held in Moscow on 7 May. With no access to suitable premises, the first day of the event took place in a communal apartment into which some 150 people were jammed, with dozens more marooned in the adjoining hallway. Repeatedly interrupted by police sorties against the outer doors, the proceedings were punctuated by a number of definitive moments, such as a summons to all from Vladimir Zhirinovskii 'to clutch copies of the Constitution in hand',[65] to which Novodvorskaya responded with a formula that would serve both as a litmus test for genuine delegates (non-subscribers were asked to leave) and as the quintessence of the party's moral–political character. 'Political struggle', she claimed, 'must be uncompromising. We can take an example here from the Bolsheviks who had one virtue: they never compromised with their enemy, autocracy.'[66]

Intensified police harassment of the congress on its second day, resulting in the arrest and deportation of most delegates from the provinces, prompted a change of venue.[67] Delegates repaired to a dacha leased by former dissident Sergei Grigoryants in Kratovo outside Moscow. Before their arrival, however, the police had appeared, arrested Grigoryants and other leaders there, and then ransacked the premises.[68]

When the remainder of the delegates arrived at midday and found the dacha surrounded by police, they drifted off in a group back toward the railway station. The proposal made *en route* to conclude the congress somewhere in the surrounding forest was rejected in favour of another to reconvene at the premises of the local soviet, permission for which had just been secured from its deputy chairperson. In more commodious surroundings, the congress completed its main business, declared itself a political party and then – since the soviet's hall had been booked for another event that evening – concluded the final details of its work on the railway platform surrounded by a troop of KGB officers.[69]

Some delegates rushed directly to Pushkin Square where they celebrated the party's founding by raising cries against police repression, distributing leaflets describing their party's goals and, of course, suffering immediate incarceration. This event was emblematic of one side of the paradox that was Democratic Union. It was a political party that steadfastly refused to behave like one. Despite its stated objective of 'organizing and enlightening the masses [by conducting] election campaigns for the local and national representative organs of power',[70] it also disdained any compromise with the Soviet order and therefore refused to participate in any elections. And since other independent groups engaged in election activity, it eschewed collaboration with them as well.[71] Yet, politically, it was anything but passive, staging some forty-eight unsanctioned demonstrations in Moscow alone by mid-summer 1988.[72] Herein would lie the key both to fixing the position occupied by Democratic Union on the field of informal politics and to explaining the other side of the paradox: namely, how a group, singularly unsuccessful by the conventional yardstick applied to political parties, could be so effective as a political organization in the context of late-Soviet politics.

Around the core leadership of Democratic Union – a few former dissidents and others repressed for offences such as forming discussion circles in the years before perestroika – there assembled a cadre of young, idealistic acolytes who constituted a standing majority for the leadership's most radical elements. The uncompromising posture that they assumed alienated more pragmatic elements in the party[73] and, indeed, made Democratic Union into an object of ridicule within the informal movement.[74] From the first, Democratic Union defined its objective in kamikaze fashion as political opposition to, and continual confrontation with, the Soviet order which it regarded as 'criminal' and 'totalitarian'.[75] This injunction became so central to the group's identity that, as the Soviet order buckled and broke, Democratic Union became more and more a political caricature, jousting with phantoms and, eventually, collapsing as an organization.[76] Although regarded by probably most informals as extremists who represented more of a liability than an asset for the movement as a whole, Democratic Union in fact contributed two indispensable elements to informal politics. The first was ideas. In this respect, the party played the role of avant-garde among informals, raising issues and proposing alternatives that others initially greeted with incredulous laughter and scorn, but which soon found broad acceptance in the movement, just as Democratic Union's particular language tended to colonize its everyday vocabulary. This list would include: open opposition to the Communist Party and to the Soviet order generally; the creation of a multi-party political system; self-determination for the nations in the USSR; the adoption of the tricolour as the Russian state flag; and the use of the adjective 'totalitarian'.[77] The second element was space. That is, by virtue of the very radicalism that often shocked and offended other informals, Democratic Union drew the wrath of the party-state upon itself. In demonstrations involving a plurality of groups, its members would invariably be singled out for the fiercest beatings and stiffest punishments.[78] By proselytizing its radical ideology of total opposition, it made other groups seem rather moderate and thus more acceptable to the authorities. And, of course, by proclaiming itself a political party, Democratic Union catalyzed the sentiment in other groups that, indeed, the time had arrived to move beyond the stage of political discussion and unite with others keen to quicken the pace and deepen the significance of perestroika.

The notion of effecting some organizational unity had been mooted in informal circles since summer of 1987.[79] It had also been lent official respectability by an article published in December of that year by a prominent legal specialist advising individual clubs to combine forces in a larger unit 'which in the beginning will be something like a popular front in support of perestroika', thereafter developing into a 'democratic union for the renewal of socialism' under the direction of the Communist Party.[80] Having migrated to the Baltic, the idea was first realized in Estonia where, inspired by the activism displayed by their counterparts in Moscow and Leningrad, informals at Tartu University formed a popular front initiative group in April 1988 that grew to include 150,000 members by June.[81] There, as in many urban areas throughout the USSR, demonstrations organized by informal groups protesting the party apparatus's lock on the selection of delegates to the Nineteenth Party Conference gave the movement a powerful boost, dramatizing the need for coordination in order to have some impact on the critical events unfolding at the time.[82]

In Moscow, just as ten months earlier when the spectre of the A-US-PCC's national conference had haunted both informal leaders and their supporters in the apparatus, the emergence of Democratic Union as a competitor poised to assume a leading role in the movement brought other quarrelling informals together. The CSI persuaded its former patrons in the Soviet Sociological Association to sponsor its call for a citywide conference, while others utilized their ties to Vadim Churbanov (who directed the Institute of Culture) to secure premises. With the consent of the CPSU's Central Committee, about 500 informals representing some twenty groups assembled on 5 June.[83] Since a cautious approach toward informals generally – as well as a divide-and-rule strategy favouring some groups over others – remained the earmarks of authorities' policy, they attached two significant provisos to their permission for the conference: first, that only groups composed of supporters of socialism would be allowed to attend; and, second, that the conference would concern itself only with the recently published 'Theses' that the CPSU's Central Committee had prepared for the Nineteenth Party Conference.[84] Having little choice in the matter, the organizers assented to these. However, the dynamics at play within the larger circle of Moscow's informals would transgress both their pledges.

The majority of those at the conference personified that very 'socialist orientation' stipulated by the authorities. Initially, they were fully prepared to police the premises themselves, turning away delegates from those groups not certifiably socialist. However, the moral suasion used by some leaders of the CSI and Perestroika–88, particularly effectively inasmuch as the leaders of the socialist groups appeared to be taking the side of the party apparatus against others in their own movement, induced the socialists to relent and to admit the others. During the conference's first session, the informals dutifully stuck to the authorities' second proviso regarding the agenda, drawing up a list of 'public demands' that were forwarded to the CPSU's Central Committee. But when the conference reconvened on 12 June, the socialist groups unfurled a project that contravened this stipulation as well. It called for the creation of the Moscow Popular Front ('Moskovskii narodnyi front' or MNF), according to whose programme the organization would be:

a union of the broad democratic movement and the progressive forces in the ranks of the CPSU. Not being a political party, neither does the [M]NF aspire to reducing itself to a non-autonomous, obedient and, therefore, impotent 'helper' of the party leadership . . . We aim to avoid the common lot that has befallen Soviet mass public organizations – statization, bureaucratization and a compromised status in relation to the party and state organs. The [M]NF's support for the progressive forces in the CPSU does not imply automatic agreement with the party's course.

The ideational orientation of the [M]NF unites various groups and movements

. . . around our common ideals of democratic socialism . . . Under the condition of the country's actual development in the direction of socialist democracy [and] self-management, the [M]NF does not compete with the CPSU for political power. [However] the question of a single- or multi-party system in the USSR must be decided by the people itself and not by the ruling party . . . At the present time, the [M]NF believes that the preconditions for a multi-party system are absent in our country.[85]

After heated debate, this programme was approved by the vast majority of those present. An organizing committee was then set up for bringing the project to fruition in Moscow, the first step toward uniting informals across the country in one popular front under the leadership of the Muscovites.

However, no sooner had the MNF been founded than it experienced its first major setback. Due to the fact that votes on the organizing committee were apportioned equally among groups irrespective of membership size, those confessing a thoroughly 'socialist orientation' commanded a majority that laid down a new condition for affiliation: only groups composed uniformly of members subscribing to a 'socialist orientation' would be allowed to remain.[86] This tactic backfired. Rather than purging their non-socialist members, seven of the largest groups in the front – Memorial, the CSI, Perestroika–88, Civic Dignity and others – simply withdrew. Indeed, the strictures on 'socialist orientation' were so stringently enforced by leaders of the Group of Socialist Initiative (a spin-off of the CSI) who envisaged the MNF as an ideologically coherent proto-party under their leadership, that Obshchina – whose 'socialist orientation' had never been questioned and whose leader, Andrei Isaev, had himself authored the front's charter – broke away as well. These events both sharpened the conflicts already prevalent within Moscow's informal movement and added new ones. This was reflected above all in the case of Obshchina, whose recoil from the authoritarian methods employed by the socialists in the MNF led it to reconsider its commitment to a socialist project and to turn toward anarchism.[87]

The knock-on effect of political organizing occasioned by the forma-tion of Democratic Union in Russia, followed by the emergence of popular fronts in the Baltic which in turn inspired the founding of the MNF, continued with mixed results through the summer and autumn of 1988. By year's end, popular fronts had appeared in over twenty Russian cities,[88] while the election campaign of 1989 stimulated a second wave of organizing in others.[89] Already in August 1988 the Muscovites attempted to realize their goal of bringing these diverse groups together under their roof. However, the conference convened in Leningrad for that purpose failed. The delegates representing scores of organizations from more than thirty cities in the USSR rejected the organizational structure proposed by the MNF's leader, itself an extrapolation to the entire country of the same formula that had provoked the split among Moscow's informals two months earlier.[90]

The role of the informals in Russia's political rebirth

During the period of perestroika, the significance of Russia's informal movement consisted in the fact that it generated the country's first organized forms of civic activity and opened alternative channels of communication wherein nascent political identities could develop. By carving out a space for interaction independent of the tutelage of the party-state, the movement was thus tantamount to the inauguration of a recognizable field of Russian politics. To be sure, this field remained tightly constricted by the authorities; but that very constriction conduced to turning the informal movement in a political direction. However, that direction remained in many respects inward, constituting a sort of self-referential activity until the election campaigns of 1989 had focused energies on the practical task of defeating the candidates of the party-state and, where possible, electing to office those associated with the democratic movement. Prior to these campaigns which enormously enlarged the circle of activists and multiplied the incidence of contact between them and the larger public, informal politics had an illusory air about it. Leadership in the movement tended to be conferred on those whose forte was philosophical–political polemic, those with a talent for formulating sweeping solutions to problems construed in equally broad terms, all at light-years' remove from implementation. The particular discursive practices, then, that typified the politics of the movement had understandably little to do with framing practical political projects. Rather, they revolved around the signification of social and political identities.

These poured forth in abundant variety: socialists and communists of every imaginable stripe; liberal democrats, constitutional democrats and Christian democrats; monarchists, greens and anarchists. Indicatively, cooperation among these groups often crossed ideological lines, as we observed in the instance of Obshchina's militant socialists joining with Civic Dignity's equally militant liberals in a series of unsanctioned street demonstrations. The attraction present between such opposites derived from the fact that none was encumbered by considerations of social *interests* that might be interpreted in opposing ways on their respective ideological calculi while, from the point of view of *identity*, avoiding close cooperation with those groups professing similar programmatic orientations meant keeping competitors at arm's length.[91] The party-state's restrictions also encouraged this 'cross-sectarian' cooperation because restrictions continually subordinated the matter of what would be communicated to the public to the more immediate issue of the *possibility* of communicating in public. Hence, diverse groups made common cause to secure that space in which to express their very diversity. As such, as one participant-observer has remarked, 'a handful of organizations, formally consisting of ideologically opposed groups, often organized rallies together – at which onlookers to the very end would never guess that they had just witnessed speeches delivered by ideological opponents'.[92] Free expression thus bore the marks of the constraints against which it protested. Restrictions on speech retarded its capacity to generate and sustain a community of speakers in which political identities could both distinguish themselves one from another and find common mooring in the reciprocal recognition presupposed by open communications. Under the conditions prevailing in Russia, then, political statements ostensibly directed against external constraints would not themselves be internally constrained by the requirement of conforming to the socially mediated identity of the speaker. Relatively detached in this way, subjects uttered things that would make sense to those in their immediate circle, but which would appear incomprehensible and bizarre to those outside it: for instance, Democratic Union's combination of the principles of liberal democracy with the uncompromising political posture of Bolshevism. As we see, below, those political parties that sprouted from the informal movement inherited this problem and channelled its disorganizing consequences directly into the post-communist Russian polity.

The political field opened by the informals was also structured by the hazily defined project for political reform ('democratization') offered by the Gorbachev leadership. On one hand, democratization required a series of compromises within the upper echelons of the party-state which would ensure the continuation of the CPSU's 'leading role', even while this role would be exercised under conditions designed to create the appearance of broad popular endorsement.[93] Therefore, at least the appearance of some political forces standing outside the party-state's ensemble of 'public organizations' would suit this purpose, lending authenticity of the overall project. Since these same forces remained dwarfed by official organizations whose control of effectively all resources enabled them to play off one group against another, a strategy of containing the informal movement recommended itself over one of unsightly, across-the-board repression.[94] But, on the other hand, the interventions of the party-state along the lines of divide-and-rule introduced a sharp differentiation within the informal movement that generated a series of chain reactions culminating in the formation of the MNF and comparable organizations in most of Russia's major cities. The division between groups enjoying the patronage of the authorities and those to whom it was denied created two sets of positions on the field of informal politics: one marked by official respectability and access to material resources; the other by independence, authenticity, innovation, free expression – in short, all those qualities that were highly valorized in the informal sub-culture. Interaction between those occupying these positions thus tended to take the movement precisely in the direction that the authorities had sought to discourage. The conjunction of these interactive dynamics within the movement with the relaxation of repression occasioned by Reagan's visit and the CPSU conference that followed it spelt the ruin of the divide-and-rule strategy and released the germs of political opposition.

It is far from certain that this political opposition was immediately conscious of itself as such. Of course, Democratic Union took up the part of an uncompromising opponent of the 'totalitarian' order, but its role was to infect others with the virus of opposition, mainly by mounting quixotic challenges to the party-state. The MNF formally disclaimed opposition to the Soviet order and explicitly rejected competing with the CPSU for power. Yet beneath the surface of its non-oppositionist self-description, the identity that it assumed would take it directly down that path. The significance of its name, 'popular front' – a term 'borrowed from France in 1936, meaning an association of people from different organizations and with different political views, with the sole aim of resisting a totalitarian regime'[95] – indicated as much. The principal tasks that the MNF set for itself – 'participation in election campaigns by nominating candidates from public organizations', 'public monitoring over the activity of soviets', 'preparing draft legislation and introducing it into soviets and for broad [public] consideration' and 'conducting mass meetings, demonstrations, assemblies and other forms of direct democracy'[96] – did so as well. During the elections of 1989, the MNF in the capital, along with equivalent groups in Leningrad and other cities, provided the shock troops for the first massed assault on the hegemons of the party-state.

Few informals would themselves emerge as leaders in the renewal of Russian political life heralded by those elections. None the less, the unsung adventures of many activists tightrope-walking the slender line separating the permitted from the proscribed – and, on frequent occasion, crossing that line – helped to prepare the way for that renewal. Two aspects of their political activity would stand out in that regard.

First, informal organizations displayed an enormous amount of resourcefulness in expressing themselves in print. Denied access to print facilities and newspulp, their efforts to communicate with one another and with a larger audience via the written word resembled the samizdat publications of the dissidents: typewritten manuscripts duplicated with carbon paper, sometimes put out in larger editions thanks to the advent of the photocopier. But the scope of the subjects that they addressed was far broader than the documenting of human rights abuses featured in the dissidents' *Chronicle of Current Events*. Many, perhaps most, politically oriented groups managed to put out information bulletins on their activities and concerns. These, along with those published by informal journalists not working directly on behalf of a political group,[97] began to constitute something of an alternative press in which even established writers would publish ideas still deemed too radical for official outlets. The interaction between these informal newspapers and liberal establishment publications had an impact on the latter, pushing outward the restrictions on press freedom that remained under glasnost. With the organization of independent information agencies in 1987, this influence was also apparent in the levels of information available in the Soviet press generally.[98] In short, the roots of a free press in Russia were in many ways nourished by informal groups. They were the first to establish fully independent newspapers. Second, there was the ground that informals broke in the area of organization. Their modal form of organization – the discussion club which gave birth to a political group – was appropriated by the leading figures in Moscow's liberal establishment who formed their own elite club, Moscow Tribune, in autumn 1988. Although their initial project was indistinguishable from that developed by, say, Perestroika a year or so earlier,[99] and despite the fact that their high social status might discourage descent into the world of mass politics, a number of Moscow Tribune's members would enter the electoral fray in early 1989. By April, they could be found in Moscow's Arbat with their counterparts from the MNF, Memorial and other informal organizations engaged in unsanctioned street assemblies.[100]

6   National elections and mass politics

Consummated by an increasingly radical press and informal political movement, midwifed by the political reforms of perestroika, Russian politics was reborn in the national elections of 1989. The birthplace itself spanned myriad sites: voters' assemblies at factories or meeting halls, often raucous, occasionally violent and sometimes lasting till the wee hours of the morning; cramped apartments where candidates huddled with their staffs and volunteers discussing tactics, composing leaflets, arguing philosophy; city streets and public squares where contestants for office engaged the public directly, holding rallies, answering questions, distributing campaign literature. By the time the electoral process had run its course, the circle of political activism had expanded enormously, fanning out from cloisters of informal groups and enclaves of democratic orientation ensconced in official organizations to include millions of citizens who, for the first time in their lives, would have the opportunity to vote.[1] Yet, for three related reasons, it would be mistaken to regard that voting as commensurate with an actual election. First, irrespective of the results of the balloting, there was no possibility whatsoever that the Communist Party could be removed from power. Its 'leading role' was still enshrined in the Soviet Constitution, while the legislature which was to be filled by successful candidates had not been designed either to choose or to control a government. The CPSU's political monopoly would remain intact; this election could neither turn it out of office nor serve as a mandate for the continuation of its rule.

Second, there was no organized challenge to its monopoly on power. Outside of the small Democratic Union (which, moreover, boycotted these elections), no other political party existed. No organizations independent of communist tutelage had the legal right to nominate candidates.[2] Thus the electorate was unable in a second sense to deliver a clear mandate either for or against the CPSU. Since political parties were not present to structure the national vote, the election resembled a collection of localized contests wherein national issues were eclipsed by local concerns and the personal qualities of individual candidates.[3] Each office-seeker did put forward his or her own electoral platform, but these were hardly distinguishable one from another,[4] regarded as altogether irrelevant by some 60 per cent of the electorate,[5] and were in no discernable way connected to what the candidates, once elected, might achieve in office for the obvious reason that no single legislator would be able to enact a programme by himself or herself.

Finally, there was the matter of procedures. Those under which the elections were conducted were instituted and interpreted by the Communist Party hierarchy. The overall organization and supervision of the elections fell to the thirty-five–member Central Electoral Commission (CEC) named by the Supreme Soviet of the USSR, while in each electoral district and public organization which was choosing deputies, a corresponding electoral commission arranged and managed the entire process. In the same way in which the Politburo staffed and directed the CEC,[6] so each lower-level electoral commission was staffed and directed by the corresponding party apparatus.[7] This arrangement encouraged procedural manipulation to the point that officials could casually confirm to newspaper reporters that their task consisted in securing the election of the 'right' candidates.[8] In the role of both contestant and referee, the organs of the CPSU behaved as one might expect, perpetrating a steady stream of illegalities and dirty tricks that would minimize competition at the polls.[9]

Although our topic cannot be properly regarded as an 'election', we shall none the less employ this term for convenience's sake. But this usage obviously raises another question, namely: if the events in question do not pertain to the category of elections *per se*, how might we construe the significance of these contests, what meanings can we ascribe to them? One meaning – associated with the notion of perestroika as 'renewal' – can be derived from what the authors of the political reform had apparently intended: that is, to force some measure of competition on the party apparatus and to arouse a certain degree of political activity in the broader public for this purpose. As Gorbachev had often opined,[10] electoral competition would (somehow) enable the CPSU to earn demonstrably its leading role in society by winning the confidence of the voters. Relatedly, the elections would restore the fitness of the Communist Party to perform its 'leading role' by identifying those of its officers who did not enjoy the support of the electorate. In this respect, the elections would serve as a surrogate party purge, with popular rejection at the polls providing added leverage to oust certain officials not identified with the reform leadership. Some, such as Politburo member Yu. F. Solov'ev, were denied safe passage to the legislature in the seats reserved for the Communist Party. Unable to survive in the seas of open electoral competition, the verdict of the voters portended their removal from positions of authority in the CPSU. Engineering the early retirements of seventy-four members and thirty-six candidate-members of the Central Committee in the immediate aftermath of these elections, Gorbachev made direct reference to this purge-like aspect of the electoral process.[11]

But if the elections represented a 'renewal of socialism' and a demonstrable 'conquest of authority' for the Communist Party in the eyes of its reform leadership, they had the reverse affect on Russia's emergent citizenry and public movement. The significance of the elections at this – the decisive – level can be divided into three aspects. First, through chicanery, deceit and crude violations of both the legal provisions governing the elections as well as any standard of elementary fairness, the Communist Party publicly and irreparably discredited itself in the eyes of a broad section of the politically active population. As a field of action, the electoral arena crystallized unmistakably in public view what had hitherto dwelt solely in the province of words, words that were fraught with ambiguity, words crafted for mutual misunder-standing: democratization, pluralism, socialism, rule-of-law and so forth. What was the real semantic content of this new vocabulary adopted by the Communist Party? When it spoke of, say, a 'socialist rule-of-law', was this merely its idiosyncratic way of saying 'rule-of-law'? The indeterminacy surrounding this question posed in the abstract was resolved in the concrete experience of the electoral contests that would show that 'socialism' could only mean what the Communist Party defined it to mean. Therefore, by affixing the adjective 'socialist' to any noun, the Communist Party had declared that noun its private property.[12] As such, it was necessarily an alien thing for those grounding their political identities in notions of citizenship and public participation in the affairs of state, for a commitment to *common* principles such as pluralism and the rule-of-law would imply a rejection of any *private* appropriation of those same principles. Never mind for the moment the sincerity of this commitment. The important thing would be that those professing it had already prepared the ground for public assessment of that avalanche of capricious one-sidedness that the CPSU displayed in the course of these elections. By advocating a rule of law and then honouring that commitment in the breach, the authorities both discredited themselves and provided a powerful impulse toward mass political development at one go.

The second aspect involved a reconfiguration of political forces. Until the onset of the electoral process, the informal movement in Russia had remained a marginal phenomenon. Securing spaces removed from the stifling structures of the party-state in order to engage in political activity, informals simultaneously ensured for themselves a certain isolation from the larger society. Their influence on Russia's political development had thus been indirect, taking the form of the information, ideas and example provided to those in official structures and to those members of the population at large who came into contact with these novel – and, perhaps in their eyes, rather peculiar – groups. Moreover, the influence of the outside world on that of the informals was also remote. The adoption of forms of organization, the selection of methods of activity and the development of political orientations were determined principally by the interplay of the individuals and groups within the informals' subculture itself. The elections changed all of this. Now there was a situation to face, an opportunity to grasp and no want of things to be done. Instead of merely talking about politics or protesting the lack thereof, here was the chance to engage in full-blooded political activity. On one hand, then, these elections revived the flagging movement, wearied by endless discussions and riddled by the disputes and schisms following thereon. New members appeared, lapsed members returned.[13] Indeed, this period of intense political activity marked the apogee of Russia's informal movement. On the other hand, however, it closed the chapter on it, depriving the informals of their political virginity. The opportunity to influence public affairs directly involved simultaneously the surrender of subcultural autonomy. Beginning with these campaigns, identities, programmes and projects could no longer be formulated in circles of political activists more or less detached from the public. The rules had changed. *Hic Rhodus, hic salta!* Accordingly, during these elections and in their immediate aftermath, informal groups would either disappear altogether, wither in isolation[14] or dissolve themselves into the new organizations thrown up in the course of the campaigns. Some of the movement's leaders would advance to the front ranks of Russia's new contingent of politicians while others would remain on the margins of political life or retreat to private pursuits.

The third feature concerned the profound changes wrought in the perspectives of Russia's emerging political subjects. Not only had the Communist Party shamed itself publicly, but the success of hundreds of independent candidates and the defeat of dozens of the CPSU's top functionaries broached the real possibility that the communists did not hold a permanent lease on power. These elections, then, deeply disturbed conventional lines of thinking anchored in the 'fact' established by some seventy years of history that there was no alternative to communism, that this system could not be overthrown and that resistance to it would be futile.[15] They brought state and society into an altogether new relationship, one in which the gulf that had theretofore divided the two was now spanned by scores of small bridges, each representing the experience of voters electing *their* deputies to public office.[16] Soon the logical extension of the vista opened by the electoral campaign would reflect itself in a new political consciousness emerging throughout the country, namely, that the Communist Party should surrender its monopoly on power and that it could be forced by the public to do just that. What had been unthinkable in the advent of the 1989 elections would become in a matter of months the principal demand of the popular movement.

Our treatment of the 1989 elections divides the topic into three phases: the period during which potential candidates were nominated to stand for office (26 December – 24 January); the cycle of pre-electoral district meetings during which those put forward in the previous round were politically vetted by the party-state apparatus (25 January – 22 February); and the election campaigns themselves (23 February – 25 March). Our intention throughout is to focus on those aspects of the process that contributed to its overall significance. To that end, the narrative oscillates between discussions of those patterns of activity that would establish empirically the significance of the elections in one phase or another, and descriptions of specific cases that contribute more detailed understanding to the patterns themselves.

First phase of the election campaign: the struggle to participate

Since we are concerned with public elections, we pass over that essentially privatized process through which the apparatus of the party-state distributed one-third of the seats in the new legislature to their own members.[17] Our focus falls on two broad groupings active in the public arena: CPSU officers and functionaries, and those affiliated with them; and informal political groups and those independent candidates who made common cause with them during the campaign. Both of these opposed groupings held one thing in common: neither had ever taken part in a competitive election. This mutual inexperience was coextensive with the relative indeterminacy of the phenomenon that unfolded, a phenomenon reciprocally constructed out of the interaction between these groupings and the reactions triggered within each camp through its interactions with the other. Each side was continually feeling its way and continually feeling the presence of the other as it did so. In the opening round, the first grouping – the incumbents, so to speak – endeavoured to close down those apparent channels for participation that the second would seek to enter. This was where the battle was joined in the initial stage. It concerned who would be able to participate in these elections.

It goes without saying that the distribution of resources between these two groups was completely lopsided. The party-state Goliath had armies of paid activists, it controlled the strategic junctures on the field of the nominations process and, by virtue of its *de facto* right to interpret the procedures governing the conduct of the participants, it dictated the terms of engagement. As nominations got under way, a rather motley collection of diminutive Davids sallied forth in Russia's larger cities to offer challenge. A measure of their initial strength can be taken from the size of the 'initiative groups' in various districts of Moscow, formed to secure places on the ballot for their preferred candidates. These initiative groups were composed of informal activists – most of whom were affiliated with the Moscow Popular Front (MNF) – who were distributed across the city's boroughs according to the figures set out in Table 6.1. Under the most favourable of circumstances, active informals in the overall population numbered fewer than 1:2,000; in the less favourable ones, the ratio was about 1:50,000. In Moscow, Leningrad and other large cities where informal activists sought to take part in the nominations process, the thinness in their ranks was made the worse by the virtual absence of coordination among them. In one Moscow sub-district, for instance, both the ecological group, Sever, and a coalition of activists from the MNF and the Committee for Social Security formed initiative groups in support of their respective candidates. It was only at the nominating assembly itself that each group became aware of the other's existence. Their potential backers thus divided, both would-be candidates failed to garner the support needed to survive this round of the nominations process.[18]

Voters' meetings

The electoral law provided two distinct channels through which a candidate might be nominated. He or she could be selected at a conference of a 'labour collective' conducted at factories, farms, schools and other institutions, or a candidate could be named by a meeting held at a residential site that required the participation of 500 voters who lived in the respective district. The choice of venue was by no means arbitrary. Officialdom, finding far firmer footing on the home ground of the institutions that it commanded, favoured the first channel. With no other alternative before them, their challengers sought to exploit the second. But since the authorities controlled this channel as well, the

Table 6.1 *Membership in initiative groups in ten boroughs of Moscow*

Borough	Population	Members of initiative group
Sovetskii	457,400	90
Krasnopresnenskii	135,200	10–15
Sevastopol'skii	287,100	200
Perovskii	453,400	20
Gagarinskii	288,200	20–30
Cheremushkinskii	510,900	200
Proletarskii	240,100	3–5
Sverdlovskii	115,100	100
Oktyabrskii	220,000	10
Volgogradskii	331,400	30

Sources: Borough population figures for 1 January 1990 were taken from *Moskva v tsifrakh* (Moscow: Statistika, 1990), p. 22. The data on initiative groups have been provided by Mikhail Shneider who served as campaign coordinator for the Moscow Popular Front.

initial round of nominations involved a struggle over whether and to what degree this channel would be open to popular participation. In Leningrad, the authorities shut it off altogether.[19] Elsewhere, local elites regularly and quite shamelessly proffered preposterous excuses to organized citizens seeking to exercise their legal rights. According to the law, an initiative group was required to produce a petition with thirty signatures in order to qualify for the use of premises in which to stage a nominations meeting. In Arkhangel's, however, one group that had collected 300 signatures was denied premises[20] while another in Stavropol that had managed to gather 1,500 signatures was likewise turned down.[21] These were not isolated incidences.[22]

When the authorities did grant permission to hold a nominations meeting in a place of residence, they usually took precautions to ensure that the meeting would produce the results that they desired. To that end, a number of tactics were regularly employed. To minimize the chances that the assembly would attract citizens other than those rehearsed by the local apparatus – usually, pensioners on whom party officials relied for 'public work' – the meeting might be held during working hours; it might be announced at the last minute and sometimes the announcement itself would bear a false address; it might be staged in an out-of-the-way place to which public transportation had suddenly and inexplicably ceased; the meeting place might be draped with phoney signs that would fool uninformed citizens into thinking that it had been closed for cleaning or repairs. Once inside the assembly, supporters of independent candidates would often have difficulty registering and sometimes would simply be refused this right because of their candidate preferences. During the most lively moments of debate over the choice of nominees, microphones would abruptly go dead or the lights might be switched off.[23]

Let us illustrate something of the style and flavour of the nominations meetings by taking the example of two convocations at which an initiative group supporting the candidacy of Vitalii Korotich – editor of *Ogonek*, one of the premier journals of the glasnost era – found themselves confronted by zealous exponents of the Stalinist–nationalist political tendency. As the first meeting got under way, shouts of 'Let Korotich speak before the voters!' rose from the noisy hall, along with replies exclaiming, 'Down with Korotich!' From the balcony, placards were unfurled with inscriptions such as: A JOURNAL READ BY A MILLION DOESN´T NEED AN EDITOR CHAMELEON! KOROTICH IS THE SUPERINTENDENT OF PERESTROIKA SCUM! DOWN WITH THE YELLOW PRESS! KOROTICH IS A LATTER-DAY GOL´DSHTYUKKER. Another placard carried the Star of David with a slash of red paint running across it. A group calling itself the Sobriety Society then began passing out photocopies of an article from 1982 in which Korotich had consigned many fine words to the honour of Leonid Brezhnev. At this point, Korotich, who had been seated in the second row, got up and left the meeting. His exit was accompanied by supporters fearing for his safety and by more shouts of 'Down with Zionists!', 'No to cosmopolitans!' and 'Long live Russia'. Then, the authorities took action – they turned off the house lights and thereby ended the proceedings.

Korotich supporters regrouped and attempted to secure his nomination some days later at another voters' meeting while Korotich himself was out of country. In anticipation of this event, people began gathering outside the gates to the premises long before the appointed hour. When an automobile with officials from the local soviet drove through the gates, the entire crowd darted after it and ran to the closed glass doors of the meeting place which they pushed and pulled to no avail. Korotich's supporters appeared and in vain attempted to make their way through those pressed up against the glass doors. Confusion reigned. Desultory shouts went up – 'We are all the initiative group!', 'We know who *you* are!', 'I just want to go to the meeting'. Then the crowd began to chant – 'The doors!' 'The doors!' Crash! The first pane of glass shattered. At this someone sardonically called out – 'Democracy, Soviet-style!' Crash! The second pane was blown out. Neither the glass doors nor the cordon of volunteer keepers of public order (*druzhina*) could staunch the tide of enthusiasm that swept the crowd into the hall and filled it to capacity.

Tele-journalist V. Tsvetov spoke on behalf of the absent Korotich. 'We have before us three paths,' he said, 'either into the abyss, either to make ourselves into a great, free, socialist country, or to become a second-rate power with a tyrannical government. Therefore, let's vote for Korotich!' Yurii Skokov – Korotich's contender for the nomination, director of Kvant (a large armaments plant) and future secretary of the Security Council in the El'tsin administration – spoke next. Those in the hall had plenty of questions for him. Here is a sample of the dialogue that ensued:

(QUESTION) Which publication is closest to your way of thinking: *Molodaya gvardiya, Nash sovremennik* or *Ogonek*? And if it's *Ogonek*, withdraw your candidacy.
(QUESTION) How do you relate to someone leaving the country?
(SKOKOV) If a person wants to go, let him go; but don't then let him ask to come back!
(QUESTION) What's your attitude toward the Democratic Union as a political party?
(SKOKOV) We need freedom and glasnost, but is something like that really necessary?

Another luminary of the glasnost press – the novelist, Yurii Karyakin – then rose on Korotich's behalf. Admitting that those who had brought up his candidate's previous panegyric to Brezhnev had, indeed, delivered a weighty and painful blow, he then rejoined with the rhetorical imperative, 'Name me one member of the TsK [Central Committee of the CPSU] who is unsullied!' An answer ricocheted back from the audience: 'Why does Korotich slander Russian writers?' Karyakin's reply was 'Down with Pamyat!' Then idly winding his head, his eyes flashing on those in the hall, he gathered himself up as a maestro vigorously gesticulating a visual rhythm to the syllables he repeated – '*Do-loi!*' ['Down with . . .']. At first the hall was silent, then with deepening courage and rising amplitude, it shot back – '*Do-loi! Do-loi!* Pamyat, out! Pamyat, out!' The people's wrath then descended on the 'patriots'. 'Bitches', they were called, 'fascists'. Pandemonium broke out. The representatives of the press scattered toward any available refuge as the audience's activity began to slide into mass hysteria. The presiding officer managed to call for the vote and it came back lopsidedly for Korotich – 780, against 145 cast for Skokov.[24]

These two voters' meetings – superficially so different in their political complexions and results – reveal a striking symmetry at the level of political culture. In the first instance, Stalinists–nationalists seem to have had the upper hand; in the second, the democrats proved the stronger. As soon as one group had established its dominance, it was concerned with more than merely nominating its candidate; rather, it aimed to obliterate the other group. In these two meetings, the validation of one's own cause was indistinguishable from annihilating one's opponents. The righteousness and triumphalism that each side displayed could only be taken by the other as insults and rude provocations that confirmed foreknowledge of its loathsome character, thus justifying the epithets hurled in reply. Neither recognized the other as such. Each 'saw through' the presentation of the self that its counterpart advanced and renamed it accordingly – 'patriots' were dubbed 'fascists', just as 'democrats' were called 'cosmopolitans'. The rhetorical strategies exhibited in these meetings – righteousness, triumphalism, mutual renaming and so on – would persist and flourish in Russia as open political contest became the norm,[25] not only exacerbating the already high levels of conflict potential stored up over years of repressive communist rule but ensuring that these conflicts would themselves persist and flourish within a communicative code that has thrived on them.

The Korotich candidacy that prevailed at the second of the meetings just discussed – like most of the other 282 nominees who succeeded in garnering the support of their respective voters' assemblies during the opening round of nominations[26] – was scratched in the subsequent stage of the nominations process. In a series of other cases, a simple and altogether arbitrary decision by the corresponding electoral commission to ignore the results of these meetings accomplished the same objective.[27] The apparatuses of the party-state, then, managed to contain their opponents in this election first and foremost by restricting to a minimum their ability to mount candidacies in those venues where their legal opportunities to do so were greatest.

Workplace assemblies

In comparison with the voters' meetings just described, the nominations conducted at workplace assemblies was quite a different affair. Here the heavy inertia of the past palpably weighed on the present, often arresting any movement toward political action. This inertia packed the meeting halls. It was printed on the broad banners draped around the room, urging workers on to greater feats of labour heroism, and reminding them of how, if not why, the party and the people were united. It hung from the stilted speeches of petty officials and their stooges who sang the praises of some nominee chosen by the bosses – as ever before. It showed itself in the ritualistic raising of hands for someone and about something that was not, after all, 'our business' but 'theirs'.[28] But when all of these icons, symbols and verbal cues failed to remind workers just where they were and what was expected of them, the bosses had at their ready disposal an ample arsenal of other persuasive devices.

The cleanest among them – since no illegalities were involved – was to control communications. Obviously, this method worked best in large factories where individuals might be familiar with their workmates but not with those in other shops. Here the authorities often found it relatively easy to manipulate delegates from shop-level by various combinations of screened information, misinformation and disinformation.[29] Sometimes the example of local notables bowing out of the contest in accession to even larger luminaries – along with reminders to other would-be candidates, issued behind closed-doors, about just whom they would be going up against – was sufficient to persuade shop-level nominees to follow suit.[30] But sterner measures were taken as well. These ranged from rather course manipulation of the nominations procedures,[31] to smear campaigns against candidates supported by informal organizations[32] – campaigns that were apparently ordered and orchestrated by local committees of the Communist Party[33] – to open threats to one's career, to criminal prosecution[34] and, indeed, to one's physical safety.[35] By the very nature of these tactics it would be impossible to determine their rate of success; but they seemed to have been effective in enough cases to conclude that failures to dissuade candidates were the exception to the rule.

However, exceptions did occur. Especially when press attention was focused on the scandalous behaviour of local elites, the chances increased that the CEC would perform its legally prescribed functions and intervene to investigate complaints and overrule improper decisions taken at lower levels.[36] Sometimes labour collectives would refuse to back down in the face of intransigent local officials and, faced with the threat of strike that had been picked up by the press, officialdom would relent.[37] In another instance, the mere presence of the press at a nominations meeting prompted its presidium to acquiesce to demands for voting by secret ballot; with the predictable result that, given the opportunity to vote against the candidacy of their boss, the workers made the most of it.[38] But even the comparatively few instances in which independent nominees were able to win out over the repression employed by the party-state apparatus did not translate into places on the ballot. Most were ambushed at pre-electoral district meetings.

Second phase of the electoral campaign: the struggle to participate continues

According to the law, district electoral commissions had the right to call pre-electoral meetings in their bailiwicks if more than two individuals had been nominated in the first round. These meetings would decide which of the nominees would be registered by the electoral commission as a candidate. In an interpretive ruling, the CEC mandated that pre-electoral meetings were to be composed of delegates drawn from those assemblies in which the original nominations had occurred and by an equal complement of delegates from some of the other labour collectives in the district (designated by the local electoral commission) that had not nominated anyone. Although this second provision would have seemed to provide sufficient opportunity to local elites to pack these meetings with their own people and thus ensure the desired outcomes, this was not always the case. Sometimes the local authorities saw fit to expand the margin of delegates from hitherto passive labour collectives from 50 to 60 per cent.[39] Sometimes they lost control of these assemblies and watched their worst fears realized before their eyes. But usually these meetings – called in 868 of the USSR's 1,500 electoral districts[40] – worked according to plan. Across the USSR, they disposed of some two-thirds of the 7,558 candidates who had been nominated in the first round.[41] Over 1,000 complaints reached the CEC concerning the way that these meetings were manipulated by local officialdom.[42] In many cases, not only were delegates from voters' assemblies or certain labour collectives denied credentials, but 'delegates' selected at closed party conferences at the workplace were seated in their stead.[43] Some of those attending complained that what they had thought to be a voters' meeting turned out to be a conference of local party-state cadres.[44] A sociological study has corroborated that impression, finding that local administrators represented the most active and influential group at the pre-electoral meetings.[45]

Local authorities complemented their control over delegate selection with control over procedures. Most effective in their quiver of rules was the arrow marked 'open voting' which, when mounted on the bow by decision of those officiating, was pointed at every delegate now required to express his or her political preference in the presence of both workplace superiors and the local power structure.[46] Perhaps symptomatic of the unrepresentative and constricted nature of these exercises was the fact that Boris El'tsin – who entered the *Guinness Book of Records* by outpolling his opponent, Evgenii Brakov, in the March balloting by a margin of 89.5 to 6.9 per cent – actually trailed Brakov by 577 votes to 532 at the pre-electoral meeting that placed them both on the ballot. But there was some room for the unexpected in these stage-managed affairs and occasionally the unexpected happened. Anatolii Sobchak, later elected as St Petersburg's first mayor, has recounted that although his supporters were hopelessly outnumbered at the pre-electoral meeting that eventually approved his nomination, he was able to place second in the balloting because of the strong impression his impromptu 'I have a dream' speech – lifted from the late Martin Luther King, Jr – had on many of the other delegates.[47] In that same city, the candidacy of Yurii Boldyrev, an activist then associated with Club Perestroika, survived this round on the strength of an eloquent and impassioned plea made on his behalf by an elderly, distinguished-looking gentleman who then collapsed and expired. His final words – 'This may be our last chance' – were apparently taken to heart by enough delegates previously pledged to Boldyrev's opponent (the city's party chief) to swing them over to Boldyrev.[48] In other locales, the course behaviour of the apparatus's dummy-delegates – whistling, shouting, foot-stamping and cat-calling – actually defamed their candidates so badly that the huge majorities that they sported on entering the hall melted away in the heat of the proceedings.[49]

Third phase of the electoral campaign: open competition for public office

The ham-handed tactics of the authorities, amply evident during the nominations process as well as in the election campaigns that followed, backfired to a considerable extent. Although they succeeded in torpedoing thousands of candidacies mounted by informal political groups and independents, their behaviour also incensed and thus activated many previously passive people who would join in to work for the defeat of apparatus-sponsored candidates. As the campaign wore on, the widening circles of activists grew into a mass political movement whose communicative code and forms of organization were the direct byproducts of its struggle with the communist regime. The experience of, and resistance to, the anti-democratic practices of that regime shaped its identity in specific ways, above all by imprinting on it an anti-communist character. From their inception, then, neither could a democratic practice nor a democratic identity be meaningfully distinguished from an anti-communist one. With respect to organization, the repressive practices of the party-state both deprived most informal groups of the candidates whom they had supported during the nominations phases and supplied for them all one common, odious opponent: the apparatus. This encouraged the many small and separate groups to act in concert. The energies of those backing candidates who were subsequently expunged from the race were usually redeployed on behalf of others, while the presence of a single arch-opponent stimulated a search for new forms of association that would enhance their capacity for conflict. In the main, this search was a spontaneous process transpiring at micro level. Campaign staffs 'found' their candidates,[50] just as small groups discovered one another at, say, voters' meetings.[51] As venues changed from the meeting hall to the streets, however, this process not only accelerated but began to assume more consciously designed shapes.

In the capital, a number of political groups with no history of previous cooperation fashioned an effective alliance as the campaign unfolded. A club of prestigious liberal intellectuals, Moscow Tribune, had formed a 'social council' under the auspices of *Moscow News*[52] which subsequently published its 'radical democratic' programme as a common platform for a number of the club's prominent members who were seeking office.[53] The MNF initially had sought to field candidates in nineteen of the city's electoral districts but the resistance of the local apparatus proved insurmountable in all but two. Memorial also played an independent role early on, but circumstances changed radically for the organization when its leading member, Andrei Sakharov, chose to contest a seat within the Academy of Sciences rather than stand in an electoral district. Finally, there were the more amorphous forces associated with the populist figures, Boris El'tsin and Tel'man Gdlyan (the anti-corruption prosecutor), and the many labour collectives backing them. As the electoral process brought these separate strands of the public movement into contact, certain of their organizers began to find grounds for *ad hoc*, and eventually more regularized, cooperation[54] which laid the basis for establishing the Moscow Voters' Association in the immediate aftermath of the elections.[55]

In Leningrad the process was broadly similar. There, a host of political groups – Club Perestroika, the Leningrad Popular Front, Alternative, Memorial and others – eventually combined forces in Elections–89. This was an especially loose coalition by most measures – it lacked a common programme, fixed membership or vertical organizational structures – but was an especially supple, adroit and effective one in the face of its primary objective, namely, to marshal the voters against the candidates of that same apparatus that had scotched the candidacies of effectively all nominees put forward by these groups.[56] With varying degrees of success, analogous coalitions were formed to contest the elections in such places as Kaliningrad, Tomsk and Sverdlovsk while local popular fronts played the same role in Kazan, Stavropol, Chelyabinsk, Yaroslavl and elsewhere.[57]

Due both to the features of the USSR's Law on Elections requiring a candidate to receive a majority of the votes cast in order to be elected and to the successful efforts of the apparatus in eliminating popular candidates during the nominations process, the 1989 campaign would feature two distinct forms of electoral competition. The first was the conventional type that pitted candidates against other candidates in a contest for voters' support. The second involved those instances in which all the candidates for a given seat were in fact candidates of the apparatus. These contests might accurately be described as a struggle between the candidates and the voters in which independent political groups functioned as catalysts for voter disapproval of all names on the ballot. Here, we present a few sketches of each type of electoral competition, beginning with the second one.

Voters versus candidates

Perhaps the single most important factor contributing to voter victory over the slates of candidates fielded by the apparatus was disgust at the shameless behaviour exhibited by the authorities during the nominations process and in the campaigns themselves. The impact of this factor in one locale or another was magnified by the press coverage afforded to similar dirty tricks perpetrated by the authorities in other places. In this respect, even the quite limited attention that liberal publications managed to focus on the machinations of local power elites served to stimulate a sense of outrage nationally.[58] And independent political groups capitalized on it. In many districts where the apparatus had monopolized the nomination process, they waged spirited campaigns urging the electorate to vote against all those who appeared on the ballot. In 199 districts, majorities voted against these candidates, thereby eliminating them from further competition and forcing new elections.[59] In Leningrad, Elections–89 mounted an exceptionally effective leafleting campaign against 'elections without choice' that convinced over 60 per cent of the voters to strike from the ballot the name of Yurii Solov'ev, the First Secretary of the Leningrad Obkom, and defeat five other leading figures in the city and regional apparatus in the first round.[60] The Popular Front of Tatariya, braving both police threats to open fire and onslaughts of snow removal equipment, rallied against apparatus candidates in front of CPSU headquarters in Kazan. They succeeded in defeating a number of them.[61] In Stavropol, local activists staged hunger strikes to draw attention to the way in which the apparatus had rigged races there. Although they decided in the end to support one apparatus candidate as the lesser of two evils, the voters sent them both down to defeat.[62]

Some interesting contests of this sort took place in Moscow. In one, Valerii Saikin – chairperson of the city soviet – went to considerable lengths to cloak his candidacy in democratic garb. His leaflets emphasized his struggles on behalf of the people against 'bureaucrats and the mafia, crime and social injustice'. His apparatus associates in the Lyublin district in which he ran not only screened out all would-be contenders but arranged for a 'running mate' – a shop leader and member of the city party committee of the CPSU who was virtually unknown to the public – to appear on the same ballot in order to create the impression that this was, indeed, a competitive race. Saikin even went so far as to distribute leaflets bearing a testimonial to him from Boris El'tsin, delivered while the latter had been Communist Party chief in Moscow. To no avail. The campaign mounted by an initiative group urging voters to strike the names of both candidates from the ballot left them both short of a majority and thus disqualified from the repeat elections that ensued.

In two other races of this type in Moscow, the voters came out on top. Just outside the city, however, in the town of Stupino, they were defeated by V. K. Mesyats, first secretary of the CPSU's Moscow Obkom. All of Mesyats' opponents had been conveniently disposed of by the district electoral commission at the pre-electoral assembly. Although targeted by a local leaflet campaign, Mesyats passed the gate on election day with 52.6 per cent of the vote. At one precinct in the district, however, when the staff of the school at which voting took place attempted to validate the returns, the authorities hastily bundled off the ballots to the local soviet. Fraud, then, may have provided him with the winning margin; what is perhaps more important, it *appeared* to have done so.[63]

Candidates versus candidates

The 'Saikin syndrome' – stooge candidates in sham competition with party-state officials – would discount the competitive character of a great many ostensible 'races' in 1989. Therefore, we turn to a sample of those contests in which genuine candidates campaigned against one another, beginning with the main event: Boris El'tsin versus Evgenii Brakov (director of the ZIL Automotive Works) in Moscow's national-territorial district no. 1 which encompassed the entire capital and included some six million voters. What accounted for El'tsin's landslide, 5.1 million votes – in a ratio of nearly 9:1 – for the maverick populist from the CPSU's own Central Committee? Firstly, the Communist Party's 'stop El'tsin' campaign. To invert an old phrase, with enemies like these, the candidate seemed scarcely to need friends. Via a combination of crude, insinuating and anonymously issued leaflets, character assassinations in the press, a host of dirty tricks ranging from threatening phone calls to vandalism, and – the clincher – a formal investigation launched by the

CPSU Central Committee, the apparatus showed itself to be as inept as it was vicious.[64] As El'tsin himself observed,

everything that has been done has given me a martyr's halo, which gets brighter every day . . . Every new move against me only makes the Moscow voters more and more indignant; and since there have been a lot of such moves, the result is that my enemies have sabotaged their own efforts . . . So obvious are the mistakes that people ask whether in fact Lev Zaikov, my enemy and successor as First Secretary of the Moscow City Committee of the Party, is perhaps not my secret supporter.[65]

Independent political groups were quick to seize the opportunities handed them by the apparatus. A week before election day, the Russian Popular Front drew some 5,000 people to a rally in Gorky Park in support of El'tsin. Though sanctioned by the authorities, police were dispatched to disperse the crowd anyway.[66] With no prior planning, those assembled simply set off on foot to the city soviet. Their numbers doubled *en route* as thousands of Muscovites abandoned their personal affairs to join this spontaneous street demonstration. On reaching their destination, the marchers staged a rally before the Moscow soviet that shut down traffic on Gorky Street and filled the city centre with the angry cries of political protest boomed out over bull-horns. A second rally followed on 22 March. It was organized by the initiative group that had supported El'tsin's nomination and was publicized all over Moscow, thanks largely to *agents provocateur* who spread rumours of impending police assault and possible massacre, and to the authorities themselves who posted statements saying that they had cancelled the rally. Some 20,000 people attended while thousands more looked on over the police cordons that blocked their way.[67] This rally inaugurated the era of mass political actions in Russia. It marked the turning point at which political society felt itself sufficiently strong to challenge openly the repressive party-state; it heralded the passing of power from the old guard of functionaries – proving themselves increasingly helpless to control, much less direct, the forces unleashed in the elections – to a new coterie of politicians who would harness them.

Who were these politicians? Almost all of them came from the ranks of the CPSU and effectively none had participated in the dissident movement. They were, of course, ambitious people who had worked to further their own careers, but they could hardly be said to have been careerists in the sense of the word as it applied to the Brezhnev era. They displayed talents and abilities but had been prevented from making full use of them by the communist system which so often rewarded cronyism and ignored, if not actually penalized, merit. They were, in short, 'new people' as the Russians say. Their time had come. The launching of one such political career – to our knowledge, more or less typical of many others – might illustrate the larger pattern. This example has been drawn from the Cheremushkinskii district of Moscow where a relatively high concentration of independent activists (see Table 6.1) and a comparatively fair and open nominations process produced four candidates for the March election. Two were put forward by the party apparatus while the other two were the lone survivors on the MNF's long list of nominees after the pre-electoral meeting had completed its work. One was Mikhail Lemeshev, an economist and ecologist who was backed by the ecologically oriented wing of the Front. The other was Sergei Stankevich, a young historian and Front leader who had just managed by his own initiative to get his name included at the bottom of the Front's initial list. To avoid internecine competition, Stankevich earlier promised to withdraw in favour of Lemeshev at the pre-electoral meeting, explaining that his sole intention was to use his candidacy temporarily as a podium for popularizing the Front. However, the favourable response to his public orations seemed to cause him to reconsider that decision.

Stankevich had applied for admission to the CPSU during the Andropov interregnum, a time at which it seemed to him that changes were possible,[68] but he was not admitted till 1987. On joining the ranks of the CPSU, Stankevich, unlike most, was not a passive member. He served on a commission of the Cheremushkinskii district party committee for counter-propaganda and kept the local authorities apprised of the activities of informal organizations there.[69] On entering informal circles, however, Stankevich was soon caught up in the spirit of his new surroundings and came to share some of the perspectives on society and the possibilities for change then being worked out by those in the MNF. Indeed, he soon became a leader of that organization and simultaneously cut his ties with the CPSU's district committee (although he remained a party member until mid-1990). This was to prove a fortunate change of allegiances, but Stankevich would need some skilful manoeuvres in order to capitalize on it.

Ecological sentiment was running high in the Cheremushkinskii district at the time, just as it was throughout the USSR.[70] Feeling hoodwinked by Stankevich's *volte face* on his pledge to withdraw in favour of their man, Lemeshev, ecological activists began plastering the precincts with anti-Stankevich propaganda. One leaflet read simply: 'JEWS! Vote for STANKEVICH, he's OUR man!' Such items, along with the favourable coverage afforded Lemeshev by the right-wing *Nash sovremennik*, dictated the counter-attack. Stankevich's campaign literature began to play up associations between Lemeshev and Pamyat. Lemeshev supporters, however, uncovered Stankevich's previous service to the district committee of the CPSU and publicized it along with some piquantly compromising prose lifted from an old article published by Stankevich in the newspaper, *Druzhba*. As Lemeshev supporters accused Stankevich of being an agent of the CPSU apparatus, so the latter's staff would shower the district with leaflets depicting Lemeshev as an unprincipled servant of the Soviet regime.

From this mutual mud-slinging, Stankevich repaired to higher ground on the wings of a timely stratagem. As election day neared, he persuaded fourteen other candidates to sign with him a telegram to the CPSU's Central Committee protesting its investigation of El'tsin. Subsequently, the telegram was reprinted as a leaflet on which also appeared El'tsin's reply thanking the signators for their support and wishing them all success. The use of this eleventh-hour association with El'tsin appeared to benefit all those involved – the fifteen signators collectively averaged some 46 per cent of the vote on 26 March, while other candidates in the capital averaged only 26 per cent.[71] Stankevich placed first among the four candidates in his district and scored a victory in the run-off that followed.

The electoral alliance formed among the El'tsin forces and fifteen other candidates spearheading the popular movement in Moscow was the culmination on a citywide basis of the same process of coalition formation begun at micro level at the advent of nominations. Political society was now beginning to assume a definite shape, three aspects of which disclose its main contours at this stage of development. The first might be called 'mobilizational'. There was precious little by way of organizations at the ready that lined up for the starter's gun and conducted races for public office; rather, organizations developed fluidly and rapidly out of the skeletal initiative groups that battled the party apparatus during the nominations phase. The stage of open campaigning brought them into contact with the larger public, a public that was often bewildered by the unprecedented spectacle of candidates stumping the hustings for their votes, debating one another on local radio and television, speaking in public places and answering voters' queries on all and sundry matters. As this spectacle unfolded, it drew in countless newcomers to politics. Having heard a candidate speak at, say, a metro station, onlookers might approach his staff thereafter with an offer to help in the campaign. Having seen a leaflet whose slogans appealed to their sympathies that was posted at some bus stop, others would ring up one of the telephone numbers printed at the bottom of it and volunteer their services. Often enough, they would simply knock on the door of the candidate's apartment and report for duty. In short, by election day campaign organizations had multiplied their numbers many times over as tens, perhaps hundreds, of thousands of spectators had turned into participants.[72]

The second aspect was 'organizational'. As activists scrambled to address the many new problems confronting them over the course of the campaign – not least of which was how to deploy effectively the waves of new recruits appearing on their doorsteps – they developed task-specific forms of organization, mastering new techniques as they went along on the basis of trial and error. Inasmuch as the principal task was victory on election day – or, when blocked in the nominations process, the defeat of the candidate(s) of the apparatus – organizational forms quite naturally favoured maximum inclusion. Here, a correspondence was evident between an amorphous mass of voters and a proliferation of amoeba-like campaign organizations. When the objective was itself congruent with loose, inclusive organizational forms, this arrangement was especially serviceable. Elections–89 – which included groups associated with the liberal democratic current (such as the Leningrad Popular Front), the radical socialist tendency (for instance, For Leninism and a Communist Orientation) and the patriotic camp (Pamyat among them) – was enormously successful in deploying this unwieldy coalition *against* the apparatus. However, cooperation could not be sustained when the task shifted to coordinating the nomination of candidates and working jointly for their election. Without the adhesive of a common opponent, Elections–89 splintered into its constituent elements that campaigned against one another in the new round of elections that was forced by voters' rejection of the apparatus candidates on 26 March. Nowhere was the weakness of these loose forms of coalition more apparent than in the repeated election staged on 14 May in Leningrad's national-territorial district no. 19. There, thirty-four candidates had been nominated, most of them on the initiative of groups affiliated with Elections–89. This internal conflict was compounded by the defection of other groups to the candidacy of Nikolai Ivanov – Gdlyan's partner from Moscow – whom Elections–89 publicly opposed. On election day, Ivanov captured 61 per cent of the vote in a field of twenty-eight (remaining) candidates.[73]

Ivanov's success in Leningrad highlights the third aspect of these elections: the 'political' one. When Elections–89 was channelling voter resentment against the apparatus, its successes were spectacular. However, when it found itself upstaged by a figure who personified the struggle against the corrupt party-state, its influence was immediately marginalized. This episode would bring into sharp relief the principal political issue driving the entire election process, the issue of the

Communist Party itself. To be sure, the issue was articulated in oblique and rudimentary forms by popular candidates at this juncture: opposition to 'privilege', opposition to the abuses of power perpetrated by the apparatus, sometimes as demands for a multi-party system. But what caused the popular movement to cohere was the same thing that marshalled the voters behind it: the presence of one overbearing enemy, the Communist Party. If independent political groups had not realized this before the elections had commenced, they could scarcely have failed to recognize it by the time that they were over.[74]

Nor would the Communist Party refrain from reminding them of this ineluctable fact. As new elections got under way in those districts where voters had rejected the candidates put before them on 26 March, the apparatus in a number of instances redoubled its efforts against contenders, illegally excluding nominees from the ballot in some places,[75] in others ordering in the police with truncheons against peaceful demonstrators, sending many to hospital and even more to jail.[76] At the polling places on election day, ballot fraud occurred often.[77] Roadblocks were thrown up to prevent the participation of independent poll watchers and commonly the only precinct monitors supervising the balloting were those selected by the local bosses.[78] In other cases in which independent poll-watchers reported apparent violations, the members of the respective electoral commissions responded by assaulting them physically or charging them with 'violations of public order' for which they would be fined in court.[79] An indicative episode of this type took place in Moscow's Proletarian Electoral District where four duly certified poll-watchers – all members of an officially registered organization, Memorial – were arrested on charges of malicious disobedience to authority and petty hooliganism for doing apparently nothing more than performing their jobs. One of them, G. P. Sinyanskaya (a surgeon), later described the event in this way:

At 10:20 [a.m.], a woman with two ballots entered and exited the polling booth. I intercepted her [asking], 'Forgive me, do you have two ballots?' I raised the ballots over my head and loudly said, 'Comrades, a violation of the law on elections has occurred! Article 52! I demand a statement for the record, and then one of the ballots must be cancelled [and] the other deposited in the ballot box!' Right away a few people came flying at me. From the executive committee of the local soviet there were Kuznetskii and Belyaev [saying], 'You are interfering with [our] work! Return the ballots immediately!' The chairperson of [the local electoral] commission, Sharapov, arrived with a policeman, Sofilkanich, who showed me his credentials and took me into custody.

Another in the party of poll-watchers, Vera Kriger, recalled her experience thus:

There was a mass of [voting] violations. I put them all down in writing and [gave the list] to the chairperson of the [local electoral] commission, Stepanov. He [responded], 'Why are you poking your nose into all of this? I am the master here, I am!!!' Other members of the commission [told me], 'You are wrecking all our work!' And then amongst themselves [they said], 'Because of her the elections are being ruined!' They began to fence me off from the ballot boxes there, casually standing up and surrounding me so that I couldn't see a thing. They threatened me [saying], 'Are you in line for an apartment? If we can't remove you from the queue, we'll transfer [your name] to the end.' On one occasion they assaulted me. A woman had deposited one ballot and with a second one in hand was quickly [heading for] another ballot box. I went up to her. From behind my back, three people struck me with their hands, calling me 'fascist' and 'sicko'. According to my notes [at the time], by 7:00 p.m. only 20 per cent of those registered had voted. [Then someone] in uniform came up to me [saying], 'Some charges have been lodged concerning your conduct. Let's go, we'll sort this out!' We left, and a black Volga with two zeros on the license plate stood waiting. I thought that we would go to the executive committee of the soviet. [But] in a few minutes I was at the police station.[80]

Election results

The 1989 elections represented a watershed in the course of Russia's political development, fundamentally redefining the relations between state and society. In place of the Communist Party's longstanding claim to authority as history's scientifically guided vanguard, the experience of these elections supplied a new one: popular sovereignty. Herein lay the subtle yet unmistakable result of the national elections that would constitute their singular importance. Millions of people got it into their heads that their state was, after all, their concern. Not 'their concern' merely as individuals musing, complaining or joking about this state, for Russians under all but the heaviest forms of repression had rarely been wanting for opinions on such matters. Rather, 'their concern' now engaged them as citizens, occupying a new status that bound them together with unseen fellows into a larger public with a capacity to act in concert. To be sure, the transformation of authority structures coincident with this change in popular mentalities was not accomplished by these elections. But the important thing was that it was begun. In order to investigate this metamorphosis, we might divide the discussion into two related topics: agency and outcome.

Agency

Among those forces contributing to the revival of political life in Russia that was manifest in the 1989 elections none was more influential than the press. Earlier we outlined some of the ways in which liberal publications had been preparing the way for the appearance of a mass public, enkindling new habits of mind inclined both toward a citizen's right to information and to the expression of his or her views on matters of common concern. We also called attention to how the readership of the country's liberal press had comprised, by the time that the 1989 elections had arrived, a distinguishable political community sustained by a liberal-populist discourse. Table 6.2 provides an illustration of how this political community expressed itself with its vote.

Some of the data reported in this table are rather unconventional: subscription rates to two newspapers – the liberal weekly, *Argumenty i fakty*, and the conservative daily, *Trud* – organized according to the number of subscriptions to each per hundred mailboxes within the twelve postal codes found in the Sevastopol'skii district of Moscow. Since individual-level data on subscriptions and voting are not available, aggregated data by postal code have been used as an indication of reading habits. These data have been collapsed into three categories – high, medium and low – each composed of four corresponding postal codes (left-hand column of the table). The Sevastopol'skii district has been selected to illustrate the relationship between reading habits and candidate preferences because it was the only election district in Moscow with a majority of working-class voters in which a liberal candidate managed to get his name on the ballot, thus enabling us to compare the effect of variable subscription rates for two newspapers against the vote for a 'liberal' (O. Bogomolov), a 'centrist' (A. Bryachikin, the party secretary in the district) and a 'conservative' (A. Seredenin, a rank-and-file worker) whose names appear at the head of the table. We would expect the correlations between our subscription data and voter preferences to be weak (due to the aggregated nature of the former)[81] but consistent in their direction. The results bear this out. The liberal vote correlates positively with subscription rates to the liberal publication and negatively with those to the conservative one; the conservative vote sustains this same pattern in reverse; and the centrist vote fluctuates in correspondence with the conservative one, suggesting that Bryachikin and Seredenin were dividing between themselves the non-liberal sector of the electorate, with the latter doing better in core conservative districts and the former in mixed ones.

In addition to preparing the way for the emergence of a mass public, the press also played no small role in stimulating its activity during the elections themselves. At the national level, this period featured a clear distinction between conservative papers, whose coverage of the elections was effectively confined to reprinting the harmless programmes of

Table 6.2 *Voting for candidates in Moscow's Sevastopol'skii district by subscription rates to* Argumenty i fakty *and* Trud *(in percentages)*

Subscription rates		Votes for candidates		
		O. Bogomolov	A. Bryachikin	A. Seredenin
Argumenty i fakty	high	52.14	13.87	15.93
	medium	49.28	20.97	20.20
	low	47.72	19.91	22.93
Trud	high	47.10	20.13	23.58
	medium	50.67	20.47	19.31
	low	51.38	24.16	16.17

regime-sponsored candidates, and liberal ones that supplied their readers with a steady stream of disclosures on how the functionaries of the party-state were so shamelessly stealing their election from them. Never mind that there were still limits to what the liberal newspapers and journals could or would report. The point would be simply that they disclosed the shenanigans of the apparatus in sufficient measure to stimulate growing levels of popular involvement as the process went forward. At the local level, party-state officials held a tighter rein on newspapers in their respective areas. But even there certain publications opened their pages to insurgent candidates and doubtless contributed to their success.[82]

The second component of agency was the informals. By supplying the initial cadres of activists for the electoral campaigns, they provided an indispensable presence on the public stage that they themselves largely constructed. Their dogged persistence in the face of innumerable defeats and disappointments during the nominations process paid off later in the more open venue of the campaigns, when that which the informals would not surrender – the claim to participate in politics – would be redeemed many thousands of times over by those who would actively join in. Subsequent surveys conducted among the population in urban centres have tapped something of the informals' political impact on the larger public registered during these elections. In one, a majority of respondents ranked informal political groups ahead of all other organizations in conducting 'energetic, intelligent and honourable' campaigns.[83] In another – a panel study covering the period December 1988 to mid-March 1989 – it was determined that the initially low level of voter attention to the upcoming elections had been superseded by the close of the campaign period by widespread interest with some 48 per cent of the sample expressing the opinion that electoral competition had raised the quality of the candidates themselves.[84] However, the mass public movement that emerged with these elections was as much a consequence as a cause of what occurred during the Russian spring of 1989.

Outcomes

We have already remarked on the principal outcome of these elections – the appearance of a mass public and what that implied for the way in which state power would be reconfigured in political discourse. It remains here to add some qualifications. First, there is the matter of the party-state authorities whose pyrrhic victory in 1989 portended the perdition of the communist regime that followed in relatively short order. Rather than winning a popular mandate for its leading role in society, the CPSU's performance in these elections provoked only society's contempt. Although muffled by the baroque mechanisms that the apparatus had emplaced, and then manipulated, for the purpose of confecting itself into the 'governing party' in the new legislature, the voting results none the less expressed this contempt quite eloquently. Dozens of the CPSU's regional personifications – the obkom and kraikom first secretaries – went down to defeat.[85] Perhaps even more indicative of voter disgust was the fact that some 90 per cent of those regional party bosses in the USSR elected to the Congress of People's Deputies had stood for election in safe rural constituencies where they ran unopposed, while over 80 per cent of those who lost were involved in competitive races.[86]

Finally, there was the manner in which the anti-apparatus sentiment that characterized Russia's emerging public consciousness meshed with the organizational forms erected to channel it into a mass political movement: loose electoral blocs whose primary plank was opposition to the ruling apparatus. Given what had hitherto existed in Russia by way of organized political activity, this in itself can be counted as a major breakthrough. Yet, while the formula first discovered in 1989 – anti-communist ideology plus inclusive forms of organization in which programmatic issues were glossed – would repeatedly prove its utility for securing the country's political liberation, it would represent a recipe for disaster once that liberation had been won. For this formula contained neither the ingredients necessary to the practice of quotidian politics – in short, organizational forms capable of articulating and adjusting conflicting social claims – nor the ideational and emotional orientations required to frame such conflicts in those pragmatic terms conducive to their resolution. Not only were the achievements of 1989 to be reproduced on an expanded scale in the months ahead, but Russia's political rebirth would be traumatized by the disorienting influence of its anti-communist inception.

Part III

Politics and revolution

The chapters in this part of the book trace the course of Russian politics over the period bounded at one end by the convening of perestroika's centrepiece, the Congress of People's Deputies, and at the other, the dissolution of this same assembly in the wake of the failed *coup* of August 1991. During this brief epoch, the scope of political life was massively enlarged and its character fundamentally transformed. What had begun as a conflict inside the Soviet tent over the pace and character of reform quickly gave way to the formation of an opposition standing outside of it, offering an alternative group of political leaders and an alternative vision for the country's future. Chapter 7, which focuses on this question, locates the genesis of this (initially reluctant) opposition in the context of a regime ('above') that systematically blocked its reformist initiatives and an emergent mass movement ('below') that radicalized the would-be reformers and summoned them to supply the leadership that the movement required.

The dynamic interaction between leaders and movement entered a new stage during the Russian elections of 1990, the topic of Chapter 8. During the electoral contest, the country's democratic movement situated itself – tentatively, uneasily – within a political–territorial and cultural space: Russia. Its opposition to the communist system took on the character of a national liberation struggle directed against the Soviet order and aimed at the establishment of a sovereign Russian state. Victory in this respect – not according to the cockeyed arithmetic of the electoral system but in terms of a public validation of the movement's then unmatched power in Russian politics – not only set the new Russian polity on a collision course with a retrenching Soviet elite but revealed at an early stage the basted seams running through the fabric of the country's hastily stitched political institutions. With full liberation achieved, these institutions would rapidly rip and unravel under the burden of governing.

Chapter 9 concerns the first differentiation of Russian political society mediated by large organizations: on one hand, political parties and the movement, DemRossiya, that subsumed them; on the other, those forces organized in reaction to the reappearance of politics, toward the purpose either of suppressing political activity or exploiting it by forming imitation parties as a kind of political capital that their leaders could trade against concessions from the party-state. With respect to the parties associated with DemRossiya, the questions that we address revolve around the issue of party formation under the particular conditions prevailing in the late-Soviet period that structured the emerging party systems in two important ways. First, there was the matter of *absences*, the fact that at this juncture the development of civil society had scarcely progressed beyond the level of intentions and hopes while the degree of socio-economic differentiation remained minimal. Under these circumstances, 'interest' would not represent a meaningful category in accounting for party formation and, accordingly, we observe that no party had been able to formulate a programme distinguishing itself from others on that basis. Second, parties derived their respective identities by means of one or another dialect – social-, Christian-, constitutional-democratic and so on – intoned by the speakers of a common language, that of anti-communism, which itself provided testimony to the overbearing *presence* of the party-state on the terrain of politics and the profound impact that it had on party formation. The separate party identities, in turn, are traced to specific stages of the party-state's disintegration in the period under review: the final one of which began with the founding of the DemRossiya movement, the coalescence of political society into an organized revolutionary force.

Chapter 10 focuses on Russia's political development under conditions of the low intensity *coup d'état* launched by the Soviet regime in autumn 1990. It outlines the structures of resistance according to which the institutions of state and political society were shaped in struggle with the party-state's attempt at restoration, how these structures induced a particular coherence within and between each set of institutions that proved decisive in defeating the August 1991 *putsch*, and notes how that same coherence would dissolve once the communist opponent – its political centre of gravity – had been broken.

7   The politics of opposition

Contrary to the pattern accompanying transitions from authoritarian rule to democracy that we discussed in Chapter 3 – in which national elections had been followed by a rapid demobilization of popular forces and a de-escalation of political demands – in the Russian case precisely the opposite occurred. In the wake of the 1989 elections, the country was rocked by an explosion of political activity that fundamentally transformed the relations of power within an already shaken communist order and brought millions of people into the political process as active participants. As this post-election mobilization gathered force, leaders of the democratic forces correspondingly altered their strategy. No longer would they attempt to influence the Gorbachev leadership to adopt one or another measure through persuasion; rather, they would oppose that leadership, adopting an increasingly radical posture in so doing. Thus demands to renew the social order were replaced by those to transform it.

How can this departure from the pattern described in the transitions literature be explained? Contextualizing the structural categories used in our earlier discussion of this question, we here call attention to the manner in which the USSR's weak structures rendered the new legislature both unrepresentative and institutionally debilitated. The following section explores these questions from a number of viewpoints, arguing that within the prevailing circumstances publicity, rather than legislative activity, was the single alternative to capitulation facing those returned to office by a sector of the electorate that was already becoming an active mass base for a revolutionary-democratic movement. Through publicity, interaction between democratic leaders and the public spiralled into the creation of a loosely organized national opposition whose objective became the destruction of the communist system in Russia. The remaining sections outline that interaction, focusing on the forms of political organization and communication engendered by it.

Why the legislature was not a legislature

Neither the USSR's Congress of People's Deputies nor the smaller Supreme Soviet that it elected from its ranks can be regarded as a national legislature in the proper sense of that term. In the previous chapter, we outlined the representational side of this matter, noting how the electoral mechanisms employed to fill the Congress discriminated heavily in favour of the candidates of party-state apparatus and severely handicapped their opponents, thus yielding a corpus of deputies that reflected the vote of the electorate like some grossly distorted image in a fun house mirror. Here, we turn to a related, yet separate, question: the institutional status of the Congress and Supreme Soviet. Our discussion is organized according to three categories or levels: the structural, the organizational and the communicative.

The structural level

For the moment, we direct our attention away from the empirical question – what did the members of the Congress and Supreme Soviet do? – in order to address the implications of the structures within which these bodies were embedded. Therefore, the question raised here might be read: what *could* the members of the Congress and Supreme Soviet have done? Our answer, in short, would be that they could not have carried on that collection of activities ordinarily associated with the functions of a legislature because that was not possible in the context of the (weak) structures of the communist system onto which this would-be legislature had been grafted. To illustrate this point, we consider the ability of the Congress and Supreme Soviet to discharge the two principal functions performed by legislatures anywhere: budgeting and legislating.

That singularly important means by which legislatures have been able to exercise control over the activities of their corresponding executives – budgeting, or the so-called 'power of the purse' – was unavailable to the USSR's newly elected assemblies for the simple reason that the USSR was not a monetized economy. Budgets may have been deliberated, appropriations passed, spending cuts introduced and so forth, but none of this amounted to the establishment of any real control over the behaviour of executive bodies because real money was not involved. Rather, the activities of the entire state apparatus were subject to physical determinations – so many tons of this to be produced, so many personnel assigned to that department – with units of an arbitrarily valued currency appended to each as no less arbitrarily set 'prices'. Not only was a rational allocation of budgeted resources thus precluded in principle, but executive bodies could alter the impact of whatever budget was passed by securing price changes that would correspondingly multiply or divide the operant sums of budget allocations.[1] Without money and non-arbitrary prices, then, there was no 'purse' over which the legislature could exercise any power. Attempts to do so merely led to absurd outcomes: excised departments increased in size,[2] while termination of a programme's budget resulted in more actual spending on it.[3] As a senior official in the Supreme Soviet remarked in this regard, 'without a market [and, thus, non-arbitrary prices] there cannot be a parliament'.[4]

From the point of view of legislative activity, things were no better. Regardless of what might occur within the walls of the would-be legislature – committee hearings, floor debates, the drafting and passage of laws – the structures of the Soviet order made impossible the implementation of any laws in the face of administrative resistance. Legislators could neither exact executive compliance by means of budgeting nor could they ensure that either the letter or the spirit of the laws that they enacted would be put into effect. The practical content of any measure passed by the Congress or Supreme Soviet depended entirely on instructions that administrative agencies issued to their performing units, those regulations, codes and standard operating procedures that represented the only means available for governing the actual behaviour of the machinery of state. In administrative practice these instructions had always taken precedence over the law(s) from which they were formally derived, no matter how they might have eviscerated, cancelled or contradicted their enabling legislation. The weak structural basis of the Soviet state evinced by this want of legality meant that the actual legislators were in fact the implementors. What is more, the overwhelming majority of administrative instructions were kept secret, thus depriving those in the would-be legislature of knowledge concerning the shape that their laws had assumed in practice.[5] This problem was insurmountable because the structures of the Soviet system provided no basis for addressing it in a practical way. To be sure, an attempt was made by the new watchdog of legality – the USSR's Committee on Constitutional Oversight which took office in autumn 1989 – that issued a ruling the following year requiring the publication of all administrative instructions that impinged on the rights and obligations of citizens within three months, after which time unpublished instructions would lose all juridical force. But the state apparatus responded to this ruling with complete non-compliance.[6]

The organizational level

The effects of the Soviet system's weak structures were amply apparent within the Congress and Supreme Soviet where personalized relations prevailed over impersonal procedures. This was evident even before the Congress had convened, inasmuch as the written procedures distributed to its members were not those that had been approved by the duly authorized deputies conference, but those arbitrarily substituted by the presidium of the outgoing Supreme Soviet.[7] The first order of business transacted at the Congress – the election of its presiding officer, the chairperson of the Supreme Soviet – was emblematic in this respect of the entire experience of the Soviet legislature. Although the Constitution specified that the head of the Central Electoral Commission was to preside over the Congress until it had named a chairperson, Gorbachev decided to ignore this regulation, along with a number of oral and written reminders about it directed to him from the floor, and supervised his own election to this office on the basis of procedures that he arbitrarily concocted on the spot.[8] From the perspective of the legislature's organization, the double-incompetence manifested thereby – for either Gorbachev was ignorant of the implications of his unconstitutional actions, or he chose to disregard them in order to display his personal authority regardless of the consequences for the new institution[9] – provided a preview of the way in which the work of the Congress and Supreme Soviet would be conducted.

At the Congress's first session, scores of motions were put forth from the floor which the presiding officer simply ignored. Moreover, he would occasionally offer his own motions or amend those advanced by others, relying on shouts of approval from the audience to signal that a rule had been adopted. This session also established certain patterns that prevailed at subsequent Congresses and Supreme Soviet sessions whereby the presiding officer would refuse to recognize deputies wishing to speak, or switch off their microphones or heckle them when displeased by their remarks. The prerogatives of personal authority left no room for the parliamentary institution of the neutrality of the chair. Gorbachev and Anatolii Luk'yanov – elected by the Congress as deputy chairperson and later as chairperson when Gorbachev assumed the presidency in March 1990 – regularly instructed the deputies on which way to vote on given questions.

Since there was no internal organization of the legislature along party lines, the executive apparatus of the Communist Party dictated organizational arrangements from without. Accordingly, the Congress was divided into delegations of deputies from territorial units – union-republics or regions in the case of the Russian Republic – in the same manner that the CPSU organized its own congresses. In most cases, top CPSU officials led their respective delegations, determining which of their members would get a chance to speak from the floor and whom the delegation would nominate for election to the Supreme Soviet.[10] They often instructed their deputies on how to vote[11] and, since those in the delegations were all seated together and most voting was accomplished by a show of hands, they were able to monitor directly the behaviour of 'their' deputies.

The Supreme Soviet's presidium with Gorbachev in command functioned as the direct agent of Communist Party control inside Congress and the Supreme Soviet. This control was accomplished along the lines of longstanding communist practice whereby the organs of the CPSU inserted their personnel into key technical positions in the executive apparatus of soviets from which these officers would be able to monitor and, when necessary, direct all activities of concern to them.[12] In like fashion, the recruitment and placement functions for technical staff were superintended by Politburo member, Anatolii Luk'yanov, in his capacity as deputy chairperson of the Supreme Soviet,[13] while staff members in sensitive spots regularly reported directly to their counterparts in the apparatus of the Communist Party's Central Committee.[14] Almost all of the draft legislation on which the deputies voted was thus written by, or approved by, scribes of the CPSU apparatus.[15] One exception to this pattern, in which a bill authored by others was reported out of committee to the Supreme Soviet, witnessed the disappearance of the bill in question and an apparatus substitute proffered in its place.[16] The same can be said for the election of the Soviet government, the Council of Ministers. Although deputies in some instances subjected nominees to considerable grilling and voted down a few of them,[17] all nominations had come from the Communist Party's Central Committee, relayed through either the Supreme Soviet's presidium or the Council of Ministers headed by Nikolai Ryzhkov. Consequently, all ministerial personnel were well aware that their appointments – and, thus, their loyalties – were owed to patrons in the Communist Party rather than to the legislature.[18]

Personalized relations of authority were reinforced by drawing deputies into a web of dependency relations in which the party-state apparatus would dole out material concessions – apartments, junkets, equipment, transportation and so on – in return for votes.[19] In the face of these practices, even the most elementary issues confronting these bodies – a sort of institutional 'To be or not to be?' – were decided in personalized and arbitrary fashion. For instance, according to the

Constitution, a 20 per cent rotation in the membership of the Supreme Soviet was required each year; yet the Congress never discharged its obligation to replace a fifth of the Supreme Soviet's membership. However, after sitting for a year and a half, some 36 per cent of those on the Supreme Soviet voluntarily resigned their positions – itself a comment on their attachment to this institution – and the Congress voted their replacements.[20] Finally, in the wake of the failed *coup* of August 1991, Gorbachev summoned all the deputies into extraordinary session and directed them to extinguish the Congress itself. Having been assured that they would none the less retain their deputies' perquisites for another three years, they did as instructed.

The level of communications

The tumult attending the first sitting of the Congress of People's Deputies – the displays of bitter invective and rancorous admonition often consummated in stormy crescendos of foot-stamping, hand-clapping and jeering whistles – indicated that more than political differences divided that body. Rather, they signalled the fact that the deputies were talking past one another, readily relying on certain discourteous forms of non-verbal communication to overcome the inadequacy of mere words. These coarse displays were symptomatic of the presence of two distinct discourses on the floor of the Congress, each vying to establish itself as the framework within which communications would proceed. The gap between them was unbridgeable. When, for instance, Yurii Karyakin spoke of honouring Lenin's last request to be buried with his relatives in the city still bearing his name and, accordingly, to close down the nightmarish mausoleum erected by Stalin, A. A. Sokolov rose in indignation to condemn this 'blasphemy'.[21] For his remarks on Soviet war atrocities committed in Afghanistan given in an interview to a Canadian newspaper, Andrei Sakharov was accused from the floor by S. V. Chervonopiskii of 'maliciously attacking the Soviet armed forces'. Sakharov's subsequent explanation that he neither insulted the armed forces nor the Soviet soldier but exclusively 'the people who issued the criminal order to send Soviet troops to Afghanistan' was met by a prolonged din of abuse from the majority.[22]

As these episodes might illustrate, one of the discourses present at the Congress can be identified generally as parliamentary speech. Although often expressed with barbed riposte and richly embroidered with metaphor, allusion and trope, the core of this discourse concerned the pragmatic question of organizing representative government. It was manifested in the narratives of a number of deputies associated with an emerging democratic wing in the Congress who employed it – in part, at least – as a means of empowerment before an 'aggressively obedient majority'[23] in the hall that seemed prepared to enact whatever directives the authorities chose to issue. To offset their numerical disadvantage, those employing parliamentary speech verbally constructed an imagined world ruled by reason and governed by sensible procedures, inviting their audience either to participate in it or to advertise their submission to unreason and arbitrary power. Although this form of speech contributed little if anything to the operations of the Congress and Supreme Soviet as legislative institutions, its appearance in these fora was none the less of seminal import for the development of politics in Russia. We therefore reserve this topic for the following section, turning here to its counterpart at the Congress: Soviet speech.

As we have noted, Soviet speech involved the enactment of an officially established mythology in which all the important secrets of social life have been mastered by an infallible vanguard whose pronouncements have been embellished with elements of the reigning sacral complex (hence the umbrage taken at the suggestion to remortalize Lenin by means of a burial). Soviet speech constituted the communicative counterpart of the Soviet system's personalized relations of authority, defining the world in one way or another by means of the words authority uttered, and prohibiting all challenges to these definitions. Whereas parliamentary rhetoric would be implicitly dialogic and political, Soviet speech is quintessentially monologic and anti-political. The truth content of its statements depended entirely on their proximity to power, a feature highlighted at the Congress by the way in which Gorbachev and others brushed aside procedural and even constitutional issues in order to do as they pleased. When authority ordained that the legislature should savage itself as an institution, the vast majority of the legislators readily complied. Although some observers have regarded the inattention to procedures as a byproduct of a fixation on substance,[24] in our understanding the deputies were simply following Soviet procedures, which meant responding on cue to the directives of authority.

Authority, of course, would invariably attempt to display itself in larger-than-personal terms. Gorbachev's preferred device in this respect was (incongruously, from the perspective of arguments appealing to reason) the 'constitution'. Despite the fact that the country's basic law had been simply dictated by the authorities, and the fact that he himself would violate, ignore or adjust its provisions as circumstances might require, Gorbachev's speech often employed the category 'constitution' as a sort of magical incantation dividing the political world into those who supported his actions and those anti-constitutional individuals who did not.[25] The category 'constitution', then, functioned in a manner analogous to its predecessors in the standard Soviet lexicon, in which 'socialism' would be deployed to stigmatize critics or opponents as 'anti-socialist', 'the party' to declare them 'anti-party', 'Soviet' to label them 'anti-Soviet' and so forth. At bottom, Gorbachev's constitution shared with these tropes the capacity to reference a community of the righteous, defending itself against those who, indeed, had placed themselves outside of that community. His illocution was replicated by numerous deputies whose statements were predicated on the interests of the people or the demands of their voters. To be sure, terms such as these have been common currency in parliamentary speech, too. But their content in that instance would depend on the relationship – in principle, subject to empirical verification – between the speaker and some community that he or she has claimed to represent. In Soviet speech, statements including the terms 'the people' or 'my constituents' would not be premised on an actual group of individuals, but on a mythical community of the righteous expressing itself through the words of the orator. Hence, deputies who had been elected in one-candidate races, or who had been named by the CPSU's Central Committee or by one of its affiliated public organizations, would all the same insist that 'the people' or 'the voters' had sent them to the Congress to solve one or another problem facing the country.[26]

Soviet speech, the dominant discourse in the Congress and Supreme Soviet, functioned both to trace magic circles around its purveyors and to stigmatize those standing outside of them. Deputies who raised elementary questions of procedure would thus be accused of engaging in empty talk in order to divert the Congress from its real tasks.[27] Simple requests to register the votes of the deputies so that constituents would have a record of their representative's behaviour were met with suspicions that these were 'attempts to draw us into something that the Congress must not be drawn into'.[28] When Gavriil Popov announced plans to organize a group of like-minded deputies committed to advancing the cause of liberal democracy, Gorbachev accused him and his associates of seeking to 'split the Congress', a remark echoed by others and amplified by one deputy who claimed that Popov and his colleagues were trying 'to turn the people against the Congress'.[29] Evidently, there was no distinction in this discourse between the institution of the Congress and the particular people who made up its ruling majority. As such, there was no room in the assembly for the very things on which legislatures depend: impersonal rules and procedures, basic information, caucuses and factions. There was also no place within

Soviet discourse for parliamentary speech, as both the frequent appeals from the floor to silence its exponents,[30] as well as the actual silencing accomplished by switching off microphones or hooting down speakers, would suggest.[31]

The Congress as a vehicle for politics

Although the structural, organizational and communicative conditions of the Soviet order militated against the development of the Congress and Supreme Soviet into legislative institutions, the convocation of the first Congress presented an occasion *sui generis* to continue the process of mass politicization that had got under way with the spring elections. Television coverage of the Congress proved to be of inestimable importance in this respect, and the decision to provide it may well have been the product of the lobbying activities of the Moscow deputies associated with the democratic movement.[32] According to survey research, an astounding 95 per cent of the country's adult population watched either all or part of the proceedings on live TV.[33] At workplaces, dinner tables, street corners and queues, the country was suddenly abuzz with discussions of what their deputies were saying and doing on the floor of the Congress. A public opinion survey revealed that most regarded the party-state apparatus as exercising the dominant influence in the proceedings but only about a third of those expressing that view considered that influence to be positive.[34] As one observer subsequently remarked, the live broadcasts of the Congress amounted to 'a crash course in political literacy for the entire country'.[35]

From this perspective, the major achievement of the first Congress was publicity – in the most literal sense of that term. A number of deputies took advantage of this novel and endlessly fascinating spectacle to generate yet more publicity, gradually undergoing a metamorphosis themselves in the process. After the March elections, they had opened an office at the Moscow party committee's House of Political Enlightenment that became an unofficial headquarters for hundreds of political activists converging on it from all corners of the USSR.[36] The core group of deputies working out of that office – especially Gavriil Popov, Yurii Afanas'ev, Tat'yana Zaslavskaya, Mark Zakharov, Arkadii Murashev and Sergei Stankevich – expected to exert considerable, even decisive, influence at the Congress. They enjoyed access to the leadership of the party-state, including Gorbachev himself, who assisted in organizing the Moscow delegation a few days before the Congress opened. They also had close connections with informal political organizations and voters' clubs in the capital. These could be tapped to bring Muscovites out onto the streets and thus used as added leverage on Gorbachev. Initially, however, the Moscow democrats stood aside from – or above – the mobilized demos presenting themselves in more respectable fashion while those in the informal movement took the lead in street organizing.

As opening day of the Congress neared, the Moscow deputies composed an appeal to that body, outlining their proposals regarding procedures and elections to the Supreme Soviet.[37] Although this initiative faltered sadly – the document was confiscated by the Supreme Soviet's staff and the Congress would reject all of their proposals from the floor – another simultaneously transpiring in the capital produced some spectacular results. On May 20–1, representatives from dozens of leading informal groups from around the country convened at a conference hosted by Democratic Perestroika to discuss perspectives on forming a social democratic party *and,* in the near term, to work out ways in which their organizations could serve as links between the public and the deputies already assembling in the city.[38] The second objective was immediately realized in the form of a mass rally staged at the Luzhniki sports complex. Sponsored by Moscow Tribune, Memorial, Democratic Perestroika, Civic Dignity, the Moscow Popular Front (MNF) and Voters' Clubs of Moscow, and well advertised by some 16,000 posted handbills, it drew considerably over 100,000 people to endorse its principal slogans: 'All power to the Soviets!', 'For a radical Perestroika!' and 'For a union of really free and sovereign people!'[39] This event inaugurated a series of rallies that would continue throughout the unexpectedly long sitting of the Congress, contributing as well to some equally unforeseen outcomes.

Thus, a remarkable synergism began to occur between the democratic minority inside the Kremlin's Palace of Congresses and their supporters in the capital's electorate that brought together two distinct modes of political expression, each bolstering the other. Badly outnumbered in the Congress by the party-state's standing majority, the democrats adopted the time-honoured tactic of avoiding defeat in the arena in which they found themselves by moving its walls outward. In so doing they could hope to increase the number of participants in the contest and thereby offset the numerical advantage initially enjoyed by their opponents.[40] Broadly speaking, they accomplished this in two ways. By focusing on procedural questions, they attacked the restrictions on publicity that prevailed inside the Congress; by raising issues concerning the rights of citizens to assemble, they targeted the restrictions on publicity that existed outside of it. Forays in either direction contributed to the success of those in the other.

Procedures as publicity

The first two addresses delivered at the Congress challenged from the standpoint of democratic principle the procedures imposed on the Congress by the presidium of the outgoing Supreme Soviet. Andrei Sakharov argued for dropping the entire idea of electing a Supreme Soviet, inasmuch as some 64 per cent of the deputies – even were that body's membership renewed annually by a fifth – would never have the opportunity to represent their voters on the Congress's law-making organ. His remarks on electing a chairperson only after candidates had been adequately discussed were reiterated by Popov, who extended this idea to elections to the Supreme Soviet, pointing out that the rule for assigning quotas to regional delegations made some sense for elections to the federal chamber (the Council of Nationalities) but not for those to the other house for which competitive elections based on programmes should be required.[41] Following a retort from E. N. Meshalkin that these proposals amounted only to 'words', whereas the people de-manded 'deeds' from the Congress, Yurii Boldyrev requested that votes be recorded so that the electorate would be able to know how their representatives had acted, while Stankevich followed with a proposal for roll-call voting when this had been requested by 100 deputies or more. These and similar procedural points made during the Congress amounted to a foolproof tactic in so far as publicity was concerned. If adopted, they would provide the public with important information on deputies' behaviour, introducing an element of accountability. Defeated, as they were either by Gorbachev's arbitrary diktat or by the Congress's ready-made majority responding to his signals, they produced publicity of another type: publicity concerning who favoured and who opposed publicity. If authority were to have its way in the face of reasonable arguments appealing to democratic principles, then it would have to do so by publicly exposing its preference for power over its pretensions to democracy.

In the voting for the Supreme Soviet on the third day of the Congress, the conservatives rose to the bait dangled before them by the Moscow delegation that had decided to set a democratic example for others by nominating all fifty-five of their number for the twenty-nine seats apportioned to them on the Supreme Soviet's Council of the Union, while the Russian delegation put up twelve candidates to fill its eleven seats on the Council of Nationalities.[42] None of the prominent democrats on Moscow's list was voted in; El'tsin placed last on the Russian list and was shut out, too. Especially since no member of the Congress held a mandate that could begin to compare with the more than 5 million votes won by El'tsin, these results amounted to self-discreditation writ large.[43]

Publicizing publicity

Attention focused by the democrats on the party-state's restriction of free expression contributed significantly to Russia's political development. The relatively liberal Law on the Press, eventually adopted in June 1990, was perhaps the outstanding achievement in this respect,[44] but it would have been difficult to imagine either the passage of this law or the assertiveness of certain segments of the press that antedated it without previous gains in this area. One of them resulted from the criticisms levelled by the democrats at a decree adopted on 8 April by the presidium of the outgoing Supreme Soviet which prohibited 'public insults or discreditation of the higher organs of state power' or their officers. The publicity afforded by the Congress, its Supreme Soviet[45] and some sections of the press[46] to the chilling effect of these passages eventually induced Gorbachev to excise them from the decree.[47]

From the floor, the democrats had discharged the first volley in the battle over restrictions on public expression within two hours of the Congress's opening. The writer, Ales Adamovich, fired off a double-barrelled summons, calling on the Congress to suspend restrictions on free assembly while it was in session and subtly suggesting to the citizenry – most of whom were, of course, watching the proceedings on live television – that they were already feeling an urge to go out in public and express their opinions on the activities of the Congress. Gorbachev, confessing no need to suspend anything, waved off Adamovich's proposal and returned to supervising his own election as chairperson.[48] However, on the Congress's second day, Tat'yana Zaslavskaya resurrected Adamovich's idea as the first order of business, delivering a report on a gathering at Pushkin Square the previous evening that had encountered police repression when the participants walked to the Kremlin's Borovitskii Gates in order to talk with deputies on their way from the Congress.[49] Interior minister Vadim Bakatin was on hand to give a sanitized version of the events in question, but his account was immediately contradicted by two eye-witnesses, Stankevich and Sakharov, whose appeals to the Congress to permit free assemblies were concomitantly appeals to the citizens to hold them.[50] Somewhat befuddled, Gorbachev resolved the matter by issuing an oblique instruction to the city authorities to reserve the grounds at Luzhniki for public gatherings during the Congress, and then informing the assembly that this had, in fact, already been done.

Just as the democrats had used the rostrum of the Congress to pry open the opportunity for public expression outside the hall, so the public would figure into the correlation of forces present within it, as deputies brought the comments of citizens into the Congress and, more importantly, delivered them in front of the TV cameras.[51] Like an alternating current, power surged back and forth between the public and those deputies enjoying their trust and support. On the evening following the decimation of the democrats in the voting for the Supreme Soviet, this power was running at Luzhniki at particularly high voltage. A rally organized by the Moscow Popular Front, Memorial and the Voters' Club of the Academy of Sciences drew a crowd of some 70,000.[52] Unlike the previous day's gathering, this one was attended by a number of democratic deputies, among them El'tsin who arrived in dramatic fashion, on foot with a large crowd at this back. This moment was pivotal. The stormy responses to the deputies' speeches indicated that an alternative to persuading Gorbachev was already becoming dimly visible: going it alone with the backing of an increasingly politicized public. To reinforce that possibility, the leaders of the informals left the rally already decided to repeat the event every day for the duration of the Congress, with the Moscow Popular Front and Memorial alternating as sponsors.

On the following morning, Popov stunned the Congress with his announcement that an inter-regional group of independent deputies was forming and that all deputies interested in advancing democracy were invited to participate. Not only was this declaration spontaneous – reflecting the ebullient reception just awarded to the deputies at Luzhniki in the wake of their rout in the voting for the Supreme Soviet – it reversed the strategy that the Moscow democrats had been pursuing since the spring elections: namely, garnering influence by employing a combination of persuasion and pressure on Gorbachev.[53] Indeed, prior to the Congress, certain leaders of the informal movement had invited Popov and others to a meeting with deputies from Lithuania and Estonia in order to discuss prospects for coordinating the work of their respective delegations.[54] The Balts attended, waited some two hours for the Muscovites to arrive, and then left after a chauffeur for the Moscow delegation appeared to inform those present that none of the Moscow deputies would be coming.

Having eschewed this invitation – as well as another one tendered two days later[55] – to initiate what would become known as an 'inter-regional group of independent deputies', Popov shortly found himself on the floor of the Congress ironically proclaiming the existence of just such a group. Its name indicated both the democrats' resolve, and their reluctance at this juncture, to form an opposition. On one hand, the innocuous adjective 'inter-regional' surmounted symbolically the barriers erected within the corpus of deputies by its regional form of organization that confined those opposing the authorities to discrete pockets that could easily be marginalized.[56] Inter-regional, then, represented a challenge to this quarantine. On the other, 'independent' connoted 'opposition', since it contained the implicit question: independent of what? The notion of opposition still carried plenty of negative connotations, and many democrats at the Congress discouraged Popov's proposal on this basis. Popov himself went to great pains to defend it by saying that he and his confederates had no intention of organizing a faction or an opposition of any sort.[57] None the less, his conservative opponents saw what was happening and immediately condemned the Muscovites for doing precisely what they claimed not to be doing: trying 'to turn the people against the Congress' (meaning, of course, against its controlling majority);[58] and engaging 'in factional activities aimed at splitting the Congress'.[59] Despite their disclaimers to the contrary and the torpid follow-up to Popov's proclamation,[60] the democrats had willy-nilly crossed this Soviet Rubicon. The spark of open political opposition had flashed on the third day of the Congress.

Politicization in the wake of the First Congress

On the Congress's final day, two of the bolder members of the incipient opposition took the floor to lay down what would become its basic planks. A. M. Emel'yanov indicted the Communist Party for its monopoly of power that had resulted in a long and depressing list of misfortunes for the country.[61] Sakharov, in the final speech made to the Congress – delivered in rather desultory fashion due to repeated prompts from Gorbachev to wind things up quickly – outlined a 'decree on power' that included the repeal of the Constitution's article 6 that underwrote the CPSU's monopoly, and a reversal of authority relations between Moscow and the union-republics such that the former's legal acts could only be implemented on the territories of the latter with their explicit authorization.[62] These two points represented a frontal assault on the authority structure of the communist system. Since they were also the only principles, other than a commitment to non-violence, on which consensus consistently prevailed within the Inter-Regional Deputies Group (I-RDG), they defined the group from the outset as an opposition organized *against* the communist system – although it may have taken most members a while to digest this fact – and they established a basic orientation for its positions on other issues. This orientation was less substantive than relational; that is, the I-RDG's position on a given matter would be determined primarily by its relevance to the communist system. As the I-RDG expanded its programmatic repertoire to include demands for a market economy and private property, it was laying more brick on its oppositionist foundation, multiplying the number of points at which it could criticize, discredit and undermine the communist order.[63]

The spiral of challenges to authority witnessed during the Congress – deputies stimulating the process of politicization in society, leading in turn to a radicalization of the deputies and so on – continued in its wake. However, the major injection of political energy now was supplied not by stormy rallies of Muscovites but by their black-faced compatriots in the provinces, the miners. On 10 July, strike committees formed in Kuzbass initiated a series of walkouts that within a week shut down the entire Soviet coal mining industry. Work stoppages had been appearing sporadically since January in protest over working conditions and the absence of basic goods such as soap. But what seemed to have galvanized the miners' resolve to take bolder measures was the abrupt change in the country's political climate brought about by the spring elections and represented vividly by the example of people's deputies appearing on their television screens, talking straight into the face of power.[64] The radical equality engendered by political speech had thus begun to reach a segment of the working class for whom the degrading deference demanded by their bosses had suddenly become an unbearable burden.[65]

Although the striking miners displayed considerable levels of organization, discipline and solidarity in the individual mining districts, there was at this juncture no national miners' organization, not to mention a nationwide workers' movement. Attempts had begun as early as 1987 to establish a national network of workers' clubs, and these attempts had continued till the very eve of the Kuzbass walkout when a Moscow meeting of representatives of clubs from around the country, held on 8–9 July, again had failed to find a way to stitch the city-based units together in some larger pattern.[66] Yet the lack of a national organization did not mean the lack of a national political presence, as deputies from mining districts shuttled between their constituents and the Supreme Soviet where they would explain the miners' grievances to both their colleagues and to a nationwide television audience.[67] The miners' demands rapidly escalated from physical necessities to political ones. On the crest of the strike wave, miner and people's deputy, Vladimir Lushnikov, delivered a speech on national television calling for the removal of article 6 from the Constitution along with many of the 'filters' that had been installed in the country's election procedures.[68]

Organizing an opposition 'above'

The magnitude of the political shocks occasioned by a workers' rebellion in the very bosom of the proletarian motherland would be difficult to exaggerate. Intervening as it did between the first formal, and relatively inconsequential, gathering of the I-RDG on 7 June and its official founding on 29 and 30 July, the miners' strike made an enormous impact on the incipient opposition. As Gavriil Popov later recalled:

[The strike] compelled us to change our general policy. In June we believed that the CPSU had to be prompted to start reforms. [By July we in the I-RDG realized that] if we did not want to lose touch with the people, we had to think not about exerting pressure on the CPSU, but about eliminating its monopoly on power.[69]

Indeed, the political example returned by the miners to the deputies contributed directly to the decision to constitute the I-RDG as an open opposition when the group met to establish itself formally.

In the auditorium of the Cinematographers' Union, some 316 deputies assembled on the morning of 29 July to thrash out the principles on which the I-RDG would be based.[70] Disputes erupted on all important questions. Should the group function as a discussion club for generating legislative proposals or should it establish a distinct identity for itself, complete with its own programme and officers? What should this programme include and should membership depend on full adherence to it? What leadership structure would be appropriate? Finally, and most importantly, should the I-RDG consider itself an opposition? Those of more radical persuasion, often citing the example set by the striking miners,[71] carried the day on most of the main points. The 269 deputies who opted for membership decided that, indeed, the I-RDG should set itself apart from the larger body of deputies with its own programme and leadership – composed of five co-chairpersons (El'tsin, Afanas'ev, Popov, Sakharov and Viktor Palm) and a Coordinating Council of twenty – authorized to represent the group and to take decisions in its name. Although a number of the leading personages continued to insist that the I-RDG was not organized as an opposition,[72] two of the group's co-chairpersons – El'tsin and Afanas'ev – characterized it in essentially those terms.[73] The buoyant effects of rhetoric were amply evident in the hall, lifting many along on a tide of oppositionist sentiment. Afanas'ev's speech – in which he castigated Gorbachev as a failed leader, derided the idea of 'renewing socialism' and proclaimed that 'Marxism–Leninism cannot be reformed' – was by far the most powerful in this respect. It drew the longest and noisiest ovations.[74]

Ironically, the initial disclaimers voiced by some I-RDG leaders that the group was not an oppositionist faction turned out to be quite accurate. The characteristics of the Soviet legislature that we reviewed would have excluded *ex definitio* the possibility that the group could have played that role. Moreover, in actual practice, the I-RDG neither mounted any factional activity in these bodies, nor did it long persist in the notion it could achieve any significant results by working within them. To be sure, a number of the ideas associated with the group were eventually passed into law: the repeal of the Constitution's article 6, a Law on the Press that abolished censorship, the removal of filters in the electoral system and restrictions on the right of movement.[75] But during that period in which the group reached its peak in membership (about 400) and organized activity, a consensus already prevailed that continuing to work within Soviet institutions was an exercise in futility.[76] Before the second Congress of People's Deputies had met in December 1989, the strategic decision had been taken to focus the energies of the I-RDG elsewhere: namely, on the upcoming elections in the union-republics that represented a separate avenue to power. Following the success of that endeavour, the I-RDG's relation to the Congress and Supreme Soviet was most clearly expressed as an unequivocal demand for their immediate dissolution.[77]

The I-RDG, then, might be best regarded as a peak association of the democratic movement in the USSR, outwardly disguised as a legislative faction.[78] Organizationally, the group was weak. Although repression might explain this in part,[79] internal factors tell the larger story. Despite generating a number of leading ideas for the democratic movement, the I-RDG proved unable to adopt a full platform for itself.[80] Its third and last try to do so in December 1989 failed for lack of a quorum, a circumstance that had plagued not only its general conferences but also meetings of its twenty-person Coordinating Council.[81] Even when a quorum was present, meetings tended to be desultory affairs, as business agendas were washed away by freewheeling discussions of 'the overall situation in the country' which, of course, accomplished nothing of substance. Internal organization was never sufficiently well defined to allow for the assignment of specific duties to the officers or to recruit a supporting staff. The chief tasks that it had set for itself – developing alternative draft legislation, organizing its own press organ – went unattended in practice, although individual members submitted dozens of draft proposals for laws and constitutional amendments.[82] With its meetings frequented by 'large contingents of permanent participant-observers [that] oriented them toward debate on broad political resolutions', the I-RDG devolved into that very 'deputies discussion club' that its founding conference had rejected as a model for the group.

None the less, from the perspective of communication, the I-RDG represented a breakthrough for the democratic movement in Russia. As Gennadii Burbulis of its Coordinating Council once confessed to a political club at the Moscow Aviation Institute, 'The I-RDG has abused publicity [and] self-advertisements, and has done most of its work through a microphone, through all kinds of appeals to get the attention of the public.'[83] Indeed, delivered before one of those politically active groups whose attention I-RDG members sought to attract, Burbulis's confession was self-validating. Although 'weak' from the perspective of organization, the I-RDG's presence on the political field transformed the structure of communications.[84] Here, now, was a leadership around which the diffuse, amorphous forces in political society that had congealed at micro-level as informal organizations and voters' clubs could begin to unite.

Organizing an opposition 'below'

Judging by the tenor of the daily mass meetings held at Luzhniki during the first Congress, this leadership was marching considerably to the rear of its most fervid backers. On the Congress's final day, the meeting marking its close shouted noisy approval for resolutions instructing the I-RDG – as yet, existing in no more than name – 'to unite all the democratic forces in the country [for a] peaceful, democratic revolution'. Moreover, these resolutions already previewed the general strategy for accomplishing this goal: namely, 'victory of the democratic forces in [elections to] the higher organs of power of Russia [leading to] a free, sovereign Russia in a Democratic Union of peoples'.[85] The issue preoccupying political society in the ensuing months pivoted on the organizational question of how to bring off that victory.

The election campaign and the appearance of an opposition in the legislature created a new field in Russian politics. The former had mobilized a fresh cohort of activists working in local voters' clubs or in support groups, such as Moscow's Committee of 19 (named for the nineteen factory assemblies that had nominated El'tsin), which provided a populist organizational base for figures such as El'tsin and Gdlyan.[86] A number of those active in the informal movement quickly grasped the possibilities for leveraging this new element, entered these associations and in most cases immediately assumed leadership roles.[87] Many in the opposition in the Congress were soon busy positioning themselves as public leaders of an opposition in society in anticipation of the Russian elections commencing in December. That prospect favoured loose, populist forms of organization, backing candidates whose programmes were essentially protests against existing conditions and those thought responsible for them.

In the capital, the MNF provided a clear illustration of the influence of these factors. Following a period of intense activity during the election campaigns, the Front's active membership had tripled (to over 600 members) by the time that it convened its official founding conference in May[88] and then climbed to about 1,000 in the period immediately after the first Congress of People's Deputies.[89] However, the elections that had occasioned this steep growth curve in membership also represented the Front's undoing. Top organizers such as Vladimir Bokser and Mikhail Shneider, sensing the opportunities presented by the Russian elections scheduled for March, joined with Lev Ponomarev of Memorial and Lev Shamaev and Aleksandr Muzykanskii of the Committee of 19 to bring together the various voters' clubs into one citywide association. The product of these efforts was the Moscow Voters' Association (MOI) which held its founding conference on 27 July. The notables on hand to address this gathering (Afanas'ev and Nikolai Travkin of the I-RDG), the decision to seek maximum inclusion by avoiding potentially divisive issues such as formulating a programme (none was adopted) or choosing a leader (a fifteen-person Coordinating Council was elected), as well as MOI's two to three thousand activists already deployed in thirty of the capital's thirty-three electoral districts indicated considerable potential for this task-specific form of organization.[90] As MOI developed, the MNF correspondingly languished. Founded in order to receive official status as a 'public organization', within a few months it was lapsing inactive and, after January 1990, was no longer convening meetings.[91]

In Leningrad, the same experience and opportunity – successful campaign activity in 1989 and the prospect for competing again in the 1990 elections – underlay the official founding of the Leningrad Popular Front (LNF) in June. Unlike its Moscow namesake, the LNF has no particular ideological orientation – save a commitment to broad democratic principles – and was headed by a number of leading intellectuals in the city: Sergei Andreev, Mikhail Chulaki and Mariya Sal'e. In this respect, it more resembled Moscow Tribune than the MNF.[92] With a relatively large membership – initially 5,000 people included in the organizations affiliated with it, growing to over 7,000 by mid-summer – practised in, or intent upon, electoral activity,[93] it formed Leningrad's equivalent of MOI. The mushrooming of popular fronts across Russia in summer and autumn of 1989 tended to follow the Leningrad pattern, supplying a potential base of constituency organizations for the projected all-union league that would unite them. However, efforts to do so produced negligible results. A conservative, if not fascist, Russian Popular Front, led by Valerii Skurlatov, had announced its existence in December 1988 and numbered among the organizations convened in Yaroslavl in October where a Popular Front of the RSFSR was to be formed. Finding no ears there for his tales of Zionist–Masonic conspiracy, Skurlatov dropped out of this meeting and the remaining delegates accomplished their appointed task.[94] But this organization was stillborn. Rather like the MNF's quest for official standing, the realization of a project that had been mooted for over two years came at a time already passed for this organizing strategy. None of the leading democratic figures who had been thrust by the elections into the limelight of national publicity had bothered to attend the founding conference of this popular front, perhaps because they had already travelled so far with the relatively light-weight organizational baggage of voters' associations unconcerned with programmes and internal leadership structures.

Concerted preparations for assembling a nationwide coalition of voters' associations began in September. In the capital, two distinct groups of organizers sought to take the lead in this endeavour. One was MOI, whose 28 September conclave that brought together most of the capital's democratic clubs to adopt an election platform and formulate a campaign strategy ended without producing a consensus on either count.[95] The other was a rival group – the Moscow City Committee of Voters' Associations, which had been publishing its own weekly, *Khronika*, since March – that convened a conference two days later that drew together some 150 delegates from over thirty cities in the USSR to found the All-Union Association of Voters (VAI). The charter presented to the delegates called for merging the affiliated groups into a single organization; in fact, a political party in all but name. However, since a majority of delegates were prepared to subscribe to no more than the minimum of centralized coordination over their city-based groups, the conference rewrote and decentralized the charter. Similarly, the relatively detailed platform was rejected *in toto*; in its place, the delegates opted for embracing whatever programme the I-RDG might eventually produce.[96] In effect, then, VAI had been transformed into a loose confederation of affiliated clubs that would serve as constituency organizations for the coming elections. The fact that this was precisely the organizational orientation of MOI – whose leaders had also participated in VAI's founding conference – breathed new life into their project. A few days later when their conference reconvened, MOI's platform and plan of action were now adopted unanimously.[97] Soon thereafter, VAI disappeared.

In Chelyabinsk on 28–9 October, an all-union voters' association was founded. A preparatory gathering in Leningrad sponsored by the LNF had already laid the conceptual groundwork for its minimalist form of organization – no central offices whatsoever; all decisions to be taken by quarterly conferences of delegates – that promised maximum inclusion for all democratic groups.[98] The organization that issued from the Chelyabinsk conference took the name 'Inter-Regional Association of Democratic Organizations' (MADO) and existed thereafter in name only. The inclusiveness built into the organization's design turned into chaos and confusion as soon as that same design was animated by actual individuals pursuing their own ends. For instance, one of MADO's prime movers, Mariya Sal'e, has estimated that three-quarters of the two-day founding conference was spent on debates about philosophical and political principles while no effort was turned to the matters at hand: the questions of strategy, tactics and organization for the campaign that lay less than two months ahead.[99]

These developments at grassroots reflected the same tendency that we noted with respect to the I-RDG: a penchant for expressive behaviour, resulting in seemingly interminable debates on abstract principles with no demonstrable bearing on anything save the gratification of speakers and their supporters. The setting of tasks, not to mention tasks themselves, seemed in either case to slip unnoticed through organizational cracks as debate on the 'big questions' steamed ahead. From one vantage, this could be regarded as a form of recreation appearing as political activity. Of course, politics anywhere would probably include some elements of recreation in its mix of ingredients, explaining in part why people have become drawn to this field of human endeavour. The serious face worn in the characteristically Russian mode of political recreation – endless discussions on 'the overall situation in the country' – has disguised somewhat this recreational component as purposive–rational action. But taken literally, recreation would hold a key to an important aspect of Russia's recovery of political life. What was here manifested as confusion or chaos in the efforts of the democratic groups to organize themselves nationally can at the same time be appreciated in terms of communication as a process by which they were taking the initial steps down this very road. All the meetings, the long-winded speeches, the quarrels over platforms and principles represented an important stage in the development of a national opposition to communism. For as those from the various democratic groups congregated in these interactive milieux, a movement was being established as a fact through the acts, and in the eyes, of its members.

Despite the persistence of state repression,[100] this 'fact' became public. On Revolution Day (7 November), the official parade was held in the capital as usual. Refused a place in it by the city authorities, democratic groups turned out tens of thousands of people for the first free march in the city since the early 1920s. Behind banners proclaiming 'Eternal glory to the first perestroikaists – the sailors of Kronshtadt'[101] and '72 Years – on the road to nowhere',[102] an enthusiastic column of Muscovites chanted for a multi-party system and full freedom of speech as they made their way across the city's north-east quarter from the Dinamo metro station to the Olympic sports complex where they staged their rally. The leading slogan of the hour was the crowd's collective announcement: 'We will live in a normal country.'[103] On that same day in Leningrad, the LNF led about 30,000 people who marched in a column parallel to the official parade, replete with banners and chants like those of their Moscow counterparts.[104]

Through interaction with an emergent national movement, the I-RDG was defining its own political identity, cementing its relations with the broader movement as it did so.[105] If its leading intellectual figures from Moscow Tribune had defined their role in early 1989 as progressive counsel to the authorities[106] and by mid-year as a loyal – albeit reluctant – opposition, then by year's end they were prepared to acknowledge that theirs was indeed an opposition aimed not at reforming the communist system but at liquidating it.[107] Afanas'ev delivered the I-RDG's proclamation to that effect to the December Congress of People's Deputies[108] in an atmosphere charged by the marginally successful two-hour national political strike called by some of its leaders to protest the continuation of the Communist Party's formal monopoly on power.[109] Fresh from another bout of political defeats at this Congress – whose proceedings they were by now subjecting to open mockery and ridicule[110] – a number of I-RDG members joined with some 107 democratic candidates standing for election to the Russian Congress, their campaign organizers and leaders of voters' associations and informal groups to found an electoral coalition aimed at realizing that 'peaceful, democratic revolution' that had been proclaimed at the Luzhniki mass meeting on the final day of the USSR's first Congress.[111]

This electoral coalition came to life over the course of the campaign, the topic of the following chapter. Here, mention need be made of only a few aspects of its founding. First, the sustained initiative that resulted in the Moscow meeting where the coalition was formed was provided by second- and third-echelon figures in the democratic movement: principally, Lev Ponomarev, Vladimir Bokser and others from MOI (and its all-union paper counterpart, MADO), and Viktor Sheinis, Mikhail Bocharov and Anatolii Shabad of the Voters' Club of the USSR's Academy of Sciences.[112] Second, the founding meeting was anything but a textbook case of organizational discipline. Individuals representing various groups or those about to launch their election campaigns arrived from all quarters of the country, wandered in and out of the meeting, and spoke to all and sundry questions.[113] Finally, the adoption of a name for the coalition turned out to be a study in serendipity. After a number of would-be monikers were screened out, the voting focused on the two remaining alternatives: 'Za Narodovlastie' ('For people's power') and 'Demokraticheskaya Rossiya' ('Democratic Russia'). The former held a preferential edge in the hall until a delegate from the Yaroslavl Popular Front rose to request its exclusion because that same name happened to belong to a right-wing group in his city that was hostile to the democratic forces there. Obligingly, many changed their votes and the coalition was thus christened 'Democratic Russia',[114] shortened in popular parlance to DemRossiya.[115] Below, we have occasion to comment on the significance assumed by this name, adopted as it were by chance.

Counter-organization on the right

Counter-organization among right-wing groups was triggered by the 1989 elections and the Congress that followed. The groups in question have contributed nothing directly to the recovery of Russia's political life; if anything, they would represent a reaction to and *against* that recovery. However, with the reappearance of politics, they came forward to act on that field, their presence thus affecting its overall structure.[116] Broadly speaking, they have occupied positions on it analogous to those held by neo-Stalinists and national-patriots as set out in Figure 2.1. As in the earlier, pre-political period, cooperation between these tendencies was easily arranged. Regardless of the differing principles proclaimed by each – internationalism and socialism in one instance, Russian patriotism and tradition in the other – both were reacting to the same thing: the political success of the democratic forces. More than the positive representations of identity that they advanced, this negative element of *opposing* and, indeed, demonizing the democrats would characterize the politics of each and account for their readiness to combine forces.

The inception of a neo-Stalinist movement occurred in direct response to the 1989 election debacle experienced by the Communist Party hierarchy in Leningrad. To stem the democratic tide in that city, the local apparatus copied the tactics of its Baltic counterparts, organizing a 'workers movement' from above to serve as a counterweight to the democrats.[117] On 15–16 July 1989, under the auspices of the Leningrad party organization, the United Front of Working People of the USSR (OFT in its Russian acronym) staged its founding congress.[118] Since this organization never managed to operate on a union-wide scale, it may be accurate to regard this Leningrad congress as a prelude to the actual founding of a Russian OFT which took place in Sverdlovsk in September. Led by people's deputy of the USSR, Venamin Yarin – an individual whose political career included leading assaults on demonstrations protesting against factory pollution as well as a recent appearance on television for the purpose of persuading striking miners to return to work[119] – the OFT adopted a programme highlighted by commitments to restore the authority of the Communist Party, return it to 'authentic Marxism–Leninism', and struggle against such 'negative phenomena' as 'social pluralism'.[120]

Only the Moscow and Leningrad branches of the OFT were able to muster memberships large enough (200–300 people in either case) to provide any political presence for the organization,[121] and the combination of working-class members (Leningrad) with intellectuals from the Association of Scientific Communism (Moscow)[122] tended to keep even these at arm's length, as each group tended to be suspicious of being used by the other.[123] Of course, the real string-puller in the piece was the Leningrad Communist Party apparatus (a number of whose functionaries sat on the OFT's Coordinating Council),[124] along with its *nomenklatura* allies across Russia, that employed the OFT as a cats-paw of reaction within the Communist Party. At the OFT's second congress, held in Leningrad in January 1990, a Movement of Communist Initiative was launched to provide the appearance of working-class enthusiasm for the creation of a Russian Communist Party, which, based on the OFT's platform,[125] would challenge the more liberal Gorbachev leadership in the CPSU.

The OFT played a key role in effecting the right-wing's response to the organization of the I-RDG and its constituency base in local voters' associations. On the OFT's initiative,[126] a conference was called for 20–1 October in Tyumen at which the combined deputies'–voters' club 'Rossiya' was formed. In terms of its organizational structure and operational tasks, Rossiya was a carbon copy of the I-RDG.[127] Its five co-chairpersons included Yarin and two other people's deputies (En Kim and Vladimir Stepanov) along with two functionaries from the Communist Party's Central Committee.[128] Anchored in a programmatic statement that recounted the many ways in which the Russian nation had been and has remained victimized,[129] supported by a coalition of effectively all neo-Stalinist and national–patriotic groups to the left of Pamyat, it would comprise the kernel of the right-wing's campaign in the upcoming Russian elections.

8   The 1990 elections and the politics of national liberation

The 1990 elections represented a critical phase in the disintegration of the communist order in Russia. Already, Gorbachev's project to renew the Communist Party – disentangling it from state administration, ending its petty administrative tutelage over every aspect of life and focusing its efforts on solving the country's 'strategic' problems which would earn for it the support of the citizenry[1] – had been racking up results quite contrary to those intended. Members were deserting the CPSU in large numbers, either actively by turning in their party cards or passively by not turning in their party dues and otherwise lapsing inactive. Circulation of the party press plummeted, activists were transferring their skills and energies to its competitors, and open political warfare among contending factions broke out within it.[2] By the time that these elections were called, the self-proclaimed vanguard was approaching total disarray.[3] Opposition foci were springing up within, around and outside of the Communist Party. Now it would take another pounding at the polls.

Our concern in this chapter is to analyse political organization under the conditions of Russian national and local elections that commenced with the nomination of candidates in December 1989 and concluded with the balloting of 4 March 1990 and the various run offs and repeated elections that followed. These elections functioned like some great centrifuge, sorting political society into distinguishable layers, separating those forms and forces whose hour had arrived from those for whom it had passed. This centrifuge, of course, had first spun a year earlier, yielding more or less distinguishable opposition groupings to the left and right of Gorbachev. These, however, had devoted their principal efforts to persuading or pressuring him to adopt as much as possible of their respective agendas: broadly speaking, either to press ahead more boldly with reforms in government and economy or to slow the pace, if not reverse course entirely. In the main, however, this was the politics of bluster and bluff, for such was the arena. Whether from high party or state rostra, through the bullhorn at street rallies or in the ringing prose of one or another manifesto, all political persuasions reserved the right to speak in the name of 'the people' and to instruct and warn others – most particularly, the Gorbachev leadership – on what 'the people' demanded or would no longer tolerate. Election results – no matter how devastating they might have been in given instances – had scarcely discouraged anyone from the use of this rhetoric.

But election results did supply credibility quotients that were manifest in the complements of legislative seats captured by the contending political forces. The 1990 elections advanced this process a giant step by converting the credibility of Russia's democrats into government, thus establishing a base of opposition within the Soviet state itself. This event radically altered the structure of communication in the polity. The category 'Russia' would begin to displace that of 'the USSR' (or the more oblique version previously preferred by the democrats, 'the country') as the field of primary significance; Gorbachev would no longer be the principal addressee for political messages, as the electorate came to represent an alternative construction of authority; the more effective messages addressed to this political constituency-in-the-making, the Russian people, would be those encoded with the negative markers 'not Soviet', 'not communist' and so forth, thus inscribing the project of liberation into its identity.

The experience of the 1990 elections also transformed the organizational dimension of Russian politics, remaking the internal constitution of each of the three principal forces then present on the political field. We might introduce this topic by providing a brief sketch of these forces and the transformation that they experienced, developing in the narrative that follows the particular factors and processes that contributed to it.

The Communist Party

At the plenary session of its Central Committee conducted on the eve of these elections, the CPSU resolved to create within itself a Russian Bureau headed by Gorbachev, rather than a full-blown Russian Communist Party as conservative spokesmen had been demanding.[4] This decision meant that there would be no national Communist Party in Russia, as there was in the other union-republics, to contest these elections. No distinct platform was issued,[5] no national slate of candidates was fielded. As of old, the call went out to nominate 'both Communists and non-party people' to stand as candidates for elections to soviets at all levels.[6] As a result, CPSU members campaigned mainly against one another, just as they had a year earlier.[7] At local level, Communist Party organizations did wage campaigns throughout most of

Russia. Their leading officers, however, would prove reluctant, if not downright afraid, to face the voters directly. In callous comment on the party's claims to proletarian pedigree, they often retreated from political battles in the urban industrial centres for the safe harbour of rural backwaters, fighting rearguard actions where the changes sweeping the rest of the country had scarcely penetrated and where challengers were not to be found. These elections underscored the fact that the CPSU was not a political party by any stretch of the imagination. Rather, it amounted to a collection of offices still possessing enormous resources – both its own property and its control of access to state offices at the all-union level and in those localities of Russia where it had not been dislodged from power – over which opposing forces within it would struggle. Thus the elections intensified the level of factional conflict within it, accelerated its disintegration in coming months, and encouraged the departure from its ranks of ambitious politicians seeking to extend their careers by joining other organizations whose future prospects appeared more promising.

Nationalists and neo-Stalinists

The elections brought together these two strands in Russian political society and simultaneously exposed them as marginal forces in the political process. As such, the 1990 contests served both as a precedent for future alliances between nationalists and neo-Stalinists and as a summary judgement on the particular leaders and organizations hitherto comprising this bloc. The implications of this latter point would prove important for the future when this space on the political field would be filled by defectors from the communist and democratic camps who would lead a new patriotic opposition movement, having elbowed the majority of first-wave 'patriots' out of the way.

The democrats

Over the course of these elections, the democratic tendency in Russian politics transformed itself into a *bona fide* national movement. The exigencies of electoral politics largely determined its form: a loose coalition of candidates and supporting voters' associations, linked to an emerging national leader (Boris El'tsin) and cemented together ideologically by anti-communism. The organization cobbled together during the campaign contained elements of both the 'popular front' and the political party, even as it displaced existing popular fronts and antedated the formation of parties themselves. These elections also marked the appearance of a new wave of leaders and functionaries in the democratic movement: professional politicians and organizers. Some had graduated from the ranks of the informals, but most arrived from other quarters, either from the CPSU or from non-political backgrounds. Concomitantly, two hitherto important components of the democratic current – the 'informals' and prestigious social actors – began to exit the stage. To be sure, neither disappeared entirely, but drifted toward the wings as centre stage became the province of another cohort building their new careers in politics.

From inception, the construction of this movement would render it prone to division. This feature of the democratic movement, organizationally incarnate as DemRossiya, resulted from the predominance of personage over institution and the attendant personalized forms of organizational relations consistent with that which we noted in our analysis of Soviet forms of organization based on weak structures propagating strong (personal) ties. Although we regularly refer in this chapter to 'organizations' such as DemRossiya, the Communist Party or the 'patriotic' bloc, these appellations should not disguise the fact that each represented a fluid, under-determined grouping of political forces built in great measure around ambitious and/or powerful individuals and certain evocative but ambiguous symbols. Especially with respect to the insurgent democrats, these forms of organization and communication will repeatedly prove themselves effective in marshalling a powerful mass movement directed against the Soviet party-state, but of considerably less utility for institutionalizing popular government.

The field of electoral struggle

As the second stage of Gorbachev's political reform unfolded in the republic and local elections of winter and spring 1989–90,[8] opposition forces under the broad umbrella of DemRossiya were poised to contest the Communist Party for control of the state. This, of course, amounted to another uphill battle for the challengers. But two outcomes of the struggles that they had waged since the elections of 1989 had already altered the terrain to their advantage. First, the attention focused by the Inter-Regional Deputies Group (I-RDG) on the anti-democratic features of the USSR's electoral system and legislative organization mobilized public opinion against their re-appearance in the reforms that the union-republics adopted in the autumn of 1989.[9] Since the outgoing supreme soviets in each of the union-republics would soon be facing the voters, and since no reasonable argument had yet been found to justify stacking the electoral deck in favour of the collective incumbent – the party-state apparatus – supreme soviets in nearly all the republics declined to incorporate in their new legislation the various filters that had been installed a year earlier at the all-union level. Although the Supreme Soviet of the Russian Federation, alone among the union-republics, did adopt the USSR's two-tiered legislative structure (a Congress of People's Deputies that would elect a smaller, full-time Supreme Soviet), like most others it rejected those two mechanisms that had been used with such effect in the 1989 races to scuttle independent candidates and thus pack the legislature with loyal supporters of the regime: the pre-electoral district meetings and the provision reserving a bloc of seats for officially sponsored 'public organizations'.[10] This greatly expanded the possibilities for getting candidates not vetted by the Communist Party apparatus on the ballot and ensured that those elected to the legislature would not confront there a ready-made communist voting majority as was the case a year earlier. Candidates would be nominated directly for the 1,068 seats in the new Congress of People's Deputies of the Russian Federation from workplaces, at voters' meetings in residential areas or by duly registered public organizations (which, in practice, meant the Communist Party and its sponsored organizations since no other applicant had been registered by either the all-union or Russian government until after the close of nominations). Since thousands of candidates had been arbitrarily denied registration by district electoral commissions in the previous year, the voters' associations that had subsequently formed in most of Russia's cities made concerted efforts this time around to get some of their members elected to these commissions.[11] In the capital, the Moscow Voters' Association (MOI) succeeded in placing one of its leaders, A. I. Muzykantskii, on the city commission[12] and had varying degrees of success securing the election of affiliates' members in the electoral districts to the commissions at that level.[13]

But even with a more level playing field and less biased referees, the 1990 elections were witness to a considerable measure of administrative meddling. A not unrepresentative example of the attitude taken by local authorities would be a document composed by the regional committee of the Communist Party in Ryazan which was purloined, reproduced and posted around the city. It instructed local officials to exercise strict control over all local mass media and printing facilities, to make every effort to eject from the race a certain candidate associated with informal organizations and, in a revealing statement on its notion of due process, to analyse the speeches of N. V. Molotkov – a people's deputy of the USSR supporting this same candidate – and to warn him about the impermissibility of a people's deputy expressing such views.[14] As was the case in 1989, local elites were generally loathe to allow voters' meetings in places of residence, preferring instead venues such as factory assemblies or meetings of official public organizations more amenable to their manipulation. Using the latitude of the law or simply various forms of connivance to prevent residential assemblies from gathering, they saw to it that the overwhelming majority of all nominations occurred in those sites where their influence was strongest.[15] As was the case a year earlier, nomination was not synonymous with the appearance of a candidate's name on the ballot. Local electoral commissions, even without the handy filter of pre-electoral district meetings, arbitrarily refused to register duly nominated candidates, thus eliminating from competition for the parliament alone some hundreds of would-be contenders.[16] At the final end of the process – vote tabulation – violations also occurred. By their nature, these would be difficult to detect and to measure. But the disproportionately high levels of reported voter turnout in rural areas where the party-state apparatus was not subject to the supervision of independent poll-watchers,[17] as well as incidences in urban districts where the authorities denied poll-watchers the right to carry out their functions, would indicate that ballot tampering probably occurred on a considerable scale.[18] Since the opposition was now better organized, however, fraud seemed less of a factor in determining the final results. Indeed, cheating was subjected to a greater degree of vigilance on the part of the central authorities who actually caught out two local officials engaged in it.[19]

The second outcome of past struggles that would aid the insurgent democrats in this contest was the politicization of the electorate. In contrast to mass indifference that had initially greeted elections the previous year, sizeable percentages of voters were now reported to be taking a keen interest in the process from the very start.[20] This interest was driven by widespread discontent with prevailing conditions and the corresponding desire to punish those regarded as responsible for them. For instance, in a mass survey conducted by the USSR's Institute of Sociology in December 1989 and January 1990, large majorities in Moscow and Gor'kii expressed their 'complete dissatisfaction' (79 and 69 per cent, respectively) with the economic situation and blamed above all the Communist Party for it.[21] Although most people did not expect the results of the balloting to improve anything, the elections did serve as an outlet for their frustrations.[22] In the capital, the public mood swung increasingly behind the idea of administering a blow to the bureau-crats,[23] while in a number of the provinces, voters would not wait till election day to change the make up of the local power structure. Staging large public protests against local elites in Volgograd, Sverdlovsk,

Tyumen, Murmansk and elsewhere, they demanded and secured the resignations of dozens of regional bosses.[24]

Just as informal organizations and the I-RDG had been fanning the flames of popular discontent by battering on the issue of *nomenklatura* privileges and ridiculing the incompetent and self-serving behaviour displayed by the party-state apparatus, so DemRossiya and its affiliates would harness the diffuse sense of anger swirling around the electorate and target it on the Communist Party.[25] A measure of the change in the country's political climate induced by these efforts can be taken from the results of a survey of candidates in the 1990 elections. Whereas a year earlier, open opposition to the Communist Party's monopoly on power had been confined to small, rejectionist circles such as the Democratic Union, some 80 per cent of all candidates running for the Russian parliament favoured an end to that monopoly by removing the Constitution's guarantee (article 6) of the CPSU's 'leading role', while only 7 per cent supported its continuation.[26]

In addition to accelerating society's politicization via the mobilization of discontent, these elections also witnessed developments in political organization and communication. Not surprisingly, those forms and methods of electioneering pioneered by democratic groups at district and city level in 1989 were rehearsed and perfected by their national coalition, DemRossiya. But they were also copied in 1990 by DemRossiya's opponents. In Moscow, for instance, the Communist Party set up its own voters' clubs in various quarters of the city.[27] Similarly, it began to use some of the language of its competitors, not only demanding 'social justice' – a shibboleth for opposition to unearned privilege – but excoriating 'bureaucratic dictate and administrative tyranny blocking the way to real democracy (*narodovlastiya*) and a root improvement in the lives of Muscovites'. Thus the communists in the capital had appropriated key terms from the vocabulary of the democrats and reversed their vectors by casting themselves as the nemesis of those 'people and little groups who are striving to monopolize glasnost [and] to confer on themselves the right to speak in the name of all the people'.[28] Although, in the West, attention has been drawn to the appearance of an electioneering manual composed for these races by Sergei Stankevich and Mikhail Shneider of Moscow's Popular Front,[29] it was not the democrats but the Communist Party that made the greatest efforts to equip its candidates with up-to-date methods of public relations (or, in plain language, voter manipulation). In addition to producing campaign manuals, CPSU organizations in cities such as Moscow, Gor'kii, Kazan and Yaroslavl conducted training sessions for perhaps thousands of their candidates that extended for as much as five days and featured psychologists, sociologists and others teaching the most advanced political technology available in Russia.[30]

Similarly, nationalist and neo-Stalinist groups adopted the coalition tactics of the democrats and actually beat them off the starting blocks by announcing their own national organization, the Bloc of Public and Patriotic Movements of Russia, nearly a month before the democrats had formed theirs. But this effort to replicate the organizational forms developed by their opponents was not based in grassroots associations. As a consequence, the coalition of nationalists and neo-Stalinists remained top-heavy and without much reach into localities, amounting to a hollow shell, if not an outright caricature, of an electoral organization. Of the thousands of candidates that it sponsored in the elections, none was elected to the Russian legislature and only an insignificant handful were elected to local soviets.

Since the 'patriotic' coalition played an ancillary role in these elections while that performed by the Communist Party was largely obstructionist, we confine our comments on these two groups to the manner in which their presences on the political field shaped its overall structure. Still in control of the machinery of state, the Communist Party represented the principal influence in this respect. As Mary McAuley has pointed out, the strategy pursued by most sub-national units of the CPSU involved avoiding open battle with the democrats. Instead, they would utilize the control that they exercised over election procedures and access to the mass media to retard the progress of DemRossiya's electoral insurgency. One variant of this strategy, pursued by the party apparatus in Leningrad, involved backing DemRossiya's other opponent – the patriotic coalition – furnishing them with professional staff and other resources.[31] Indeed, if one consults the newspaper *Rossiya*, the organ of the deputies' and voters' clubs of that same name that functioned as the patriotic bloc's principal print medium for disseminating its message during this campaign, one notices that the majority of its content was authored by officials in the pay of the CPSU's Central Committee.[32]

Another communist strategy was gerrymandering. It took two forms. The first promoted the over-representation of rural areas, brought about by malapportionment among regions compounded by additional malapportionment between urban and rural districts within them. This practice yielded a plethora of safe rural districts where the campaigns of party-state candidates would not be burdened by the bothersome presence of actual opponents. The second – which would have caused Elbridge Gerry himself to blush – occurred 'in a series of regions [in which] the boundaries of electoral districts were tailored for the purpose of guaranteeing the predominance of specific political forces in the electoral process . . . [by] *composing electoral districts out of non-adjacent territories*.[33] This produced more safe seats for the candidates of the party-state apparatus. However, in those instances in which the apparatus chose to engage its democratic opponents directly and on terms not altogether lopsided, a string of defeats ensued. Moscow was probably the best example of this. There, despite their huge edge with regard to material resources, the city party committee could manage to stage no more than a lacklustre campaign and its candidates were trounced at the polls.[34]

For their part, the nationalist and neo-Stalinist coalition consisting of (formally) twelve separate organizations[35] announced its existence in late December 1989 with the publication of an election platform in the right-wing *Literaturnaya Rossiya* and *Sovetskaya Rossiya*.[36] Dubbing themselves the Bloc of Public and Patriotic Movements of Russia, this assemblage proclaimed for itself an independent role in combating the odious tendencies of separatism and 'radical' democracy – inasmuch as the CPSU had already shown itself inadequate to these tasks – and vowed to curtail these and other flagitious phenomena by introducing a law on state morality making it a crime 'to do as one pleases'. Interestingly, those in the patriotic bloc reached their decision on the futility of attempting to 'correct' the course pursued by the CPSU at roughly the same time as had their opponents in the democratic camp. But whereas the democrats had a cadre already experienced in political organizing, the patriotic bloc was at a clear disadvantage in that respect. Only the United Front of Working People (OFT) and the legislative faction 'Russia' could be counted on to contribute much to their campaign[37] – excepting, of course, self-gratifying speeches and counter-productive propaganda from which those in the bloc's cultural associations never managed to refrain. As a result, such practical activities as composing and distributing leaflets, setting up pickets or canvassing door-to-door went almost entirely missing. For the patriots, the elections seemed primarily an occasion for reprising at rallies that rhetoric that so delighted the faithful.

In Moscow, the television complex at Ostankino – regarded by the patriots as a hotbed of Russophobic treachery polluting the airwaves with Zionist–Masonic propaganda – was a preferred site for holding rallies, although they also used the officially sanctioned grounds of the Luzhniki sports facility. In order to convey something of the flavour of these affairs, we might consider one more or less typical meeting. It convened on 27 January and was conducted under the slogans 'Private property is the path to civil war', 'Restorers of capitalism – to the pillory' and 'I-RDG is Zionist power'. The leading orators included the candidates for parliament Nikolai Bondarenko, Valentin Terekhov, Viktor Anpilov, and others. For their part, OFT representatives accused the USSR's government of 'killing the revolutionary essence of Marxism', causing 'the collapse of the world socialist system', and singled out Gorbachev as one who collaborates with the 'murderer-president, Bush' to those ends. Other speakers repeated the familiar right-wing injunctions against 'insulting soldier-internationalists [the Afghan veterans]', 'spitting on socialist ideals' and 'creating Zionist military gangs' in the country. Bondarenko called for debunking the 'lies [being told] about Russian fascism', reiterated the bloc's plank on eliminating financial assistance from the RSFSR to other union-republics and advocated the dissolution of the Russian Bureau of the CPSU since, in his opinion, it was composed of non-Russians.[38]

The meaning of these and similar propositions cannot be located on that plane of communication where statements admit to factual verification. Rather, their significance derives from the discursive categories on which they have been predicated, categories such as 'treachery' and 'betrayal' that construct the Russian nation as victim, preyed upon by dark forces from without – capitalism (a metonymn for the West), the 'murder-president, Bush', Zionism – which are in league with domestic malefactors (Gorbachev and the I-RDG). Consequently, the play of terms in the discourse drives it toward a resolution of the opposition that it has established between 'Russia' and those forces bent on her destruction, a resolution that occurs in the cathartic moment of naming the treacherous ones. At this juncture, the nationalists and neo-Stalinists had regularly singled out Politburo member Aleksandr Yakovlev as the personification of treachery and, accordingly, the 27 January rally at Ostankino would adopt by acclamation a resolution recording the charges that:

[He] is the old filth of stagnation converted into the pseudo-brilliant scum of perestroika. Tolerating his leadership and that of similar degenerates, the party is signing its own death warrant. Tolerating Yakovlev at the steering wheel of the country, we are signing our own death warrant and that of our children and grandchildren. Tolerance has come to an end. We demand Yakovlev's removal from all his duties and the creation of an independent public commission to investigate his activities.[39]

In one version or another, the national idea that the patriots had been stressing became in the course of these elections the lingua franca of Russian politics. Its salience was apparent in the fact that all three of the main contenders in these races advocated the idea of sovereignty for the Russian Federation. This notion had followed a more or less identifiable path from the popular fronts in the Baltics to their Russian allies in the

I-RDG, thence to communists and neo-Stalinists and, of course, to the nationalists for whom this formulation was easily assimilated into their overall credo. Of course, each group had its own interpretation of what sovereignty would mean for Russia, and each interpretation reflected the political strategy of the respective group. For the democrats, the idea also had reciprocal effects. By the beginning of the 1990 campaign, they had begun to identify themselves with a specific cultural, geographic and political space: Russia. Hitherto, their discourse had elided mention of their exact territorial coordinates. Their admiration of, and proclaimed affinity with, Western institutions and practices, their announced subscription to 'all-human values', their repeated references to 'civilized countries', had all served to construct for them a discursive platform from which they could survey the situation in their own country, compare it against a foreign or abstract standard, find it grossly deficient and then lay the blame for this on the Communist Party. Since their discourse directly associated the USSR with the CPSU, they tended to refrain from even using the words 'Soviet Union' or 'USSR', preferring instead to designate their spatial location simply as 'the country'. Now, as the very name that they had selected for themselves would indicate, they had discovered a home. To be sure, their construction of 'Russia' was a strategic use of language *par excellence*. Much like the patriots, the democrats portrayed the nation as the victim of predatory forces. However, their construction of victim and villain linked Russia to their images of the West while simultaneously counterposing the nation to their arch-opponent, the Communist Party. In their rendition of the suffering nation, the democrats pictured Russia as an otherwise normal, civilized, democratic country but for the fact that the nation had been robbed of its history and potential by an alien power, communism. Yet in deploying this strategic language, the democrats were willy-nilly calling forth the category 'nation' that reached deeply into the store of cultural memory, opening what would later become a site of bitter contestation for a variety of political forces. For the moment, however, our purpose would be simply to note how the struggle waged by the democrats against their communist opponents had transformed them in a matter of months from rootless liberals into champions of national liberation.

The election campaign and the making of DemRossiya

During the period considered here, DemRossiya represented the principal dynamic animating Russia's political rebirth. Its leaders had already seized the initiative from Gorbachev, eclipsing his 'revolutionary perestroika' with calls for far deeper and more extensive changes in government and economy, thus setting a political agenda to which he was forced to respond.[40] Similarly, the innovations accomplished by those under the DemRossiya umbrella in the areas of political organization and communication evoked a number of comparable responses from its competitors, although their efforts to copy the new forms that it had introduced brought them small success. The bulk of our discussion of the 1990 election campaign therefore will focus on that which in context amounted to Russia's engine of political development, DemRossiya.

As an electoral bloc, DemRossiya was comprised of three basic elements. At the top stood the public leaders of the I-RDG; at the next level were the organizers who had emerged from the informal movement, the constituency organizations that sprang up during the 1989 elections and the voters' associations established in their wake; below them, the mass of volunteer activists contributing the indispensable resources of energy, enthusiasm and hard work. With respect to the first group, their position in the bloc and the role that they played were more or less axiomatic. These were the acknowledged leaders of Russia's democratic movement, luminaries such as El'tsin, Popov, Afanas'ev, Travkin and others. Their authority within the coalition was unquestioned. The draft platform that they had composed for the I-RDG was thus adopted wholesale by DemRossiya.[41] The exigencies of the election promoted outward unity among the leadership, but certain fault lines running beneath the surface consensus could be detected as well. Perhaps the foremost was the fracture already present between the indisputable champion of Russia's democratic movement and DemRossiya itself. Initially, El'tsin had acquiesced with some reluctance to the very idea of forming a nationwide electoral coalition, preferring instead to rely on the same forms and methods of campaigning that had served him so well in 1989: individual campaign organizations that might support one another in *ad hoc* fashion.[42] In his 1990 race, he spent relatively little time in Sverdlovsk where he was standing for office. Instead, he was stumping around the entire country, attempting to build for himself a national constituency,[43] launching in effect a campaign for the Russian presidency,[44] despite the fact that that office would not be established for more than a year. Moreover, his attempts to expand his potential voter appeal found him articulating a number of themes that were neither consistent one with another nor always in tune with the rhetoric of his coalition partners.[45] He was demonstrably seeking to build a personal presence in the electorate by transcending the organizational base supplied him by DemRossiya. The relationship between

El'tsin and DemRossiya was from the first, then, 'mutually-parasitic'.[46] The public leader required at the time – and would again require on occasion – a political organization, just as that organization benefited by its association with El'tsin. However, El'tsin would detach himself from his host as soon as his immediate objectives had been accomplished; in this instance, suspending his membership in DemRossiya following his election to the post of chairperson of Russia's Supreme Soviet. The persistence of a half-relationship or sometimes-relationship between the leader of the country's democratic movement and the organized forces of that same movement would confound the construction of a Russian polity. This relationship was present from the very outset.

The second echelon of DemRossiya – the organizational leaders – directed the activities of an electoral coalition that, with small exaggeration, existed on a nationwide basis in name only. Its actual operating units were coalitions of groups that existed exclusively in the country's larger cities. This feature of the coalition was to a considerable degree a product of timing and time. DemRossiya had not held its founding conference until nearly three weeks *after* the nominations period had already expired. Thus, it could only appear as a coalition among candidates already nominated and smaller, city-based coalitions of constituency organizations already conducting their campaigns. Many of these city-based units in DemRossiya's national coalition declined to adopt its name, retaining their own monikers more familiar to voters in their respective areas: 'Democratic Elections–90' in Leningrad, 'Democratic Choice' in Sverdlovsk, 'Democratic Bloc' in Yaroslavl', 'New Wave' in Novosibirsk, 'Democratic Movement of Kuban' in Krasnodar, or simply 'popular front' in places such as Kostroma and Khabarovsk. Moreover, since only six weeks separated DemRossiya's inauguration from election day, there was an acute shortage of time and no compelling reason to attempt to build this coalition into an actual national entity. The imperative of the moment was unmistakably clear: 'We must elect our people to the parliament!' Precisely who 'our people' were in a given instance was thus a matter already decided in the main by those in the localities. DemRossiya had no resources to pump into local campaigns, save its own endorsement and the consequent association of individual candidates with its public leaders. Except for the public funding of five staff assistants allotted by the state to each candidate (often used to employ organizers from DemRossiya's affiliated voters' organizations), it had little to throw into the effort of building the machinery of an electoral organization. Its skeletal staff – supplied by MOI and some seventy members of the voters' club of the USSR's Academy of Sciences – was located exclusively in the capital. Its ability to vet candidates running under its label was exercised almost entirely by its city-based affiliates and their screening mechanisms were usually slipshod at best. Thus heterogeneity in the second echelon added another unsettling potential to the tension between leader (El'tsin) and organization. Before two years had passed, a number of those elected to parliament with the backing of DemRossiya and its affiliates would sport national reputations as some of its most bitter enemies.[47]

For the races to the Russian parliament and those to local soviets, some 5000 candidates received the endorsement of DemRossiya or its local members.[48] In Moscow – where DemRossiya was built on the organizational base of MOI, the centre of a network of voters' associations functioning in all thirty-three of the capital's districts[49] – its capacity to recruit and deploy candidates far exceeded that of its counterparts elsewhere in the country.[50] Even so, the democratic forces encountered serious problems here. As the nominations process commenced, MOI began receiving applications from a number of organizations whose membership either overlapped it or with which cooperative work had already become the norm: Moscow Tribune, Shchit (the unofficial military association), Communists for Perestroika and, most importantly, Elections–90 (a coalition that included eighteen separate democratic groups in the city).[51] MOI channelled the candidates to its district-level counterparts in order to secure their nominations in places of residence or, more often, in workplaces. Imbalances were immediately apparent: there was a serious deficit of potential candidates for local soviets and a glut of hopefuls for slots on the ballot for the parliamentary races. MOI was able to do very little to correct this problem.[52] As a result, it sometimes found itself cancelling the force of its own endorsements by backing more than one candidate in a given race; in other instances, it would drop its support for one candidate at the last minute in order to throw it behind another who had secured the personal endorsements of I-RDG notables.[53] In a few cases, candidates were coopted onto its city list without their knowledge.[54] Unable to induce any candidate to drop out of a race in order to unify the democrats' constituency in a given district around a single nominee, MOI's overall role in recruiting and assisting candidates more resembled that of a fireman than a traffic cop.

In other cities, the nominations process was broadly similar. In Leningrad, Democratic Elections–90 – formed in December 1989 by the Leningrad Popular Front, the Leningrad Voters' Union, Memorial, Democratic Platform in the CPSU, Club Perestroika and a host of other associations – created a five-member working group that solicited nominations from member organizations and distributed these potential candidates across electoral districts in the city. Although the Leningrad democrats seemed to have had a little more success than did their Moscow counterparts in supplying each district with no more than one candidate, they were able neither to ensure representation in all districts nor to prevent potentially fratricidal competition from occurring (about one-third of the races for the city soviet featured competition between two or more candidates affiliated with the coalition).[55] In Yaroslavl, an especially active local popular front that endorsed and supported the candidates of the Democratic Bloc had difficulty finding standard-bearers for local and regional races, fielding, for instance, only seventy-five candidates in the 200 districts electing deputies to the provincial legislature.[56] In places such as Ivanova and Kostroma where local democratic organizations had just begun to function[57] – or in those such as Krasnodar where they remained hampered by the repressive actions of the local authorities[58] – nomination efforts showed correspondingly more meagre results.

On the basis of its performance in recruiting and distributing candidates we might easily reach the conclusion that DemRossiya was a rather weak organization. It had effectively no presence in rural areas, a rather marginal one in many provincial capitals and towns, and where its strength was greatest – in Moscow, Leningrad, Sverdlovsk and a few other large cities – it scarcely functioned as a well-oiled political machine matching its candidates to each and all constituencies. Moreover, certain individuals were able to bypass the established arrangements whereby the candidates chosen by its district-level voters' associations had their names entered on its city-wide lists. In Moscow, this led to the inclusion on the list of a KGB officer active in the repression of the 'Young Socialists' in the early eighties, the recent director of the Komsomol's surveillance-informant squads at Moscow State University and other candidates with less than spotless democratic credentials.[59] From the perspective of those functions that electoral organizations perform in democratic politics, then, DemRossiya was weak. But recalling the specific context and actual significance of these elections, this conclusion should be qualified. Contextually, we might note that DemRossiya faced competition from only two other organized contenders – the Communist Party and the Bloc of Public and Patriotic Movements of Russia – and these displayed considerably lower degrees of energy and effectiveness than it did.[60] In the overwhelming majority of the races conducted in urban areas where all three sides had the capability of putting their troops into the field, DemRossiya would scotch its opponents. *Relatively* speaking, then, DemRossiya was a powerhouse.

This point would deserve to be underscored with regard to the elections' significance. Viewing them through the lenses of conventional contests for seats in legislative institutions, Gavin Helf and Jeffrey Hahn have observed that 'the victories of the opposition [DemRossiya], although striking in their novelty, were actually quite isolated and almost entirely limited to cities'.[61] In this respect, Mary McAuley has pointed out that DemRossiya scored well where a strong political presence had already been established by informal organizations (Leningrad) and poorly where such had not been the case (Perm and Arkhangel'sk).[62] These geographical determinants of electoral success revealed at a point in time the spatial coordinates of mass politicization. In those areas where the process had advanced the furthest, DemRossiya's candidates scored their major victories; conversely, where politicization had not gone very far, those of the party-state apparatus scored theirs. But these considerations should not obscure another side of the question. These were national elections, representing the first round in an ongoing struggle between the democratic movement and the Communist Party for control of Russia. From that vantage, it would matter little whether the communists had captured every seat in every rural legislature or had garnered majorities in regional soviets from one end of the country to the other. The critical unit at this juncture was the national one, and the major cities represented the strategic approaches to it. The primary significance of the elections, therefore, consisted in the fact that, by constructing a field for a national political contest, they conduced to the formation of a national political movement. Having captured the key sites in this round of struggle, this movement would later go on to wrest control of the Russian government from the Communist Party and establish in the process a Russian state.

As Vladimir Pribylovskii has noted, the emergence of this movement as something more than the mere sum of its parts took place during the 1990 campaign.[63] In order to account for this result, especially remarkable inasmuch as it transpired within an abbreviated time span, we might begin with the question of agency. The relative division of labour that we have mentioned came about more or less spontaneously in the crucible of the campaign. El'tsin and Afanas'ev performed the function of public leaders – providing the new organization with a face, building a popular presence for it via association with their own prestige and charisma – while Popov, Stankevich and Travkin played more the role of organization leaders, coordinating campaign activities and making the major decisions regarding how resources would be deployed, which candidates would appear on DemRossiya's Moscow ticket and liaising with affiliates in the provinces. As this public presence developed, the great bulk of DemRossiya's leadership began to identify themselves with the new organization rather than with the various associations among its constituent parts from which they had come. This appeared to be equally true for rank-and-file activists campaigning for its candidates. A measure of the change introduced into the affiliations of those in the democratic movement can be taken from the fact that whereas popular fronts arguably had been the leading form of political organization prior to the onset of the 1990 campaign, they effectively disappeared from the scene after these elections.[64]

As would be the case with any organization, DemRossiya developed into a real entity over the course of engaging in practical activities and symbolically mediating its actions. Given the things to be done in an election campaign, these aspects of the organization's ontology were closely joined. Ironically, the party-state authorities contributed to its progress in this respect by attempting to circumscribe its activities. As its members managed to overcome the various barriers thrown up against their campaign efforts, they were simultaneously forging a sense of combat, comradeship and capability for their fledgling organization, concatenating their struggles against the communists with the nation's liberation from communism.

The principal barrier erected by the authorities concerned access to the means of mass communications. During the 1990 campaign, something approaching a blackout of campaign coverage took place.[65] Even liberal publications, such as the weekly, *Ogonek*, scarcely mentioned the election campaigns that were under way or said a word about DemRossiya itself.[66] In a few instances, local newspapers did break ranks with their formal superiors and published materials that aided the democrats.[67] But instances of this sort were rare and they hardly offset the campaigning performed by other publications on behalf of the Communist Party.[68] DemRossiya managed in many places to overcome this by putting out its own campaign leaflets, an action that, under the rules governing electioneering, was patently illegal. However, since electoral commissions encharged with supplying candidates with printed campaign statements and posters tended to discharge their tasks sluggishly,[69] DemRossiya and its affiliates decided to take on this job themselves. The other two contenders in the race did so as well, but neither would begin to match the amount or the effectiveness of the weaponry deployed by DemRossiya in the war of the leaflets. Wherever they found the printing facilities to do so, city-based units of DemRossiya blanketed their respective territories with campaign handbills, plastering them in public places and stuffing them into residents' letter boxes.[70] In the language employed in one of its initial leaflets distributed in Moscow, we have a clear illustration of how the new organization was constructing itself symbolically. The leaflet read:

DEAR FRIENDS! The old apparatus has made every effort to impede your vote. They have nominated a few obvious or disguised henchmen of the nomenklatura to stand against each democratic candidate. Surely, you have noticed that open campaigning in these elections has been limited severely. Everything, as if by accident, is being done so that you will cast your ballot only on the basis of the scanty information provided on the ballot itself. But there is one clear-cut indicator by which you can distinguish the candidates standing for decisive democratic and socio-economic transformation. It's their membership in the bloc 'DemRossiya'. The list of candidates of this bloc will be publicized in a few days. On it are deputies of the USSR – members of the Inter-Regional Deputies Group – running in the current elections. Only by electing candidates from the bloc 'DemRossiya' will you get in the Russian, Moscow and district soviets those who share our views and are our comrades-in-arms. According to public opinion data not published in the official press, over 75 per cent of Muscovites support the position of the Inter-Regional Deputies Group. Should we really award election victory to the candidates of the apparatus and right wing conservative forces?

WE ARE VOTING FOR DEMROSSIYA!

WE HOPE YOU ARE TOO

B. El'tsin	S. Stankevich	L. Ponomarev
G. Popov	O. Orlov	I. Bogantseva
Yu. Afanas'ev	V. Bokser[71]	

Obviously, this leaflet reprised the tactic that had proven so successful when first employed in Moscow a year earlier: in this case, using notables to personify a new organization hitherto unknown to the vast majority of voters. Expanding on the use to which it had been put on behalf of some individual candidates in 1989, DemRossiya standardized this practice for those receiving its endorsement in the 1990 races. A typical example of this tactic appeared in a leaflet distributed prior to the run-off elections of 18 March, which read:

Esteemed voters of the Taganskii District!!
We thank you for supporting the candidates of democratic orientation, who have received the greatest number of votes in the district. We ask you to support the candidates of 'DemRossiya' in the runoff – candidates for People's Deputies of the RSFSR: Leonid Volkov, known in democratic circles as a champion of the rule-of-law [pravovogo gosudarstva] and the social security of the citizenry, [and] Valerii Korolev, a working-class democrat, and other candidates of the bloc.

B. El'tsin   S. Stankevich   Yu. Afanas'ev[72]

In addition to positive messages on behalf of its candidates, DemRossiya's campaign literature also extensively propagated negative images of its communist opponents, utilizing certain stereotypes that resonated broadly in popular consciousness. Here, its electoral agitation was directed toward expressing, reiterating and amplifying one central idea: 'We are against the powers that be!'[73] This 'negative' campaigning was, in fact, indistinguishable from DemRossiya's positive self-representation as the people's instrument for smiting the forces of evil: the *nomenklatura*. One typical campaign leaflet presented the matter thus:

> The apparatus has done everything in order that the representatives of democratic organizations won't enter the body of candidates for people's deputies . . . [A]mong the candidates about 80 per cent are members of the CPSU. The people can realize the idea of democracy [*narodovlastiya*] in only one way, to vote *against* a candidate if he belongs to the party apparatus or is one of its henchmen, with the exception of those cases when he by his own actions has proven his devotion to democracy . . . We do not summon the voters to vote 'For soviets without communists', we summon them to vote 'For soviets *without* the party *nomenklatura*'.[74]

Similarly, El'tsin's election platform, often reproduced as a campaign leaflet, demanded that those 'who have brought Russia to a crisis be made to answer [for their actions]' and that 'all privileges, including the use of state transportation, be removed [while] transferring state dachas, private residences and other specially allotted social properties to children and the least-provisioned strata of the population'.[75]

The effectiveness of this rhetoric derived from its resonance with the egalitarian norms valorized by society's cultural code, and its foregrounding of certain cultural stereotypes. In this latter respect, the figure of Boris El'tsin was immensely important. He personified the simple man of the people, cast down from the heights of power by nefarious forces, victimized and forced to suffer by those who have victimized the people generally, yet possessed of enormous energy, will and force, thus inspiring hope that these dark forces could, indeed, be overcome.[76] But if these cultural norms were pressed into service by DemRossiya as a form of strategic communication – soliciting popular support by speaking in a language available to, and evocative for, broad strata of the population – it would likewise be obvious that by propagating these forms DemRossiya was also accelerating the development of political language in Russian society. Its attacks on the minions of the party-state for the restrictions that they imposed on political activity and the privileges that they appropriated to themselves were, of course, simplistic and one-sided. But the point, here, would be that they were addressed to a new audience: not to the authorities, as had been evident in the language of the dissidents; not to the reformers, as had been the case with the informals and the liberal wing of the CPSU; but to an imagined public. By speaking to this audience in its own language, by rhetorically framing it as a community of equal persons abhorring special privileges and contemptuous of those seeking to impose restrictions on its right to participate in its own governance, DemRossiya's forms of communication were actively positing political community, calling it into existence.[77]

This political community would manifest itself corporeally in the form of mass demonstrations, the other of DemRossiya's principal methods of campaigning. Here, again, the party-state authorities threw up obstacles to contain the insurgency-via-the-vote that was unfolding in Russia, limiting access to public places for staging street demonstrations and rallies. Where the democratic forces were too weak to defy a ban on such activities, such a ban could be effectively imposed.[78] In most instances, however, the authorities would permit public gatherings but attempt to reduce their size and impact, either by restricting them to areas away from the city centre[79] or by cranking up the rumour mill to churn out ominous tales of impending pogroms and mass violence[80] that would discourage attendance.

The authorities success in these endeavours proved marginal at best. *Pravda* reported later that over 200,000 public actions were staged in the USSR during these elections, only some ninety of which had been called by local units of the Communist Party.[81] In at least one instance, a communist rally became the occasion for citizens to mount the platform and denounce the *nomenklatura*;[82] in other cases in which sanction or access to the city centre were denied, masses of citizens rallied in front of Communist Party headquarters.[83] In the capital, DemRossiya staged its first march and rally at Manege Square on 3 February, drawing about 200,000 people who echoed back their leaders' demands to the CPSU's Central Committee – many of whose members, in town for a plenary session, were occupying hotel rooms abutting the square – to end the Communist Party's constitutionally guaranteed monopoly on power. Two days later, the Central Committee obliged. By the close of the contest, DemRossiya had staged the largest political rally in the country's history, drawing to its 25 February campaign finale as many as one million people. On that same day, it turned out over 30,000 people in Sverdlovsk and more than 20,000 in Volgograd, while mounting demonstrations for the first time in Saransk, Tomsk, Arkhangel'sk, Pavlodar, Khabarovsk, Ufa, Vladivostok, Kostroma and Chelyabinsk.[84]

The rapid coalescence of a national movement during this campaign both completed a decisive stage in Russia's political rebirth and inaugurated another. The objective inscribed in the first was liberation. Here action was directed primarily toward obliterating restrictions on action itself. Accordingly, its salient self-representations were expansive

– the people, the nation, the civilized world, universal human values –
and at the same time negative: ' "No" to those who deny us!' Among
those involved with this process of becoming, a sense developed that
removing the barriers to, and the fetters on, activity would be equivalent
to securing the preconditions for the actual participation of a people in
its own governance. It may well be the case that individuals reflecting on
this matter would detect the fact that institutions capable of sustaining
this participation had yet to be established, and thus would recognize as
spurious the putative equivalence between practices specific to the stage
of political liberation and those involved with normal politics. But that,
for us, would be beside the point. Rather, at issue here would be the
particular construction of social actors engendered by the very activity in
which they were engaged, a construction manifested in their forms of
organization and communication.

From this vantage, it would be obvious that DemRossiya's organizational forms were shaped by the state socialist context from which it
emerged and against which it defined itself. On the one hand, the
absence of a civil society structured by the institution of property meant
that it, too, would consist of an ensemble of personalized relations
analogous to those characteristic of the party-state that it opposed. With
respect to such elementary matters as mediating its existence physically
by setting up a headquarters, branch offices and a publishing arm, it was
forced to rely either on personal contacts with its members and
supporters in official organizations or – as was more often the case for
task-centred meetings – simply the private apartments of its activists. On
the other, although it appeared as a national movement, its corpus was
not a coalition of social interests expressing themselves as voluntary
associations – say, trade unions or professional associations – but
overlapping networks of personal acquaintances among its leaders,
organizers and activists developed as far back as the dissident period and
extending through the informal movement, the 1989 election campaigns, work in the I-RDG, voters' associations and the 1990 campaign
itself. DemRossiya was thus vulnerable to a number of internally
disorganizing influences: friendly relations can turn sour; rivalries and
feuds may develop; leading individuals might stake out certain programmatic areas and gather around them followers who see themselves as
representing the true interests of the movement in distinction from their
counterparts portrayed as misguided or worse. In fact, all three of these
influences would show themselves before long, sometimes in combined
form. At this juncture, however, they were submerged in the overriding
objective of defeating the party-state. This task promoted DemRossiya's
coherence by providing its members with both a limitless number of

things to do and a clear indicator of success. Yet the ethos of solidarity accompanying their collective efforts was insufficient for task-effectiveness, as we noted with respect to the weak influence displayed by DemRossiya's city-based affiliates in recruiting candidates and distributing them efficiently among electoral districts.

The forms of communication displayed by DemRossiya during the 1990 elections likewise bristled with the personalized and the negative. The authenticity of its campaign tracts derived primarily from the names that they included (especially El'tsin's), while their imperatives tended to be formulated in the negative, such as the summons 'to vote *against* a candidate if he belongs to the party apparatus or is one of its henchmen'. Although DemRossiya extensively employed the term 'Russia' in its campaign messages, it too appeared in negated fashion as that which had been denied by the communist system.[85] Rallies and demonstrations simply enacted these same texts with live performers and a proximate audience. These personalized and negative features of DemRossiya's forms of communication were, then, congruent with the relations internal to it as an organization. Each can be traced to its context and to the task that it set for itself. Crossing the divide separating the politics of liberation from the normal politics of public governance with this ordnance in tow would thus prove an especially difficult and hazardous passage for Russia's emerging political society and its newly created state.

Some results of the election

We focus here on three specific outcomes of the 1990 elections. The first concerns the complement of deputies elected to the national legislature; the second examines the major actions taken by those in the Russian Congress of People's Deputies that bear on the issue of national liberation; the third involves the continuation of political struggles fought out now at the level of contending state structures, thus introducing the question of governability.

The new legislators

Turnover indicated the changes accomplished by the 1990 elections. When the Congress of People's Deputies convened on 16 May, some 94 per cent of its members were taking their seats in Russia's national legislature for the first time.[86] The new parliament was in many respects a direct reflection of Russia's social structure. In contrast to the communist practice of reserving large blocs of seats for those at the lower end of the social ladder – workers, peasants and women – thereby disguising the social hierarchies of power and status in the formally supreme organ of government, these elections reproduced those same hierarchies within the corpus of legislators returned to the parliament. Perhaps the clearest illustration of this would be the fact that some 92.7 per cent of those elected possessed that singularly important status characteristic prevalent in state socialist societies: higher education.[87] It would be equally apparent in the low proportions of workers and peasants (from 5 to 10 per cent, depending on how this category has been constructed) and women (5.3 per cent) on whom mandates were conferred.[88] In terms of occupation, the largest single bloc of legislators consisted of executive personnel from the industrial sector (35 per cent),[89] followed by party-state officials and functionaries (30.4 per cent),[90] and professionals and those engaged in academic or artistic pursuits who together accounted for about 20 per cent of the deputies.[91]

Since close association obtains in virtually every competitive political system between social standing and access to higher office, these results would not be remarkable. But specific features of the Russian situation invite comment. One concerns working people who – in terms of available time, cultural capital, experience with public speaking and other factors relevant to vote-getting – are relatively disadvantaged in the electoral arena. In the Russia of 1990, however, this group in the population faced additional handicaps. Not only were they unable to rely on voluntary associations to offset the social biases of electoral democracy – as trade unions and/or labour-oriented political groups were virtually unknown outside the mining areas – but the management of factories and farms still exercised police functions over their respective workforces, visiting threats and penalties on those choosing to participate in 'unsanctioned' political activities.[92] Relatively unencumbered by these constraints, many of those entering the electoral arena from other social locations were responding to the new opportunities presented by representative democracy. Here, we might underscore a certain change already apparent in the composition of the Russian Congress in comparison with its all-union counterpart. Whereas a large contingent of deputies to the Soviet legislature were individuals who had already attained high social status before involving themselves with politics, the Russian elections produced an even larger group who had not particularly distinguished themselves in professional life, entering now into political careers as an alternative – and, for some, much faster – track to social advancement.

The political composition of the Russian Congress would resist precise specifications. Some 86 per cent of the deputies were still members of the Communist Party,[93] but this denominator can disclose very little. With respect to legislative factions, about one-third of the members were associated with DemRossiya,[94] a slightly smaller contingent formed a voting bloc of conservative communists, while a recrudescent patriotic tendency and a sizeable complement of fence-sitters filled out the remainder. We should not, however, attach much importance to these proportions. Mechanisms that might ensure disciplined voting were far too weak and the overall situation far too fluid to translate these initial leanings into established legislative groupings.

An agenda for national liberation

The two principal acts of the first Russian Congress – the election of a chairperson and the adoption of a Declaration on Sovereignty – charted a course toward national liberation. The Congress's first order of substantive business was set by outgoing Supreme Soviet chairperson, Vitalii Vorotnikov, who presented a legislative draft addressed to an issue that had already acquired near-acclamatory status in the hall: sovereignty for Russia. However, his version of 'sovereignty' stood in marked contrast to that offered by the second speaker on this question, El'tsin, whose more radical proposals provided for the supremacy of Russian law on Russian soil and allowed for relations with the USSR solely on the basis of formal treaties concluded between the two governments.[95] Below the surface of these rival conceptions of sovereignty stood three political tendencies vying for power.

   Vorotnikov's plan was in fact a concession to those forces on the right who had been peppering the Gorbachev regime with criticism for its alleged inattention to Russian national interests. It was these forces that sought to loosen Gorbachev's grip on power within the CPSU – if not dispose of him entirely – by creating a Russian Communist Party that they expected to dominate. Gorbachev's recent conversion to the concept of sovereignty, then, represented an attempt to diffuse right-wing attacks and to discredit El'tsin's position by portraying it as politically irresponsible and destructive.[96] Since the right's conception of sovereignty involved a strong, assertive Russia that would play the dominant role in the USSR – just as the Russian Communist Party would within the CPSU – and thus directly reinforce the central government's efforts to save the Soviet empire, Gorbachev's plan had much to recommend it in their eyes. This same logic, in inverted form, underlay the orientation evinced by El'tsin and the insurgent democrats. Rather than a Russia that would dominate the USSR, their concerns were with a USSR that would continue to dominate Russia. Therefore, for those in the democratic camp, liberation from communism meant national liberation via the route of maximum state sovereignty. Theirs was an unusual variant of nationalist ideology, one that tended less to celebrate the nation's history than to valorize the country's current potential for overcoming it. Unlike the right wing, offended by those insufficiently appreciative of Russia's past accomplishments, the democrats argued that, 'We are going toward a democratic state [which can have nothing in common with empire] . . . Today, it is necessary *to create* Russia, as it were, *de novo*. To separate Russia from [the control of the party-state] apparatus, which we must do, is to separate Russia from the [Soviet] Union.'[97]

The question of which version of 'sovereignty' the Russian Congress would adopt thus became inextricably connected to the matter of whom it would choose as its chairperson.[98] El'tsin led in the initial balloting, but his base of support, DemRossiya and independent deputies, proved insufficient to defeat an anti-El'tsin coalition orchestrated by Gorbachev himself. The stalemate was only broken on the third ballot when – thanks to Gorbachev's departure for a summit with the US president, the persistence of El'tsin supporters who formed a 'living corridor' through which the deputies had to pass into the Hotel Rossiya where they stayed or the Kremlin where they deliberated[99] and, finally, no small amount of horse-trading on El'tsin's part – El'tsin was elected by a margin of four votes.[100] Apparently in return for the votes that they delivered – and thanks to the room for manoeuvre provided him by a disorganized and unassertive DemRossiya faction[101] – Russia's new parliamentary chairperson quickly adopted a more conciliatory posture toward representatives of the very party-state apparatus against which he had waged his popular campaign. His support for their candidates to the Supreme Soviet and its offices helped to install in the country's full-time legislature majorities composed of members of that same group, the *nomenklatura*, that had served him so well as a butt for his populist rhetoric.[102] Having thus distanced himself from DemRossiya and forged working relations with erstwhile opponents, El'tsin got his way on the sovereignty issue: his Declaration on Sovereignty was passed on 12 June by a margin of 907 to 13, with 9 abstentions.[103]

Out of this play of parliamentary manoeuvre, Russia's political field was being remapped. El'tsin would pursue the outlines of his original programme – state sovereignty making possible (in rhetoric, at least) radical economic reform – but not necessarily with those from the democratic camp with whom he had kept close company *en route* to becoming leader of the Russian state. Rather, he was already building his own base of power within the legislature, using his position to dish out favours right and left, thus drawing others into relations of personal dependency on him. Some favours went to DemRossiya, as El'tsin helped to secure certain key committee chairs for the faction, thus offsetting their opponents' numerical advantage on the Supreme Soviet. He also arranged for the appointment of prominent democrats such as Gennadii Filshin, Grigorii Yavlinskii, Viktor Yaroshenko, Mikhail Poltoranin and Boris Fedorov to ministerial posts.[104] Having failed to secure the confirmation of his first choice for Russian prime minister – fellow I-RDG member, M. A. Bocharov, an economist associated with the so-called '500 days' plan for a radical restructuring of the USSR's economy – he threw his weight on the second ballot behind Ivan Silaev, then deputy prime minister of the USSR and an individual who had thitherto no reputation as a market-oriented reformer.[105] He would have to be a quick-study. Some ten days after Silaev's election as prime minister, El'tsin announced at a press conference that the Russian government would implement the '500 days' programme on its own territory, and was prepared to issue a Russian national currency to control economic activity in the republic and thus overcome any sandbagging by the central authorities.[106] In effect, he had fired the first shot in the 'war of the laws' that symbolized the ensuing struggle for power between Russia and the USSR.

Governability

At the level of state structures, the crisis of governability that resulted from the 1990 elections was most clearly manifest as two governments laying mutually exclusive claims to sovereignty on the territory of Russia. The struggle between them tended to overshadow, and thus conceal, a no less significant crisis already breaking out in political society. Insurgent democrats represented the largest single group in the Russian Congress and their acknowledged leader held the top position in the country. Yet El'tsin's suspension of his membership in DemRossiya,[107] as well as his readiness to employ patronage to extend his personal authority, meant that the rewards of office would neither be available for promoting the coherence of factions in the legislature nor for instilling cohesion into DemRossiya, whose formal inauguration as a political movement lay some months in the future.[108] But if the politics of national liberation contained for the time being the fissiparous tendencies within the broad coalition of democrats at the national level, subnational developments augured ominously what lay in store for Russia's democratic movement once liberation had been won.

In those city soviets captured by DemRossiya's affiliates, the heady enthusiasm engendered by their spectacular victories at the polls rapidly dissolved into rancour and internecine conflict once the democrats assumed office. In Moscow, where the DemRossiya faction accounted for over 60 per cent of the seats on the city council (290 out of 465), Popov and Stankevich were easily elected chairperson and deputy-chairperson. However, the loose electoral coalition of democrats proved unable to survive the first act of its leaders in government: staffing the municipal administration. Arguing both for the need to place competent and experienced people in charge of running the city and for the necessity of reaching some *modus vivendi* with the Moscow Committee of the Communist Party that in the wake of the democrats' victory had arrogated to itself the bulk of municipal property and all publications theretofore belonging to the Moscow Soviet, Popov reappointed the old apparatus.[109] Deprived by their own leadership of the spoils of office, many (and soon most) deputies elected on the DemRossiya ticket became hardened opponents of the reigning authorities in Moscow. As one lamented,

All the previous officials have remained in their posts. G. Popov has proposed to give them a chance, which has come to mean that they isolate committees [of the soviet] from information and [deprive us] of the possibility of exercising any influence on the course of events . . . Some deputies have the impression that the leaders of the Moscow Soviet have composed a staff for deciding questions that consists of a narrow group intent on appeasing those still holding on to power: the Moscow City Committee of the Communist Party and the executive organs from the old city administration.[110]

Thus divided into supporters and opponents of the city soviet's new leadership, the DemRossiya contingent splintered further into a collection of smaller factions, neither much inclined to seek consensus on a given question nor capable in most cases of maintaining their own internal discipline.[111]

With different sequencing, the same situation developed in Leningrad where DemRossiya's affiliate, Democratic Elections–90, had also taken about 60 per cent of the seats on the city soviet. Badly split and immobilized,[112] the democrats sought exit from their impasse by turning to I-RDG notable, Anatolii Sobchak, whom they persuaded to stand for a vacant seat with the promise that, once elected as a deputy, they would immediately use their voting majority to make him chairperson. However, ensconced in office, Sobchak infuriated the majority of his erstwhile patrons by following the same appointments pattern practised by his counterpart in Moscow. Ironically, this did produce a perverse form of order in the city soviet as the squabbling democrats closed ranks to make common cause against their new 'leader'.[113] These same divisions were replicated in the October district's soviet in central Moscow where DemRossiya had staged its most effective campaign for office at this level.[114] There, I-RDG notable, Il'ya Zaslavskii, was elected chairperson of the soviet by DemRossiya's commanding majority and then rapidly alienated the bulk of his supporters by transacting the business of the district's government over their heads and behind their backs.[115]

The executive–legislative conflicts that broke out within the democratic camp in these three instances provided disturbing previews of the struggle that would rage within the Russian state after liberation and result in the violent end of the first republic. Consequently, we might enquire into the aetiology of this tragedy-to-come by examining the factors that contributed to the problem of governability as experienced by the democrats 'in power' in Moscow and Leningrad. In terms of organization, we have already observed how the loose, inclusive coalition form adopted by DemRossiya in the election campaign was well suited to accomplishing the purpose of mobilizing a mass electorate. Its lowest-common-denominator style of communication – ' "No" to the apparatus' – was congruent with this organizational form and effective in marshalling votes for its candidates. These same assets in the campaign, however, would become liabilities after the elections when the problem of governing had to be addressed. Accordingly, the crisis of governability was more than a contest over whose authority – Gorbachev's or El'tsin's – would prevail in Russia. It was also an outgrowth of deeper problems in political society: its amorphous, movement-like character, and the weakness of its organizational structures that were based on a citizens' movement rather than on a civil society.[116] In their turn, both of these features of political society derived from the communist order from which DemRossiya had emerged. Its officials provided a splendid target for opposition, thus enabling the movement to cohere in a negative way, but its institutional structures had left no room for the formation and articulation of social interests and identities capable both of conflict and the resolution thereof. Thus, the only mandate that DemRossiya could have sought in these elections was a *political* mandate to *undo* that order; it housed no identifiable *social* interests endeavouring to *do* anything else.[117]

Reflecting the personalized patterns of authority prevalent in the communist system, relations between leaders and the larger body of DemRossiya privileged the position of the former. We might imagine the sense of outrage experienced by many in the Moscow soviet, for example, when the man that they had elected chairperson took to running the city without their advice and consent. But we might equally imagine Popov's chagrin at these protests from deputies elected on 'his' ticket, who had featured the endorsement of his name on their campaign literature. From his point of view, as well as from that of Sobchak and Zaslavskii,[118] the problem of governability resulted precisely from these people, the deputies. There were too many of them; their internal organization was appalling (vote after vote would be suspended for lack of a quorum while deputies sipped tea in the buffet or jawed with one another outside the legislative chambers); they seemed entirely unprepared to act in a timely and effective manner. As executives responsible for governing, the natural thing to do would be to clear away these cumbersome, obstructive bodies and get down to the matter at hand. Consequently, they quickly reappraised the utility of soviets and endorsed the idea of strong, popularly elected executive authority capable of tackling the task of governing.[119] But by restructuring governmental institutions in this way, these municipal executives were simultaneously emancipating themselves from responsibility toward the democratic movement, thereby reshaping the contours of political society. They would coopt some segments into their spheres of authority while pushing others into an opposition which, without a civil society and coherent political structures, would organize themselves on the only basis available: namely, state and legislative offices under their control.

The politics of liberation masked this problem within political society. Since the defeat of communism remained the overriding objective for those in the democratic movement, the rationale for empowering democratic executives and thus securing a sovereign Russia set solidly on the path of 'reform' was convincing for many. But the patterns of conflict already visible at this juncture suggested that the coherence of political society was conditioned by the type of politics in which its members were engaged. High-stakes struggles in which the issues appeared in black and white engendered one pattern: a national movement, solidarity, grand drama and heroism. However, when the stakes involved more prosaic matters, such as whom to appoint to municipal departments, this solidarity unravelled and political society immediately fractured, not along the lines of issues, policy or ideology – although conflicts would often be thus expressed (and disguised) – but according to which state offices belonged to whom.

9   Parties in movement: the articulation of Russian political society at the close of the Soviet period

By lifting the constitutional ban on political parties in March 1990, the USSR's Congress of People's Deputies opened the way for the next step in the logical sequence of political organizing. It seemed that those amorphous, fluid and *ad hoc* forms that had hitherto populated Russian political society – informal groups and voters' associations, loose electoral and legislative coalitions – would now give way to the genuine article: political parties. However, the rather motley collection of groups that came forth to claim this title scarcely measured up to the expectations that their leaders, as well as many observers, had entertained for them. While a few managed to attract more than 10,000 members, most numbered their followers in the hundreds. Measuring even their collective roster against that of the multi-million CPSU made them appear all the more insignificant. Their programmes were top-heavy with platitudes, neither specifying concrete measures to be implemented nor doing much to distinguish one party from another. It seemed anyone's guess just whom and what they represented.

Much of this confusion resulted from timing. Since the authorities had not removed the prohibition on parties until *after* the 1990 elections, all the new parties were latecomers, arriving on the scene only after the ball had ended. With neither identifiable constituencies to represent nor upcoming elections to prepare for, the development of Russia's political parties was ingrown. In each instance, it amounted to a collection of leaders and activists consciously pursuing the project of being a political party in the absence of clear connection to events in the world. Congresses were called, platforms debated, charters adopted and officers elected – all to the effect that there were now these 'parties'. Understandably, this spectacle left Russians wondering whether it was meaningful to regard any of these new organizations as the real thing.[1]

Was it? Measuring our Russian parties against the standards used in the comparative politics literature on parties and party systems would appear to be a straightforward way to settle the issue. Unfortunately, it provides surprisingly little help. Scholars in this field have employed diverse conceptions in their studies of political parties. Although definitions pertaining to the essential features of a party abound, they cancel out one another since an organization meeting one scholar's criteria would not necessarily measure up to those of another.[2] Exploring the two basic dimensions of this literature – one concerning 'external' forces that shape party formation, another that inquires into the 'internal' side of party activity, focusing on those things that parties do – for additional clues does not get us much further. To be sure, the comparative analysis of political parties has produced a wealth of data and conceptual frameworks on either count. But, although couched in theoretic language, the mode of analysis evinced in these studies is uniformly empirical-analytic, yielding generalizations that sum up that which has been regarded as significant in given cases, then framing these generalizations as discrete propositions confirmed through empirical analyses. This method has produced universal propositions about political parties, but they do not travel well from their areas of origin. This is apparent in the most ambitious effort of this type to be found in the literature on parties – that by S. M. Lipset and S. Rokkan – that accounts for party genesis and development in Europe in terms of social cleavages introduced by the national and industrial revolutions of the eighteenth and nineteenth centuries. Their typology is, of course, specific to the European experience, but more troubling is the fact that the number of categories that it contains nearly equals the number of phenomena (parties) to be categorized.[3] Rather than general classes, the categories function as names for discrete things. Similar efforts along these lines have gained in empirical range only at the expense of conceptual precision.[4] The associations between socio-economic and political cleavages on one hand, and the constellation of parties in a given system on the other, is therefore limited to the instances from which the associations have been drawn. They tend to spoil in transit.[5]

With respect to the work of those who approach the issue of political parties on the basis of their primary activities or functions, we confront a different problem. As Angelo Panebianco has pointed out, such studies can be reduced to two types. One holds that a party seeks to win office in order to implement a programme; the other, that a party adopts a programme in order to improve its chances for winning office. In addition to the 'teleological prejudice' that informs this approach,[6] the relationship between programme and electoral success is in principle unknowable. Despite apparent exceptions to the contrary, we simply have no means to determine which is the tail and which the dog. Is programme a means to the goal of winning, or is winning important because a programme can then be enacted? In the face of this conundrum, Panebianco recommends defocusing the essence of the concept 'political party'. He simply regards parties as particular organizations, distinct from others by reason of 'the specific *environment* in which they carry out a specific *activity*'.[7] This formulation harkens back to Maurice Duverger's classic study in which a political party appeared as 'a community with a particular structure [predicated] essentially on unwritten practice and habit'.[8] Since the 'specific environment' and 'specific activity' characterizing Russia's parties differs qualitatively from the West European systems studied by Panebianco, training the sights of his sophisticated version of organization theory on Russia's fluid and clamorous groupings would result in little more than analytic overkill. Likewise, we do not have before us the sort of established entities investigated by Duverger in which 'practice and habit' would weigh heavily. None the less, the concepts advanced by these scholars can be adapted to the study of Russia's parties to demonstrate that they can be meaningfully regarded as parties in the context of their specific environment which had called forth a specific activity.

We begin by recalling the model introduced above (Table 1.1). Locating its categories in the period under consideration – roughly, from the emergence of a national movement opposed to the Soviet regime in late 1989 to that regime's overthrow in August 1991 – we can specify the axes of conflict that structured party formation. Since the concept 'civil society' would refer far more to the project of bringing one about than to an extant set of relationships in society, the category 'interest' would be much less helpful than 'identity' in mapping these lines of conflict. Russian society remained largely undifferentiated; only a few groups – say, those active in the cooperative sector or the self-organized coal miners – had begun to emancipate themselves from the tutelage of the party-state. This condition militated against the formation of socially relevant interests and impressed on identity formation a transcendent quality. Identity referred not to the present state of being but to a projected or anticipated future (often derived from a suitably reconstructed past). It concerned becoming. As such, social-political identities constructed by ostensibly distinct communities – social democrats, Christian democrats, constitutional democrats, and others – shared an overriding commonality. Their mutual interest in becoming bound them together in a struggle to overcome the principal impediment to realizing their projected identities: the Soviet party-state. Consequently, the first axis of conflict was not a division *within* civil society mediated by the institutions of political society and the state; it was a division *between* political society and the state itself. Since the

Soviet party-state was framed in the discourse of political society as that overbearing and odious 'other' that stifled the very existence of political and civil society, the parties that formed in Russia in this period as discrete organizations collectively comprised a single social-political movement structured by its relations of opposition to the communist order.[9] To use a military metaphor, they represented the various regiments – each hoisting its distinctive colours – of the anti-communist army. Overlaid on this line of conflict was another drawn between the Russian state and the USSR. This second axis formed after the 1990 elections and straddled the issue of sovereignty: Russia versus the USSR, El'tsin versus Gorbachev. Struggles joined at the state level thus triggered contests in Russian political society for control of the Russian state, just as the resolution of those contests intensified the conflict between the Russian and Soviet states that led, ultimately, to the latter's annihilation.

The formation of political parties

Returning to our proposition that the rebirth of politics in Russia was historically coextensive with the collapse of Soviet communism, we can specify at this juncture the temporal sequences at which this double-sided process unfolded by focusing on the stages of the CPSU's disintegration and the dynamics of party formation that accompanied them. Within the time-frame of this chapter, three stages of disintegration can be distinguished, commensurate with which were three waves of political mobilization.[10] Each of these waves crested with the founding of organizationally distinct parties sharing certain characteristics that set them apart from those tossed up by the other waves. We shall therefore subdivide this section according to the stages of CPSU disintegration and identify the types of parties that formed in correspondence to each of them.

Stage 1: Identity-based parties

This stage of disintegration appeared in the discourse of the party-state as 'democratization', 'political perestroika', 'socialist pluralism' and so forth. Important was the fact that it opened up opportunities for organizing outside of official structures, thus enabling a number of informal groups to coalesce around various leaders articulating one or another variety of identity-based politics.[11] As noted, above, a host of groups crystallized out of the dynamic interactions occurring between party-state and informal organizations each proclaiming a distinct political identity: anarchism (Obshchina), democratic socialism (Group of Socialist Initiative), social democracy (Democratic Perestroika), constitutional democracy (Civic Dignity), liberal democracy (Democratic Union) and so on. The 1989 elections and the prospect of another round of balloting in Russia in 1990 enlarged the opportunity structure for political mobilization, stimulating some of these groups to convert themselves into organizing committees that would go on to found political parties. Here, we shall consider the three most significant identity-based parties to emerge from the informal movement: the Social Democratic Party of Russia, the Russian Christian Democratic Movement and the Constitutional Democratic Party.

The Social Democratic Party of Russia

The 237 delegates representing over 100 social democratic clubs from around Russia who gathered in Moscow on 4–6 May 1990 to found the Social Democratic Party of Russia (SDPR)[12] were mainly survivors. Some – such as Pavel Kudyukin, V. M. Chernetskii and Yu. L. Khavkin – had survived imprisonment in the pre-perestroika era for forming political discussion circles.[13] Others had endured lesser degrees of repression for their activities in the country's informal movement. To one degree or another, all had subjected themselves to innumerable organizational meetings and philosophical–political debates – often extending into the small hours of the morning in cramped and dingy quarters – that comprised the prenatal history of this party. The organizational sources that fed it were many and varied: the Social-Democratic Union that emerged from the January 1988 collapse of the All-Union Social-Political Club; the social-democratic faction of the Democratic Union; Moscow's Democratic Perestroika and Perestroika of Leningrad, as well as similar groups in dozens of Russia's larger cities whose memberships and levels of activity had been highest in Volgograd, Saratov, Sverdlovsk and Yaroslavl; the Social Democratic Confederation formed in Leningrad in February 1989; and the May 1989 Moscow meeting of informals mentioned, above, in the context of political mobilization on the eve of the first Congress of People's Deputies.[14] Due to the prohibition against forming political parties, the SDPR was first configured as an organizing committee within the Social Democratic Association of the Soviet Union (SDA) founded in January 1990 in Tallinn where that prohibition was no longer enforced. Its leaders dominated the SDA's top ranks, just as the number of social-democratic groups that it represented dwarfed the contingents of their counterparts from the non-Russian republics.[15] From the first, the

SDPR asserted its financial independence from the SDA,[16] in part to assure an organizational autonomy that would insulate its interpretation of social-democratic principles from others within the alliance.[17] Whereas the SDA had endorsed 'democratic socialism' and regarded worker-owned enterprises as the preferred form of property arrangement,[18] most SDPR leaders insisted that social democracy should not be confused with socialism of any sort.[19] Once the SDPR had staged its own founding congress, it effectively broke with the SDA, limiting its operational horizons to Russia, even though its political vision was 'European'.

The SDPR was a 'community with a particular structure'. That structure was a discourse that had gestated within its pre-party prototypes that had populated the informal movement. Its identity was pitched against all things Soviet, relying on its images of Western social democracy to supply the requisite positive markers. Identity was the party's obsession. At its founding congress, members groped for the proper form of address to apply to one another, eventually adopting a formal decision to use 'Mr' and 'Ms' but often lapsing into 'comrade'.[20] The matter of composing a 'social-democratic' analysis of 'the situation in the country' became so vexed that adoption of the party's programme was delayed for a year.[21] The version that was finally approved read like a philosophical–political treatise on the essence of social democracy. As one pragmatic party official later remarked,

We have not done well in reaching people. Take the party's programme. The cadets [Constitutional Democrats] have a six-page programme; people can read it and understand it. Our programme is over sixty pages long. This is not a programme but a dissertation. Nobody will read this. Maybe someone at Harvard or Oxford would find this interesting, but your man-on-the-street here in Russia won't bother to read it. So what good is such a programme?[22]

One of the few straightforward statements in the programme appeared under the subsection: 'What do we want?' The first item in reply was 'we want to return Russia to the channel of world civilization'.[23] Informed readers would know that this 'channel' referred to the Rhine, not to the Ganges.

The political trajectory of the SDPR was the correlate of its preoccupation with identity. Here were people who wanted to construct a Western-style social-democratic party in Russia, and construct one they did. Declaring themselves opposed to any form of class-based politics, they portrayed themselves as the bearer of all putative social interests, with the exception of the *nomenklatura* which they, naturally, opposed.[24] They explicitly rejected the 'tradition of social-democracy in

Russia' and embraced what they regarded as 'contemporary . . . social-liberal orientations (in the European sense)'.[25] They expended countless hours at congresses and conferences debating just what that meant, without ever reaching enough closure to derive a practical plan of action[26]. However, within their own community they did replicate those institutions and acted out those modes of behaviour associated with their conception of a Western-style social-democratic party. SDPR members working in Russian legislatures generally constituted the most disciplined and effective factions, while party leaders claimed credit for penning landmark pieces of legislation, such as Russia's Declaration of Sovereignty and the Supreme Soviet's draft of a new constitution.[27] The party formed its own (white-collar) trade union affiliate (Sotsprof), its own publishing house (Sotsium) and established its own internal financing operations.[28] It put out the widest array of both national and regional newspapers of any political party in Russia.[29] With respect to the animus of these activities, party leader Oleg Rumyantsev captured the common devotion to building a social-democratic identity in his remark, 'We must be pure etymologically in our self-naming. We need a purity of party symbology with which we can achieve our own programme and face [the next] elections.'[30] Unfortunately, as was true of the other parties surveyed in this section, for the SDPR these elections would never come.[31]

The Russian Christian Democratic Movement

The Western orientation of the SDPR was a thousand miles and a hundred years apart from that assumed by the Russian Christian Democratic Movement (RCDM). If the former cut its anti-communist identity from the cloth of secular, humanist values, the latter constructed its on eschatological scaffolding retrieved from Russia's past. No less attentive than the SDPR to the 'purity of symbols', the RCDM reached back in time for its organizational lexicon. Rather than a 'congress' (*s"ezd*), its national assembly was called a '*sobor*'; instead of 'conferences' (*konferentsii*), its sub-national units held *sobraniya*; while other parties proposed convening another constituent assembly to complete the work interrupted by the Bolsheviks in 1918, the RCDM harkened back to an even earlier era, issuing in the programme adopted at its founding congress (8–9 April 1990)[32] a call to convoke a *Zemskii Sobor* (Assembly of the Lands) to *restore* the 'supreme legal power in Russia' that had been suspended by the 1917 Revolution.[33]

The idea of forming a political organization in Russia based on Christian-democratic principles had already been consummated prior to the RCDM's appearance. In August 1989, a number of religious circles grouped around their respective samizdat publications had come together to found the Christian Democratic Union of Russia. Fractious from the first, this organization divided into two separate ones by May 1990, each declining in membership thereafter[34] as many former supporters left to join the newly formed RCDM.[35] To distinguish themselves from their rivals, the initiators of the RCDM – a number of Russian Orthodox circles, the leading one of which had been publishing the religious-literary journal *Vybor* ('Choice') since 1987 – constructed for the RCDM a revivalist identity portraying the organization as committed to the restoration of a Russian state based on tradition and, most importantly, on Russian Orthodoxy.[36] Defining itself in this way, the RCDM inserted a double-contradiction into the very centre of its self-concept. Not only had it substituted Orthodoxy for Christianity in general while maintaining that it subscribed to the common principles of Christian democracy, but its claim to speak for Russian tradition was contradicted on its face by the fact that there had never been a tradition of Christian-democratic politics in Russia. These contradictions drove the discourse of the party's non-clerical leadership (especially Viktor Aksyuchits and Gleb Anishchenko) toward fundamentalism, and that fundamentalism was sustained within its ranks by authoritarian methods of organization.

From the first, Aksyuchits controlled the party's material resources: funds derived from commercial operations and assistance from the Christian-Democratic International. These he manipulated to his own advantage, rewarding supporters while punishing and expelling his opponents.[37] Within a year after the party's founding, the internal dispute occasioned by these practices prompted the resignation of the RCDM's most prominent public figure, Gleb Yakunin. His exit roughly coincided with the RCDM headlong plunge into fundamentalism,[38] a solution of sorts to the contradictions lodged within the organization's identity construct. Prior to the overthrow of the Soviet regime, the RCDM's identity was stabilized by the CPSU, characterized in party literature as the embodiment of evil on earth which the RCDM had been summoned by God to dispatch.[39] Once this actual *bête noire* disappeared, RCDM discourse dived deeply into political mysticism,[40] enriching its identity construct to the point that it appeared as the single authentic saviour of the Russian people against whom were arrayed a formidable assembly of enemies both within the country and outside it: the 'international lumpen regime' that had seized power in Russia in 1917 and was still ruling despite cosmetic changes; liberals purveying universal human values which offend against, and corrupt, Russia's 'organic mode of life'; foreign powers pouncing on an exsanguinated Russia, poised to drain whatever strength might remain.[41] Measured against the standards of its own previous fundamentalism, declarations such as these would appear extreme. But alterations in the RCDM's rhetorical strategies reflected a certain continuity as well, one derived from its own identity construct projected against its rivals and opponents at one or another stage of the country's political development. While marching in the democratic column before August 1991, the party featured its anti-communist – ergo, 'democratic' – credentials.[42] Thereafter, when it lost out in a struggle to assert control over the democratic movement, it quickly repaired to the anti-democratic camp, adjusted its political posture accordingly, and redeployed against its erstwhile allies that truculence which had always informed its rhetoric.[43] The RCDM played the principal role in organizing the Congress of Civic and Patriotic Forces of Russia in February 1992, from which issued the 'white–brown' (colours symbolizing nationalist and fascist organizations) alliance known as the Russian National Assembly.[44] Apparently because of the salience of anti-communism for its political identity, the RCDM was the only member of this bloc not to enter the 'red–brown' coalition, the Front for National Salvation (FNS), that coalesced in October 1992. Despite the absence of formal affiliation, however, the party was connected to the Front via Il'ya Konstantinov who served simultaneously as the FNS's chairperson and as deputy head of the RCDM.[45]

The Constitutional Democratic Party

The two parties thus far considered inverted traditional Russian political identities: one, by rejecting the Russian tradition of social democracy and proclaiming itself a Russian social-democratic party of the West European type; the other, by styling itself a traditional Russian Christian-democratic party in full recognition of the fact that there had never been a Christian-democratic tradition in Russian politics. The final group of interest to us, here, turned out to be two political parties: the Party of Constitutional Democrats (PCD) and the Constitutional Democratic Party (CDP). In this instance, political identity was anchored securely in Russian political traditions, the pre-revolutionary Constitutional Democrats.[46] The problem of identity formation which split this group in two involved the *interpretation* of that heritage.

In October 1989, the informal group, Civic Dignity, joined with the 'democratic faction' of the Moscow Popular Front to host a conference – attended by some 100 representatives from informal associations in the

USSR – at which the Union of Constitutional Democrats was founded. After the fashion of their political forebears,[47] Russia's new 'Cadets' attempted to position themselves between (and in opposition to) the regime, on the one hand, and revolution, on the other. Thus, the programme that they adopted was filled with references to gradualism and evolution. While it demanded an end to the CPSU's political monopoly, it also referred to the necessity of dialogue with the communists.[48] Above all, its leaders referenced the traditions of Russian constitutional democracy that they intended to revive in the form of a political party.[49]

At its founding in May 1990, the PCD announced its desire 'to act in the traditions of [Russia's] native free-thinking liberalism and constitutional democracy . . . affirming the priority of all-human values over any type of national, class or other interests'.[50] But in the wake of disputes within the party's organizing committee over the meaning of these traditions, a conflict over 'constitutional democracy' erupted at the founding congress, resulting in a large walk-out led by one of the group's principal figures, G. V. Deryagin.[51] From the perspective of the disaffected, the PCD was unable to distinguish constitutional democracy from liberalism and, as such, flirted dangerously with populism.[52] To rescue their endangered principles, they immediately formed the Constitutional Democratic Party (CDP) which proclaimed itself the legitimate heir to the Cadet tradition; a claim, of course, categorically denied by the PCD.[53]

By September 1990, the PCD had taken a position against any reunification of the two Cadet parties. For its part, the CDP had succeeded in recruiting a few prominent political figures – among them, Mikhail Astaf'ev, a people's deputy in the Russian Congress – and was rapidly expanding its membership.[54] Within a few months, the CDP was preaching a constitutional-democratic philosophy that was all but indistinguishable from the variety of Christian democracy purveyed by the RCDM. Indeed, as these two parties moved toward coalition, the CDP newspaper – entitled *Rech'* after that of the pre-revolutionary Cadets – was published as an insert within the RCDM's *Put'*. As one PCD commentator astutely observed, the associations established between his CDP rivals and the CPSU on one hand, the RCDM on the other, already had laid the basis for a 'red–brown imperial guard'.[55] While the PCD remained an insignificantly small party, attracting at most a few hundred members, the CDP claimed a few thousand members by 1991[56] and became a serious player on the field of Russian politics, incongruously bearing the standard of Russian constitutional democracy within the communist–fascist camp.[57]

Stage 2: Programmatic factions in the CPSU

The second stage in the CPSU's disintegration was marked by the appearance of openly organized factions within it, despite the strictures against such activity that continued to exist in its charter. Like the parties that formed outside the CPSU, these factions and the parties that issued from them wrestled with the question of political identity. However, since they originated within the Communist Party, the identity issue for them did not involve distinguishing themselves from the Soviet order *in toto*. Rather, they drew distinctions between themselves and Gorbachev's CPSU – as well as from the other political parties that were appearing at the time – by valorizing certain thematic elements drawn from the corpus of socialist and/or communist thought and weaving these into alternative discourses, each of which spoke a particular language of communism. Initially, at least, the programmes that these factions put forward can be regarded as efforts to persuade others in the Communist Party to adopt the discourse – and the identity – embedded in each.

By early 1990, three principal factions had coalesced within the CPSU. While it would be difficult to specify their precise ideological-programmatic coordinates – for reasons related to the viscid character of these political formations functioning within the equally fluid context of Russian politics – we might hazard some approximations along those lines.[58] The smallest of the three factions, the Marxist Platform, subscribed to a radical (but non-violent) version of democratic socialism, programmatically oriented toward, say, that future social order sketched by Lenin in his *State and Revolution*. A considerably larger faction, the Democratic Platform, projected a brand of reform-communism that eschewed the notion of going back to Marxist–Leninist basics, preferring instead the vistas opened by Eurocommunism. The third faction, the Movement of Communist Initiative, took shape as the neo-Stalinist reaction to the democratic movement in Russia and to the Democratic Platform in the CPSU. Since this faction and the Russian Communist Party that it spawned represented the last political redoubt of the Soviet party-state, we shall discuss these organizations later in this chapter.

The Marxist and Democratic Platforms both originated in the Moscow inter-club party group, formed by communists active in the informal movement on the eve of the CPSU's Nineteenth Conference for the purpose of transmitting to that conclave various ideas then current in informal circles. Thereafter, the inter-club group began staging semi-regular meetings, thus becoming something of an informal presence within the Communist Party, attracting into the circumference of relatively open political expression many CPSU members for whom the outside world of the informals for one reason or another had remained off limits.[59] Both factions issuing from the inter-club group subsequently claimed that it was the failure of the Communist Party to enact the programme adopted at the Nineteenth Party Conference that led to their decision to organize themselves as separate groups within the CPSU, each aiming its critical darts at those features of the Conference's resolutions that it considered paramount and whose unfulfilment, therefore, engendered their most acute sense of disappointment and concern.[60]

For the Marxist Platform, the CPSU's dilatory and limited implementation of its programme on democratization constituted the principal problem. Having shown itself unprepared to dismantle the existing 'bureaucratic-authoritarian' form of socialism, the Communist Party had ceded the political initiative to 'bourgeois-liberal' and 'social-democratic' groups. These forces, they argued, could capitalize on the country's current economic crisis, eventually sweeping away the discredited 'bureaucratic-authoritarian' system and introducing capitalism in its place.[61] In order to avert that result, the Marxist Platform advocated a programme for the CPSU that would not only steal the democratic thunder of their anti-communist adversaries – one providing for multi-party parliamentary democracy – but raise the democratic ante beyond their reach by introducing direct forms of democracy in the workplace, consumer cooperatives, neighbourhood self-governing associations and so forth.[62]

Aware that the proposals of a small band of radical socialists had little chance of influencing the CPSU's Twenty-Eighth Congress (set for July), the Marxist Platform scoured the Communist Party for allies.[63] Although unable to find common ground with the Democratic Platform – for which the hangover of rivalries from the period of informal politics would appear to weigh as heavily as principled differences[64] – they did reach an accord with one group within it[65] and scored a few symbolic victories at the Congress.[66]This spaghetti-like pattern of political associations – two distinct factions (platforms), one with a sub-faction allied to the other – became even more complicated in the aftermath of the CPSU Congress as the Marxist Platform looked for confederates outside the Communist Party. Some members entered the Socialist Party, formed in June 1990 by elements from the radical socialist tendency in the Moscow Popular Front;[67] others called for partnership with it[68] and formed voting blocs with the socialists in a few city soviets. In September 1990, this alliance was broadened to include the

Confederation of Anarcho-Syndicalists.[69] By the year's end, when both this alliance and the Socialist Party had become historical footnotes, those in the Marxist Platform who remained politically active involved themselves with a mooted Labour Party,[70] which eventually they helped to found in autumn 1992,[71] and with that Russian Communist Party which appeared in December 1991[72] and occupied with new faces this old political niche until a re-legalized Communist Party of the Russian Federation nudged it back into obscurity about a year later.

Although the journey from faction to political party undertaken by those in the Democratic Platform reached a somewhat more consequential destination, it traced a no less twisted path. The point of departure was a nationwide invitation, sent out by the Moscow party club in August 1989 via the informals' communications network, to participate in a conference at which supporters of both multi-party democracy and democratization of the CPSU would constitute themselves a distinct programmatic group.[73] By year's end, this summons had been answered by similar party clubs in 102 cities of the USSR.[74] More than 400 delegates from these clubs convened in Moscow on 20–1 January 1990 formally to declare themselves the Democratic Platform in the CPSU.

Portentously, the question was raised at this conference as to whether the Democratic Platform *should* remain in the CPSU. The argument for setting up an independent political organization was made most forcefully by Igor Chubais (a young scholar-activist), and rebutted most effectively by Vladimir Lysenko and Sergei Stankevich (two others) who argued for remaining in the CPSU in order to reform it from within or, failing that, in order to claim (somehow) a share of its property when they did leave.[75] These ostensibly moderate views prevailed, testifying more to inertia and the fear of unemployment within the group – the threat of which hung over a great many of its leading figures whose positions in the academic world would probably not survive a collective political break with the Communist Party – than to its political acumen. As subsequent events demonstrated, the faction's founding conference represented the hour of its greatest potential. On board at the time was the full complement of the country's democratic leadership – El'tsin, Afanas'ev, Popov, Travkin – a day away stood the formation of DemRossiya, and already under way were the 1990 election campaigns. Announcing itself as an opposition outside of the CPSU at this time may well have paid greater political dividends than did the wait-and-see approach, justified by the autistic plan to reform the CPSU from within, and the vain hope of acquiring some of its property. The decision to remain in the CPSU at the time represented the first of the major missed opportunities in Russia's political rebirth.[76]

The programme adopted at the January conference – a combination of measures already widely publicized by the Inter-Regional Deputies Group (I-RDG) (such as transferring all power to the soviets, establishing full freedom of the press and instituting a market economy) and a de-Leninization of the CPSU itself[77] – stood little or no chance of acceptancy by the CPSU. Any doubts were quickly laid to rest by the party apparatus, which conducted a typical 'election' of delegates for its July Congress – 68 per cent of whom were party-state officials[78] – and unleashed a counter-attack on the Democratic Platform, expelling a few of its members from the Communist Party[79] and ordering a purge of the entire faction in a directive issued first by Egor Ligachev in March[80] and soon reiterated in the Central Committee's 'Open letter to all communists'.[81] The fact that local CPSU bodies almost uniformly failed to carry out these instructions indicated ironically that the party's disintegration had already rendered moot the debate over whether or not it should retain 'democratic-centralism' as its principle of organization.[82]

None of this destroyed the resolve of the majority in the Democratic Platform to remain in the CPSU. At its Moscow city and regional conference in May the debate over forming a separate party or remaining as a faction in the Communist Party was rehearsed again,[83] as it was at the second national conference of the Democratic Platform held in June which witnessed the same arguments, championed by the same speakers along with the same outcome.[84] The Democratic Platform would go to the Twenty-Eighth Congress of the Communist Party, fight for its programme and, if defeated, would then leave to form a separate party of its own. At the Congress, its main proposals on party organization, on ending internal party control of state bodies and so forth were all voted down. Yet its leaders went suddenly mute on their previous threats to leave. Only with the dramatic resignations from the CPSU on the Congress's final day – El'tsin announced his before the Congress itself, while Popov, Sobchak and others cabled in their decisions to call it quits[85] – did the Democratic Platform come forward with its own statement. And here the leadership hedged again. At the 13 July press conference called to announce their decision, nothing was said about 'leaving' the CPSU. Instead, references were made to 'splitting' (with or, perhaps, within) it, glossing this decision with the now familiar phrases about securing some slice of the Communist Party's property.[86] On the following day, when the Democratic Platform convened a conference at the Cinematographer's Union to discuss the question of its post-Congress destination, members thrashed out the old questions yet again: whether to form a separate party, to join with other groups in a larger democratic movement, or to remain a part of the CPSU. Eventually, and without a formal vote, the 'separatist' position originally advocated by Chubais was adopted.[87]

On route to constituting itself as an independent political party, the Democratic Platform evinced the same diligence toward the narrow questions of organization, finances and material resources that it had displayed theretofore.[88] However, since its caution had cost it time – in particular, a timely and decisive exit from the CPSU – the number of its supporters who entered the Republican Party of Russia (RPR) that it founded on 17–18 November 1990 proved embarrassingly small.[89] Indeed, the bulk of its *members* failed to join, remaining in the Communist Party as the faction 'Communist-Reformers for the Democratic Platform in the CPSU'[90] that would become yet another separate party a year later. The shadow of its previous indecisiveness appeared at the RPR's founding congress as an attempt to compensate for missed opportunities. Since the incipient RPR shared the SDPR's 'social-democratic' orientation, Chubais and the SDPR leaders invited to address the congress proposed merging the two small parties into a larger one then and there.[91] A majority of the delegates favoured union, but they deferred to the proposal of the RPR's *de facto* co-chairpersons – Vyacheslav Shostakovskii, Vladimir Lysenko and Stepan Sulakshin[92] – to establish a RPR–SDPR commission to work out the details of merger and present them to a joint congress of the two parties in February.[93] Although their Moscow organizations consummated a marriage in January,[94] the February joint congress ended in divorce. Negotiations continuing over the next six months failed to produce a formula for reconciliation and were finally broken off by the RPR.[95]

What explains this failure to unite? Ideologically compatible and with the obvious strategic advantage to be gained through merger – since a combined RPR–SDPR would probably have become the most influential party inside DemRossiya[96] – union would have appeared to be in the interest of each party. M. Steven Fish has provided part of the explanation by noting that the merger failed because it threatened the still precarious political identities that each of the groups, drawn from different milieux and composed of discrete inter-personal networks, was attempting to establish.[97] But this pertains more to the SDPR[98] – the more persistent suitor[99] – than to the RPR. Indeed, it was only after the RPR had rejected union that it began to cultivate its own liberal-capitalist orientation.[100] When the idea of merger was in the air, the RPR had no distinct political identity, unless one can take seriously its intention to combine elements of Eurocommunism, Christian democracy and the ideology of the US Republican Party.[101] Anything, it would seem, that was not 'social democracy'.[102]

The organizational perspective, advanced by Panebianco[103] and adapted to Russian circumstances, would supply a more convincing explanation. From this vantage, the dominant coalition in the RPR's leadership accomplished two tasks by averting a merger with the SDPR. First, they laid to rest an internal challenge represented by Chubais, whose position on party formation in January 1990 had proven prescient and who alone among the leaders spoke for immediate union with the SDPR the following autumn. After the February 1991 joint congress rejected the idea, Chubais soon left the RPR.[104] Second, the dominant group reduced its own uncertainty on the issue of leadership by maintaining the RPR as a separate party. Whereas each and all might have lost out to their counterparts in the SDPR – or, for that matter, to Chubais who already had distinguished himself as the champion of RPR–SDPR unity – for the top positions in a combined organization, they could be much more sure of retaining their status within a separate RPR. Remembering that in Russia at this time, status in the world of politics did not necessarily correlate with actual influence in the affairs of government, this was no small consideration. As a leader of a political party, one had far more access to the means of mass communication, higher standing in the pecking order of the democratic movement and greater social prestige than a mere party member or political activist. For those individuals, none of whom sported the reputation or enjoyed the personal authority of, say, Afanas'ev or Travkin, the resources available to them as party leaders were critical to the political careers on which they had embarked.

Stage 3: The anti-communist party

Two distinct political currents, brought together by the opportunities and exigencies of the winter election campaigns of 1990, converged in Moscow in late May to found the Democratic Party of Russia (DPR).[105] One consisted of DemRossiya's organization leaders who had emerged from the informal movement to head voters' associations that had sprung up in Russia's large cities. In Leningrad, the popular front's Mariya Sal'e and Il'ya Konstantinov had initiated the formation of a political party in summer 1989, roughing out a draft programme for it by October.[106] Following the 1990 election campaigns, an organizing committee was assembled in Moscow under the direction of the leader of the Moscow Voters' Association (MOI), Lev Ponomarev, which supplied a draft charter for the prospective party.[107] The second current was made up of DemRossiya's public leaders, Afanas'ev (whose relations with the DPR would be both tenuous and tentative) and Travkin (whose name would become synonymous with that of the new party itself), along with the I-RDG's Gennadii Burbulis, Arkadii Murashev and others active in the Democratic Platform. Sensing that the moment had arrived to leave the Communist Party and expecting to pull out with them those fast losing faith with Gorbachev's ability, if not intention, to democratize the CPSU, they joined the DPR's organizing committee in late April.[108]

Although the DPR could claim at inception to be the largest of the Russian parties,[109] it utterly failed to realize the announced hopes of its organizers to unite the country's democratic forces – both those still inside the CPSU as well as those organizing outside it – into a single mass party capable of toppling the Communist Party from power. The anticipated flood of defectors from the CPSU turned out to be a mere trickle, while the explosions that rocked the party at launch burst the alliance between the two groups that had come together to found it. The absent exodus from the CPSU can be accounted for in part by the fickle behaviour of some of DemRossiya's public leaders whose attenuated association with the DPR, and subsequent severing of all ties to it, deprived the party of notables whose presence might have brought over to it some sizeable cohort of CPSU members.[110] Moreover, the stridently anti-communist profile assumed by the new party scarcely conduced to easing the prospective passage of those still in the Communist Party. But a contest among party organizers for control of the new organization was even more damaging, depriving it of a mass base in the country's new voters' associations. Drawing on their recent experience in stitching together voters' clubs into larger alliances via the medium of collective leadership, Ponomarev's organizing committee had proposed a three-person leadership structure for the DPR. This provision, they believed, would broaden the base of the party and fit with their plan to make party membership available to both individuals ('individual membership') and to those belonging to other organizations affiliated with the DPR ('collective membership').[111] One or more of the affiliates was likely to be represented among the three co-chairpersons; and given the numerical weight of the voters' associations, the odds favoured Ponomarev of MOI and, probably, Sal'e of the Leningrad Popular Front. Travkin and his supporters, however, produced an alternative single-leader scheme, one that they claimed would equip the new party with the discipline, decisiveness and dispatch required to overthrow the CPSU.[112] In one respect, the dispute sprang from a clash of ambitions and simple arithmetic. Travkin was already recognized as the DPR's pre-eminent figure.[113] Either he would direct the party as its single leader or his would be one of three voices on its directorate. In other regards, however, the issue was much more ramified, reflecting both the communist past and the anti-communist trauma of Russia's political rebirth.

From its opening, the DPR's founding congress resembled a diminutive version of, say, the USSR's Congress of People's Deputies. Delegates claiming to speak on behalf of all Russia (or, in one instance, all of Moscow's Red Guard district) jostled, pushed and punched one another in order to grab the microphone, responding in choruses of verbal abuse to comments not meeting their approval.[114] From the point of view of procedures, the congress failed to measure up to Soviet standards. Neither did the presidium submit themselves even to a perfunctory election, nor did those serving on the credentials committee. Protests from the hall over one or another arbitrary ruling on procedures were answered by threats of expulsion, while agreed upon rules and procedures were discarded in equally arbitrary fashion. On the key issue of whether to adopt single or collective leadership, a tie vote was subjected to recount by Travkin supporters who broke the deadlock in Travkin's favour. This resulted in the exit of most of the party's prime movers – Ponomarev, Sal'e, Konstantinov, Vera Kriger (a leader of MOI), Murashev, Mikhail Tolstoi (a people's deputy of Russia), Garri Kasparov (chess champion of the world) and others. The last three of these individuals shortly returned and organized a 'liberal faction' in the DPR[115] that remained in the party until its April 1991 congress when Murashev and Kasparov left for good, charging Travkin and the majority with insufficient anti-communism.[116] The others formed a new organizing committee on the spot, recruited a few other political notables (such as Astaf'ev who had not yet converted to 'constitutional democracy')[117] and founded the Free Democratic Party of Russia (FDPR) a few months later.[118] This project came to very little, since these refugees from the DPR, along with the leaders of its rival 'liberal faction',[119] were busied with efforts to outflank Travkin in the battle to lead the country's democratic forces by converting the electoral coalition, DemRossiya, into an organized movement that would subsume all groups of democratic orientation, the DPR included.

The struggles waged by the principals in Russia's democratic movement had little or nothing to do with the principles that they proclaimed. In view of the rapid disintegration of the democratic column in the wake of its election victories as reviewed in the previous chapter, as well as the bounty of débâcles in store for it in the period that followed, this point should be underscored. In this respect, we recall the importance of adapting the concept 'opportunity structures' to Russian conditions, paying particular attention to the forms of communication and organization employed by those responding to the opportunities occasioned by the CPSU's disintegration and how these were conditioned by the state socialist order in which they functioned. On the side of communication we notice a form reminiscent of communism's split discourse in which subjects would participate publicly in the alien speech of the official ideology while reserving for familiar face-to-face venues the expression of their 'authentic' identities. This bifurcated pattern of communication was replicated in the democratic movement as a common discourse of 'democracy' – defined negatively as anti-communism – along with a jumble of mutually-unintelligible argots, each supplying some positive markers by which the various parties within the movement confected their separate identities. At inception, the parties' public communications provided little if any basis for drawing distinctions among them. The DPR's programme, for instance, could be read as a version of the programmes put forth by, say, the SDPR or the PCD, but not as an alternative to them.[120] Since prospects for their actual implementation were, to say the least, remote, a given programme might have served as a means for announcing the existence and identity of the respective party before the public, setting out distinctions of a symbolic sort. The similarity of these texts, however, foreclosed that possibility. Instead, distinctions were signalled internally via a recondite language reminiscent of 'indifferent variety' whose initiates communicated through the esoteric codes of their respective political micro-societies: constitutional, social, free or, *sans* adjoining adjective, democratic party. The only common language available to these parties was the language of anti-communism, the lingua franca of the movement in which they were embedded. Anti-communism, in turn, was not a political–philosophical discourse but a medium for channelling amorphous animosities and frustrations. As such, it could easily be turned against anyone, much like the protean categories of official communist ideology had served generations of rulers in identifying 'anti-socialist' elements. The spasm of hysterical hatred that splattered Ponomarev, Sal'e and the others who walked out of the DPR congress echoed decades of the Soviet regime's hate-mongering against the country's 'enemies'; it also presaged a comparable outburst of hysteria that deluged DPR delegates some eighteen months later when they walked out of a DemRossiya congress, with Ponomarev, Sal'e and others looking on.

Turning to the organizational dimension of party formation, it was apparent that the personalized forms of authority characteristic of state socialism structured the manner in which opportunities to organize were realized in practice. The DPR epitomized one pattern in this respect, that of personalized authority *within* the organization.[121] From inception, the DPR was known publicly as 'the party of Travkin'. The leadership type that he practised within 'his' party reminded many of that very Bolshevism that he claimed the party had been summoned to extirpate from the country. With a standing majority of delegates to DPR congresses at his back, Travkin regularly discarded elementary democratic procedures and dictated decisions to the party's would-be deliberative body.[122] The directions in which he took it at one time or another were charted on the compass of the leader's sense of opportunity, however much it may have compromised the integrity of the DPR as an institution. Two critical episodes in the party's early history place this pattern of leader-over-institution in sharp relief. The first involved the DPR's alliance with the RCDM and the CDP in early 1991 that constituted an opposition bloc within DemRossiya. The second was its exit, along with those same partners, from DemRossiya later in that same year. In each instance, the direction taken by the DPR flew directly in the face of the political principles that it had theretofore proclaimed and, in the second case, amounted to a repudiation of its own organizational charter.[123]

Bases of political differentiation

The DPR's readiness to abandon principles fundamental to its integrity can be traced to the weak structures of the Soviet order from which it sprang and within which it operated. Like the other parties emerging in this period, it was unable to differentiate itself politically by serving as a vehicle for the expression of organized social interests. And like those parties, its identity construct was fashioned under conditions of indifferent variety, wherein the absence of mutual recognition meant that no identity could become secure and stable. Rather, the parties considered up to this point crystallized around identity constructs that posited some future society in which organized interests would come into existence. Political differentiation, then, did not correspond to a social differentiation structured by property relations and manifest as associations pursuing specific interests; rather, it was the residue of interaction among individuals who flocked together in various associations (parties) that appeared as distinct discursive communities.

The process of differentiation characteristic of party formation amounted to a continuation – on an expanded scale – of those tendencies evinced by informal associations in the pre-party period. Much like their informal predecessors, the identity constructs of the emerging political parties tapped valorized elements in the symbolic worlds of those entering them from more or less discrete 'spaces' in Soviet society. Data generated by a survey of delegates to congresses of the DPR and SDPR in April 1991 (about a year after each had been founded)[124] enable us to demonstrate this point via a comparison of the composition of the respective party elites. The samples drawn include just under half of the DPR's top leaders, activists and functionaries (190 out of some 400 delegates) and a little over half of their counterparts in the SDPR (109 out of about 200 delegates).

In terms of standard indicators of social differentiation in industrial societies – levels of income and education – DPR and SDPR elites evinced nearly identical profiles. Both were more or less equally distinguished from the larger population as sub-groups of 'over-educated' and 'under-paid' individuals.[125] Differences between the two party elites, however, were evident in their respective occupational mixes, a category representing a first approximation of our notion of spaces in Soviet society from which individuals entered political parties. Whereas 46 per cent of the SDPR's elite consisted of those involved in intellectual pursuits, the comparable figure for the DPR was only 30 per cent. Similarly, 54 per cent of the DPR's elite was engaged in business, engineering, service sector activities or were either retired or unemployed while only 37 per cent of the SDPR's elites fell into those categories. A second approximation of distinct social spaces would concern family background. Here a marked disparity was evident in levels of parents' education, indicating that the SDPR elite more frequently had come from higher-status family backgrounds.[126] Taken together, these comparisons would suggest a collection of more or less discrete social traits imprinted on each party's elite. Those drawn to the SDPR tended to have come from higher-status social groups and were more often pursuing careers characteristic of the Russian intelligentsia; those entering the DPR were more upwardly mobile and more often evinced career patterns remote from those of the intelligentsia.

These distinctions based on passive social characteristics are further amplified by considering the time at which – and, therefore, the context within – party elites had become politically active. Whereas the majority of those in the DPR reported no political involvement before their party had been founded, some 85 per cent of those in the SDPR had been active in some form of political organization (excluding the CPSU) before their party had been inaugurated. In other words, the SDPR elite contained an overwhelming majority of individuals who had been politicized prior to the advent of parties, while most of those in the DPR had sat out the entire perestroika period, becoming politically active only when political parties had been legalized. As such, the DPR elite had little or no experience in the non-conformist subculture of the informal movement. Only when palpably practical prospects for political activity – parties and (expectedly) elections – had appeared did the majority of its members become involved in politics. The SDPR elite, on the other hand, had been immersed in the informal sub-culture for years developing over time a social-democratic 'community' among themselves prior to launching their political party.

The diverse spaces from which these two elites entered their respective political parties thus tell us a good deal about their contrasting character and political style. The political orientation of the SDPR pivoted on abstract (social-democratic) principles that defined them as a community. These principles, and the endless debates over their proper interpretation at congresses and plenary sessions of the SDPR's executive bodies, served as the basis for factional activities within the party.[127] Moreover, this preoccupation with abstract ideas restricted the size of the party membership: in part, because after its failed courtship of the RPR, the SDPR eschewed raiding the disintegrating CPSU, regarding affinity groups within it as 'Eurocommunist' and therefore unreceptive to its definition of 'social democracy';[128] in part, because the social-democratic community, in the words of one member, consisted of 'a lot of theoreticians, but very few people who knew how to build a political party'.[129]

For the DPR, things were quite the reverse. Its leaders regarded the behaviour of intellectually oriented parties such as the SDPR as the windbaggery of political dilettantes who had no notion of what real party-political activity involved.[130] As we have seen, party principles proved expendable when circumstances seemed to dictate it and factions in the party were based on support for particular leaders – mainly pro- or anti-Travkin – rather than on abstract ideas. Not surprisingly, given the upwardly mobile cohort represented in this party's elite, politics for the DPR was above all about action, about getting things done. In discussing their work, party officials would regularly point with pride to that which they regarded as concrete accomplishments: the acquisition of fax machines and telephones for party offices, the discipline displayed by the party's factions in legislatures, and the steady energy of its organizational and recruitment activities in localities. These mundane matters underscored by the orientation of DPR leaders would seem something of an afterthought, if not a distraction, to many of their counterparts in the SDPR[131] whose efforts were more devoted to working out theoretical analyses of the country's political economy.[132]

The differences between the DPR and SDPR elites with respect to the spaces in Soviet society from which they entered these parties and the diverse political identities that these parties outwardly manifested were reflected within each as a particular 'ethos' or 'internal context'. By internal context, we have in mind a set of mutually reinforcing expectations embedded in the discursive practices characteristic of each party – a normative-rational mode in the case of the SDPR, a pragmatic disposition oriented toward achieving concrete results in that of the DPR – that structured the manner in which party business was transacted. These internal contexts determined how the two parties managed the critical issue of leadership selection and its attendant problems of ambition, competition and rivalry.

As noted, Travkin's successful bid to be the DPR's sole leader was commensurate with the decimation of the party's leadership corps, the alienation of its would-be base in the network of voters' associations and the subsequent departure of other party notables. The DPR was 'Travkin's party', not only because his name was affixed to it in popular parlance and because he directed it with a firm hand, but because his forceful persona resonated with the ethos of the party itself.[133] The premium placed on decisiveness, action and results within the party's internal context meant that challengers to Travkin's authority were afforded two options: either submit to it or leave.[134] Consequently, the DPR experienced an enormous amount of turnover in its top elite and either failed to attract, or rather quickly lost, political figures enjoying some degree of prominence in the country.

Conflicting ambitions and rivalries were also part of the SDPR's history, but they were mediated by the party's internal context in an altogether different way. For the first two years of its existence, the SDPR maintained a collective leadership, and a number of individuals rotated through the troika at the top without leaving the party on replacement.[135] When this arrangement gave way to the single-leader pattern at the party's fourth congress in May 1992, the change had already been exhaustively debated within the party for months.[136] The adoption of the new leadership arrangement was coincident with a bitter rivalry that developed between Boris Orlov, the chairperson elected at the SDPR's fourth congress, and Oleg Rumyantsev, the party's most prominent public figure. Their quarrel centred on Rumyantsev's contention that although the party had chosen Orlov as its highest organizational officer, it should recognize Rumyantsev himself as its public leader because of his important role in Russia's Supreme Soviet as executive secretary of its constitutional commission and therefore untether him from the dicta of the party's programme.[137] The terms in which this leadership conflict was expressed, as well as its eventual outcome, were altogether congruent with the party's internal context. The issue of leadership took the form of a debate over the type of federalism that should be incorporated into Russia's new constitution, Rumyantsev arguing one position and Orlov another.[138] Even the insults that accompanied the exchange of views were distinctly 'social-democratic'.[139] Eventually, the conflict was resolved in consonance with the normative structure of the party's ethos in which principles counted for more than personality. Since Rumyantsev refused to endorse the SDPR's concept of federalism, he was stripped of the rank of party deputy co-chairperson. Thereafter, he left the SDPR and founded another social democratic party, the Social Democratic Centre.

DemRossiya: the movement

In contrast to the 'under-articulated' political parties forming in the Russia of 1990, that organized movement with which they would affiliate, DemRossiya, was 'over-articulated'. Given the degree of organization that it displayed, DemRossiya constituted something more than a mere clearing-house for coordinating the efforts of its member units. It also displayed a far greater level of organizational coherence than those modern social movements, surveyed by Sydney Tarrow and others, whose actual basis would reside in 'invisible communities' comprised of a myriad of interlocking networks of individuals capable of harnessing extant 'structures of solidarity'.[140] The strange symmetry obtaining between under-articulated political parties and an over-articulated movement into which they were enfolded resulted from two sets of considerations. First, to varying degrees, all political parties participated in a discourse of anti-communism which facilitated their entry into a larger coalition – or, as DemRossiya was often referred to in their vernacular, a 'super-party' – that would concentrate their energies on the overriding objective confronting them all: removing the Communist Party from power. In this respect, the movement's organizers doubtless struck a common chord by remarking that the 1990 elections had ushered in an entirely new situation in Russian politics. Whereas the democratic forces both inside and outside the CPSU had been arrayed against the Communist Party's conservative apparatus in the pre-election period, the election itself, the formation of a new Russian government and the appearance of political parties had fundamentally redrawn the battle lines. Now, they announced, the fight was between the democratic forces and the CPSU as a whole.[141] In the face of that objective, the movement uniting those forces would tend to subsume, and thus eclipse on the political field, the separate parties that comprised it.

Second, alongside this common language and shared objective stood the enduring quest to unite the country's democratic forces, as well as the bitter rivalries that it had unleashed among those seeking a leading role in that project. In this respect, the pre-history of the DemRossiya movement stretched back to the many false starts begun during the period of informal politics: the attempts at establishing a national centre for those in the informal movement; the formation of the Democratic Union; the efforts to found a unionwide or Russian popular front; the stillborn national voters' associations and, most recently, the divisive inauguration of the DPR. Indeed, it was this last event that provided the immediate impetus to organize DemRossiya as a national movement.

Within a few weeks after the DPR's stormy entry onto the political scene, those alienated from 'Travkin's party' convened a conference in Moscow where delegates from over fifty cities in the Russian Federation sought to revive the project of creating an inclusive organization whose purpose consisted in marshalling the democratic forces against the Soviet party-state.[142] Some three weeks later, on 14 July, this conference reconvened to elect an organizing committee charged with preparing for a formal congress, set for 20–1 October, at which the movement, DemRossiya, would be founded.[143] These conferences consisted of outsiders. That is, the only party leaders on hand were either refugees from the DPR – such as Ponomarev and four other members of his FDPR who were elected to DemRossiya's twenty-seven-member organizing committee – or DPR refugees-to-be, like Murashev who was named as the organizing committee's chairperson. Almost all of the other positions on the committee were occupied by leaders of MOI (10) and/or by members of the DemRossiya legislative factions in the Russian Congress of People's Deputies (10) and the Moscow city soviet (5).[144] The fact that no other political parties were represented among the organizers indicated that the DemRossiya movement was launched by a particular segment of Russian political society, one consisting almost entirely of individuals who, for one reason or another, had not found their way into any of the newly formed parties.

The addition of an incipient movement organization to Russia's political field prompted a number of party leaders to take counter-measures. By September, the DPR, SDPR and the Democratic Platform entered into a formal (albeit, short-lived) alliance which, in principle, registered its 'support of the broad popular movement, "Democratic Russia"'.[145] Thereafter, the DPR sought, but ultimately failed, to form a similar coalition with the CDP and the small, but relatively well-financed, Party of Free Labour.[146] Travkin's opponents in the DPR then dealt a serious blow to his efforts to craft a coalition of parties outside of DemRossiya (whose reincarnation as an organized movement lay just weeks ahead) by transferring the DPR's principal material resource – its twelve million dollar printing facility, rumoured to have been acquired thanks to the generous donations of chess champion and Travkin-rival, Garri Kasparov[147] – to the 'union of democratic forces'.[148] In practice, this meant that the party's handsome newspaper, *Demokraticheskaya Rossiya*, became the property of DemRossiya, while the DPR was left scrambling to replace its loss. Within about three months it managed to publish its own (smaller and far less attractive) newspaper, *Demokraticheskaya gazeta*, the first issue of which announced that the party's deputy co-chairperson, Georgii Khatsenkov, had been stripped of all responsibilities because of his 'dirty work' and 'treason' in relinquishing control of the DPR's first media organ to forces outside the party.[149] On 20–1 October, these same forces – in the persons of 1,181 delegates from 71 regions, to whose numbers were added 121 delegates representing the organizing committee, 23 USSR people's deputies and 104 of their counterparts in the Russian legislature[150] – came together to found the new movement. Only a small fraction of the delegates (14 per cent) were drawn from nascent DemRossiya groups in the localities. Most represented its thirty-three affiliated organizations: political parties, voters' associations, public organizations such as Memorial and April, trade unions and strike committees. This ratio would later change, and with critical consequences for Russian politics in general. But at this stage, DemRossiya was principally a coalition of political parties with the largest among them, the DPR (although not yet a formal member), exercising 16 per cent of the votes at the congress.[151]

In addition to declaring that its primary aim was to liquidate the communist order in Russia,[152] DemRossiya's inauguration was noteworthy on two counts. The first was the conspicuous absence of the acknowledged leaders of the country's democratic movement itself. Neither El'tsin nor Popov put in an appearance, while the vast majority of those in the DemRossiya deputies' faction, like their intellectual counterparts in Moscow Tribune, were also truant. Afanas'ev arrived on the congress's second day, but declined to address it.[153] The standoffish attitude thus displayed became a defining characteristic of DemRossiya, inaugurating a pattern of political leadership 'outside the organization'. This pattern, too, would be fraught with critical, and arguably tragic, consequences for the development of Russian politics. The second noteworthy aspect concerned the organizational structure appropriate for the movement, to which was loosely appended a (muffled) dispute on strategy. Travkin, arguing the minority view, reprised his thesis on the need to create a tight, disciplined organization which, in his opinion, could force new parliamentary elections and defeat the CPSU in a two-party contest. Although his position was rejected – unsurprisingly, since those initiating the DemRossiya movement regarded this approach as wrongheaded if not 'Bolshevist' – he and his party continued to propound it until their break with DemRossiya the following year.[154] The organizational scheme approved by the congress was the over-articulated version of a movement organization. DemRossiya would adopt no specific programme; but it would house affiliated parties and organizations – all of which remained free to pursue their own strategies and tactics – and, at the same time, form its own regional organizations which both deputies and citizens unattached to any of its member groups could join. DemRossiya thereby consisted of an organizational structure distinct from its affiliates,[155] complete with its own funds, newspaper and dues-paying individual, as well as collective, members.[156]

The goal of this inclusive strategy – to topple the communist order – would be achieved by means of presidential, rather than parliamentary, elections[157] in which El'tsin was already understood to be DemRossiya's candidate.[158] In certain respects the strategy was unquestionably successful: DemRossiya's membership soon climbed into the hundreds of thousands[159] and its successful presidential campaign for El'tsin in the following spring broke the back of the communist system. The momentum that it gathered even forced a reluctant Travkin to abandon his principles and bring his DPR into DemRossiya as a full member in January 1991.[160] Yet the choice already made to attack the CPSU with the executive, rather than (or also with) the legislative, branch of government, coupled with the fact that the individual who would lead the assault was neither accountable to DemRossiya nor to any other organization in Russian political society was, indeed, fateful. As an SDPR leader, Galina Rakitskaya, observed on the eve of the democrats' triumph, the organizational weapon thus forged by the union of a single-minded movement in support of the Russian head of state meant that the democrats were poised not so much to extirpate the legacy of communism but 'to repeat the criminal mistakes of the CPSU'.[161]

Parties in the backwash

We conclude with a brief excursus on those political parties formed in the backwash churned up by the conflict between the country's democratic forces and the disintegrating Soviet party-state. These parties were all derivatives of that conflict, but the particular positions that they assumed in relation to it would divide them into two groups:

'opportunists' and 'restorationists'. Opportunists took advantage of the CPSU's disintegration to found independent political organizations that amounted to caricatures of parties, posing as competitors to DemRossiya and its affiliates in order to parlay that posture into political capital that they could exchange with the Communist Party against material resources and grants of authority. Restorationists were also by-products of the CPSU's disintegration, but their position on the country's political field and, accordingly, the thrust of their efforts were fundamentally different. Theirs was the politics of anti-politics; they organized politically in order to put an end to opportunities to form political organizations. Rather than accommodation with the CPSU's leadership, they sought to capture it for the purpose of turning back Russia's political clock to some pre-perestroika past.

If the opportunists were competitors with respect to Russia's democratic parties, then the restorationists occupied an analogous position *vis-à-vis* the CPSU. These relationships structured the question of identity for both groups in quite different ways. For the opportunists it implied the capacity to counterfeit; the knack of forging democratic identities. The beauty of these identities consisted in the fact that they were not even skin-deep and, therefore, could be readily donned and discarded as circumstances might warrant. The restorationists, on the other hand, were scions to that great inventory of hand-me-down identities from Russia's tsarist and communist past. Although decidedly out of fashion in political society, these get-ups – resplendent with the majesty of empire and adorned with the ornaments of a righteous social order to be recaptured via 'workers' power' coiled into the fist of the celebrated 'strong hand' – symbolized a social visage as 'natural' and, for that reason, compelling as any version of fundamentalism. Despite their differences, however, opportunists and restorationists shared three related characteristics: first, unlike the parties within the democratic movement, identity constructs played no discernible role in structuring the internal lives of these organizations; second, their leadership corps consisted of marginal elements, the flotsam of political society, while their respective memberships were either fluid, fictive or both; and, third, their organizational structures and the norms governing their internal procedures were no more than episodic residues of power struggles within them.

Opportunist parties

The first such party in this category – the Democratic Party of the Soviet Union – was founded in August 1989 at a Moscow conference initiated by Lev Ubozhko, Vladimir Bogachev and R. Semenov, all of whom had been expelled from the Democratic Union in the previous year for publishing caustic criticisms of that organization's *de facto* leader, Valeriya Novodvorskaya.[162] This conference commenced a sequence of events that spun out a number of 'democratic parties' in the following months. Semenov's apparently unexpected election to the chairperson-ship of the new party led a disappointed Ubozhko and Bogachev to withdraw from it and to form another 'Democratic Party' with Ubozhko as its leader. By the autumn, Bogachev had quit 'Ubozhko's party' and joined with Vladimir Zhirinovskii – orphaned by the Democratic Union rather than expelled from it – in an effort to organize yet another 'Democratic Party'. Before very long, Ubozhko was expelled from 'his' party at its second congress in October 1990 for his unauthorized announcement on prime-time Soviet television that his Democratic Party had been renamed the Conservative Party and was in the process of negotiating an alliance with the CPSU and for ripping the microphone from the congress's presiding officer to summon para-military police (OMON) to suppress delegates expressing opinions contrary to his own.[163] Thereafter, Ubozhko and his handful of followers declared themselves the Conservative Party.

No less fractious and sadly comical results attended the organizing efforts of Bogachev and Zhirinovskii. Recycling a programme that the latter had prepared for an aborted Social-Democratic Party of Russia[164] and assembling in March some 250 individuals who were signed up on the spot as party members and 'delegates' to its founding congress,[165] they uncorked a parody of democratic procedures that gave birth to the Liberal Democratic Party of the Soviet Union (LDPSS). Although altogether separate from the various parties coalescing in Russia in the wake of the 1990 elections, the LDPSS's image was fashioned into an indistinguishable likeness of their demo-cratic competitors expressed concisely in the remarks of its chair-person, Zhirinovskii: 'We want to be a European industrial society.'[166] Although this posture may have increased the attractiveness of the LDPSS to sponsors in the CPSU and KGB attempting to blunt the assault of Russia's democratic forces by means of the diversionary tactics of fielding and/or supporting certain opportunist parties, Zhirinovskii was already testing other waters, previewing certain aspects of his future political persona in addresses delivered at Pamyat rallies.[167] His collaboration with the KGB, which was apparently funding him personally, led Bogachev and others to expel him from the LDPSS in October 1990. But Zhirinovskii retorted by disgorging these same individuals from 'his party'.[168] Although the country was graced for the moment by the presence of two LDPSSs, Zhirinovskii's proved the more durable.

It was Zhirinovskii's rump party that later entered the so-called Centrist Bloc, an alliance formed among a number of DemRossiya's competitors disposed toward participating in a bogus coalition with the CPSU.[169] In a bizarre burlesque of consensus building, Soviet Prime Minister Nikolai Ryzhkov and chairperson of the USSR's Supreme Soviet Anatolii Luk'yanov conducted two days of 'negotiations' with these paper parties toward the purpose of forming a 'coalition government of national accord'.[170] Ryzhkov and Luk'yanov soon lost interest in this plan and by early 1991 the Centrist Bloc had collapsed along with effectively all its constituent organizations,[171] excepting Zhirinovskii's LDPSS that would form the nucleus of his bid for the Russian presidency in spring, repositioning itself on the far right of the political field.

Restorationists

Organizations in this category would include the Peasant Union and the Soyuz (Union) deputies' group in the USSR Congress of People's Deputies. In the words of one of its founders, the Peasant Union was 'in fact subordinated to the presently existing apparatus of management in the agrarian sector'.[172] It thus represented officialdom's reaction to the appearance of the Association of Peasant Farms and Cooperatives of Russia (AKKOR) formed in July 1989 by Aleksei Emel'yanov, Vladimir Tikhonov and others to advance the prospects for private farming in the country, as well as to the Peasant Party of Russia that emerged from AKKOR in March although not formally inaugurated until September.[173] The Peasant Union was both a successor to the party-state's organizational form in the countryside (the collective farm councils) through which the rural apparatus had long coordinated its operations, and a political device for emancipating local officials from the tutelage of the central government, enabling them to exercise the dominion of an 'estate' in the agricultural sector.[174]

Similarly, the Soyuz deputies' group, which included many members of the Peasant Union, was formed in February 1990 as a restorationist response to the appearance of the I-RDG. Incensed by the I-RDG's campaigns for multi-party democracy and sovereignty for the union-republics, as well as by Gorbachev's apparent receptivity to pressure on these issues – whose consequences were epitomized by the national-democratic revolutions that had just swept East Europe – the reactionary elements in the Soviet legislature set aside their much-touted principles against factionalism and formed one of their own. Consonant with other restorationist groups, the formation of this legislative faction did not entail any reciprocity on the part of its members. As its name 'union' would indicate, the group neither constructed itself discursively as a mere part of the deputies' corpus, nor did it authorize the division of that corpus into parts. After the pattern of Soviet speech, it presented itself as the whole, arithmetic considerations notwithstanding. Consisting of some 560 deputies almost exclusively named to the legislature by 'public organizations' or elected to it from safe districts, Soyuz represented no popular constituencies. Rather, its position in the legislature served as a rostrum to express the view of its respective estates within the Soviet order, namely, the officers' corps and the military-industrial complex.[175] Just as the Peasant Union championed the full restoration of the Soviet order in the countryside, so Soyuz stood for the full restoration of the Soviet empire.

Each of these groups maintained close ties and overlapping memberships with that right-wing insurgency within the CPSU that culminated in the creation of the Russian Communist Party[176] and its attempt to take power in the USSR. Activists and supporters of an Initiative Committee for the Creation of a Russian Communist Party were distributed across the country among many in the CPSU apparatus, ideologists in their employ and the 'workers' organization', OFT (the United Front of Working People). However, the centre of operations was clearly the CPSU's Leningrad regional committee headed by Boris Gidaspov. The Initiative Committee arose and gathered force on the heels of three events. The first was Gorbachev's failed compromise of December 1989, a plan to assuage his conservative and neo-Stalinist opponents in the CPSU by creating a Russian Bureau within the CPSU's Central Committee. This Bureau met rarely and, when it did, carried out no real business of its own.[177] The second was the February 1990 decision of the CPSU's Central Committee to remove the constitutional ban on party formation. The alarm among CPSU restorationists occasioned by this development was manifest in a leaflet distributed in Moscow immediately after that decision had been taken. Referring to the Central Committee's resolution as 'a massed attack on the Communist Party' and castigating Gorbachev in particular for 'capitulating' to that 'fig leaf for the shadow economy', the Democratic Platform of the CPSU, the leaflet instructed communists 'not to wait for instructions from above' but to elect delegates at once to an extraordinary conference of the Moscow city committee,[178] a preparatory stage *en route* to creating a Russian Communist Party. The third event propelling the Initiative Committee along its course of restorationist insurgency was the débâcle experienced by their standard bearers, the Bloc of Public and Patriotic Movements of Russia, in the March 1990 elections. Defeated in the political arena, the conservatives and neo-Stalinists would attempt to close down that arena by seizing control of the CPSU and using it to restore the Soviet order.

Rejecting another compromise offered by Gorbachev in March – according to which, delegates from the Russian Federation who had been selected for the CPSU's Twenty-Eighth Congress would hold their own prior conference on 19 June – the Initiative Committee organized a separate Congress for Reviving the Russian Communist Party on 21–2 April. At that gathering, the 600 delegates chosen specifically for it – whose neo-Stalinist orientation coincided with the procedures effecting their 'election' – declared themselves a 'new party'.[179] In the face of this challenge to their authority, the central leadership of the CPSU capitulated. In early May the Politburo met the Initiative Committee half way by placing the question of creating a Russian Communist Party within the CPSU on the agenda of the 19 June conference; as that date approached, the Central Committee's Russian Bureau went the rest of the way and declared that the conference would be the site for founding the Russian Communist Party.[180]

The founding itself would rival or surpass any of the organizational peculiarities that we have encountered among Russian political parties in this chapter. Composed of both delegates selected from within Russia to the upcoming CPSU Congress and those installed (that seems the most accurate word) by the Initiative Committee's network for this specific congress, they encompassed almost the entire range of political orientations in the country – from Eurocommunist liberals to hidebound Stalinists – assembled now for the ostensible purpose of uniting in a new political party. About two-thirds of those assembled were members of the CPSU apparatus (1,171) or of its industrial (210) and agricultural (130) counterparts.[181] To this number were added hundreds of 'guests' and, simply, other people who functioned on a par with the delegates themselves, addressing the Congress and standing for the offices that it would fill.[182] Although the formal purpose was to form a party, nothing along these lines was accomplished, save the elections of a leader – Ivan Polozkov, the CPSU's Krasnodar boss whose Stalinist proclivities had already earned him a broad reputation as perhaps the country's foremost restorationist[183] – and a few members of its Central Committee. The energies of the Congress were channelled primarily into speech-making, which often simply meant firing vituperative broadsides at the leadership of the parent organization, the CPSU.[184] Although many sounded alarms against the spectre of capitalism menacing the country, neither at this juncture nor in the future would this concern find its way into the new party's criticism of their parent, despite the fact that the CPSU was undoubtedly the country's principal capitalist at the time.[185] In the end, the Russian Communist Party's influence within the CPSU did not prove sufficient to enact the major anti-democratic measures that it advocated – the formation of parallel legislatures known as 'soviets of workers' deputies' and the annulment of the results of previous elections, thus dissolving the legislatures that had issued from them.[186] None the less, by spearheading the restorationists' assault on Russian democracy, it prepared the way for the *coup d'état* of August 1991.

10   Restoration and revolution

Faced with politically mobilized societies in most of the union-republics mustered behind their respective sovereign states, the Soviet regime responded with a politics of restoration. In autumn 1990, it launched a 'low-intensity' *coup d'état,* menacing, probing and pressuring the national-democratic movements on a variety of fronts in a war of manoeuvre. From the standpoint of political organization, this meant a reassertion of *nomenklatura* rule by relying on those state agencies with the capacity for physical violence: the KGB, the army, paramilitary forces (OMON) and the police. From that of communication, it involved a reassertion of the regime's longstanding prerogative to define and interpret the world. Each figured centrally in the politics of restoration: violence and intimidation directed against bodies on the one hand; lies, disinformation and blackouts inflicted on minds on the other. In Russia, the low-intensity *coup* was punctuated by two ostensible efforts at compromise. The first, in summer 1990 involving economic reform, came to nothing.[1] The second, a negotiated revision of the federal system, precipitated the seizure of power by the self-proclaimed State Committee for the State of Emergency (SCSE) on 19 August 1991.

The protracted siege imposed by the party-state established a particular context for the development of Russia's nascent political society, erasing any possibility of 'normal' politics and inscribing into it the martial virtues of solidarity, resistance and heroism. This chapter analyses the political struggle that prevailed in Russia under the tacit 'state of emergency' that lasted from autumn 1990 till the defeat of the August *coup.* Its aim is to situate state-building and political development within it, demonstrating that structures of resistance, and those alone, brought cohesion and form to political relations. These same structures accounted for the particular shape assumed by the Russian state in this period, coiled as a fist in combat with communism, bereft of the dexterity required for normal government once the communist regime had been smashed. The first section examines the low-intensity *coup* in terms of three inter-related sites of repression/resistance: political manoeuvre and mobilization, the struggle for the means of communication and the contest for authority waged between Russia and the USSR. The second focuses on the spring breakthrough of the democratic forces, their reversal of the restorationist offensive in the Russian legislature and the ensuing counter-offensive that established a Russian presidency poised to dismantle the Soviet order. The denouement of the anti-communist revolution appears in the third part as that last-ditch effort to save the communist system results in its overthrow.

Low-intensity coup

Manoeuvre, resistance and dress rehearsals

The first signs of an impending *coup* appeared in September 1990. Reprising the standard Soviet scenario implemented to restore communist rule in certain East European states, RKP (Russian Communist Party) first secretary Ivan Polozkov called for a 'committee of national salvation' to seize power in the USSR while divisions of the Soviet army decamped and assumed positions around the capital.[2] The Centrist Bloc appeared, was duly introduced over national television[3] and entered into negotiations with the Soviet government. By the time of their December congress in the Kremlin, at which they reiterated Polozkov's demand for instituting dictatorship via a 'committee of national salvation',[4] the 'centrists' had been joined by the Soyuz deputies group[5] and enjoyed direct access to KGB chief, Vladimir Kryuchkov.[6] By January, they had presumptively assumed the title of national saviours themselves.[7] Although the Soviet authorities had no immediate need for their services in this capacity – there seemed at the time another, cleaner method to depose Boris El'tsin and recapture the Russian government – they did retain one centrist leader, Vladimir Zhirinovskii, whom they fielded and funded for the presidential race in spring.[8] Zhirinovskii eventually repaid his debt by declaring his 'full support' for the SCSE on the first day of the August *coup*.[9]

The forced resignation of Interior Minister Vadim Bakatin in October 1990 and his replacement by Boris Pugo – head of the Latvian Communist Party till political perestroika swept him from that post in 1988 – signalled the unfolding of the central government's *coup* strategy. Along with administrative reorganizations centralizing government control in the hands of the president,[10] directives from that office removed legal restrictions on the police and secret police in the areas of search and arrest and underwrote a *de facto* installation of marshal law in Soviet cities as local police were integrated into command structures including units of the Soviet army and the paramilitary OMON.[11] In January these elements of the coup machinery – army, OMON, committees of national salvation and Soviet president protesting his uninvolvement – were put to use in Lithuania and Latvia in a blood-stained dress rehearsal for August. Determined civil resistance in the Baltic, supported by mass protests around the country, stopped the coup in its tracks.

Under ashen skies and the blows of police truncheons, hundreds of thousands of Muscovites – along with their counterparts in seven other major Russian cities – massed on 13 January to jam the coup machinery with their bodies.[12] As Boris El'tsin appealed to Russian officers and soldiers to disobey orders to turn their weapons against peaceful civilians,[13] DemRossiya launched a political strike demanding the immediate resignation of the Soviet president, Cabinet of Ministers and legislature. Within three days, fifty enterprises and institutions in Moscow had joined it.[14] By 20 January, strike committees in 110 enterprises publicly endorsed DemRossiya's demands, adding their numbers to its 700,000-person show of force in Moscow and to comparable actions that day in twenty-six other Russian cities.[15] The insurgency triggered by Soviet restoration snowballed through the winter, enlisting Russia's miners as well as millions of workers in other sectors (often with the support of the official trade unions) using strikes and mass meetings to press their demand for the dissolution of the Soviet state and the transfer of power to the union-republics.[16] Thus mobilized, these forces would play a decisive role in foiling the legislative coup mounted by the party-state against El'tsin in late March.

'War of laws'

The expression 'war of laws' captured in oxymoronic fashion the status of legal relations with the Soviet order: law was a medium for the expression of personalized authority structures, no more and no less. As these authority structures disaggregated in the late Soviet period, sections of the state captured by groups ascendant on the early waves of popular mobilization utilized the formal mechanisms of law to stake out their own claims. These were met by a series of annulling acts, decrees and decisions from the central authorities which, when ignored or annulled themselves, spiralled into battles over sovereignty expressed as a war of laws.[17]

The Russian state was already well practised in this peculiar martial art by the time that the Soviet coup was launched in the Baltic. In autumn of 1990, its Supreme Soviet passed a number of laws making legal acts of the USSR conditional on the approval of the corresponding branches of the Russian government and establishing private enterprise rights and banking prerogatives sharply at odds with all-union legislation.[18] Moreover, Russia had concluded a number of political, economic and civil treaties with most union-republics, bypassing the central authorities entirely.[19] Gorbachev's efforts to bring this war of laws to an end by concluding a new 'Union Treaty' defining the rights and obligations of members of the federal system[20] was rejected wholesale by DemRossiya[21] and stood little chance of a better reception from the Russian government as long as El'tsin was in charge. Accordingly, the Soviet leadership devised a two-fold strategy to clear away the obstacles: a unionwide referendum on the *idea* of 'renewing' the federal system; and an attempt in the Russian parliament to remove El'tsin from the leadership. These set the stage for endgame in the struggle between Russia and the USSR already previewed by the actions of the Russian and Soviet leaders during the Baltic *coup*. On January 13 and 14, El'tsin had signed with the leaders of the Baltic governments in Tallinn a joint statement condemning the actions of the USSR[22] and pledging mutual assistance against threats from the Soviet government.[23] Two days later, Gorbachev had appeared before the USSR's Supreme Soviet to recommend suspension of the country's six-month-old law guaranteeing press freedom.[24]

The struggle to control communications

Control of mass communications was, of course, vital to the *coup* strategy, and Gorbachev's recommendation derived its significance from that fact. Two points would pertain, here. First, the Law on the Press had been a symbolic victory for press freedom that encouraged publishers and journalists to assert their newly codified rights. But it did not itself ensure press freedom. Not only had the Commission on the Press formed by the USSR's Supreme Soviet been docile in this area,[25] but the Soviet government never provided the law with an enforcement mechanism.[26] Consequently, the ability to exercise the rights proclaimed in law hinged in the first instance on official registration with the authorities, a process that for many involved a protracted, and often unsuccessful, struggle.[27] Those denied registration by the USSR's State Committee on Publications could turn to a more hospitable Russian Ministry of the Press and Mass Communications, but the disposition of administrators, rather than juridical relations, governed the process in either case.[28] Second, the Soviet government used a variety of means to curtail or extinguish those independent sources of information legally functioning in Russia.

With respect to electronic media, the appointment of Leonid Kravchenko to head the USSR's State Committee on Television and Radio (Gosteleradio) inaugurated a return to pre-glasnost conditions. In accord with his philosophy that 'the interests of state power must be first for television, and only after that [those] of the people',[29] Kravchenko substituted for lively public affairs programming a combination of chauvinism and schmaltz. Programmes such as *Vzglad*, whose free-wheeling discussions had made it the country's most popular weekly show, were cancelled; a Brezhnevian forgery appeared in its place,[30] pending the advent of Aleksandr Nevzorov's *Nashi* ('Ours') that broadcast unadorned Russian nationalism to a mass audience for the first time in the history of the USSR. Official registration provided protection neither for the independent news agency Interfaks – evicted from its premises by Gosteleradio which confiscated its property as well[31] – nor for Radio Rossiya and Mayak whose air time was cut and whose broadcasts were jammed in many areas.[32]

For print media, the authorities used a number of measures to restrict, if not extinguish, free expression. Its agencies refused to print certain registered newspapers, contractual obligations notwithstanding.[33] Its distribution network, Soyuzpechat, often refused to handle others[34] or, when they did, simply warehoused, and later returned, them as 'unsold'.[35] Police harassment of street vendors,[36] arson[37] and assassination[38] also occurred. But the most effective means to contain the printed word was to control access to the paper on which it would appear. Thus a multi-tiered pricing system was introduced whereby the party-state press purchased newsprint at 10 per cent of the rate available to independents, who saw their costs for paper climb by a factor of fifty during the first year of formal press freedom,[39] forcing either abbreviated print runs and less frequent – or, in some cases, full suspension of – publication. Rather than press freedom, a patronage arrangement prevailed in publishing whereby organs of the party-state enjoyed incomparable advantages – possession of nearly all print facilities, allocations of the lion's share of newsprint at reduced rates, immunity from taxes and unimpeded distribution – that they would often parlay through commercial operations and black market ties into handsome profits for themselves and associates.[40] This appropriation of state offices, and the corrupt practices that stemmed from it, was, of course, completely consistent with the Soviet order's basis in weak structures and strong (personal) ties, an observation sustained by the fact that many of Russia's democrats, now ensconced in their own offices, behaved in comparable fashion. Commercial operations blossomed inside the state organizations that the democrats controlled;[41] loyalty was expected from those publications that they sponsored;[42] no distinctions were drawn between 'state' and 'political' functions when it came to the use of resources or personnel.[43] Certainly the scale of these practices was vastly reduced among the democrats, if only for the reason that their access to state resources was still quite limited. At this juncture it would be important to note, however, that democrats were not distinguished from communists by some qualitatively different set of political practices. Patronage and appropriation of office were common to both. Rather, the principal distinctions consisted in the fact that the democratic forces had assumed an anti-communist identity symbolically mediated by those markers – freedom, rule-of-law and so forth – antagonistic to the presumed essence of the Soviet regime. Communist restoration validated and vastly reinforced this identity, sharpening its image of the opponent, confronting it with outrageous actions to which it was compelled to respond, offering it the opportunity to enact its identity construct in various modes of resistance.

In the struggle to control the means of communication, this resistance was considerable. The Russian government began publishing its own daily, *Rossiiskaya gazeta*, in November 1990 and later added *Rossiiskii vestnik* and the weekly *Rossiya*. It also registered scores of small, independent publications. The Moscow city soviet underwrote two new daily newspapers in late 1990 (*Kuranty* and *Nezavisimaya gazeta*) and their Leningrad counterparts did the same for *Nevskoe vremya* in early 1991. Journalists organized their own independent union in September 1990 and began publishing a weekly (*Golos*) in 1991 devoted primarily to exposing the lies and disinformation purveyed in the Soviet mass media, especially Gosteleradio[44] whose director the journalists expelled from their union in April.[45] For their part, the Cinematographer's Union had been striking Soviet TV since February.[46] At *Izvestiya*, paragon of 'responsible' establishment journalism in the USSR, a battle for control of the editorial board broke out in January 1991, pitting the newspaper's staff against the USSR's Supreme Soviet whose committees and commissions had been duly, if illegally, purged by Chairperson Luk'yanov of their remaining democrats.[47] Laws, decrees, petitions and hunger strikes settled nothing. But the defeat of the August *coup* provided *Izvestiya* with a new patron, the Russian government, and the newspaper duly employed its 'independence' on its behalf. The sustained attempts begun by Russia's Supreme Soviet in April 1992 to reappropriate *Izvestiya* along with the ensuing legal battles and court cases remind us of the continuity of structural relations between the

Soviet and post-Soviet periods, highlighting the subordination of both legal relations and professional journalism to the prevailing configuration of state power.[48]

From resistance to revolution

Restoration foiled

In March 1991, the Russian legislature became the focus of the Soviet *coup*. An extraordinary Third Congress of People's Deputies was called into session by a petition effort orchestrated by the *nomenklatura* for the sole purpose of hearing a report from Chairperson El'tsin, a ritual portending his planned removal from that office.[49] Following El'tsin's televised remarks on 19 February calling for Gorbachev's immediate resignation, the 'dump-El'tsin' campaign gathered more momentum as six members of the presidium of Russia's Supreme Soviet published an open letter calling for his dismissal.[50] As the 28 March opening approached, Gorbachev proclaimed a state of emergency in Moscow, forbad political meetings, placed the police under the direct authority of Pugo's Ministry of Internal Affairs and flooded the city with 50,000 troops in battle dress.[51] Although all the restorationist pieces appeared to be in place, the Third Congress reversed the *coup*'s direction entirely and resulted in a resounding victory for El'tsin and the democratic movement.

To mark the Congress's opening, DemRossiya and Moscow's Union of Labour Collectives staged mass demonstrations at city centre, defying the ban imposed by the Soviet authorities and raising a million voices in support of El'tsin. This action made a critical difference inside the Congress itself which passed by a margin of one vote a resolution demanding the cancellation of the state of emergency. Proceedings were then adjourned while deputies left for the streets to place their bodies between the troops and the demonstrators[52] physically enacting the very relations among state, political and civil society as specified in our analytic model (see Table 1.1). When the Congress reconvened, momentum had shifted decisively behind El'tsin and the democrats. Not only did the urgency of the hour resolidify their fragmented voting bloc, but the Communists of Russia faction, which had been the decisive force at the Congress's last meeting in December, crumbled.[53] The shift in the voting balance resulted from Aleksandr Rutskoi's *coup de théâtre*: although a leader of Communists of Russia and a member of the RKP's Central Committee, Rutskoi turned on his erstwhile colleagues, denounced their attempts to discredit El'tsin and DemRossiya and marched his 179 supporters – calling themselves 'Communists for Democracy' – over to the El'tsin column.[54] This reshuffling of parliamentary alignments betrayed the presence of a new force in the legislature: public opinion. While association with El'tsin, unquestionably the country's most popular political figure,[55] might aid one's political career, connections with his restorationist foes – whose ratings were disastrous – was bound to hurt.[56]

El'tsin's victory at this Congress was consummated by its endorsement of his proposal – backed by his threat to resign – to set 12 June as the date for elections to the Russian presidency. This event speaks volumes about the establishment of that office and its significance for Russian politics. By delaying convention of the Third Congress for some three weeks, El'tsin and supporters had allowed the 17 March all-union referendum to take place first. They had piggy-backed onto it their own question, asking voters whether they favoured 'the introduction of the position of President of the RSFSR, elected by universal suffrage?' At the First Congress, deputies from across the political spectrum would have answered that question in the affirmative. However, as the likely surname of a Russian president became clear, things changed dramatically. Just as Communists of Russia reversed themselves on the issue, sandbagging initiatives to establish the office at the Second Congress,[57] so DemRossiya could warn the Third Congress that since 70 per cent of the voters had endorsed the office of the presidency in the referendum, they now had no right to depose El'tsin.[58] At that Congress, proposals to establish the presidency were thrice defeated prior to El'tsin's threat to resign, suggesting again that the legislature depended for its internal organization on his ability to frame issues in sharply conflictive terms, solidifying otherwise amorphous voting blocs around either/or alternatives.[59] As such, the Russian presidency before its legal inception was already 'El'tsin's presidency'; not only an identification of an institution with an individual, but the virtual disappearance of the institution behind the person himself.[60]

Presidential election

To siphon off as many votes as possible from El'tsin and thus force a run off that might delay a final result till, perhaps, autumn, the party-state fielded five candidates to run against him. To no avail: El'tsin captured 57.3 per cent of the vote on the first round.[61] This result undoubtedly reflected his broad popularity in Russia, boosted by his battles with Gorbachev[62] and resonant with the oscillating images that he projected at the time as a 'man of action' in his element among the people yet strong enough to bear alone the burdens of national leadership.[63] El'tsin's candidacy may also have benefited some by his selection of Rutskoi as his running mate, but ambiguities surround that question.[64] Above all, his first-round win was brought about by the national campaign waged by DemRossiya that poured 150,000 activists into the effort: collecting nomination signatures, setting up pickets at metro stations and in public squares, distributing leaflets in neighbourhoods and factories, canvassing door to door, staging mass rallies and poll-watching on election day. In return for their labours, DemRossiya received nothing save the satisfaction of victory.

The relationship between El'tsin and DemRossiya – what we have described, above, as leadership *outside* the organization – was critical for the development of Russian politics. If the presidency was less an institution than a popular consecration of El'tsin's personal authority, then the distance put by El'tsin between himself and his organizational base would mean that the president's political responsibilities were every bit as weak as his legal ones. Since its organization as a movement, El'tsin had been meeting with DemRossiya's leadership to map political strategy.[65] After his televised address of 19 February in which he called for the creation of a 'powerful party' to unite all democratic forces, he dropped this project directly in their laps.[66] However, he showed no indication that he would lead, or even join, such a party.[67] To make matters worse, in April – once DemRossiya had grown into this role and was mounting protests and political strikes nationwide in hope of bringing down the communist order there and then – El'tsin pulled the rug from under them by cutting a deal with Gorbachev that commenced negotiations with eight other republics (the 'nine-plus-one' process) to rescue the federal union and restore civil peace. While his presidential bid depended entirely on DemRossiya for mounting an election campaign, El'tsin named their opponent Rutskoi, without bothering to inform, much less consult with, his organized base of support. Even more remarkable, however, was the fact that DemRossiya – at the peak of its power – made no demands on 'their' candidate.[68] This departure from 'normal' politics was mediated in the democratic camp by its established discourse of crisis and the absence of alternatives. For instance, Sergei Yushenkov, having outlined his deep disagreement with El'tsin's actions in a number of critical areas, explained that without immediate, radical action 'we will have to continue to drag out our miserable existence under the old Bolshevik power structures because Boris El'tsin may be a good man or bad but there is no other real candidate of the democratic forces. And . . . if we remain in the present condition? Chaos, full-blown crisis and all the more real are the chances for military dictatorship.'[69] The leader's avoidance of responsibility to his base, along with the latter's reluctance to demand it, can be counted as the second missed opportunity to provide structure to Russian political society. It directly contributed to DemRossiya's disintegration,[70] to the power struggle between executive and legislature in communism's aftermath and to the fall of the first Russian republic.

El'tsin's election as president heralded the end of the communist system in Russia. Toward that end, he quickly set in motion two processes: building up Russia's state apparatus and tearing down that of the Communist Party. The former had in fact been under way since summer of 1990 when El'tsin began assembling various policy-making organs. These not only operated at great remove from the legislature but, in terms of membership and patterns of influence, they amounted to another personalization of power: networks formed around El'tsin when he was party boss in Sverdlosk and Moscow, others from the democratic movement coopted into his administration.[71] Their authority derived from El'tsin's; their responsibilities were to him. A month after assuming the presidency, El'tsin established by decree the rudiments of an executive apparatus that would rapidly grow to dominate politics and government in Russia. In its first incarnation at federal level, it consisted of: the State Council of the RSFSR, a policy group headed by Gennadii Burbulis composed of the president, vice-president, prime minister and six other top members of the government; the Administration of the President that included the heads of the various apparatuses of government functioning as administrative coordinators for presidential rule; and the Council of the Federation and Affairs of the Territories which, along with the Control Commission, would superintend the implementation of presidential rule in the country's regions.[72] In this last respect, El'tsin's plan called for two new offices. One was 'presidential representatives', initially a communist proposal that appealed to Gorbachev's desire to end the war of laws by dispatching a plenipotentiary to each region to ensure the implementation of the president's policy.[73] El'tsin created the office of his representatives some two weeks before he was elected president.[74] The other was 'head of administration', at first intended as the top administrative official elected in each subnational government – and, as such, endorsed by DemRossiya[75] – and realized in June via presidential decrees recognizing the elected mayors of Moscow, St Petersburg and Severnodvinsk as heads of administration in those cities.[76] Moscow's and St Petersburg's mayors – Popov and Sobchak – were awarded extensive powers over city government by resolutions issued by the presidium of Russia's Supreme Soviet that reduced the role of their corresponding soviets to approval of the budget.[77] Popov extended his authority still more during the August *coup*, transferring to the ten prefects that he appointed to newly created sub-regions[78] the entire stock and personnel of the capital's thirty-three district soviets.[79] Although the legal standing of heads of administration remained unsteady, since the July Congress of People's Deputies rejected the draft legislation put before them on this score,[80] El'tsin would unilaterally push ahead with his project in the wake of the August *coup*, thereby reconfiguring power relations in the Russian state and changing its relations to political society.

The attack on the Communist Party apparatus was launched via a presidential decree issued on 20 July that – with the exception of certain of the USSR's governmental bodies operating on Russian soil[81] – required all party organizations formed in enterprises or institutions to be dissolved within two weeks.[82] 'Departization', as this measure was called, aimed to secure the power and authority of the Russian state by ripping the rival structures of the communist order out at their roots. El'tsin's minister of justice, Nikolai Fedorov, explained that the mandate won by El'tsin that spring provided the authority for this decree,[83] yet its provisions contradicted existing Russian law,[84] and the USSR's Committee of Constitutional Oversight declared it null and void.[85] None the less, departization steamed ahead with the appointment of commissions in various localities to enforce compliance.[86] Results were mixed. Many Communist Party organizations voluntarily dissolved themselves at factory level,[87] but the territorial apparatus dug in its heels, threatened to go underground[88] and appealed to the Soviet president for relief.[89] The stakes here were very high, for at a stroke departization removed some 30 per cent of the party apparatus from the state payroll.[90] Simultaneously, DemRossiya launched a petition drive for a referendum on nationalizing the CPSU's property in Russia. Half of the necessary one million signatures had been gathered in Leningrad alone,[91] while in Moscow the petition campaign was restarted after the half-million signatures collected there had been incinerated in the 16 May bombing of DemRossiya's headquarters.[92] If departization would chop the party-state's power structure off at the knees, then nationalizing the CPSU's property would crush its organizational spine.

Centrists without a centre

Restoration and revolution had polarized Russia's political field, producing thereby a vacant 'centre' whose putative existence was reinforced by the suspension of hostilities between Russia and the USSR as the 'nine-plus-one' process went forward. But there was no centre to occupy, a fact illustrated by June's presidential race in which the lone centrist candidate, Bakatin, finished last with a mere 3.4 per cent of the vote. Indeed, the absence of a centre derived from the very structure of political activity in this period: on one hand, the party-state's desperate attempts to save the Soviet order by renewing the use of its instruments of domination – physical coercion and control of communications; on the other, resistance to those same attempts. On this field, politics appeared, in common journalistic parlance, as 'Olympian battles', titanic struggles at the heights of state power with the fate of an anxious nation hanging in the balance. These contests were framed by the cultural stereotypes of heroism, honour and pride. They were frozen on the faces of the guards at the Lenin mausoleum and just as much on those of the defenders of the White House in August, posing on the barricades for snapshots to record their moment of triumph. They had been enacted at countless legislative sessions broadcast over television and so had become the recognizable form of serious political engagement. The structure of the political field as well as the prevailing practices on it precluded a centre. All the same, splinters from both DemRossiya and the CPSU sought to create one.

Although their immediate objective proved illusory, the organizations created in communism's twilight would for the most part survive its collapse, jockeying for position around a no less illusory centre on the field of post-communist politics.[93] Among those notables lending their efforts to the centrist cause, Rutskoi, the right-wing communist-turned-democrat, was a central actor. Rutskoi had attempted to straddle the chasm separating communists from democrats as long as it was there to straddle, a posture advertised by the names borne by the legislative faction that he organized and the extra-parliamentary network (in fact, that section of the Democratic Platform that did not leave the Communist Party in 1990) adjoined to it: 'Communists for Democracy' and 'Democratic Movement of Communists', respectively. Throughout, Rutskoi and his organizational leader, Vasilii Lipitskii, contended that remaining in the CPSU in order to reform it would place its organizational and resource base at the disposal of 'responsible' reformist forces.[94] This version of centrism persisted even after they were expelled from the RKP in August, since their new Democratic Party of Communists of Russia claimed to be a constituent member of the CPSU.[95] When the CPSU had disappeared as well, the would-be centre migrated (temporarily) to the democratic camp, Rutskoi announcing his a 'pro-presidential' party.[96] Renamed in October 1991 the People's Party of Free Russia, it soon joined one of the opposition blocs arrayed against El'tsin and his government, but displayed a certain consistency by selecting the centrist one.

Rutskoi also collaborated with the remnants of perestroika's vanguard – whom Gorbachev had deserted during the first phase of the low-intensity *coup* – to found in July another would-be centrist organization, the Movement for Democratic Reform (MDR). Despite its name, the MDR was not a movement at all but the first attempt to field a political organization by one of the networks in control of government offices.[97] Besides Rutskoi, its top leaders included mayors Popov and Sobchak, former Politburo members Eduard Shevardnadze and Aleksandr Ya-kovlev, Russian Prime Minister Ivan Silaev, spokespersons for state industry Arkadii Vol'skii and Aleksandr Vladislavlev, and other high office holders and advisers associated with the liberal wing of the CPSU or the moderate wing of DemRossiya.[98] Shopping for an organizational base, they had first turned to the Democratic Party of Russia (DPR)[99] before inviting DemRossiya to join their movement, an invitation interpreted by the latter as an attempt simply to annex their membership and organization.[100] Among DemRossiya's constituent parties, only the Republican Party of Russia (RPR) broke ranks and affiliated temporarily with the MDR.[101] Thus the new centrist organization remained a top-heavy amalgam of notables, attracting not the following that they had anticipated but the interested indifference of rivals on the political field who had already made niches for themselves that they were intent on expanding.[102] Within a matter of months, however, both the DPR and DemRossiya would form coalitions with sections of MDR spun off by its disintegration. These and other[103] organizational initiatives on the eve of the August *coup* bore frenetic witness to the tumult and uncertainty attending the final days of the communist order in Russia: projects launched amid abundant signs that the conditions on which they were predicated were vanishing.

Showdown

Despite the shock, the early morning broadcast on 19 August that a State Committee for the State of Emergency (SCSE) had assumed power in the USSR did not come as a surprise. In July the CPSU's official journal had opened its pages to I. I. Antonovich – RKP secretary and leading ideologue – who reprised his party's call for a 'committee of national salvation' with an appeal for a union of socialist and patriotic forces to stop the destruction of 'our Fatherland' wrought by DemRos-siya.[104] In that same month, *Sovetskaya Rossiya* published 'A Word to the People', a more grandiloquent manifesto signed by twelve leaders of those socialist and patriotic forces referenced by Antonovich (three of whom would be included in the SCSE) that demanded the immediate introduction of emergency rule.[105] Two days prior to its imposition, one signator, Aleksandr Prokhanov, made similar pronouncements over Radio Moscow while his liberal counterpart, Aleksandr Yakovlev, publicly warned of a *coup*'s imminence.[106] The El'tsin government had a plan to resist it,[107] just as many democratic activists had grown accustomed to its eventuality, interpreting certain commonplaces – such as telephone lines suddenly going dead – as a possible sign that a *coup* had begun.[108]

Perhaps the clearest indication that Soviet restoration was unprepared to countenance Russia's revolution was the series of positions taken by the USSR's government and Supreme Soviet in blatant contradiction to the line that Gorbachev had (at least publicly) adopted after a million Muscovites and a majority of Russia's legislators had foiled the attempt to unseat El'tsin in March. As Yurii Kon outlined the matter on the eve of the August *putsch*, since June Gorbachev's Cabinet of Ministers had not only been issuing decrees that nullified those of their formal superior, but Prime Minister Valentin Pavlov publicly justified this practice of subverting Gorbachev's authority at an 13 August press conference.[109] For its part, the Supreme Soviet detected mortal danger in the 'nine-plus-one' process and the new federal arrangement that it had produced.[110] Concerned for the survival of the USSR and, therefore, their own positions, the deputies seemed fully prepared to grant Pavlov's 17 June request for emergency powers to restore order in the country by putting paid to Russian sovereignty and that of the other republics. This ploy was apparently only foiled by an alert from the legislature that reached Gavriil Popov who relayed it to US Ambassador Jack Matlock, whence by secure telephone lines to US President Bush who, by informing Gorbachev of the *coup* then under way, robbed him of his accustomed deniability and prompted his intervention to secure that last political asset which he possessed: his international reputation as a democratic leader.[111]

Was Gorbachev, indeed, party to this restorationist cabal that formally would have decoupled his office from a government awarded extraordinary powers and, apparently, prepared to take drastic measures to save the Soviet state? Was he party to the August *coup* itself, conveniently cloistered in his villa, leaving the dirty work of restoration to others? The glaring inconsistencies in his subsequent denials would only fuel suspicions that he was.[112] However, as John Dunlop has noted, a conclusive answer to these and related questions may ever escape us, since the Russian government's prosecution of the entire affair relied on a legal premise – an 'anti-constitutional' seizure of power – that would have been compromised were it shown that the Soviet president had approved the SCSE's actions. A more aggressive investigation mounted by a commission of the Russian Supreme Soviet was terminated prematurely, an early victim of post-communist power struggles.[113] Faced with these lacunae at the very centre of the August *coup*, we shall not attempt to add to the literature on its anatomy.[114] Instead, we place the event within the categories of our model and examine its significance both for the immediate problematic of restoration and revolution and for the larger issue of Russia's political rebirth.

As far as the Soviet state was concerned, the *coup* succeeded. With the exception of the absent president and two uncooperative ministers, all its central institutions and officers either openly endorsed the SCSE's seizure of power or tacitly consented to it.[115] The SCSE also drew support from the CPSU apparatus and from those regional soviets where it had reproduced itself as the governing elite in the 1990 elections,[116] although in a few regions a mobilized citizenry discouraged any expression of pro-*coup* sentiment.[117] Initially, the military appeared to have been on board, but loyalties quickly unravelled in that quarter.[118] Indicatively, no effective public manifestations of support were organized.[119] From the perspective of political organization, the *putsch* represented the culmination of the restoration that had begun in autumn: *nomenklatura* rule resting solely on the agencies of state violence.

The *coup*'s failure cannot be attributed to a lack of resolve on the part of the SCSE to achieve its ends by violent means. In anticipation of civil resistance, some 300,000 warrants had been delivered to the Moscow Commandant in the small hours of August 19, each with a large blank spot for inscribing the name of the unfortunate.[120] The KGB had also prepared lists of individuals to be incarcerated immediately, although the length of these lists remains unclear.[121] Moreover, the order to seize the seat of resistance – the Russian White House – was given more than once, despite the fact that its execution would have meant a bloodbath. Rather, failure was procured by the weak structures of the Soviet order, represented in the first instance by the incompetence of the plotters. The upper echelon of both the KGB and the Ministry of Internal Affairs had been packed with Communist Party careerists, abjectly dependent on professionals at lower levels for the operational functioning of their agencies. Ordinarily, this had presented no serious problems – professionals did the work. But the secrecy required to stage a *coup* interrupted that pattern, leaving operational issues in hands that would botch the effort.[122] In addition to such fatal omissions as leaving telephone and fax lines open, orders were sloppily prepared, thus opening ample room for discretion on the part of those expected to carry them out. As a result, armed KGB units belatedly dispatched to seize the White House would reconnoitre, reinterpret their instructions and return to base,[123] while the KGB itself seemed to have sat on its hands[124] or, in a few cases, actively lent them to the Russian resistance.[125] This breakdown on the side of the civilian organizers provided the time and space to military commanders to reinterpret their own instructions and to reconfigure their own loyalties, accounting in part for the Russian government's success in winning them over.

With respect to the communicative dimension of the *coup*, matters for its principals were even worse. The plan seemed simple enough: shut down all mass communications not in tune with the SCSE; use the remaining ones – Central Television, TASS and a number of newspapers (*Pravda, Izvestiya, Sovetskaya Rossiya* and others) – to convey at least the futility of resistance to, if not foster active support for, the USSR's new government. In addition to failing in the first endeavour, the *coup* forces bungled the second one. From their vapid 'Appeal to the Soviet People' that crowded all functioning media outlets on 19 August to that evening's SCSE news conference, the public was treated to stale prose, self-incriminating statements and the spectacle of the press's open ridicule of the junta, amplified by camera shots of the new president's trembling hands.[126] Moreover, administrative incompetence enabled the resistance's message to reach a mass audience over those 'official' news outlets still functioning. Perhaps the most amazing episode in this respect took place on the news programme *Vremya* on the first evening of the *coup*. Following a few soothing spots suggesting that order and tranquillity now prevailed in the country, footage appeared of DemRossiya's march from Manege Square to the White House, El'tsin delivering his famous 'Appeal to the citizens of Russia' from atop a tank there and of interviews with those erecting barricades around the building, informing viewers that 'Vilnius had taught us [what to do]', and beckoning them with hands on hearts to assemble there in defence of Russia.[127]

From the perspective of organization, the Russian government and its supporters fared no better than the SCSE; they simply profited from the latter's blunders. Their defence of the White House was scarcely formidable in material terms: a few tanks perched outside, lacking firing mechanisms and ammunition; a gaggle of lightly armed Moscow OMON and police within, along with a few soldiers, Afghan veterans and private detectives; barricades tossed together with materials secured from a nearby construction site, representing perhaps two minutes' work for an assaulting tank or bulldozer. In his 'Appeal', El'tsin had called for a general strike to face down the junta, and this summons resounded periodically in speeches delivered from the back balcony of the White House to the crowd assembled below. But no one in authority did anything to stimulate or coordinate strike actions.[128] DemRossiya immediately put out the word for a public demonstration, but confusion among the organizers resulting in splitting it between two sites instead of massing at one.[129]

From the perspective of communication, however, this miscue proved fortunate. By midday, the 10,000–15,000 Muscovites gathered on Manege Square were busy fraternizing with the thousands of troops taking up positions there, thus commencing a withering psychological offensive whose heavy weaponry was surely the face-to-face admonishments delivered to the soldiers by many a Moscow babushka: 'Does your mother know what you're doing?' 'Are you going to shoot us? No, I don't think you will, but you look hungry. Here, I have some eggs.'[130] By 2:00 p.m., word had reached this rally that the plan had been to mass at the White House, and so the 80,000 assembled by then marched two miles down New Arbat street to that destination in critically visible mass defiance of the state of emergency.[131] This episode was the first significant communicative blow struck against the junta. Its message echoed immediately around Moscow and was broadcast nationwide that evening via *Vremya*'s inadvertent inclusion of that footage in its transmission.

Communication would prove the key to the outcome. We might examine that question by proceeding along the concentric communicative circles that comprised Russia's resistance to the SCSE. At the centre, of course, stood El'tsin projecting classically Russian images of the leader,[132] issuing proclamations which – albeit purely symbolic – were unmistakably effective in reinforcing the reality of that 'imagined community', Russia, all of whose institutions he declared subordinate solely to the Russian government. In so doing, he invited an uncertain and divided military over to Russia's side; inspiring them, as it were, not to mutiny but – on the contrary – to come to the defence of their homeland.

Along the next ring, we might place those 250 or so deputies who remained in the White House during the siege. When circumstances required, some staged peaceful forays on columns of tanks and APCs dispatched against them, explaining the situation – copies of the constitution in hand – to commanding officers, either turning them back or bringing them over to their side.[133] Many took copies of El'tsin's 'Appeal' to airports and railway stations, whence they could be disseminated around the country. Others worked the telephones and fax machines and organized radio transmission from inside the White House.[134] Those with party affiliation kept a two-way channel going between the White House and their colleagues elsewhere in the capital, who also relayed information to and from their counterparts in the provinces.[135] The temporary pairing of the RPR and MDR proved fortuitous in this respect, coupling the former's network of activists with the latter's bank of equipment and access to premises. The communications system thus established brought information on such things as troop movements and resistance organization in key regions where the RPR had capable organizers, while the link to their colleagues at the centre underscored the national significance of local acts.[136] Similarly, the DPR was intensely active. Its members in some 500 cities and towns were connected by telephone and fax with the party's central offices, accounting for a huge portion of the information travelling between Moscow and the provinces during the *coup*.[137]

Around the next ring were the journalists, divided into four broad categories by the SCSE's ban on independent mass media. The first group consisted of those working in agencies sanctioned by the junta and serving as its mouthpiece. The second group also worked in these agencies but stepped outside of assigned tasks and expectations to contribute subversive information to official news reporting, as we have seen in the case of some of Central Television's coverage of events.[138] *Izvestiya*, alone among those nine dailies in the capital permitted to function by the SCSE, played an especially important role, publishing a condensed version of El'tsin's 'Appeal' in its 20 August number that informed the entire nation of the very resistance that the junta sought to conceal. In Moscow, *Izvestiya*'s staff threw spanners into the military machinery, putting out leaflets that they distributed to the troops clogging city centre, informing them of El'tsin's 'Appeal' and urging them to refrain from violence against their fellow countrymen.[139] The third group were those working in cities outside the control of SCSE and its local supporters.[140] In Novosibirsk and Yaroslav, for instance, regional publications placed their facilities at the disposal of their embattled colleagues in the capital.[141] Since the military seizure of Leningrad was thwarted early on, that city's television, radio and press – especially the Union of Journalists' *Chas pik* – functioned freely and doubtless contributed to the massive public demonstrations of resistance mobilized in that city.

But the critical contribution to the *coup*'s defeat was made by those in the fourth group, Moscow journalists who defied the SCSE. Those at Interfaks and Postfaktum simply ignored the order to cease operations, delivered on the morning of 19 August by armed men. Rather, they linked their national networks of correspondents to the White House's information centre, supplying information and relaying messages for the duration of the *coup*.[142] Much of this information was broadcast in the capital over radio *Ekho Moskvy*, transmitting clandestinely from a series of sites, and by the makeshift 'Radio White House' transmitting from the roof of its namesake. Many print journalists also refused to be silenced and continued to function during the *coup*, despite the menacing presence of APC's ringing their premises. They put out both agitational flyers and limited editions in photocopy that were plastered on the walls of metro stations and at other intersections of pedestrian traffic, keeping millions of Muscovites informed of events and summoning them to the defence of Russia's government. The most notable achievement along these lines was the publication of *Obshchaya gazeta* – a joint effort undertaken by eleven banned newspapers to run the information blockade – whose first four-page edition put out on the *coup*'s second day was visible on the walls of innumerable metro stations in Moscow and other large cities. Six- and then eight-page editions followed, now on standard typeset.[143]

The journalists' acts of resistance fused seamlessly with those on the last of our concentric circles, the mobilized population. Indeed, resistance erased conventional classifications and produced for the moment a synthesis of political and civil society. Political parties gathered news while journalists composed and distributed agitational flyers; the individual instructing his comrades on the proper way to erect a barricade or on how to form up in human chains may have been a party activist, an Afghan veteran, a private detective or simply a student or worker responding to the exigencies of the moment. It was this synthesis that created those tactile presences fixing and reinforcing the reality of national resistance: citizens anxiously crowded around newspapers posted in public places; individuals leafleting the many thousands of soldiers in the capital, often attempting to block the movement of their tanks with their bodies, just as often conversing amiably with them as their children played atop those same tanks; tens of thousands in vigil around the White House, cheering the sounds of some radio bulletin boomed out by loudspeakers. This reality was in many respects carnivalesque – a commodity brokers' street demonstration that stopped at McDonald's *en route* to the White House to procure rations for its defenders, thousands of young people around the barricades reproducing scenes reminiscent of outdoor rock festivals – but certainly neither carefree nor wanting in that clarity of purpose demanded by the situation. Those who came to the defence of the White House had come with the knowledge that death lay there. That realization was written especially vividly on fear-braced faces during the critical night of 20–1 August when some movement or commotion near the circumference of the barricades would set off shouts that skipped through the crowd with lightning speed: 'They've come!' 'The attack has started!' 'They're already shooting!' The carnival was thus saturated with the macabre, death as near and palpable as the heavy sky dropping its gentle rain. Miraculously, it came but thrice.[144]

The drama enacted at the White House represented a relentless assault on the order that the SCSE had sought to impose, breaking chains-of-command, severing formal allegiances and insistently dissuading armed men in uniform from discharging their appointed tasks. Perhaps a million persons took some part in breathing life into it.[145] Why did they risk so much to do so? Adopting Craig Calhoun's insightful analysis of a comparable phenomenon (the readiness of Chinese students to face massacre at Tiananmen Square), we would answer that the lived experience of the identities that they had assumed prevented them from not (re)enacting those identities at the critical hour in precisely the spot where it mattered.[146] Identity – that which would require 'me' to behave like 'me' – for those in Russia's democratic movement had been constructed in binary opposition to the communist order and to all things associated with it. At mass meetings, the word most frequently hurled against that order had been 'shame'. It came from the orators, it appeared on innumerable placards and, at the mention of some party-state official and his latest chicanery or malevolence, it welled up spontaneously from the crowd in choruses of opprobrium: '*Po-zór* [shame], *po-zór, po-zór* . . . ' Those who refer to others with this word reflexively mark themselves as 'honourable', as those who recognize and condemn those who are 'shameful'. To recall that this ritual of collective shaming had been taking place regularly in Moscow for nearly a year would be to apprehend something about its participants: how they had taken their own 'walks out onto the square' and identified themselves as the honourable ones. Certainly, honour was not the only factor propelling people to the barricades. Adventure was there, so was curiosity and the sense of fulfilment to be had by taking part in a manifestly historic moment. Yet none of those impulses could substitute for the cumulative effect of resistance to the low-intensity *coup* and the particular personal–collective identity that had been galvanized by it.

The collapse of the SCSE on 21 August confirmed that Russia's structures of resistance had become stronger than the order that they opposed. At the moment of triumph, the Russian state, political and civil society seemed to form a seamless whole, confident and eager to set about the task of building that normal, civilized society so often contrasted with the now-dead communist order. Expectedly, that moment was but a moment. More tellingly, the configuration assumed by the Russian political system during its struggle with communist restoration would reproduce that struggle within state and political society, thus already foreshadowing the conflict that would break out among the victors and consume both the republic that they founded and the White House where they had defended it.

Part IV

Ground up: politics in post-communist Russia

The word-play in this part's title both underscores the perspective that we have employed to frame Russia's political rebirth and suggests something about the fate of those forces in political society that brought it about. On one hand, our interpretation of the recovery of political life – as much as it may have depended in its early stages on certain dispensations issued by the Gorbachev leadership – has emphasized the fact that it was a mass phenomenon involving countless choices, risks, sacrifices and acts of courage by individuals and groups of people. Politics, that is, came from the 'ground up'. On the other, the particular path followed by political society, the path of struggle against the Soviet party-state, also shaped its institutions and its relations with the Russian state in critical and, perhaps, fatal ways. In the end, those forces accounting for Russia's political rebirth have been 'ground up' themselves; defeated, coopted or marginalized by the executive apparatus of the state.

Organized as a reverse-order counterpart to Part I, the chapters here are laid out along diachronic and synchronic lines. The narrative in Chapter 11 traces political society's division to the statist/monetarist strategy of transformation adopted by Russia's post-communist leadership. Ironically, this strategy progressively undermined the coherence of state institutions while it simultaneously contributed to the political capital of the most extreme forces arrayed against the government. The violent termination of that struggle inaugurated a new constitutional order in Russia inscribed with executive dominance. Chapter 12 surveys that order by returning to the themes introduced in Chapter 1 and substantively assessing from a synchronic perspective those problematics associated with its Soviet predecessor that have been altered (or not) in the course of Russia's political rebirth.

11 Reform, reaction and rebellion: the calamity of the first republic

On the morning after the August *coup*'s defeat, a special session of the Russian Supreme Soviet shelved a motion to replace the national flag with the tricolour – unofficial ensign of the democratic resistance to communism – on the grounds that the Constitution had consigned the designation of state symbols solely to the Congress of People's Deputies. That afternoon, however, El'tsin – who had sat sphinx-like during the Supreme Soviet's deliberations – interrupted the progression of distinguished officials addressing the rally from the back balcony of the White House to put that same question directly to the crowd. Thus an acclamatory chorus adopted the new flag which fluttered from state buildings, including the Kremlin, on the following day. During that evening, Gorbachev appeared before Russia's Supreme Soviet to take unwitting part in a ritual marking the passage of power from the Soviet president to the Russian one. Here, El'tsin publicly humiliated his nemesis, answering his appeal not to blame the CPSU for the *coup* with a decree signed on the spot that suspended all CPSU activities on Russian soil, bullying him to read aloud the minutes of the recent meeting of the USSR's Cabinet of Ministers at which one after another of his ministers had betrayed him. The television cameras zoomed in on the *dramatis personae*, capturing a forceful Russian leader in full control of the situation and a spent Soviet president, confused, indecisive and unable to control his own slackened and quivering jaw that testified to his new, subordinate status.

These vignettes at the dawn of Russia's post-communist transformation previewed the authoritarian-populist strategy employed to effect it. Instrumentally, this approach involved loading extraordinary powers onto the executive agencies of the state for the purpose of pushing through an economic reform in the face of anticipated resistance. Symbolically, this statist turn was justified on the basis of El'tsin's overwhelming popularity in the wake of the *coup*'s defeat,[1] providing the executive with the political capital it required to secure *carte blanche* from the legislature and to govern in spite of the legislature once its indulgences had been rescinded. Instead of building a base of support in political society via consultation and concession, the executive generally ignored organized political forces altogether, except to acknowledge their pressure on it by coopting leaders into the executive itself. With rare exceptions, those from Russia's political parties and movements appointed to state offices never looked back. Access to the resources of the state thus traced a path of particularism through the corridors of power via personal contacts among the holders of executive office. Concomitantly, Russia's infant legislatures and courts – institutions within which a public component could be brought to bear in formulating and adjudicating rules and procedures that would resolve conflicts according to generalizable criteria – suffered crib death. Personalized relations thus would characterize Russian politics every bit as much as they had the Soviet order. Moreover, executive rule divided political society into insiders and outsiders, those with access to state power and those who would overcome their lack of same by warring on those who had it. Without a neutral mechanism for deciding the issue of access, the institutions of government themselves would be converted into weapons of political struggle.

The seizure of power

Communism's collapse temporarily orphaned the Russian presidency. The establishment of the office itself had represented a particular moment in the contest between democrats and communists, its subsequent development tempered by ensuing rounds of political battle with the Soviet state. Its genesis had imprinted on it – to borrow Lenin's term for his party – the character of a 'fighting organization' whose experience and consequent combat ethos had elided attention to the mundane matters of government.[2] The Russian presidency would assume the functions of government in the wake of the *coup*, but would come to this responsibility via the familiar path of struggle, now against two opponents: the remnants of the Soviet state that Gorbachev was trying desperately to rescue; and other institutions laying competing claim to the exercise of political power, legislatures at all levels and those political forces animating them.

Dismantling the Soviet system

Immediately after the *coup*'s collapse, citizens under the belated direction of the Russian and Moscow authorities shut down and sealed off the CPSU's national and city offices. Gorbachev resigned as its general secretary and called for dissolution of its Central Committee. Russian authorities also closed down the USSR's Cabinet of Ministers, a fact duly recorded by a Gorbachev decree dismissing his entire government and appointing an interim committee whose composition had been all but dictated by El'tsin.[3] Within a few days, the USSR's Supreme Soviet suspended the activities of the CPSU; a week later the USSR's Congress of People's Deputies followed Gorbachev's recommendations to abolish itself and authorize its replacement,[4] a temporary legislature composed of deputies from both the union and the republics, chosen in part by virtue of the negative correlation between their voting records and that of the Congress's communist majority.[5]

These events illustrated two important features of the new reality ushered in by the *coup*'s defeat. First, the Communist Party and Soviet state were already dead,[6] their officers enjoined to publicize that fact through acts of ritual suicide. Second, all of the funeral arrangements were made without the advice and consent of political society.[7] Rather, a narrow circle of Russia's government leaders commissioned the Soviet president to act as golem, demolishing all of the USSR's party-state structures save his own office. The Soviet presidency, in turn, would expire when another round of high-level agreements had abolished the country over which it (now nominally) presided. By the time that El'tsin had met with Ukrainian and Belarusan leaders Leonid Kravchuk and Stanislav Shushkevich to drive the final nail into that coffin, its only occupant was Gorbachev. El'tsin had already abolished the CPSU entirely and confiscated its property; his autumn decrees had annexed the government of the USSR to the Russian state.[8] The Soviet president endeavoured to recreate some semblance of a state to house his office via televised appeals to public opinion and modifications in the draft union treaty still under consideration by the leaders of the republics.[9] If anything, these efforts backfired. In late November, the republic leaders withdrew from the treaty negotiations;[10] on 1 December Ukraine voted independence; one week later the USSR was dissolved. Although Russian politics would soon be convulsed by a furore over the 'unconstitutional' termination of the Soviet Union, it would be well to remember that many making this change had themselves ratified that decision in Russia's Supreme Soviet on 12 December by a vote of 188 to 6.[11]

Seizing power in Russia

The margin of approval for extinguishing the USSR and joining an undefined Commonwealth of Independent States was roughly indicative of the Russian legislature's indulgent attitude toward the executive until the onset of economic reform. The lawmakers thus participated in their own 'Mossovietization', a term derived from the emasculation of the Moscow City Council by Mayor Popov and its subsequent conversion into an anti-executive forum, pure and simple.[12] Indeed, Russia's Supreme Soviet contributed directly to Mossovietization in the first instance, rejecting the city council's appeal to overturn Popov's illegal appointment of Arkadii Murashev as police chief[13] and endorsing almost unanimously El'tsin's decree instituting mayoral rule in the capital.[14] To be sure, some legislators were prepared to guard their prerogatives, as evinced at the Supreme Soviet's first session after the *putsch* when a number of them spoke out against the 'authoritarian' tendencies of Russia's president. Reprising Soviet speech on the floor of the legislature, El'tsin's advocates merely admonished them to 'stop it and get back to work'.[15] This work consisted primarily of enacting presidential rule into law. The first dimension of that enterprise involved cancelling the elections scheduled for December to the office of head of administration in each of Russia's regions, and awarding the president the power to name his viceroys with the consent of their respective soviets. Although the Supreme Soviet refused to cancel these elections,[16] the Congress of People's Deputies acceded to El'tsin's plan when it convened two weeks later. This Congress also underwrote the second dimension of presidential rule, awarding El'tsin full power over the entire national government for a period of one year.[17]

On the heels of this grant of authority and a constitutional amendment declaring him the head of a 'unified system of executive power' in the country,[18] El'tsin issued a decree on presidential rule centralizing all policy-making in a collegium of top governmental officials headed by the president himself.[19] The internal management of the collegium, and its overall direction in El'tsin's absence, was assigned to the first deputy prime minister, Gennadii Burbulis, the chief architect of this reorganization.[20] Together with Sergei Shakhrai – El'tsin's chief legal advisor and drafter of most presidential decrees – Burbulis composed a thoroughly statist strategy for effecting Russia's economic transformation. Their plan embraced the notion that rapid and radical economic reform was an urgent necessity whose resulting hardships and dislocations in the short term would be justified by future prosperity. Since those same short-term difficulties could be expected to induce a popular backlash, even an insurrection, the situation required a unified executive prepared to subdue the population and administer the painful economic cure.[21] Moreover, resistance was expected from officialdom, from the *nomenklatura* still entrenched as the government of most regions, and a unified executive whose power reached directly into the localities would be needed to overcome it.[22] But if the economic reform required this sharp turn toward statism, the turn itself required the creation of a new ideology to justify the suspension of democracy by Russia's new government of democrats.

This ideology drew deeply from the combat ethos that had accumulated around El'tsin's leadership and in the larger democratic movement during the struggle with the Soviet party-state. Following their August victory, its proponents claimed that 'we are on the attack [and ready to go where] it is dangerous for tanks'.[23] Accordingly, Burbulis christened his a 'kamikaze government'[24] whose members would sacrifice themselves for the sake of an uncomprehending nation, ramming through the needed measures before an ungrateful public excised them permanently from the affairs of state. Prior to the 'attack', this government already was describing itself as a 'club of victims', a 'team of the dead'.[25] El'tsin wrapped his appeal to the Congress of People's Deputies for extraordinary powers in precisely this language, explaining that no one in his government could expect to continue in politics once the kamikaze mission had been completed.[26] However, since the 'dead' still walk, we might enquire into these self-ascriptions, investigating how they functioned at this critical juncture to launch the Russian state on the path toward disaster.

First, terms such as 'team of the dead' located this government outside the world of the living and debased that same world, reframing it as a mere object for them to transform. Those joining this team had already proven themselves worthy to rule by their putative sacrifice on behalf of the unappreciative nation for which it was made. As such, the palpable expressions of this world – in particular, democratic elections – could be ignored or suppressed as part of this very sacrifice. New elections to parliament or those scheduled for heads of administration in the regions appeared as a luxury in which this government would not indulge.[27] Considerable energies were spent convincing one another – as well as outsiders – that elections would prove damaging to democracy in Russia. Presidential counsellor, Sergei Stankevich, laid down the universal proposition that 'a period of root-level reform has never been a period of blossoming for parliamentary democracy'.[28] Shakhrai, ideological pointman in the effort to cancel December's regional elections,[29] enlisted political analysts Aleksandr Sobyanin and Dmitrii Yur'ev to make the case to El'tsin on one hand[30] and the public on the other, that permitting the luxury of an election would end in the political catastrophe of communist restoration.[31] RPR leader and now presidential representative in Tomsk, Stepan Sulakshin, explained that elections could not be relied on to accomplish the main task: 'the liquidation of opposition to the president in the executive organs'.[32]

The second side of the new government's ideology – an unqualified endorsement of monetarism – complemented its professions of worthiness via sacrifice. Those prepared to lay down their own lives for the greater good commanded the authority to institute generalized austerity. Moreover, monetarism resonated with the anti-communism of the larger democratic movement, appearing as that economic philosophy that represented communism's polar opposite, even as it replicated communism's 'complete disdain for all that exists'[33] and its eagerness to make over both social relations and the 'interiors' of individuals. Its proponents never hesitated to utter their convictions that their reform measures were the product of 'thoroughly-tested, professional economics', any compromise with which would lead only to disaster.[34] Their plan for freeing prices and achieving 'macroeconomic stabilization' via restrictions on money supply and credit was a carbon copy of that produced in December 1990 for the Soviet economy by specialists from the International Monetary Fund, World Bank and other international financial institutions, with the exception that Russia's 'shock therapy' would be even more austere.[35] Despite the fact that this brand of economics had been 'thoroughly tested' in Latin America – which, regardless of outcomes, represented an economic situation in no meaningful way comparable to that prevailing in Russia[36] – and applied to only one state socialist country, Poland, advantaged by a relatively generous stabilization loan and the large private sector already in operation (but none the less still reeling from the effect of the shock), the urgent implementation of this policy overshadowed all other considerations.

In its basic contours, then, the new government's ideology replicated the core features of communist doctrine: in place of the monolithic party – the unified executive; instead of scientific Marxism–Leninism – professional economics. Moreover, since this ideology pivoted on the desideratum of socio-economic transformation and the anticipated resistance to it, it etched enemy images into its picture of the world. Now the *nomenklatura* entrenched in soviets, prepared to sabotage the reform and to take revenge on the democrats, occupied the position held earlier by such furtive forces as kulaks, class enemies and wreckers. Like its communist predecessors, the new government's ideology captured the world *in camera obscura*, its mythic categories turning real relations upside down. With respect to the alleged scientific or professional basis for its economic policy, 'reform' functioned from the first as a magic word.[37] It lacked a practical, discursive dimension and, therefore, simply could not be discussed; in part, because governmental and economic structures presupposed in the monetarist plan did not exist in Russia, while that which did exist could not be thematized without undercutting the entire logic of the reform. The crux of the issue, here, involved a plan predicated on autonomous firms that would adapt their behaviour to market conditions, responding to price liberalization with profit-maximizing strategies that would rapidly rationalize relations throughout the economy. In fact, actual relations in Russia's economy were of quite a different order: monopoly producers were relatively impervious to market forces; mutual dependencies existed between local governments and firms on their territory from which protective responses to reform measures would be crafted, thus vitiating the reform's logic by setting off a spiral of high inflation, steep drops in production and, above all, a demonetization of the entire economy.[38] In the face of this incongruence, attempts to expound on the conception of the government's plan in a practical way – such as those displayed by officials and sympathetic economists at the December 1991 Congress of Reform Supporters – created nothing but confusion.[39]

The 'unified executive' inverted the practical world every bit as much as the mundane referent of 'monolithic' Communist Party had been a collection of rival administrative cliques and patronage networks. The principal groups comprising El'tsin's government consisted of those with whom he had made personal association during his earlier career in the CPSU (the communist *nomenklatura*) and his more recent one in the democratic movement (the democratic *nomenklatura*). The first group was headed by Yurii Petrov, a longstanding associate from Sverdlovsk who had worked in the CPSU's Central Committee before being recommended by El'tsin to succeed him as party boss in the region when El'tsin was tapped for a post in Moscow. Petrov became head of the Administration of the President (auspiciously) on the opening day of the August *coup*, quickly relying on his network of associations to assemble a staff of some 300 to manage and coordinate the internal operations of the presidency.[40] The flow of personnel from the communist *nomenklatura* into the new government was further augmented by Oleg Lobov, another El'tsin confederate from Sverdlovsk who had served as first deputy premier in the Russian government since 1990 but was sidelined to the post of Chairperson of the Council of Experts (a presidential advisory group) when the post-*coup* government was formed in November.[41] Lobov's patronage appeared to account for another influx of communist *nomenklatura*, especially from the military-industrial sector.[42]

Burbulis headed the democratic *nomenklatura*, selecting personally or through his chief aide, Aleksei Golovkov, the key players for the new government's reform team: Egor Gaidar (deputy prime minister for economic policy), Aleksandr Shokhin (deputy prime minister for social policy), Petr Aven (minister of foreign trade) and Vladimir Lopukhin (minister of energy).[43] One indication of Burbulis's prerogatives in this area was the fact that Gaidar – a thirty-five-year-old economist, recent editor at *Pravda* and complete stranger to government employment – was named to the cabinet's critical post without El'tsin's involvement.[44] Another would be the reorganization decree that Burbulis had authored which excluded vice-president Rutskoi from membership in the government's top organ, the collegium, and assigned to him other 'organization and control functions' which the president may later commission. As a member of neither *nomenklatura*, Rutskoi found himself isolated under the new arrangements, complaining publicly by year's end that he had been unable to speak with El'tsin since the *putsch*.[45]

The first public manifestation of hostility between the groups headed by Petrov and Burbulis appeared toward the end of September when Shakhrai officially informed the president that nineteen of his recent decrees violated the constitution.[46] It would seem that most, or all, of these decrees had been prepared under Petrov's auspices, probably by Viktor Ilyushin's staff. This problem for the democratic *nomenklatura* – mysteriously authored presidential decrees affecting their united government – was substantially reduced (albeit not eliminated) when the Main Legal Administration, which would prepare all presidential legal documents, was created in the Administration of the President in December with Shakhrai at its head.[47] Subsequent signals of struggle within the executive concerned governmental staffing as the communist *nomenklatura* poached on the democrats' preserve. Golovkov remarked publicly about the deleterious impact made on the 'unified' government by 'parallel persons' joining the cabinet and sowing division:

Whether [this involves just individuals or] teams, I can only guess. Certainly, someone has been working in parallel. There were some things that were unclear about some of the candidates [for government positions]. But [our] team then was in a very difficult position – either we work with these people or we don't work at all. And during the November [1991] holidays all their appointments were confirmed.[48]

An even stronger indictment appeared in a document prepared for El'tsin by the analytic centre, RF-politika, that outlined the flow of officials from the CPSU apparatus into the new government, the abortion of appointments authorized by El'tsin (the relevant documents had a habit of getting 'lost'), the rewriting of some presidential decrees after they had been signed and the mysterious appearance of others such as the ill-fated combination of all security and police agencies in one ministry.[49]

The divisions apparent within the 'unified' executive reflected the fact that the alliance on which the Russian state initially rested – the so-called 'August bloc' of democrats and those communists who had come over to the winning side in the *coup*'s wake, annexed *en masse* as the Russian government absorbed the Soviet one – was inherently untenable in the absence of general elections. By loading all power onto the executive, the new authorities had drained the public arena of the potential for meaningful political conflict and consigned it to the interior of the executive itself. In that arena, it appeared as administrative in-fighting and intrigue, debasing the authoritative character of state communication, disrupting the coherence of state organization. Moreover, that development within the state had profound consequences for political and civil society, attenuating the connections between emerging interests and those parties that might represent them in legislatures, instead encouraging the direct lobbying of executive officials, an activity commonly known as 'corruption'. Unable to form up for elections, the elements of political society would divide themselves into that minority enjoying some access to the government – and, accordingly, offering its support – and a majority, the outsiders, who occupied positions in Mossovieticized legislatures. Since these institutions did not have the capacity to control the executive in any significant way, oppositionist currents within them had nothing to do except to utilize these institutions as bases to attack and destroy the government.

The impact of statization on political society

State and political society: 'Kto kogo?'

Lenin's timeless question – 'Who [will dominate] whom? – was decided by the *coup*'s outcome. The democrats had bested the communists. In the post-communist period, however, it reappeared with respect to the relationship between state and political society in Russia. Would political society control the state or would the state dominate political society? Although a clear answer would emerge slowly, factors working in the direction of state domination were quick to appear. The first of these was the failure to call new elections. That failure would count as the third missed opportunity to provide structure to political society, to establish clear and consistent terms of intercourse between it and the state, and to institute avenues of influence between emerging socio-economic interests and agencies of public representation such as parties and parliament. The power transferred to, or usurped by, the executive was at best weakly constrained by legislatures elected in 1990 when neither party competition nor procedures guaranteeing fair outcomes had prevailed. Their internal organization was chaotic; their authority tarnished.

Following the August *coup*, the victorious democrats expected new elections shortly. The DPR–RCDM–CDP bloc, Popular Accord, began preparing in September for elections to a new all-union parliament.[50] Simultaneously, DemRossiya readied itself for those anticipated in Russia. Warning of a 'new authoritarianism' issuing from the 'uncontrolled strengthening of executive power' that must be countered by a 'democratically law-bound state', DemRossiya called for immediate elections to fill gubernatorial posts in the regions and elections to legislatures at all levels by spring.[51] But DemRossiya's supine posture toward its leader 'outside the organization' and its disinclination to alter it now meant that its demands could be safely ignored. Denied for a month an opportunity to speak with El'tsin himself, DemRossiya's officers met on 19 September with Burbulis, Rutskoi, Press Minister Mikhail Poltoranin and head of the Control Commission for regional personnel, Valerii Makharadze. Burbulis flatly rejected all their demands then and there; Poltoranin and Makharadze suggested that DemRossiya contribute names to the new *nomenklatura*.[52] DemRossiya went along, but soon began to grumble publicly that their nominees to executive positions were being systematically passed over in favour of candidates from the old party-state apparatus.[53] Finally, nearly two months after their August victory, DemRossiya's leaders got an audience with the president. Consensus emerged on awarding the government extraordinary powers to implement 'radical economic reform', forming that government through consultation with DemRossiya, and staging parliamentary elections in spring. The president's side honoured neither of these last two commitments. Similarly, El'tsin signed an agreement with nine parties on 2 November (later expanded to include twenty), according to which he would meet monthly with them and include their counsel in policy and personnel decisions.[54] This agreement broke down at once. Until he needed their support at April's Sixth Congress of People's Deputies, El'tsin only met once with the party leaders, and that meeting resolved nothing.[55] Burbulis and Gaidar kept some contact with the democratic factions in the Supreme Soviet but, with exceptions that showed the rule,[56] they denied them any hand in shaping the composition of the new government and ignored their advice on policy matters.[57] For their part, those parties prepared to support the government seemed especially timid in pressing their claims.[58] The government's only significant reciprocation for party support involved transmitting to them confidential documents on upcoming privatization arrangements, inside information that the parties could use to supplement their finances.[59]

Although a goodly number of politicians in the democratic camp shortly began to be favoured with executive appointments,[60] it would be important to emphasize that these were not party appointments to the executive but the cooptation of party and legislative elites into it. Although in most instances appointees had been nominated for these posts by their respective parties, they were required to suspend their party membership on assuming office. Personalized forms of clientelism usually ensued thereafter, as yesterday's party activists embarked on government careers in which ties to very different sets of patrons mattered more. Consequently, the vast majority of these individuals quickly acclimatized themselves to the prevailing ways of Russian officialdom, going along in order to get along. As Yurii Boldyrev observed at the onset of these migrations, 'As "ours" have come to power it has become clear according to their *modus operandi* that there is very little to distinguish them from those whom they have replaced.'[61] Unable to control 'their' members in government and cut off from any appreciable influence over it, Russia's organized political forces quickly began to wither and disintegrate.[62]

Political society fragmented

In a number of respects, Russian political society fell victim to the politics of appropriation. Although the struggles raging within it after the August *coup* were fought under an assortment of lofty principles – the self-determination of peoples versus the maintenance of national-territorial integrity, the freedom of the individual versus the collective rights of groups, and so on – the positions taken by participants correlated closely with their access to state offices and the resources that they disposed. To an extraordinary degree, post-communist political society in Russia has thus been defined by state power rather than by autonomous interests in civil society; to that same degree, impersonal modes of social and political interaction have been displaced by the personalized character of relations prevalent in the Soviet and, now, Russian state. The appropriation of state offices has been something of a constant in the transition, fragmenting the political society that has come into being in Russia.

The Russian Movement for Democratic Reforms (RMDR)[63] would illustrate one aspect of this proposition. Its primary base was the mayors' offices in Moscow and St Petersburg which supplied administrative jobs to a number of activists in the democratic movement. In Moscow, DemRossiya organizational leaders Vladimir Bokser, Mikhail Shneider, Vera Kriger and others – all on the mayor's payroll – as well as Popov clients Arkadii Murashev and Il'ya Zaslavskii, had taken control of the capital's branch of DemRossiya in July 1991. Their opponents – party leaders with neither access to the national government nor entrée at the mayor's office – bolted and set up their own 'Democratic Moscow' bloc in October, a development presaging the schism in DemRossiya that occurred a month later.[64] At the root of DemRossiya's ruptures nationally, in Moscow and in St Petersburg,[65] was the use of state offices to capture organized forces in political society.[66] These, in turn, would be deployed as 'public committees for reform', injecting themselves into the privatization process and providing access to state property at bargain prices for supporters and clients;[67] or as political organizations campaigning in society for increasing executive power.[68] Erstwhile allies certainly assessed these stratagems in this way and formed counter-organizations either to battle their own way into the state's larder or to close down the channels of access to it enjoyed by those controlling the executive.

For those networks jockeying for position in post-communist Russia, words connoted far more – and denoted much less – than they ordinarily might. DemRossiya – the first major casualty in the war of words, the battle *not* to be understood – exemplified the point. At its second congress in November 1991, the three-party bloc Popular Accord walked out for good, accusing DemRossiya of 'national state nihilism', the ruin of the union and the impending disintegration of the Russian Federation. Although the critical importance of preserving the union was repeatedly emphasized by those in the bloc, neither Popular Accord nor its constituent members made any attempt to cooperate in this endeavour with the MDR – for whom the matter was also paramount and portrayed in often identical language[69] – until after the union had been dissolved. The barrier dividing the pro-union forces among the democrats was the same one that delineated their respective networks. For Popular Accord, the maintenance of these networks was placed in jeopardy by the attempt of DemRossiya's leadership to convert their organization from a loose coalition of political forces into a unified political party in all but name, thereby subsuming the individual parties within it.[70] Membership expansion over the previous year and the inclusion of a number of small organizations had placed the larger parties at a glaring disadvantage in delegate selection to the congress. Relying on delegates chosen by non-party members or those supplied by small affiliates, as well as their control of the credentials commission,[71] DemRossiya's leadership steamrollered Popular Accord on every programmatic and organization issue.[72]

The long-fought battle over the leadership of a united democratic movement was finally decided at the expense of the movement itself. Trumpeting their commitment to save the union, Popular Accord staged a stormy walkout. Similarly, DemRossiya's majority faction bathed their power play in familiar anti-communist rhetoric whose pitch seemed to ascend on the occasion of communism's actual defeat. Russia, it was claimed, was perched on the precipice of imminent counter-revolution, threatened by 'elemental rebellions' and 'fascism',[73] the *nomenklatura* underground' and the 'communist hydra'.[74] Petition drives were launched to stage public referenda: the first (in early 1992), for elections to a constituent assembly from which communists would be barred;[75] the second (a few months later), to dissolve their putative stronghold, the Congress of People's Deputies.[76] Neither came to pass, yet each campaign generated considerable heat around what top officials candidly admitted was 'just a slogan'.[77] As militant market–liberal discourse established itself as the prevailing orthodoxy inside DemRossiya, social democrats – charter members of the organization – found themselves tarred with the same anti-communist brush.[78] This was the rhetoric of a movement already in shambles, marginalized by the president's refusal to call new elections and his assertion of executive authority, its remnants signalling their readiness blindly to back the government and its policies by conjuring and attacking ghosts.

The pro-reform stance assumed by the dominant ('pragmatic') group in DemRossiya opened opportunities for creating new distinctions on the political field. Accordingly, a section of DemRossiya that had already staked out the liberal high-ground for itself[79] moved further upward in moral–political space by claiming disassociation – that is, neither support nor opposition – from the El'tsin government. Rather, as Yurii Afanas'ev proclaimed at DemRossiya's second congress, they intended to support El'tsin's reform course by heading off that mass opposition that it was bound to trigger, somehow serving as the voice 'of those for whom [life has become] bad' even while they would exhort the government to abide by strictly liberal-economic principles.[80] Although the practical effect that this tendency had on either objective was minimal at most, their position on the political field proved as attractive in certain circles of the intelligentsia as had Democratic Union's politics of moral protest a few years earlier. However, in this instance, the proximate target of protest was DemRossiya itself.

At the plenary session of DemRossiya's Council of Representatives in January 1992, Afanas'ev's 'Radical Faction' squared off with the pragmatic – or in his word, 'opportunist' – group in command of the organization. A second schism thus occurred when the radical's resolution prohibiting state agencies from using 'tax revenues [to engage in] commercial and entrepreneurial activity' was voted down, opponents arguing that such activity was not only permissible but necessary for organs of the state. Similarly, the voting for a new Coordinating Council added to the pragmatist/opportunist majority, removing any question about DemRossiya's complete support for executive power in Russia.[81] The radicals – Afanas'ev, Leonid Batkin, Yurii Burtin and Mariya Sal'e – then suspended their membership in DemRossiya while rank-and-file members left in droves.[82] The radicals made a final effort to recapture their influence by calling an extraordinary congress in July 1992, but failed for lack of a quorum.[83] Thereafter they drifted away from DemRossiya which, deserted by both its constituent parties (except the RPR) and by most of its members,[84] splintered again into two groups: Reform, which counselled the government to modify its monetarism; and Democratic Choice which demanded a purer version of it.[85] In November 1992, the revival of a united democratic movement flashed briefly, and for the last time, on the political horizon as El'tsin addressed a conclave of leaders from all groups – the Forum of Supporters of Reform – with a call to unite in one 'democratic party of reform', vowing that he would be 'with it and in it'.[86] However, that pledge turned out to be no more than a tactic, momentarily replaced by others as El'tsin manoeuvred against his opponents who by then commanded an overwhelming majority in the legislature.

Oppositions

To the same degree that the government's statist/monetarist reform strategy undermined the coherence of those forces initially supporting it, it contributed to the cohesion of those that for one reason or another opposed it. Although roles were now reversed, post-communist patterns of political alliance in Russia closely resembled their late-Soviet predecessors. Once again, political society would split into warring camps – complete with a fictive 'centre' organized to exploit that division – each deriving its identity and purpose negatively as the self-proclaimed nemesis of the other. The Russian legislature would form the opposition's critical pivot. Although it had generally acquiesced to presidential claims on its authority prior to the implementation of reform,[87] it rapidly reversed course thereafter, drawing strength for a reassertion of its institutional interests from opposition factions within it. Thus the opposition's political struggle with the government was transformed into war between legislature and executive.

Opposition forms

In large measure, the formation of the various opposition groupings to El'tsin's government was effected by refugees from the democratic camp either denied positions in, or access to, the state apparatus. One section took the lead in organizing the so-called 'irreconcilable' opposition that sought to overthrow El'tsin's regime. Another, less extreme group, sought to 'correct' its policies. This second group consisted of two tendencies. The first, and milder variant, included the Social Demo-cratic Party of Russia (SDPR), the People's Party of Russia, the Peasant Party of Russia and the Social-Liberal Association (defectors from the RPR) who formed the left-democratic opposition bloc, New Russia, in January 1992 in protest over the government's statist/monetarist course and its enrichment of *nomenklatura* groups, old and new.[88] Unable to abide its uncritical support for the government and its new alliance with the RMDR – regarded as *nomenklatura* incarnate – New Russia effectively parted ways with DemRossiya in March.[89] This decision sprang from the identity politics central to the bloc's principal player, the SDPR, and would count as one of those rare instances in post-communist Russia in which articulated principles actually informed political behaviour.

The second tendency, represented by the DPR's path toward opposition, was a case closer to the norm. Its rivalry with DemRossiya had already reconfigured 'Travkin's party' as *gosudarstvenniki*[90] – champions of 'statehood' or the 'state principle' – and after the *coup* that meant preserving the union at all costs. At the DPR's third congress (December 1991), when his hold on the organization was at its apex, Travkin engineered the replacement of liberal-individualism with the state principle (*gosudarstvennost'*) as the party's supreme value.[91] Fresh from this triumph, Travkin participated in a rally on Manege Square featuring Zhirinovskii and other patriotic leaders from the embryonic red–brown movement, drawing censure from his DPR colleagues for this and for other unauthorized actions inspired by *gosudarstvennost'*.[92] This rift inside the DPR destroyed Popular Accord. To contain internal frictions, the DPR leadership decided in January to cease participation in the bloc's efforts to unite democratic and patriotic *gosudarstvenniki* in a single political movement.[93] Here, the road forked for democrats-turned-*gosudarstvenniki*.

One fork led rightward. Along that road travelled Popular Accord's other members – the RCDM and CDP – who inaugurated the white-brown opposition bloc, the Russian Popular Assembly (RPA), at the Congress of Civic and Patriotic Forces that they staged in February. The largest openly Russian chauvinist gathering yet convened, the congress included (ex-democrat) Sergei Barburin's recently organized Russian Public Union (RPU),[94] restorationist factions from the Russian legislature, the Union of Cossack Hosts of Russia, the Union of Officers for the Rebirth of Russia, the (openly fascist) National Republican Party and Pamyat, now marginalized on the right by the new wave of patriotic politicians.[95] The programme adopted at this congress was a collection of symbols and slogans marshalled against the government and its supporters, fevered animosity toward whom supplied the indispensable glue cementing incoherence and inconsistency into a political philosophy for the patriots. Vowing to redirect their struggle against totalitarianism toward the rootless democrats who had come to power prepared to wreck Russian civilization and state, the RPA stipulated that neither personal interests nor ambitions, but the Motherland herself, had summoned them to restore the empire,[96] replace both the reforms and the reformers with a 'war economy', end any special status for ethnic minorities in Russia while securing the same for Russians living outside the Russian Federation, restore state religion and eliminate all phenomena offensive to the 'healthy majority'.[97] Although these forces did not officially consummate their alliance with the communists till autumn – the so-called red–brown bloc – by late winter they were already marching shoulder-to-shoulder in street demonstrations drawing upward of 100,000 people.[98]

The other fork led toward the centre. The first milestone along that route was the bloc formed in March 1992 by the DPR and the People's Party of Free Russia (PPFR) whose head, the country's vice-president, had been positioning himself as an opposition leader as soon as he had been severed from any participation in the affairs of state by the Burbulis government,[99] a brief respite in that condition notwithstanding.[100] Rutskoi had actually delivered the keynote address to the Congress of Civic and Patriotic Forces, but strong sentiment in his party against association with the 'browns' encouraged him to keep his distance from the RPA.[101] Like Travkin's party, then, the PPFR had neither a foot in the government nor one in the bloc opposed to it. That circumstance proved sufficient to overcome recent differences such as the PPFR's reluctance to relinquish its ties to the CPSU or the DPR's virulent anti-communism. Regardless of claims to the contrary,[102] the DPR hereafter dropped its liberal-capitalist orientation and found a common language with its new partner, privileging state forms over private ones in every respect.[103] Despite vast differences in the political leanings of their respective memberships,[104] the alliance of these strange bedfellows became the core of the centrist opposition that formed in April at the Sixth Congress of People's Deputies.

Legislative opposition

The onset of shock therapy coincided with the legislature's conversion to opposition. Before two weeks had gone by, the Supreme Soviet's chairperson, Ruslan Khasbulatov, was informing the president – his erstwhile patron and partner – that unless he dismissed his government immediately the parliament would step in to do so.[105] Within another two weeks, the Supreme Soviet was discussing a number of bills that would strip El'tsin of his extraordinary appointments powers – both nationally and regionally – and assert the legislature's prerogatives in those areas.[106] Both supporters and opponents of the reform braced for an anticipated showdown at the April Congress, on whose eve each side paraded its respective determination to uphold or to bring down the government, thus producing again a putative centre around which another regrouping would occur. The democrats invited some 2,000 delegates from parties and associations thought hospitable to the reform course to their Assembly of Citizens of the Russian Federation, but their efforts were marred by both bitter debates and a walkout by representatives of effectively all sizeable organizations save DemRossiya and the RMDR, protesting the latter's joint resolution for a referendum on the Constitution that would dissolve the legislature.[107] The RPA sponsored a street rally with Labouring Russia, a militant neo-Stalinist movement, that drew a crowd of 50,000 in spite of the boycott by their communist-patriotic rivals cultivating at the moment a more centrist image.[108]

At the Congress, three broad blocs of deputies emerged, but since there was no necessary correspondence between a deputy's party membership and his or her factional affiliation (some deputies were simultaneously members of different, even opposing, factions and blocs[109]) voting patterns were fluid. The four factions combined in Coalition in Support of Reform accounted for about 30 per cent of the deputies; the five anti-government factions making up the Russian Unity bloc represented over 40 per cent; the remainder, a centrist Bloc of Creative Forces formed during the Congress itself, was comprised of fence-sitters and splinters from the other camps.[110] Although the three-bloc alignment in the

Congress endured,[111] the ranks of reform-supporters suffered attrition, reducing the government's actual margin of firm backers to about a quarter of the deputies.[112]

To offset their dwindling measure of support in parliament, El'tsin's government sought to coopt milder opponents, passing out promises of appointments in the executive[113] and offering certain compromises on economic policy.[114] As he had intimated to the Congress, El'tsin reshuffled his cabinet a few weeks after it had adjourned. Burbulis was demoted a rung on the official ladder while Gaidar and Vladimir Shumeiko – deputy chairperson of the Supreme Soviet, member of both the pro-reform and centrist blocs at the Sixth Congress, currently advancing his career via association with Arkadii Vol'skii's industrial lobby[115] – topped the hierarchy as first deputy prime ministers. The remainder of the cabinet was filled by the retention of Shokhin and the additions of State Property Committee head and Gaidar ally, Anatolii Chubais, whose elevation coincided with impending broad-scale privatization; and Georgii Khizha and Viktor Chernomyrdin, representing the military-industrial and energy sectors, respectively. Under pressure from the centrist opposition, El'tsin agreed to some modifications in the course of reform.[116]

Two aspects of the compromise between El'tsin and the centrists concern us here. First, the galvanization of industrial executives and local government administrators in support of Vol'skii's Russian Union of Industrialists and Entrepreneurs – formed in January 1992 on the basis of the Scientific-Industrial Union of the USSR, the industrial sector's first incarnation as a political lobby which metamorphosed again into the political party, Renewal, after the Sixth Congress[117] – was the predictable consequence of the reform's disastrous impact on these constituencies. Freeing prices had immediately produced steep inflation (over 400 per cent in the first month) while the government's insistence on tight credit and holding down the money supply meant that firms continued to function on the basis of either barter or inter-enterprise 'credit', non-payment for filled orders.[118] The spiral of non-payments in the first quarter of 1992 increased the overall amount of enterprise debt by a factor of twenty-three[119] while the real value of the money supply had dropped by 70 per cent.[120] To extricate the economy from this impasse, industrial and agricultural subsidies were gradually renewed in April, pending a full reversal of monetary policy in July when Viktor Gerashchenko replaced Georgii Matyukhin as head of Russia's Central Bank, that would remonetize the economy (in which inter-enterprise debt already stood at 80 per cent of GNP) by opening the sluices of state credits and reflating the money supply.[121] The reform was thereby reversed even as the 'kamikazes' retained four of seven positions in the cabinet.

Second, the compromise engineered between the executive and the producers' lobby resulted in further disjunctions between and within state and political society. El'tsin's government was prepared to make tactical, even strategic, concessions, but none restricting its room for subsequent manoeuvre. Eschewing power sharing with parliament,[122] it instead parcelled out positions and access to decision-making to corporatist representatives from the industrial sector in exchange for their support. This redefined the political field yet again, enabling representatives of the industrial lobbies and their partners in local administration to convert their positions in government and economy into influence within the state that was out of all proportion to their actual political strength.[123] By thus designating the administrative arena as the site for political accommodation, the El'tsin strategy largely removed practical issues from the public sphere, reducing politics therein to the choice between either assenting to, or protesting against, that which had been decided 'above'. Moreover, by politicizing the state in this way, providing access to Soviet-era networks of enterprise directors and local officials, national policy-making and implementation became even more incoherent. And since there was no identifiable industrial interest beyond the facilitation of production for individual enterprises, the directors' lobby thrived under arrangements that encouraged particular solutions – credits, licensing, tax breaks, contracts and so forth – for particular problems.

Within the context of El'tsin's accommodation, Vol'skii's industrial executives emerged as a potent political force. His Renewal party absorbed the important Change and Industrial Union factions in parliament, and was joined in June by the DPR and PPFR in a coalition christened Civic Union, a self-professed centre positioning itself between the democrats at one end of the spectrum and the emerging red–brown coalition at the other.[124] Immediately submitting lists of candidates for government appointment to El'tsin[125] and forming its own 'shadow cabinet',[126] it made bold to announce that it was prepared to assume the full burden of government.[127] Negotiations with El'tsin along the lines of that proposal continued during the summer.[128] By autumn, Civic Union unveiled its 'corrective' to the 'mistaken' statist/monetarist policy of the government, namely, a statist/productionist programme featuring price controls plus liberal state credits to enterprises.[129] Simultaneously, Civic Union worked the other side of the street, supporting Khasbulatov's power plays in the Supreme Soviet that were fast subordinating that institution to his personal control[130] as well as his bid to place the Russian Central Bank solely within the Supreme Soviet's jurisdiction.[131] As Khasbulatov prepared legislation reasserting parliament's control over the government,[132] Civic Union advertised not only its readiness to populate it but its intention to ensure that 'its' ministers were subordinated neither to the president nor the legislature, but to Civic Union itself.[133] With the Seventh Congress of People's Deputies a month away, El'tsin was again prepared to trade appointments for support, dumping Burbulis from his cabinet and elevating figures more congenial to the industrial lobby such as Oleg Lobov and Yurii Skokov. But Civic Union refused to cash in its politically lucrative position as a would-be centre holding the balance between legislature and executive, securing concessions from each. In reply, El'tsin would turn the tables on what was a paper tiger outside of the 'corridors of power' by using the Seventh Congress of People's Deputies to return the political struggle back to the streets.[134]

The intemperate opposition

The seeds of cooperation between the patriotic and communist movements sown on the streets of Moscow, St Petersburg and other large cities during the winter and spring blossomed in summer's violent protests at the Ostankino television centre[135] and ripened in autumn with the formation of a united left–right opposition, the Front for National Salvation (FNS). This organization constituted the purest expression of the tendency in Russian politics to derive an identity construct from hyperbolic representations of a nefarious other, against whom would be deployed the 'indifferent variety' of the collective: symbols and markers comprising an internally incoherent system held together by enemy images deployed to heap opprobrium on opponents and heroicize those calling the nation to righteous battle against them. The Front's founding, for instance, witnessed a breathtakingly desultory parade of slogans and symbols: summons to restore the Russian empire and to prosecute the international proletarian revolution to its final victory; the old imperial flag hoisted alongside the hammer-and-sickle; Orthodox priests and uniformed Nazis; crucifixes and swastikas; portraits of Stalin and portraits of Christ.[136] Hatred for the other – referred to as the 'Judas regime', the 'occupation government' and so forth – stabilized the volatile mix of elements, enabling each to contribute its force, undiminished by the qualifications of logical relationships, to the discourse of the 'united opposition'. The loss of Russia's greatness was the opposition's gravamen; its correlate of popular appeal was the implicit restoration of those things associated with it – material security, national pride, lifeworlds made familiar, if not intelligible, again. The Front's principal components included the parliamentary bloc Russian Unity, the RPA and RPU, the overtly fascist Russian National Union (RNU), the Russian Communist Workers' Party, the Union of Officers, some elements of Labouring Russia, and other small groups, with the ultra-nationalist daily, *Den'*, serving as semi-official organ. El'tsin immediately issued a decree outlawing the FNS, but the Front successfully contested it in court, thus validating its self-styled image of a potent force capable of bringing down the El'tsin regime. Indeed, its expectations for doing so at the Seventh Congress of People's Deputies were high enough to obviate the need for tactical alliance with the other opposition bloc, Civic Union.[137]

Despite hosannas of unity and selflessness in the cause of national salvation, the FNS evinced a measure of colliding ambitions and conflicting agendas at least equal to that displayed by the democrats two years earlier in their efforts to unite against the Soviet regime. On the patriotic side of this hyphenated opposition, rivalries were apparent with Civic Union's *gosudarstvenniki*, particularly because of the attention commanded by its most potent voice of patriotism, the country's vice-president. Another competitor, the Union for the Rebirth of Russia, soon appeared, positioning itself between Civic Union and the FNS.[138] More significantly, however, efforts to revive the banned communist party reached fruition when a marathon of maneouvres, competing congresses, internal schisms and raids on one another's membership[139] resulted in the February 1993 founding of the Communist Party of Russian Federation (KPRF).[140] Although the new party neither subsumed all organized communist forces nor established fraternal relations with them,[141] its roster of 500,000 made it the pre-eminent force on this quarter of the political field. Moreover, its leader, Gennadii Zyuganov, had long cultivated the image of Russian patriot. His signature had appeared under the pre-*coup* summons, 'A word to the people'; more recently, he had been one of the RNU's most visible leaders.[142] Rewriting communist ideology along the lines of Russian nationalism – 'The communist idea is the Russian idea' as he later expressed it[143] – his KPRF could campaign for the support of both the communist and patriotic constituencies in the FNS. But while conflicting ambitions within the Front sapped its unity, conflict with the El'tsin government breathed purpose across the entire field of communist and patriotic opposition, personified by the joint actions – reminiscent of DemRossiya's in form if not size – conducted daily on Red Square during the Seventh Congress of People's Deputies by the FNS and its arch-rival, Labouring Moscow.[144]

Political conflict engulfs the state

Constitutional collapse

The Seventh Congress of People's Deputies coincided with the end of constitutional government in Russia. To be sure, what had passed for a constitutional arrangement during the Russian state's first year of independent existence had little in common with constitutionalism – the conduct of government according to established rules based on a broad consensus among participants, hallowed by history and tradition. Russia had never enjoyed that. Written constitutions had arrived there with Soviet power as decorative trappings embellishing the Communist Party's monopoly on the state. As the Soviet order began to disintegrate, constitutions became weapons of political struggle. The Russian Federation 'constitutionally' proclaimed the superiority of its jurisdiction on Russian soil, regardless of the provisions of the Constitution of the USSR, the state in which it was then housed. In summer 1990, its Supreme Soviet ordained a commission to write a new constitution for the country, but thereafter lost interest in acting on the draft, apparently because the existing constitution – especially its provisions vesting supreme power in the Congress of People's Deputies – suited the political purposes of the majority in the legislature. Competing drafts were authored by individual politicians, more to boost their images as latter-day Solons than to set out the ground rules of government as an invitation to political dialogue, compromise and consensus.[145] El'tsin took a somewhat different tack by summoning a Constitutional Convention in June 1993. But his was less a commission to produce a new basic law for Russia than an effort to use their product to decommission his adversary, the Congress of People's Deputies.

During its first year, the Russian state none the less bore traces of constitutional government, at least as a potential to be realized, a direction to be pursued. Certainly, imperfections abounded. The Fifth Congress had empanelled a Constitutional Court with a make-up mirroring the distribution of factional forces in the legislature[146] and an activist inclination that quickly inserted it into the vortex of political controversies.[147] The Congress sought advantage against the executive branch by reinterpreting the ground rules of government, amending the constitution no less than 320 times between April 1992 and March 1993.[148] Yet, until the Seventh Congress, a shaky constitutional order had prevailed. It had been predicated on the Fifth Congress's temporary grant of extraordinary powers to the president to effect radical economic reform. El'tsin had the power that he wanted; but the Congress had the constitutional right to take it back. El'tsin refused to permit that outcome, a decision that was both cause and consequence of the legislature's reassertion of its authority: 'cause' in the sense that the legislature would remain unable to control the government in a significant way without recovering those powers it had transferred to the president for a year; 'consequence', inasmuch as the composition of *this* legislature – drained of El'tsin's previous supporters who had migrated to the executive branch or to the opposition – fairly guaranteed that the reassertion of the legislature's authority would be indistinguishable from the elimination of the president's.[149] In tragic irony, then, the political force appearing as the most potent bearer of parliament's institutional interests and advocate for constitutionally based government was the left–right opposition.[150]

This group's programme, spearheaded by its most militant wing, those 290 deputies affiliated with the FNS,[151] dominated the agenda at the Seventh Congress. Khasbulatov immediately set about enacting it, presenting the house with a battery of constitutional amendments that would replace presidential rule with a parliamentary regime, all of which passed easily. However, the assertion of parliament's prerogatives was accomplished by a mockery of parliamentary procedures. Contrary to the Congress's own by-laws, the voting on the constitutional amendments was conducted by secret ballot,[152] an innovation that sparked fisticuffs on the floor. The procedural parody continued with an information blackout in the press section, denying both journalists and, through them, the public, knowledge of that which was being voted on at a given time. Khasbulatov orchestrated the proceedings in the manner of his Soviet predecessors, arbitrarily rejecting some deputies' proposals, rewording others, regularly instructing the house on the correct way to vote.[153] Inside the Congress, if not actually in the country, parliamentary sovereignty prevailed until the tenth day of the session when El'tsin made an unscheduled appearance to inform the legislature that he no longer would abide its authority and would soon call a referendum to dissolve it.

El'tsin's announcement stunned Congress, particularly since he had spent the previous few days in negotiations with its various factions – something that he had neglected to do before the session opened[154] – that had apparently arrived at a political solution acceptable to most of them.[155] But his attempt to immobilize it on the spot, by summoning his supporters to walk out with him and thus deprive the Congress of a quorum, misfired badly. Fewer than 100 deputies responded and many of them drifted back into the hall within the hour.[156] That evening a televised rally at a Moscow factory found the president reprising Soviet-style rituals, receiving the near-unanimous endorsement (one member of the collective abstained) of the workers for his stand against the parliament and accepting congratulations for it from life-long communists. A few hours later, however, he accepted an invitation from Valerii Zor'kin, chief justice of the Constitutional Court, to meet with a congressional delegation the next day in order to resolve the crisis by compromise. And compromise was reached on the basis of Zor'kin's proposal to freeze the constitutional amendments just passed (thus restoring the president's powers), to suspend the Constitution's provisions for referenda (thus protecting the deputies from the voters) and to call a special referendum on the Constitution (without specification of the question to be put to the population) for 11 April.[157] On the following day, the Congress endorsed this bargain almost unanimously and without debate, vigorously applauding the spectacle of president, speaker and chief justice – hands clasped and raised upward – beaming broadly at one another in celebration of their new-found consensus.

By striking this compromise, the three branches of the Russian state placed themselves outside the framework of the Constitution, never to return to it. Its immediate trade-off – suspending the right of referendum and freezing duly adopted constitutional amendments – was patently unconstitutional.[158] Its third provision, a referendum on the Constitution itself, promised to make matters even worse. On one hand, there was no constitutional provision for amending the basic law via referendum. On the other, the compromise had begged the question of what this referendum would actually concern. Khasbulatov, who soon stated publicly that it would not involve the issue on which El'tsin insisted – whether the Congress should be dissolved[159] – unveiled the Supreme Soviet's version of the constitutional referendum in late January: twelve questions, all either obfuscating or distracting attention from the basic dispute that the referendum was supposed to solve.[160] Meanwhile, and despite the fact that he had himself authored the December compromise, Zor'kin was busy orchestrating a public campaign against staging any referendum. Informed by a series of roundtables that he organized with certain politicians and legal specialists,[161] Zor'kin began issuing appeals to cancel the project for the sake of Russia's fragile stability.[162]

Although originally summoned to extraordinary session to ratify the referendum's question(s), the Eighth Congress cancelled it. This event was epiphenomenal, a consecration of Khasbulatov's February announcement that the abolition of the presidency was the current task of legislatures throughout the country – stripping that office of all functions save the nomination of the prime minister, the immediate objective[163] –

and his appropriation of Zor'kin's roundtable to the Supreme Soviet as a 'permanently acting organ'.[164] December's constitutional amendments were now in effect. El'tsin replied with a threat to institute presidential rule and to hold the referendum that his supporters, who had organized their own roundtable,[165] had been demanding. His announcement provoked the Constitutional Court into a new series of self-discrediting judicial debacles,[166] and the Congress into convening yet another extraordinary session.

Meeting a few days later, the Ninth Congress voted to dissolve both the president's Federal Information Centre (which controlled television and radio programming) and his representatives in the regions. El'tsin ignored these acts. However, he did agree to the Ninth Congress's decision to call for a referendum on 25 April, despite the fact that the legislature reserved the right to compose the questions. They composed four: whether the voter had confidence in the president; whether he or she supported the government's policies; whether new elections should be called for the presidency; and whether new elections should be called for the Congress. Given the hardships inflicted by some sixteen months of economic 'shock therapy', this stratagem seemed guaranteed to produce a 'no' vote on the second item. Perhaps this 'no' would then influence the voters' decision on the first item. At any event, El'tsin's approval ratings in opinion polls at the time, hovering around the 25 per cent mark, seemed to indicate that his opponents could expect to win on this question, too. The final two questions on early elections would remain moot: not only was there no implementation clause in the referendum, but an improvising Constitutional Court had ruled that these were constitutional issues requiring the approval of two-thirds of all *eligible* voters.

Astoundingly, El'tsin scored victories in the referendum on all four questions. Since he had been touting the proceedings as a national decision on something that had not appeared on the ballot – the Constitution – he used the occasion of his success to take constitution-making out of the hands of the legislature and awarded it to a Constitutional Assembly that he summoned in June.[167] By early July this assembly had crafted a new constitution, merging the president's project with the most recent version produced by the Supreme Soviet's Constitutional Commission.[168] However, a new constitution was more by-product than purpose in this affair; El'tsin's strategy was plainly to eliminate the Congress via the adoption of a new basic law containing no provision for its existence. In order to secure the means to that end, he would require the support of the country's regional elites for his project. They would deny it.

Disintegration of the federation

El'tsin's efforts to scuttle the legislature by dissolving its constitutional basis foundered on the results of his own policies in the regions. Just as his government's statist/monetarist course had structured patterns of interest representation at national level by galvanizing one set of its victims into an industrial lobby that would be more or less pacified by *ad hoc* concessions doled out by the executive, so it stimulated the development of regional lobbies whose interests were advanced by senior administrators in the localities around whom elites at that level would coalesce. In either instance, the formation, articulation and accommodation of interests primarily took place *outside* of the institutions of political society in which the interaction of contending forces could shape the content and mix of interests expressing themselves through general rules (laws) conjoining, if not harmonizing, a number of (initially) separate demands. Instead, the transaction of interest politics *within* the executive machinery of the state produced an altogether different pattern. Here, interests might be accommodated, but not aggregated. Thus the common interest of the participants could appear only as the maintenance of a general situation conducive to the satisfaction of their particular claims. At the Constitutional Assembly's closing session on 12 July, it was precisely this 'common bond' among regional delegations that underlay their solidarity in rejecting the proposed constitution.[169] El'tsin's gambit fell foul of regional representatives intent on perpetuating the executive–legislative impasse on which their particular interests had thrived.

By dividing central authority, executive–legislative conflict in 1992–3 accelerated the disintegration of the federal system. Eager to enlist allies, both president and Supreme Soviet tendered various concessions and inducements to regional elites which – given the competitive bidding – forced each side to jack up its offers and induced regional leaders to stake out expanded spheres of authority for themselves. These developments represented the continuation of a comparable process of disintegration initiated by the struggle between Russia and the USSR. In the wake of the democrats' success in spring 1990, El'tsin's election to chair Russia's Supreme Soviet and the ensuing declaration of Russian sovereignty, Gorbachev had played the sovereignty card against his opponents by encouraging communist elites in the autonomous republics of the Russian Federation to declare sovereignty for their national-territorial units.[170] Not to be outbid, El'tsin instructed them to 'take as much sovereignty as [they] could swallow'. During the 'nine-plus-one' negotiations, both leaders agreed to accord them the same 'sovereign' standing as that enjoyed by the USSR's union republics[171] and Russia's Supreme Soviet reaffirmed their privileged status soon after the union had collapsed.[172] In March 1992, a 'federal treaty' was concluded between the Russian state and its constituent units, but it represented no more than a temporary cease-fire in the 'war of laws'. On one hand, key provisions in the treaty were honoured by all parties in the breach.[173] On the other, it sanctioned the crazy-quilt of claims to economic resources and rights over licensing and revenue gathering that had emerged with two-tiered federalism. The asymmetric distribution of authority among the federation's members codified in the treaty – to say nothing of the additional privileges bestowed by bilateral agreements on Tatarstan and Bashkortostan who had refused to sign it – thus served as incentive to the non-privileged regions to seek an upgrade in their status commensurate with that accorded the sovereign republics.[174] In addition to consistently pressing for a single standard of rights for all subjects of the federation,[175] many regions that lacked republic status solved this problem unilaterally by staging referenda on the issue and then declaring themselves 'sovereign' republics.[176] Threatened by equality, most of the original twenty sovereign republics no less consistently maintained that they had no intention of agreeing to a new constitutional order whose provisions failed to incorporate their privileged standing.[177]

The issue of sovereignty expressed in juridical terms the power struggles raging throughout the Russian Federation. Their form derived from the unified executive, and thus appeared as conflicts between governments. In the face of the president's control of regional offices, this would at first appear puzzling. Following the August *putsch*, presidential rule had been extended to Russia's regions by dissolving the executive structures of soviets and placing all administrative authority in the hands of heads of administration selected personally by El'tsin, Burbulis and Shakhrai,[178] and formally approved in most instances by the corresponding soviet.[179] The vertical line of presidential authority was completed by awarding these heads of administration the power to appoint their counterparts at lower levels[180] and by instituting the parallel structure of presidential representatives – hand-picked by Burbulis and Makharadze who supervised their performance[181] – encharged with overseeing the implementation of presidential policy in the regions. The powers granted to these offices, and the mechanisms for central control over them, were continually enhanced. Supervision of the presidential representatives, for example, was transferred directly to Sergei Filatov, head of the Administration of the President, following steep increases in support staff at both central and regional levels.[182] By February 1993, presidential decrees had transformed his representatives from monitors reporting on implementation to prefects actively engaged in it.[183] Similarly, the heads of administration were brought directly into the national government in March 1993 as the Council of the Heads of Administration chaired by El'tsin himself.[184]

However, despite the apparent strengthening of the vertical line of authority in the federation, the purely administrative forms relied on to achieve top-down integration revealed precisely the reverse result. Two general considerations accounted for that outcome. First, the deep disruption of production/distribution relations around the country effected by the economic reform had reinforced the importance of inter-elite ties within and among regions. With survival at stake – the survival of enterprises, meaning in turn the survival of schools, hospitals, transport, indeed, entire cities and towns – local and regional actors adapted by developing broad, intersecting barter networks that would keep their economies afloat,[185] by issuing local 'currencies'[186] and by juggling accounting and budgeting procedures to curtail the extractive capacities of the centre.[187] In short, these adaptations bound each of the respective regional elites more tightly together. Second, at the hub of these regional elite networks stood the administrators appointed by the centre. Once installed in office, presidential representatives and heads of administration were confronted by existing elite networks that they could either cultivate as bases of support or oppose and consequently face the retributive capabilities of that phalanx of officials representing elite interests. Although their decisions were by no means foreordained, the relevant arithmetic – two agents of the centre, each of whom would be courted by local cliques, thereby providing each with an incentive to strike a bargain before the other had – worked in the direction of collaboration with existing networks of officials. By summer 1992, the available evidence would indicate that nearly all of the centre's men had 'married the natives'.[188]

That pattern was counterpart to the results of the macroeconomic stabilization policy pursued at the national level. In either instance, the disjunction between a uniform policy in principle and an heterogenous mix of *ad hoc* arrangements, concessions and special indulgences in practice can be traced to the statist strategy of reform and the consequent retention of personalized authority relations inherited from the Soviet order. That aspect of authority was apparent in staffing procedures at all levels, as we have seen. It was even more obvious in the sacking of Yurii Boldyrev, who had replaced Makharadze as head of the Control Commission, for taking his responsibilities seriously enough to secure the dismissals of a number of regional officials for criminal wrongdoing despite the fact that many of the wrongdoers were clients of those in El'tsin's circle.[189] Although disguised by state insignias, personalized relations of authority also stood at the centre of the reform's second phase, privatization. At the level of national agencies,[190] regional committees,[191] and individual enterprises,[192] state officials regularly 'privatized' their own offices, using their control over the distribution of state assets to build dependency networks – and lucrative arrangements – for themselves. Configurations of power thereby produced would account for the ludicrous redistributive patterns witnessed in taxing and spending whereby wealthy regions contributed to the state's coffers at drastically reduced rates – when not withholding revenue payments altogether – yet benefited disproportionately from state subsidies.[193]

In the face of this real accretion of power to regional elites, it would seem rather improbable that the assembly of their representatives – the Council of the Federation, first formed in March 1993 as a potential interim parliament were the Congress of People's Deputies dissolved – would serve as an instrument to repair the divided centre of the Russian state and reknit the frayed federal system. Particularly after El'tsin's surprising success in the April referendum, regional elites closed ranks and dug in their heels against the president, fearing a loss of leverage should he capitalize on that victory, vanquish his opponents in the legislature and institute a new constitutional order.[194] They had already rebuffed him once, issuing a *de facto* veto over his draft constitution in July. None the less, he summoned them into session in September in an attempt to salvage some semblance of legitimacy for his efforts to decommission the Congress of People's Deputies with an offer to the Council of the Federation to assume the status of the upper house of a new parliament whose lower chamber would be elected after the Congress had been dissolved. The majority, however, balked at the idea, declining further participation in the Council even in an advisory capacity.[195] Three days later, on 21 September, El'tsin decreed the Constitution null and void.

The logic of extremes

Much has remained unclear with respect to the events of 15 September–4 October that brought Russia's first republic to a tragic and bloody end. Since – as part of the compromise underlying the amnesty of February 1994[196] – the State Duma nullified its earlier decision to empanel a commission to investigate those events, a definitive account may never appear.[197] Consequently, inconsistent and contradictory information has continued to surround the entire episode, from El'tsin's decree that triggered it[198] to his decree commissioning the armed forces to conclude it.[199] In the face of that problem, we shall follow again the approach taken to the August 1991 *coup*, framing the significance of this one by means of some of the categories developed hitherto. In this instance, the focus will fall on the consequences of the oppositional relationship between legislature and executive that developed after independence which set the terms for political struggles. Our argument, in short, will be that, within the structure of this relationship, each side in the conflict constructed itself and its other in analogous ways that entrapped both parties in a logic of extremes, *requiring*, in the end, the use of violence against the other as a purgative act of self-affirmation.

The counterpart to the social chaos and economic collapse under way in late-Soviet Russia and accelerated by Gaidar's reform in the post-communist period had been a political discourse that valorized certainty, consistency and closure. Regardless of the particular identity mediating it in a given instance – democrat, *gosudarstvennik*, patriot or communist – the discourse constructed some absolutized community ('the civilized world', 'the traditions of Russian state and civilization' and so on) in which the identities of its subjects were embedded. These identities, as we have seen, were formed in the course of political struggles, first against the Soviet regime and then against opponents on the political field formed in its aftermath. The positive content of any of the identities appearing in the post-communist period was therefore flimsy; rather, identities were weighted toward the negative, toward the capacity of subjects to account for social distress within the absolutized community by naming others regarded as responsible for it. Correspondingly, these systems of representation also absolutized the other – as enemy of the nation – and the self as its protector and saviour, a status enacted by doing battle with the enemy/other.[200]

El'tsin has explained his decision to annul the Constitution in precisely these terms. At the first session of his Constitutional Convention at which Khasbulatov and others took strong issue with the procedures laid down by his organizers, he confessed to 'once again . . . experiencing an overwhelming desire to break up this entire gang'.[201] After issuing the decree designed to do so, he claimed to have been required to reject any meaningful negotiations with the parliamentary leadership because the people 'would have lost trust in me forever'.[202] Although he later allowed his representatives to conduct negotiations with a delegation from the Supreme Soviet, he placed no stock in the possibility of reaching an agreement.[203] Throughout the two-week crisis, El'tsin steadfastly resisted efforts by some of his top advisers and supporters in the legislature,[204] a broad array of political parties and groups[205] and the Council of the Federation[206] to accept some formula

– principally, simultaneous new elections to both branches of government – that would represent a peaceful way out of the crisis.

The parliament's leadership was every bit as adamant about resisting any accommodation with the executive.[207] Since the onset of the latter's statist/monetarist policy in 1992, Khasbulatov had compensated for the flow of power to the presidency by building in the legislature a personalized network of dependencies around himself, using his office's arsenal of rewards and punishments – and supplementing it in rather creative ways – to connect the career interests of its members with the corporate interests of legislatures at all levels for which he, of course, was the spokesperson.[208] With that leverage at his disposal, Khasbulatov was able time and again during the crisis of September and October to quash efforts toward initiating negotiations,[209] to restaff the parliament's negotiating team with obstructionists once talks were under way,[210] or to marshal votes in the Congress to kill those agreements that had been reached at the bargaining table.[211] Indicative of the Khasbulatov group's orientation toward dialogue with the presidential side would be their portrayal of the killings accomplished by the Union of Officers – a leading element among those defending the White House – at the Commonwealth of Independent States' defence headquarters on the night of 22–3 September.[212] Khasbulatov blamed both deaths on El'tsin.[213] Later, during their negotiations with the presidential delegation, his representatives justified parliament's harbouring of the offenders by either denouncing the blockade of the White House effected in response to that violence or by accusing (*sans* evidence) the Moscow police for the killings.[214]

Between the president's inner circle and their opponents in the parliament's leadership lay a no-man's-land in which would-be neutrals were systematically cut down. Having announced his intention to refrain from taking sides in the conflict, for instance, procurator general Valentin Stepankov immediately became anathema to each.[215] Sadder still was the way in which certain actors representing institutions that might have interceded between the antagonists clumsily attempted to exploit the crisis for their own purposes, thus cancelling their credibility as mediators. Zor'kin repeatedly offered the services of the Constitutional Court in that respect, but his behaviour throughout the affair indicated his collusion with Khasbulatov and Rutskoi. On the first day of the crisis, he met with them in the White House to plan a response to El'tsin's decree.[216] On the second day, he engineered a court decision branding the decree unconstitutional and grounds for impeachment, thus legitimizing the Congress's vote to remove El'tsin from office and to install Rutskoi.[217] Moreover, not only did he continually turn a blind eye to the unconstitutional acts of the Congress,[218] but he secured the expulsion from the court of those justices not in tune with his brand of jurisprudence.[219] Similarly, Kirsan Ilyumzhinov – the president of Kalmykiya authorized by the Council of the Federation to persuade the antagonists to accept its plan for a resolution of the conflict – immediately torpedoed the Council's neutrality. Speaking to the parliament on the night of 30 September, he gave every indication that the council had taken the parliament's side in the dispute, referring to El'tsin as 'the former president' and to Rutskoi as 'acting president'.[220]

The leaders of the parliament recognized from the outset of the crisis that they lacked any meaningful support in society.[221] Consequently, they welcomed without hesitation those fascist formations arriving at the White House in the role of 'defenders', distributing arms to them – but not to their left-wing counterparts from Labouring Russia who also took on that role from the first – and thereby alienating the bulk of their own security forces who simply went home and never returned.[222] Equally, the complement of deputies remaining within the walls of parliament listed heavily rightward as the conflict continued. Some departed for political reasons; many others took advantage of the job-placement service initiated by presidential decree on 23 September which offered – in eloquent testimony to the feebleness of the identity constructs projected by both sides in the struggle – appointments in the executive to all deputies willing to surrender their mandates.[223] Thus the fatal logic of legislative–executive confrontation entered its penultimate stage, incongruously fusing the most extreme elements of the red–brown coalition with the cause of parliamentary democracy. This was the trap that Khasbulatov and Rutskoi prepared for themselves. Convinced that the army would either remain neutral or intercede on their behalf,[224] they stuck to a strategy of no concessions, no compromises. Rather, they would hold out in the White House until its supporters had gathered sufficient strength to achieve victory by force of arms.[225]

Within the logic of extremes, it remained for the presidential side to bait this trap and then to spring it.[226] The matter of baiting primarily involved inaction. As parliament's supporters began staging disruptions around Moscow in late September, police and paramilitary units (OMON) would scuffle with them but make no arrests.[227] On 2 October, violent demonstrations broke out in the heart of the capital on Smolensk Square, complete with barricades, Molotov cocktails and particularly brutal OMON assaults on demonstrators (who were some-times protected from them by regular police).[228] During the following day's rematch, a thin line of police and OMON rapidly retreated before an incensed crowd of about 7,000 under the direction of Labouring Russia's leader, Viktor Anpilov. Rather than rushing in reinforcements, the authorities removed nearly all forces that had been cordoning off the White House, abandoning their weapons and vehicles (keys in ignitions) to the crowd.[229] As the demonstrators advanced to the White House itself, shots rang out – apparently from the mayor's office across the square where hundreds of heavily armed security troops and OMON had established a base – striking police officers still envigilating before the parliament who were then negotiating with those in the front ranks of the march.[230] Militants immediately commandeered trucks and crashed into the ground floor of the mayor's office, mysteriously abandoned by the president's forces.[231] Armed largely with weapons left them by OMON, and riding in vehicles that OMON 'supplied', detachments under Anpilov and Al'bert Makashov set off to seize the television studios at Ostankino.

More violence occurred there, but accounts conflict as to which side commenced the shooting. For our purposes it would be important to record the fact that the presidential side effectively manipulated those events for their purposes. Vyacheslav Bragin, director of Central Television, ceased broadcasting after the majority of insurgents had left and while the building was still protected by some 500 well-armed troops and six armoured personnel carriers.[232] It would appear that his reasons for doing so were two-fold. First, as in August 1991, television journalists had been reporting on events with some measure of objectivity. Better, therefore, a blackout than running the risk of airing dispatches departing from the presidential script.[233] Second, the notice that was displayed thereafter on Central Television stations – BROAD-CASTS ON CHANNELS ONE AND FOUR HAVE BEEN CUT BY AN ARMED CROWD THAT HAS BURST INTO THE BUILDING – was part of the script. It amplified the dimensions of the armed insurgency, creating the impression that without the army's intervention it would succeed.

Springing the trap hinged on that impression. Units of the army ordered into Moscow on the evening of 3 October – as well as the Ministry of Security's crack counter-terrorist troops already stationed in the capital – continued to refuse to take sides in the battle.[234] Into the small hours of 4 October, another television station (Russian TV) continued in-studio broadcasts appealing to the population to defend the country from the insurgents. Some 15,000 people responded to Gaidar's summons to mass in front of the Moscow City Council where they erected symbolic barricades.[235] Relying on these images of the unarmed citizenry rallying to Russia's defence against an armed mob of 'bandits, fascists and criminals',[236] El'tsin finally persuaded his generals to follow his orders and attack the parliament. After a prolonged artillery barrage, the building was taken in the late afternoon.

Exploiting the logic of extremes paid handsome dividends to the presidential side in the short term. By allowing their opponents in the legislature to discredit themselves thoroughly and then crushing them with overwhelming force, El'tsin's team emerged from the conflict as undisputed masters of the country. Initially, public opinion supported the decision to use violence against parliament.[237] Trade unions that had greeted his decree nullifying the constitution with calls for a nationwide political strike[238] now pledged their loyalty, as did regions which had steadfastly opposed his *coup d'état* prior to the devastating cannonade trained on the White House that doubtless had a demonstrative effect for them as well.[239] To capitalize on their political monopoly of the moment, the presidential side attempted to legitimate it through parliamentary elections (neither very free nor very fair) that included a referendum on a new constitution (adopted despite the voters' failure to endorse it) that instituted a modified form of dictatorship.[240] Many hundreds of lives were claimed by the violent termination of the first republic.[241] But, in the longer term, the cumulative damage to state and society was even greater.

12   Neither democracy nor dictatorship

The face of contemporary political life in Russia combines both democratic and dictatorial features. Their co-presence has been inscribed by the victors of October 1993 into the country's constitution which retains institutions and practices associated with modern democracy – freedom of expression and association, public elections and popular assemblies – but drastically restricts their influence on the executive agencies of the state. The legislative power of the popularly elected lower house of the Federal Assembly (the State Duma) is hemmed in by the upper chamber (the Council of the Federation) the vast majority of whose members owe their seats directly or indirectly to the president, the president's own law-making and veto prerogatives, and a nominally independent Constitutional Court, whose loyalties have leaned toward the justices' patron – the president – as evinced, for instance, in the way in which they have freighted the legislative process with a definition of the majority required to pass a bill: half-plus-one of all *seats* in the Duma, no matter how many are vacant at a given time owing to truancies, assassinations or failure to hold elections in certain districts. Consequently, the executive's power dwarfs that of the legislature. This distribution of authority in the constitutional order calls to mind the pattern of 'delegative democracy' as described by Guillermo O'Donnell, a sort of elected dictatorship unencumbered by a legislative counterweight that enables the president to enact his putative popular mandate to perform surgery on an ailing body politic ('reform').[1] However, that concept would have limited purchase in contemporary Russia where two of its key components go partly or entirely missing. First, the 'delegation' of democracy is predicated on the residual restraints that law and the courts exercise over executive power, curbing its arbitrary and undemocratic use. In Russia, not only are these institutions decidedly deficient in that department,[2] but the executive, when so disposed, acts in ways unencumbered by the rules that it promulgates itself.[3] Second, the constraints supplied by organized interests or the executive's own base of organized support seem to count for very little in Russia where interests are primarily serviced *within* the machinery of state in particularistic fashion and where the executive – when experiencing the need for a base in political society – simply uses its resources to create one. To be sure, the influence of public opinion or the criticisms levelled at the government by leading actors in political society should not be discounted entirely. But bearing in mind that influence, we should overlook neither the fact that the executive represents the dominant force on the field of politics itself – its voice is amplified over state television and radio, it shapes electoral outcomes by administrative intervention and ballot fraud – nor the fact that it can silence, inhibit and restrict other voices. Local authorities confiscate critical newspapers just as the president may dissolve the Duma should it exercise either of its two direct constitutional controls over the government: withholding confirmation from the president's designee for the post of prime minister or sustaining a vote of 'no confidence' in the government for a period of three months.

The interplay between political society and the state would suggest that the system's democratic features are not without influence to curb its dictatorial potential. The publicity generated by the press and electronic media, the actions of both civic groups and parliament and, particularly at elections time, the criticisms voiced by politicians have sustained a public sphere and the implicit notion of the government's accountability before the citizenry. From this perspective, democracy and dictatorship cohabit uneasily. However, the development of the Russian polity in the late-Soviet and post-Soviet periods to date has not produced any mechanisms by which this accountability can be realized directly in practice – if anything, the trend has been in the opposite direction – thus indicating that dictatorship and democracy do not so much cohabit as maintain separate residences. Although an end to the Soviet state's active prohibition of social communication has provided that space in which identities and interests can form, they are weakly mediated by the institutions of political society since parties and parliament are not meaningfully linked to the exercise of state power. As such, interests gravitate toward the agents of their satisfaction – executive organs – a pattern that both inhibits their mediation in civil and political society and undermines the coherence of state institutions, retarding their capacities to penetrate and regulate society, and to extract and appropriate resources. Here, we survey the ongoing development of politics in Russia, organizing our discussion along the lines of the four problematics introduced in the first chapter: the problem of state structures; the problem of social communication; the problem of interest; and the problem of social and political identity. This survey is certainly made no easier by the fact that the transformation begun by perestroika is still under way. Political relations remain in flux, just as the visage of a stable outcome continues to elude participants and observers alike. None the less, flux and instability do not equate with chaos. Indeed, they are as enduring as the remarkably durable conditions that generate them.

The problem of state structures

The statist strategy for transforming the socio-economic order has reproduced in the Russian state the weak structures of its Soviet predecessor. This outcome is reflected most immediately in the relative incoherence of state organizations that have themselves been penetrated by power groups at all levels of the federal system. In turn, that incoherence has sharply diminished the state's capacities to regulate, extract and appropriate resources. Although weakness expresses itself in physical terms (declining output, declining revenues and so on), its origins lie elsewhere: namely, in the structure of relations among holders of state office. Accordingly, whereas the size of government has increased substantially in recent years,[4] formal rules governing the civil service effectively still do not exist.[5] Size, then, contributes not to enhanced capacity but to increasing incoherence.[6]

Incoherence is itself the product of rules; not formal ones that are based on impersonal relations but widespread informal understandings that shape actual behaviours. For instance, the formal rules governing the state's fiscal policies pale into insignificance in light of the regularized practices of non-payment of taxes and non-remission of funds to cover state purchases. Since tax rates are often set at confiscatory levels, firms engage in a variety of avoidance schemes, from bribing tax collectors to perpetrating physical assaults against them, a practice sufficiently common in the capital in 1995 to have prompted the formation of a paramilitary auxiliary unit that subdues by force of arms those subject to taxation before the inspectors arrive to make their assessments.[7] Strapped for revenues and mindful of the demands of international lending agencies to balance budgets and control inflation, the government regularly reneges on payment for its purchases and thus directly exacerbates the country's non-payments crisis (non-payments by mid-1994 stood at four times the level of liquid assets in the entire economy) which, in turn, compounds the problem of revenue collection.[8] Taxing and spending practices, then, would have little to do with a rational policy pursued according to impersonal rules governing the interaction between state agencies and private firms; rather, they reflect the *sub rosa* presence of another set of rules according to which officials effectively appropriate their offices and engage in various sorts of personalized exchanges – from straightforward payoffs to highly articulated forms of resource acquisition[9] – all at the expense of the state itself.

Comparable economies on diminished scale exist in the legislature as well, reflecting in that institution those personalized authority relations characteristic of the executive. On one hand, participant-observers in the legislative process point to a powerful tendency among deputies to refrain from enacting legislation, especially bills concerning such cardinal issues as government responsibility toward parliament and legislative control over its actual spending.[10] As one has remarked, 'In fact, the government does as it pleases and most deputies want that situation to continue.' This aspect of legislative–executive relations stems from a number of factors: the avoidance of institutional responsibility by deferring decisions to the executive whose actions then become convenient targets for legislative criticism; a widespread inclination among deputies against enacting laws that would establish unambiguous rules, in the belief that they and their associations will benefit more through personal connections in the legal netherworld of state and economy;[11] the persistence of those tendencies that flourished in the Soviet and Russian Congresses of People's Deputies[12] whereby loyalty to those in influential positions is repaid with concrete, albeit illicit, favours.[13] Contrary, then, to everyday assumptions regarding rational action among legislators, most deputies in the Russian Duma have willingly surrendered their formal rights and actively collaborated in violations of the rules of their chamber in order to enable officers – such as Ivan Rybkin, chairperson of the Fifth Duma (1993–5) – to usurp power within the institution which they employ to pay off individual deputies[14] as well as to parlay it into privileged access to executive agencies.[15] Comparable patterns have prevailed in the Council of the Federation.[16] In 1994, the appointment of the chairpersons of both chambers to the president's Security Council had reinforced and extended the practices of influence trading and the appropriation of public offices even while the appointments represented rather clear violations of constitutional provisions regarding the separation of legislative and executive powers.

The formal division of powers in the federal system and the separation of powers within its units have likewise fallen victim to executive usurpations. Along the lines of the former, a presidential decree on 'Strengthening the unified system of executive power' has saddled all regional heads of administration – whether appointed or elected – with direct responsibility to the president, therefore making them liable to dismissal on his initiative.[17] In the wake of the president's October 1993 dissolution of local legislatures, the reconstitution of legislative bodies throughout Russia has been generally synonymous with their capture by administrative elites together with their associates in the worlds of business and organized crime, between whom boundaries are porous when they exist at all.[18] Consequently, the formal separation of powers has become almost entirely fictive; legislatures do not so much control the exercise of executive authority as facilitate it; government does not appear as a regulator of economic relations but as that site where the major players congregate to appropriate state resources to themselves.[19] Deprived of the material sustenance that access to, or influence over, the resources disposed of by executive bodies provides, the organizations of political society wither and decompose. The power monopolies established by local cliques in control of executive offices and their attendant resources are thus able to subdue potential resistance to their rule by exchanging those resources – subsidies to the press, premises for the courts and so on – for preferred behaviours. The clumsy methods of federal control – appointments to, and monitoring of, regional administration – have proven sadly inadequate to the task of taming these tendencies among regional elites to pocket power and to use it as they see fit.[20]

These tendencies are integral to the particular political-economy emerging in post-communist Russia, one rather aptly dubbed 'merchant capital' by Michael Burawoy and his associates[21] who have highlighted the role of state-centred exchange/distribution networks populated primarily by officials from the old communist *nomenklatura*. These networks service their respective sectors of putatively privatized firms[22] – whether arranging barter relations, cheap state credits or international transactions – and, of course, skim proceeds for themselves. Thus the directing forces in the economy are primarily parasitic ones, deriving their profits from the movement of goods and services – licensing, duties, taxes, mark-ups on turnover, bribes and protection payments – rather than from production. Consequently, production stagnates and contracts. Resources appropriated from it are not reinjected as investments for future growth but either are relocated in the West[23] or set to work in Russia to renew the turnover in trade and the profits derived (quickly) from it.[24]

In this context, the term 'privatization' carries few if any of the connotations that accompany its usage in the West: detached from the state sector, refitted for market competition, animated by entrepreneurial spirit and so forth. Instead, the pointed substitute commonly employed in Russian parlance – *prikhvatizatsiya*, or 'ripping off' – would more accurately describe that which has been transpiring in the national economy: the use of state offices to appropriate state assets and to enhance their potential for income generation, as well as to reappropriate those privatized by one group when control of office has passed to another.[25] The epitome of this process involves the privatization of privatization itself. This has taken the form of an exchange brokered by behemoths in the energy sector and their attendant financial institutions – whose singular 'representative' in the state has been Prime Minister Viktor Chernomyrdin – that places the economy's most lucrative enterprises in the hands of a consortium of big banks which, in return for temporarily storing assets in the state treasury in order to offset immediate shortfalls in revenue, determine how, to whom and at what prices these firms will be sold off to private buyers.[26]

Just as certain networks emerging from the state and economic apparatuses of the Soviet order have laid hands on its remunerative assets, so other groups that had thrived outside the 'laws' of that order but had, in fact, riddled its formal organizations,[27] have enlarged their niche during the transformation. Indeed, the tight-knit structures of the Soviet underworld, the money that they had amassed and the associations that they had established with (corrupt) state officials provided the criminal subculture with enormous advantages for its brutal entrance into the Russian market.[28] There would be perhaps no clearer indication of the weakness, if not impotence, of the current Russian state than the hypertrophy of criminal activity in the country, expressed as a steady tide of business-related assassinations[29] and the take-over of some 40 per cent of the entire economy by organized crime.[30] The collapse of the state's ability to protect its citizens generally is reflected in mushrooming armies of private bodyguards and security services, numbering 800,000 according to one 1995 estimate and thought to outnumber the police by a factor of 1.5.[31] Indeed, levels of lawlessness and violence have even destroyed the particular order that had earlier prevailed in criminal society as newcomers have appeared to shoot their way into the worlds of crime, protection rackets and business activity.[32] To date, the principal response of the authorities to the burgeoning levels of lawlessness has taken the form of more lawlessness, especially the presidential decree[33] authorizing – in contradiction to the constitution and a number of laws – warrantless arrests of both suspects and their associates, a thirty-day period of internment before any charges need be brought, and special courts wherein procedural rights are severely diminished.[34] It may well be the case, as human rights advocates have argued, that these measures award extraordinary powers to law enforcement agencies that have already been corrupted, powers that they then employ against sectors of the business community that have either remained outside the ambit of corrupt practices or, at least, have not yet become beholden to these particular officials and their associates in the underworld.[35]

The mysterious origins of this decree[36] are symptomatic of the ongoing confiscation of state power by highly personalized networks within the executive. Accordingly, the machinery of state comes to resemble its Soviet predecessor as a collection of 'wheels within wheels'. The outer ones are the established agencies of government that often turn or not according to the momentum supplied by less-visible bodies within the presidency (the Security Council, the Administration of the President) whose function would be comparable to that of the old CPSU apparatus. Rather like Stalin's personalized ('inner') secretariate formed within the CPSU's formal organizations, another wheel turns within the two just mentioned, namely, the Presidential Security Service (PSS), a multi-functional praetorian guard assembled by Aleksandr Korzhakov who headed it till June 1996. Naturally, information concerning this innermost group is exceptionally sparse. Even the November 1993 decree that chartered it remains an official secret.[37] In the words of Sergei Filatov, the president's chief of staff (1993–6), 'I know neither the composition of [this] service nor its structure, nor what these people do. Although it is known that they are strengthening their influence in the administration and the government, they are expanding, bringing personnel under their control and much else.'[38] Filatov's mention of the personnel function by the PSS would refer to vetting all top government officials,[39] a capability later extended while Korazhakov's lieutenant, Mikhail Barsukov, headed the Federal Security Service (1995–6). Its lines of administrative responsibility were redrawn, linking it directly to the PSS and thus to effectively all positions in government.[40] The Korzhzkov–Barsukov network built its power within government by controlling and manipulating finances and information.

By inserting certain provisions into the licenses of firms exporting petroleum, weapons, gold and gems, the PSS has been able to siphon off substantial sums of money for which it accounts to no one.[41] Reportedly, it uses the proceeds to finance its activities in government and politics (for example, subsidizing certain election campaigns). Its influence has been amplified further by gaining access to, and control over, information. With the creation within the PSS of the Federal Agency of Governmental Communication and Information (FAPSI) – a successor to its 'analytic department'[42] – the PSS has now centralized information gathering and analysis for all areas of government work.[43] The personnel comprising these inner wheels of the Russian state are almost exclusively former KGB officers who, despite reorganizations and changes in titles in the post-communist period, have maintained essentially their old networks,[44] their previous functions gradually restored along with organizational coherence now centred around the PSS.[45]

Statism, the consequent evisceration of political society and the resulting appropriation of office in the executive account for an overall deterioration of state capacities that has accompanied the enhanced positions of power and influence enjoyed by certain groups and individuals. Although the presidency has emerged as the pre-eminent power centre in the Russian state, considerable uncertainty surrounds the issue of who actually controls (directs, influences) whom within that institution and how groups within it articulate with other power centres in government, the military, business and finance. For instance, corrupt practices in the military – from illicit sales of weapons and supplies to providing transport for automobiles stolen in Europe and then sold in Russia – have been both rampant and effectively unpunished. Does this suggest that El'tsin has become hostage to those generals on whom he relied in October 1993 to vanquish his opponents, or would it indicate a reprise of Soviet patterns whereby the prosecution of known offenders is suspended in order to establish a relation of personal dependency between the wrongdoers and a president (or someone in or near the presidency) protecting them from retribution?[46]

The problem of social communication

Under communism, the problem of social communication was conditioned by the party-state's active prohibition against social communication that constricted the formation of social interests and identities, aborting their development by removing possibilities for their mediation across the population. Although that condition has vanished in post-communist Russia, its long-term effects on social consciousness, together with the massive dislocations engendered by the socio-economic transformation and consequences of the statist orientation in government and politics, have combined to reproduce the problem in new ways. To take an obvious example, a free press now exists, yet the spiral of prices and the deterioration of general living standards have severely circumscribed its place in society. By mid-1995, the overall circulation of newspapers and periodicals had declined to a mere 7 per cent of the figure posted in 1990.[47] Considering that this statistic includes government publications that have benefited disproportionately from state subsidies[48] and thus have escaped precipitous declines in circulation,[49] the situation for independents has been even worse. Moreover, state subsidies are not doled out without strings attached. Consequently, independent publications – especially (but not exclusively)[50] regional or city newspapers – are forced to exchange editorial autonomy for government financing.[51] The contracted circulation of the printed word has meant that most citizens have come to rely exclusively on electronic media for news. Although independent television and radio stations now compete with, and thus influence the broadcast content of, their government counterparts, the direct role now played by FAPSI in overseeing state television and radio programming,[52] the blatant use of these media to further the government's political agenda,[53] and the harassment visited on independent stations presenting unflattering portraits of top officials – such as that directed in 1995 against the weekly lampoon 'Kukly' (Puppets') – suggest that the democratic/dictatorial balance lists heavily toward the latter.

With respect to the qualitative aspect of social communications, we encounter a number of phenomena that, on the surface, appear nothing short of bizarre. Taken together, they indicate an enormous proclivity in the population to seek escape from the desperate and worsening circumstances of everyday life. Thus large segments of society seem keenly receptive to messages in which elements of the miraculous have been encoded, a response to pressing problems in its own way rational, given the apparent hopelessness of instrumentally oriented courses of action to bring relief (paychecks, often withheld for many months, do not keep pace with prices; the government sometimes confiscates savings).[54] Along these lines, the miracle informs the significance of the many foreign soap operas that have become the most popular television fare in post-communist Russia. It colonizes the world of business and finance in the form of seemingly preposterous and self-parodying images featured in the television advertising campaigns of bunko artists that persuade many millions of people to part with their savings.[55] It intrudes – comically and tragically – in politics and government.[56] On the financial ruins of countless families victimized by various 'investment' scams, a number of 'shareholder associations' have appeared, channelling the anger of hundreds of thousands of the dispossessed directly into the political arena. The principal exponent of the politics of miracles placed first in the national balloting of December 1993, thereafter relying on the sufficient receptivity in the population to *outré* antics to fix himself firmly in the public eye.[57] From Zhirinovskii's calculated outrageousness to the counter-theatrical politics of groups such as the Sub-Tropical Russia Movement[58] – with all manner of costumed Cossack,[59] communist and patriot in between – social communication seems in many respects carnivalesque. Significations subdue their social referents on the communicative plane, not so much integrating society as reproducing new forms of indifferent variety.

This aspect of social communications is readily illustrated by the configuration of organized forces on the political field. Despite the enormous gravitational shifts surveyed in this book – communists turned democrats, democrats turned *gosudarstvenniki* or patriots, and so on – the basic parameters of the field of cultural politics in the pre-political period (Figure 2.1, above) have persisted. To be sure, permutations – in the form of 'left-', right-' and even 'centrist-centres'[60] – have multiplied. But the overall shape of the political field would not be supplied by these derivative hybrids but by the primary oppositions structuring it, as set out in Figure 12.1. Since the spaces separating the four terms in the chart would be populated by scores of groups claiming greater or lesser affinity with two or more of the terms in the square – all subject to further regroupings, migrations and permutations – it would be pointless to specify the relations mediating the primary identities themselves (as we have done in Figure 2.1). In this instance, a characterization of the practical relations among the primary terms would be precluded by the fact that the many compound identities derived from them mediate those relations, each with a potential for collaboration and conflict with others, all shifting in time. Rather than attempting to map this kaleidoscopic field, Figure 12.1 isolates the (apparently quite durable) primary identities informing political communications. The oppositions among them establish those differences enabling political subjects to make sensible statements, even while these same subjects combine the terms in ways calculated to enlarge their respective audiences – say, the KPRF's 'patriotic communism' or the Congress of Russian Communities' purported syntheses of liberal economic and 'traditional Russian mentality'[61] – and thus generate contradictory or nonsensical messages.

The key to this structure of political communications lies with the state. With the exception of those political organizations fielded at election time by the dominant group within the state itself – Russia's Choice in 1993,[62] Our Home Is Russia in 1995[63] – organized forces in political society have had neither a direct claim on state power nor responsibility for its use. Consequently, identities manifest themselves by thematizing one or another desideratum that government allegedly has neglected, negated, perverted or betrayed. The democratic identity is reinforced by calling attention to those ways in which the state appears undemocratic; the patriotic one, by railing against a government regarded as anti-Russian; and, since the communist idea has been

Figure 12.1   Primary identities on the field of post-communist
Russian politics

broadly discredited, most communists piggyback on that same nationalist notion, distinguishing themselves from patriots by speaking in
'social democratic' dialect about the importance of 'social protection'.
With respect to the advantages enjoyed by compound identities on this
field, the mutual unintelligibility among the three primary discourses
that structure it actually favours impossible combinations and grafts.
Communication need not require a coherent synthesis available to all,
rather, it may replicate forms of indifferent variety whose separate
elements appeal either to discrete sections of the electorate or to those
simply spellbound by signification.[64]

This peculiar stability of the primary identities on the field of political
communication corresponds to a comparable stability in the electorate.
To be sure, stability in this respect need not connote firm links between
espoused principles and preferred practices. Most people have evinced
solid attachments to certain symbols – among which, the 'strong hand'
of authority seems the perennial favourite – while remaining equivocal or
even contrarily disposed toward enacting what the symbols appear to
imply.[65] Although interpreting voting patterns is difficult – because of
both the character of the elections in question (only in 1993 did party
differentiation begin to organize the vote in a meaningful way) and the
high levels of ballot falsification (by one estimate, accounting for as
much as 20 per cent of the 'vote' in 1993)[66] – a number of separate
studies have converged in the conclusion that the respective sizes of the
constituencies corresponding to the three primary identities on the
political field have remained quite stable across those elections in which
they have been measured: the 1991 presidential elections, the 1993
referendum and the 1993 and 1995 parliamentary elections.[67] Both the
democratic and communist poles have attracted from 20 to 25 per cent
of the electorate, (with a diminution of a few percentage points for the
former and a corresponding increase for the latter in 1995); the patriotic

one, usually from 10 to 15 per cent; and the remainder reflects no clear or consistent orientation (the 'swing vote' in Western parlance, the 'swamp' in Russian).[68] It would appear that the dominant voter coalition in the first two of these elections – the so-called 'El'tsin majority' – had been a combination of the democratic and patriotic constituencies, a coalition that unravelled in December 1993 when El'tsin himself was not in the race[69] and which collapsed altogether in 1995 as a consequence of the war in Chechnya.[70] Whether the fiercely anti-communist campaign that secured El'tsin's re-election in 1996 has actually revived it remains unclear at this writing.

Since politics involves interaction, the stability evinced by the structure of the political field and voting patterns in the mass electorate readily produces its opposite in political life. This apparent paradox dissolves on recollecting the particular character of the stability in question: one exhibiting strong significations and weak referents such that parties package immediate objectives as battles for absolute truth, then shift sides without hesitation when doors leading to those objectives close. To illustrate, take the lopsidedly 'presidential' constitution sponsored by Russia's Choice in autumn 1993 which undermined the possibility that the legislature could serve as a counterweight to executive power. Within weeks of the constitution's 'adoption', however, Russia's Choice leaders Egor Gaidar and Boris Federov resigned from the cabinet and announced that they would lead the 'democratic opposition' to Chernomyrdin's government, a notion whose practical import the constitution had already cancelled.[71] Similarly, the Party of Russian Unity and Accord (PRES) campaigned in 1995 on the promise to combat 'illegal actions to create regional and all-Russian associations of local authorities out of the ranks of the appointed heads of local administrations'.[72] These remarks pledged PRES to oppose the very organizations created by its leaders – Sergei Shakhrai and Aleksandr Kotenkov – some two years earlier when they headed the State Committee for the Affairs of the Federation,[73] but which had moved into other orbits after Shakhrai and Kotenkov had left those posts. These events underscore the fact that in interaction no single force can control outcomes, while the strong but shallow representations issuing from actors on a political field characterized by indifferent variety confuse interest with intention and thus continually destabilize the conditions for political action itself.

The problem of interest

The principal conditions restricting the formation and mediation of social interests that characterized the Soviet order – a low degree of socio-

economic differentiation and an active prohibition of social communication policing all sites for expression and association – have been overcome
in Russia's transformation.[74] Accordingly, thousands of associations
advancing one or another interest have appeared: trade unions and
business groups, professional associations and amateur societies, organizations affiliated with religious, ethnic, gender, humanitarian and
ecological concerns, and more. At the same time, however, the structural
transformation under way has ushered in conditions affecting interest
formation and mediation that yield patterns that diverge significantly
from either those encountered in capitalist states (whether democratic or
authoritarian in form) or that which would be specified on the basis of our
model (Table 1.1). The particular problem of interest in post-communist
Russia would derive from, and contribute to, three aspects of the political
and moral economy surveyed, above: the interpenetration of state and
economic institutions (the appropriation of offices); the institutional
weakness of political and civil society; and the confused, segmented
character of social communication (indifferent variety). Here, we
examine interactions among three principal sectors – labour, capital and
the state – in order to illustrate how conditions structuring the formation
of interests array them 'vertically' along the hierarchic lines of state power
while militating against 'horizontal' forms of association with a capacity
to mediate themselves in political and civil society.

We begin with an absence. In the face of tremendous difficulties,
autonomous working-class organizations had rapidly coalesced to contribute critical energies to the recovery of political life in Russia.
However, in communism's aftermath, they decomposed just as fast,
effectively ceding their space on the political field to workplace superiors,
certain business lobbies and their confederates in the old trade union
apparatus.[75] Emblematically, the Union of Labour – an electoral bloc
founded by the Federation of Independent Trade Unions (FITU) and
the political reincarnation of the RUIE, the Russian United Industrial
Party (RUIP) – contested the 1995 elections on a platform homoge-
nizing working-class interests and those of industrial capital. That
formulation concealed the overriding coincidence of interests between
FITU and RUIP elites that defined workers' interests for them. In the
same way that the FITU has been as much a business organization as a
trade union,[76] so the cadres of industry directors forming the backbone
of the RUIP have performed welfare functions at the workplace that
ordinarily do not appear on the job descriptions of business executives.
Working in tandem, these elites have protected the jobs (if not the
incomes) of workers,[77] cushioning the blows dealt to living standards by
the reform via the provision inside the factory gates of a broad range of

consumer goods obtained through barter networks.[78] But this administrative arrangement has not resonated politically among those whom
these elites would presume to represent. Although the FITU includes
some 60 million members, its Union of Labour garnered less than 2 per
cent of the vote in the 1995 elections, indicating the effective absence of
a link between the vehicle for interest representation and the political
identities assumed by the Russian working class.

This relationship between labour and capital has precluded significant
differentiation and thematization of their respective interests. Rather
than a horizontally negotiated agreement arrived at by autonomous
subjects, the coincidence of interests appears here as vertical subordination, as a form of patronage extended by the privileged partner. In the
same way that organized labour formulates working-class interests in
conjunction with, rather than in opposition to, industrial capital, so the
paternal character of the relationship appears in the consciousness of
most business executives as a 'code of honour' obligating them in
particularistic ways to employees and associates in their respective
networks, thus inhibiting that impersonal rationality associated with
market structures.[79] Industrial executives and their trade union partners
therefore articulate the interests of *their* workers in the same way that
their counterparts in the rural sector have consolidated *their* peasant
constituencies by employing their offices against the rival form of
economic and political activity represented by private farming.[80]

The epoxy of this labour–capital alliance has been supplied by the
state. Organizationally, it has appeared as a Tripartite Commission on
the Regulation of Social and Labour Relations, a federally structured set
of commissions instituted by El'tsin to achieve a 'social partnership'[81]
along the lines of West European corporatist practices whereby
representatives of labour, management and government negotiate solutions to industrial disputes. However, unlike the European experience of
government mediation between opposing interests advanced by unions
and business associations, Russia's Tripartite Commission has functioned almost exclusively as a forum in which a labour–management
alliance (principally, the FITU and the RUIE) has taken sides against
the government mediators. That pattern of conflict has grown directly
out of the state's role in the industrial sector, especially its supply of
subsidies to industry for which the business–union tandem lobbies.[82]
Workers, protected from unemployment by this arrangement, contribute
to its maintenance by carrying out industrial actions, typically calling
strikes to collect unpaid wages, which translate in practice into a form of
mass pressure on government to release the funds required to pay for its
industrial orders.

If state protection for weak producers has shaped the formulation of interests in the manufacturing and agricultural sectors – sustaining Soviet-era networks that appear on the present political field as unlikely alliances of organized labour and capital – then direct associations between holders of state office and their counterparts in the stronger sectors of the economy (such as banking and certain extractive industries) have tended to blur, if not erase, state/private distinctions. As such, the category 'interest' would lose its usual connotations of a socio-political association attempting to influence state actions, and would refer more to either power groups penetrating the state or, conversely, emanating from the state to set up shop in the private sector. In both instances, interests would be weakly mediated on the field of politics; they instead crowd the corridors of power.

Along the lines of Burawoy's 'merchant capital' model of the Russian economy, banks have appeared primarily at key nodes in the structure of trade, to service, and thus to exact profits from, domestic and foreign transactions. In the main, these banks have been formed on the basis of state institutions that have been privatized and typically retain a substantial portion of state ownership.[83] Banking has become the single most remunerative occupation in Russia and banks overwhelmingly dominate the country's roster of leading enterprises.[84] They funnel the flow of state subsidies to ailing industries, often diverting substantial portions of these funds, sometimes absconding with them entirely, to their own purposes.[85] They have derived windfall profits from their intermediary role in foreign trade circuits, financing the import of manufactured items against the export of raw materials and energy.[86] Their money-making capabilities have drawn organized crime directly into the world of high finance, as witnessed by the epidemic of assassinations in the banking community and the share of the country's financial capital – according to some reports, over one-half of it[87] – that has fallen into the hands of the mafia.

The interlocking of state and economic power is most pronounced precisely where business is most lucrative, namely, in the energy sector. There, the profits derived from export sustain a complex of producers, their attendant financial institutions and control of top government posts that facilitate – through licensing, tax regulations, suspension of anti-monopoly laws and so forth – money-making operations. This complex represents the premier power bloc in politics and government whose branches run directly into other sectors of the economy with profit-making potential, suturing together a collection of state–private conglomerates that channel their 'interests' directly into the state organs, bypassing publics, parties and parliament.[88] As a result, patron–client relations are reproduced within the state and, through them, between the principal economic sector and the dependent ones. This pattern would be readily apparent in the manner in which business interests have organized themselves politically.

After the collapse of communism, hundreds of business associations sprang to life in Russia. In large measure, their origins lay in the realization among business leaders that the institutions of political society were poor vehicles for translating their demands into state policies, and that organizing at closer proximity to state power itself promised better results. Accordingly, business interests began to group themselves into larger associations, each distinguished from the other by its particular association with the state. Those firms most injured by the 1992 reforms and, initially at least, enjoying least entrée in the corridors of power, affiliated with the Russian Union of Industrialists and Entrepreneurs (RUIE) and/or the Russian Confederation of Manufacturers, both based on the remnants of the Soviet *nomenklatura*. Others, enjoying closer links to top officials, were organized by the democratic *nomenklatura* into the Association of Privatizing and Private Enterprises (APPE) and, less importantly, Entrepreneurs for a New Russia. Banks, interlocked with state functions and finances, enrolled in the Association of Russian Banks.[89] In their respective ways, these associations attached business interests directly to the state. For instance, the RUIE's position within the Tripartite Commission extended the lifeline of state subsidies directly to its members.[90] The APPE, which was formed on the basis of the State Property Committee parcelling out its holdings to a new class of owners, tithed its members to finance its political organization – Russia's Choice – and used its control of state offices to channel foreign assistance, allocated for the Russian economy generally, directly and exclusively to its own members.[91] The upshot of government–business interpenetration has been a confusion of interest formulation within business associations themselves, as executives in one branch or another of the economy enlist in as many associations as possible in order to multiply their chances for access to those offices where decisions affecting their firms are made.[92] As such, interests surrender the capacity for public mediation. In the same way that distinctions between labour and capital disappear in their organized representation, so differences among various business sectors are muted within their attendant associations. Differences, of course, remain. But they lose both the need and capacity to articulate themselves publicly. The capacity for satisfying their needs resides in the various networks linking state offices to positions in the private sector. Interest-based politics, therefore, is less a public phenomenon than an exercise in Byzantine intrigue conducted inside the state.

The problem of identity

The problem of identity appears as the reverse aspect of those conditions inhibiting the formation and mediation of distinct interests in the polity. If interests gather like so many barnacles attached to the underside of the state, feeding themselves from the moorings that it provides, then identities parade in the open air of political society as various forms of protest against that entire arrangement. The detaching of state from political society that we have discussed tends to decouple interest and identity, establishing more or less separate sites for their formation and mediation. In the Russian political vernacular, the 'parties of power', concealed behind state titles and working through their respective networks in the economy, encase the practical dynamics of 'interest'. The symbolic mediation of identity transpires among the 'parties of society'. As Bill Lomax has observed with respect to post-communist transformations generally, the organized forces of political society have not 'formed for the rational pursuit of desired ends, but [appear as] communities formed on the basis of affect rather than interest or reason'.[93]

The potential to combine interest and identity in reasonably coherent patterns of political organization was present at communism's collapse. The refusal to call national elections, along with the statist course of transformation adopted by the government, eclipsed it in two respects. First, the postponement of elections at this critical juncture denied political society the opportunity to thematize issues of identity and interest linked by political parties as programmes competing for voter support and aimed at steering the practical course of state action. Since elections were not called, symbolically mediated 'communities' – democrats, *gosudarstvenniki*, patriots and communists – were not supplanted by pragmatically oriented constituencies. Second, the particular association that developed at that time between the democratic forces and the state led directly to the former's undoing. Paralleling the failure to institutionalize a relationship of support and responsibility between the democratic movement and 'their' leaders at the top of the state hierarchy, a comparable pattern appeared within the democrats' organizations, especially inside DemRossiya and its *de facto* successor, Russia's Choice. In either instance, leaders with access to state positions simply ran roughshod over their supporting organizations, arbitrarily awarding positions and favours as they saw fit.[94] As a consequence, the democratic identity was undermined. Communism's collapse was the first blow, depriving democrats of that nefarious 'other' against which their identity had been projected. Post-communist political practice was the second, as the democrats' worldly orientation toward securing a normal life – social and material progress within a new political order based on a rule of law – amounted to a promise soon forfeit when 'their' government embarked on a statist course of economic reform. While individual democrats were in many instances spectacularly successful in securing their own career interest, the democratic identity was drained of significance, as signalled in popular parlance by terms such as 'democratic *nomenklatura*', '*prikhvatizatsiya*' or '*demokrator*' (literally an agent of democracy used in slang to denote a policeman's truncheon). A measure of the impact of that development can be taken from efforts to revive the democratic identity, such as the appearance in 1994 of the Party of Popular Conscience whose membership has been open only to 'highly moral and law-abiding citizens'.[95] Signification and practice, identity and interest, pull apart and in opposite directions.[96]

Pushing upward to claim some influence over state action, 'parties of society' have tended to confect strong representations of their respective identities, portraying themselves as communities based on moral concerns, prepared to render whatever sacrifices that the nation might require, ready to champion the cause of the dispossessed, and so forth. On the other hand, 'parties of power' – pushing downward into political society at the advent of elections to secure popular mandate for their rule – have experienced glaring deficits in that respect. Although the premier party of power in the 1993 elections, Russia's Choice, enjoyed every material advantage in that contest (its members set, changed and with impunity broke the election rules; it received the lion's share of campaign financing and had full control of state television), it was routed nationally by a stronger symbology marshalled by Zhirinovskii. Civic Union, a power bloc of enterprise directors and state officials, projected an anaemic identity based on a combination of know-how and moderate temperament: it captured less than 2 per cent of the vote. With the approach of the 1995 elections, parties of power regrouped. Following two unsuccessful attempts to field a political organization for those races,[97] the Administration of the President created and managed its own self-proclaimed two-party system: Our Home Is Russia (NDR), headed by Prime Minister Chernomyrdin, and the Bloc named for Rybkin, led by the Duma's speaker.[98] The strategy, here, involved an ambitious but ill-fated effort to distribute both governmental and legislative posts at national, regional and local levels between these two parties of power in staggered fashion – if one received, say, a ministerial appointment, then the position of deputy minister would go to the other – thus assembling a two-party government prior to the elections themselves.[99] Again the overwhelming material advantage of office proved no match for the assault of symbols. Rybkin's Bloc sputtered to a disastrous showing at the polls, attracting about 1 per cent of the vote. Chernomyrdin's received 10 per cent but, even under the dubious assumption that its tallies were clean, the 'ruling party' was outpolled by the KPRF (22 per cent) and the Liberal Democratic Party of Russia (LDPR) (11 per cent). Were the democrats less fractured into competing parties and blocs in those races – resulting in only one democratic group, Yabloko, surmounting the 5 per cent threshold for representation in the Duma – it would appear that that political identity, too, would have enjoyed the advantage over the parties of power in the national voting. These events illustrate in another way the detachment of state from political society and the corresponding separation of the politics of interest from that of identity. Since ballots appear to have no purchase at the state/interest emporium, it is left to voters to redeem them at one of the kiosks where identities are displayed. And here parties of power such as NDR have been no match for the competition. Unlike their democratic, communist or patriotic opponents, they appear iconically on the political field, unable to signify anything but themselves. Thus NDR's overwhelming material advantages in mass communications in 1995 – unlimited free access to state television plus nearly 2 million dollars for paid spots, amounting in itself to 605 times more than the (victorious) KPRF's television budget[100] – failed to compensate for the poverty of its symbology which simply was unable to mediate any identity other than that of a peak association conjoining state power and big capital.

At this writing, some among the parties of power appear to be seeking solutions to their painful deficit of signification by scripting and promulgating a new official state ideology to combat those forces alleged to 'desacralize and discredit' state power in the eyes of the population.[101] Whatever course those efforts might take, they seem to be inspired by the need to replace the current Babel generated by contending political identities with a common national discourse, something that Russia has not experienced since Marxism–Leninism was dethroned. A new synthesis would probably feature traditional religious and militaristic elements, inasmuch as the Orthodox Church and the army have been among those rare institutions still enjoying the confidence of the population.[102] A statist solution to the problem of identity thus portends a return to the triadic construct of the Soviet era, awaiting at the moment that leader with sufficient cult or charisma to hold its disparate elements together and a degree of political mobilization sufficient to support a full return to those repressive practices required to secure its sacral character.

But there are at least two alternatives to that outcome: continued disintegration and a revival of political life. Here, we make no predictions, but close by restating our principal theme in comparative perspective. Throughout this study we have treated 'politics' in an old-fashioned way, refusing to reduce it to the more sophisticated concept of elite competition and bargaining against the backdrop of public elections, registering an implicit protest against the tyranny of reality that sustains that view. From a positivist vantage, our conception would appear as utopian or ideal. But there is an important distinction to be made between those adjectives. Whereas utopias might rightly be regarded as paving the road to ruin, ideals point the way toward a future more worth living than the life that we have known. As such, ideals do not stand apart from political practice; however imperfectly, they inform it, thus breaking reality's tyrannical grip. Russia's December 1995 elections would illustrate this directly. Despite the fact that their president had reminded the country over national television at the very beginning of the balloting that election results were absolutely unrelated to the policies that his government would pursue,[103] some 65 per cent of the electorate came out to vote anyway. This unrealistic or irrational behaviour signified the fact that the great majority of eligible voters would continue to act as if they were, indeed, political subjects. No matter the immediate consequences of their votes, they would express themselves all the same. Unfortunately, that moment has been too much missing from those comparative analyses of democratization in post-communist countries that insert that experience into categories drawn from other 'transitions', while remaining indifferent to the possibility that post-communist cases 'may not simply refine the common wisdom, they may overturn it'.[104] One contribution that Russia's political rebirth makes to either refining or overturning that wisdom consists in the fact that the political struggles surveyed in this book have been in the end outgrowths of another, ongoing struggle 'merely' to have politics.

Notes

1. POLITICS AND COMMUNISM: FIGURE AND GROUND

1　For a number of reasons, we wish to refrain from supplying a substantive definition of 'politics'. The closure that such a definition provides – if it were to be of much use at all as a definition – could easily preclude many phenomena important to our purposes. It would also run the risk of smuggling culture-bound conceptions directly into the heart of the analysis as well as reinforcing, rather than restraining, our own normative biases. But the possible consequences of indulging this wish – not being understood, being misunderstood – could make matters even worse. In order to escape this predicament, we offer the view that politics is a form of activity that involves the population, in Thomas Jefferson's words, as 'participators in the government of affairs'. In the same vein, Hanna Pitkin has referred to politics as 'the activity through which relatively-large and permanent groups of people determine what they will collectively do, settle how they will live together, and decide their future, to whatever extent that is within human power'. While subscribing to these general definitions, however, we should note the grave imperfections evinced by any political practice in the face of these high standards. Pitkin's definition can be found in her 'Justice: On Relating Private and Public', *Political Theory* 9 (August 1981), pp. 327–52, esp. p. 343. Jefferson's words are quoted by Hannah Arendt, *On Revolution* (New York: Viking, 1963), pp. 124–5.

2　Our discussion draws on Andrew Arato's essay, 'Social Movements and Civil Society in the Soviet Union', in J. B. Sedaitis and J. Butterfield (eds.), *Perestroika from Below* (Boulder, CO: Westview, 1991), pp. 197–214.

3　A discussion of these types of communicative action can be found in Jürgen Habermas, *Communication and the Evolution of Society* (Boston: Beacon, 1979); *The Theory of Communicative Action*, vol. I (Boston: Beacon, 1984).

4　The addition of 'threats' to the category of communicative action in the sphere of civil society might at first seem to contradict the stipulation that communication here involves a normative discourse oriented toward reaching understanding. When it is remembered, however, that this is precisely the form taken by threats in the sphere of civil society – trade unionists, for example, walk picket lines with placards that read 'management unfair' rather than 'we want more' – this objection is overcome. A more serious problem for this model – indeed for the entire issue of civil society – concerns the fact that the so-called 'voluntary associations', especially those that tend to exercise power and influence, also exercise it over their own members, thus drastically qualifying the adjective 'voluntary'. On this matter, see Theodore Lowi, *The End of Liberalism* (New York: Norton, 1969); Claus Offe, 'Political Authority and Class Structure – an Analysis of Late Capitalist Societies', *International Journal of Sociology*, 2 (Spring 1972), pp. 73–108; Adam Przeworski, *Democracy and the Market* (Cambridge: Cambridge University Press, 1991), esp. pp. 1–12.

5 For a stimulating discussion of the interrelations obtaining between state and civil society, see Michael Walzer, 'The Civil Society Argument' in Chantal Mouffe (ed.), *Dimensions of Radical Democracy* (London: Verso, 1992), pp. 89–107.

6 At issue here is the phenomenon of 'statization', a term connoting the break up of all spontaneous or subject-initiated forms of social interaction along with the provision of new forms by the state. On the history of this process, see Lewis H. Siegelbaum, 'State and Society in the 1920s' in R. Crummy (ed.), *Reform in Russia* (Urbana, IL: University of Illinois Press, 1989), pp. 126–43; Moshe Lewin, *The Making of the Soviet System* (New York: Pantheon, 1985), esp. pp. 209–85.

7 A. L. Unger, 'Stalin's Renewal of the Leading Stratum: a Note on the Great Purge', *Soviet Studies* 20 (January 1969), pp. 321–30; Lewin, *The Making of the Soviet System*, pp. 209–85.

8 Mark Von Hagen, 'Civil–Military Relations and the Evolution of the Soviet Socialist State', *Slavic Review* 50 (Summer 1991), pp. 268–85.

9 For an analysis of labour relations in the Stalin period that effectively unmasks this fact, see Donald Filtzer, *Soviet Workers and Stalinist Industrialization* (Armonk, NY: M. E. Sharpe, 1986).

10 Whether these results followed 'logically' as a stage in the development of this system is a question that does not concern us. For varying accounts that make arguments along the lines of developmental logic, see Chalmers Johnson (ed.), *Change in Communist Systems* (Stanford, CA: Stanford University Press, 1970); Seweryn Bialer, *Stalin's Successors* (Cambridge: Cambridge University Press, 1980); Ken Jowitt, *New World Disorder* (Berkeley: University of California Press, 1992).

11 Jean Piaget, *Structuralism* (London: Routledge & Kegan Paul, 1971), pp. 5–16; see also Marc Barbut, 'On the Meaning of the Word "Structure" in Mathematics' in Michael Lane (ed.), *Introduction to Structuralism* (New Work: Basic Books, 1970), pp. 367–388.

12 Examples of this concept of structure are not hard to come by in the human world. The numbers system, a game of cards and the language we use all organize and define their elements in determinate ways, all consist of internal rules that relate these elements one to another, all include transformation possibilities (say, the addition or subtraction of numbers, drawing fresh cards in a hand of poker or the construction of plural nouns in a language) that are implicit in the rules of ordering themselves. These examples also illustrate another aspect of structure. In each case, what appears in the 'outer' world of experience – whether it is numbers written on a chalkboard, words on a piece of paper or cards lying on a table – serves

to represent, to reproduce and to reinforce that which corresponds to it in the 'inner' world of the subject. Although people produce structures, structures also 'produce' people – as mathematicians, as card players and as language users, to mention only those practices relevant to the cases at hand. Structure is no more apart from us than we are apart from it. For a discussion of these points, see Yuri Lotman, *The Universe of the Mind: a Semiotic Theory of Culture* (London: I. B. Tauris, 1990).

13 Although our explanation of structure as a dynamic concept leans heavily on social exchange theory, it also seems to be fully compatible with that offered by William H. Sewell, Jr which is based on a tension among non-homologous relations established by the intersection of different structures – say, kinship, religion and education – functioning simultaneously. For Sewell's approach, see his 'Theory of Structure: Duality, Agency and Transformation', *American Journal of Sociology* 98 (July 1992), pp. 1–29.

14 In the literature on social exchange, the category 'general' or 'generalized' has also been used in reference to a non-property order in which exchanges among individuals in fact take the form of exchanges between individuals and the entire community. For a discussion of this type of 'generalized exchange', see Claude Levi-Strauss, *The Elementary Structure of Kinship* (2nd ed.; Boston: Beacon, 1969), esp. chapter 15.

15 For an extended discussion of these aspects of market exchange, see I. I. Rubin, *Essays on Marx's Theory of Value* (Detroit: Black and Red, 1972).

16 C. B. MacPherson, 'The Meaning of Property' in C. B. MacPherson (ed.), *Property* (Toronto: University of Toronto Press, 1978), pp. 1–13; Gary Libecap, *Contracting for Property Rights* (Cambridge: Cambridge University Press, 1989), pp. 1–7; Steven A. Gilham, 'State, Law and Modern Economic Exchange' in D. Willer and B. Anderson (eds.), *Networks, Exchange and Coercion* (New York: Elsevier, 1981), pp. 129–51.

17 Max Weber, *Economy and Society* (3 vols.; New York: Bedminster, 1968), vol. III, p. 946.

18 *Ibid.*, esp. pp. 224–5, 1,394–5.

19 Fernand Braudel, *The Structures of Everyday Life* (New York: Harper and Row, 1981), *The Wheels of Commerce* (New York: Harper and Row, 1982), and *The Perspective of the World* (New York: Harper and Row, 1984).

20 Michel Foucault, *Discipline and Punish* (New York: Pantheon, 1977) and *The History of Sexuality* (vol. 1; New York: Random House, 1978); Marc Raeff, *The Well-Ordered Police State* (New Haven, CT: Yale University Press, 1983).

21 These questions are discussed in detail in: Harry Braverman, *Labor and Monopoly Capital* (New York: Monthly Review Press, 1974); Richard Edwards, *Contested Terrain* (New York: Basic Books, 1979); Graeme Salaman and Kenneth Thompson (eds.), *Control and Ideology in Organizations* (Cambridge, MA: The MIT Press, 1980); Mary Zey-Ferrell and Michael Aiken (eds.), *Complex Organizations* (Glenview, IL: Scott, Foresman, 1981).

22 Michael Urban, *The Ideology of Administration* (Albany, NY: State University of New York Press, 1982); Gerald E. Fruge, 'The Ideology of Bureaucracy in American Law', *Harvard Law Review* 97 (April 1984), pp. 1,276–88.

23 For example: Frederick W. Taylor, *The Principles of Scientific Management* (New York: Harper, 1911); Luther Gulick and L. Urwick (eds.), *Papers on the Science of Administration* (New York: Columbia University, Institute of Public Administration, 1937); Herbert A. Simon, *Administrative Behavior* (2nd ed.; New York: Macmillan, 1960), esp. pp. 110–11; Amatai Etzioni, *Modern Organizations* (Englewood Cliffs, NJ: Prentice Hall, 1964).

24 For an extended treatment of 'strong' and 'weak' structures from the perspective of exchange – a treatment on which much of the foregoing has been based – see David Willer, 'Quality and Network Structure' in Willer and Anderson (eds.), *Networks, Exchange and Coercion*, pp. 109–27; and also his *Theory and the Experimental Investigation of Social Structures* (New York: Gordon and Beach Science Publishers, 1987), esp. chapters 6 and 8; 'Exclusion and Power: a Test of Four Theories of Power in Exchange Networks', *American Sociological Review* 58 (December 1993), pp. 801–18. For a related argument showing that rational calculation in exchange relations is more a product of the structure in which exchange occurs than an attribute belonging to the parties themselves, see Barry Hindess, 'Rational Choice Theory and the Analysis of Political Action', *Economy and Society* 13(3) (1984), pp. 255–77.

25 Hillel H. Ticktin, *Origins of the Crisis in the USSR* (Armonk, NY: M. E. Sharpe, 1992), pp. 12–13, 83–6.

26 Lewis H. Siegelbaum, 'Norm Determination in Theory and Practice, 1917–1941', *Soviet Studies*, 36 (January 1984), pp. 45–68; Bob Arnot, 'Soviet Labour Productivity and the Failure of the Shchekino Experiment', *Critique* 15 (1981), pp. 31–56.

27 Vladimir Anderle, *Managerial Power in the Soviet Union* (Westmead: Saxon House, 1976); Timothy Dunmore, *The Stalinist Command Economy* (New York: St. Martin's, 1980); David Granick, *The Red Executive* (Garden City, NY: Doubleday, 1960).

28 On the mass production of waste as a central characteristic of the Soviet economy, see Ticktin, *Origins of the Crisis in the USSR*, pp. 10–13, 117–18. The ecologically disastrous results of this economy of waste have been vividly described by Murray Feshbach and Alfred Friendly, Jr, *Ecocide in the USSR*, (New York: Basic Books, 1992).

29 The Soviet economy was, of course, renowned for poor quality products. For an illustration of the relationship between particularized exchange relations and the production of shoddy goods, see S. Ovdienko, 'Nikomu ne nuzhnaya produktsiya', *Izvestiya* (8 January 1983).

30 Jan Pakulski, 'Bureaucracy and the Soviet System', *Studies in Comparative Communism*, 19 (Spring 1986), pp. 3–24; Don Van Atta, 'Why There Is No Taylorism in the Soviet Union', *Comparative Politics* 18 (April 1986), pp. 327–37; Filtzer, *Soviet Workers and Stalinist Industrialization*.

31 Jerry Hough, *The Soviet Prefects* (Cambridge, MA: Harvard University Press, 1969).

32 Michael Urban, 'Conceptualizing Political Power in the USSR: Patterns of Binding and Bonding', *Studies in Comparative Communism* 18 (Winter 1985), pp. 207–26; William DiFranceisco and Zvi Gitelman, 'Soviet

Political Culture and "Covert" Participation', *American Political Science Review* 78 (September 1984), pp. 603–21.

33 Zygmunt Bauman, 'Officialdom and Class: Bases of Inequality in Socialist Society' in Frank Parkin (ed.), *The Social Analysis of Class Structure* (London: Tavistock, 1974), pp. 129–48; Jowitt, *New World Disorder*, pp. 121–58; David Willer, 'Max Weber's Missing Authority Type', *Sociological Inquiry* 37 (Spring 1967), pp. 231–40.

34 For a discussion of this pattern of generating personal dependencies, see Urban, 'Conceptualizing Political Power in the USSR', esp. pp. 216–21.

35 Aleksandr Zinov'ev, *Kommunizm kak real'nost'* (Lausanne: Editions L'Age D'Homme, 1981).

36 For example: Merle Fainsod, *Smolensk Under Soviet Rule* (Cambridge, MA: Harvard University Press, 1985); J. Arch Getty, *Origins of the Great Purges* (Cambridge: Cambridge University Press, 1985); J. H. Oliver, 'Turnover and Family Circles in Soviet Administration', *Slavic Review* 32 (Fall 1973), pp. 527–545. Also articles by Gabor Tamas Rittersporn, 'Soviet Politics in the 1930s: Rehabilitating Society', *Studies in Comparative Communism* 19 (Summer 1986), pp. 105–28; 'Stalin in 1938: Political Defeat Behind the Rhetorical Apotheosis', *Telos* 46 (Winter 1980–1), pp. 6–42; 'The State Against Itself: Social Tensions and Political Conflict in the USSR: 1936–1938', *Telos* 41 (Fall 1979), pp. 87–104; *Stalinist Simplifications and Soviet Complications* (Chur, Switzerland: Harwood, 1991).

37 John P. Willerton, *Patronage and Politics in the USSR* (Cambridge: Cambridge University Press, 1992); Michael Urban, *An Algebra of Soviet Power* (Cambridge: Cambridge University Press, 1989), esp. pp. 59–135; T. H. Rigby, 'Early Provincial Cliques and the Rise of Stalin', *Soviet Studies* 33 (January 1981), pp. 3–28; R. V. Daniels, 'Evaluation of Leadership Selection in the Central Committee, 1917–1927' in W. Pintner and R. Rowney (eds.), *Russian Officialdom* (Chapel Hill: University of North Carolina Press, 1980), pp. 355–68; Joel C. Moses, 'Regional Cohorts and Political Mobility in the USSR: the Case of Dnepropetrovsk', *Soviet Union* 3(1) (1976), pp. 63–89. On similarities between clientelism in the Soviet and tsarist periods, see Daniel Orlovsky, 'Political Clientelism in Russia: the Historical Perspective' in T. H. Rigby and B. Harasymiw (eds.), *Leadership Selection and Patron-Client Relations in the USSR and Yugoslavia* (London: Allen and Unwin, 1983), pp. 3–28.

38 Mark Granovetter, 'The Strength of Weak Ties', *American Journal of Sociology* 78 (May 1973), pp. 1360–80; 'The Strength of Weak Ties: a Network Theory Revisited' in P. Marsden and N. Lin (eds.), *Soviet Structure and Network Analysis* (Beverly Hills, CA: Sage Publications, 1982), pp. 105–30; N. Lin *et al.*, 'Analyzing the Instrumental Use of Relations in the Context of Social Structure' in R. Burt and M. Minor (eds.), *Applied Network Analysis* (Beverly Hills, CA: Sage Publications, 1983), pp. 119–32.

39 These forms of interaction would count as instances of what Barry Markovsky *et al.* have identified as 'weak power' within and between certain network structures. See their 'The Seeds of Weak Power: an Extension of Network Exchange Theory', *American Sociological Review* 58 (April 1993), pp. 1–13.

40 Joel Migdal, *Strong Societies and Weak States* (Princeton: Princeton University Press, 1988), esp. pp. 3–41.

41 Nicholas Timasheff, *The Great Retreat* (New York: E. P. Dutton, 1946); Robert Tucker, *The Soviet Political Mind* (rev. ed.; London: Allen and Unwin, 1972), esp. pp. 121–3.

42 Migdal, *Strong Societies and Weak States*, p. 4 (italics in original).

43 See, for instance, N. Pastukhov, 'Pravda nepobedima', *Izvestiya* (26 July 1986).

44 G. A. E. Smith, 'The Industrial Problems of Soviet Agriculture', *Critique* 14 (1981), pp. 41–65; Hillel Ticktin, 'Andropov: Disintegration and Discipline', *Critique* 16 (1983), pp. 111–22; Gertrude Schroeder, 'The Slowdown in Soviet Industry', *Soviet Economy* 1 (January–March 1985), pp. 42–74.

45 Examples in the sphere of economic production can be found in: Gertrude Schroeder, 'The Soviet Economy on a Treadmill of "Reforms"', *Soviet Economy in a Time of Change* (Joint Economic Committee of the US Congress; Washington, D.C.: GPO, 1979), pp. 312–40; George Feiwel, 'Economic Performance and Reforms in the Soviet Union' in D. Kelley (ed.), *Soviet Politics in the Brezhnev Era* (New York: Praeger, 1980), pp. 70–103; William Conyngham, *The Modernization of Soviet Industrial Management* (Cambridge: Cambridge University Press, 1982). For illustrations in the area of territorial coordination of planning and plan implementation, see: Ronald J. Hill, 'Local Government since Stalin' in E. Jacobs (ed.), *Soviet Local Politics and Government* (London: Allen and Unwin, 1983), pp. 18–33; Michael Urban, 'Local Government and Popular Needs: Where the Official Ideology Meets Everyday Life' in S. White and A. Pravda (eds.), *Ideology and Soviet Politics* (London: Macmillan, 1988), pp. 136–58.

46 Roy Medvedev, *Let History Judge* (New York: Vintage Books, 1973), pp. 192–239, 344–55; Lewin, *The Making of the Soviet System*, pp. 209–51.

47 According to Aleksandr Solzhenitsyn's account of the terror perpetrated in the 1930s, '75 per cent of the time the particular choice of *whom* to arrest . . . was determined by human greed and vengefulness; and of that 75 per cent, half were the result of material self-interest on the part of the local NKVD.' See his *The Gulag Archipelago*, vol. I (Glasgow: Collins Harvill, 1974), p. 152 (emphasis in original). Similarly, under the more stable conditions of the Brezhnev years, Vladimir Shlapentokh recounts numerous episodes in which members of the intelligentsia would toady to the authorities in order to enlist the repressive power of the state against their rivals in the academic world. See his *Soviet Intellectuals and Political Power* (Princeton: Princeton University Press, 1990), esp. pp. 172–202.

48 Jürgen Habermas, 'Hannah Arendt's Communications Concept of Power', *Social Research* 44 (Spring 1977), pp. 3–24; esp. p. 8.

49 Jürgen Habermas, 'On Social Identity', *Telos* 19 (Spring 1974), pp. 91–103.

50 On the subject of Marxism as doctrine in the USSR, see Alvin Gouldner, *The Two Marxisms* (New York: Seabury, 1980); Herbert Marcuse, *Soviet Marxism* (New York: Vintage Books, 1961); Leszek Kolakowski, *Towards a Marxist Humanist* (New York: Grove, 1968); James P. Scanlan, *Marxism in the USSR* (Ithaca: Cornell University Press, 1985).

51 Nina Tumarkin, *Lenin Lives! The Lenin Cult in Soviet Russia* (Harvard: Harvard University Press, 1983).

52 In 1936, for instance, the Central Committee of the Communist Party of the Soviet Union issued a special decision concerning the production of Borodin's opera 'Bogatyri' (which contained a farcical libretto written by Dem'yan Bednyi), that condemned it for its 'indiscriminate blackening of the great warriors of the Russian folk epics' and called the baptism of Russia 'a positive epoch in the history of the Russian people'. *Protiv fal'sifikatsii narodnogo proshlogo* (Moscow: Iskusstvo, 1937), pp. 3–4. Similarly, in this same period, a nationwide competition launched by Stalin led to the publication of the authoritative textbook *Kratkii kurs istorii SSSR* in 1937 which dethroned the erstwhile reigning school of Marxist historiography, headed by M. N. Pokrovskii, and resurrected from its rogues' gallery a wide collection of Russian tsars, princes and generals who were now declared to have been 'progressive'. 'Revolyutsiya v soznanii: Beseda s doktorom istoricheskikh nauk professorom Diplomaticheskoi Akademii MID SSSR Vladlenom Sirotkinym' (an interview conducted by V. Igrunov), *Vek XX i mir* 7 (1988), pp. 18–23.

53 Edward Keenan, *Ethnic Russia in the USSR* (New York: Pergamon, 1980).

54 One illustration of this conscious exploitation of traditional forms of social communication would include the Soviet regime's use of the Russian folkloric idiom. Although folklore was initially disdained by the authorities as embodying the 'backward' nature of Russian culture, its forms were deliberately appropriated by the propaganda apparatus in the 1930s, substituting communist figures, especially Lenin and Stalin, for past heroes and changing the plot, setting and content to reflect the regime's industrial priorities, thus yielding an official Soviet state socialist 'folklore' that persisted in the USSR until its final years. See: Frank O. Miller, 'The Image of Stalin in Soviet Russian Folklore', *The Russian Review* 39 (January 1980), pp. 50–67; Felix Oinas, 'The Political Uses and Themes of Folklore in the Soviet Union', *Journal of the Folklore Institute* 12 (1975), pp. 157–75; Stephen White, 'The USSR: Patterns of Autocracy and Industrialism' in A. Brown and J. Gray (eds.), *Political Culture and Change in Communist States* (New York: Holmes and Meier, 1977), pp. 25–65.

55 Michael Cherniavsky, *Tsar and People* (New Haven: Yale University Press, 1961).

56 To illustrate, consider the letter to Stalin written by shock workers (Stakhanovites), in which they remark that 'when you mounted the rostrum, we were filled by a powerful sense of joy . . . We nestled closer one to another and felt some kind of magical, heroic strength flowing into us' (quoted in R. Maier, 'O chudesakh i chudovishchakh: Stakhanovskoe dvizhenie i stalinizm', *Otechestvennaya istoriya* 3 (1993), pp. 3–4). Even if the content of *this* letter was purely apocryphal, its composition would none the less reflect precisely the non-rational forms of social integration via the medium of sacral authority.

57 Here we rely on A. J. Greimas' concepts of 'mythic' and 'practical' as the fundamental dimensions of semantic structures. See his *Structural Semantics* (Lincoln, NB: University of Nebraska Press, 1983).

58 Michael Urban, 'The Structure of Significance in the General Secretary's Address: a Semiotic Approach to Soviet Political Discourse', *Coexistence* 24(2) (1987), pp. 187–210.

59 Rachel Walker, 'Marxism–Leninism: the Politics of the Empty Signifier and the Double Bind', *British Journal of Political Science* 19 (April 1989), pp. 161–89; also her 'Language and the Politics of Identity in the USSR' in M. Urban (ed.), *Ideology and System Change in the USSR and East Europe* (London: Macmillan/New York: St. Martin's Press, 1992), pp. 3–19.

60 Moshe Lewin, *The Gorbachev Phenomenon* (2nd ed.; Berkeley, University of California Press, 1991), pp. 63–71. Similarly, Grzegorz Ekiert uses the term 'domestic society' to describe this site of human interaction in the face of weak state and social structures; see his 'Democratization Processes in East Central Europe: a Theoretical Reconsideration', *British Journal of Political Science* 21 (July 1991), pp. 285–313; esp. pp. 299–303.

61 Jadwiga Staniszkis, 'Forms of Reasoning as Ideology', *Telos* 66 (Winter 1985–6), pp. 67–80.

62 For example, Jerry Hough and Merle Fainsod, *How the Soviet Union is Governed* (Cambridge, MA: Harvard University Press, 1979), pp. 284–93; Alfred E. Evans, 'Developed Socialism and the New Programme of the CPSU' in White and Pravda (eds.), *Ideology and Soviet Politics*, pp. 83–113.

63 Jürgen Habermas, *Legitimation Crisis* (Boston: Beacon, 1975), p. 108; also his *Communication and the Evolution of Society*, p. 178; and *The Theory of Communicative Action*.

64 Raymond Taras, 'The Crisis of Ideology and the Ideology of Crisis: Marxist Critiques of the Polish Socialist System 1956–90' in Urban (ed.), *Ideology and System Change*, pp. 162–82.

65 Leszek Kolakowskii, 'Mind and Body: Ideology and Economy in the Collapse of Communism' in K. Z. Poznanski (ed.), *Constructing Capitalism* (Boulder, CO: Westview, 1992), pp. 9–23; esp. pp. 11–15.

66 Antonio Carlo, 'The Crisis of Bureaucratic Collectivism', *Telos* 43 (Summer 1980), pp. 3–31.

67 Eugene Huskey, 'Government Rulemaking as a Brake on *Perestroika*', *Law and Social Inquiry* 15 (Summer 1990), pp. 419–32.

68 Frances Foster, 'Procedure as a Guarantee of Democracy: the Legacy of the Perestroika Parliament', *Journal of Transnational Law* 26 (April 1993), pp. 1–109.

69 Dario Melossi, 'Weak Leviathan and Strong Democracy, or Two Styles of Social Control', *International Journal of Contemporary Sociology* 31(1) (1994), pp. 1–15.

70 Arendt, *On Revolution*, pp. 229–30; Alvin Goulder, *The Dialectic of Ideology and Technology* (New York: Seaburg, 1976), pp. 210–28; Charles E. Lindblom, *Politics and Markets* (New York: Basic Books, 1977), pp. 134–9.

71 Examples of these approaches can be found in Jerry Hough, *The Soviet Union and Social Science Theory* (Cambridge, MA: Harvard University Press, 1977); Gordon Skilling and Franklyn Griffiths (eds.), *Interest Groups in Soviet Politics*, (Princeton: Princeton University Press, 1971); Valerie

Bunce and John M. Echols III, 'Soviet Politics in the Brezhnev Era: "Pluralism" or "Corporatism"?' in Kelley (ed.), *Soviet Politics in the Brezhnev Era*, pp. 1–26.

72 This qualitative difference is analysed by John Gray, 'Post-Totalitarianism, Civil Society and the Limits of the Western Model' in Z. Rau (ed.), *The Reemergence of Civil Society in Eastern Europe and the Soviet Union* (Boulder, CO: Westview, 1992), pp. 145–60.

73 Ferenc Feher, Agnes Heller and Gyorgy Markus, *Dictatorship over Needs* (Oxford: Blackwell, 1983), pp. 111–12.

74 Although it would seem correct to suppose that the cultural intelligentsia was the social group most involved with these enterprises, it would not follow that they were the only group taking part. Take, for instance, the fact that over the decade 1968–78, ownership of tape recorders among working people increased from 13 per cent of households to 68 per cent (*Formirovanie potrebnostei sovetskikh lyudei* (Tula, 1980), p. 66). Nearly a decade before glasnost, then, most Soviet working families possessed the technical means to participate in the unsanctioned cultural economy, taping and listening to such things as protest songs by Vysotskii and others far more often, we can surmise, than lectures on Marxist–Leninist ideology.

75 For an organizational account, see Sheldon Wolin, *Politics and Vision* (Boston: Little, Brown, 1960), pp. 421–9 and A. J. Polan, *Lenin and the End of Politics* (Berkeley, CA: University of California Press, 1984), esp. pp. 27–85, 93–101. Another tack to the 'end of politics' in Russia, one emphasizing state socialism's peculiar social structure and attendant absence of autonomous social forces capable of both formulating and pursuing their own interests in opposition to others, can be found in M. V. Malyutin, 'Perspektivy demokratii v Rossii' (Report to the Higher Consultative-Coordinating Council under the Chairperson of the Supreme Soviet of Russia, August, 1991); and in Sergei Mitrokhin, 'Novye partii v politicheskom spektre Rossii' (Moscow: Institute of Humanities and Political Studies, June 1991). Finally, studies focusing on the communicative aspects of politics have arrived at the same conclusion. See Urban, 'Conceptualizing Political Power in the USSR', esp. pp. 216–19 and his 'From Chernenko to Gorbachev: a Repoliticization of Official Soviet Discourse?', *Soviet Union* 13(2) (1986), pp. 131–61; Maria Markus, 'Overt and Covert Modes of Legitimation in Communist States' in T. H. Rigby and F. Feher (eds.), *Political Legitimation in Communist States* (New York: St Martin's Press, 1989), pp. 82–93.

76 Jean L. Cohen, 'Strategy or Identity; New Theoretical Paradigms and Contemporary Social Movements', *Social Research* 52 (Winter 1985), pp. 663–716; Alain Touraine, 'An Introduction to the Study of Social Movements', *Social Research* 52 (Winter 1985), pp. 749–87.

77 Claus Offe, 'Capitalism and Democratic Design? Democratic Theory Facing the Triple Transition in East Central Europe', *Social Research* 58 (Winter 1991), pp. 863–92, esp. p. 883.

78 Jadwiga Staniszkis, 'Main Paradoxes of the Democratic Change in Eastern Europe' in Poznanski (ed.), *Constructing Capitalism*, pp. 178–97.

2. REGIME AND OPPOSITION IN THE PRE-POLITICAL PERIOD

1 Peter Reddaway has estimated that, at its highwater mark in the early 1970s, membership in the dissident movement for the entire USSR numbered no more than 2,000. See his *Uncensored Russia* (New York: American Heritage Press, 1972), p. 23.

2 A. I. Solzhenitsyn, *Arkhipelag Gulag, 1918–1956. Opyt khudozhestvennogo issledovaniya*, vol. II (Paris: YMCA Press, 1989), pp. 28–33.

3 *Ibid.*, p. 164.

4 Address by N. Korzhavin at the Moscow State Historical-Archival Institute (March,1989).

5 Another case would be that of Revol't Pimenov who was interned in a psychiatric hospital for resigning from the Komsomol in protest over the party-state's anti-Yugoslav campaign in the late 1940s. Boris Vail', *Osobo opasen* (London: Overseas Publication Interchange, 1980), p. 154.

6 A. V. Zhigulin, *Chernye kamni: avtobiograficheskaya povest'* (Moscow: Moskovskii rabochii, 1989), pp. 32, 48, 204.

7 V. Iofe, 'Obzor Leningradskikh politicheskikh protsessov (periodizatsiya i istochniki)' (paper presented at the International Conference on 'The Dissident Movement in the USSR, 1950–1980', Moscow, 24–6 August 1992), p. 40 (Archive of the Moscow Bureau of Information Exchange [hereafter, M-BIO]).

8 Zhigulin, *Chernye kamni*, pp. 28, 33.

9 *Ibid.*, p. 28.

10 Zhigulin (*ibid.*, p. 75), for instance, recounts how the son of a provincial party secretary managed to acquire a copy of Lenin's letter to the Thirteenth Congress of the Communist Party which called for Stalin's removal from the post of General Secretary, and how this radicalized the views of those in his underground circle.

11 Having been arrested with others in his group for distributing subversive leaflets, Vladimir Gershuni greeted the inmates on his arrival at a prison camp by exclaiming, 'Now we again are revolutionaries . . . only [this time] against Soviet power!' (quoted in Solzhenitsyn, *Arkhipelag Gulag*, p. 44); Georgii Pomerants related similar incidents in his conversation with V. Igrunov and S. Mitrokhin, (manuscript, M-BIO archives), p. 1. I. V. Mazus has remarked of the times that 'our groups were isolated and as defenseless as children, but we combined fundamentally the old Russian revolutionary traditions, including that of Nechaev, with everything that we ourselves were able to understand and see for ourselves'. See his *Gde ty byl?* (Moscow: Vozvrashchenie, 1992), p. 100.

12 Zhigulin, *Chernye kamni*, p. 31. Another group, led by Maya Ulanovskaya, Susanna Pechuro and Evgenii Gurevich, called itself the Union for the Struggle for the Cause of Revolution but was similarly Marxist in orientation. N. M. and M. A. Ulanovskii, *Istoriya odnoi sem'i* (New York: Chalidze, 1982), pp. 305–6; A. A. Yakobson, *Pochva i sud'ba* (Moscow: Vest', 1992), pp. 240–2, 340–1.

13 R. D. Orlova, *Vospominaniya o neproshedshem vremeni* (Moscow: Slovo,

1993), p. 386; Yu. A. Gastev, 'Sud'ba "neshchikh sibaritov"', *Pamyat'* 1 (1976), pp. 232–68; also his 'Letter to the Editor', *Pamyat'* 3 (1978), pp. 539–57.

14 M. Ivanovich, 'Molodezhnaya terroristicheskaya organizatsiya (1944–1945)', *Pamyat'* 1 (1976), pp. 219–31; E. I. Neizvestnyi, *Govorit Neizvestnyi* (Perm: Permskie Novosti, 1991), pp. 30–3.

15 Amongst others, M. K. Mamardashvili, 'Nachalo vsegda istorichno, t. e. sluchaino', *Voprosy metodologii* 1 (1991), pp. 44–52; A. M. Pyatigorskii and V. N. Sadovskii, 'Kak my izuchali filosofiyu. Moskovskii universitet, 50-e gody', *Svobodnaya mysl'* 2 (1993), pp. 42–54.

16 For documents concerning student actions in these years, see E. Taranov, '"Raskachaem Leninskie gory!" Iz istorii "vol'nodumstva" v Moskovskom universitete (1955–1956 g.g.)', *Svobodnaya mysl'* 10 (1993), pp. 94–103. The reminiscences of Grigorii Pomerants have been set out in 'Korzina tsvetov nobelevskomu laureatu', *Oktyabr* 11 (1990), pp. 144–6, and in the conversation cited above (M-BIO), pp. 14–15.

17 K. M. Simonov, *Glazami cheloveka moego pokoleniya* (Moscow: Novosti, 1989), p. 261.

18 V. K. Bukovskii, *I vozvrashchaetsya veter* (Moscow: Demokraticheskaya Rossiya, 1990), pp. 77–8.

19 S. I. Osipov, 'Za kulisami velikikh torzhestv', *Izvestiya* (6 November 1992), p. 3.

20 S. D. Rozhdestvenskii [V. Iofe], 'Materialy k istorii samodeyatel'nykh politicheskikh ob"edinenii v SSSR posle 1945 g.', *Pamyat'* 5 (1981), p. 232.

21 N. Yanevich [Elena Evnina], 'Institut mirovoi literatury v 1930-e – 70-e gody', *Pamyat'* 5 (1981), p. 115.

22 Yanevich continues thus in her memoir: 'Young people, having heard the story of the consequences of "the cult" wanted to examine the reasons for this phenomenon . . . People began to think, to compare, to criticize and to draw far-reaching conclusions.' In the case of her Institute, this led to an open 'uprising' against its director. *Ibid.*, pp. 115–17.

23 Rozhdestvenskii, 'Materialy k istorii samodeyatel'nykh politicheskikh ob"edinenii', p. 251.

24 Orlova, *Vospominaniya o neproshedshem vremeni*, pp. 210, 223–6; Yu. A. Orlov, *Opasnye mysli*, (Moscow: Argumenty i fakty, 1991), pp. 114–17.

25 Geoffrey Hosking, *The First Socialist Society: a History of the Soviet Union From Within* (Cambridge, MA: Harvard University Press, 1985), pp. 329–32.

26 Yakobson, *Pochva i sud'ba*, p. 240.

27 Rozhdestvenskii, 'Materialy k istorii samodeyatel'nykh politicheskikh ob"edinenii', p. 232.

28 *Ibid.*, p. 237.

29 The poet F. Chuev, of Stalinist persuasion, recounts how the crushing of the 'anti-party' group inspired him at age sixteen to compose a panegyric to the fallen party leaders (Lazar Kaganovich, Vyacheslav Molotov, *et al.*) entitled 'We don't believe it'. This, he says, was his 'first verse not coinciding with the official point of view'. See his *Tak govoril Kaganovich* (Moscow: Otechestvo, 1992), p. 15.

30 Roy Medvedev, *Kniga o sotsialisticheskoi demokratii* (Amsterdam and Paris: Grasset and Fasquelle, 1972), pp. 53–5, 216–18.
31 The organization that Bukovskii joined was a conspiratorial network preparing terrorist actions. Bukovskii, *I vozvrashchaetsya veter*, pp. 85–6.
32 Rozhdestvenskii, 'Materialy k istorii samodeyatel'nykh politicheskikh ob"edinenii', p. 251.
33 Osipov, 'Za kulisami', p. 3.
34 In Moscow, the group formed principally of students from the Library Institute decided overwhelmingly to pursue only underground, conspiratorial activity. One member, Revol't Pimenov, has claimed that his was the only voice advocating an open organization. A similar situation occurred in Leningrad at the Forestry Institute. See Pimenov's 'Vospominaniya. Chast' 1. Odin politicheskii protsess', *Pamyat'* 2 (1977), pp. 160–260 and part 2 of his article in *Pamyat'* 3 (1978), pp. 7–119.
35 Non-Marxists also joined these groups, attracted by their atmosphere of intellectual freedom. Rozhdestvenskii, 'Materialy k istorii samodeyatel'nykh politicheskikh ob"edinenii'.
36 M. Kheifets, 'Russkii patriot V. Osipov', *Kontinent* 27–8 (1981), p. 165.
37 Among them were Vladimir Bukovskii, Yurii Galanskov, Vladimir Osipov, Viktor Khaustov and Eduard Kuznetsov. Bukovskii, *I vozvrashchaetsya veter*, p. 113.
38 Kheifets, 'Russkii patriot V. Osipov', p. 180.
39 The major literary forms of samizdat at this time included the journals edited by Aleksandr Ginzburg ('Sintaksis') and Yurii Galanskov ('Feniks'). See also the collection of materials published in *Novoe literaturnoe obozrenie* 5 (1993), pp. 186–290.
40 For instance, V. Ronkin and S. Khakhaev, 'Ot diktatury byurokratii k diktature proletariata', (M-BIO archives).
41 An example of the former would be the journal, *Kolokol*, (*The Bell*) (1962–5), put out by graduates of the Leningrad Technical Institute who named it after Alexander Herzen's famous revolutionary newspaper of the previous century. See N. Peskov, 'Delo "Kolokola"', *Pamyat'* 1 (1976), pp. 260–84; V. Sazhin, 'Druz'ya-tovarishchi', *Ierusalim* 43 (1988), pp. 135–53. For examples of the latter, see the materials in *Novoe literaturnoe obozrenie* 5 (1993), pp. 186–290, and S. M. Dovlatov, 'Remeslo' (manuscript, M-BIO archives).
42 Leonid Rendel' and Vladimir Osipov would be among the leading examples. Bukovskii has observed that by the time that the gatherings at Mayakovskii Square had come to an end, 'already there were practically no socialists among us.' (*I vozvrashchaetsya veter*, p. 113).
43 Andrei Amal'rik has applied a similar approach to cultural production during the USSR's dissident period in the areas of unofficial artistic life, including its intrusions into official theatre. See his *Zapiski dissidenta* (Moscow: Slovo, 1991), esp. pp. 13–19.
44 Pierre Bourdieu's concepts are set out in his *The Field of Cultural Production* in Randal Johnson (ed.), (New York: Columbia University Press, 1993); also in Bourdieu, *In Other Words* (Cambridge, MA: Polity Press, 1990) and

Distinction: a Social Critique of Judgement and Taste (Cambridge, MA; Harvard University Press, 1984).

45 For the history of the journal during the Khrushchev years, see V. Lakshin, *Novyi mir vo vremya Khrushcheva* (Moscow: Knizhnaya palata, 1991). For a more extended historical treatment, see Dina Spechler, *Permitted Dissent in the USSR: Novyi Mir and the Soviet Regime* (New York: Praeger, 1982).

46 Bourdieu, *The Field of Cultural Production*, pp. 42–67, 75, 82–6; also his *Distinction*. Craig Calhoun, 'Habitus, Field and Capital: the Question of Historical Specificity' in C. Calhoun *et al.* (eds.), *Bourdieu: Critical Perspectives* (Cambridge, MA: Polity Press, 1993), pp. 61–88.

47 Another innovation in the media available in the cultural–political field was the so-called author's song (*avtorskaya pesnya*) pioneered as early as the 1940s and 1950s by M. L. Ancharov and B. Sh. Okudzhava, but which developed into a genuine cultural phenomenon in the 1960s: the 'bard movement'. These compositions, sometimes employing the verse of poets denied official recognition, exhibited varying degrees of protest against, and criticism of, social conditions, expressed usually in lyrical images. Some 'bards' participated directly in dissident activities (for instance, Aleksandr Galich and Yulii Kim); others refrained, thus protecting their standing within the establishment (Okudzhava, Vladimir Vysotskii). The high-water mark of this movement occurred in the latter half of the 1960s when an unofficial Club of Free Song was founded by (primarily) members of the urban intelligentsia which, under the aegis of the Siberian Division of the Academy of Sciences, staged a festival ('Pesnya–68') in March 1968 where artists performed uncensored compositions before a large audience. The songs of dissident Aleksandr Galich – 'Karaganda', 'Staratel'skii val'sok' and 'Pamyati Pasternaka' – took top honours. Within weeks, a newspaper and administrative campaign was launched against the festival's organizers and participants, ensuring that such a venue for free expression would not be available again in the USSR for nearly a generation. Our information on the festival and its aftermath comes from: a speech by V. Turiyanskii at an evening in remembrance of Aleksandr Galich, Meridian House of Culture (October 1993); Nina Geitner (ed.), *Zaklinanie dobra i zla* (Moscow: Progress, 1991), p. 446; L. I. Bogoraz and A. Yu. Daniel, 'V poiskakh nesushchestvuyushchei nauki (dissidentstvo kak istoricheskaya problema)', *Problemy Vostochnoi Evropy* 37–8 (1993), p. 143.

48 Amal'rik, *Zapiski dissidenta*, pp. 43–44.

49 I. A. Brodskii, *Sochineniya* (St. Petersburg: Pushkinskii fond, 1992), p. 7.

50 Amal'rik, *Zapiski dissidenta*, p. 13.

51 For instance, the circle around Vladimir Osipov and Yurii Ivanov laid plans for terrorist actions, including an assassination attempt on Khrushchev in the early 1960s. Kheifets, 'Russkii patriot V. Osipov', p. 191. This also held true for the All-Russian Social-Christian Union for the Liberation of the People, an organization discussed below.

52 Quoted in Bukovskii, *I vozvrashchaetsya veter*, p. 176.

53 *Ibid.*, pp. 123–4, 176–8.

54 Il'ya Kudryavtsev, 'Oppozitsiya i totalitarizm v SSSR' (Moscow: Institute for Humanities and Political Studies, June 1993), pp. 5–8.

55 E.g., Bogoraz and Daniel, 'V poiskak nesushchestvuyushchei nauki', p. 145.
56 Reddaway, *Uncensored Russia*, p. 61.
57 See M. A. Naritsa's testament in *Al'manakh samizdata*. *Nepodtsenzurnaya mysl' v SSSR* 1 (1974), pp. 55–6.
58 Bukovskii, *I vozvrashchaetsya veter*, pp. 182–4.
59 Roy Medvedev, *On Soviet Dissent* (New York: Columbia University Press, 1980), p. 56.
60 In 1977, the date for the demonstration was changed to 10 December in order to coincide with International Human Rights Day.
61 L. I. Bogoraz, V. G. Golitsyn and S. A. Kovalev, 'Politicheskaya bor'ba ili zashchita prav? Dvadtsatiletnii opyt nezavisimogo obshchestvennogo dvizheniya v SSSR' in A. N. Zav'yalova and N. K. Sazanovich (eds.), *Pogruzhenie v triasinu* (Moscow: Progress, 1991), pp. 530–1.
62 Amal'rik, *Zapiski dissidenta*, p. 45.
63 Amal'rik (*ibid.*) has described this moment of truth thus: 'a person placing his own signature [on a petition] was by that very act taking a step toward inner emancipation, and for many this step became decisive. For the political situation in the country one or another signature may not have had any significance, but for the signator himself it became a catharsis *sui generis*, a break from the system of double thinking in which "soviet man" has been brought up since childhood.'

    In the case of the Sinyavskii–Daniel affair alone, some twenty-two protest petitions are known to have been circulated. Aleksandr Ginzburg, *Belaya kniga po delu Sinyavskogo i Danielya* (Frankfurt: Posev, 1967), pp. 64–7, 80–7, 95–100, 117–30, 148–66, 341–4, 385–7; *Tsena metafory ili prestuplenie i nakazanie Sinyavskogo i Danielya*, compiled by E. M. Velikanova, L. S. Eremina (ed.), (Moscow: Kniga, 1989).
64 Reddaway, *Uncensored Russia*, p. 18.
65 Bukovskii, *I vozvrashchaetsya veter*, pp. 210–12.
66 Andrei Amal'rik, *SSSR i Zapad v odnoi lodke* (London: Overseas Publication Interchange, 1978), p. 25; L. M. Alekseeva, *Istoriya inakomysliya v SSSR* (Moscow: Vest', 1992), p. 206.
67 Andrei Amal'rik, *Prosushchestvuet li Sovetskii Soyuz do 1984 goda?* (Amsterdam: Hertsen Foundation, 1974) pp. 26–8.
68 Larisa Bogoraz and Pavel Litvinov, *Protsess chetyrekh: sbornik materialov po delu Galanskova, Ginzburga, Dobrovol'skogo i Lashkovoi* (Amsterdam: Hertsen Foundation, 1971).
69 R. D. Orlova, *Vospominaniya o neproshedshem vremeni*, pp. 378–9.
70 Vladimir Shlapentokh, *Soviet Intellectuals and Political Power* (Princeton: Princeton University Press, 1991), pp. 172–185.
71 Andrei Sakharov, *Thoughts on Progress, Peaceful Coexistence and Intellectual Freedom* (Petersham, UK: Foreign Affairs Publishing, 1968).
72 Reddaway, *Uncensored Russia*, esp. pp. 20–3.
73 The participants in the demonstration on Red Square included Konstantin Babitskii, Larisa Bogoraz, Vadim Delone, Vladimir Demlyuga, Pavel Litvinov, Viktor Fainberg and Natalya Gorbanevskaya. All but the last of these were arrested, tried in consonance with standard Soviet practices and duly sentenced to either punitive labour or exile.

74 Reddaway, *Uncensored Russia*, pp. 95–126. Additional materials are available in the journal *Karta* 3 (1993), pp. 5–9.

75 In his letter, Victor Krasin urged dissidents to recognize that the 'movement had collapsed and that there was only one thing to be done, to lay out its whole history for the future. The KGB has nobly taken on itself the role of historian. Everyone must honestly tell [everything] to the KGB and in so far as everyone voluntarily disarms, the KGB will not punish anyone.' Quoted in Amal'rik, *Zapiski dissidenta*, pp. 298–9.

76 It would appear that suspicions about the moral reliability of members increased in the wake of this episode. For examples, see Medvedev, *On Soviet Dissent*, pp. 5–6, 132–3; Valerii Chalidze, 'Pravozashchitnoe dvizhenie: problemy i perspektivy', *SSSR: Vnutrennie protivorechiya* 9 (1987), pp. 15–16.

77 A Moscow Helsinki Group headed by Yurii Orlov was announced on 12 May 1976, and regional affiliates were soon set up in Ukraine and Lithuania. The Moscow Helsinki Group actively investigated the regime's use of psychiatry for political purposes and collaborated in this respect closely with the Christian Committee for the Defense of the Rights of Believers, headed by Gleb Yakunin (Orlov, *Opasnye mysli*, pp. 189–90).

78 Peter Reddaway, 'Dissent in the Soviet Union', *Problems of Communism* 32 (November–December 1982), pp. 1–15.

79 *Ibid.*, p. 13.

80 In the 1970s, some dissidents began rethinking strategy and tactics, arguing that appeals for human rights were irresponsible without a practical plan for reforms in the economic, societal and cultural spheres that an enlightened Soviet regime might implement in future. Examples of these arguments circulated in samizdat include: Amal'rik, *Prosushchestvuet li Sovetskii Soyuz do 1984 goda?*, esp. p. 41; L. Ventsov [B. Shragin], 'Dumat'!' (manuscript, M-BIO); and Ego [V. V. Igrunov], 'K problematike obshchestvennogo dvizheniya' (manuscript, M-BIO). Their arguments failed to persuade many others. Perhaps a representative example of the counter-position within the movement would be the sentiments voiced by Tat'yana Khodorovich who, along with Tat'yana Velikanova and Sergei Kovalev, assumed responsibility for resuming production and distribution of the movement's principal organ, the *Chronicle of Current Events*, in 1974. 'There are no "differently minded people [*inakomyslyashchikh*]", no "dissidents"', she wrote, 'there are only people, on the one hand, and, on the other, a faceless, organized and trained [*vydressirovannoe*] violence with one single well-developed instinct: to stifle each and every thought . . . [Therefore] I don't desire to enter into dialogue with an organization that doesn't recognize the existence of moral rights' (T. Khodorovich, 'Po veleniyu sovesti', *Al'manakh samizdata* 1 (1974), pp. 37–8).

81 One such achievement was the appearance of a new samizdat journal, *Poiski*, in 1979 that partially realized a stillborn project of V. V. Igrunov called 'Almanakh–77' which would have eschewed the publication of more materials on repression in order to devote its pages to articles on history, sociology, politics and economics. *Poiski* was put out by Valerii Abramkin,

Petr Abovin-Egides, Pavel Pryzhov (Gleb Pavlovskii), Victor Sokirko and others. Interview with V. V. Igrunov (6 March 1994; M-BIO).

82 On two occasions, V. Igrunov was solicited by the KGB to write up proposals for reform of the socio-economic and governmental order in the USSR. The first took place in May 1979 when – following a number of interrogations and 'conversations' at the KGB office in Odessa during which Igrunov presented his views on the urgency of initiating a process involving broad sections of the intelligentsia in working out an evolutionary plan mindful of the stability of state and society that any meaningful reform was liable to place under stress – KGB captain N. A. Filippskii proposed a paid work leave enabling Igrunov to compose such a project and submit it to him. Personal circumstances required Igrunov to decline this offer.

The second solicitation occurred three years later, occasioned by the arrest on 6 April 1982 of Gleb Pavlovskii with whom Igrunov had very close ties through dissident activities, having collaborated with him as co-editor of the samizdat journal *Poiski*. On 8 April, KGB major L. V. Kulyabichev visited Igrunov in hospital recovering from a bout of tuberculosis in order to record Igrunov's reaction to Pavlovskii's arrest. As the discussion turned to other issues, Kulyabichev expressed a keen interest in many of Igrunov's ideas and proposed that Igrunov draft an extended outline for reform with two principal goals in view: curtailing the level of internal repression and setting out alternative paths for socio-economic development in the USSR. Igrunov this time accepted the KGB offer, but stipulated that acceptance was contingent on his freedom to consult with other dissidents. Kulyabichev agreed.

Consultations with other members of the movement began in late May when Igrunov was released from hospital. A number of leading figures in the movement – among them Larissa Bogoraz and Mikhail Gefter – consented to participate in the project and a protocol for negotiations and consensus-building around the planned text was worked out (M-BIO archives). A copy of these protocols and a prospectus were transmitted in mid-June to Kulyabichev who expressed great interest in the project's ideas. For reasons unknown to us, however, the KGB then closed down this channel of communication. Thereafter, the KGB maintained surveillance on Igrunov, but lifted the prohibition introduced after his arrest in the 1970s against working in his profession (economist). Since Igrunov committed most of his major ideas to letters sent to Pavlovskii, who was then in a labour camp, the KGB none the less obtained a large portion of the work that would have been done under the aborted contact.

83 A. J. Greimas and F. Rastier, 'The Interaction of Semiotic Constraints', *Yale French Studies* 41 (1968), pp. 86–105. For application of this model to various cultural–political systems of representation, see: Frederic Jameson, *The Political Unconscious* (Ithaca, NY: Cornell University Press, 1981); Claude Levi-Strauss, *The Naked Man* (New York: Harper and Row, 1981), esp. pp. 649–50; Michael Urban, 'The Structure of Signification in the General Secretary's Address: a Semiotic Approach to Soviet Political Discourse', *Coexistence* 24 (1987), pp. 187–210.

84 See Medvedev, *Kniga o sotsialisticheskoi demokratii*, pp. 52–6, 63–7.

85 We refer here to the group 'Young Socialists' that emerged at the beginning of the 1980s. Led by such individuals as Pavel Kudyukin, Boris Kagarlitskii and Andrei Fadin, the group's samizdat journals *Levyi povorot* and *Varianty* featured social science analyses heavily influenced by European neo-Marxism. This tendency assumed a certain salience in the 'informal' movement in 1986.

86 Alexander Yanov, *The Russian Challenge and the Year 2000* (New York: Basil Blackwell, 1987), p. 185. On this same point in theoretic perspective, see Bourdieu, *The Field of Cultural Production*, esp. pp. 34–43.

87 On this group generally, see: *VSKhSON: Programma. Sud. V tyur'makh i lageryakh* (Paris: YMCA Press, 1975); Alexander Yanov, *The Russian New Right* (Berkeley: Institute for International Studies, University of California, 1978), pp. 21–38; N. Mitrokhin, 'Istoriya russkogo natsional'nogo dvizheniya v SSSR. 1940–80-e gody' (senior thesis; Moscow: Russian State Humanities University, 1994)(M-BIO archives); and for a sympathetic treatment, John Dunlop, *The New Russian Revolutionaries* (Belmont, MA: Nordland, 1976).

88 According to one account, members of the VSKhSON who were arrested and tried by the authorities evinced degrees of 'extremism' in their respective commitments to the national–religious postulates of the VSKhSON 'in direct dependence on the degree of their previous faith in the ideals of communism'. *VSKhSON: Programma. Sud. V tyur'makh i lagerakh*, p. 94.

89 Quoted in John Dunlop, *The Faces of Contemporary Russian Nationalism* (Princeton: Princeton University Press, 1983), p. 45 (emphasis in original).

90 Yanov, *The Russian New Right*, pp. 62–80, esp. p. 80. On *Veche* generally, see Yanov's *The Russian Challenge and the Year 2000*; Dunlop, *The Faces of Contemporary Russian Nationalism*.

91 Yanov, *The Russian Challenge and the Year 2000*, p. 155.

92 The description of the Fetisov group offered by *The Chronicle of Current Events* is available in Reddaway, *Uncensored Russia*, pp. 431–3.

93 The text of this leaflet appears in Yanov, *The Russian New Right*, pp. 170–2.

94 Sergei Soldatov, *Zarnitsy vozrozhdeniya* (London: Overseas Publication Interchange, 1984), pp. 183–95.

95 Dunlop, *The Faces of Contemporary Russian Nationalism*, pp. 32–6.

96 Yanov, *The Russian New Right*, pp. 39–61.

97 Stephen Carter, *Russian Nationalism: Yesterday, Today, Tomorrow* (London: Pinter 1990), pp. 108–16.

98 *Ibid.*, p. 83; Yanov, *The Russian New Right*, pp. 49–51.

99 L. A. Alekseeva, *Istoriya inakomysliya v SSSR* (Moscow: Vest', 1991), p. 206.

100 Both episodes are recounted in Yanov, *The Russian New Right*, pp. 52–60.

3. PERESTROIKA: RENEWAL, TRANSITION OR TRANSFORMATION?

1 Mary McAuley, *Soviet Politics, 1917–1991* (Oxford: Oxford University Press, 1993), p. 90.

2 The text of this address appeared in *Izvestiya* (26 February 1987).

3 For discussions of democracy as the centrepiece of perestroika, see John Gooding, 'Gorbachev and Democracy', *Soviet Studies* 42 (April 1990), pp. 195–232; Joel C. Moses, 'Democratic Reform in the Gorbachev Era: Dimensions of Reform in the Soviet Union, 1986–1989', *Russian Review* 48 (July 1989), pp. 235–69.

4 Thane Gustafson and Dawn Mann, 'Gorbachev's First Year: Building Power and Authority', *Problems of Communism* 35 (May–June 1986), pp. 1–19; 'Gorbachev's Next Gamble', *Problems of Communism* 36 (July–August 1987), pp. 1–20; 'Gorbachev and the Circular Flow of Power' in D. Lane (ed.), *Elites and Political Power in the USSR* (Aldershot: Edward Elgar, 1988), pp. 21–48. Also, Jerry Hough, 'Gorbachev Consolidating Power', *Problems of Communism* 36 (July–August 1987), pp. 21–43.

5 For interesting insights into this problem from the viewpoint of someone directly involved with it, see I. Usmankhodzhaev, 'Rukovodstvo cherez kommunistov', *Sovety narodnykh deputatov* 10 (October 1987), pp. 17–26.

6 Mikhail Gorbachev, *Perestroika* (New York: Harper and Row, 1987), pp. 27–35.

7 A useful outline of this appears in Neil Robinson, *Ideology and the Collapse of the Soviet System: a Critical History of Soviet Ideological Discourse* (Aldershot: Edward Elgar, 1995), pp. 6–16.

8 Richard Sakwa, *Gorbachev and his Reforms, 1985–1990* (New York: Prentice Hall, 1990), pp. 126–44; also his *Russian Politics and Society* (London: Routledge, 1993), pp. 2–5; Stephen White, *After Gorbachev* (4th ed.; Cambridge: Cambridge University Press, 1993), pp. 29–43.

9 Sakwa, *Gorbachev and his Reforms*, p. 390.

10 For a critique of these assumptions about politics, see the following works by Murray Edelman, *The Symbolic Uses of Politics* (Urbana, IL: University of Illinois Press, 1964); *Politics as Symbolic Action* (Chicago: Markham, 1971); *Political Language* (New York: Academic Press, 1977); *Constructing the Political Spectacle* (Chicago: University of Chicago Press, 1988).

11 See also Martin Crouch, *Revolution and Evolution: Gorbachev and Soviet Politics* (London: Philip Allan, 1989), pp. 100–2.

12 Vaclav Havel, *The Power of the Powerless* edited by John Keane (London: Hutchinson Educational, 1985), p. 45.

13 The authors were Andrei Sakharov, Roy Medvedev and Valerii Turchin. A text of the letter can be found in Alexander Dallin and Gail Lapidus (eds.), *The Soviet System in Crisis* (Boulder, CO: Westview, 1991), pp. 81–6.

14 Examples include Anatolii Butenko, 'Protivorechiya razvitiya sotsializma kak obshchestvennogo stroya', *Voprosy filosofii* 10 (1982), pp. 20–7; Vadim Semenov, 'Problema protivorechii v usloviyakh sotsializma', *Voprosy filosofii* 7 (1982), pp. 17–32 and 9 (1982), pp. 3–2; Evgenii Ambartsumov, 'Analiz V. I. Leninym prichin krizisa 1921 g. i putei vykhoda iz nego', *Voprosy istorii* 4 (1984), pp. 130–40.

15 This document, authored by Tat'yana Zaslavskaya, has been published in the West as 'The Novosibirsk Report', *Survey* 28, (Spring 1984), pp. 88–108.

16 In his autobiography, *Moi vybor* (Moscow: Novosti, 1991), pp. 58–79,

Eduard Shevardnadze recounts his acquaintance with Mikhail Gorbachev that began in the 1970s while he was KGB chief and, later, party leader in Georgia and Gorbachev was first secretary of the Communist Party's regional organization in Stavropol. According to Shevardnadze, both men had often shared ideas about the situation in the country that were informed by dissident critiques and both had reached the conclusion by the winter of 1984 that, in Shevardnadze's words to Gorbachev at the time, 'Everything is rotten. It must be changed' (p. 79).

17　Zhores Medvedev, *Andropov* (New York: W. W. Norton, 1983), pp. 63–70.

18　On the creation of this commission and its role in writing the Andropov reform, see Nikolai Ryzhkov, *Perestroika: Istoriya predatel'stv* (Moscow: Novosti, 1992), pp. 41–8.

19　See Yurii Andropov, 'Uchenie Karla Marksa i nekotorye voprosy sotsialis-ticheskogo stroitel'stva v SSSR', *Kommunist* 3 (January 1983).

20　On 'the human factor', see Gorbachev, *Perestroika*, pp. 29–36.

21　Ryzhkov, *Perestroika: Istoriya predatel'stv*, pp. 70–73.

22　Aleksandr Yakovlev, *Predislovie. Obval. Posleslovie* (Moscow: Novosti, 1992), pp. 127, 148.

23　Gorbachev, *Perestroika*, p. 25.

24　Vadim Bakatin, *Osvobozhdenie ot illyuzii* (Kemerovo: Kemerovskoe knizhnoe isdatel'stvo, 1992), pp. 7–9; Yakovlev, *Predislovie*, p. 141.

25　Oleg Bogomolov, 'I Can't Absolve Myself of Guilt' in Dallin and Lapidus (eds.), *The Soviet System in Crisis*, pp. 352–4.

26　E.g., K. Jowitt, *New World Disorder* (Berkeley: University of California Press, 1992), pp. 121–58, 220–48; Grzegorz Ekiert, 'Democratization Processes in East Central Europe: a Theoretical Reconsideration', *British Journal of Political Science* 21 (July 1991), pp. 286–7.

27　Leszek Kolakowski, 'Mind and Body: Ideology and Economy in the Collapse of Communism' in Kazimierz Poznanski (ed.), *Constructing Capitalism* (Boulder, CO: Westview, 1992), pp. 9–23.

28　Yakovlev, *Predislovie*, p. 146.

29　Cf. Bakatin, *Osvobozhdenie ot illyuzii*, pp. 10–11.

30　Guillermo O'Donnell and Philippe Schmitter, *Transitions from Authoritarian Rule: Tentative Conclusions about Uncertain Democracies* (Baltimore: The Johns Hopkins University Press, 1986), p. 65.

31　Russell Bova, 'Political Dynamics of the Post-Communist Transition: a Comparative Perspective', *World Politics* 44 (October 1991), p. 113. Other studies arguing for this approach include Rasma Karklins, 'Explaining Regime Change', *Europe-Asia Studies* 46(1) (1994), pp. 29–45; Giuseppe Di Palma, *To Craft Democracies* (Berkeley: University of California Press, 1990), pp. 35–9, 78–95, 157–81; Philippe Schmitter, 'Reflections on Revolutionary and Evolutionary Transitions: the Russian Case in Comparative Perspective' in Alexander Dallin (ed.), *Political Parties in Russia* (Berkeley: University of California, International and Area Studies, 1993), pp. 29–33.

32　Examples include Chalmers Johnson (ed.), *Change in Communist Systems* (Stanford: Stanford University Press, 1970); Moshe Lewin, *The Gorbachev Phenomenon* (2nd ed.; Berkeley: University of California Press, 1991); Jerry

Hough, *Soviet Leadership in Transition* (Washington, DC: Brookings Institution, 1980); Donna Bahry, 'Society Transformed? Rethinking the Social Roots of Perestroika', *Slavic Review* 52 (Fall 1993), pp. 512–54.

33   Di Palma, *To Craft Democracies*, p. 4.

34   Adam Przeworski, 'Some Problems in the Study of Transitions to Democracy' in Guillermo O'Donnell, Philippe Schmitter and Laurence Whitehead (eds.), *Transitions from Authoritarian Rule: Comparative Perspectives* (Baltimore: The Johns Hopkins University Press, 1986), pp. 47–50, esp. p. 49.

35   Thomas Remington, 'Regime Transition in Communist Systems: the Soviet Case', *Soviet Economy* 6(2) (1990), pp. 160–90.

36   O'Donnell and Schmitter, *Transitions from Authoritarian Rule: Tentative Conclusions*, p. 3.

37   *Ibid.*, pp. 3–5; Di Palma, *To Craft Democracies*, pp. 6–9.

38   Michel Foucault, *Discipline and Punish* (New York: Pantheon, 1977); *The History of Sexuality*, vol. I (New York: Random House, 1978); and his *Power/Knowledge*, Colin Gardner (ed.), (New York: Pantheon, 1980).

39   It would be the ongoing and reciprocal interactions between social science and society that had gone missing in the USSR. The capacity of the former to rationalize the life-world of the latter, thus making it susceptible to conventional social science methods had been, at most, a marginal phenomenon in the history of the Soviet Union. We return to this point below.

40   Philippe Schmitter with Terry Lynn Karl, 'The Conceptual Travels of Transitologists and Consolidologists: How Far to the East Should They Attempt to Go?', *Slavic Review* 53 (Spring 1994), pp. 173–84.

41   Alvin Gouldner has developed this aspect of social theory in *Against Fragmentation* (Oxford: Oxford University Press, 1985), pp. 176–258.

42   This paleosymbolic element is most detectible in its classic formulation, Dankwart Rustow's, 'Transitions to Democracy: Toward a Dynamic Model', *Comparative Politics* 2 (April 1970), pp. 337–63.

43   Adam Przeworski, *Democracy and the Market* (Cambridge: Cambridge University Press, 1991), p. 54. For the Soviet case, see Bova, 'Political Dynamics of the Post-Communist Transition', pp. 119–20; and in a critical vein, Hillel Ticktin, 'The Year After General Secretaries: Change Without Change', *Critique* 17 (1986), pp. 113–35 and 'The Contradictions of Gorbachev', *Journal of Communist Studies* 4 (December 1988), pp. 83–99.

44   This would appear to be axiomatic. See O'Donnell and Schmitter, *Transitions from Authoritarian Rule: Tentative Conclusions*, pp. 7–8.

45   Steven Fish, 'Who Shall Speak For Whom? Democracy and Interest Representation in Post-Soviet Russia' in Dallin (ed.), *Political Parties in Russia*, p. 38; White, *After Gorbachev*, p. 99.

46   For an analysis portraying these events as a bona fide pact, see Neil Robinson, 'Parliamentary Politics under Gorbachev: Opposition and the Failure of Socialist Pluralism', *Journal of Communist Studies* 9 (March 1993), pp. 93–4; for one that refers to elements of pacting, see Bova, 'Political Dynamics of the Post-Communist Transition', pp. 122, 131; for arguments against regarding this 'democratization' as equivalent to a pact, see Brendan

Kiernan, *The End of Soviet Politics* (Boulder, CO: Westview, 1993), pp. 2–8; Michael McFaul, 'Party Formation After Revolutionary Transformation: the Russian Case' in Dallin (ed.), *Political Parties in Russia*, pp. 10–11.

47 O'Donnell and Schmitter, *Transitions from Authoritarian Rule: Tentative Conclusions*, p. 37; Schmitter, 'Reflections on Revolutionary and Evolutionary Transitions, p. 30.

48 Amongst others, Rustow, 'Transitions to Democracy', pp. 344–5; Przeworski, *Democracy and the Market*, pp. 20–6; Di Palma, *To Craft Democracies*, pp. 11–14, 76–108.

49 G. V. Barabashev, 'Izbiratel'naya kampaniya: tseli i sredstva', *Sovetskoe gosudarstvo i pravo* 4 (April 1987), pp. 3–12; also his 'Resurs neposredstvennoi demokratii', *Sovety narodnykh deputatov* (July 1987), pp. 17–24; Stephen White, 'Reforming the Electoral System', *Journal of Communist Studies* 4 (December 1988), pp. 1–17; Jeffrey Hahn, 'An Experiment in Competition: the 1987 Elections to the Local Soviets', *Slavic Review* 47 (Fall 1988), pp. 434–47; Michael Urban, *More Power to the Soviets: the Democratic Revolution in the USSR* (Aldershot: Edward Elgar, 1990), pp. 40–3.

50 For an extended analysis, see Baruch Hazan, *Gorbachev's Gamble: the 19th All-Union Party Conference* (Boulder, CO: Westview, 1990).

51 For details, see Urban, *More Power to the Soviets*, pp. 21–87.

52 *Ibid.*, pp. 68–82.

53 Di Palma, *To Craft Democracies*, pp. 10–16.

54 On the significance of a 'founding election' and the institutionalization of rules for elite competition, see O'Donnell and Schmitter, *Transitions from Authoritarian Rule; Tentative Conclusions*, pp. 57–62.

55 *Ibid.*, p. 49.

56 Darrell Slider, 'The First Independent Soviet Interest Groups: Unions and Associations of Cooperatives' in Judith Sedaitis and Jim Butterfield (eds.), *Perestroika from Below: Social Movements in the Soviet Union* (Boulder, CO: Westview, 1991), pp. 145–64; 'Embattled Entrepreneurs: Soviet Cooperatives in an Unreformed Economy', *Soviet Studies* 43 (September 1991), pp. 797–821.

57 Analyses of the USSR that treat 'civil society' in this way include: Bova, 'Political Dynamics of the Post-Communist Transition', pp. 117, 134; Marcia Wiegle and Jim Butterfield, 'Civil Society in Reforming Communist Regimes: the Logic of Emergence', *Comparative Politics* 25 (October 1992), pp. 1–23; Gail Lapidus, 'State and Society: Toward the Emergence of Civil Society in the Soviet Union' in Dallin and Lapidus (eds.), *The Soviet System in Crisis*, pp. 130–50; S. Frederick Starr, 'Soviet Union: a Civil Society', *Foreign Policy* 70 (Spring 1989), pp. 26–41; and, for post-communist politics generally, Vladimir Tismaneanu, *Reinventing Politics* (New York: The Free Press, 1992).

58 The adjective 'civil' is not a frivolous one in this respect, for it is by no means unimaginable that social relations outside the sphere of the state could assume 'uncivil' forms.

59 John Keane, *Democracy and Civil Society* (London: Verso, 1988), pp. 46–69; esp. p. 69.

60 Foucault, *Discipline and Punish*, pp. 75–89, 218–23.
61 C. B. MacPherson, 'The Meaning of Property' in C. B. MacPherson (ed.), *Property* (Toronto: University of Toronto Press, 1978), pp. 1–13; Gary Libecap, *Contracting for Property Rights* (Cambridge: Cambridge University Press, 1989), pp. 1–7.
62 H. Demsetz, 'Toward a Theory of Property Rights', *American Economic Review* 62(2) (1967), p. 347.
63 Franz Neuman, *Behemoth* (London: Oxford University Press, 1942), pp. 442–7. We leave aside the issue of whether some other social institution could perform the role that property has assumed in modern societies, recognizing that the limits of our experience and imagination scarcely represent a window onto the future.
64 Przeworski, 'Some Problems in the Study of Transitions to Democracy', p. 63; Di Palma, *To Craft Democracies*, pp. 22, 78–9; John Sheahan, 'Economic Policies and the Prospects for Successful Transitions from Authoritarian Rules in Latin America' in O'Donnell, Schmitter and Whitehead (eds.), *Transitions from Authoritarian Rule: Comparative Perspectives*, pp. 154–5.
65 Przeworski, *Democracy and the Market*, p. 66.
66 Jadwiga Staniszkis, 'Forms of Reasoning as Ideology', *Telos* 66 (Winter 1985–6), pp. 67–80.
67 Marc Garcelon, 'The Shadow of Leviathan: Public and Private in Communist and Post-Communist Society' in Jeff Weintraub and Krishan Kumar (eds.), *Public and Private in Thought and Practice* (Chicago: University of Chicago Press, 1994).
68 Grzegorz Ekiert, 'Peculiarities of Post-Communist Politics: the Case of Poland', *Studies in Comparative Communism* 25 (December 1992), pp. 341–61; George Kolankiewicz, 'The Reconstruction of Citizenship: Reverse Incorporation in Eastern Europe' in Poznanski (ed.), *Constructing Capitalism*, pp. 141–58; Jadwiga Staniszkis, 'Main Paradoxes of Democratic Change in Eastern Europe' in Poznanski, *Constructing Capitalism*, pp. 179–97; Reinhard Bendix, 'State, Legitimation and "Civil Society"', *Telos* 86 (Winter 1990–1), pp. 143–52.
69 Jowitt, *New World Disorder*, p. 292.
70 Igor' Kon made these remarks at a panel of the American Association for the Advancement of Slavic Studies, Miami, Florida, November 1991.

4. GLASNOST, MASS MEDIA AND THE EMERGENCE OF POLITICAL SOCIETY

1 Aleksandr Yakovlev, *Predislovie. Obval. Posleslovie* (Moscow: Novosti, 1992), pp. 127–9.
2 Examples of this view can be found in Richard Sakwa, *Gorbachev and his Reforms, 1985–1990* (2nd ed.; Englewood Cliffs, NJ: Prentice Hall, 1991), p. 72; Owen V. Johnson, 'The Press of Change: Adaption and Transformation' in S. P. Ramet (ed.), *Adaptation and Transformation in Communist and Post-Communist Systems* (Boulder, CO: Westview, 1992), pp. 209–39; Vera

Tolz, 'The Role of Journalists and the Media in Changing Soviet Society' in David Lane (ed.), *Russia in Flux* (Aldershot: Edward Elgar, 1992), p. 103.

3   Natalie Gross, 'Glasnost: Roots and Practice', *Problems of Communism* 36 (November–December 1987), pp. 69–80: Tolz, 'The Role of Journalists', p. 102.

4   Brian McNair, *Glasnost, Perestroika and the Soviet Mass Media* (London: Routledge, 1991), p. 52.

5   Ellen Mickiewicz, *Split Signals* (Oxford: Oxford University Press, 1988), pp. 27–30.

6   Thomas Remington, 'A Socialist Pluralism of Opinions: *Glasnost* and Policy-Making under Gorbachev', *Russian Review* 48 (July 1989), pp. 271–304; esp. p. 271. Also, David Wedgewood Benn, *From Glasnost to Freedom of Speech* (New York: Council on Foreign Relations, 1992), pp. 11–16.

7   Tolz, 'The Role of Journalists', p. 101.

8   For instance, A. T. Leizerov, *Konstitutsionnyi printsip glasnosti raboty Sovetov narodnykh deputatov* (Minsk: BGU, 1981).

9   *Moscow News*, begun by the American communist, Anna Louise Strong, in 1930 did not appear in the Russian language during the first fifty years of its existence. For a history of *Moscow News* during perestroika, see Elizabeth Schillinger and Catherine Porter, 'Glasnost and the Transformation of *Moscow News*', *Journal of Communication* 41 (Spring 1991), pp. 125–49.

10   For a sketch of Karpinskii's career that reads like a collective biography of this age-cohort, gripped with enthusiasm during the Khrushchevian thaw, marginalized and/or coopted by power during the years of the Brezhnevian glaciation, then provided with a second lease on their youthful dreams in the age of glasnost, see David Remnick, 'The Pioneers of Perestroika: Back to the Intellectual Roots of Soviet Reforms' in A. Dallin and G. Lapidus (eds.), *The Soviet System in Crisis* (Boulder, CO: Westview, 1991), pp. 87–93. Remnick has also presented some poignant material on this age-cohort, the *shestidesyatniki* ('sixties people') which conveys the notion that, having been trapped between 'dissidence and surrender' during most of their adult lives in the Brezhnev administration, they seized on glasnost – in the words of Sergei Zalygin – as a 'last chance' to redeem themselves after having 'played the game' for so long. See his *Lenin's Tomb* (New York: Random House, 1993), pp. 162–79, 267.

11   *KPSS o perestroike, sbornik dokumentov* (Moscow: Politizdat, 1988), p. 135.

12   Quoted in McNair, *Glasnost, Perestroika and the Soviet Media*, p. 54.

13   Benn, *From Glasnost to Freedom of Speech*, p. 14.

14   Remnick, *Lenin's Tomb*, p. 46.

15   Quoted in Andrei Karaulov, *Vokrug kremlya (Kniga politicheskikh dialogov)* (Moscow: Novosti, 1990), p. 438.

16   G. Vachnadze, *Sekrety pressy pri Gorbacheve i El'tsine* (Moscow: Kniga, 1992), p. 121.

17   V. E. Vuchetich (ed.), *Demokratizatsiya – sut' perestroiki, sut' sotsializma* (Moscow: Politizdat, 1988), p. 18.

18   Egor Ligachev, *Zagadka Gorbacheva* (Novosibirsk: Interbuk, 1992), p. 87.

19   Egor Yakovlev reports that Gorbachev was especially irritated by the

publication of this article because, in Yakovlev's recollection of his words, 'It cannot be that some journalist knows what I don't. If I had any documents on this I would have published them long ago. This is all rubbish.' Egor Yakovlev and A. Mal'gin, 'Smotrite kto ushel – dialog o sud'bakh "shestidesyatnikov"', *Stolitsa* 4 (April 1993), p. 10.

20 Vachnadze, *Sekrety pressy*, p. 130. Stephen White, *Gorbachev and After* (3rd ed.; Cambridge: Cambridge University Press, 1992), p. 258. The readers' poll appeared in *Argumenty i fakty* 40 (7–13 October 1989), p. 1.

21 Quoted in White, *Gorbachev and After*, p. 101.

22 'President Wants to Suspend the Law on the Press', *Moscow News* 4 (27 January–3 February 1991), p. 6.

23 Ligachev, *Zagadka Gorbacheva*, pp. 85–6. According to Boris El'tsin, Gorbachev regularly received complaints against newspaper transgressions during 1986, complaints that he regarded quite seriously. See El'tsin's *Against the Grain* (New York: Summit, 1990), pp. 113–14.

24 *Argumenty i fakty* 42 (21–7 October 1989), pp. 1, 3.

25 See McNair, *Glasnost, Perestroika and the Soviet Mass Media*, pp. 94–6.

26 *Ibid.*, p. 59.

27 According to subscription rates, readers' appetites appear to have peaked in 1988 and 1989, as subscriptions generally began to drop drastically after these years. However, some liberal publications were still expanding their lists of subscribers in this period (for instance, *Literaturnaya Gazeta* increased in this department from some 3,800,000 in 1988 to 4,234,000 in 1990 while *Ogonek* in those same years jumped from about 1,700,000 to over 4,000,000). The steepest declines were suffered by conservative and Stalinist publications (*Pravda* subscribers fell from some 10,700,000 in 1988 to 6,480,000 in 1990, *Sovetskaya Rossiya* from 5,250,000 to about 3,000,000) while *Argumenty i fakty* became the most popular publication in the country with over 31 million subscribers. For figures, see *Moscow News* 8 (21 February 1988), p. 2; *Moscow News* 47 (19 November 1989), p. 4.

28 White, *Gorbachev and After*, pp. 78, 97.

29 'Postanovlenie Tsk KPSS o zhurnale "Kommunist"', (16 August 1986) in *KPSS o perestroike*, p. 147.

30 Yurii Afanas'ev, 'Energiya istoricheskogo znaniya', *Moskovskie novosti* 2 (10 January 1987), p. 6.

31 For instance, 'Po povodu stat'i Yu. N. Afanas'eva' (a letter from teachers in the social sciences, members of the Academy of Social Sciences of the Central Committee of the Communist Party), *Moskovskie novosti* 19 (10 May 1987), p. 6; and 'Istoriya i sovremennost', *Moskovskie novosti* 21 (24 May 1987), p. 6.

32 Quoted in Sakwa, *Gorbachev and his Reforms*, p. 66.

33 For instance, see the remarks of Igor Karpenko, an editor with *Izvestiya*, and Vitalii Korotich, editor of *Ogonek*, made in interviews conducted by John Murray in 1988, in Murray's *The Russian Press from Brezhnev to Yeltsin*, (Aldershot: Edward Elgar, 1994), pp. 172–3, 176–8.

34 *Ibid.*, pp. 177–8.

35 Remnick, *Lenin's Tomb*, p. 45.

36 Vladimir Padunov and Nancy Condee, 'The Outposts of Official Art:

Recharting Soviet Cultural History', *Framework* 34 (1987), pp. 59–107; Andrew Horton and Michael Brashinsky, *The Zero Hour: Glasnost and Soviet Cinema in Transition* (Princeton: Princeton University Press, 1992); Anna Lawton, *Kinoglasnost: Soviet Cinema in Our Time* (Cambridge: Cambridge University Press, 1992); Ian Christie, 'The Cinema' in J. Graffy and G. Hosking (eds.), *Culture and the Media in the USSR Today* (London: Macmillan, 1989), pp. 43–77.

37   Julian Graffy, 'The Literary Press' in Graffy and Hosking (eds.), *Culture and the Media in the USSR Today*, pp. 107–57; esp. p. 107.

38   Mickiewicz, *Split Signals*; Remnick, *Lenin's Tomb*, pp. 143–50; James Dingley, 'Soviet Television and *Glasnost*' in Graffy and Hoskings (eds.), *Culture and the Media in the USSR Today*, pp. 6–25.

39   Stephen White, Graeme Gill and Darrell Slider, *The Politics of Transition: Shaping a Post-Soviet Future* (Cambridge: Cambridge University Press, 1993), pp. 193–210.

40   Ellen Mickiewicz, *Media and the Russian Public* (New York: Praeger, 1981), p. 67.

41   For a broad sampling of letters to the editor published by a variety of newspapers during the Gorbachev years, see Jim Riordan and Sue Bridger (eds.), *Dear Comrade Editor* (Bloomington, IN: Indiana University Press, 1992).

42   Stephen White, 'Political Communications in the USSR: Letters to Party, State and Press', *Political Studies* 31 (March 1983), p. 52; Mark Hopkins, *Mass Media in the Soviet Union* (New York: Pegasus, 1970), pp. 302–7.

43   Vladimir Nadein, 'Zachem pisat' v gazetu', *Izvestiya* (9 May 1987).

44   *Ibid.*

45   *Izvestiya* (26 May 1987).

46   These remarks were quoted from a reader's letter in an article by Nikolai Bondarchuk, 'Trudno proshchat'sya s proshlym', *Izvestiya* (25 April 1987).

47   We do not mean to imply that *Izvestiya* had become an open forum for any and all views. Rather, our point concerns both the unprecedented criticism of the Soviet system and calls for real democracy that began to appear in the letters column at this time and *Izvestiya*'s own admission that, indeed, it is not such an open forum and that readers should be apprised of that fact. On this latter point, see Vladimir Nadein's column in *Izvestiya*, 18 April and 9 May 1987, as well as the letter from M. Kushnarev in the 6 March 1987 number.

48   Letter from N. Yurchenko, *Izvestiya* (6 March 1987).

49   *Izvestiya* (18 April 1987).

50   Letter from P. Stromenko, *Izvestiya* (6 March 1987).

51   Letter from I. Sidorov, *Izvestiya* (25 May 1987).

52   Letter from P. Zuev, *Izvestiya* (28 April 1987).

53   Letter from E. Devyatisil'nyi, *Izvestiya* (26 May 1987).

54   On the pre-perestroika period, see Nick Lampert, 'Petitioners and Patrons: Citizens' Complaints in the Soviet System', *Coexistence* 22(1) (1985), esp. pp. 54–65; Jan S. Adams, 'Critical Letters to the Soviet Press' in D. E. Schulz and J. S. Adams (eds.), *Political Participation in Communist Systems* (New York: Pergamon, 1981), pp. 108–36.

55 Vitalii Korotich's view of these forces on the cultural–political field was probably typical for many in the liberal establishment. In 1988, he opined in an interview that 'today, for the first time ever, the conservatives are on the defensive . . . We, the liberals, have been defending ourselves all our lives; they've never had to defend themselves, *all* their lives they've spent screaming and shouting and attacking. Today, they're not in such a position . . . among the people, they're becoming more and more unpopular.' Concerning his 'informal' competitors, he remarked, 'I disagree with the entire principle of unofficial publications . . . These unofficial writers ought to try and get published in the existing organs of the press . . . Let them bring their articles to me.' His comments appear in Murray, *The Russian Press from Brezhnev to Yeltsin*, pp. 179, 181–2.

56 V. Aksenov *et al.*, 'Pust' Gorbachev predostavit nam dokazatel'stva', *Moskovskie novosti* 13 (29 March 1987), p. 10.

57 On the furore created by this publication in the higher circles of the Communist Party, see Ligachev, *Zagadka Gorbacheva*, pp. 83–6.

58 Egor Yakovlev, 'Dokazatel'stva ot obratnogo', *Moskovskie novosti* 13 (29 March 1987), p. 10. Two features of this statement bear mention. First, the word '*samOizdat*' is a mutilation of the central institution of the dissident subculture, 'samizdat'. Second, Yakovlev's reference to what had been 'written in corners' carries a nuance that would slight the importance of dissident writing by marginalizing it. The tenor of his statement would be consistent with the activities of many in the liberal establishment at this time, seeking to fend off competition from former dissidents who had, after all, accumulated considerable stores of 'symbolic capital' in the past while establishment figures had reached their own *modus vivendi* with the regime. One such episode involved a foray into the stronghold of dissident ideology – the defence of human rights – led by the liberal publicist, Fedor Burlatskii, which attempted in 1988 to organize a human rights programme within the Soviet Committee for the Defence of Peace. Some former dissidents attended many of these meetings but the organizers made concerted efforts to prevent them from speaking (S. Mitrokhin, personal observations).

59 V. Lur'e, 'Nasha obshchestvennaya pozitsiya', *Merkurii* 6 (1987), p. 2.

60 See, for instance, Gavriil Popov's articles, 'Izvlekaya uroki' and 'Kakaya perestroika nam nuzhna', that appeared in *Moskovskie novosti* 47 (22 November 1987), p. 3 and 51 (20 December 1987), p. 15.

61 For instance, statements by the Club of Social Initiative appeared in *Merkurii* 7 (1987), pp. 3–4; the Club Perestroika position was published in *Otkrytaya zona* 2 (November 1987), pp. 1–2.

62 Lev Sukhanov, personal assistant to El'tsin during this period, recounts how the Communist Party prevented the publication of interviews that El'tsin had given to various official publications after his fall from power. He also details how the information blockade was skirted in summer of 1988 when El'tsin was interviewed by a local newspaper in Latvia, *Sovetskaya molodezh'*, that passed the text to a national publication for broader distribution (although the party apparatus intercepted and confiscated most copies of the newspaper containing this interview), and in autumn of that same year when El'tsin spoke at the Moscow Higher Komsomol School. There

El'tsin's remarks were tape recorded, and the transcripts were then boot-legged around the country – often by airline pilots – and either sold on the street or reprinted in sympathetic provincial newspapers. See his *Tri goda s El'tsinym* (Riga: Vaga, 1992), pp. 61–73.

63 Vitaly Abramkin, 'The Soviet "Unofficial" Press', *Critique* 22 (1990), p. 115.

64 A consummate example of this collaboration involved an article written by a co-founder of the Leningrad 'informal' group, Al'ternativa, that dissected the power structure of the USSR along the lines of Milovan Djilas's concept of 'the new class', arguing that Soviet social science was afraid even to mention, much less analyse, the existence of a parasitic 'ruling class' of party-state officials whose dislodging from power required the introduction of a multi-party system. See Sergei Andreev, 'Struktura vlasti i zadachi obshchestva', *Neva* 1 (1989), pp. 144–73.

65 See, in particular, A. Arkhangel'skii, 'Mezhdu svobodnoi i ravenstvom: obshchestvennoe soznanie v zerkale "Ogon'ka" i "Nashego sovremennika"', 1986–1990', *Novyi mir* 2 (February 1991), pp. 225–41.

66 Indicative of this surrender would be the tendency among both liberal politicians and publicists to avoid speaking about the nation state in which they lived in other than oblique terms. Thus, they rarely provided a specific locus for, say, current events or ongoing processes by using the 'Soviet Union', the 'USSR' or 'Russia', instead situating them 'in our country'.

67 An outstanding example of this process can be found in Nikolai Shmelev's return to Leninist principles via free market economics. See his 'Avansy i dolgi', *Novyi mir* 6 (June 1987), pp. 142–58; and also his 'New Worries', reprinted from *Novyi mir* 4 (April 1988) in I. J. Tarasulo (ed.), *Gorbachev and Glasnost: Viewpoints from the Soviet Press* (Wilmington, DE: Scholarly Resources, 1989), pp. 117–25.

68 Arkhangel'skii, 'Mezhdu svobodnoi i ravenstvom'.

69 P. G. Bunich, 'Iskat', borot'sya, pobezhdat'', *Moskovskie novosti* 27 (5 July 1987), p. 12.

70 Andrei Nuikin, 'O tsenakh, zakone stoimosti i tsentnere zerna za 10 minut', *Moskovskie novosti* 25 (21 June 1987), p. 11.

71 Gavriil Popov, 'Pora prakticheskikh shagov', *Moskovskie novosti* 35 (30 August 1987), p. 8.

72 L. Popkova, 'Gde pyshnee pirogi?', *Novyi mir* 5 (1987), p. 240.

73 Quoted in Karaulov, *Vokrug kremlya*, p. 429.

74 Gorbachev frequently compared perestroika to the October Revolution. For instance, see his *Perestroika: New Thinking for our Country and the World* (New York: Harper and Row, 1987), pp. 49–55.

75 'Govorim o proshlom, no reshaetsya budushchee sotsializma', *Moskovskie novosti* 19 (10 May 1987), p. 11. Similarly Egor Yakovlev, 'Perestroika: promedlenie pagubno', *Moskovskie novosti* 32 (16 August 1987), p. 3.

76 By the end of 1986, these themes were prominent in journals on law and government. See M. Piskotin, 'Strategiya upravleniya', *Sovety narodnykh deputatov* 12 (December 1986), pp. 10–16; Yu. A. Rozenbaum, 'Sistema raboty s kadrami v usloviyakh perestroiki', *Sovetskoe gosudarstvo i pravo* 12 (December 1986), pp. 11–20; A. V. Obolonskii, 'Byurokraticheskaya

deformatsiya soznaniya i bor'ba s byurokratizmom', *Sovetskoe gosudartsvo i pravo* 1 (January 1987), pp. 52–61; B. Markov, 'Byurokratizm-antipod demokratii', *Kommunist* 11 (July 1987), pp. 110–19. Examples of these themes in the popular press, include G. Shipit'ko, 'Priroda ne proshchaet oshibok', *Izvestiya* (14 August 1986); G. Ni-Li, 'Provintsial'naya istoriya', *Izvestiya* (11 December 1986).

77 N. Andreeva, 'Ne mogu postupat'sya printsipami', *Sovetskaya Rossiya* (13 March 1988).

78 For an account of this episode detailing the orchestrating role of Politburo member, Egor Ligachev, see Remnick, *Lenin's Tomb*, pp. 72–7.

79 The author of the rebuke appearing in *Pravda* (5 April 1988) was apparently Aleksandr Yakovlev.

80 Eric Green, *The 19th Conference of the CPSU: Politics and Policy* (Washington, DC: American Committee on US–Soviet Relations, 1988), pp. 5–7; Nikolai Shishlin, 'Perestroika and the Party' in R. J. Kingston (ed.), *Perestroika Papers* (Dubuque, IA: Kendall/Hunt, 1988), pp. 40–5.

81 McNair, *Glasnost, Perestroika and the Soviet Media*, pp. 101–2.

82 A. Gel'man, 'Vremya sobiraniya sil', *Sovetskaya kul'tura*, (9 April 1988), p. 5.

83 Otto Latsis, 'Drugogo i ne nado', *Moskovskie novosti* 21 (24 March 1987), p. 12.

84 E. Yakovlev, 'Drugogo net puti', *Moskovskie novosti* 39 (27 September 1987), p. 2.

85 Yu. N. Afanas'ev (ed.), *Inogo ne dano* (Moscow: Progress, 1988).

86 Yu. Levada (ed.), *Est' mnenie!* (Moscow: Progress, 1990).

87 *Ibid.*, pp. 115–18.

88 *Ibid.*, pp. 14–15.

89 *Ibid.*, p. 15.

90 *Ibid.*, pp. 56–7.

91 *Ibid.*, p. 57.

92 *Ibid.*, pp. 131, 282.

93 *Ibid.*, p. 284.

94 *Ibid.*

5. THE INFORMAL MOVEMENT: POLITICS ON THE MARGINS OF THE SOVIET ORDER

1 S. N. Yushenkov, interviewed by Georgii Dolgov, 'Deti totalitarnogo podzemel'ya', *Soyuz* 7 (12–18 February 1990), pp. 8–9.

2 Marcia Wiegle and Jim Butterfield, 'Civil Society in Reforming Communist Regimes: the Logic of Emergence', *Comparative Politics* 25 (October 1992), p. 23, note 41.

3 M. V. Malyutin, 'Neformaly v perestroike: opyt i perspektivy' in Yu. N. Afanas'ev (ed.), *Inogo ne dano* (Moscow: Progress, 1988), pp. 210–11; V. N. Berezovskii and N. I. Krotov, *Neformal'naya Rossiya* (Moscow: Molodaya gvardiya, 1990), pp. 11–20.

4 This disaffection took a variety of forms, from 'internal emigration' to gang violence. The former involved youth attracted to Western popular culture

or Eastern mysticism who constructed for themselves micro-worlds modelled on their knowledge of these things and so journeyed to and lived within other cultural milieux without leaving home. The latter included an increasing number of young people drawn into gang activity, itself falling under the direction of hardened criminals whose presence in a gang had become a mark of status within this subculture. On this topic, see Vera Pisareva, 'Formirovanie agressivno-konformistskoi molodezhnoi subkul'tury v Rossii' (Moscow: Institute for Humanities and Political Studies, July 1991) and I. Yu. Sundiev, 'Neformal'nye molodezhnye ob"edineniya: opyt ekspozitsii', *Sotsiologicheskie issledovaniya* 5 (1987), esp. pp. 56–8.

5 Vyacheslav Igrunov, 'Public Movements: From Protest to Political Self-Consciousness' in B. Roberts and N. Belyaeva (eds.), *After Perestroika: Democracy in the Soviet Union* (Washington, D.C.: Center for Strategic and International Studies, 1991), pp. 15, 27.

6 Berezovskii and Krotov estimate that prior to autumn 1987, when politicization set in among the informals, only about 10 per cent of those in the movement had an interest in political activity (*Neformal'naya Rossiya*, p. 21).

7 Cited in Victoria Bonnell, 'Voluntary Associations in Gorbachev's Reform Program' in A. Dallin and G. Lapidus (eds.), *The Soviet System in Crisis* (Boulder, CO: Westview, 1991), p. 156.

8 Quoted in D. V. Ol'shanskii, *Neformaly: gruppovoi portret v inter'ere* (Moscow: Pedagogika, 1990), p. 84.

9 *Ibid.*, p. 88.

10 A. V. Gromov and O. S. Kuzin, *Neformaly: kto est' kto?* (Moscow: Mysl', 1990), p. 255; Sergei Mitrokhin, 'Molodezh i politika v epokhu pereotsenki tsennostei (rossiiski opyt)' (Moscow: Institute for Humanities and Political Studies, August 1991), pp. 1–3.

11 Our discussion of this club is based on relevant materials in the M-BIO archives.

12 'Ustav Fonda sotsial'nykh initsiativ' (Moscow, 12 June 1987; M-BIO archives).

13 'Spravochnik po "neformal'nym" obshchestvennym organizatsiyam i presse', *Informatsionnyi byulleten' IAS* 5 (May 1988), p. 26.

14 V. M. Voronkov, E. A. Zdravomyslova and V. V. Kastyushchev, *Obshchestvennye dvizheniya Leningrada* (Leningrad: Lenuprizdat, 1989), pp. 114–17.

15 Berezovskii and Krotov, *Neformal'naya Rossiya*, p. 115.

16 *Ibid.*, pp. 97, 212.

17 Dmitrii Levchik, personal communication (10 May 1991).

18 Berezovskii and Krotov, *Neformal'naya Rossiya*, pp. 236–7; A. Stepovoi, 'Brateevski fenomen', *Izvestiya* (26 January 1989)

19 Thomas Remington, 'A Socialist Pluralism of Opinions: *Glasnost*' and Policy-Making Under Gorbachev', *Russian Review* 4 (July 1989), pp. 271–304. M. Steven Fish, *Democracy From Scratch: Opposition and Regime in the New Russian Revolution* (Princeton: Princeton University Press, 1994), p. 32.

20 The list, here, would include Communist Party organizations (such as that in the Sevastopol'skii district of Moscow which sponsored the club, Perestroika), academic ones (such as the Soviet Sociological Association

which sponsored the Club of Social Initiative) and others involved in culture and politics such as the Soviet Peace Committee and its journal, *XX vek i mir* (which sponsored the mystical–philosophic clubs, Federation of Common Concern and Cosmos, and the Moscow Bureau for Information Exchange, respectively).

21 Igrunov, 'Public Movements', pp. 15, 22, 27–31. National newspapers, such as *Pravda* and *Komsomol'skaya Pravda* launched their campaigns against the informals in the latter half of 1987. For a typical example, see A. Pyzhov's letter to the editor that appeared in *Pravda* (25 November 1988).

22 V. Ponomarev *et al.*, *Samodeyatel'nye obshchestvennye organizatsii SSSR (Spravochnik)* (Moscow: Informatsionnyi tsentr Moskovskogo narodnogo fronta, 1988), p. 60.

23 *Ibid.*, p. 58.

24 Berezovskii and Krotov, *Neformal'naya Rossiya*, p. 101.

25 Vladimir Pribylovskii, *Slovar' oppozitsii: novye politicheski partii i organizatsii Rossii* (Moscow: Postfaktum, 1991), pp. 26–8.

26 Walter Laqueur, *Black Hundred* (New York: HarperPerenial, 1994).

27 Joel Moses, 'The Challenge to Soviet Democracy From the Political Right' in R. Huber and D. Kelley (eds.), *Perestroika-Era Politics: Soviet Legislature and Gorbachev's Political Reforms* (Armonk, NY: M. E. Sharpe, 1991), pp. 105–27; Robert Orttung, 'The Russian Right and the Dilemmas of Party Organization', *Soviet Studies* 44(3) (1991), pp. 445–78; Michael Cox, 'After Stalinism: the Extreme Right in Russia, East Germany and Eastern Europe' in P. Hainsworth (ed.), *The Extreme Right in Europe and the USA* (London: Pinter, 1992), pp. 270–5.

28 Donna Bahry and Brian Silver have written that 'most [informals] had been politically active before the Gorbachev era', either in official organizations or as dissidents. This characterization does not appear to fit the facts. Richard Sakwa's description of the association between dissidents and informals also glosses the very different character evinced by these movements. Bahry and Silver, 'Soviet Citizen Participation on the Eve of Democratization', *American Political Science Review* 84 (September 1990), p. 842; Sakwa, *Gorbachev and his Reforms 1985–1990* (New York: Prentice Hall, 1991), p. 203. Other studies implying a direct lineage between dissidents and informals include Nicolai Petro, 'Perestroika from Below: Voluntary Socio-political Associations in the RSFSR' in A. J. Rieber and A. Z. Rubinstein (eds.), *Perestroika at the Crossroads* (Armonk, NY: M. E. Sharpe, 1991), p. 104; Marcia Weigle, 'Political Participation and Party Formation in Russia, 1985–1992: Institutionalizing Democracy?', *Russian Review* 53 (April 1994), p. 243.

29 For example, Gleb Pavlovskii and V. Igrunov joined the informals in 1986.

30 Pavlovskii and Igrunov were the individuals in question.

31 These contacts were largely due to an informal activist, Galina Rakitskaya, who attended a December 1987 Doverie seminar. Her husband – Boris Rakitskii, vice-chairperson of the Institute for Sociology in the Academy of Sciences – had done much to sponsor informal associations within the academic establishment. Subsequent meetings between them and dissidents

such as Timofeev, Larissa Bogoraz and Sergei Koval'ev opened up direct contacts between the Democracy and Humanism group and the informal association, Perestroika, discussed below.

32 A partial exception would be 'Young Socialists' such as Boris Kagarlitskii, Pavel Kudyukin and Andrei Fadin who had been incarcerated and internally exiled in the early 1980s and who played leading roles in Moscow's informal movement. However, it is doubtful that these individuals would identify themselves as 'dissidents' or would be so regarded by others.

33 Personal observations of S. Mitrokhin.

34 This account is based on the personal observations of S. Mitrokhin. The generalizations at the end of this paragraph are based on his observations and those of V. Igrunov and M. Urban.

35 Hannah Arendt, *The Human Condition* (Chicago: University of Chicago Press, 1958), esp. pp. 176–85, 194, 232–3.

36 Quoted in I. Kudryavtsev, 'Oppozitsiya i totalitarizm v SSSR' (Moscow: Institute for Humanities and Political Studies, June 1993), p. 15.

37 Malyutin, 'Neformaly v perestroike', p. 214.

38 Kudryavtsev, 'Oppozitsiya i totalitarizm v SSSR', pp. 11–16.

39 Petro has mentioned instances in which local television stations in Yaroslavl, Sverdlovsk and Ryazan aired favourable spots on informal organizations over the objections of regional CPSU bosses ('Perestroika From Below', pp. 118, 124). Malyutin has also referred to cases in which CPSU and Komsomol bodies cooperated closely with certain informal groups ('Neformaly v perestroike', pp. 214, 224).

40 Malyutin, 'Neformaly v perestroike', p. 220; Igrunov, 'Public Movements', pp. 15–16.

41 Berezovskii and Krotov, *Neformal'naya Rossiya*, pp. 33–4.

42 Grigorii Pel'man should also be mentioned in this respect. According to one member of Nash Arbat, it was Pel'man – who had ties with certain officials in the Ministry of the Interior – who nudged other members of the club toward political activity by convincing them that repression would be relaxed enough to permit it. Interview given to M. Urban by Vladimir Stratanovich, 18 July 1989.

43 Geoffrey Hosking, Jonathan Aves and Peter Duncan, *The Road to Post-Communism: Independent Political Movements in the Soviet Union 1985–1991* (London: Pinter, 1992), p. 14.

44 M-BIO archives, fond I.G., no. 4.

45 V. Igrunov, 'CSI and Others', *XX Century and Peace* 6 (1988), pp. 26–30.

46 The most significant addition of this sort was the club Obshchina, a student discussion circle organized in the history faculty of Moscow State University, whose growing activism had put them at loggerheads with the University's Komsomol organization by 1986 and, by 1988, had made the group the focus of a movement against the Komsomol on that campus.

47 Voronkov, Zdravomyslova and Kostyushev, *Obshchestvennye dvizheniya Leningrada*, p. 46.

48 *Ibid.*

49 This list would include Yurii Levada, Viktor Klyamkin, Alla Nazimova, Ernest Ametisov, Gavriil Popov and Viktor Shenis.

50 Igrunov, 'Public Movements', p. 20.

51 *Pravda* (11 August 1987). El'tsin's motives for these remarks remain unclear, but he may have been attempting to diffuse the scandal occasioned by the audience that he had granted to leaders of Pamyat in early May, a meeting reported quite favourably by *Moskovskaya pravda* (7 May 1987) which portrayed the Pamyat delegation as progressive civic forces participating in perestroika. A month later, however, *Izvestiya* (3 June 1987) described Pamyat as a group of dangerous extremists opposed to the Soviet order and, in that context, mentioned the El'tsin meeting.

52 At the November plenum of the Moscow city committee of the CPSU at which El'tsin was savaged by all and sundry, Yu. A. Prokofiev, then a secretary of the city committee, castigated him for his cordial reception of Pamyat's leaders the previous May (*Izvestiya* (14 November 1987)).

53 Among the informals, the prime movers appear to have been Mikhail Malyutin and Pavlovskii of the CSI and Sergei Skvartsov of the FSI. Their counterparts in the CPSU were Nikolai Krotov of the propaganda department and instructors in the Sevastopol district committee.

54 After the Taganrog conference, at which the A-US-PCC changed its name to the All-Union Socio-Political Club (A-US-PC), the group was joined by a liberal faction of the Democracy and Humanism seminar. The A-US-PC's Marxist–Leninist wing objected strenuously to the inclusion of these anti-socialist elements and called for the expulsion of the liberals, a call to which the A-US-PC's social democratic wing objected with equal verve, seeing in it a ban on criticism and thus a violation of the 'spirit of the club'. At the A-US-PC's third, and final, conference held in Moscow in January 1988, the Marxist–Leninist faction secured the expulsion of the liberal one, thus triggering a walkout by the social democratic group and for all intents and purposes the end of the A-US-PC. Igrunov, 'Public Movements', pp. 20–2.

55 This is a speculative proposition, but it deserves consideration. Although the Moscow-based informals never succeeded in organizing a nationwide movement, their actions in the summer of 1987 did contribute to the eclipse of just such an organization, the A-US-PCC, based in the provinces. This group, composed predominantly of young people (20–30 years of age) with little social status, would have made an unlikely partner for those high-status liberal intellectuals who entered the arena of politics in the 1989 elections. However, the coupling of Moscow's informal leadership with those liberals had profound effects on the course of politics generally, radicalizing the liberal intellectuals-turned-politicians.

56 Igrunov, 'CSI and Others', p. 28.

57 The idea that led to the creation of the Memorial society – initially, to realize a proposal once made by Nikita Khrushchev to erect a monument to the victims of Stalin's terror – had been mooted by a number of figures in the cultural sphere in 1985–6. Action on it began in Moscow in May 1987 when Yurii Samodurov and Pavel Kudyukin urged meetings of the CSI and Perestroika to form a public organization to accomplish this goal, and in Leningrad in July when Elena Zelinskaya initiated a petition campaign (quickly repressed by the police) for that same purpose. At the August conference of informals where an initiative group was formed to found the

society 'Pamyatnik' (Monument), its scope had already expanded to include an archive and research-education centre. Thereafter, the initiative group launched a petition drive at the workplaces of its activists and, in November, took this campaign to the streets. By then, the organization's name had evolved into 'Memorial'.

The authorities responded to the street-level campaign with repression. Those collecting signatures were detained by the police and KGB and were fined. After heated arguments over whether to continue in the face of this repression, the group decided on a compromise whereby signature collection would continue, but in less exposed public places such as theatres. During the winter, groups in the provinces affiliated with Memorial also circulated petitions. In the capital, 113 notables in the cultural and scientific spheres added their names to the petition and addressed over their signatures a letter appealing to Gorbachev to assist in the project. The support of these establishment figures led to a new stage of development. The initiative group turned Memorial into a 'public organization' seeking official registration and took their petitions back to the streets.

In June 1988, with repression relaxed for the Nineteenth Party Conference, Memorial staged its first mass meeting at which the 50,000 signatures that had been gathered to date were passed to conference delegates Yurii Afanas'ev (rector of Moscow's Institute of Historical Archives) and Elem Klimov (head of the Cinematographers Union) who delivered them to the party conference a few days later. In his final remarks to the conference, Gorbachev offhandedly endorsed the idea of erecting a memorial to the terror's victims. This endorsement represented a new strategy of containment deployed against Memorial. As its membership and level of activity increased exponentially over the summer of 1988 – leading to the establishment of a Public Council in August, composed of such luminaries as Afanas'ev, Andrei Sakharov and Boris El'tsin, and the founding of a research and information centre in September – the authorities employed a variety of devices to retard Memorial's progress. These included: commissioning certain official organizations to serve as sponsors, thus inserting a conservative wedge into Memorial's organizing committee; pressure on independent sponsors and leading organizers to adopt the conservative orientation of the new 'sponsors'; the use of repressive measures against many activists in the provinces; repeated retraction of commitments to allow an official founding conference in autumn 1988; the Ministry of Culture's hijacking of the proposal to build the monument along with the funds already collected by Memorial for doing so; and, after Memorial had jettisoned all its official sponsors and staged its own founding conference in January 1989, the creation of rival 'Memorial' societies in a number of cities. It was only at Andrei Sakharov's funeral in December 1989 that Gorbachev acceded to his widow's request to issue an official registration to Memorial. Andrei Vasilevskii, 'Khroniki Memoriala', *Panorama* 10 (October 1989), pp. 6–7; Gromov and Kuzin, *Neformaly*, pp. 107–12; Berezovskii and Krotov, *Neformal'naya Rossiya*, pp. 282–5.

58 Novodvorskaya's speech to the August 1987 conference has been published

as 'Zemskoi Sobor ili Gosudarstvennaya Duma?', *Valeriya Novodvorskaya: sbornik statei* (Moscow: Svobodnoe Slovo, no date), pp. 22–3.

59 Obshchina was the prime mover in the creation of FSOK, which adopted in autumn a programme calling for free elections, an end to censorship and democratic planning based on market relations. All member groups claimed to have a 'socialist orientation'. In addition to Obshchina, they included: the CSI, Perestroika, Red Sail, Forest People, the Che Guevara Brigade, the Folk-Rock Association (Moscow), Salvation and Outpost (Leningrad), the Committee of Collaboration for Perestroika (Krasnoyarsk), Worker (Sverdlovsk) and a few others. Outside Moscow, FSOK amounted to an information network at most. In Moscow, however, the federation's members collaborated closely, putting out in September 1987 their own samizdat journal, *Svidetel'* (*Witness*, later changed in name to *Levyi povorot* or *Left Turn*). After El'tsin's sacking, FSOK set up a picket at the metro station '1905 Street' whose placards demanded 'Full glasnost in the El'tsin affair' and 'An end to information apartheid'. Obshchina also organized meetings to discuss the matter at Moscow State University but the authorities broke up these gatherings. Although previous relations between El'tsin and the informals had been less than fraternal, FSOK's actions appear to have been the only public statement of support on his behalf in the immediate aftermath of his fall from power. El'tsin soon became a *cause célèbre* among informal circles, thus preparing the way for his return to the political limelight as a democratic leader.

60 We regard that line of activity represented by Novodvorskaya and her young confederates as related to the struggle over identity issues within the movement, distinguishing them sharply and invidiously from their pro-socialist competitors (FSOK). This characterization makes no comment on their sincerity; it merely attempts to situate the group on the field of the informal movement. See Viktor Panomarev, 'Novodvorskoe veche', *Sobesednik* 44 (October 1987), pp. 12–13.

61 The following paragraphs lean on the observations of V. Igrunov and S. Mitrokhin. Some elements appear in Igrunov, 'Public Movements', pp. 17–20, 28–30; Michael McFaul and Sergei Markov, *The Troubled Birth of Russian Democracy: Parties, Personalities, and Programs* (Stanford, CA: Hoover Institution Press, 1993), pp. 27–9, 88–90.

62 The repression – involving preventive detention and mass arrests in places such as Yaroslavl and Kuibyshev – was sanctioned under decrees issued by the Supreme Soviet's Presidium popularly known as 'the July ordinances'. Mikhail Malyutin, 'Kak v odnoi strane pravovoe gosudarstvo vvodili (da, slava bogu, poka ne vveli)', (Moscow: mimeo, October 1988).

63 Synopses of this party's history can be found in Vera Tolz, *The USSR's Emerging Multiparty System* (New York: Praeger, 1990), pp. 56–60; Pribylovskii, *Slovar' oppozitsii*, pp. 9–11; Berezovskii and Krotov, *Neformal'naya Rossiya*, pp. 250–53.

64 Pribylovskii, *Slovar' oppozitsii*, p. 9; (anon.), 'Sensatsiya, kotoruyu zhdali', *Khronograf* 4 (18 May 1988), p. 1.

65 Zhirinovskii joined the Democratic Union and was elected to its Central Coordinating Council. However, regarded as an outsider by the core

group, he was seldom notified about meetings and other events and before long drifted away to form his own party. D. Starikov, 'Korotkye vstrechi' (Moscow; manuscript, 27 December 1993)(M-BIO archives, fond D.S.).

66 Quoted in N. N., 'Den' pervyi: doktrina', *Khronograf* 4 (18 May 1988), pp. 2–3.

67 S. Mitrokhin, 'Den' vtoroi: demokratiya i med', *Khronograf* 5 (25 May 1988), pp. 1–3.

68 See the interview with Viktor Kuzin in McFaul and Markov, *The Troubled Birth of Russian Democracy*, pp. 33–4.

69 S. Mitrokhin, 'Den' tretii: est' takaya partiya', *Khronograf* 6 (28 May 1988), pp. 1–3.

70 'Deklaratsiya, pervogo s"ezda DS', *Demokraticheskii soyuz: paket dokumentov* (Moscow: mimeo, 9 May 1988), p. 10.

71 M. Malyutin, 'Za kem poidut massy', *Narodnyi deputat* 5 (1990), pp. 40–2.

72 Petro, 'Perestroika from Below', pp. 114–15.

73 The first defection from the Democratic Union occurred in autumn 1988 when some members left to form the Libertarian and Transnational Radical parties. In the same period, a number of factions appeared within Democratic Union: liberal democrats, social democrats, Eurocommunists, Christian democrats, constitutional democrats and others. By June 1989, many from these factions – excepting the liberal democrats – had joined electoral organizations or the organizing committees formed to establish other political parties. Pribylovskii, *Slovar' oppozitsii*, p. 10; Berezovskii and Krotov, *Neformal'naya Rossiya*, pp. 251–52.

74 According to Dmitrii Leonev, this was apparent on the first day of the Democratic Union's founding congress. In an item contributed to *Khronograf* (no. 4 (18 May 1988), p. 3), he observed, 'The gong was struck . . . the audience took their places. The actors came out onto the stage and began reciting verse. The hall fell silent: we didn't know whether we should laugh or cry. Gentlemen and comrades, dramatis personae and performers! We presently don't know the main thing – the genre of your songs (it isn't Vaudeville, is it!) and therefore . . . [since] we cannot evaluate either the songs or the act, we shall refrain from both whistles and applause.'

75 The political programme adopted by the Democratic Union at its founding congress appears in McFaul and Markov, *The Troubled Birth of Russian Democracy*, pp. 41–3.

76 P. Anatol'ev, 'Raspad DS, raspad KPSS', *Novaya zhizn'* 15 (June 1990), p. 2.

77 *Al'ternativa KPSS* (September 1989), pp. 7–9.

78 Igrunov, 'Public Movements', pp. 28–30.

79 This is mentioned in an item in *Khronograf* 5 (25 May 1988), p. 6.

80 B. P. Kurashvili, 'Aspekty perestroiki', *Sovetskoe gosudarstvo i pravo* 12 (December 1987), pp. 3–12; esp. p. 8.

81 Michael Urban, 'Popular Fronts and "Informals"', *Detente* 14 (1989), pp. 4, 27.

82 *Ibid.*, pp. 4, 6; Vladimir Brovkin, 'Revolution From Below: Informal Political Organizations in Russia 1988–1989', *Soviet Studies* 42 (April

1990), pp. 233–57; esp. p. 236; Weigle, 'Political Participation and Party Formation in Russia', pp. 248–9.

83 This account is based on the participant-observation of V. Igrunov and S. Mitrokhin. See Igrunov, 'Public Movements', pp. 22–3; Vladimir Pribylovskii, 'Pouchitel'naya istoriya Moskovskogo narodnogo fronta', *Panorama* 28 (July 1991), pp. 6–7.

84 'Tezisy Tsentral'nogo Komiteta KPSS k XIX Vsesoyuznoi partiinoi konferentsii', *Izvestiya* (23 May 1988).

85 'Proekt programmy moskovskogo narodnogo fronta' (Moscow: mimeo, June 1988), pp. 1–5.

86 Pribylovskii, *Slovar' oppozitsii*, p. 41.

87 In January 1989, Obshchina played the central part in the formation of the Confederation of Anarcho-Syndicalists. *Ibid.*, p. 14.

88 Two of the larger ones formed in Yaroslavl and Kuibyshev where mass demonstrations against the local authorities, catalysed by rigged delegate selection to the Nineteenth Party Conference, contributed significantly to organizing efforts. On the formation of popular fronts in Russia, see Berezovskii and Krotov, *Neformal'naya Rossiya*, pp. 89–226, 357–8; Gromov and Kuzin, *Neformaly*, pp. 180–225; V. Levicheva, 'Anatomiya neformal'nogo dvizheniya', *Izvestiya Tsk KPSS* 4 (April 1990), pp. 150–6.

89 Berezovskii and Krotov, *Neformal'naya Rossiya*, pp. 136, 184–5.

90 Gromov and Kuzin, *Neformaly*, p. 198. The proposed organizational structure of the all-union popular front appears in 'Printsipy organizatsii i osnovye tseli narodnogo fronta' (mimeo; no date), p. 2.

91 Malyutin, 'Za kem poidut massy', pp. 41–6.

92 Kudryavtsev, 'Oppozitsiya i totalitarizm v SSSR', p. 16.

93 Michael Urban, *More Power to the Soviets: the Democratic Revolution in the USSR* (Aldershot: Edward Elgar, 1990), pp. 39–53.

94 Sakwa, *Gorbachev and his Reforms*, p. 121; Brovkin, 'Revolution From Below', pp. 248–9.

95 This definition was offered by leading MNF organizer, Mikhail Shneider, in an interview that appeared in McFaul and Markov, *The Troubled Birth of Russian Democracy*, p. 142.

96 These four items appeared first on a list of eleven 'basic activities' set down in 'Proekt programmy Moskovskogo narodnogo fronta', pp. 2–3.

97 Examples include *Ekspress-Khronika*, *Glasnost'*, *Khronograf* and *Merkurii*.

98 Berezovskii and Krotov, *Neformal'naya Rossiya*, pp. 47–8.

99 Moscow Tribune's draft charter, signed by Yurii Afanas'ev, Andrei Sakharov, Leonid Batkin, Yurii Burtin and six others, outlined the purposes of the club as assisting the leadership of the Communist Party by supplying them with 'independent, sober and critical assessments', and uniting intellectuals to work for perestroika by supporting the course of democratization and radical economic reforms. 'O sozdanii politiko-kul'turnogo obshchestvennogo kluba "Moskovskaya Tribuna" (proekt zayavleniya)' (Moscow: mimeo, no date; M-BIO archives).

100 Viktoriya Chalikova, '"Moskovskaya Tribuna" vpervye vyshla na miting', *Soglasiya* 7 (30 April 1989), p. 8.

6. NATIONAL ELECTIONS AND MASS POLITICS

1 Obviously, we are denying that voting existed under the oxymoronic institution of single-candidate elections that had been the standard practice in the USSR from its inception. In addition to the de-politicizing functions of these 'elections' as outlined by Viktor Zaslavsky and Robert Brym ('The Structure of Power and the Functions of Local Soviet Elections' in E. Jacobs (ed.), *Soviet Local Politics and Government* (London: Allen and Unwin, 1983), pp. 69–77), we would note the double insult handed the population by the regime at election time: '*We* have chosen *your* candidate and now *we* compel *you* to vote for him!'

2 Of course, the situation was fundamentally different in the Baltic republics where popular fronts challenged and effectively defeated the Communist Party in these elections. But our concern is with Russia.

3 See, for example, the data reported in: V. Levanskii, A. Obolonskii and G. Tokarevskii, 'Chto dumayut lyudi o vyborakh?', *Argumenty i fakty* 10 (11–17 March 1989), p. 2; N. Popov, 'Obshchestvennoe mnenie i vybory', *Izvestiya* (22 April 1989).

4 A. V. Berezkin *et al.*, 'The Geography of the 1989 Elections of People's Deputies of the USSR (Preliminary Results)', *Soviet Geography*, 30 (October 1989), pp. 610–11.

5 V. Komarovskii and E. Dugin, 'Do i posle vyborov', *Izvestiya* (12 May 1989).

6 The Politburo awarded this task to A. I. Luk'yanov who arranged for the appointment of the CEC's members and attended all save one of its meetings. M. Urban's interview with CEC member, G. V. Barabashev (6 May 1989).

7 Arno Al'mann, 'Aktual'nye politicheskie voprosy', *Kommunist Estonii* 2 (1989), pp. 97–102; I. Fonyakov, 'Ravnodushnykh net', *Literaturnaya gazeta* 2 (11 January 1989), p. 10; G. Obreskov, 'Izbrany dlya podpisi?', *Izvestiya* (16 January 1989).

8 See the interview given by Yu. I. Ryzhov to V. Saklakov, *Izvestiya* (29 December 1988). See also V. Tolstenko, 'Kollektiv otstoyal svoego pretendenta', *Izvestiya* (13 February 1989).

9 For an overview, see I. Butko and M. Stavniichuk, 'Vzglyad na komissii. Chto bylo i chto dolzhno byt', *Sovety narodnykh deputatov* 12 (December 1989), pp. 43–5.

Egor Ligachev has written that during the campaign, the Central Committee of the CPSU issued 'one after another directive to [party organizations in] the localities: Don't interfere, Don't interfere! Keep your distance! In many party committees confusion set in. But the [Central Committee] refrained from providing any political directions . . . [Instead, the secretary encharged with supervising the campaign, G. P.] Razumovskii, telephoned the obkoms and kraikoms, giving the instructions "Don't interfere! Don't interfere!" ' In view of the blatant illegalities and crude interventions perpetrated by local organs of the CPSU, one can only wonder what might have occurred had the Central Committee or Razumovskii taken a different attitude. Ligachev's comments appeared in his

Zagadka Gorbacheva (Novosibirsk: Interbuk, 1992), pp. 76–8. Vladimir Brovkin has argued that the central leadership in fact sent contradictory signals to its local counterparts – to control and guide the elections in addition to Ligachev's 'Don't interfere!' – throughout the process. See Brovkin 'The Making of Elections to the Congress of People's Deputies (CPD) in March 1989', *Russian Review* 49 (October 1990), pp. 418–22.

10 See, for example, M. S. Gorbachev's 'On Progress in Implementing the Decisions of the 27th CPSU Congress and the Tasks of Promoting Perestroika', *19th All-Union Conference of the CPSU: Documents and Materials* (Moscow; Novosti, 1988), esp. pp. 42, 49; see also his speech in *Izvestiya* (1 July 1988).

11 'Zaklyuchitl'noe slovo M. S. Gorbacheva na Plenume Tsk KPSS 25 aprelya 1989 goda', *Izvestiya* (27 April 1989).

12 Neil Robinson, 'Parliamentary Politics Under Gorbachev: Opposition and the Failure of Socialist Pluralism', *Journal of Communist Studies* 9 (March 1993), pp. 91–108.

13 To take one example – Russia's premier informal organization, the MNF. By autumn of 1988 active membership had declined rather steeply but rebounded and expanded with the onset of the campaigns it waged in winter 1989. Vladimir Pribylovskii, 'Pouchitel'naya istoriya MNF', *Panorama* 1 (January 1991), pp. 6–7.

14 This was true for Democratic Union which declined to participate in elections conducted under the aegis of the CPSU.

15 Leszek Kolakowski, 'Mind and Body: Ideology and the Collapse of Communism' in K. Z. Poznanski (ed.), *Constructing Capitalism* (Boulder, CO: Westview, 1992), pp. 9–23.

16 Max Mote was among the first Western analysts to draw attention to the deep changes caused by these elections in the psychological climate in the country. See his 'Electing the USSR Congress of People's Deputies', *Problems of Communism* 38 (November–December 1989), pp. 51–6.

17 Almost invariably, these 'elections' in the thirty-nine official public organizations authorized to select deputies (ranging from the 100 deputies allotted to both the Communist Party and the All-Union Council of Trades Unions, at one end, to the single seat assigned to such organizations as the All-Union Society of Philatelists, at the other) were in fact rubber-stamp affairs in which the central bodies confirmed the lists of candidates drawn up by their corresponding executive organs. The major exception occurred in the Academy of Sciences in which a widespread mutiny forced a second round of nominations and elections that resulted in such prominent figures as Andrei Sakharov, Roald Sagdeev, Dmitrii Likhachev and Nikolai Shmelev winning seats. On these and other nominations and elections in the USSR's public organizations, see Michael Urban, *More Power to the Soviets: the Democratic Revolution in the USSR* (Aldershot, UK: Edward Elgar, 1990), pp. 93–7; Brendan Kiernan, *The End of Soviet Politics* (Boulder, CO: Westview, 1993), pp. 65–6: A. V. Berezkin *et al.*, *Vesna–89* (Moscow: Progress, 1990), pp. 93–103.

18 This instance was reported in 'Moskovskie initsiativnye gruppy', *Panorama* 3 (1989), p. 3.

19   Robert Orttung, 'Democratization in Leningrad' (doctoral dissertation, University of California at Los Angeles, 1992), p. 41.
20   *Izvestiya* (19 January 1989).
21   Anatolii Papp, 'Stavropol'' in Anatolii Papp (ed.), *Vybory–1989* (Moscow: Panorama, 1993), part 2, p. 44.
22   See the cases reported in the telegrams published by *Izvestiya* (20 January 1989). See also A. Davydov *et al.*, 'Kandidaty nazvany – bor'ba vperedi', *Izvestiya* (25 January 1989) and I. Korolikov. 'My tak schitaem', *Izvestiya.* (17 January 1989).
23   Mikhail Shneider has documented in Moscow alone dozens of cases involving one or more of these tactics. See his 'Pervyi etap: vydvizhenie kandidatov' in Papp (ed.), *Vybory–1989*, part 1, pp. 5–9.
24   These accounts of the two voters' meetings involving the candidacy of Korotich are based on eye-witness reports, some of which can be found in *Khronograf* 21 (1989), pp. 1–2 and V. Chernov, 'Deti Sharikova', *Ogonek* 3 (January 1989), p. 31.
25   The meetings described here were replete with more or less typical elements characterizing innumerable encounters of this sort that have taken place in Russia since the return of open political activity. To take one more example from a long list, consider a voters' meeting with the candidates for a vacant seat in the Russian Congress of People's Deputies in Moscow some two years later (23 May 1991). The two principal contenders were Yurii Afanas'ev, then co-chairperson of Democratic Russia, and Ivan Antonovich, then a secretary of the Russian Communist Party. While Afanas'ev addressed the assembly, Antonovich supporters – about half the hall – bellowed abuse ('fascist', 'traitor') that rose to such a din that Afanas'ev's remarks became inaudible, his use of a microphone notwithstanding. Afanas'ev's supporters – fairly the other half of the hall – took to chiding the catcallers for their rudeness, asking them to behave in a 'civilized' way and reminding them that their man will get his turn. When Antonovich's turn did come, however, a complete role reversal occurred. Now Afanas'ev backers created the din of abuse while the Antonovich people reprimanded them for not behaving in a 'civilized' way. The voters' meeting looked very much like two opposing rallies held simultaneously, the symmetry between them so complete that soon each side was insistently accusing the other of being the reason for what they held to be an impending civil war. As epilogue, a member of the Communist Party USA rose to deliver some remarks on the dangers of anti-communism as he had witnessed it during the McCarthy era. His speech was punctuated by shouts from the floor of 'Communist, go back to America!' (Personal observations, M. Urban.)
26   This figure of 282 comes from Jeffrey W. Hahn, 'Developments in Local Soviet Politics' (unpublished paper, Villanova University, Villanova, PA, 1990), p. 27
27   Shneider, 'Pervyi etap', pp. 5–7; Korolikov, 'My tak schitaem'.
28   For examples see V. Nikolaeva, 'Luchshego – iz odnogo', *Izvestiya* (14 January 1989).
29   V. Kalugin, 'Po vcherashnim retseptam', *Izvestiya* (24 January 1989); V. Solyanik, 'Vetry peremen i starye prepony', *Sovety narodnykh deputatov 2*

(February 1989), pp. 36–8; 'V tekh zhe dvukh okrugakh', *Sovety narodnykh deputatov* 3 (March 1989), pp. 27–30.

30   *Izvestiya* (20 January 1989).
31   Tolstenko, 'Kollektiv otstoyal svoego pretendenta'.
32   V. Istomin, 'Skazka dlya izbiratelei', *Leningradskaya pravda* (17 January 1989); Andrei Romanov, 'Po 132–i stat'e', *Moskovskie novosti* 9 (26 February 1989), p. 13.
33   Andrei Nuikin, 'Stat'e deputatom', *Moskovskie novosti* 10 (5 March 1989), p. 13.
34   *Izvestiya*, (10 January 1989).
35   Aleksandr Bolotin and Lev Sherstennikov, 'Raskovanost'', *Ogonek* 7 (February 1989), pp. 1–2; L. Annus, 'O glasnosti – glasno', *Sovetskaya Estoniya* (23 February 1989).
36   Kathleen Mihailisko, 'Alla Yaroshins'ka: Crusading Journalist From Zhitomir Becomes People's Deputy', *Radio Liberty Report on the USSR*, 247/ 89 (24 May 1989), pp. 17–19.
37   Vladimir Pribylovskii, 'Kazan'', in Papp (ed.), *Vybory–89*, part 2, p. 19.
38   Revol't Pimenov, 'Syktyvkar' in Papp (ed.), *Vybory–89*, part 2, pp. 51–2.
39   Sergei Mitrokhin, 'Grazhdanskie voiny: ot okruzhnykh sobranii do podscheta golosov' in Papp (ed.), *Vybory – 1989*, part 1, p. 10.
40   *Izvestiya* (21 March 1989). Since no meetings were called in Estonia and since the Central Asian republics staged thoroughly 'Soviet elections' (one-candidate), by inference the bulk of these meetings were held in Russia.
41   *Izvestiya* (11 March 1989).
42   *Izvestiya* (21 March 1989).
43   Mitrokhin, 'Grazhdanskie voiny', p. 11; Letter from Yu. Karyakin, *Ogonek* 12 (1989), pp. 4–5.
44   S. Troyan, 'Nadezhnye lyudi v zale', *Izvestiya* (6 February 1989).
45   Levanskii, Obolonskii and Tokarevskii, 'Chto dumayut lyudi o vyborakh?', p. 2.
46   See: the interview given by G. V. Barabashev to V. Shchepotkin, *Izvestiya* (9 February 1989); Yu. Perepletkin, 'Pretendentov bylo odinnadtsat'', *Izvestiya* (21 February 1989); A. Krivchenko, 'Edinodushie ravnodush-nykh', *Izvestiya* (14 February 1989); M. Ovcharov and V. Shchepotkin, 'Portret protokola na fone demokratii', *Izvestiya*. (18 February 1989); A. Ivanov, 'Turnir pretendentov: zachem lomalis' Kop'ya', *Sovety narodnykh deputatov*, 3 (March 1989), pp. 30–2.
47   Anatoly Sobchak, *For a New Russia* (New York: The Free Press, 1992), pp. 9–10.
48   Orttung, 'Democratization in Leningrad', pp. 44–5.
49   Mitrokhin, 'Grazhdanskie voiny', p. 11; Pimenov, 'Syktyvkar', pp. 53–4.
50   Sobchak provides an example of this in his *For a New Russia*, pp. 14–15.
51   Mitrokhin, 'Grazhdanskie voiny', pp. 10–14.
52   The 'social council' members are listed in *Moskovskie novosti* 2 (8 January 1989).
53   'Predvybornye platformy', *Moskovskie novosti* 4 (22 January 1989), p. 12; Nina Belyaeva, 'Moskovskaya tribuna', *Moskovskie novosti* 7 (12 February

1989); Antaras Burachas, 'Zayavlenie kluba "Moskovskaya tribuna"', *Vozrozhdenie* 12 (10 March 1989), p. 2.

54 One of us (V. Igrunov) participated directly in negotiations between El'tsin's campaign staff, led by Lev Sukhanov, and candidates of the liberal intelligentsia represented in these discussions by Yurii Afanas'ev's staffers. Initially, Sukhanov eschewed all cooperation with other candidates, announcing that El'tsin expected to win his own race without their assistance and stated that his position was 'every man for himself'. This resistance was eventually overcome by pointing out that a El'tsin victory would mean very little should the democrats suffer defeat, leaving El'tsin with few allies in the new legislature. Since El'tsin had already taken a step toward the liberals by joining Memorial, these arguments made the second step easier and led to the collaborative campaign efforts.

55 M. Steven Fish, *Democracy From Scratch* (Princeton: Princeton University Press, 1995), pp. 35–8.

56 A possible exception was Yurii Boldyrev's nomination. Although Boldyrev was associated with Club Perestroika, he was never an actual member. On the formation of Elections–89, see E. A. Zdravomyslova and A. A. Temkina, 'Izbiratel'naya kampaniya i obshchestvennoe dvizhenie v Leningrade' in Papp (ed.), *Vybory–89*, part 2, pp. 2–4.

57 Their activities are described in Papp (ed.), *Vybory–89*, part 2.

58 On this question see Levanskii, Obolonskii and Tokarevskii, 'Chto dumayut lyudi o vyborakh?', p. 2; V. Komarevskii and A. Usol'tsev, 'Protivoborstvo? Net, sotrudnichestvo', *Argumenty i fakty* 22 (3–9 June 1989), p. 5. In the main, liberal publications tended to shy away from supporting candidates or advocating political positions, save the importance of observing procedures and ensuring fairness. This neutral posture afforded them a splendid stance from which to attack their conservative opponents for transgressing the rules. Examples would include: the roundtable, 'Vybory, pervye uroki', *Literaturnaya gazeta* (5 April 1989), p. 10; A. Stepovoi, 'Kak eto bylo, ili ob odnom nesostoyavshemsya sobranii izbiratelei', *Izvestiya* (18 January 1989). Conservative publications often tended to support regime-sponsored candidates, drawing attention to their programmes for 'improving the life' of people. Examples can be found in 'Opravdat' doverie' in *Sovetskaya Rossiya* (28 March 1989). Interestingly, some local newspapers used the same tactics as liberals, in one instance claiming to have unmasked the 'intrigues' of the Nizhegorod Popular Front and the candidates whom they supported. See V. Barmin and V. Kiselev, 'Predvybornye igry' in *Gor'kovskii rabochii* (10 March 1989).

59 L. Lazerov, interviewed by Dmitrii Ostal'skii, *Moskovskie novosti* 15 (9 April 1989).

60 Zdravomyslova and Temkina, 'Izbiratel'naya kampaniya i obshchestvennoe dvizhenie v Leningrade', pp. 4, 13.

61 Pribylovskii, 'Kazan'', pp. 21–22.

62 Papp, 'Stavropol'', p. 44.

63 Mitrokhin, 'Grazhdanskie voiny', p. 14.

64 On the CPSU's 'stop El'tsin' campaign, see: Stephen White, 'The Soviet Elections of 1989: From Acclamation to Limited Choice', *Coexistence* 28

(December 1991), pp. 513–39; Dawn Mann, 'El'tsin Rides a Political Roller Coaster', *Radio Liberty Report on the USSR*, 253/89 (9 June 1989), p. 3; John Morrison, *Boris Yeltsin: From Bolshevik to Democrat* (New York: Dutton, 1991), pp. 90–4.

65 Boris Yeltsin, *Against the Grain: an Autobiography* (New York: Summit, 1990), p. 104.

66 *Izvestiya* (20 March 1989).

67 *Vybory v Moskve. Kak eto bylo* (Moscow: M-BIO, 1989), pp. 17–18.

68 Interview given by Sergei Stankevich to S. Mitrokhin (27 April 1989).

69 Vladimir Pribylovskii, *Sto politikov Rossii* (Moscow: Panorama, 1992), p. 30.

70 See Charles E. Ziegler, 'Ideology, Postcommunist Values and the Environment' in M. Urban (ed.), *Ideology and System Change in the USSR and East Europe* (London: Macmillan/New York: St. Martin's Press, 1992), pp. 121–37.

71 On the 'El'tsin factor' in the 1989 elections, see Brendan Kiernan and Joseph Aistrup, 'Moscow's 1989 Elections to the Congress of People's Deputies', *Soviet Studies* 43(6) (1991), pp. 1049–64; Berezkin *et al.*, *Vesna–89*, pp. 225–6.

72 For descriptions of the mobilization of erstwhile onlookers, see: Sobchak, *For a New Russia*, pp. 11–15 and Mikhail Shneider, in an interview published in Michael McFaul and Sergei Markov, *The Troubled Birth of Russian Democracy* (Stanford, CA: Hoover Institute, 1993), pp. 143–7.

73 Zdravomyslova and Temkina, 'Izbiratel'naya kampaniya i obshchestvennoe dvizhenie v Leningrade', pp. 4–5, 7, 17.

74 Illustrative of the voter rebellion against officers of the party-state is a case in southern Russia during the local elections of 1990 where one candidate – an airport dispatcher – lodged a stiff protest against the local authorities who mistakenly listed his occupation as 'director' on the official voters' bulletins. Although most people in the small district in which he was running for office knew him personally, he none the less was convinced that the typographic error was the kiss of death for his candidacy. See Berezkin *et al.*, *Vesna–89*, pp. 104–5, note 1.

75 *Izvestiya* (13 May 1989).

76 Pribylovskii, 'Kazan'', pp. 21–22; Papp, 'Stavropol'', p. 45; N. Kiselev, 'U paradnogo pod''ezda', *Komsomolskaya pravda*, (26 April 1989).

77 Kiernan, *The End of Soviet Politics*, p. 64.

78 Sergei Mitrokhin, 'Izbiratel'naya kampaniya Samsonova' in Papp (ed.), *Vybory–89*, part 1, p. 47.

79 *Ibid.*, pp. 47–8.

80 Both episodes have been recounted in V. Krylovskii, 'Est' li chem gordit'sya?', *Pravo golosa* 3 (1990), pp. 4–5.

81 One postal code (the Tsarskoe selo sub-district) both epitomizes the problem here and confounds our overall statistical results. This area is composed of nearly equal proportions of intelligentsia, party-state officials and staff, and industrial workers. It recorded the highest number of subscribers to *Argumenty i fakty* (56.3 per 100 mailboxes), the lowest number to *Trud* (21.9 per 100 mailboxes) *but* the lowest percentage of the liberal vote (41.03 per cent).

82 Subterfuge or stupidity would often come into play in this respect. In
    Leningrad, for instance, the daily *Leningradskaya pravda* published some of
    Election–89's propaganda for the explicit purpose of warning voters against
    it. See Mary McAuley, 'Politics, Economics and Elite Realignment in
    Russia: a Regional Perspective', *Soviet Economy* 8 (January–March 1992),
    p. 55. On the resistance of another daily, *Vechernaya Kazan'*, to the
    intimidation of local party organs, see Pribylovskii, 'Kazan'', p. 19. For a
    discussion of local press assistance to democratic forces in four provinces,
    see Fish, *Democracy From Scratch*, chapter 5.
83 V. Komarovskii and A. Usol'tsev, 'Protivoborstvo? Net, sotrudnichestvo',
    Argumenty i fakty 22 (3–9 June 1989), p. 5.
84 Geoffrey Hosking, Jonathan Aves and Peter Duncan, *The Road to Post-
    Communism: Independent Political Movements in the Soviet Union, 1985–1991*
    (London: Pinter, 1992), p. 70.
85 Various figures have been cited in the literature on these elections regarding
    the number of regional first secretaries of the CPSU who suffered defeat at
    the polls. For instance: Kiernan (*The End of Soviet Politics*, p. 68) lists
    twenty-nine; Brovkin ('The Making of Elections', p. 441), claims thirty-
    eight; Otto Cappelli ('Comparative Communism's Fall', *The Harriman
    Institute Forum* 3 (June 1990), p. 5) puts the figure at 49 per cent of those
    who ran. We rely on the number thirty-one, provided in Berezkin *et al.*,
    Vesna–89, p. 68.
86 Berezkin *et al.*, 'The Geography of the 1989 Elections', p. 629.

7. THE POLITICS OF OPPOSITION

1 Stuart Goldman, 'The New Soviet Legislative Branch' in R. Huber and
   D. Kelley (eds.), *Perestroika-Era Politics: the New Soviet Legislature and
   Gorbachev's Political Reforms* (Armonk, NY: M. E. Sharpe, 1991), pp.
   69–70.
2 See Anatolii Sobchak's address to the second Congress of People's Deputies
   of the USSR, *Izvestiya* (18 December 1989).
3 See A. B. Yablokov's address to the second Congress of People's Deputies
   of the USSR, *Izvestiya* (16 December 1989).
4 Quoted by Thomas Remington, 'Parliamentary Government in the USSR'
   in Huber and Kelley (eds.), *Perestroika-Era Politics*, p. 186.
5 Eugene Huskey, 'Legislative–Executive Relations in the New Soviet
   Political Order' in Huber and Kelley (eds.), *Perestroika-Era Politics*, pp.
   162–3.
6 *Izvestiya* (4 March 1991).
7 K. A. Antanavichius, speech to the Congress, *Izvestiya* (26 May 1989).
8 A stenographic record of this episode appeared in *Izvestiya* (26 May 1989).
9 This 'double-incompetence' with respect to legislative organization was
   altogether congruent with the personalized relations of authority characteristic of state socialism. Executive bodies issuing instructions irrespective of
   the laws that formally commission their activities accorded fully with the
   leader's arbitrary behaviour at the Congress. Neither was bound by legal
   relations; both did whatever they could get away with. The hierarchic

ordering of the Soviet system led to the (mistaken) impression that it was subalterns who disobeyed directives, disregarded the law and so forth. They did. But hierarchy tended to evoke the notion that they *shouldn't*, that it was *wrong* to defy the authority of those at the top. In fact, subordinate officials were enacting the same (personalized) authority within their respective spheres of activity that those at the top enacted within theirs.

10 Ann Sheehy, 'The Non-Russian Republics and the Congress of People's Deputies', *Radio Liberty Report on the USSR*, RL270/89 (16 June 1989), p. 22; I. A. Kazannik interviewed by L. Novikova, *Argumenty i fakty* 24 (17–23 June 1989), pp. 1–2.

11 Remington, 'Parliamentary Government in the USSR', p. 183.

12 Michael Urban, 'Technical Assistance and Political Control: a Research Note on the Organization–Instruction Department of Local Soviets', *Comparative Politics* 17 (April 1985), pp. 337–50.

13 Georgii Barabashev, personal communication to M. Urban (14 July 1990).

14 Mikhail Forin, personal communication to M. Urban (8 July 1990).

15 V. Kurasov, 'Vneocherednye sessii Sovetov', *Izvestiya* (7 August 1989); V. Dolganov and R. Lynev, 'Sdelan vazhnyi shag', *Izvestiya* (7 August 1989); V. Dolganov and M. Kushtapin, 'Debaty v pol'zu peremen', *Izvestiya* (20 July 1989); E. Gonzal'ez, *et al.*, 'S"ezd i mir', *Izvestiya* (20 June 1989).

16 Remington, 'Parliamentary Government in the USSR', pp. 186–94.

17 For an account, see Michael Urban, *More Power to the Soviets: the Democratic Revolution in the USSR* (Aldershot: Edward Elgar, 1990), pp. 135–7.

18 B. Kruzhkov, 'Net uzhe mesyatsev, ostalis' nedeli', *Narodnyi deputat* 15 (1990), pp. 44–7; Eduard Cherny, 'The Minister Ignores the USSR Constitution', *Moscow News* 41 (21–8 October 1990), p. 6.

19 Huskey, 'Legislative–Executive Relations in the New Soviet Political Order', p. 165.

20 Goldman, 'The New Soviet Legislative Branch', p. 66.

21 *Izvestiya* (2 June 1989).

22 *Ibid.*

23 Yurii Afanas'ev coined this phrase in a speech to the Congress, *Izvestiya* (29 May 1989).

24 Goldman, 'The New Soviet Legislative Branch', p. 66.

25 Robert Sharlet, 'The Path of Constitutional Reform in the USSR' in Huber and Kelley (eds.), *Perestroika-Era Politics*, pp. 24–5.

26 Victor Sergeyev and Nikolai Biryukov, *Russia's Road to Democracy: Parliament, Communism and Traditional Culture* (Aldershot: Edward Elgar, 1993), pp. 130–3.

27 *Ibid.*, pp. 112–18.

28 This was Gorbachev's reply to a request to record the voting, *Izvestiya* (26 May 1989).

29 *Izvestiya* (29 May 1989).

30 Within an hour and a half of the Congress's first session, two deputies called for restrictions on the speaking rights of Andrei Sakharov and Yurii Boldyrev who – for raising procedural issues related to the election of the Supreme Soviet and its chairperson – were described as 'actively disorga-

nizing the work of the Congress', *Izvestiya* (26 May 1989). Periodically, demands came from the floor to deny all deputies in the Moscow delegation the right to speak.

31 An indicative illustration of the dominance of Soviet speech was the practice adopted at the first Congress (and continued thereafter) whereby deputies not afforded the opportunity to deliver their remarks to the assembly could submit them in writing for inclusion in the record of the proceedings. This practice, of course, had nothing in common with legislative debate for, perhaps, obvious reasons. However, it conformed to standard Soviet practices – such as the publication, irrespective of their degree of banality, of the speeches and writings of one or another Politburo personage – producing in this instance a sort of 'collected works of the entire collective'. Sergeyev and Biryukov, *Russia's Road to Democracy*, pp. 165–6.

32 Arkadii Murashev has claimed that persuasion and pressure from the Moscow group reversed the authorities' previous decision not to broadcast the Congress on live television. See his 'Mezhregional'naya deputatskaya gruppa', *Ogonek* 32 (4–11 August 1990), p. 6.

33 'S″ezd glazami zritelei', *Izvestiya* (18 August 1989).

34 In that nationwide poll, 63 per cent of respondents reported that the apparatus was the dominant influence at the Congress; of these 46 per cent labelled this influence 'negative' while 36 per cent thought it 'positive'. T. Zaslavskaya and Ya. Kapelyush, 'Obshchestvennoe mnenie ob itogakh S″ezda', *Argumenty i fakty* 26 (1–7 July 1989), p. 1.

35 Interview given by Mikhail Malyutin to M. Urban, 13 July 1990.

36 Interview given by Boris El'tsin to N. Selnorova and L. Novikova, *Argumenty i fakty* 23 (10–16 July 1989), p. 6.

37 'Glubokouvazhaemyi narodnyi deputat' (mimeo, no date; M-BIO archives).

38 'Kommyunike' of the Inter-City Working Conference of Democratic Clubs of Social Orientation (Moscow, no date; M-BIO archives).

39 Sponsors and slogans for this meeting are contained on the leaflet 'Sograzhdane!' (no date; M-BIO archives).

40 The classic statement on this subject is E. E. Schattschneider's *The Semisovereign People: a Realist's View of Democracy in America* (New York: Holt, Rinehart and Winston, 1960).

41 *Izvestiya* (26 May 1989).

42 The only delegation choosing to follow this example was the one from Sakhalin which put up two of its members for one seat in the Supreme Soviet, *Izvestiya* (27 May 1989).

43 A deal was subsequently worked out whereby A. I. Kazannik who was elected to the Council of Nationalities, voluntarily relinquished his seat so that El'tsin could fill it, *Izvestiya* (31 May 1989).

44 Although this law represented a watershed in official policy – from state-sponsored glasnost to full press freedom – it was more a recognition of changed circumstances than a reason for that change. Moreover, the Soviet state continued to employ a number of restrictive and oppressive practices in the field of publications until the defeat of the *coup d'état* of August 1991. On this law and those practices, see Michael Urban, 'The Russian Free

Press in the Transition to a Post-Communist Society', *Journal of Communist Studies* 9 (June 1993), esp. pp. 21–2, 29–31.

45 V. Dolganov *et al.*, 'Im stoyat' na strazhe zakona', *Izvestiya* (7 July 1989).

46 For a range of interpretations, from positive to negative, on the implications of this decree for freedom of expression, see: V. N. Kudryavtsev, interviewed by V. Itkin, *Sovetskaya Rossiya* (11 April 1989); Aleksandr Yakovlev, 'Trudnosti zakonotvorchestva', *Moskovskie novosti* 16 (16–23 April 1989), p. 1; A V. Sakharov, interviewed by Oleg Shcherbakov, *Stroitel'naya gazeta* (16 April 1989); A. Churganov's letter to the editor, *Ogonek* 21 (May 1989), p. 6; Egidiyus Bichkauskas, 'A vdrug ispugaemsya?', *Soglasie* 6 (19 April 1989), p. 1.

47 *Izvestiya* (1 August 1989).

48 Adamovich's proposal and Gorbachev's response to it appear in *Izvestiya* (26 May 1989).

49 Zaslavskaya's report and the ensuing discussion appear in *Izvestiya* (27 May 1989).

50 This seems to have been sensed immediately by the democrats' opponents, one of whom accused Sakharov and Stankevich of engaging in 'demagoguery', *Izvestiya* (27 May 1989).

51 One such episode involved A. E. Sebentsov who used citizens' remarks to blow the whistle on the authorities' method for fixing the vote: a show of hands by the presidium that cued the hall. Sebentsov's comments on voters' complaints about this appear in *Izvestiya* (30 May 1989).

52 Mikhail Malyutin, 'Za kem poidut massy', *Narodnyi deputat* 5 (1990), p. 38.

53 This strategy was apparent in a 27 April telegram to Gorbachev composed at a meeting in their Moscow office and signed by Popov, Murashev, Il'ya Zaslavskii and three others. While this missive was a polite request for a meeting, the purpose – to discuss the 'anti-constitutional counter-investigation of Tel'man Gdlyan' for exposing corruption among the high officials' with Gdlyan' himself present to tell his side of the story – was evidently less so (M-BIO archives).

54 V. Igrunov was among those who organized this meeting at the offices of the journal, *XX vek i mir*, held on May 20.

55 On May 22 V. Igrunov met with Popov on this matter. Popov claimed that the Moscow deputies were working with Gorbachev, not the Balts, and that the latter should follow the Muscovites.

56 Neil Robinson, 'Parliamentary Politics Under Gorbachev: Opposition and the Failure of Socialist Pluralism', *Journal of Communist Studies* 9 (March 1993), pp. 97–8. Marginalization took two forms. In most delegations, a deputy opposing the authorities was restricted by the party-state official who headed it – buttressed by its conformist members – from getting his or her name on the lists for addressing the Congress or standing for election to the Supreme Soviet. The remaining delegations – say those from the Baltic or from Moscow – were stigmatized as a handful of 'radicals' or 'separatists' out of step with prevailing opinion in the country.

57 See Popov's remarks at the next day's session, *Izvestiya* (29 May 1989).

58 See V. N. Stepanov's remarks, *Izvestiya* (28 May 1989).

59 See E. N. Meshalkin's remarks, *Izvestiya* (28 May 1989).

60 On the morning following Popov's announcement, V. Igrunov stood with two other informal leaders (Andrei Fadin and Yurii Permyakov of Perestroika–88) near the Kremlin entrance to the Palace of Congresses inviting deputies to a meeting to organize the very group mentioned by Popov. The meeting was held at the House of Learning – from late morning till about 6:00 p.m. – with Lev Ponomarev acting as moderator. Neither Popov nor El'tsin attended; Afanas'ev and Zaslavskaya did, but soon left. The main participants among the deputies were Sakharov, Zaslavskii, Evgenii Kogan from Estonia and Yurii Shcherbak from Ukraine. Although the discussion was in some ways rather timid – for instance, Sakharov's wife, Elena Bonner, accused the informal organizers of attempting to involve the deputies in 'politics' – a consensus did emerge among the deputies present that they were, indeed, a faction and should organize themselves along those lines.

61 *Izvestiya* (10 June 1989).

62 *Izvestiya* (11 June 1989).

63 Since the free market ideology that came to prevail within the I-RDG and the democratic movement was not an expression of class interests – for the simple reason that a class of property owners did not exist at this time – this ideology reflected another set of contingencies and circumstances summed up in (deepening) opposition to the communist authorities. As the prospects for renewing the Soviet system diminished in the face of a series of disappointments (among which the first Congress of People's Deputies represented a milestone) a radicalization set in among the democrats that valorized those socio-economic and political concepts most at odds with the extant order. If I-RDG leaders in early 1989 were still speaking about humane socialism, a socialist market and so forth, by the end of the year their narratives had enshrined bourgeois virtues at the centre of their preferred social ontology. This ideational transformation was a variant of Marx's much-disputed epigrams: 'life is not determined by consciousness, but consciousness by life' and 'consciousness is . . . a social product'. The consciousness in question was that of an emergent group of political leaders locked in a struggle for power with the communist authorities. Accordingly, the acquisition of ideas serviceable to them in that struggle – irrespective of either their recent profession of loyalty to socialism or the obvious lack of thought given to the practical implications of free-market nostrums that they now tossed about like chips off the philosopher's stone – should come as no surprise. Karl Marx and Frederick Engels, *The German Ideology* (London: Lawrence and Wishart, 1965), pp. 38, 42. For an account of I-RDG narratives at the second Congress of People's Deputies (December 1989) which exemplified the use of capitalist ideology in discrediting communist authorities and the communist system, see Michael Urban and John McClure, 'Discourse, Ideology and Party Formation in the USSR' in M. Urban (ed.), *Ideology and System Change in the USSR and East Europe* (New York: St. Martin's Press, 1992), pp. 92–120.

64 Theodore Friedgut and Lewis Sigelbaum, 'The Soviet Miners' Strike, July 1989', *The Carl Beck Papers* 804 (Pittsburgh: University of Pittsburgh Center for Russian and East European Studies, 1990), pp. 5, 11; Russell

Bova, 'Worker Activism: the Role of the State', J. B. Sedaitis and J. Butterfield (eds.), *Perestroika From Below: Social Movements in the Soviet Union* (Boulder, CO: Westview, 1991), pp. 33–4.

65 Friedgut and Sigelbaum, 'The Soviet Miners' Strike', pp. 14–17.

66 Aleksandr Verkhovskii, 'Rabochie kluby nakanune Kuzbassa', *Panorama* 7 (August 1989), p. 4.

67 V. Dolganov *et al.*, 'Deputaty ishchut reshenie', *Izvestiya* (24 July 1989).

68 Peter Rutland, 'Labor Unrest and Movements in 1989 and 1990', *Soviet Economy* 6 (October—December 1990), pp. 359–60.

69 Gavriil Popov, 'The Fifth Anniversary of the Miners' Strike', *Moscow News* 29 (22–8 July 1994), p. 2.

70 *Informatsionnyi byulleten'*, published by the I-RDG of the USSR (15 September 1989); Andrei Vasilevskii, 'Demokraty v parlamente', *Panorama* 8 (September 1989), p. 6; Valentin Logunov, 'Mezhregional'naya deputatskaya gruppa: god v oppozitsii', *Narodnyi deputat* 12 (1990), pp. 19–27; *Foreign Broadcast Information Service (FBIS)* SOV–89–145 (31 July 1989), pp. 49–56.

71 In his address to the conference, Popov claimed that the miners' strike has indicated that 'the people have come onto the stage' and that it is up to those in the I-RDG to lead them to 'a new type of socialism because, more and more, the voters are falling in behind us. We represent the opinions of the majority of the people.' Similarly, El'tsin argued that the miners' strike committees have shown the way by 'seizing real power from the party and state organs'. At least two deputies from mining regions were present to deliver the appeals of their constituents to the deputies in the hall. These speeches can be found in the I-RDG's *Informatsionnyi byulleten'* (15 September 1989), esp. pp. 2–4, 13–14, 17.

72 Statements to that effect, made by Popov, Stankevich and Gennadii Filshin, appear in the *FBIS* summaries, SOV–89–145 (31 July 1989), pp. 50, 55–6.

73 At the conference El'tsin expressed this conception of the group: 'We understand that our group must have not only its own approaches to problems, but also its own leadership structure, system of connections with the electorate and, possibly, some sort of fund of material support.' Quoted in A. Ivanov, 'Rassudit zhizn'', *Sovety narodnykh deputatov* 9 (1989), p. 31.

74 The success of Afanas'ev's address seemed entirely due to its coupling of political–symbolic categories that produced strong rhetorical effects by playing on the tension inherent in the binary opposition – Soviet system/ civilized world – that underlay his narrative. Accordingly, he proposed retaining the 'socialist idea' shorn of its 'Russian, Bolshevik, plebiscitary content', attaching it to a market – which 'is not a capitalist category' – and to the teachings of 'Jesus Christ and the brotherhood of man', suggesting that with the proper leadership the country would soon be enjoying the blessings of life as they have been experienced in Sweden or Denmark. The fact that the most enthusiastic reception at this meeting was reserved for that muddle would indicate something about the disposition of the deputies. *Informatisionnyi byulleten'* (15 September 1989), pp. 8–10.

75 Logunov, 'Mezhregional'naya deputatskaya gruppa', pp. 22–3.

76 *Ibid.*, p. 24.

77 Murashev, 'Mezhregional'naya deputatskaya gruppa', p. 8.
78 To illustrate, consider the I-RDG's approach to one of the tasks that it set
    for itself at its founding conference: the drafting of a new constitution for the
    USSR. The I-RDG's approach to this project was entirely geared to the
    publicity that a constitution might generate rather than to a process that
    might produce a constitution. Accordingly, the constitutional project
    produced three forms of publicity (but no constitution): appeals to the
    authorities to convene a constitutional convention; a draft constitution
    written by one man (Andrei Sakharov), that more resembled a moral–
    political testament than it did a juridical basis for government; and a national
    competition for the 'best draft constitution' involving prize money of 14,000
    rubles to be distributed to first, second and third place contestants. This
    competition was outlined in 'Vestnik sekretariata Mezhregional'noi gruppy
    narodnykh deputatov SSSR' (Moscow: mimeo, 27 March 1990).
79 For instance, the authorities rebuffed a number of I-RDG requests to use
    print facilities in order to publish a newspaper and closed the bank account
    which the group had set up. 'Pechat' za sem'yu pechatyami', *Golos izbiratelya*
    4 (1989), p. 1. They also saw to it that the mass media portrayed I-RDG
    leaders such as Afanas'ev, El'tsin and Gdlyan in anything but favourable
    light. See *ibid.*, p. 4; *Golos izbiratelya* 5 (1989), pp. 1–4; *Golos izbiratelya* 7
    (1989), p. 1.
80 The closest the I-RDG came to a platform was the list of platitudes and
    generalities 'Tezisy na programmu' appearing in the single issue of its
    newspaper, *Narodnyi deputat*, published as a special edition of the Kurchatov
    Institute's *Sovetskii Fizik* (no date) in summer 1989.
81 The information in this paragraph, and all quotations appearing in it, can be
    found in a report of the I-RDG's secretary, Arkadii Murashev, 'Vestnik
    sekretariata Mezhregional'noi gruppy narodnyk deputatov SSSR' (Moscow:
    mimeo, 14 March 1990).
82 M-BIO archives.
83 Burbulis's remarks appeared in the club's *Svobodnoe padenie* 3 (March
    1990), p. 1.
84 Another perspective was offered by I-RDG member Yurii Boldyrev in an
    interview given to M. Urban (20 September 1994). He distinguished
    sharply between the orientation of the group's membership – in his views,
    one emphasizing legislative activity and reform through parliamentary
    action – and that which he attributed to the I-RDG's leadership: the use of
    legal and constitutional issues as a 'rostrum from which to appeal to the
    population' in order to advance their 'destructive purposes . . . of tearing
    down the Soviet order'.
85 'Rezolyutsia mitinga v Luzhnikakh (g. Moskva) 12 iun'ya 1989 g.' (mimeo,
    no date; M-BIO archives).
86 T. Andreeva, 'Svobodnym grazhdanam – svobodnaya strana', *Golos
    izbiratelya* 2 (1989), p. 1.
87 V. Pribylovskii and I. Vasilevskii, 'Moskovskoe Ob''edinenie Izbiratelei
    (MOI)' (Moscow: mimeo, 4 June 1991), pp. 1–3.
88 I. Krudryavtsev, 'Oppozitsiya i totalitarizm v SSSR' (Moscow: Institution
    for Humanities and Political Studies, 19 June 1993), p. 16.

89 Vladimir Pribylovskii, 'Pouchitel'naya istoriya Moskovskogo narodnogo fronta', *Panorama* 28 (July 1991), pp. 6–7.

90 The bitter debates over 'socialist orientation' reprised at MOI's founding conference probably facilitated adoption of its draft statement of objectives eschewing a specific programme and inviting all groups of democratic orientation to cooperate toward common objectives, 'Tezisy k deklaratsii Moskovskogo ob"edineniya izbiratelei (proekt)' (mimeo, 11 July 1989; M-BIO archives). MOI's charter defined it as a union of clubs and committees devoted to promoting civil society and democracy whose efforts would be coordinated, but in no way directed, by MOI itself. The functions envisaged for MOI were confined to publicity and electioneering: organization of public discussions, publication of information bulletins, service on electoral commissions, nomination of candidates, conducting election campaigns and contributing to the legislative process by drafting bills, 'Ustav Moskovskogo ob"edineniya izbiratelei (proekt)' (mimeo, no date; M-BIO archives). Aside from its work in the 1990 elections, MOI's major accomplishments included the support group that it formed on behalf of *Argumenty i fakty* in autumn 1989 when its editorial board was attacked by Gorbachev (*Pravo golosa* (December, 1989), p. 1), its campaign to prevent the installation of 'filters' in Russia's electoral law ('Obrashchenie II Konferentsii Moskovskogo ob"edineniya izbiratelei [MOI] k narodnym deputatam SSSR' (mimeo, no date; M-BIO archives); 'Obrashchenie II Konferentsii Moskovskogo ob"edineniya izbiratelei [MOI] k narodnym deputatam Verkhovnogo Soveta RSFSR ob izmeneniyakh konstitutsii i vyborakh v RSFSR' (mimeo, no date; M-BIO archives)), and the spirited defences of I-RDG leaders – who had been targeted by the official mass media – in its monthly newspaper, *Golos izbiratelya*, and in the protest rallies that it helped to organize. See Pribylovskii and Vasilevskii, 'Moskovskoe ob"edinenie izbiratelei (MOI)'; and the interview with MOI co-founder, Lev Shamaev, that appeared in *Golos izbiratelya* 1 (August 1989), pp. 1–2.

91 Pribylovskii, 'Pouchitel'naya istoriya Moskovskogo narodnogo fronta', p. 7.

92 Vladimir Pribylovskii, 'Pervyi narodnyi front v Rossii', *Panorama* 6 (June 1989), p. 1.

93 Vadim Lifshits, 'Leningradskii spektr', *Panorama* 8 (September 1989), p. 4.

94 Ya. Gorbadei, 'Uchreditelnyi s"ezd narodnogo fronta RSFSR', *Golos izbiratelya* 2 (1989), p. 1; V. N. Berezovskii, N. I. Krotov and V. V. Chervyakov, *Rossiya: partii, assotsiatsii, soyuzy, kluby*, vol. I, part 1 (Moscow: RAU-PRESS, 1991), p. 96; Vladimir Pribylovskii, *Slovar' oppozitsii: novye politcheskie partii i organizatsii Rossii* (Moscow: Postfaktum, 1991), pp. 21–2.

95 'Budet li izbiratel'nyi blok?', *Panorama* 10 (October 1989), p. 7.

96 Aleksandr Verkhovskii, 'VAI – Vsesoyuznaya assotsiatsiya izbiratelei', *Panorama* 10 (October 1989), p. 7.

97 'Budet li izbiratel'nyi blok?', *Panorama* 10 (October 1989).

98 Aleksandr Verkhovskii, 'Na puti k edinoi oppozitsii', *Panorama* 10 (October 1989), p. 1.

99 M. Sal'e, 'Novyi uroven' razvitiya demokraticheskikh dvizhenii strany', *Demokratiya i my* 14 (1990), pp. 18–26; esp. pp. 19–22.

100 For instance, in Kharkov a number of individuals were arrested and fined in

succession in autumn 1989 for activities such as reading the Soviet Constitution aloud in public places, collecting money for the striking miners and unauthorized participation in the Revolution Day Parade. These cases are listed in *Khroniki* 37 (1989), p. 1.

101 This banner refers to the insurrection against the Bolshevik dictatorship but in favour of Soviet power staged by the sailors at the naval base at Kronshtadt in March 1921.

102 This slogan was apparently taken from Yurii Afanas'ev's remarks to the Leningrad meeting on 16 September convened to prepare the larger conference in Chelyabinsk where MADO was founded. According to *Pravda* (17 September 1989), Afanas'ev had remarked in Leningrad that the Communist Party for the past seventy years 'had led the country nowhere'.

103 V. Krilovskii, 'Cherez 72 goda', *Pravo golosa* 3 (December 1989), p. 7.

104 Robert Orttung, 'Democratization in Leningrad' (doctoral dissertation, University of California at Los Angeles, 1992), p. 116.

105 In addition to ties between I-RDG notables and democratic groups evinced by the regular attendance of the former at conferences held by the latter, the I-RDG's Coordinating Council decided on 26 November to invite representatives of informal groups to the I-RDG's conference on 9–10 December with a view toward forging close links to the democratic movement (Yu. Panyushkina, 'Na poroge s"ezda', *Pravo golosa* 3 (December 1989), p. 1).

106 A. Morozov, 'Kul'tura i oppozitsiya', *Panorama* 6 (June 1989), pp. 4–5.

107 A turning point came at the I-RDG's second full conference on 23–4 September. Afanas'ev, reporting for the leadership, called for the overthrow of the communist system. Andrei Vasilevskii, 'Gorbachevu net al'ternativy, no . . . ', *Panorama* 10 (October 1989), p. 3.

108 Murashev, 'Mezhregional'naya deputskaya gruppa', p. 8.

109 The strike was called for 11 December when it had been learned that the issue of the Constitution's article 6 would not be included on the agenda for the Congress. Apparently, about one million people took part in it (*Ibid.*, p. 8). The leaflet put out to advertise the strike and its purpose was signed by five members of the I-RDG: Sakharov, Popov, Vladimir Tikhonov, Arkadii Murashev and Yurii Chernichenko. It was reprinted in *Khroniki* 37 (December 1989), p.1.

110 Urban and McClure, 'Discourse, Ideology and Party Formation', pp. 99–110.

111 Vladimir Pribylovskii, 'Izbiratel'nyi blok "Demokraticheskaya Rossiya"', *Ekspress Khronika* 6 (25 January 1990), pp. 1–2.

112 *Ibid.*

113 *Ibid.*; Berezovskii, Krotov and Chervyakov, *Rossiya*, vol. I; part 1, pp. 92–4.

114 Pribylovskii, 'Izbiratel'nyi blok "Demokraticheskaya Rossiya"', p. 2.

115 Hereafter, we use the popular form – DemRossiya – to refer to this organization.

116 E.g., at DemRossiya's founding as an electoral coalition, Gleb Yakunin described it as a 'democratic front *against* the apparatus, Pamyat, Otchestvo and the OFT'. Quoted in Pribylovskii, 'Izbiratel'nyi blok "Demokraticheskaya Rossiya"', p. 1 (emphasis added).

117 Mikhail Malyutin, 'Za kem poidut massy', pp. 46–7. On the creation of so-called 'internationalist' movements among some Russian workers in various large factories in the Baltic republics during the late 1980s, see Michael Urban, 'Popular Fronts and "Informals"', *Detente* 14 (1989), p. 5.

118 Geoffrey Hosking, Jonathan Aves and Peter Duncan, *The Road to Post-Communism: Independent Political Movements in the Soviet Union 1989–1991* (London: Pinter, 1992), pp. 125, 145–6.

119 Yurii Lesunov, 'Rabochii pri dvore prezidenta: za kulisami odnoi politicheskoi kar'ery', *Stolitsa* 6 (December 1990), pp. 10–13.

120 *Svobodnoe padenie* 3 (March 1990), pp. 8–10; Berezovskii, Krotov and Chervyakov, *Rossiya*, vol. I, part 1, p. 99.

121 Pribylovskii, *Slovar' oppozitsii . . .* , p. 24.

122 Berezovskii, Krotov and Chervyakov, *Rossiya*, p. 98.

123 Interview given by Sergei Skvartsov to Michael Urban (11 July 1990).

124 Aleksandr Verkhovskii, 'Sovetskii chelovek – aktivnaya zhiznennaya pozitsiya', *Panorama* 7 (August 1989), pp. 6–7.

125 Pribylovskii, *Slovar' oppozitsii*, p. 24.

126 See the interview given to Andrei Vasilevskii by Venamin Yarin, *Panorama* 1 (January 1990), p. 9; see also Berezovskii, Krotov and Chervyakov, *Rossiya*, p. 19.

127 'Ustav kluba "Rossiya"', *Rossiya* 1 (November 1989), p. 1.

128 *Ibid.*, p. a.

129 'Zayavlenie narodnykh deputatov', *IIIii Rim'* 1 (December 1989), p. 8.

8. THE 1990 ELECTIONS AND THE POLITICS OF NATIONAL LIBERATION

1 Mikhail Gorbachev, 'Sotsialisticheskaya idea i revolyutsionnaya perestroika', *Pravda* (26 November 1989).

2 The Lithuanian Communist Party declared its independence from the CPSU at its congress on 20 December 20 1989. For discussions of the CPSU's disintegration, see: Ronald Hill, 'The CPSU: From Monolith to Pluralist?', *Soviet Studies* 43(2) (1991), pp. 217–35; Stephen White, 'Rethinking the CPSU', *Soviet Studies.* 43(3) (1991), pp. 405–28; Rita Di Leo, 'The Soviet Union 1985–1990: After Communist Rule the Deluge?', *Soviet Studies* 43(3) (1991), pp. 429–49.

3 For example, at a rally staged by the conservative Leningrad party organization on 22 November 1989, numerous speakers openly opposed the CPSU's Politburo and Central Committee (*Pravda* (23 November 1989)).

4 See Gorbachev's speech to the plenary session, *Izvestiya* (10 December 1989).

5 The CPSU's Central Committee published an election statement – 'K sovetskomu narodu', *Pravda* (12 December 1989) – but this was not a platform, unless one will admit to this category summonses to 'communists and non-party candidates to move perestroika forward, improve the people's welfare and [promote] national concord and cohesion'. To our knowledge, this statement played no role in the campaigns of any communists or non-party candidates.

6   Gorbachev in *Izvestiya* (10 December 1989).

7   In the 1990 races, some 86 per cent of all candidates belonged to the Communist Party. Thomas Remington, 'The 1990 RSFSR Elections' (paper presented at Soviet Nationalities Workshop, Duke University, Durham, NC, 11–12 May 1990), p. 18.

8   On these elections generally, see Stephen White, Greame Gill and Darrell Slider, *The Politics of Transition: Shaping a Post-Soviet Future* (Cambridge: Cambridge University Press, 1993).

9   Arkadii Murashev, 'Mezhregional'naya deputatskaya gruppa', *Ogonek* 32 (4–11 August 1990), p. 7. The Moscow Voters' Association also helped to focus the attention of Russia's Supreme Soviet on this matter by meeting with the deputies in their respective districts before the session, and, once it had begun, visiting the Hotel Rossiya where most deputies stayed in order to deliver leaflets, flowers and advice. I. Vasina, 'Tsvety deputatam?', *Pravo golosa* 3 (December 1989), p. 2.

10 The text of the Russian electoral law appeared in *Izvestiya* (28 October 1989).

11 'Vopros voprosov', *Pravo golosa* 3 (December 1989), p. 7.

12 A. Luk'yanchikov, 'Uroki nedavnego proshlogo', *Narodnyi deputat* 1 (1990), p. 60.

13 In those districts in the capital wherein voter organizations included a number of active clubs, from a third to a half of the corresponding electoral commissions were composed of their members. 'MOI (Moskovskoe ob"edinenie izbiratelei)' (manuscript, M-BIO archive, 1990).

14 *Vybory–90* 9 (Moscow: Vybory–90, February 1990).

15 The available data on nominations in the various authorized venues are not completely consistent, but there is no question that administrative manipulation directed the nominations process away from residential assemblies. A. Shiryaev, a staff member of Russia's Central Electoral Commission, has provided the figures of 3.2 per cent and about 20 per cent for the proportions of nominees coming from residential meetings and 'public organizations', respectively. These figures indicate that 70–5 per cent of nominations took place in workplace assemblies. A. Davydov has supplied different percentages for nominees coming from residential meetings: 4.7 per cent of all candidates and 7 per cent of all candidates to the Russian parliament. Shiryaev's data appear in his 'Dva vzglyada na vybory', *Narodnyi deputat* 9 (1990), pp. 27–8; Davydov's in his 'Predstoit ostraya bor'ba', *Izvestiya* (14 January 1990).

16 Shiryaev, 'Dva vzglyada na vybory', pp. 28–9.

17 In a typical instance in the Yaroslavl region, turnout on 4 March was 89.5 per cent in rural districts and 62.3 per cent in the provincial capital. Gavin Helf and Jeffrey Hahn, 'Old Dogs and New Tricks: Party Elites in the Russian Regional Elections of 1990', *Slavic Review* 51 (Fall 1992), p. 526.

18 A. Kabakov, 'Tak bylo v Khabarovske', *Narodnyi deputat* 7 (1990), pp. 44–6. A partial list of election irregularities noted by foreign observers appears in *Elections in the Baltic States and Soviet Republics* (Commission on Security and Cooperation in Europe, Washington, D.C.: Government Printing Office, December 1990), p. 107.

19 *Izvestiya* (10 May 1990); *Izvestiya* (2 June 1990).

20 *Izvestiya* (30 January 1990).

21 Darrell Slider, 'Soviet Public Opinion on the Eve of the Elections', *Journal of Soviet Nationalities* 1 (Spring 1990), pp. 156–7.

22 *Izvestiya* (30 January 1990.) A national survey conducted after the elections also brought this out. Identifying the best way to secure their interests, over 25 per cent mentioned public protests, 17 per cent said strikes and demonstrations and 'no small number' replied 'guns' (V. Komarovskii, 'Optimisty i pessimisty', *Narodnyi deputat* 14 (1990), pp. 15–21). Jeffrey Hahn's opinion survey (March 1990) in the city of Yaroslavl found both high levels of disaffection with governmental institutions and equally high levels of interest in politics and support for the basic ideas of electoral democracy. See his 'Continuity and Change in Russian Political Culture', *British Journal of Political Science* 21 (October 1991), pp. 393–421.

23 Alexei Levinson, 'Predictable Surprises', *Moscow News* 10 (18–25 March 1990), p. 4.

24 Remington, 'The 1990 RSFSR Elections'.

25 Irena Fomicheva pointed out that 'public opinion' existed at a very rudimentary level, appearing in black and white categories and expressing itself primarily as 'No' or 'Down with . . .'. See her 'Chas udachnykh reshenii', *Soyuz* 4 (22–8 January 1990), p. 17.

26 *Vybory–90* 7 (February 1990).

27 Brendan Kiernan, *The End of Soviet Politics* (Boulder, CO: Westview, 1993), chapter 9.

28 Moscow City Committee of the Communist Party 1990 campaign leaflet (M-BIO archives).

29 S. Stankievich and M. Shneider, 'Rekomendatsii po taktike kandidatov demokraticheskogo bloka i ikh kommand v izbiratel'noi kampanii 1989–90 g.g.' (Moscow: Informatsentr MNF, no date) (M-BIO archives).

30 N. Mikhaleva and L. Morozova, 'Pobedil tot, kto luchshe gotovilsya', *Narodnyi deputat* 7 (1990), pp. 34–40; esp. pp. 35–6.

31 Mary McAuley, 'Politics, Economics and Elite Realignment in Russia: a Regional Perspective', *Soviet Economy* 8 (January–March 1992), p. 52; Robert Orttung, 'Democratization in Leningrad' (doctoral dissertation; University of California at Los Angeles, 1992), pp. 144–58.

32 Interestingly, one such article written by an instructor of the CPSU's Central Committee went so far as to claim that the Communist Party was no longer capable of leading perestroika. See D. Barabashov, 'Vo imya otchizny, za pravoe delo', *Rossiya* 3 (January 1990), p. 1.

33 Letter from A. Berezkin (on behalf of the Electoral Geography Group of the Geography Faculty at Moscow State University) to V. Sheinis, chairperson of the Subcommission for Questions and Politics and the Electoral System, Supreme Soviet of the RSFSR, 7 October 1990 (emphasis added).

34 Timothy Colton, 'The Politics of Democratization: the Moscow Elections of 1990', *Soviet Economy* 6 (October–December 1990), pp. 304–7.

35 The most important of these twelve organizations was the United Council of Russia, a roof for five other members of the bloc (the All-Russian Cultural Fund, the Public Committee to Save the Volga, the Society of Russian Artists, the Russian Division of the International Fund of Slavic

Literature and Culture, and the Union for the Spiritual Rebirth of the Fatherland), and a link to two others (the United Association of Lovers of Russian Literature and Art, and the Fund for the Restoration of the Cathedral of Christ the Saviour). Overlapping memberships tied these eight groups to two others: the All-Russian Society for the Preservation of Historical and Cultural Monuments, and the Russian Republic's Voluntary Society of Book Lovers. The other two affiliates were the United Front of Working People (OFT) and the 'Russia' faction formed in the USSR's legislature together with its voters' associations. Overlaps occurred here as well, both at the level of their top officials and at that of the organizations (such as the All-Russian Cultural Fund) that were included as 'founding organizations' in the 'Russia' association. Thus, the bloc was not a coalition of like-minded, but independent groups; it was an inter-locking network of patriotic organizations kept separate on paper in order to supply distinct titles to the various leaders. 'Ustav kluba "Russia"', *Rossiya* 1 (November 1989), p. 1; interview given by V. Skripko to N. Solyanik, *Narodnyi deputat* 7 (1990), pp. 54–6.

36 'Za politiku narodnogo soglasiya i rossiiskogo vozrozhdeniya', *Literaturnaya Rossiya* 52 (December 1989); *Sovetskaya Rossiya* (30 December 1989).

37 The one patriotic association that had acquired some practical experience in political organizing, Pamyat, was excluded from the coalition.

38 'Rezolyutsiya obshchemoskovskogo mitinga bloka obshchestvenno-patrioti-cheskikh dvizhenii Rossii', 27 January 1990 (M-BIO archives). The rally at Ostankino on 18 February amplified these themes. There, the poet, Vyacheslav Dolganov, delivered encomia to Ivan the Terrible and Stalin while succeeding orators heaped opprobrium on the right's entire rogues' gallery, blaming Russia's misfortunes on Zionists, democrats, imperialists, the mass media and so on. *Izvestiya* (22 February 1990).

39 *Vybory–90* 6 (February 1990), p. 9.

40 For instance, Gorbachev had regularly rejected as 'rubbish' the I-RDG's demand for a multi-party system – in February 1989 associating its advocacy with 'demagogues and irresponsible elements' yet less than one year later sponsoring this very idea himself before the plenary session of the CPSU's Central Committee that resolved to end the monopoly on power. Richard Sakwa, *Gorbachev and his Reforms 1985–1990* (New York: Prentice Hall, 1991), pp. 180–8.

41 Murashev, 'Mezhregional'naya deputatskaya gruppa', p. 8.

42 Yitzhak Brudny, 'The Dynamics of "Democratic Russia"', 1990–1993', *Post-Soviet Affairs* 9 (April–June 1993), p. 146.

43 Remington, 'The 1990 RSFSR Elections'.

44 Interview given to Michael Urban by Mikhail Shneider (13 May 1991).

45 El'tsin's election platform – issued for his constituency in Sverdlovsk on 1 February 1990 (M-BIO, archives) – called for both the transfer of 'all full power to the soviets' and the establishment of a 'presidential republic'. It also advocated a Russian Communist Party based on 'apparatus-free structures' and oriented toward 'humanistic and democratic socialism'. Although he would presumably lead this party, his campaign statements often emphasized the importance of instituting private property and setting

up free economic zones. He also stressed reviving Russia's spiritual traditions and called for dialogue with Pamyat (Remington, 'The 1990 RSFSR Elections').

46 Samuel Eldersveld thus described relations between organized interests and party units in the US party system in *Political Parties: a Behavioral Analysis* (Chicago: Rand McNally, 1964).

47 This list would include Il'ya Konstantinov, Nikolai Pavlov, Sergei Baburin, Viktor Aksyuchits, Mikhail Astaf'ev, Andrei Golovin and Nikolai Travkin.

48 Brudny, 'The Dynamics of "Democratic Russia"', 1990–1993', p. 143.

49 'MOI', p. 2.

50 Murashev, 'Mezhregional'naya deputatskaya gruppa', p. 8.

51 MOI representatives attended Election–90's organizational conference but refused to enter the coalition, stating that since most of their affiliates were supporters of El'tsin or Gdlyan, they feared internal rupture should candidates on Elections–90's list criticize these individuals, a prospect that they could by no means discount at the time. V. Pribylovskii, 'Vybory–90' (mimeo, no date, M-BIO archives). After long negotiations with MOI, Elections–90 dropped its demand that its forty candidates would run under its label, thus merging them with those of MOI.

52 'MOI', p. 4.

53 This was true in the case of Oleg Poptsov who got El'tsin's and Afanas'ev's endorsement at the end of the campaign. MOI's support was withdrawn from the other democratic candidate in that race, Ernest Ametisov.

54 Colton, 'The Politics of Democratization', p. 310.

55 Orttung, 'Democratization in Leningrad', pp. 162–8.

56 Helf and Hahn, 'Old Dogs and New Tricks', p. 518.

57 M. Ovcharov, 'Krushenie illyuzii', *Narodnyi deputat* 6 (1990), pp. 20–3.

58 Lyudmila Telen', 'Zapovednaya zona?', *Narodnyi deputat* 10 (1990), pp. 53–61.

59 Vladimir Pribylovskii, 'Golosovanie po shpargalke', *Panorama* 6 (June 1990), p. 3.

60 For Moscow, see Colton, 'The Politics of Democratization', esp. pp. 311, 314–15. The patriotic bloc appeared to have small success in matching its candidates to available districts. In Moscow, it was unable to field a candidate for all seats in the national legislature while supplying two candidates in twelve electoral districts and three candidates in two others (*Rossiya* 4 (February 1990), p. 1).

61 Helf and Hahn, 'Old Dogs and New Tricks', p. 511.

62 McAuley, 'Politics, Economics and Elite Realignment in Russia', pp. 59–66.

63 Vladimir Pribylovskii, 'Kandidaty v parlament Rossii', *Panorama* 4 (March 1990), p. 9.

64 In Leningrad, the popular front had waged a struggle for two years with local authorities over the right to register. Authorized by the new city government, the Leningrad Popular Front held its founding congress in July 1990 and then immediately fell into inactivity. McAuley, 'Politics, Economics and Elite Realignment in Russia', p. 61.

65 Richard Sakwa, *Russian Politics and Society*, (London: Routledge, 1993), p. 56.

66 In the eight issues of *Ogonek* that appeared during the 1990 campaigns, six articles had some relevance to the elections. Of these: one was an interview with Anatolii Sobchak concerned primarily with the Second Congress of People's Deputies of the USSR (2 (January 1990), pp. 30–3); another by Edmund Iodkovskii criticized the 'patriots', praised Andrei Sakharov's draft constitution and advocated a liberal-democratic political orientation (4 (January 1990), pp. 20–1); a third featured an anti-communist tract by Igor Klyamkin that called for following East Europe toward capitalism and democracy (5 (January 1990), pp. 5–8); a fourth was by Aleksandr Bolotin on the democratic movement in Khar'kov (6 (February 1990), pp. 1–3); and a fifth was a photo display with commentary on the democratic rally on Manege Square on 4 February that rebutted *Pravda*'s coverage of that event (8 (February 1990), p. 5). Only one piece, then, concerned the election directly or mentioned DemRossiya by name. This was 'Sozdan izbiratel'nyi blok "Demokraticheskaya Rossiya"' appearing in issue no. 6 (February 1990), pp. 17–18, which outlined DemRossiya's platform, mentioned its leading names and – importantly – characterized the new organization as an alternative to CPSU reformers who were unable to withstand the pressure from conservative forces.

67 The organ of the Leningrad Komsomol, *Smena*, published in its 2 March 1990 number the list of candidates endorsed by Democratic Elections–90. *Smena* had asked all associations in Leningrad that supported candidates to submit their own lists for publication, but the communists and patriotic bloc declined to do so (Orttung, 'Democratization in Leningrad', p. 168). An asymmetrically comparable episode occurred in Ivanova where the local youth paper published the names of party-state officials – most of whom were candidates – who had recently purchased automobiles without having to undergo the usual waiting period (Ovcharov, 'Krushenie illyuzii', p. 21).

68 In Moscow, both *Moskovskaya pravda* and *Vechernaya Moskva* featured election appeals from the Communist Party on the day before the first balloting, thus violating the election law (Colton, 'The Politics of Democratization', p. 321).

69 This sluggishness was widespread, and consonant with the CPSU's strategy to limit campaigning. On Moscow, see *ibid.*, p. 293; on Russia generally, see Shiryaev, 'Dva vzglyada na vybory', p. 30.

70 Colton has described this for Moscow ('The Politics of Democratization', pp. 314–15); Orttung for Leningrad ('Democratization in Leningrad', p. 169); and Ovcharov for Yaroslavl ('Krushenie illyuzii', p. 21). Vitalii Skripko, chairperson of the United Council of Russia, the 'patriotic' bloc's centre of gravity in this election, paid a backhanded compliment to his opponents in this respect, complaining in an interview that a fresh DemRossiya leaflet had been turning up in his postbox almost daily (Interview given to N. Solyanik, *Narodnyi deputat* 7 (1990), p. 56).

71 'To the Citizens of Moscow' (leaflet, M-BIO archives).

72 Leaflet (M-BIO archives).

73 The campaign literature put out by individual candidates was diverse on this

score. For example, two politicians who would soon become close political allies – Viktor Aksyuchits and Mikhail Astaf′ev – composed platforms that ranged from calls to overthrow the communist system (Aksyuchits) to a subdued form of anti-communism encoded as support for 'all-human values' (Astaf′ev). Aksyuchits's campaign statements endorsed the unrestricted right of all nations to self-determination and Astaf′ev's, the full exercise of Russian sovereignty; yet within a year each would enter a coalition inside DemRossiya opposing the disintegration of the USSR and, after the August 1991 *coup*, would join the ranks of the national-patriotic forces for whom the ideas contained in these 1990 leaflets represented nothing short of treason. The 1990 leaflets are contained in the M-BIO archives.

74 'MOI', p. 5 (emphasis in original).

75 M-BIO archives.

76 El′tsin's autobiography is replete with these themes. See his *Against the Grain* (New York: Summit Books, 1990).

77 We note in this respect the parallels that appear to obtain between the emergence of the political in modern Russia and in ancient Greece. These would include: the development of persuasive speech into an instrument of power; the production of equality among those engaged in political speech, establishing the category 'citizen' over and above distinctions of social rank; the consecration of public spaces for assembly and deliberation; the transformation of the media of authority from sacred texts and ritualized words conveying the commands of the sovereign into (in principle) logical persuasive argument submitted to the judgement of the people; and, along those same lines, the codification of law and procedures implying equality of treatment. Jean-Pierre Vernant develops these points regarding politics and community in ancient Greece in his *The Origins of Greek Thought* (Ithaca: Cornell University Press, 1982), esp. pp. 46–65.

78 Such was the case, for instance, in Krasnodar. Telen′, 'Zapovednaya zona?', p. 59.

79 This tactic was used in Saratov (*Izvestiya* (10 February 1990)) and Leningrad (Orttung, 'Democratization in Leningrad', pp. 155–8).

80 This has been reported in Yaroslavl (Ovcharov, 'Krushenie illyuzii', p. 21) and Leningrad (Orttung, 'Democratization in Leningrad', pp. 157–8). A DemRossiya activist has described the atmosphere in Moscow prior to the major rally staged a week prior to election day in these words:

School teachers had forbidden the children to go out on the street on [that] Sunday, fearing pogroms. Doctors were given instructions to communicate to the patients their need to prepare places in the hospitals for the thousands of wounded and traumatized people that were expected . . . The police were informing us day after day about the stores of weapons they had readied . . . Rumours flew about the city about gangs lurking in every basement.

These comments appeared in 'Ot Moskvy do samykh do okrain, 25 fevralya-reportazh s mitinga', *Golos* 6 (February 1990), p. 2.

81 *Pravda* (26 March 1990). Certainly, DemRossiya did not stage all of the public gatherings not sponsored by the CPSU. Many were held outside of

the Russian Republic, of course, and many that took place in Russia were organized by the patriotic bloc. None the less, DemRossiya and its affiliates were much more active on this front than were their opponents, accounting by conservative estimate for perhaps tens of thousands of these public gatherings.

82 Ovcharov ('Krushenie illyuzii', p. 22) describes such a scene in Kostroma.

83 A rally of this type occurred in Saratov where premises had been granted only on the city outskirts (*Izvestiya* (14 February 1990)); in Sverdlovsk, DemRossiya forces brought out some 30,000 people to an unsanctioned rally ('Ot Moskvy do samykh do okrain', p. 2).

84 With the exception of the Kostroma rally (on which see Ovcharov, 'Krushenie illyuzii', p. 23) the data in this paragraph appear in 'Ot Moskvy do samykh do okrain', p. 2.

85 In a DemRossiya leaflet put out just before the vote ('4 marta – Den' vybora puti Rossii!', (no date; M-BIO archives, fond 049–008), 'Russia' appears thrice: as a nation which has a 'fate', as a nation which should be 'sovereign', and as a nation which should be 'rich'. The latter two are negative markers inasmuch as the context makes clear that Russia is neither sovereign nor rich while fate frames these alternatives as desirable. Not for another year would the discourse of the democrats begin to supply Russia with more of a positive content by referring to history, culture, traditions, and so forth. One illustration of this is the visual images used in Gavriil Popov's campaign for mayor in Moscow, employing the visage of V. M. Vasnetsov's 1898 painting 'Bogatyri' – depicting three massive Russian warriors on horseback, legendary for their feats of strength and bravery in the cause of the people – onto which Popov's head had been superimposed over that of the central figure while those of his partners, Sergei Stankevich and Yurii Luzhkov, appeared on the shoulder of the horsemen on either flank.

86 *Pravda* (17 May 1990).

87 Shiryaev, 'Dva vzglyada na vybory', p. 32.

88 The figure for women and the high figure for workers and peasants appears in *ibid.*; the lower one for workers and peasants comes from Sakwa, *Russian Politics and Society*, p. 57.

89 Remington, 'The 1990 RSFSR Elections'.

90 Shiryaev, 'Dva vzglyada na vybory', p. 32.

91 Remington, 'The 1990 RSFSR Elections'.

92 This point is made by M. Steven Fish, *Democracy From Scratch* (Princeton: Princeton University Press, 1995), pp. 162–70. See also L. Diskova, 'Dialog cherez bar'er', *Narodnyi deputat* 3 (1990), pp. 49–56, esp. p. 50.

93 *Pravda* (17 May 1990).

94 Vladimir Pribylovskii, *Slovar' oppozitsii: novye politicheskie partii i organizatsii Rossii* (Moscow: Postfactum, 1991), p. 7.

95 *Pravda* (23 May 1990).

96 See Gorbachev's 23 May address to the Russian Congress, *Izvestiya* (25 May 1990).

97 These remarks were made by Viktor Mironov, then editor of an information bulletin associated with DemRossiya, in a roundtable (led by M. Baima-

khanov) held on the opening day of the Russian Congress (*Narodnyi deputat* 8 (1990), p. 18 (emphasis added)). A comparable formulation appeared in the platform and summons to voters issued by Democratic Elections–90 in Leningrad. Here, 'Russia' is twice defined only by means of the negative: it is counterposed to the 'Soviet empire' whose maintenance will only continue the 'discrimination' that Russia has endured; and it is the site for 'a complete change of the existing social order'. *Nevskii kur'er* (1–18 February 1990), p. 3.

98 Ruslan Khasbulatov, *The Struggle for Russia* (ed. by Richard Sakwa; London: Routledge, 1993), pp. 30–1, 87–8.

99 The effect of the 'living corridor' – those leafleting, hunger striking, reading poetry aloud, and beseeching the deputies to heed the 'voice of the people' and vote for El'tsin – should not be underestimated in wearing down some fence-sitters and throwing the needed margin behind the eventual winner (M. Alinina, 'Dym otechestva razveyan unizhen'em', *Golos izbiratelya* 11 (27 May–5 June 1990), p. 1).

100 On Gorbachev's attempts to derail El'tsin's candidacy, see John Dunlop, *The Rise of Russia and the Fall of the Soviet Empire* (Princeton: Princeton University Press, 1993), pp. 24–6.

101 Over 200 deputies attended the first organizational conference of the DemRossiya faction, held in Moscow, March 31–April 1. They rejected short draft programme – 'Blok Demokraticheskaya Rossiya' (mimeo, no date) – because it lacked specifics, although its provisions on sovereignty for Russia, economic reform, democratization and non-violence represented the group's core principles. An alternative programme submitted on behalf of sixty-three deputies by Nikolai Travkin – 'Obrashchenie k izbiratelyam, deputatam vsekh urovnei RSFSR ot gruppy deputatov bloka "Demokraticheskaya Rossiya"' (mimeo, no date) – spelled out these same principles in more detail but it was also rejected, apparently because of its provisions on factional discipline. This meeting reached agreement only on one issue: a request to the presidium of the outgoing Supreme Soviet to call an organizational conference of all deputies to prepare for the Congress's opening ('Obrashchenie deputatov bloka "Demokraticheskaya Rossiya" k Prezidiumu Verkovnogo Soveta RSFSR' (mimeo, 1 April 1990). The presidium declined. Matters scarcely improved for DemRossiya once the Congress began. Faction leader, Sergei Filatov, admitted later in an interview (*Panorama* 7 (1990), p. 2) that DemRossiya's six-person coordinating council in the legislature was not even formed until the Congress had been in session for two weeks.

102 While members of the *nomenklatura* packed into the Supreme Soviet, electing the conservative communist, Vladimir Isakov, to chair of one of its chambers, not one member of the Moscow or Leningrad delegations – together accounting for eighty-two members of the DemRossiya faction – won a seat in the standing legislature (*Izvestiya* (9 June 1990)). The DemRossiya faction was also led down the garden path by their opponents in the Communists of Russia faction. Having agreed to support one another's choices for the Supreme Soviet, DemRossiya kept its side of the bargain while Communists of Russia did not. See Andrei Vasilevskii, 'Nashi

i vashi', *Panorama* 7 (July 1990), p. 2; Dmitry Ostalsky, 'Is a Coalition Possible', *Moscow News* 24 (24 June–1 July 1990), p. 4.

103 *Izvestiya* (12 June 1990).

104 Andrei Vasilevskii, 'Tekhnologiya pobedy', *Panorama* 9 (August 1990), pp. 1–2.

105 *Izvestiya* (16 June 1990).

106 *Izvestiya* (26 June 1990).

107 El'tsin's escape from responsibility to DemRossiya was aided by a temporary resolution passed by the Russian Congress on 21 June, adopted *in lieu* of a Decree on Power. This resolution, like the draft decree, forbad any head of a state body to hold office in a party or political organization (*Izvestiya* (21 June 1990)).

108 One case involved Sergei Baburin, a radical democrat who failed to receive a key committee assignment and then migrated toward the patriotic pole in the parliament, becoming a leader of the 'intemperate' opposition to El'tsin and the democrats. See Aleksei Kazannik's interview given to Oleg Bondarenko, *Segodnya* (16 June 1993), p. 11.

109 Popov's views appeared in an interview with Valerii Vyzhutovich, *Izvestiya* (28 June 1990).

110 A. Savel'ev, 'Mossovet: vzglyad iznutri', *Al'ternativa* 3 (September 1990), p. 2.

111 A. Dikhtyar', 'Na osnove edineniya', *Narodnyi deputat* 8 (1990), pp. 22–4; Terry Clark, 'A House Divided: a Roll-Call Analysis of the First Session of the Moscow City Soviet', *Slavic Review* 51 (Winter 1992), pp. 674–90.

112 Andrei Chernov, 'Leningrad City Soviet: a Pitfall for Democracy', *Moscow News* 19 (20–7 May 1990), p. 5; O. Belikova, 'Trudnaya vesna Lensoveta', *Narodnyi deputat* 8 (1990), pp. 27–8.

113 Vladimir Gel'man and Mary McAuley, 'The Politics of City Government: Leningrad/St. Petersburg, 1990–1992' in T. Friedgut and J. Hahn (eds.), *Local Power and Post-Soviet Politics* (Armonk, NY: M. E. Sharpe, 1994), pp. 17–31.

114 Mikhaleva and Morozova, 'Pobedil tot, kto luchshe gotovilsya', p. 35.

115 A. Davydov, 'Strasti po Zaslavskomu', *Izvestiya* (17 July 1991); Vladimir Orlov, ' "Pavlovian Reflex" on a District Scale', *Moscow News* 2 (13–20 January 1991), p. 6.

116 M. Steven Fish, 'The Emergence of Independent Associations and the Transformation of Russian Political Society', *Journal of Communist Studies* 7 (September 1991), pp. 299–334.

117 Although individuals and groups associated with DemRossiya espoused proposals to institute private property, support civil society and so on, these were about *constructing* such a social order and thus were not the products of extant social interests and identities themselves. Moreover, it would be difficult to distinguish the degree to which these projects to create a 'normal' society were more than strategic communication against the communist opponent, despite the sincerity of their intentions.

118 Zaslavskii's views appear in Davydov, 'Strasti po Zaslavskomu'; Popov's in *Izvestiya* (28 June 1990); Sobchak's in an interview with Sergei Krayukhin, *Soyuz* 49 (December 1990), p. 5.

119 Popov's deputy, Stankevich, made this point in a roundtable on local government, *Pravda* (29 June 1990); Popov's and Sobchak's views appeared in the interviews detailed in n. 118, above, and in Popov's interview with Yegor Yakovlev, *Moscow News* 42 (28 October–4 November 1990), p. 7.

9. PARTIES IN MOVEMENT: THE ARTICULATION OF RUSSIAN POLITICAL SOCIETY AT THE CLOSE OF THE SOVIET PERIOD

1 For example, see Michael Urban (moderator), 'The Soviet Multi-Party System: a Moscow Roundtable'. *Russia and the World* 18 (1990), pp. 1–6.

2 E.g., Giovanni Sartori defines a political party as 'any political group identified by an official label that presents at elections, and is capable of placing through elections (free or nonfree), candidates for public office'. Kenneth Janda advances a similar definition but drops the criterion that 'placing their avowed representatives in government positions' is accomplished by electoral means. Complaining that such constructions fail to distinguish between parties and interest groups, Alan Ware adopts the notion that 'parties are bodies that intend to exercise some control over a state, and that its [sic] members are not simply the representatives of a single interest in society'. It is therefore not at all obvious that what would constitute a political party for one of these scholars would meet the critera employed by the other two. Sartori's definition appears in his *Parties and Party Systems: a Framework for Analysis*, vol I (Cambridge: Cambridge University Press, 1976), p. 63; Janda's in his *A Conceptual Framework for the Comparative Analysis of Political Parties* (Beverly Hills, CA: Sage, 1970), p. 83; and Ware's, in his *Citizens, Parties and the State* (Cambridge: Polity Press, 1987), p. 16.

3 Seymour Martin Lipset and Stein Rokkan, 'Cleavage Structures, Party Systems and Voter Alignments: an Introducti on' in their *Party Systems and Voter Alignments: Cross-National Perspectives* (New York: The Free Press, 1967), pp. 1–64.

4 For instance, regarding the conditions germane to the maintenance of party competition, Joseph LaPalombara and Myron Weiner write: 'Where the incorporation [of extra-parliamentary mass parties] has been relatively imperfect, where the central values concerning the political process are not adequately shared, we often find unstable political systems in which a continuation of competitive parties is somewhat problematical.' 'The Origin and Development of Political Parties' and 'The Impact of Parties on Political Development' in their *Political Parties and Political Development* (Princeton: Princeton University Press, 1966), pp. 3–42 (esp. p. 28), 399–435.

5 Herbert Kitschelt's application of this methodology to party systems in postcommunist East Europe illustrates this. The cleavages that he detects and the vectors that he draws seem perfectly plausible on the basis of West European experience, but break down entirely when transposed onto East Europe ('The Formation of Party Systems in East Central Europe', *Politics and Society* 20 (March 1992), pp. 7–50).

6 Angelo Panebianco, *Political Parties: Organization and Power* (Cambridge: Cambridge University Press, 1988), pp. 3–6.

7 *Ibid.*, p. 6 (italics in original).

8 Maurice Duverger, *Political Parties* (3rd ed.; London: Methuen, 1964), pp. xv–xvi.

9 We exclude, here, those parties that the Soviet party-state itself sponsored.

10 We intend neither to suggest that the three stages were rigidly bounded in time nor that they completed the disintegration/formation process. A fourth wave that occurred in 1991 will be considered in the following chapter.

11 Our discussion of stages of disintegration and corresponding opportunities for political mobilization is informed by Sidney Tarrow's *Power in Movement: Social Movements, Collective Action and Politics* (Cambridge: Cambridge University Press 1994). The title of this chapter acknowledges his influence on our thinking.

12 On the SDPR's founding congress, see: *Alternativa* 1 (30 May–12 June 1990); Dmitrii Khrapovintskii, 'Partiya sotsial-demokratov', *Soyuz* 19 (May 1990), p. 10; N. Solyanik, 'Pomen'she by ambitsii', *Narodnyi deputat* 12 (1990), pp. 75–7. SDPR membership stood at 4,000 at the party's inception, grew to some 7,000 by the end of 1990 and declined thereafter. Mikhail Malyutin, 'Sushchestvuet li v SSSR mnogopartiinost'?' (Moscow: mimeo, May 1991).

13 D. A. Pankin, *Sotsial-demokraticheskaya partiya Rossiiskoi Federatsii: kratkii spravochnik* (Moscow and Petrozavodsk: Inform-sluzhby, Board of SDPR, 1991), p. 28.

14 On the SDPR's pre-history, see: Vladimir Pribylovskii, *Slovar' oppozitsii: novye politicheskie partii i organizatsii Rossii* (Moscow, Postfactum, 1991), p. 40; 'Esdeki', *Panorama* 8 (September 1989), pp. 1–2; Pankin, *Sotsial-demokraticheskaya partiya Rossiiskoi Federatsii*, pp. 28–30.

15 'Informatsionnaya set' SDA' (mimeo, 6 April 1990).

16 'Soglashenie po organizatsionnomu i khozyaistvenno-finansovomu vzaimodeistviyu SDA i SDPR' (document, no date); 'Akt sdachi-priemki del po finansovym operatsii Sotsial-demokraticheskoi partii Rossiiskoi federatsii (SDPR)' (document, no date).

17 Vladimir Pribylovskii, 'Samizdat i novye partii', *Sodeistve* 10 (1–15 June 1990), p. 4; Vadim Lifshits, 'Mysly posle s"ezda', *Esdek* 6 (April–May 1990), p. 6.

18 For the SDA's version of social democracy, see *Esdek* 6 (April–May 1990), pp. 2–3.

19 See *Al'ternativa* 1 (30 May–12 June 1990), p. 2 and Lifshits, 'Mysly posle s"ezda'.

20 Solyanik, 'Pomen'she by ambitsii', p. 75.

21 See the position paper composed by party leaders and the intra-party disputes occasioned by it, 'Situatsiya v strane', *Al'ternativa* 3 (September 1990), pp. 1–2.

22 Interview given by Vladimir Nyrko to M. Urban (17 November 1991).

23 'Put' progressa i sotsial'noi demokratii: programme SDPR' (Moscow: Sotsium, 1991), p. 10. SDPR leader Andrei Fadin put to himself the party's preoccupying question – 'What is going on in our country today?' – and

answered that 'we are attempting to break out of the old vicious circle of imperial history, to find a way out of our impasse to the road of world development, *to become part of the world* . . . There is no other way' ('Vstupaya na dorogu', *Otkrytaya zona* 13 (January 1990), p. 4 (emphasis in original)).

24 *Al'ternativa* 1 (30 May–12 June 1990), p. 2; V. E. Lyzlov in Dmitrii Khrapovitskii's 'Partii nachinayut i . . .', *Soyuz* 17 (April 1990), p. 19.

25 Oleg Rumyantsev, 'Nash put' k sotsial'noi demokratii', *Narodnyi deputat* 2 (1991), p. 86. A left-wing current in the SDPR that would not concur with this definition of social democracy was formed around Galina Rakitskaya. Its position paper, 'Levaya fraktsiya v SDPR' (19 April 1991), set out a counter-identity for the party, harkening back to when the unionized working class in the West formed the backbone of social-democratic and labour parties. This faction left the SDPR in 1993.

26 Y. Ushenin, 'More About the Social Democratic Party of the Russian Federation' in M. A. Babkina (ed.), *New Political Parties and Movements in the Soviet Union* (Commack, NJ: Nova, 1991), pp. 71–3; Sergei Andreev, 'Opredelenie tseli', *Ogonek* 10 (1991), pp. 9–10; M. Steven Fish, *Democracy From Scratch: Opposition and Regime in the New Russia Revolution* (Princeton: Princeton University Press, 1995), pp. 83–6.

27 'Sotsial-demokraty v Rossiiskom parlamente', *Novosti sotsial-demokratii* 2 (1990), pp. 2–6; interview given by Denis Pankin (SDPR executive secretary) to M. Urban (23 April 1991).

28 'Ob utverzhdenii polozheniya o tsentral'noi finansovo-kommercheskoi komissii pri Pravlenii SDPR', Reshenie 2-go plenuma Pravleniya SDPR (Moscow: mimeo, 5 August 1990).

29 Pankin, *Sotsial-demokraticheskaya partiya Rossiiskoi Federatsii*, pp. 35–6.

30 Rumyantsev, 'Nash put' k sotsial'noi demokratii', p. 86.

31 By the time that elections were held in December 1993, Rumyantsev had thrown in his lot with Civic Union, a coalition based on that very *nomenklatura* that he had spent his earlier years attacking. The left faction, United Social Democrats, had broken away, joined with the Party of Labour and the Socialist Party of Working People but failed to qualify for the ballot. The remainder of the SDPR entered the Yabloko bloc, receiving one slot on its national list.

32 Sergei Gryzunov *et al.*, 'Novye partii', *Soyuz* 24 (June 1990), p. 11.

33 'Osnovnye polozheniya politicheskoi programmy Rossiiskogo Khristians-kogo Demokraticheskogo Dvizheniya (RKhDD)' in *Rossiiskoe Khristianskoe Demokraticheskoe Dvizhenie: Sbornik materialov* (Moscow: Duma Khristians-kogo Demokraticheskogo Dvizheniya, 1990), pp. 38–9. The programme suggests that the RCDM had in mind, here, turning back the political clock not to October, but to February 1917.

34 Pribylovskii, 'Samizdat i novye partii', p. 5; V. F. Levichev and A. A. Nelyubin, 'Novye obshchestvenno-politicheskie organizatsii, partii i dvizhe-niya', *Izvestiya TsK KPSS* 8 (1990), pp. 154–5.

35 Fish, *Democracy From Scratch*, p. 106.

36 E.g., 'Dvizhenie Khristianskoi Demokratii v Rossii', in *Rossiiskoe Khris-tianskoe Demokraticheskoe Dvizhenie*, p. 3.

37 Urban, 'The Soviet Multi-Party System', pp. 4–5; *Ekspress khronika* 13 (1992), p. 7.

38 Vladimir Todres, personal communication to M. Urban (2 August 1992). Yakunin and Polozin – Orthodox priests – were less enamored with the Orthodox Church hierarchy than were Aksyuchits and Anishchenko. Yakunin sharply criticized it at the RCDM's founding congress – *Obshchestvennoe dvizhenie: lyudi, sobytiya, dokumenty* (10 April 1990), p. 4 – while Aksyuchits apologized for its collaboration with the regime in an interview with *XX Vek i mir*, reprinted in *Khristianskaya Demokratiya* 13 (May–June 1991), pp. 17–28; esp. pp. 21–2.

39 'Dvizhenie Khristianskoi Demokratii v Rossii', pp. 7–9; interview given by Viktor Aksyuchits to Nataliya Izyumova, *Moscow News* 21 (3–10 June 1990), p. 6.

40 In an interview with M. Urban (31 July 1992), Aksyuchits explained that Russia's historical mission – to realize the divine plan on earth – could only be apprehended by 'apostolic consciousness'.

41 Michael Urban, 'Contending Conceptions of Nation and State in Russian Politics', *Demokratizatsiya* 4 (1993), pp. 9–11.

42 Except for a mention of 'enlightened patriotism', Aksyuchits's 1990 campaign broadsheet was indistinguishable from that of other DemRossiya candidates. (We are indebted to M. Steven Fish for this material.)

43 The RCDM's Manichaean stance derived from its role as a temporal agent of Russian Orthodoxy, the only 'true' version of Christianity (e.g., Aksyuchits in *Khristianskaya Demokratiya*, pp. 17–18.) It was reprised by Anishchenko at DemRossiya's counter-demonstration to the party-state's Revolution Day celebrations on 7 November 1990 where he claimed that 'today is the day of the victims. But today is also the day of the executioners. Their spirit is alive now in the offices [of CPSU headquarters] on Old Square and [the KGB's] in the Lubyanka, among those who parade today under red flags and who sit beneath portraits of Lenin' (*Put'* 1 (1990), p. 3).

44 V. Aksyuchits, 'Vystuplenie na Sobore RKhDD', *Put'* 7 (1992), p. 3. His speech to that congress appears in *Put'* 2 (1992), p. 3.

45 B. I. Koval' and V. B. Pavlenko, *Partii i politicheskie bloki v Rossii* (Moscow: Narodnaya neftenaya investitsionno-promyshlennaya evroasiatskaya korporatsiya, 1993), pp. 136, 203.

46 A. Zolotareva, 'Soyuz Konstitutsionnykh Demokratov' in B. I. Koval' (ed.), *Rossiya segodnya: politicheskii portret v dokumentakh, 1985–1991* (Moscow: Mezhdunarodnye otnosheniya, 1991), pp. 154–5.

47 Terrance Emmons, *The Formation of Political Parties and the First National Elections in Russia* (Cambridge, MA: Harvard University Press, 1982), esp. p. 22.

48 'Soyuz Konstitutsionnykh Demokratov: paket programmnykh dokumentov' (Moscow: mimeo, 1989).

49 *Inter alia*, G. V. Deryagin's comments in Khrapovitskii, 'Partii nachinayut i ...'.

50 'Manifest o sozdanii Partii Konstitutsionnykh Demokratov', *Grazhdanskoe dostoinstvo* 21 (June 1990), p. 1.

51 Ol′ga Golenkina, 'Zapiski na mandatakh', *Grazhdanskoe dostoinstvo* 21 (June 1990), p. 3.

52 Levichev and Nelyubin, 'Novye obshchestvenno-politicheskie organizatsii', pp. 149–50.

53 For details, see 'O pretenziyakh na kadetskoe nasledstvo', *Grazhdanskoe dostoinstvo* 3 (23–30 May 1991), p. 8.

54 'V mire Kadetov', *Panorama* 12 (October 1990), p. 6.

55 M. Globachev, 'Aromat progressiruyushchikh konservov', *Grazhdanskoe dostoinstvo* 3 (23–30 May 1991), p. 8.

56 Koval′ and Pavlenko, *Partii i politicheskie bloki v Rossii*, pp. 126–33.

57 In 1992, the PCD joined the Russian National Assembly and Front for National Salvation. Its leader, Astaf′ev, was co-chairperson of the former and sat on the latter's executive bodies.

58 Synopses of their programmes appeared in 'Est′ mnenie', *Izvestiya* (10 June 1990).

59 Yu. Gladysh, 'Ot partiinogo kluba k "Demokraticheskoi platforme"', *Narodnyi deputat* 6 (1990), pp. 59–62; M. Malyutin, 'Za kem poidut massy', *Narodnyi deputat* 5 (1990), pp. 45–6. In June 1989 this group, renamed the Moscow party club, began meeting at the premises that the Sevastopol district CPSU committee had previously afforded to the informals. 'Zayavlenie o sozdani Moskovskaya partiinaya kluba (kommunisty za perestroiku)' (mimeo, no date; M-BIO archives, fond DP 079–052); 'K kommunistam v pervichnykh partiinykh organizatsii raikomakh MGK KPSS' (mimeo, no date; M-BIO archives, fond DP 079–053).

60 For the Democratic Platform's reaction, see Vyacheslav Shostakovskii, 'Partapparat: imitatsiya perestroiki', *Kar′era* (March 1990), pp. 8–9. For the Marxist Platform's, see 'Zayavlenie konferentsii storonikov Marksistskoi platformy v KPSS (14–15 aprelya 1990)' (Moscow: mimeo, no date) and 'Marksistskaya platforma k XXVII S″ezdu KPSS' (Moscow: mimeo, 14–15 April 1990), p. 3.

61 'Marksistkaya platforma k XXVIII S″ezdu KPSS', pp. 3–6.

62 *Ibid.*, pp. 7–8.

63 Interview given to M. Urban by Marxist Platform leader, Sergei Skvatsov (11 July 1990).

64 Many in the Marxist and Democratic platforms had been rivals in the Moscow Popular Front. After its founding in April, personal spats within the Marxist Platform led to the exit of some leaders (e.g., V. Tryukin). From personal observations (M. Urban, 10 July 1990) of one of this group's caucuses during the CPSU congress, the discursive practices prevalent in the Marxist Platform did not conduce to consensus-formation but to sectarian squabbles over theoretic points, yielding both walkouts and (temporary) unanimity among those remaining.

65 This group did not leave the CPSU after the Twenty-Eighth Congress. Its alliance with the Marxist Platform was announced in 'Sovmestnoe zayavlenie koordinatsionnogo soveta Marksistskoi platformy v KPSS i rabochei gruppy sektsii kommunist-reformatorov Demokraticheskoi platformy v KPSS' (Moscow: mimeo, 28 June 1990; M-BIO archives, fond DP 079–005).

66 It contributed to the language of the CPSU's programme and one of its leaders, Aleksandr Buzgalin, was elected to the Central Committee.

67 Il'ya Kudryavtsev, 'Eti vechno novye sotsialisty', *Panorama* 7 (July 1990), pp. 4–5.

68 'Nashi drug druga', *Panorama* 7 (July 1990), p. 5.

69 V. N. Berezovskii, N. I. Krotov and V. V. Chervyakov, *Rossiya: partii, assotsiatsii, soyuzy kluby*, vol. I, part 2 (Moscow: RAU-Press, 1991), p. 322.

70 O. Grigor'ev, V. Lepekhin and M. Malyutin, *Partiya truda v sovremennoi Rossii: neobkhodimost' i vozmozhnost'* (Moscow: Institute for the Study of Extraordinary [*ekstremal'nykh*] Processes, 1991).

71 Vladimir Pribylovskii, *Sto politikov Rossii* (Moscow: Panorama, 1992), p. 11; Koval' and Pavlenko, *Parti i politicheskie bloki v Rossii*, pp. 80–5.

72 Koval' and Pavlenko, *Parti i politicheskie bloki v Rossii*, pp. 103–8.

73 The flyer announcing this event was put out on 8 August 1989 with the title 'Sozdadim Demokraticheskuyu platformu v KPSS' (M-BIO archives, fond DP 1079–017).

74 Gladysh, 'Ot partiinogo kluba k "Demokraticheskoi platforme"', pp. 59–60.

75 Il'ya Kudryavtsev, 'Reformatory v KPSS: demokratiya ili raskol?', *Panorama* 3 (February 1990), pp. 6–7.

76 This, of course, is speculative. But since we are concerned with opportunities, it seems appropriate to include those that appear to have been missed. Above, we noted the disorganization that ensued when DemRossiya's leaders, elected to higher offices, severed affiliation with their supporting organizations. El'tsin, Popov and other national leaders had flirted with an insurgent organization within the CPSU, but no more. Had they declared themselves for taking the Democratic Platform out of the CPSU at this juncture, there is reason to suppose that they could have taken with them some sizeable percentage of that one-third of its members reported to be in support of the group (Dawn Mann, 'Cracks in the Monolith', *Radio Liberty Research Reports*, RL 257/90 (10 June 1990), p. 4), who were likely the most politically conscious and active contingent in its ranks. Months later, when the Democratic Platform decided to leave the CPSU, El'tsin *et al.* were no longer associated with it and the third-echelon leaders now in charge commanded no comparable influence within the CPSU. Vladmir Zharikin, a member of the Democratic Platform who remained in the CPSU till 1991, made this point in an interview with M. Urban (15 July 1993).

77 Democratic Platform called for converting the CPSU into a parliamentary party, dissolving party organizations within all state bodies and eliminating 'democratic-centralism'. 'Deklaratsiya Vsesoyuznoi konferentsii partiinykh klubov i partorganizatsii' (Moscow, 20–1 January 1990 (M-BIO archives, fond DP 079–101)).

78 Stepan Troyan, 'A Congress or a Party Apparat Conference', *Moscow News* 24 (24 June–1 July 1990), pp. 8–9. Over 40 per cent of the delegates were CPSU functionaries, almost twice the number attending the Twenty-Seventh Congress in 1986. John Gooding, 'The XXVIII Congress of the CPSU in Perspective', *Soviet Studies* 43(2) (1991), p. 246.

79 The most significant involved Igor Chubais. *Krasnaya presnya* 11 (April 1991), pp. 1–2.

80 Ronald J. Hill, 'The CPSU: From Monolith to Pluralist?', *Soviet Studies* 43(2) (1991), p. 226.

81 *Pravda* (11 April 1990).

82 Georgii Khatsenkov, 'A Purge', *Moscow News* 18 (13–20 May 1990), p. 7.

83 'Pis'mo koordinatsionnogo soveta "Demokraticheskoi platformy v KPSS" k storonnikam Demplatformy o perspektivakh nashego dvizheniya' (Moscow: no date (M-BIO archives, fond DP 079–003)); Alexander Mekhanik, 'The Last Frontier for the Democratic Platform', *Moscow News* 22 (10–17 June 1990), p. 6.

84 Pavel Gutiontov, 'Demokraty pred"yavlyayut trebovaniya', *Izvestiya* (18 June 1990).

85 El'tsin's, Popov's and Sobchak's statements, were reprinted in *Pressbyulleten' oppozitsii* 4 (1990), pp. 1–2. On 19 July, other notables (Yurii Ryzhov, Sergei Stankevich, Aleksei Yablokov, Vladimir Tikhonov and Aleksei Emel'yanov) held a press conference to publicize their resignations ('Ob"yavili o vykhode iz KPSS', *Izvestiya* (19 July 1990)).

86 Viktor Sadikov, 'Nazad k dvoemysliya?', *Soyuz* 29 (July 1990), p. 3; interview given by Vyacheslav Shostakovskii to Igor' Korol'kov, *ibid.*, p. 23.

87 Personal observations (M. Urban, 14 July 1990).

88 In September 1990, the Democratic Platform instructed all members who were deputies in soviets to form their own party groups. 'Predlozhenie KS DP o napravleniyakh deyatel'nosti fraktsii v Sovetakh rasnykh urovnei (proekt)' (Moscow, 9 September 1990 (M-BIO archives, fond DP 079–001)). Another circular instructed members to cease paying dues to the CPSU, to pay them instead to the Democratic Platform and to undertake court actions, press appeals and civil demonstrations to force the Communist Party to hand over some if its property ('Poryadok deistvii Demokraticheskoi platformy v perekhodnom periode razdeleniya KPSS' (no date)).

89 At the time, the RPR claimed a membership of 10,000. *Materialy uchreditel'nogo s"ezda Respublikanskoi partii Rossiiskoi Federatsii* 1 (Moscow, 17–18 November 1990), p. 3.

90 'Katekhizis. Demokraticheskaya platforma v KPSS (kommunisty-reformatory)' (Moscow, 26 October 1990 (M-BIO archives, fond DP 079–031)).

91 *Ibid.*, p. 4.

92 Their views on merger, and those of Chubais, appeared in *Byulleten' Partiino-Politicheskoi Informatsii* 3 (Moscow: Independent Centre of Party-Political Information, January 1991).

93 Sergei Mulin, 'Mensheviks Turn Republican. Only for Three Months?', *Moscow News* 47 (2–9 December 1990), p. 6.

94 'Kommyunike "O sozdanii Ob"edinennoi moskovskoi organizatsii SDPR/ RPR' (Moscow: mimeo, 19 January 1991).

95 V. Lyzlov, 'Ob"edinyaemsya', *Alternativa* 6 (March 1991), p. 3; Aleksandr Verkhovskii, 'Demokraty na poroge novoi epokhi', *Panorama* 28 (July 1991), pp. 4–5.

96 The largest party in DemRossiya was the Democratic Party of Russia (DPR)

but the RPR had the second largest number of delegates to DemRossiya's congress and SDPR was rated the second most influential party (after the DPR) in the movement. It thus appeared plausible – especially in view of their sizeable deputies' faction in the Russian Congress – that a united RPR/ SDPR could have claimed the leading role in the democratic movement. Figures on delegates, deputies and party influence in DemRossiya can be found in Vladimir Lysenko, 'Sodoklad na uchreditel'nom s''ezde RPR', *Byulleten' Partiino-Politicheskoi Informatsii* 3 (Moscow: Independent Centre of Party-Political Information, January 1991), pp. 9–10.

97 Fish, *Democracy From Scratch*, pp. 88–93.

98 At the joint congress, merger was voted down by provincial delegates who balked at uniting with another party whose leaders and political orientations were largely unknown to them. Interviews given to M. Urban by Denis Pankin (23 April 1991) and Mikhail Malyutin (10 May 1991).

99 Lyzlov, 'Ob''edinyaemsya', p. 3; D. Mikailov, 'Demokraty ob''edinyayutsya', *Epokha* 10 (May 1991), p. 1.

100 Interview given to Vladimir Todres by Vyacheslav Shostakovskii, *Nezavisimaya gazeta* (6 February 1992), p. 2.

101 V. P. Gaiduk and S. S. Sulakshin, 'O chem umolchala "Pravda"', *Gospodin Narod* 4 (1991), p. 10.

102 During the merger debate, RPR leaders rejected 'social democracy' because, they claimed, the CPSU was turning to it, a fact 'which demonstrates the futility of that approach and which, by the way, correlates with the experience of social democracy in East Europe' (*ibid*). Later, RPR leaders shunned 'social democracy' as unrealistic until the advent of a market economy – interviews given to M. Urban by Sergei Trunov (15 November 1991) and Igor Yakovenko (19 November 1991) – but instituting a market economy was also salient for the SDPR.

103 Panebianco, *Political Parties*, esp. pp. 6–45.

104 Chubais never seemed completely comfortable among the RPR leadership. At the July conference, he sat apart from the other notables and was described off-handedly by one of them as 'our cross [to bear]'. M. Urban, personal observations, 14 July 1990.

105 Pavel Dmitry Mikhnev, 'Democratic Party of Russia (DPR)', *Moscow News* 21 (3–10 June 1990), p. 6.

106 'Programma Demokraticheskoi partii' (mimeo, 6 October 1989 (M-BIO, fond DP(R))).

107 V. Kriger, 'Pochemu ya ne mogu vstupit' v partiyu kotoruyu sama sozdavala', *Golos izbiratelya* 12 (1990), p. 4.

108 'Novosti partiinogo stroitel'stvo' (M-BIO archives, fond DPR 1, 37).

109 Party membership could be counted in tens of thousands at this time. B. Popov, in an interview given to Aleksei Mazur, *Novaya zhizn'* 16 (July 1990), p. 2.

110 Cases in point would include Afanas'ev and Burbulis. The following December, Travkin laid the blame on Afanas'ev, El'tsin, Popov and Sobchak for leaving the CPSU too late and for not joining the DPR once they had done so (Berezovskii, Krotov and Chervyakov, *Rossiya* vol. I, part 2, p. 325).

111 Lev Ponomarev interview with M. Urban (30 May 1991).

112 Interviews given by Nikolai Alyabiev (chairperson of the DPR's Moscow regional organization) and Eduard Lorkh-Sheiko (personal assistant to Travkin) to M. Urban, 14 May 1991 and 24 August 1991, respectively.

113 E.g., Valerii Zaikin, 'DPR – Partiya bez apparata', *Izvestiya* (8 May 1990).

114 Transcribed proceedings of the DPR's founding appear in Konstantin Zavoiskii and Vladimir Krylovskii, *S chego nachinaetsya partiya* (Moscow: Ekspress-Khronika, 1990).

115 Andrei Vasilevskii, 'Metamofozy "partii Travkina"', *Panorama* 6 (June 1990), pp. 1–2.

116 At the DPR's second congress (April 1991), Kasparov cued his faction's exit with a speech likening the DPR's anti-communism to that of Willy Brandt and Jimmy Carter. He preferred the Reagan–Thatcher variety (personal observations, M. Urban, 26 April 1991).

117 Vladimir Pribylovskii, 'Svobodnaya Demokratiya vnutri i snaruzhi', *Panorama* 6 (June 1990), p. 2; Vladimir Reikin, 'Obshchestvo chistykh pelenok', *Panorama* 9 (August 1990), p. 5.

118 Pribylovskii, *Slovar' oppozitsii*, p. 38.

119 'Zayavlenie o sozdanskii liberal'noi fraktsii v Demokraticheskoi partii Rossii' (Moscow: no date (M-BIO archives, fond DPR 1, 10, 11, 12)). As this document made clear, Travkin's main rivals – Murashev and Kasparov – remained in the DPR to argue the case for DemRossiya that would realize the goal that Travkin had set for 'his' party – uniting all Russia's democratic forces.

120 The DPR's programme was not adopted until its second congress in April 1991. Its provisional programme simply sloganized about multi-party democracy, the market and so forth, and was indistinguishable from those of the other democratic groups ('Prilozhenie k vypusku no. 1', *Demokraticheskaya Rossiya* 1 (July 1990), pp. 2–6). The programme of the SDPR appeared as 'Nashi printsipy' and 'Deklaratsiya' in *Sotsial-Demokratiya: Informatsionnyi byulleten' 1990g.*, pp. 1–4; the PCD's can be found in Koval' (ed.), *Rossiya segodnya*, pp. 123–4, 162–4. The actors themselves were aware of the uniformity among programmes: Oleg Rumyantsev, '"My" – partiya "oni"?', *Demokraticheskaya Rossiya* 1 (22 March 1991), p. 9; Pavel Kudyukin, 'Sotsial-Demokraty v Rossii: Byli. Kazhetsya est', *Demokraticheskaya Rossiya* 4 (12 April 1991), p. 5; and Lev Ponomarev's remarks quoted in Andrei Vasilevskii's, 'Novosti partiinogo stroitel'stva', (Moscow: mimeo, May 1990 (M-BIO archives, fond DPR)).

121 Personalized authority *outside* the organization is discussed in the next chapter.

122 Such incidences at the DPR's founding appear in Zavoiskii and Krylovskii, *S chego nachinaetsya partiya*, pp. 6–15; 'Antikommunizm – novaya vyveska KPSS' (Moscow: manuscript, 23 October 1990 (M-BIO archives, fond DPR 1, 36)). The same occurred at the DPR's second congress (personal observations, M. Urban, 26 April 1991).

123 The DPR cited two reasons for its exit from DemRossiya in November 1991: first, that DemRossiya's position on the self-determination of peoples was promoting a break-up of the USSR; and, second, that DemRossiya's

provision for both individual and collective membership was unfair to the parties within it. Since the DPR maintained both types of membership itself, it did not in principle oppose their combination. With respect to its stand against self-determination in 1991, the DPR departed from its own programme and 'Declaration' that recognized 'the unspoken right of all entering the Union of Republics to self-determination, including secession' ('Prilozhenie k vypusku no. 1', pp. 1, 4). The announcement of the DPR–RCDM–PCD alliance – Popular Accord (*Narodnoe soglasie*) – for safeguarding the USSR from the destructive politics of the larger democratic movement appeared as 'Deklaratsiya konstruktivno-demokraticheskogo bloka "narodnoe soglasie"', *Demokraticheskaya gazeta* 5 (1991), p. 2. For an outline of Travkin's manoeuvring on other programmatic issues, at one time or another basic to the DPR's profile, see Nikolai Kas'yanov, ' "Novye gorizonty" Nikolaya Travkina', *Soyuz* 20 (15–22 May 1991), p. 7.

124 S. Mitrokhin and M. Urban participated in carrying out this survey under the auspices of Moscow's Institute for Humanities and Political Studies in April 1991. For an extended discussion of its findings, see Sergei Mitrokhin and Michael Urban, 'Social Groups, Party Elites and Russia's New Democrats' in D. Lane (ed.), *Russia in Flux: the Political and Social Consequences of Reform* (Aldershot: Edward Elgar, 1992), pp. 62–81.

125 For an elaboration on this point, see *ibid.*, pp. 66–72.

126 Some 38 per cent of the fathers and 30 per cent of the mothers of those in the SDPR sample held degrees from institutions of higher education; the corresponding figures for the DPR respondents were 28 and 20 per cent, respectively.

127 On SDPR factions at the time of the party's second congress, see L. Byzov, 'Rossiiskie sotsial-demokraty: kto one?', *Epokha* 10 (May 1991), p. 6.

128 'Mnenie lidera', *Al'ternativa* 9 (June 1991), p. 1.

129 Interview given to M. Urban by Nyrko (17 November 1991).

130 Interviews given to M. Urban by Alyabiev (14 May 1991), Lorkh-Sheiko (24 August 1991) and DPR executive director Valerii Khomyakov (31 July 1992). See the interview given by Travkin to Andrei Karaulov, *Nezavisimaya gazeta* (8 August 1991), p. 6.

131 Both parties financed themselves in large measure by 'commercial activities'. One SDPR staff member rather ashamedly outlined in an interview with M. Urban (21 May 1992) how this worked in a given instance. 'We have sources in and around the government', he remarked, 'that often pick up important information. Let's suppose a trainload of scrap iron has crossed the border and is now in Khabarovsk. Our source reports this to us and we send the information to someone interested in buying the scrap iron. Our source receives a percentage of the money and another percentage goes to finance the party.' Conversation with DPR officials on similar topics were much more matter-of-fact, with the practices in question regarded as 'normal' and in no way a deviation from principles.

132 See, for instance, 'Situatsiya v strane', *Al'ternativa* 3 (September 1990), pp. 1–2.

133 Travkin's pre-political career was built in the Soviet construction industry where he began as a common labourer and rose through the ranks to

become the director of one of the largest, and most highly touted, construction trusts in the USSR. His experience in this regard – in which hard work, pragmatism and the capacity to direct others paid off in the accomplishment of physical tasks – seemed to define his political style and was emblematic of the DPR's notions of political activity and party building.

134 Zavoiskii and Krylovskii, *S chego nachinaetsya partiya*, pp. 3, 7–8; M. Urban, personal observation, 26 April 1991.

135 The only (possible) exception to this pattern involved Leonid Volkov who had been one of the party's co-chairpersons for about a year prior to leaving the SDPR in May 1992.

136 The SDPR held a conference two months prior to its fourth congress to thrash out the issue. The proposals and position papers that this conference produced were then circulated within the party in the form of a 116-page booklet, *Sbornik materialov konferentsii po partiinomu stroitel'stvu* (Moscow: Social-Democratic Party of the Russian Federation, 1992).

137 Interview given to M. Urban by Dmitrii Levchik (29 May 1992).

138 Rumyantsev outlined his views in an interview given to Andrei Sharapov, *Rossiiskaya gazeta* (15 January 1992), p. 3; and in a statement to the SDPR's fourth congress, 'Sotsial-demokraty za otvetstvennoe partnerstvo v novoi Rossii (tezisy vystupleniya pri otkrytii IV-go S″ezda SDPR)', that appeared in *Al'ternativa* 6 (June 1992), pp. 2–3. Boris Orlov set out the SDPR's position in 'Ispytanie derzhavnost'yu', *Nezavisimaya gazeta* (15 September 1992), p. 5; to which Rumyantsev responded in 'Rasstavanie s illyuziyami', *Nezavisimaya gazeta* (1 October 1992), p. 2; to which Orlov replied in 'Sotsial-demokratiya khronit' ranovato', *Nezavisimaya gazeta* (15 October 1992), p. 2.

139 For instance, in a circular letter addressed to the members of the SDPR's executive council in which he outlined his case against Rumyantsev, Orlov included a postscript that read: 'I only just now had the thought – in Russia everything repeats itself. I remembered how old G. Plekhanov [the pre-revolutionary social-democratic leader and professor, thus representing in this context Orlov himself] quarrelled with the young, energetic V. Ul'yanov [Lenin, standing in here for Rumyantsev] when he had arrived in Geneva. Is it possible that the outcome [of the present conflict] will be like that one?' Boris Orlov, 'Chlenam Pravleniya SDPR. Konfidentsial'noe pis'mo' (Abramtsevo, 30 May 1992).

140 Tarrow, *Power in Movement*, esp. pp. 8, 51–7, 146, 188–9; Jean L. Cohen, 'Strategy or Identity: New Theoretical Paradigms and Contemporary Social Movements', *Social Research* 52 (Winter 1985), pp. 663–716; Alain Touraine, 'An Introduction to the Study of Social Movements', *Social Research* 52 (Winter 1985), pp. 749–87.

141 'Obrashchenie orgkomiteta po sozdaniyu dvizheniya "Demokraticheskaya Rossiya"' (Moscow: photocopy, no date (M-BIO archives, DR, fond no. 1, doc. 17)).

142 Andrei Sashin, 'MOI: redkii primer stabil'nosti', *Panorama* 7 (July 1990), p. 4; V. Pribylovskii and A. Vasilevskii, 'Moskovskoe Ob″edinenie Izbiratelei (MOI)' (Moscow: mimeo, 4 June 1991 (M-BIO archives)).

143 'Soobshchenie No. 1 Organizatsionnogo komiteta (OK) po sozdaniyu dvizheniya "Demokraticheskaya Rossiya"' (Moscow: photocopy, no date).
144 'Spisok chlenov orgkomiteta po sozdaniyu dvizheniya "Demokraticheskaya Rossiya"' (Moscow: photocopy, no date).
145 'Sovmestnoe zayavlenie Demokraticheskoi partii Rossii, Demokraticheskoi platformy Rossiiskoi Federatsii i Sotsial-Demokraticheskoi partii Rossii', *Demokraticheskaya Rossiya* 3 (September 1991), pp. 1–2.
146 'Novyi demokraticheskii blok', *Panorama* 12 (October 1990), p. 6.
147 Interview given to B. Popov by Aleksei Mazur, *Novaya zhizn'* 16 (July 1990), p. 2; Vladimir Pribylovskii, 'Zakrytoe soveshchanie "levykh"', *Panorama* 9 (August 1990), p. 8.
148 This announcement appeared in *Demokraticheskaya Rossiya* 3 (September 1990), p. 1.
149 Igor' Sergeev, '"Bomzh" v politike', *Demokraticheskaya gazeta* 1 (10 November 1990), pp. 4–5.
150 'Itogi uchreditel'nogo S"ezda dvizheniya "Demokraticheskaya Rossiya"', *Demokraticheskaya Rossiya* 5 (November 1990), p. 1.
151 These calculations are based on the figures in *ibid.* and the preliminary quotas awarded to parties and other organizations prepared by I. Kharichev, 'Orientirovochnaya chislennost' partii i obshchestvenno-politicheskikh organizatsii, iz"yavivshikh zhelanie prinyat' uchastie v rabote S"ezda, i kvoty delegatov' (Moscow: photocopy, no date).
152 Koval' and Pavlenko, *Partii i politicheskie bloki v Rossii*, pp. 171–9.
153 Elena Bonner, 'Trevoga moya – ot kakogo-to ranee nebyvalogo chuvstva razriva', *Soyuz* 47 (November 1990), p. 15; Natalya Davydova, 'Not Everybody Takes a Break', *Moscow News* 50 (23–30 December 1990), p. 4.
154 Following this congress, Travkin stuck to his view, assuring supporters that soon those embarked on DemRossiya's mistaken course 'will come to us' (Nikolai Travkin, 'Kazhdyi dolzhen sdelat' vybor!', *Demokraticheskaya gazeta* 1 (10 November 1990), pp. 1–2). When this did not happen, he recommended dissolving the individual parties inside DemRossiya and converting that organization into a disciplined party. See his 'O raskole kotoryi nam prorochat', *Demokraticheskaya gazeta* 5 (1991), pp. 1–2. The DPR always held that DemRossiya should be either a united party or a simple coalition of parties, but *not* the 'super-party' that it became. *Inter alia*, Sergei Zimin, 'Konsolidatsiya: mif ili real'nost', *Demokraticheskaya gazeta* 1 (10 November 1990), pp. 3–4.
155 Political parties and other affiliated organizations were represented on DemRossiya's Council of Representatives, whose membership, numbering at various times between 200 and 300, also included delegates from DemRossiya's regional units who were not party members. Parties were also represented on the more important Coordinating Council, but there they were a distinct minority (eleven representatives on a body of forty-eight members in spring 1991). The Coordinating Council, which elected the co-chairpersons, was thus the real stronghold of those in DemRossiya making political careers outside of its affiliated parties, as indicated by the roster of the first six co-chairpersons elected in December 1990: Afanas'ev, Popov,

Ponomarev, Murashev, Yakunin and Viktor Dmitriev. 'Demokraticheskaya Rossiya' (M-BIO archives, DR fond no. 1, doc. 167.)

156 'Soobshchenie N 2 Orgkomiteta po sozdaniyu dvizheniya "Demokraticheskaya Rossiya"' (Moscow: photocopy, no date).

157 The fact that the presidency had not been established yet in Russia did not dissuade DemRossiya's organizers from this view. See Arkadii Murashev's remarks quoted in Aleksandr Davydov's 'Otkrylsya s″ezd "Demokraticheskoi Rossii"', Izvestiya (20 October 1990).

158 Andrei Vasilevskii, 'Demokraty: ob″edinenie i razmezhevaniya', Panorama 13 (December 1990), p. 3.

159 Membership estimates vary from the 200,000–300,000 cited by Pribylovskii (Slovar' oppozitsii, p. 8) to a figure of 1.3 million that appeared in Nezavisimaya gazeta (25 April 1991), p. 1.

160 Since most DPR regional units were joining local DemRossiya organizations, Travkin's 'choice' was forced. Vasilevskii, 'Demokraty: ob″edinenie i razmezhevaniya', p. 3.

161 Rakitskaya's comments appeared in 'O polozhenii v strane', Epokha 10 (May 1991), p. 2.

162 This paragraph is based on Pribylovskii, Slovar' oppozitsii, pp. 7, 13, 17.

163 N. V. Proselkov and A. V. Cherepanov, 'Informatsionnoe soobshchenie ob itogakh II S″ezda Demokraticheskoi partii', Zona: gazeta neravnodushnykh (November 1990), p. 4.

164 Stepan Orlov and Vadim Prokhorov, 'PervoAprel'skaya partiya', Panorama, no. 7 (July 1990), p. 5.

165 'Coup or Operetta?', Moscow News 45 (18–25 November 1990), p. 6.

166 Quoted in Natalya Izyumova, 'LDP Set to Hold Congress in Kremlin', Moscow News 17 (6–13 May 1990), p. 7. Zhirinovskii himself said that the LDPSS's orientation was indistinguishable from that of the other democratic parties (Izvestiya (1 April 1990)).

167 Orlov and Prokhorov, 'PervoAprel'skaya partiya', p. 5.

168 'Coup or Operetta?'; 'Raskoly, raskoly, raskoly . . .', Soyuz 13 (27 March– 3 April 1991), p. 10.

169 This group included Ubozhko's Conservative Party, the Soyuz faction in the USSR Congress of People's Deputies and a number of even less significant, if not altogether unknown, organizations such as the Party of Peace, the A. D. Sakharov Democratic Union (a naming that deeply offended Sakharov's widow) and Valerii Skurlatov's Russian Popular Front.

170 'Coup or Operetta?'; G. Alimov, 'A. Luk'yanov: "My otkryty dlya dialoga"', Izvestiya (2 November 1990). DemRossiya regarded the Centrist Bloc as either the creatures or the tools of the KGB ('Demokraticheskie sily o perspektivakh demokraticheskogo razvitiya', Demokraticheskaya Rossiya 3 (September 1990), p. 4).

171 'A est' li tsentristskii blok?', Izvestiya (29 March 1991).

172 A. Aidak, 'S″ezd krest'yam gotovitsya . . . apparatom', Izvestiya (25 April 1990).

173 Don Van Atta, 'Political Mobilization in the Russian Countryside: Creating Social Movements from Above' in J. Sedaitis and J. Butterfield (eds.),

Perestroika from Below: Social Movements in the Soviet Union (Boulder CO: Westview, 1991), pp. 53–7, 62.

174 *Ibid.*, pp. 57–62.

175 Aleksei Kiva, ' "Soyuz" oderzhimykh', *Izvestiya* (11 May 1991); Joel C. Moses, 'The Challenge to Soviet Democracy from the Political Right' in R. Huber and D. Kelley (eds.), *Perestroika-Era Politics: the New Soviet Legislature and Gorbachev's Political Reforms* (Armonk, NY: M. E. Sharpe, 1991) esp. pp. 109–10.

176 Neil Robinson, 'Parliamentary Politics under Gorbachev: Opposition and the Failure of Socialist Pluralism', *Journal of Communist Studies* 9 (March 1993), p. 102.

177 Robert Orttung, 'The Russian Right and the Dilemmas of Party Organization', *Soviet Studies* 44(3) (1992), p. 459.

178 'K kommunistam Moskvy' (Moscow: leaflet, 7 February 1990, M-BIO archives, fond KI, doc. 001).

179 Andrei Chernov, 'The Party Which Claims to be Saving Marxism', *Moscow News* 17 (6–13 May 1990), p. 4.

180 Orttung, 'The Russian Right', p. 463.

181 P. Gutiontov, 'Konferentsiya stanovitsya uchreditel'nym s"ezdom', *Izvestiya* (20 June 1990).

182 Orttung, 'The Russian Right', pp. 464–6.

183 For a political portrait of Polozkov, see Lyudmila Telen', 'Zapovednaya zona?', *Narodnyi deputat* 10 (1990), pp. 52–61.

184 Examples can be found in Orttung, 'The Russian Right', p. 465.

185 Nikolai Kapanets (of the CPSU's Business Department), 'Novoe v finansovo-khozyaistvennoi deyatel'nosti partii', *Izvestiya Tsk KPSS* 10 (October 1990), pp. 100–1.

186 Orttung, 'The Russian Right', pp. 467–9.

10. RESTORATION AND REVOLUTION

1 Ruslan Khasbulatov, *The Struggle for Russia* (London: Routledge, 1993), pp. 88–90.

2 V. Filin, 'Kogo spasaet "Komitet natsional'nogo spaseniya"?', *Novaya zhizn'* 3–4 (1991), pp. 1, 8; 'Po afganskomu variantu', *Novaya zhizn'* 3–4 (1991), p. 3.

3 Sergei Sysoev, 'Triumfal'noe shestvie sovetskoi mnogopartiinosti', *Grazhdanskoe dostoinstvo* 2 (15–22 May 1991), p. 4.

4 *Dvizhenie 'Demokraticheskaya Rossiya': Informatsionnyi byulleten'* 1 (January 1991), p.4.

5 Filin, 'Kogo spasaet "Komitet natsional'nogo spaseniya"?', p. 8.

6 Mark Deich, 'Tsentristskii blok igraet v politiku', *Golos* 7 (16–22 February 1991), p. 2.

7 Mikhail Malyutin, 'Chto takoe "Tsentristskii blok" i nado li s nim borot'sya?', *Gospodin Narod* 3 (1991), p. 3.

8 Gleb Yakunin has stated that Zhirinovskii's candidacy was launched by Kryuchkov and Anatolii Luk'yanov in an interview appearing in *Novaya zhizn'* 14 (1991), p. 3. Zhirinovskii's nomination, the only one effected via

the legislature, was due to the 477 votes that he received (more than double the required number) at the Fourth Congress of Peoples Deputies (*Respublika* 1 (1991), p. 3).

9   John Dunlop, *The Rise of Russia and the Fall of the Soviet Empire* (Princeton: Princeton University Press, 1993), p. 157.

10 Alexander Rahr, 'Further Restructuring of the Soviet Political System', *RFE/RL Research Institute: Report on the USSR* 3(14) (1991), pp. 1–4.

11 *Dvizhenie 'Demokraticheskaya Rossiya': Informatsionnyi byulleten'* 4 (February 1991), p. 3.

12 *Grazhdanskoe dostoinstvo* 1 (10–17 January 1991), p. 7; *Solidarnost'* 10 (1991), pp. 1–2, 9.

13 *Dvizhenie 'Demokraticheskaya Rossiya': Informatsionnyi byulleten'* 2 (January 1991), pp. 1–3. The legal basis of El'tsin's appeal was first laid in a resolution of Russia's Supreme Soviet, 21 September 1990, establishing a number of conditions for the use of Russian troops outside the borders of the republic. *Novye zakony Rossii* (Moscow: Za i protiv, 1991), pp. 82–3. The substance of this resolution was passed into law on 11 December 1990.

14 *Solidarnost'* 10 (1991), p. 2.

15 *Ibid.*, p. 2.

16 *Kuranty* 80 (27 April 1991), p. 1; *Grazhdanskoe dostoinstvo* 2 (15–22 May 1991), p. 2; *Demokraticheskaya Rossiya* 1 (22 March 1991), p. 8; *Dvizhenie 'Demokraticheskaya Rossiya': Informatsionnyi byulleten'* 8 (April 1991), p. 2; *Dvizhenie Demokraticheskaya Rossiya': Informatsionnyi byulleten'* 9 (April 1991), p. 1.

17 Michael Urban, *More Power to the Soviets: the Democratic Revolution in the USSR* (Aldershot: Edward Elgar, 1990), pp. 75–9.

18 *Novye zakony Rossii*, pp. 171–3; *Sbornik zakonodatel'nykh aktov RSFSR o gosudarstvennom suverenitete, soyuznom dogovore i referendume* (Moscow: Sovetskaya Rossiya, 1991), pp. 7–19; *Byulleten': Moskovskii yuridicheskii tsentr mosgorispolkoma* 1 (1991), pp. 3–27, 39.

19 Evgenii Kozhokin interviewed by E. Leont'eva, *Rossiiskaya gazeta* (28 January 1992), p. 2.

20 The draft appeared in *Izvestiya* (24 November 1991).

21 *Dvizhenie 'Demokraticheskaya Rossiya': Informatsionnyi byulleten'* 1 (January 1991), pp. 1–2.

22 *Dvizhenie 'Demokraticheskaya Rossiya': Informatsionnyi byulleten'* 2 (January 1991), p. 4.

23 *Grazhdanskoe dostoinstvo* 1 (10–17 January 1991), p. 7.

24 'President Wants to Suspend the Law on the Press', *Moscow News* 4 (27 January–3 February 1991), p. 6.

25 John Murray, *The Russian Press From Brezhnev to Yeltsin* (Aldershot: Edward Elgar, 1994), p. 214.

26 *Golos* 16 (22–28 April 1991), p. 1.

27 G. Alimov, 'Bitva titanov', *Izvestiya* (23 August 1990); 'Bitva titanov prodolzhaetsya', *Izvestiya* (2 September 1990); 'Zhurnal "znamiya" zaregistrirovan', *Izvestiya* (4 September 1990).

28 Artyom Karapetyan, 'Readers For, City Soviet Against', *Moscow News* 35

(9–16 September 1990), p. 2; Alexander Mostovshchikov, 'The Fourth Power in Russia', *Moscow News* 36 (16–23 September 1990), p. 4.

29 Quoted in O. Shemchuk, 'Kak Kravchenko demokratom byl', *Novaya zhizn'* 3–4 (1991), p. 2.

30 *Kuranty* 6 (11 January 1991), p. 2.

31 'Zayavlenie agentstva "Interfaks"', *Izvestiya* (12 January 1991); Mikhail Komissar, 'Konfikt Gosteleradio-"Interfaks": Politika ili bukhgalteriya', *Izvestiya* (16 January 1991).

32 *Novaya zhizn'* 5–6 (1991), p. 1; *Kuranty* 9 (28 May 1991), p. 1.

33 *Grazhdanskoe dostoinstvo* 2 (15–22 May 1991), p. 1; *Novaya zhizn'* 1–2 (1991), p. 1.

34 *Doverie* 3 (April 1991), p. 9.

35 Andrei Kolesnikov, 'Return', *Moscow News* 31 (4–11 August 1991), p. 5; interview given by Vladimir Nyrko to M. Urban (17 November 1991).

36 'Slovo k chitatelyam', *Al'ternativa* 3 (September 1990), p. 1.

37 Michael Urban, 'The Russian Free Press in the Transition to a Post-Communist Society', *Journal of Communist Studies* 9 (June 1993), pp. 29–30.

38 *Novaya zhizn'* 3–4 (1991), p. 1.

39 A. Shadrin, 'Tak kto vse-taki povysil tseny na pressu?', *Argumenty i fakty* 29 (July 1991), p. 1.

40 Leonid Prudovsky, 'A Paper Problem', *Moscow News* 44 (11–18 November 1990), p. 5; Mikhail Poltoranin, 'This Land Is My Land', *Moscow News* 44 (11–18 November 1990), p. 14; Georgii Bovt, 'Net nichego khuzhe korruptsii v politike', *Golos* 16 (22–8 April 1991), p. 4.

41 Leonid Batkin, 'Nepriyatnaya tema', *Nezavisimaya gazeta* (7 May 1991), p. 2.

42 Urban, 'The Russian Free Press', p. 30.

43 M. Urban, personal observations at Boris El'tsin campaign offices (May–June 1991).

44 E.g., Vladimir Tsvetov, 'Televidenie – zagovor . . . protiv naroda', *Golos* 15 (15–21 April 1991), p. 7.

45 *Golos* 16 (22–8 April 1991), p. 1.

46 *Kuranty* 61 (2 April 1991), p. 3.

47 Mark Deich, 'Anatolii Ivanovich beretsya za karandash', *Demokraticheskaya Rossiya* 5 (1991), pp. 1–2.

48 Frances Foster, '*Izvestiya* as a Mirror of Russian Legal Reform: Press, Law, and Crisis in the Post-Soviet Era', *Vanderbilt Journal of Transnational Law* 26 (November 1993), pp. 675–748.

49 Khasbulatov, *The Struggle For Russia*, p. 109; G. Koval'skaya and V. Niki-tina, 'Chego nam zhdat' ot nikh', *Demokraticheskaya Rossiya* 1 (22 March 1991), p. 12.

50 *Pravda* (22 February 1991).

51 *Kuranty* 61 (2 April 1991), p. 1.

52 *Dvizhenie 'Demokraticheskaya Rossiya': Informatsionnyi byulleten'* 8 (April 1991), pp. 1–2.

53 A. Sobyanin and D. Yur'ev, *S"ezd narodnykh deputatov RSFSR v zerkale poimennykh golosovanii* (Moscow, 1991), pp. 18, 20.

54 *Ibid.*, pp. 7–9, 19, 46. Roy Medvedev has noted that Rutskoi's voting support for El'tsin in the Russian legislature began at the first Congress; Yitzhak Brudnyi has shown its amplification at the second. Medvedev, 'Yeltsin's Rival Awaits in Wings', *In These Times* 14 (31 May 1993), pp. 31–2; Brudnyi, 'Ruslan Khasbulatov, Aleksandr Rutskoi, and Intraelite Conflict in Postcommunist Russia, 1991–1994' in T. Colton and R. Tucker (eds.), *Patterns in Post-Soviet Leadership* (Boulder, CO: Westview, 1995), p. 80. Thus, the voting for chairperson at the first Congress provided ample precedent for Rutskoi's jump at the third. Rutskoi has maintained that his move was intended as a surprise and that El'tsin and his forces did not suspect that it was coming. See his interview with Vadim Kantor, *Srez* 1 (1991), p. 3.

55 'Kto i kak golosoval', *Gospodin Narod* 4 (1991), p. 3.

56 Leotii Byzov, Director of the Sociological Service of the RSFSR's Supreme Soviet, emphasized in an interview with M. Urban (15 May 1991) that popular ratings played a crucial role in the calculations of many deputies, especially the imperative 'not to be associated with *them* [restorationists], since a new law on recall would soon be passed'.

57 Sobyanin and Yur'ev, *S"ezd narodnykh deputatov RSFSR*, pp. 7–9.

58 *Dvizhenie 'Demokraticheskaya Rossiya': Informatsionnyi byulleten'* 8 (April 1991), p. 1.

59 Sobyanin and Yur'ev, *S"ezd narodnykh deputatov RSFSR*, pp. 20–3.

60 In addition to the identification of office and incumbent from the outset, El'tsin's election campaign was formally launched nearly three weeks before the office had been established.

61 Unless otherwise indicated, this section is based on Michael Urban, 'Boris El'tsin, Democratic Russia and the Campaign for the Russian Presidency', *Soviet Studies* 44(2) (1992), pp. 187–207.

62 Aleksei Levinson, 'Kto nam meshaet krasivo zhit'', *Izvestiya* (12 May 1991).

63 El'tsin's two most ubiquitous campaign posters – one in which he appeared smiling, in shirt-sleeves, surrounded by enthusiastic citizens; another in which he stood alone, solemn, clenched fist raised with Kremlin wall to his back – captured succinctly this double image so resonant with Russian authority constructs. On that subject, Mikhail Yampolsky, 'The Rhetoric of Representation of Political Leaders in Soviet Culture', *Elementa* 1(1) (1993), pp. 101–13 and Dmitrii Levchik, 'Nauka pobezhdat' na vyborakh' (Moscow: Russian State Humanities University, 1993).

64 El'tsin stated the 'pluses' during the campaign in an interview (*Srez* 1 (1991), p. 8) and before DemRossiya's Council of Representatives (1 June 1995): Rutskoi appealed to constituencies in which El'tsin was weak and he split the RKP as an administrative force in Russia. The issue would remain moot, however, since it is entirely possible that another running mate – such as Vadim Bakatin, El'tsin's first choice – may have helped as much or more.

65 *Dvizhenie 'Demokraticheskaya Rossiya': Informatsionnyi byulleten'* 3 (February 1991), p. 1.

66 *Demokraticheskaya Rossiya* 1 (22 March 1991), pp. 1, 8–9.

67 *Ibid.*, p. 8.

68 Lev Ponomarev, interview given to M. Urban (30 May 1991).

69 *Demokraticheskaya Rossiya* 11 (7 June 1991), p. 2. See also Leonid Batkin, 'Golosovat' za El'tsina – no s otkrytymi glazami', *Demokraticheskaya Rossiya* 5 (19 April 1991), pp. 1, 4–5.

70 There were already signs of just this during the spring campaign, as DemRossiya candidates competed fratricidally in the mayor's race in Moscow and in a by-election there. In these instances, DemRossiya activists either worked against one another or lapsed into passivity, while rank-and-file members were often confused about which of 'their' candidates to support.

71 Vladimir Gel'man, 'Evolyutsiya predstavitel''nykh organov vlasti v sovremennoi Rossii', *Politicheskii monitoring* 11 (December 1992), p. 157; Gennadii Burbulis, interview given to Yu. Zvyagin, *Narodnyi deputat* 8 (1991), pp. 14–18.

72 Stepan Kiselyov, 'How to Capture the White House', *Moscow News* 39 (29 September–6 October 1991), pp. 8–9.

73 William Clark, 'Central Authority and Local Governance in Post-Communist Russia', (paper presented at 26th National Convention of the American Association for the Advancement of Slavic Studies, Philadelphia PA, 17–20 November 1994), p. 6.

74 Gennadii Vladimirov, 'Rossiiskii tsentr i mestnaya vlast'', *Politicheskii monitoring* 4 (April 1993), pp. 7–8.

75 *Dvizhenie 'Demokraticheskaya Rossiya': Informatsionnyi byulleten'* 11 (1991), p. 1.

76 Clark, 'Central Authority and Local Governance', p. 6.

77 Yu. A. Nikolaev, 'Gavriil Popov brosaet perchatku Mossovetu', *Al'ternativa* 9 (June 1991), p. 3; 'Verkhovnyi Sovet Rossii o vlasti v Leningrade', *Izvestiya* (9 July 1991).

78 Natalya Davydova, 'Prefects go to work', *Moscow News* 30 (28 July–4 August 1991), p. 3.

79 D. A. Levchik *et al.*, 'Putch 18–21 avgusta 1991g.: mestnye organy vlasti' (report to the Krasnogvardeiskii district soviet, Moscow, 17 October 1991), p. 23.

80 Vladimirov, 'Rossiiskii tsentr i mestnaya vlast'', pp. 7–8.

81 In May El'tsin came close to signing a similar but more inclusive decree that would have also outlawed party organizations operating in units of the army, KGB and Ministry of Internal Affairs located in Russia. Olga Bychkova, 'Non-party president issues decree', *Moscow News* 30 (28 July–4 August 1991), p. 3.

82 Text appears in *Argumenty i fakty* 29 (July 1991), p. 2. See also *Izvestiya* (22 July 1991).

83 Nikolai Fedorov, interview given to Yu. Feofanov, *Izvestiya* (23 July 1991).

84 Nikolai Kas'yanov, 'Voprosov bol'she chem otvetov', *Soyuz* 30 (24–31 July 1991), p. 2.

85 *Izvestiya* (30 July 1991).

86 Sergei Stupar', 'Mer v storone ne ostalsya', *Kuranty* 151 (10 August 1991), p. 1; *Respublika* 1 (1991), p. 5.

87 *Izvestiya* (5 August 1991); *Kuranty* 149 (8 August 1991), p. 1.

88 *Izvestiya* (26 July 1991); *Rossiiskaya gazeta* (27 July 1991), p. 1.

89 *Izvestiya* (27 July 1991).

90 A. Binev, 'Sekretari vne zakona', *Argumenty i fakty* 29 (July 1991), p. 2.

91 *Grazhdanskoe dostoinstvo* 2 (15–22 May 1991), p. 3.

92 Urban, 'Boris El'tsin, Democratic Russia', p. 205, note 40.

93 Michael Urban, 'State, Property and Political Society in Postcommunist Russia: In Search of a Political Center' in C. Saivetz and A. Jones (eds.), *In Search of Pluralism: Soviet and Post-Soviet Politics* (Boulder, CO: Westview, 1994), pp. 125–50.

94 V. S. Lipitskii, 'K reformirovannoi partii', *Izvestiya TsK KPSS* 1 (1991), pp. 37–40; Yu. Bychkov's interview with Rutskoi, *Gospodin Narod* 5 (1991), p. 10.

95 Aleksei Chernyshev, 'Est' takaya partiya!', *Soyuz* 32 (7–14 August 1991), p. 11.

96 Nikolai Kas'yanov, 'Demokraty-kommunisty nakonets-to ob"edinilis' v rabochee vremya', *Soyuz* 33 (14–21 August 1991), p. 6.

97 O. V. Grigor'ev and M. V. Malyutin, *Vlast'i sobstvennost' v Rossii: osen'yu 1991: Kto pobedil i chto dal'she* (Moscow: Public Centre of Moscow City Soviet, 1991), pp. 8–11; Aleksandr Verkhovskii, 'Demokraty na poroge novoi epokhi', *Panorama* 28 (July 1991), pp. 4–5.

98 Nikolai Kas'yanov, ' "Dvizhenie demokraticheskikh reform": istoki, politika, perspektiva', *Soyuz* 28 (10–17 July 1991), p. 6; *Izvestiya* (13 July 1991).

99 V. E. Lyzlov, 'Ob"edinennaya Demokraticheskaya partiya strany: kommentarii zainteresovannogo cheloveka', *Demokraticheskaya gazeta* 8 (July 1991), p. 3.

100 *Dvizhenie 'Demokraticheskaya Rossiya': Informatsionnyi byulleten'* 12 (July 1991), pp. 1–4.

101 Yurii Bychkov, 'Sokhranyat li respublikantsy svoyu partiyu?', *Respublika* 7 (1991), p. 9.

102 In Moscow, DemRossiya was already tangling with Popov over sinecures for its supporters and preparing candidates for national elections to regional and city executive positions expected shortly (*Kuranty* 149 (8 August 1991), p. 4). Meanwhile, the DPR was attempting to expand its base to the USSR in anticipation of elections at that level following the signing of a new Union Treaty (*Demokraticheskaya gazeta* 8 (July 1991), p. 1).

103 The principal initiatives in this respect were the founding of the People's Party of Russia and the creation of the quasi-party, the Liberal Union. The former was headed by Tel'man Gdlyan, Igor Chubais and other notables who aspired for it the status of a disciplined mass party that would dislodge the *nomenklatura* from power *and* intercept the misguided approach of the Liberal Union and others whose insistence on immediate 'marketization' would primarily benefit the *nomenklatura* itself. For their part, the Liberal Union brought together notables, small parties and party factions united by their commitment to the immediate establishment of a free market system in Russia as the *conditio sine qua non* for solving the country's problems. On the People's Party of Russia, see: Vladimir Todres, 'Radikaly ovladevayut massami?', *Nezavisimaya gazeta* (21 May 1991), p. 2; M. Volodina and V. Pribylovskii, 'Narod i narodnaya partiya Tel'mana Gdlyana – Ediny', *Panorama* 28 (July 1991), p. 7; 'Eshche odna partiya obizhennykh kommunistov', *Novaya zhizn'* 14 (1991), p. 1. On the Liberal Union see:

M. Volodina, 'Liberalnye Konservatory – eto ochen' ser'ezno', *Panorama* 28 (July 1991), p. 7; Konstantin Katanyan, 'Znakomye vse litsa', *Kuranty* 151 (10 August 1991), p. 2.

104 I. I. Antonovich, 'Patrioticheskie sily Rossii: vozmozhnost' ob"edineniya', *Izvestiya TsK KPSS* 7 (July 1991), pp. 67–9.

105 'Slovo k narodu', *Sovetskaya Rossiya* (23 July 1991).

106 'Zayavlenie A. Yakovleva', *Izvestiya* (16 August 1991).

107 Dunlop, *The Rise of Russia*, p. 213.

108 A published warning about *coup* preparations appeared in Vladimir Nyrko's 'Idet podgotovka k perevorotu?', *Al'ternativa* 9 (June 1991), p. 1.

109 Yurii Kon, 'Gorbachev–Pavlov: khronika protivostoyaniya', *Rossiskaya gazeta* (16 August 1991), p. 1.

110 Sergei Parkhomenko, 'Na poroge konstitutsionnogo krizisa', *Nezavisimaya gazeta* (30 May 1991), pp. 1–2; Lyudmila Telen, 'Parliament Opposes Accord Signed by Gorbachev and Nine Republics', *Moscow News* 22 (2–9 June 1991), p. 7.

111 Gavriil Popov, 'Taina treugol'nika', *Izvestiya* (2 February 1993).

112 'Neskol'ko voprosov byvshemu politzaklyuchennomu Gorbachevu, M.S.', *Kommersant* 34 (19–26 August 1991), p. 6; 'Kak zaderzhali Gorbacheva', *Golos* 33 (26 August–1 September 1991), p. 2; S. Merin, 'Gorbachev i zagovor protiv Gorbacheva', *Gospodin Narod* 9 (1991), p. 4; Yu. Burtin, 'Forosskie novosti', *Demokraticheskaya Rossiya* 32 (3 November 1991), p. 2.

113 Dunlop, *The Rise of Russia*, pp. 189, 202–6.

114 Accounts in English include: *ibid.*, pp. 186–255; Ruslan Khasbulatov, *The Struggle for Russia* (London: Routledge, 1993), pp. 145–223; V. Bonnell, A. Cooper and G. Freidin (eds.), *Russia at the Barricades: Eyewitness Accounts of the August 1991 Coup* (Armonk, NY: M. E. Sharpe, 1994); James Billington, *Russian Transformed: Breakthrough to Hope* (New York: The Free Press, 1992); Anatoly Sobchak, *For a New Russia* (New York: The Free Press, 1992), pp. 173–83.

115 On the role played by Luk'yanov and the USSR's Supreme Soviet, see *Izvestiya* (22 August 1991) and *Izvestiya* (24 August 1991).

116 Dunlop, *The Rise of Russia*, pp. 199–201; Andrei Berezkin, 'Rossiya: Koordinaty putcha', *Rossiiskie vesti* 20 (28 September 1991), p. 8, and the items in *Soyuz* 34 (21–8 August 1991), pp. 3, 6; Nikolai Kas'yanov, 'Byla takaya partiya', *Soyuz* 35 (28 August–4 September 1991), p. 20.

117 Lyudmila Gur'eva, 'Tipichnyi gorod provintsii: uroven' politizatsii naselenya', *Rossiiskaya gazeta* (4 January 1992).

118 On the disposition of the military during the *coup*, see John Lepingwell, 'Soviet Civil–Military Relations and the August Coup', *World Politics* 44 (July 1992), pp. 539–72 and Viktor Litovskii, 'Voennye uroki', *Soyuz* 35 (28 August–4 September 1991), p. 17.

119 Some twenty OFT activists staged a picket supporting the *coup* near Moscow's Lenin Museum on the morning of 20 August. Citizens gathered there to fraternize with the military massed on Manege Square rapidly broke it up, seizing their placards and destroying them on the spot. Police on the scene intervened only to inform the participants that their activities must be conducted in an 'orderly' way (personal observation, M. Urban.)

120 *Izvestiya* (26 August 1991).
121 Dunlop, *The Rise of Russia*, pp. 207–10 has stated that the KGB list included seventy names. S. Mostovshchikov has put the number at about 7,000 (*Izvestiya* (26 August 1991)).
122 Inga Prelovskaya, 'V te goryachie dni?', *Soyuz* 35 ((28 August–4 September 1991), p. 6.
123 N. Burbyga, 'Pochemu gruppa "Al'fa" ne stala shturmirovat' "Belyi dom"', *Izvestiya* (26 August 1991).
124 'Na Lubyanke tri dnya pili chai, a na chetvertyi zhdali shturma', *Golos* 33 (26 August–1 September 1991), p. 10; Nikolai Aleksandrov, 'Ya rodom ne iz 37–go!', *Soyuz* 35 (28 August–4 September 1991), p. 14.
125 Yevgeniya Albats and Natalia Gevorkyan, "What's to become of the KGB?", *Moscow News*, nos. 34–5 (1–8 September 1991), pp. 8–9.
126 On the failure of SCSE strategy of television management, see Victoria Bonnell and Gregory Freidin, '*Televorot*: the Role of Television in Russia's 1991 Coup', *Slavic Review* vol. 52 (Winter 1993), pp. 810–38.
127 This episode apparently resulted from the slipshod examination given to the footage by the editorial censor at Central Television. Yelena Chekalova, 'Has Central TV Collapsed?', *Moscow News*, nos. 34–5 (1–8 September 1991), p. 6.
128 Learning of this surprising fact on 20 August, V. Igrunov, S. Mitrokhin and about five colleagues from the Institute for Humanities and Political Studies arrived at the Moscow city soviet on the following morning in order to use the extensive telephone lists and the large phone bank there to begin making contacts with activists and workers' collectives around the country. Having received authorization from the White House, they organized those deputies and staff on the premises into a coordinating centre for a national political strike. By the time that a dozen or so factories in the Moscow region had been enlisted, calls began to come in from far and wide with requests for instructions. Later in the day, workers arrived to form a guard and students turned up asking to be recognized as 'officially' part of the strike effort in order to agitate among transport personnel and to take their own direct actions to shut down city transport. By day's end, a communications network for a national strike was in place but, fortunately, was no longer needed.
129 Interview given by Larisa Vladimirova to M. Urban (13 November 1991).
130 Personal observations at Manege Square, 20 August 1991 (M. Urban).
131 *Ekspress-Khronika* 34 (20 August 1991), pp. 1–2.
132 For analyses of El'tsin projection of leadership images – apotheosized in the iconography of his tank-top 'Appeal' with papers (the tsar's scrolls of sacred writ?) in hand and voice booming against a stiff wind, see Bonnell and Freidin, '*Televorot*', pp. 824–5 and Yampolsky, 'The Rhetoric of Represen-tation', pp. 105–110.
133 Dunlop, *The Rise of Russia*, pp. 218, 246.
134 Khasbulatov, *The Struggle for Russia*, pp. 145–51.
135 Synopses of the activities of political parties during the *putsch* appear in *Panorama* 2 (September 1991), pp. 1, 3.
136 *Gospodin Narod* 9 (1991), p. 2; 'Informatsionnoe soobshchenie ob uchastii RPRF v sobytiyakh 19–21 avgusta' (Moscow: mimeo, no date).

137 Eduard Lorkh-Sheiko, then an officer in the DPR, stated in an interview given to M. Urban (24 August 1991) that the DPR network carried the majority of information travelling between Moscow and the provinces. Our knowledge of the DPR and personal observations at one of its relay points in Moscow during the early hours of 21 August 1991 (M. Urban) dissuades us from quarrelling with Lorkh-Sheiko's estimate.

138 For a discussion of subversive elements in Central Television broadcasts during the *coup*, see Bonnell and Freidin, '*Televorot*', pp. 810–31.

139 I. Ovchinnikova, 'Pri svete sovesti', *Izvestiya* (22 August 1991); 'Nashi novye starye "Izvestiya"', *Izvestiya* (24 August 1991).

140 Some of these cities are identified in *Izvestiya* (22 August 1991).

141 'We Are United!', *Moscow News* 34–5 (1–8 September 1991), p. 6.

142 M. Berger, 'Fakt, kotoryi nashel Interfaks', *Izvestiya* (31 August 1991).

143 'Kak vypuskali "Obshchuyu gazetu"', *Kommersant* 34 (19–26 August 1991), p. 3.

144 Accounts of the deaths of three young men suggest that either the troops involved were disobeying orders to attack the White House or lost their nerve and their bearings when civilians responded to their assault. The first version appeared in *Izvestiya* (28 August and 9 September 1991), the second in *Nezavisimaya gazeta* (18 August 1992), p. 5.

145 Dunlop, *The Rise of Russia*, p. 29, has reported that the number of defenders did not appear 'to have exceeded 50,000–70,000 at any one time'. This estimate, in our view, seems very conservative. Even if correct, it includes neither those *en route* to or from the nearest metro station (Barrikadnaya) – who on the evening of 20 August would have added approximately another 30,000 to that number – nor those not in the area at a given time. Since the defence was conducted for three days most invigilators had been able to sleep in their own beds and attend to at least some of their normal affairs while contributing their presence at the barricades episodically. Others appeared to have dropped by briefly for a look and no more.

146 Craig Calhoun, 'The Problem of Identity in Collective Action' in J. Huber (ed.), *Macro-Micro Linkages in Sociology* (Newbury Park, CA: Sage, 1991), pp. 51–75 (we are grateful to Victoria Bonnell for this reference).

11. REFORM, REACTION AND REBELLION: THE CALAMITY OF THE FIRST REPUBLIC

1 In one poll in which respondents registered their approval on a scale from – 100 to +100, El'tsin's scores climbed from +58 (before the August *putsch*) to +89 (after it). *Gospodin Narod* 9 (1991), p. 3. In another using a five-point scale, El'tsin's rating in large cities after the *putsch* stood at 4.44. Leontii Byzov, 'Gotova li Rossiya podderzhat' svoyu novuyu vlast'?', *Nezavisimaya gazeta* (25 September 1991), p. 2.

2 Gennadii Burbulis, in an interview published in *Izvestiya* (26 October 1991).

3 Maksim Sokolov, 'Kak zhe my budem zhit' bez kommunistov?', *Kommersant* 34 (19–26 August 1991), p. 2; *Izvestiya* (26 August 1991).

4   *Izvestiya* (6 September 1991); *Nezavisimaya gazeta* (5 September 1991), p. 2.

5   *Izvestiya* (28 September 1991).

6   This fact was apparent at the December session of the interim Supreme Soviet, at which no quorum obtained to vote its own dissolution. *Rossiiskaya gazeta* (25 and 28 December 1991).

7   Lilia Shevtsova, 'Russia's Post-Communist Politics: Revolution or Continuity?' in G. Lapidus (ed.), *The New Russia: Troubled Transformation* (Boulder, CO: Westview, 1995), pp. 8–9; Timothy Colton, 'Politics' in T. Colton and R. Levgold (eds.), *After the Soviet Union: From Empire to Nations* (New York: Norton, 1992), pp. 20–1.

8   See his decrees: 'Ob organizatsii raboty s likvidatsiei ministerstv i drugikh organov gosudarstvennogo upravleniya SSSR', *Kuranty* (29 November 1991), p. 5; 'O reorganizatsii tsentral'nykh organov gosudarstvennogo upravleniya RSFSR', *Rossiiskaya gazeta* (5 December 1991), p. 2.

9   Andrei Grachev, 'Shipwreck', *Moscow News* 45 (8–15 November 1992), p. 8.

10 *Rossiiskaya gazeta* (26 November 1991), p. 1; *Nezavisimaya gazeta* (27 November 1991), p. 1.

11 John Dunlop, *The Rise of Russia and the Fall of the Soviet Empire* (Princeton: Princeton University Press, 1993), p. 272.

12 This term is used by A. Sobyanin and D. Yur'ev, *S"ezd narodnykh deputatov RSFSR v zerkale pomennykh golosovanii* (Moscow, 1991), p. 27.

13 In spring 1991, Popov, the Moscow City Council and Russia's Supreme Soviet had all backed the appointment of V. Komissarov but were blocked by USSR Minister of Internal Affairs Pugo, deputies' hunger strikes notwithstanding. After the *putsch*, Komissarov's appointment was derailed by Popov naming his political crony, Murashev. Hunger strikes were renewed, appeals made, but to no avail. See *Izvestiya*, (10 and 20 September 1991) and *Nezavisimaya gazeta* (5 and 14 September 1991, p. 2 and 1, respectively).

14 Sobyanin and Yur'ev, *S"ezd narodnykh deputatov RSFSR*, p. 25.

15 *Nezavisimaya gazeta* (19 September 1991), p. 1.

16 *Izvestiya* (18 October 1991).

17 *Rossiiskaya gazeta* (2 November 1991), p. 1; Resolution of the Supreme Soviet, RSFSR, 'Ob organizatsii ispolnitel'noi vlasti v period radikal'noi ekonomicheskoi reformy', *Rossiiskaya gazeta* (5 November 1991), p. 1.

18 'Ob izmeneniyakh i dopolneniyakh Konstitutsii (Osnovogo Zakona) RSFSR', *Rossiiskaya gazeta* (12 November 1991), p. 6.

19 'Ob organizatsii raboty Pravitel'stva RSFSR v usloviyakh ekonomicheskoi reformy', *Rossiiskaya gazeta* (12 November 1991), p. 2.

20 *Nezavisimaya gazeta* (12 October 1991), p. 1; interview given by Yurii Petrov to Tat'yana Malkina, *Nezavisimaya gazeta* (14 February 1992), pp. 1–2.

21 This thinking was expressed in El'tsin's December decree combining all security and police organs in one superministry with 'rapid reaction' units to put down the riots anticipated to follow the price rises. This decree was annulled in January 1992 by the Constitutional Court. On its history, see:

Rossiiskaya gazeta (25 December 1991), p. 1; *Rossiiskaya gazeta* (16 January 1992), p. 1; *Nezavisimaya gazeta* (21 December 1991), p. 2; *Nezavisimaya gazeta* (10 January 1992), p. 1; *Nezavisimaya gazeta* (16 January 1992), p. 1.

22 *Rossiiskaya gazeta* (4 March 1992), p. 2.

23 Quoted in *Nezavisimaya gazeta* (16 October 1991), p. 1.

24 Quoted in *Nezavisimaya gazeta* (17 October 1991), p. 1.

25 Quoted in *Nezavisimaya gazeta* (5 November 1991), p. 2.

26 *Nezavisimaya gazeta* (29 October 1991), p. 1.

27 Quoted in *Nezavisimaya gazeta* (16 October 1991), p. 1.

28 Quoted in *Nezavisimaya gazeta* (17 October 1991), p. 1.

29 *Demokraticheskaya Rossiya* 32 (3 November 1991), p. 4; *Nezavisimaya gazeta* (5 October 1991), p. 2.

30 Apparently the analysis presented to El'tsin consisted exclusively of voting patterns from 1990 and 1991 extrapolated into the future, without provision for the effect of the democrats' August triumph (personal communications from Vladimir Gel'man, 28 September 1994; Andrei Berezkin, 1 October 1994). El'tsin was shown a map of the country whose regions were shaded according to past voting patterns. This produced the (spurious) impression of overwhelming communist strength, since the democratic vote was geographically confined to population centres dwarfed by the vast expanse of steppe and tundra shaded as communist strongholds.

31 Aleksandr Sobyanin and Dmitrii Yur'ev, 'Demokraty proigrayut, esli vybory glav administratsii provesti nemedlenno', *Nezavisimaya gazeta* (17 October 1991), p. 2.

32 S. Sulakshin, 'Neprosty prostye resheniya', *Izvestiya* (4 October 1991).

33 Peter Murrell, 'What is Shock Therapy? What Did it Do in Poland and Russia?', *Post-Soviet Affairs* 9 (April–June 1993), p. 113.

34 See the articles by Georgii Lvov and Mikhail Leont'ev, *Nezavisimaya gazeta* (22 October 1991), pp. 1–2; and by Leont'ev, *Nezavisimaya gazeta* (9 November 1991), p. 1.

35 *The Economy of the USSR* (Washington, DC: The World Bank, 1990); Aleksandr Buzgalin and Andrei Kolganov, 'The Influence of the International Monetary Fund and the Internal Causes of the Socioeconomic Crisis in Russia' in their *Russia: Winter 1994/1995: Economic and Political Shifts* (Moscow: Economic Democracy, 1995), pp. 64–76.

36 Hillel Ticktin, 'Permanent Chaos Without a Market: the Non-Latinamericanization of the USSR', *Studies in Comparative Communism* 25 (September 1992), pp. 242–56.

37 Vladimir Gel'man, Vyacheslav Igrunov and Sergei Mitrokhin, 'Krizis politiki v Rossii', *Politicheskii monitoring* 1 (January 1993), pp. 7–8.

38 Murrell, 'What is Shock Therapy?', pp. 113–18; David Woodruff, 'The Barter of the Bankrupt: the Politics of Demonetization in Russia's Federal State' (paper presented at the Annual Meeting of the American Political Science Association, Chicago, 31 August–3 September 1995).

39 *Nezavisimaya gazeta* (24 December 1991), p. 2.

40 Yurii Petrov, interviewed by G. Shipit'ko, *Izvestiya* (9 October 1991).

41 Vladimir Pribylovskii, *Sto politikov Rossii* (Moscow: Panorama, 1992), p. 2.

42 *Nezavisimaya gazeta* (24 January 1992), p. 2.

43 Pavel Gazukin, 'Sud'ba truboukladchika', *Panorama* 2 (May 1992), pp. 4–5.
44 El'tsin first met Gaidar some days after appointing him. See Gaidar's interview with M. Gurevich, *Moskovskii komsomolets* (10 July 1993), p. 2.
45 Aleksandr Rutskoi, interviewed by A. Karaulov, *Nezavisimaya gazeta* (18 December 1991), pp. 1–2.
46 *Nezavisimaya gazeta* (24 September 1991), p. 1.
47 In certain respects, the creation of this organ simply blurred lines of responsibility and led to a more articulated field of intra-governmental intrigue. See Eugene Huskey, 'The State-Legal Administration and Politics of Redundancy', *Post-Soviet Affairs* 11(2) (1995), pp. 115–43.
48 Aleksei Golovkov, interviewed by A. Zuichenko, *Nezavisimaya gazeta* (22 January 1992), pp. 1–2.
49 *Nezavisimaya gazeta* (24 January 1992), p. 2.
50 *Nezavisimaya gazeta* (17 September 1991), p. 1.
51 *Dvizhenie 'Demokraticheskaya Rossiya': Informatsionnyi byulleten'* 14 (August–September 1991), pp. 1–3.
52 *Ibid.*, pp. 3–4.
53 See the interview given by Yurii Afanas'ev, Lev Ponomarev and Gleb Yakunin to V. Vyzhutovich, *Izvestiya* (7 October 1991).
54 *Kommersant* 43 (4–11 November 1991), p. 23; *Nezavisimaya gazeta* (28 November 1991), p. 1.
55 Boris Orlov, interviewed by P. Anokin, *Rossiiskaya gazeta* (1 April 1992), p. 6.
56 These included the appointment of the PPFR's Aleksandr Titkin as minister of industry, the SDPR's Pavel Kudyukin as deputy minister of labour, and Aleksandr Shokhin as deputy prime minister on the SDPR's recommendation. None of these party-initiated appointments produced even the semblance of party government. Shortly after implementation of 'shock therapy', the PPFR and SDPR declared themselves in opposition to the government but 'their' ministers refused to be recalled while Kudyukin resigned on that account.
57 *Nezavisimaya gazeta* (20 November 1991), p. 1; *Nezavisimaya gazeta* (16 January 1992), p. 2; *Rossiiskaya gazeta* (7 December 1991), p. 2; *Rossiiskaya gazeta* (29 February 1992), p. 1.
58 At a meeting of the RPR's governing board (19 November 1991), for example, discussion of the appointments question ended in reluctant agreement with the remark made by one member, 'We can't recommend anyone to El'tsin's team. They have the right to decide whom to include' (personal observation, M. Urban).
59 *Nezavisimaya gazeta* (4 January 1992), p. 2.
60 By March 1992, some 200 deputies identified with the democratic column had taken jobs in the executive. Sergei Filatov, interviewed by O. Burkaleva, *Rossiiskaya gazeta* (19 March 1992), p. 2.
61 Quoted in Galina Koval'skaya, 'Intelligentsiya i vlast'', *Demokraticheskaya Rossiya* 32 (3 November 1991), p. 5.
62 Oleg Vite, '"Ekonomicheskii" krizis demokraticheskogo dvizhenie', *Nezavisimaya gazeta* (27 February 1992), p. 2.
63 Although not founded officially until February 1992, the RMDR repre-

sented essentially the Russian (and largest) section of the all-union MDR which collapsed with the USSR in 1991.

64 Vladimir Pribylovskii, 'Treshchina', *Panorama* 3 (December 1991), pp. 4–5.

65 *Nezavisimaya gazeta* (16 November 1991), p. 2.

66 In Moscow, Popov's confiscated the CPSU's palatial Higher Party School and transferred much of it to the MDR which, in turn, rented a portion of those premises to private business concerns. *Demokraticheskaya gazeta* 19 (31 October–6 November 1991), p. 3.

67 A successful proposal to sponsor these committees with government financing – 'Struktura obshchestvennogo komiteta rossiiskikh reform' – was made at DemRossiya's January 1992 plenum by M. Shneider, V. Kriger, K. Ignat'ev, L. Ponomarev and L. Bogdanov (M-BIO archives, fond DR-2).

68 *Nezavisimaya gazeta* (5 November 1992), p. 2.

69 *Nezavisimaya gazeta* (14 December 1991), p. 2.

70 Lev Ponomarev, interviewed by A. Verkhovskii, *Panorama* 3 (December 1991), p. 4.

71 Vladimir Pribylovskii, 'Agressivnaya oppozitsiya i poslushnoe bol'shinstvo', *Panorama* 3 (December 1991), p. 6.

72 'Ustav Dvizheniya "Demokraticheskaya Rossiya"' and speeches at the second congress of DemRossiya (Moscow: photocopy, no date).

73 *Kuranty* (13 November 1991), p. 4.

74 N. M. Sirota (ed.), *Informatsionnyi byulleten'* 2 (St. Petersburg: Dvizhenie Demokraticheskaya Rossiya, 1992), pp. 1–2, 5.

75 *Ibid.*, p. 5.

76 With the petition drive under way, El'tsin changed his position and instructed DemRossiya to limit the referendum question to individual ownership of land. They did, collected nearly twice the required one million signatures, but El'tsin was by then locked in combat with the legislature and the 'successful' petition went unattended. Yitzhak Brudny, 'The Dynamics of "Democratic Russia", 1990–1993', *Post-Soviet Affairs* 9 (April–June 1993), pp. 162–3.

77 Vladimir Bokser made this statement, presciently predicting in April 1992 that the Congress of People's Deputies would be dissolved within a year and a half, and all soviets within two years, to make way for unobstructed presidential rule. His colleague, Kiril Ignat'ev, disagreed in part, saying that legislatures should be retained, but only to approve budgets and monitor implementation. See their interviews with G. Tochkin, *Panorama* 2 (May 1992), pp. 1–3.

78 Personal observations at DemRossiya's second congress (M. Urban, 10 November 1991). Related incidents are reported in: G. S. Ivantsov, 'Buinaya porosl' novoi nomenklatury', *Al'ternativa* 11 (September 1991), p. 3 and A. S. Savel'ev, 'Detskie bolezni demokratii', also in *Al'ternativa* 11 (September 1991).

79 This group was initially comprised of DPR refugees Garii Kasparov and Arkadii Murashev who joined Yurii Afanas'ev, Leonid Batkin, Il'ya Zaslavskii, Vasilii Selyunin, Larisa Piyasheva and others in June 1991 to create the Independent Civic Union and the Liberal Union (both founded

in August). On their efforts to distil a politics from their understanding of Western countries, see 'Rossiya ne namerena bolee nesti na sebe imperskoe yarmo', *Panorama* 3 (December 1991), pp. 1–3.

80   *Kuranty* (13 November 1991), p. 4.

81   *Nezavisimaya gazeta* (21 January 1992), pp. 1–2.

82   *Nezavisimaya gazeta* (25 January 1992), p. 2; *Rossiiskaya gazeta* (25 January 1992), p. 2.

83   *Nezavisimaya gazeta* (28 July 1992), p. 2.

84   A. Glubotskii, ' "Demorossy" podenie posle vzleta', *Narodnyi deputat* 5 (1993), pp. 51–2.

85   *Rossiiskaya gazeta* (27 October 1992), pp. 2,4.

86   Quoted in *Izvestiya* (30 November 1992).

87   The single exception was the Supreme Soviet's annulment of El'tsin's decree on credit and banking. As the lopsided vote would indicate (182:1), this action concerned the decree's substance far less than it did its own institutional prerogative: El'tsin's earlier promise to consult with the legislature in this one area of economic policy before issuing his own decrees. *Nezavisimaya gazeta* (23 November 1991), p. 1.

88   *Nezavisimaya gazeta* (14 January 1992), p. 2; *Nezavisimaya gazeta* (16 January 1992), p. 2; *Rossiiskaya gazeta* (26 February 1992), p. 2; *Rossiiskaya gazeta* (28 March 1992).

89   *Nezavisimaya gazeta* (17 March 1992), p. 2.

90   B. I. Koval' and V. B. Pavlenko, *Partii i politicheskie bloki v Rossii* (Moscow: Narodnaya neftenaya investitvionno-promyshlennaya evroaziatskaya korporatsiya, 1993), p. 28.

91   For instance, Travkin's report reversing the priorities of state and market consumed two-thirds of all programmatic discussion and was endorsed by all but 26 of the 700 delegates (Travkin asked those voting incorrectly to leave the party) while changes in party rules *de facto* removed the possibility for forming factions. *Materialy III S''ezda DPR (7–8 dekabrya 1991 g.)*, (Moscow, 1992); *Nezavisimaya gazeta* (10 December 1991), p. 2.

92   *Nezavisimaya gazeta* (12 December 1991), p. 2; *Nezavisimaya gazeta* (17 December 1991), p. 2.

93   *Nezavisimaya gazeta* (18 January 1992), p. 2.

94   Barburin's political career – from radical democrat to patriotic anti-democrat – was punctuated by El'tsin's denial of a key committee appointment in the Russia legislature in 1990 (Aleksei Kazannik, interviewed by O. Bondarenko, *Segodnya* (16 July 1993), p. 11). His RPU was organized in December 1991, the first attempt at forging a state-patriotic movement from a democrat-patriot alloy whose officers included Soyuz leader, Viktor Alksnis, and ex-democrat Nikolai Pavlov (*Nezavisimaya gazeta* (24 December 1991), p. 2). The RPU did not attract a popular base, but became an influential legislative faction. Tat'yana Shavshukova, 'Sotsialisticheskie i kommunisticheskie dvizheniya v fevrale–marte 1992 goda', *Politicheskii monitoring* 3 (1992), p. 123.

95   *Rossiiskaya gazeta* (10 February 1991), p. 1.

96   'Zavyavlenie Kongressa grazhdanskikh i patrioticheskikh sil Rossii' (M-BIO archives, no date).

97 'Rossiiskoe narodnoe sobranie: Politicheskie printsipy i blizhaishchie zadachi', *Obozrevatel'* 2–3 (February 1992), pp. 11–17.

98 Garem Razh, 'S″ezd lyubitelei rodina', *Panorama* 1 (April 1992), pp. 5–7; Shavshukova, 'Sotsialisticheskie i kommunisticheskie dvizheniya v fevrale– marte 1992 goda', pp. 117–18.

99 *Nezavisimaya gazeta* (3 December 1991), p. 2; *Nezavisimaya gazeta* (7 December 1991), p. 2.

100 Rutskoi finally got an audience with El'tsin in February 1992, at which he exchanged a pledge to support the government for responsibilities in the agricultural sector and the promise of bi-weekly conferences with the president. *Rossiiskaya gazeta* (14 February 1992) devoted three articles to that subject (pp. 1–3). Within a matter of days, however, Rutskoi described the new arrangement as a 'humiliation' (*Manchester Guardian Weekly* (23 February 1992), p. 9).

101 *Rossiiskaya gazeta* (17 December 1991), pp. 1–2.

102 'DPR–NPSR: shagi k konstruktivnomu dialogu' *Demokraticheskaya gazeta* 11 (March 1992), p. 2.

103 See the survey published in *Nezavisimaya gazeta* (22 July 1992), p. 2.

104 *Segodnya* (16 March 1993), p. 2.

105 *Nezavisimaya gazeta* (14 January 1992), p. 1.

106 *Rossiiskaya gazeta* (8 February 1992), p. 1.

107 *Nezavisimaya gazeta* (7 April 1992), p. 2. The statement of those who walked out appeared in *Demokraticheskaya gazeta* 16 (April 1992), p. 2.

108 *Nezavisimaya gazeta* (7 April 1992), p. 2.

109 For details, see Vladimir Pribylovskii, 'Bloki i fraktsii rossiiskogo parla- menta', *Panorama* 2 (May 1992), pp. 14–18.

110 *Nezavisimaya gazeta* (1 April 1992), p. 2; Olga Bychkova, 'Boris Yeltsin's Government Can Stand Up for Themselves', *Moscow News* 16 (19–26 April 1992), p. 6.

111 *Nezavisimaya gazeta* (24 April 1992), p. 2.

112 *Izvestiya* (11 November 1992).

113 *Nezavisimaya gazeta* (14 March 1992), p. 2; Olga Bychkova, 'The Winner Takes Nothing', *Moscow News* 17 (26 April–3 May 1992), p. 7.

114 These included wage indexation and subsidies for agriculture. Lyudmila Telen, 'Power Versus Power', *Moscow News* 16 (19–26 April 1992), p. 6.

115 Andrei Vasilevskii (ed.), *Who Is Who in the Russian Government* (Moscow: Panorama, 1992), pp. 80–1.

116 *Izvestiya* (3 June 1992).

117 Vladimir Pribylovskii, 'Konkurs naslednikov', *Panorama* 4 (August 1992), pp. 4–7; *Nezavisimaya gazeta* (13 May 1992), p. 2.

118 'Yeltsin's Administration Loses First Round in the Fight Over Reform', *Moscow News* 5 (2–9 February 1992), p. 10; Alexei Ulyukaev, 'The Reform: Headway in Spring', *Moscow News* 16 (19–26 April 1992), p. 11.

119 *Rossiiskaya gazeta* (24 April 1992), p. 1.

120 Murrell, 'What is Shock Therapy?', p. 35.

121 Barry Ickes and Randi Ryterman, 'Roadblock to Economic Reform: Inter- Enterprise Debt and the Transition to Markets', *Post-Soviet Affairs* 9 (July– September 1993), pp. 231–8.

122 Apropos that attitude, Burbulis remarked publicly on the eve of the sixth
    Congress that should 'the socialist position gain the upper hand, we will not
    cry "help" . . . or be forced up against a wall. Our morality means we will
    do what needs to be done in uninvited conditions.' Interview given to Len
    Karpinsky, *Moscow News* 14 (5–12 April 1992), p. 7.

123 Michael McFaul, 'Russian Centrism and Revolutionary Transitions', *Post-
    Soviet Affairs* 9 (July–September 1993), pp. 206–8.

124 *Partinform* 0 (1–7 June 1992), p. 1; Aleksandr Vladislavlev, interviewed by
    G. Melikants, *Izvestiya* (22 April 1992).

125 Aleksandr Vladislavlev, interviewed by S. Parkhomenko, *Nezavisimaya
    gazeta* (2 June 1992), p. 2.

126 *Nezavisimaya gazeta* (26 May 1992), p. 2.

127 *Partinform* 1 (15–21 June 1992), p. 3.

128 *Nezavisimaya gazeta* (28 June 1992), p. 2.

129 *Rossiiskaya gazeta* (6 October 1992), p. 3.

130 A watershed in this respect was Khasbulatov's illegal, but successful,
    dismissal of Sergei Filatov from his post as deputy chairperson of the
    Supreme Soviet. *Partinform* 4 (20–6 August 1992), p. 2.

131 *Nezavisimaya gazeta* (19 September 1992), p. 2; *Nezavisimaya gazeta* (22
    September 1992), p. 2.

132 *Partinform* 5 (27 August–2 September 1992), p. 1.

133 *Nezavisimaya gazeta* (16 October 1992).

134 Brudny, 'The Dynamics of "Democratic Russia" 1990–1993', pp. 162–5;
    Shevtsova, 'Russia's Post-Communist Politics', pp. 13–17.

135 *Partinform* 1 (15–21 June 1992), p. 8.

136 Garem Razh, 'Frontovye vospominaniya', *Panorama* 1 (July 1993), pp.
    13–14.

137 Koval' and Pavleno, *Partii i politicheskie bloki*, pp. 203–6, 209.

138 *Nezavisimaya gazeta* (16 January 1993), p. 2.

139 Tat'yana Shavshukova, 'Kommunisticheskie i sotsialisticheskie organizatsii
    v dekabre 1992 goda', *Politicheskii monitoring* 12 (1992), pp. 176–92; also
    her 'Kommunisty i sotsialisty v yanvare 1993 goda', *Politicheskii monitoring* 1
    (1993), pp. 167–79.

140 *Nezavisimaya gazeta* (16 February 1993), p. 1.

141 Significant communist organizations remaining outside the KPRF and
    usually in rivalry with it included: The Russian Communist Workers' Party
    led by Viktor Anpilov; the Union of Communists led by Aleksei Prigarin;
    the All-Union Communist Party of Bolsheviks led by Aleksandr Lapin; and
    the Union of Communist Parties led by Oleg Shenin.

142 Vladimir Sirotin, 'National Communism', *Moscow News* 35 (2–8 September
    1993), p. 6.

143 Quoted by Viktor Khamraev, 'Lidery oppozitii esche raz potreboval
    edinstva', *Segodnya* (14 May 1994), p. 3.

144 Shavshukova, 'Kommunisticheskie i sotsialisticheskie organizatsii v dekabre
    1992 goda', p. 184.

145 The clearest example of this was the draft constitution prepared by Anatolii
    Sobchak and others on behalf of the RMDR, which paraphrases from
    another draft written by Andrei Sakharov, defining the highest goal of the

Russian nation as 'a happy, full life, material and spiritual freedom, well-being, peace and security for the citizens of the country [and] for all people on earth, regardless of their race, nationality, sex, age and social position' (*Konstitutsiya Rossiiskoi Federatsii (Proekt): Al'ternativnyii variant* (Moscow: Novosti, 1992), p. 3).

146 *Segodnya* (2 March 1993), p. 3.

147 Robert Sharlet, 'Chief Justice as Judicial Politician', *East European Constitutional Review* 2 (Spring 1993), pp. 32–7; also his 'The Russian Constitutional Court: the First Term', *Post-Soviet Affairs* 9 (January–March 1993), pp. 1–39.

148 *Izvestiya* (6 March 1993).

149 By September 1992, the 'united [left–right] opposition' had declared its intention to topple El'tsin and had acquired enough support in the deputies' corpus to make this a realistic possibility (*Nezavisimaya gazeta* (18 September 1992), p. 1), in large part because some 40 per cent of previously pro-El'tsin deputies had defected to the opposition. Vladimir Gel'man, 'Evolyutsiya predstavitel'nykh organov vlasti v sovremennoi Rossii', *Politicheskii monitoring* 11 (December 1992), p. 165.

150 On the eve of the seventh Congress, the democrats – in the words of Sergei Yushenkov – no longer constituted a 'qualified minority' in parliament (*Partinform* 11 (8–14 October 1992), p. 2). The larger centrist bloc, Democratic Centre, consisted of about 250 deputies. The 'left–right opposition', Russian Unity, represented a clear majority. *Izvestiya* (11 November 1992); *Rossiiskaya gazeta* (11 November 1992), p. 2; *Nezavisimaya gazeta* (12 November 1992), p. 2.

151 Mikhail Malyutin *et al.*, 'Sedmoi S"ezd nardeputatov: rozhdenie i gibel' konstitutsionalizma v Rossii' (Moscow: Parliamentary Service of the Legislative Faction, 'Smena – Novaya Politika', December 1992); Aleksandr Sobyanin and Eduard Gel'man, 'Politicheskie pozitsii i sostavy deputatskikh fraktsii na VII S"edze', (Moscow: Independent Information-Analysis Group, February 1993). We are indebted to Eugene Huskey for this latter reference.

152 *Izvestiya* (4 December 1992); *Rossiiskaya gazeta* (10 December 1992), p. 4.

153 *Izvestiya* (10 December 1992). Maksim Solokov reported serious irregularities in the voting, including a surfeit of 'loose' ballots in and around the voting booths and mistallies in the results. See his 'S"ezd lopnul prezidenta', *Kommersant* 45 (7–13 December 1992), p. 2.

154 Lyudmila Telen, 'The Play Behind the Scenes', *Moscow News* 5 (13–20 December 1992), pp. 6–7.

155 *Izvestiya* (8 December 1992).

156 Some eye-witnesses put the figure at about 100 deputies (personal communications to M. Urban from Vladimir Todres (13 December 1992) and Mikhail Forin (15 December 1992)); Nikolai Travkin put the number at 53 (interview given to V. Dyudin, *Rossiiskaya gazeta* (19 January 1993), pp. 1–2); Malyutin *et al.* ('Sedmoi S"ezd nardeputatov', p. 22) have claimed that it was only 40.

157 *Izvestiya* (11 December 1992).

158 Yurii Feofanov, 'Skhvatka vlastei na fone predstoyashchego referenduma', *Izvestiya* (28 December 1992).

159 *Ibid.*
160 *Rossiiskaya gazeta* (30 January 1993).
161 *Nezavisimaya gazeta* (16 January 1993), pp. 1–2; Valerii Zor'kin interviewed by L. Nikitinskii, *Izvestiya* (27 January 1993).
162 *Rossiiskaya gazeta* (3 February 1992), p. 1; *Izvestiya* (9 February 1993).
163 *Izvestiya* (9 February 1993).
164 *Izvestiya* (6 February 1993); *Nezavisimaya gazeta* (6 February 1993), p. 1.
165 *Izvestiya* (7 February 1993).
166 The most ludicrous were, first, Zor'kin's 21 March speech at the Supreme Soviet labelling El'tsin's decree unconstitutional and an 'attempted *coup d'état*' and, second, the court's 23 March ruling that repeated the unconstitutional claim and added that the decree was contrary to the Federal Treaty. These actions violated provisions in the court's charter prohibiting judges from discussing outside of session any issue before the court, and others requiring them to adjudicate only on the basis of signed legal documents, which in this instance did not exist. Moreover, the court's ruling that the non-existent decree violated the Federal Treaty was another canard, inasmuch as the Treaty had not been incorporated into the constitution and thus was not within the court's jurisdiction. Finally, the court's decision that El'tsin's call for a referendum on the constitution was a violation of legality smacked of inconsistency since precisely such a referendum had been engineered earlier by Zor'kin himself. For details, see: *Izvestiya* (24 March 1993); *Izvestiya* (26 March 1993); *Nezavisimaya gazeta* (24 March 1993), p. 1.
167 For an outline of the various groups of delegates invited to participate in the Constitutional Assembly, see *Nezavisimaya gazeta* (25 May 1993), p. 1 and *Izvestiya* (2 June 1993). Discussions of the methods of selection can be found in *Izvestiya* (10 June 1993) and in *Rossiiskaya gazeta* (9 June 1993), p. 2.
168 *Segodnya* (13 July 1993), p. 1.
169 The draft constitution was approved by 74 per cent of the 588 voting delegates, the missing quarter of support comprised almost entirely of regional delegations. Interview given by Viktor Kolomiets (official observer at the Constitutional Convention) to M. Urban (13 July 1993). See the items in *Segodnya* (13 July 1993), pp. 1, 2; *Nezavisimaya gazeta* (13 July 1993), p. 1.
170 Ol'ga Senatova and Aleksandr Kasimov, 'Federatsiya ili novye unitarizm? Povtorenie proidennogo', *Politicheskii monitoring* 1 (January 1994), p. 11.
171 *Grazhdanskoe dostoinstvo* 2 (15–22 May 1991), p. 2.
172 Olga Glezer, 'Russian Republic: No Longer Soviet Socialist Federative', *Moscow News* 7 (16–24 February 1992), p. 7.
173 Darrell Slider, 'Federalism, Discord and Accommodation: Intergovernmental Relations in Post-Soviet Russia' in T. Friedgut and J. Hahn (eds.), *Local Power and Post-Soviet Politics* (Armonk, NY: M. E. Sharpe, 1994), pp. 247–51.
174 See the reports featured in *Moscow News* 48 (29 November–6 December 1992), p. 4.
175 *Nezavisimaya gazeta* (18 June 1993), p. 1; *Izvestiya*, (15 June 1993).

176 *Segodnya* (9 July 1993), p. 2; *Segodnya* (6 July 1993), p. 2.
177 Andrei Zhukov, 'No Agreement on Draft Constitution Yet', *Moscow News* 34 (20 August 1993), p. 2.
178 Interview given to M. Urban by Stanislav Kulakov, officer in the Control Administration of the President (6–7 August 1992).
179 Instances in which appointments were made over the strenuous opposition of soviets are discussed in *Izvestiya* (5 November 1991).
180 William Clark, 'Central Authority and Local Governance in Postcommunist Russia' (paper presented at the Annual Convention of the American Association for the Advancement of Slavic Studies, Philadelphia, PA, 17–20 November 1994), p. 8.
181 Gennadii Vladimirov, 'Rossiiskii tsentr i mestnaya vlast'', *Politicheskii monitoring* 4 (1993), p. 9.
182 *Rossiskaya gazeta* (28 October 1992), p. 1.
183 Slider, 'Federalism, Discord and Accommodation', p. 255.
184 *Ibid.*, p. 262.
185 Richard Ericson, 'The Russian Economy Since Independence' in Lapidus (ed.), *The New Russia*, pp. 37, 44.
186 Sergei Khrushchev, 'The Political Economy of Russia's Regional Fragmentation' in D. Blum (ed.), *Russia's Future: Consolidation or Disintegration?* (Boulder, CO: Westview, 1994), pp. 92–3.
187 Beth Mitchneck, 'The Changing Role of the Local Budget in Russian Cities: the Case of Yaroslavl'' in Friedgut and Hahn (eds.), *Local Power and Post-Soviet Politics*, pp. 73–95.
188 Some observers have attached great import to the fact that heads of administration had in many cases been leading members of the old *nomenklatura* in their respective regions. While that circumstance may have conduced toward cooperation with local power networks, it cannot account for it in those instances in which democrats and outsiders installed in that post behaved in the same way. See the interview given by Mikhail Kislyuk to A. Ermakov, *Rossiskaya gazeta* (6 January 1992), pp. 1, 3; Ol'ga Senatova and Vladimir Gel'man, 'Poisk zolotoi serediny', *Rossiiskaya Federatsiya* 13 (1995), p. 27. For that reason, our argument is based not on the personal attributes of the actors but on the structure of the situation. Along those lines, see Vladimirov, 'Rossiiskii tsentr i mestnaya vlast', pp. 10–16 and Sergei Mitrokhin, 'Politicheskie otnosheniya v rossiiskoi provintsii', *Politicheskii monitoring* 4 (1992), pp. 28–44.
189 On this episode, see *Rossiiskaya gazeta* (10 March 1993), p. 2 and *Nezavisimaya gazeta* (10 March 1993), p. 1. See also the interviews given by Boldyrev to L. Telen, *Moscow News* 9 (25 February 1993), p. 4 and to O. Kondrat'eva, *Rossiiskaya gazeta* (6 April 1993), p. 4.
190 Regarding personalized administration at national level, Petr Filippov, author of the law on the privatization of state and municipal enterprises, included a parallel set of committees attached to local soviets in order to offset the control of local committees subordinated to his opponent in the central government, Mikhail Malei, head of the State Property Committee. Disputes between local committees would then be referred upward for resolution to the Fund of Federal Property headed by Filippov. See

Gel'man, 'Evolyutsiya predstavitel'nykh organov', p. 58. For illustrations of corrupt practices at this level, see *Rossiiskaya gazeta* (2 March 1992), pp. 1–2; *Rossiiskaya gazeta* (4 July 1992), p. 2.

191 Senatova and Gel'man, 'Poisk zolotoi serediny', p. 27; Khrushchev, 'The Political Economy of Russia's Regional Fragmentation', p. 94.

192 *Rossiiskaya gazeta* (22 February 1992), p. 2; David Holloway and Michael McFaul, 'Demilitarization and Defense Conversion' in Lapidus (ed.), *The New Russia*, pp. 193–222.

193 Rastam Narzikulov, 'New Privileges: Post-Perestroika Variant', *Moscow News* 42 (18–25 October 1992), pp. 10–11; Oksana Dmitriyeva, 'Political Games around the Budget', *Moscow News* 28 (9 July 1993), p. 2.

194 Personal observations, V. Igrunov, then head of the Department of Information and Research, Russian State Committee for Affairs of the Federation. Also, *Nezavisimaya gazeta* (11 June 1993), pp. 1–2.

195 See the articles by Radik Batyrshin in *Nezavisimaya gazeta* (18 September and 21 September 1993).

196 Donald Barry, 'Amnesty Under the Russian Constitution: Evolution of the Provision and Its Use in February 1994', *Parker School Journal of East European Law* 1(4) (1994), pp. 437–61.

197 *Nezavisimaya gazeta* (24 February 1993), pp. 1–2; *Segodnya* (24 February 1994), pp. 1, 2.

198 In his autobiographical *The Struggle for Russia* (New York: Times Books, 1994), pp. 242–3, Boris El'tsin has said that the decree was composed in mid-September by his aide, Viktor Ilyushin, with the assistance of legal advisor, Yurii Baturin. However, Maksim Meier, Oleg Solodukhin and Aleksandr Yusupovskii have claimed that the decree had been written by February and that so many individuals were involved with its composition that the question of authorship would be moot. See their 'Intellektual'nye tsentry vliyaniya v rossiiskom politicheskom krizise', *Vek XX i mir* (October 1993), p. 84.

199 El'tsin, *The Struggle for Russia*, pp. 278–9, has written that he did not authorize the armed forces to storm the parliament until after 3:00 a.m. on 4 October when he ordered the composition of a decree to that effect. However, his minister of defence, Pavel Grachev, has stated that El'tsin had ordered this action on 2 October and had issued his decree at 2:00 p.m. on 3 October. Lev Sigal, 'Sostav prestupleniya: oshibki', *Vek XX i mir* (October 1993), p. 147.

200 For a fuller discussion, see Michael Urban, 'The Politics of Identity in Russia's Postcommunist Transition: the Nation against Itself', *Slavic Review* 53 (Fall 1994), pp. 733–65; Igor' Ambrosov, 'Dvadtsat' mesyatsev vrazhdy', *Vek XX i mir* (October 1993), pp. 36–43.

201 El'tsin, *The Struggle For Russia*, p. 10.

202 *Ibid.*, p. 259.

203 In his journal entry for 1 October 1993, El'tsin said that already 'the bridges were burned'. *Ibid.*, p. 11.

204 *Vek XX i mir* (October 1993), p. 4.

205 Timofei Dmitriev and Mikhail Lukin, 'Polnyi proval', *Vek XX i mir* (October 1993), pp. 115–19.

206 *Izvestiya* (28 September 1993); *Nezavisimaya gazeta* (28 September 1993), p. 1.

207 On the refusal of both sides – despite the strenuous efforts displayed by secondary figures in each – to pursue a course of mutual accommodation, see Yurii Solodukhin, 'Pryamye peregovory storon protivostoyaniya', *Vek XX i mir* (October 1993), pp. 163–6.

208 Gel'man, 'Evolyutsiya predstavitel'nykh organov', pp. 162–71.

209 Veronika Kutsyllo, *Zapiski iz Belogo doma* (Moscow: Kommersant, 1993), pp. 33–4, 51–2.

210 *Ibid.*, p. 104; Igor Malov, 'Parallel'naya vlast' v Dome Sovetov', *Vek XX i mir* (October 1993), pp. 105–7; Yurii Luzkov, 'Oktyabr'skaya drama ili kto sorval peregovory?', *Tishaishie peregovory* (Moscow: Magisterium, 1993), p. 373.

211 See the remarks of Viktor Aksyuchits, *Nezavisimaya gazeta* (12 October 1993), p. 2. Also, Malov, 'Parallel'naya vlast'', p. 108.

212 *Izvestiya* (25 September 1993).

213 Kutsyllo, *Zapiski iz Belogo doma*, p. 31.

214 Valentina Domina took the first tack; Yurii Voronin, the second (*Tishaishie peregovory*, pp. 179–82).

215 El'tsin, *The Struggle for Russia*, pp. 260–1; Kutsyllo, *Zapiski iz Belogo doma*, p. 27.

216 Kutsyllo, *Zapiski iz Belogo doma*, p. 8.

217 *Vek XX i mir* (October 1993), pp. 11–12; *Izvestiya* (25 September 1993).

218 Luzhkov, 'Oktyabr'skaya drama', pp. 364–6; *Nezavisimaya gazeta* (28 September 1993), p. 1.

219 *Izvestiya* (30 September 1993).

220 Solodukhin, 'Pryamye peregovory', p. 165.

221 Kutsyllo, *Zapiski iz Belogo doma*, pp. 32–4.

222 Vladimir Platonenko, 'Kommunisty i sotsialisty v sentyabre 1993 goda', *Politicheskii monitoring* 9 (1993), pp. 179–81; Sigal, 'Sostav prestupleniya', pp. 146–7.

223 *Los Angeles Times* (1 October 1993).

224 Kutsyllo, *Zapiski iz Belogo doma*, pp. 9, 139; *Vek XX i mir* (October 1993), p. 223.

225 The view that Rutskoi and Khasbulatov temporarily lost their heads on the afternoon of 3 October, calling for insurrection only when their supporters had apparently succeeded in liberating the parliament, would be contradicted by the fact that some hours prior to that event Khasbulatov, Rutskoi and others in the leadership had made statements concerning a total victory predicated on the use of force. See Kutsyllo, *Zapiski iz Belogo doma*, p. 112.

226 Aleksandr Tarasov, 'Kto vinovat?', *Novaya ezhednevnaya gazeta* (28 September 1994), p. 4.

227 Sigal, 'Sostav prestupleniya', p. 147.

228 Vladimir Platonenko, 'Kommunisty i sotsialisty: 21 sentyabrya–31 oktyabrya 1993 goda', *Politicheskii monitoring* 10 (1993), pp. 275–6.

229 Jonathan Steele, 'Chaos Theory', *Manchester Guardian Weekly* (13 November 1993), pp. 26–7.

230 Dmitrii Muratov, '"Ya Rodon-22, komandir sofrinskoi brigady, pere-

khozhu na storonu Belogo doma! . . ."'", *Novaya ezhednevnaya gazeta* (3 November 1993), pp. 1–2; Sigal, 'Sostav prestupleniya', pp. 148–9; Kutsyllo, *Zapiski iz Belogo doma*, pp. 111, 113–16.

231 Although an armed detachment led by Al'bert Makashov soon secured the entire building, the assault that took it was conducted by militants without firearms. Personal communication to M. Urban from Mikhail Forin, an eyewitness (14 December 1993); *Vek XX i mir* (October 1993), p. 225.

232 Steele, 'Chaos Theory', p. 28; Sigal, 'Sostav prestupleniya', p. 150.

233 V. Vasil'ev, 'O tselyak i organizatorakh zakhvata TV "OSTANKINO" 3 oktyabrya 1993 goda', *Vek XX i mir* (October 1993), pp. 220–2.

234 *Vek XX i mir* (October 1993), pp. 229–30; El'tsin, *The Struggle for Russia*, pp. 11–12, 274–8.

235 *Vek XX i mir*, (October 1993), pp. 226, 229.

236 El'tsin, *The Struggle for Russia*, pp. 276–7.

237 Most respondents in a nationwide poll conducted in early October said that the decision to use violence was either timely (20 per cent) or overdue (35 per cent) (Yuri Levada, 'Civic Culture' in D. Shalin (ed), *Russian Culture at the Crossroads: Paradoxes of Postcommunist Consciousness* (Boulder, CO: Westview, 1996)).

238 *Vek XX i mir* (October 1993), pp. 165.

239 *Ibid.*, p. 222; Aleksandr Kasimov and Ol'ga Senatova, 'Moskovskoe porazhenie rossiiskogo federalizma', *ibid.*, pp. 183–91.

240 Michael Urban, 'December 1993 as a Replication of Late-Soviet Electoral Practices', *Post-Soviet Affairs*, 10 (April–June 1994), pp. 127–58.

241 The government has claimed that the number of lives lost in the violence of 3–4 October was 145 (*Izvestiya* (28 Dec, 1993)). However, an intensive investigation conducted by Memorial's Human Rights Centre found that, while information from hospitals, funeral agencies, crematoria and victims' families does not add up to one indisputable statistic, at a minimum 500–600 lives were taken in the violence, the overwhelming majority of whom were victims of the government's forces (Oleg Yurchenko, presentation to a conference on the events of September–October 1993 (Dom medikov, Moscow, 30 September 1994)).

12. NEITHER DEMOCRACY NOR DICTATORSHIP

1 Guillermo O'Donnell, 'Delegative Democracy', *Journal of Democracy* 5 (January 1994), pp. 55–69.

2 Peter Solomon, Jr, 'The Limits of Legal Order in Post-Soviet Russia', *Post-Soviet Affairs* 11 (April–June 1995), pp. 89–114.

3 A representative example would include the Ministry of Justice's sacking of the Moscow city procurator in violation of the constitution, the law on local governments *and* a presidential decree (*Segodnya* (15 March 1995), p. 1).

4 According to Deputy Prime Minister Oleg Soskovets, the number of federal bureaucrats in Russia exceeded the number of their 1989 Soviet counterparts by a factor of 1.7 (*Segodnya* (13 January 1995), p. 7).

5 Although a law on civil service employment was passed and signed in spring

1995, neither the president nor the government have issued decrees to implement it.

6 V. Igrunov, who served as head of the Department for Information and Research in the State Committee for Affairs of the Federation (1992–3), has considerable experience of this problem both within his organization and among others in the national government. Its symptoms would include: non-performance of duties (a widespread pattern of reporting for work and nothing more); lack of direction (superiors devote little, if any, time to managing their organizations, they are rarely to be found and impossible to contact); waste (the product of work performed is not appropriated by the agency for its use, although it is sometimes exchanged by subalterns with their counterparts in other organizations for various considerations).

7 *Segodnya* (13 January 1995), p. 7, has reported that this practice was being utilized in about one half of tax inspections in Moscow during early 1995.

8 Viktor Al'bert, Leonid Kosals and Rosalina Ryvkina, 'Gosudarstvo – sozdatel' mekhanizma neplatezhei', *Segodnya* (31 December 1994), p. 11.

9 One instance of this would include transactions associated with the energy sector, whereby firms are only required to pay a small fraction of their fuel bills because creditors use the debts incurred as a form of capital to finance other ventures. In this 'particularized economy', all actors reap benefits – production continues, bankruptcies are avoided, energy suppliers and their attendant banks reap profits – at the expense of diminished state revenues and capacities. For examples, see Yelena Matveyeva, 'The Far East Demands Moscow's Attention', *Moscow News* 51 (23–9 December 1994), p. 13 and Aleksandr Bekker, 'Krizis neplatezhei sprovotsirovan korystnymi direktorami', *Segodnya* (4 February 1995), p. 2.

10 In addition to the direct experience of V. Igrunov and S. Mitrokhin, members of the Duma, these remarks are based on interviews with legislative staff conducted by M. Urban (23 and 29 July 1995).

11 An important case illustrating these two tendencies would involve a series of executive–legislative manoeuvres on the second stage of privatization during the summer of 1994 that culminated in Duma inaction and a presidential decree governing the sell-off of substantial state assets. See Irina Demchenko, 'Chubais has outplayed Chubais', *Moscow News* 28 (15–21 July 1994), p. 2 and *Segodnya* (19, 21, 22, 23 and 27 July 1994).

12 Vladimir Kovalevskii, 'Skandal pod grifom "sekretno"', *Soyuz* 28 (10–17 July 1991), p. 8.

13 Viktor Perushin, 'Skrytaya vzyatka dlya deputatov', *Argumenty i fakty* 7 (February 1995), p. 2.

14 Examples include providing access to information that formally belongs to the institution as a whole but has been appropriated by officers responsible for its storage and distribution or, more venally, privileging certain claims to such amenities as apartments, travel and so forth.

15 For instance, neither the president's representatives nor those of the Council of the Federation were attending sessions of the commission formed to resolve differences between them and the Duma regarding the draft law on elections in June and July 1995, thus paralyzing the commission and derailing the legislative process. However, a complaint to that effect

made by Vladimir Isakov, head of the relevant Duma committee, to Rybkin led the latter to ring the head of the President's Administration, Filatov, who sent instructions both to 'his' people and to Vladimir Shumeiko, chair of the Council of the Federation, that they were required to attend the commission's next session – which they did. Interviews with legislative staff conducted by M. Urban (23 and 29 July 1995).

16 Vasilii Tarasenko interviewed by M. Leont'ev, *Segodnya* (9 August 1995), p. 5.

17 *Segodnya* (5 October 1994), p. 2.

18 For reportage, see: Tatyana Mikhalskaya, 'Local government: no new-comers', *Moscow News* 13 (1–7 April 1994), p. 2; *Segodnya* (22 and 30 March 1994), p. 2 in each number; Mikhail Afanas'ev, ' "Poetapnaya konstitutsionnaya reforma" kak obraz zhizni', *Segodnya* (6 May 1994), p. 9.

19 Leonid Smirnyagin, 'Razdeleniya vlasti na mestakh bol'she ne sushchest-vuet', *Segodnya* (2 August 1994), p. 3.

20 Ol'ga Senatova and Vladimir Gel'man, 'Poisk zolotoi serediny', *Rossiiskaya Federatsiya* 3 (1995), pp. 25–8 and their 'Russian Local Politics in Post-Communist Transition: Institutional Changes and Their Consequences' (Moscow: Institute for Humanities and Political Studies, August 1995).

21 Michael Burawoy and Kateryn Hendley, 'Between *Perestroika* and Privatiza-tion: Divided Strategies and Political Crisis in a Soviet Enterprise', *Soviet Studies* 44(3) (1992), pp. 371–402; Michael Burawoy and Pavel Krotov, 'The Soviet Transition From Socialism to Capitalism: Worker Control and Economic Bargaining in the Wood Industry', *American Sociological Review* 57 (February 1992), pp. 16–38; also Burawoy and Krotov,, 'The Economic Basis of Russia's Political Crisis', *New Left Review* 198 (March–April 1993), pp. 49–70; Michael Burawoy, 'Why Coupon Socialism Never Stood a Chance in Russia: the Political Conditions of Economic Transition', *Politics and Society* 22 (December 1994), pp. 585–94.

22 Overwhelmingly, the privatization of sizeable firms in Russia has taken the form of 'insider' or 'directors' privatization whereby those who 'possessed' the means of production under socialism – enterprise directors and related state officials – have converted their control into a (restricted) property right. See: Simon Johnson and Heidi Knoll, 'Managerial Strategies for Spontaneous Privatization', *Soviet Economic* 7 (October–December 1991), pp. 281–316; Simon Clarke, 'Privatization and the Development of Capitalism in Russia' in S. Clarke *et al.* (eds.), *What About the Workers? Workers and the Transition to Capitalism in Russia* (London: Verso, 1993), pp. 199–241; Darrell Slider, 'Privatization in Russia's Regions', *Post-Soviet Affairs* 10 (October–December 1994), pp. 367–96; Pekka Sutela, 'Insider Privatization in Russia: Speculations on Systemic Change', *Europe–Asia Studies* 46(3) (1994), pp. 417–35; Michael McFaul, 'State Power, Institu-tional Change and the Politics of Privatization in Russia', *World Politics* 47 (January 1995), pp. 210–43.

23 At this writing, net capital export from Russia has been continuing at the rate of 1–1.5 billion dollars per month. *Rossiiskaya gazeta* (4 July 1995), p. 4.

24 Investments have steadily declined in the post-communist period.

According to the relatively reliable figures available (a report to the Federal Assembly authored by Sergei Galz'ev) capital investments in 1994 declined by 26 per cent from their 1993 level (*Segodnya* (15 February 1995), p. 2).

25 For instance, see the items in *Moscow News* 17 (5–11 May 1995), p. 9.

26 On the history of this project, see Azer Musaliyev, 'Chernomyrdin Rising to the Top', *Moscow News* 20 (26 May–1 June 1995), p. 6; Boris Boiko, 'Idei "konsortium" poluchat zakonodatel'nuyu bazu', *Kommersant daily* (21 July 1995), p. 2; Lynnley Browning, 'Russian Banks in High Stakes Capital Gains', *The Moscow Tribune* (1 August 1995), p. 8; Andrei Grigor'ev, 'Konsortium bankov vyrabotal okonchatel'nyi proekt', *Segodnya* (18 May 1995), p. 3; Rustam Narzikulov, ' "Gruppy zakhvata" v bor'be za chetvertyi peredel kapitala', *Segodnya* (23 May 1995), p. 7; also his 'Merrill Lynch potrebovala ot Rossii otkaz ot suvereniteta', *Segodnya (23 May 1995)* p. 1; *Segodnya*, (6 September 1995), p. 1.

27 Arkady Vaksberg, *The Soviet Mafia* (New York: St. Martin's Press, 1991).

28 Stephen Handelman, *Comrade Criminal: the Theft of the Second Russian Revolution* (London: Michael Joseph, 1994).

29 According to UNICEF, murders in Russia in 1993 more than doubled the comparable total in the US. In the Russian case, however, victims were far more likely to have been, bankers, business persons or state officials than would be true in the US (Tom Hundley, 'East Europe death rate soars', *San Francisco Examiner* (12 February 1995)). In 1995, the Moscow State Administration of Internal Affairs published extensive crime statistics for the first time, revealing that 86,937 serious crimes in the capital had been reported in 1994, an increase of 74 per cent over the figure for 1993 (Georgii Sanin and Elizaveta Blinova, 'U nas v Rossii mafiya est'', *Segodnya* (1 February 1995), p. 7).

30 Ol'ga Kryshtanovskaya, of the Russian Academy of Science's Institute of Sociology, has arrived at this estimate, a figure coinciding with that yielded by studies done by Russian law enforcement agencies, the US Federal Bureau of Investigation and Interpol. *Prism* (Jamestown Foundation), part 3 (25 September 1995).

31 Oleg Bogomolov, quoted in *Nezavisimaya gazeta* (11 May 1995).

32 The mainstay of the older criminal subculture was the 'thief in the law' (*vor v zakone*) who functioned as an arbiter within his respective clan and as its envoy to inter-clan councils. With the appearance of even more ruthless criminal groups in 1992–3, these thieves in the law became prime targets for assassination, their elimination undoing their respective criminal societies and offering occasion for rival groups to invade their turf. In 1994, fourteen thieves in the law were murdered in this way (*Segodnya* (6 January 1995)).

33 Apropos the issue of lawlessness, Sergei Stepashin, then Director of the Federal Security Service, remarked on the occasion of this decree that he was 'for the violation of the rights of a person if the person is a bandit or criminal'. Quoted in *Segodnya* (24 June 1994), p. 1.

34 Leonid Krutakov, 'Specialists Skeptical of Yeltsin Crime Plan', *Moscow News* 25 (24–30 June 1994), p. 3; *Segodnya* (25 June 1994), p. 2.

35 *Segodnya* (5 October 1994), p. 2.

36   According to one journalist who has investigated the matter, 'If my information is correct, neither the State legal department, nor the Security Council, nor corresponding presidential aides had seen the decree at the preparatory stage.' Nataliya Gevorkyan, 'Attention: the President's Decree Works', *Moscow News* 26 (1–7 July 1994), p. 2.

37   Sergei Parkhomenko, 'Modern Day Rasputin', *Moscow News* 16 (28 April–4 May 1995), p. 6.

38   Interview given to *Argumenty i fakty* 9 (March 1995), p. 3.

39   Valerii Vyzhutovich, 'Boris Yeltsin Joins the Party of Force', *Moscow News* 52 (30 December 1994–5 January 1995), p. 4.

40   *Monitor* (Jamestown Foundation), vol. I, no. 107 (2 October 1995).

41   Evgeniya Al'bats, 'Vlast' taino sozdaet svoyu tenevuyu ekonomiku', *Izvestiya* (1 February 1995); Sergei Parkhomenko, 'Merlin's Tower' (part 3), *Moscow News* 18 (12–18 May 1995), p.6.

42   Sergei Parkhomenko, 'Merlin's Tower' (part 2), *Moscow News* 17 (5–11 May 1995), pp. 1, 6.

43   *Segodnya* (18 April 1995), p. 2.

44   Yevgenia Albats, *The State Within a State: the KGB and Its Hold on Russia – Past, Present and Future* (New York: Farrar, Straus, Giroux, 1994); J. Michael Waller, *Secret Empire: the KGB in Russia Today* (Boulder, CO: Westview, 1994.

45   Nataliya Gevorkyan, 'KGB's Offspring Strengthens its Position', *Moscow News* 15 (21–7 April 1995), p. 3; Ellen Barry, 'Korzhakov Wins Still Greater Powers', *The Moscow Times* (3 August 1995), p. 2.

46   Aleksandr Zhilin, 'Corruption Keeps Generals in Line', *Prism* (Jamestown Foundation), part 3 (25 September 1995).

47   *OMRI Daily Report*, part 1 (6 July 1995).

48   Almost 50 per cent of all funds allocated to support the press in 1994 went to three government publications (Irina Frolova, 'How to Justly Divide Unjust Money', *Moscow News* 24 (17–23 June 1994), p. 2).

49   For example, from 1992 to 1993, subscriptions to three leading independent dailies had dropped enormously, *Izvestiya* by 75 per cent, *Komsomolskaya Pravda* by 85 per cent and *Nezavisimaya gazeta* by 61 per cent. However, heavy subsidies from the Supreme Soviet for its organ, *Rossiiskaya gazeta*, enabled it to retain 94 per cent of its subscribers in that same period. Figures cited in Mikhail Gulyaev, 'Mass Media and Power in Contemporary Russia' (unpublished manuscript, California State University, Fresno, CA, April 1995), p. 3.

50   On the use of state subsidies to influence editorial postures at national level, see 'Conscription on the Ideological Front', *Moscow News* 27 (8–14 July 1995), p. 3.

51   When financial inducements prove insufficient for their purposes, local authorities have been known simply to confiscate the offending publication, as was the case for *Vechernii Peterburg*, which was placed under the jurisdiction of St Petersburg's mayor in 1994 (*Segodnya* (12 July 1994), p. 3).

52   *Nezavisimaya gazeta* (23 February 1994), p. 2.

53   For a discussion of its use in the autumn 1993 parliamentary campaign, see

James Hughes, 'The "Americanization" of Russian Politics: Russia's First Television Election, December 1993', *Journal of Communist Studies and Transition Politics* 10 (June 1994), pp. 125–50 and Michael Urban, 'December 1993 as a Replication of Late-Soviet Electoral Practices', *Post-Soviet Affairs* 10 (April–June 1994), pp. 139–45.

54 Andrei Grachev, 'No One Can Shake Our Beliefs', *Moscow News* 32 (12–18 August 1994), p. 6.

55 The principal – but by no means only – case of this would involve Sergei Mavrodi's MMM, which bilked hundreds of thousands of people by running television commercials that charted the progress of a simpleton-hero from his initial 'investment' in the pyramid scheme through the subsequent stages of his increasing wealth, culminating in an episode in which the former star of the Mexican soap opera 'The Rich Also Cry', Veronica Castro (the most popular personage in Russia at the time), rejects a number of film-star suitors in favour of this fool. Indicatively, when MMM collapsed, 'shareholders' blamed the government, not Mavrodi. On this topic, see: Viktoriya Dubitskaya, 'Ya i Lenya Golubkov. Takie kak vse', *Segodnya* (9 August 1994), p. 9; *Segoduya* (11 August 1994), pp. 2, 7; Azer Mursaliyev and Stepan Kiselyov, 'Mavrodi is Done, But He Won't Go Yet', *Moscow News*, 31 (5–11 August 1994), p. 12.

56 In 1992, the leading television show in Russia was the Mexican soap opera 'The Rich Also Cry'. Although out of production for ten years, its popularity in Russian induced some entrepreneur to capitalize on its success by converting televised episodes into a book, the early distribution of which involved a consignment of some 1,000 copies delivered to the Supreme Soviet on 15 December 1992 (M. Urban, personal observation).

57 Michael Urban, 'The Politics of Identity in Russia's Postcommunist Transition: the Nation against Itself', *Slavic Review* 53 (Fall 1994), pp. 761–5.

58 This 'movement' – a grand parody of Russian politics whose principal goal is to use the president's limitless constitutional authority to raise the mean temperature and thus establish a sub-tropical climate in Russia – contested the 1995 parliamentary elections as a faction within the Party of Beer Lovers.

59 Barbara Skinner, 'Identity Formation in the Russian Cossack Revival', *Europe–Asia Studies* 46(6) (1994), pp. 1017–37.

60 The Trade Unions and Industrialists of Russian-Union of Labour Bloc, formed to contest the 1995 elections has described itself as 'the most centrist'. *Segodnya* (7 September 1995), p. 2.

61 Quoted in *Segodnya* (26 September 1995), p. 2.

62 Urban, 'December 1993 as a Replication', pp. 129–32.

63 M. Steven Fish, 'The Advent of Multipartism in Russia, 1993–1995', *Post-Soviet Affairs* 11(4) (1995), pp. 340–83; Michael Urban and Vladimir Gel'man, 'Elections and the Development of Political Parties in Russia' in Bruce Parrott and Karen Dawisha (eds.), *Authoritarianism and Democratization in Post-Communist Societies*, vol. 3 (Cambridge: Cambridge University Press, forthcoming).

64 For instance, in their analysis of public opinion data collected before and

after the 1993 elections, Aleksei Levinson and Vladimir Shokarev have found that LDPR voters attached little or no instrumental significance to their ballots, casting them instead for magical formulations – 'Russia is special' – that gloss the conditions accounting for their agitated states, thus reinforcing their affinity for those same magical formulations. See their 'Novaya real'nost'', *Segodnya* (26 February 1994), p. 10.

65 I. M. Klyamkin, 'Politicheskaya sotsiologiya perekhodnogo obshchestva', *Polis* 5 (1993), pp. 49–54; 'Rossiskoe obshchestvo v preddverii 21 sentyabrya', Polis 5 (1993), pp. 55–78; Aleksei Levinson, 'Znachimye imena', *Segodnya* (11 April 1995), p. 9; Yuri Levada, 'Threat or Bogus?', *Moscow News* 12 (31 March–6 April 1995), pp. 1–2.

66 Kronid Lyubarskii and Aleksandr Sobyanin, 'Fal'sifikatsiya – 3', *Novoe vremya* 15 (April, 1995), p. 11. See also Valerii Vyzhutovich, 'Tsentrizbirkom prevrashchaetsya v politicheskoe vedomstvo', *Izvestiya* (4 May 1994) and Tatyana Skorobogatko, 'Were the election returns rigged?', *Moscow News* 29 (22–8 July 1994), p. 1.

67 A. V. Berezkin, A. V. Karyagin and M. G. Shartse, 'Rossiya pered vyborami: analiz i prognoz elektoral'nogo povedeniya' in E. P. Smirnov (ed.), *Rossiya i mir: politicheksie realii i perspektivy* (Moscow: Avtodidakt, 1995), pp. 19–34; Gavin Helf, 'All the Russias: Center, Core and Periphery in Soviet and Post-Soviet Russia' (Doctoral dissertation; University of California, Berkeley, CA, 1994), pp. 67–74; Lyubarskii and Sobyanin, 'Fal'sifikatsiya – 3', p. 12.

68 Leontii Byzov, 'Rossiiskie natsional-patrioty i ikh elektorat' in A. I. Ioffe (ed.), *Analiz elektorata politicheskikh sil Rossii* (Moscow: Komtekh, 1995), pp. 52–4; Igor Klyamkin in *Segodnya* (19 May 1995), p. 3.

69 Berezkin, Karyagin and Shartse, 'Rossiya pered vyborami', pp. 23–6; Mikhail Afanas'ev, 'Ch'e zerkalo pryamee?', *Segodnya* (25 March 1994), p. 9.

70 Presentations by Leontii Byzov and Andrei Ryabov at Carnegie Foundation seminar (Moscow, 31 July 1995).

71 Vladimir Gel'man, 'Pravyashchii rezhim i problema demokraticheskoi oppozitsii v postsovetskom obshchestve: k popytke analiza', *Politicheskii monitoring* 1 (1994), pp. 33–8.

72 *Segodnya* (26 September 1995), p. 2.

73 Petr Sidorov, 'Tendentsii rossiiskoi politiki v avguste 1993 goda', *Politicheskii monitoring* 8 (1993), pp. 17–18; *Izvestiya* (19 August 1993).

74 Olga Kryshtanovskaya, 'Rich and Poor in Post-Communist Russia', *Journal of Communist Studies and Transition Politics* 10 (March 1994), pp. 3–24.

75 Simon Clarke, Peter Fairbrother and Vadim Borisov, 'The Workers' Movement in Russia 1987–1992', *Critique* 26 (1994), pp. 55–68.

76 As the successor to the official Soviet trade unions, the FITU has retained the lion's share of organized labour, accounting for some 60 million members while other trade unions collectively claim only about 5 million. Accordingly, it collects and disposes of worker contributions to the state social insurance fund, a flow of monies that augments the capital derived from its state socialist inheritance (hotels, resort property and so on). Thomas Remington, 'Democratization and the New Political Order in

Russia' (paper presented at a workshop of the Project on Democratization and Political Participation in Post-Communist Societies, 16–17 November 1995), pp. 26–7.

77 Guy Standing, 'Employment Restructuring in Russian Industry', *World Development* 22(2) (1994), pp. 253–60; also his 'Labor Market Implications of "Privatization" in Russian Industry in 1992', *World Development* 22(2) 1994), pp. 261–70.

78 Stephen Crowley, 'Barriers to Collective Action: Steel Workers and Mutual Dependence in the Former Soviet Union', *World Politics* 46 (July 1994), pp. 589–615.

79 Oleg Kharkhordin and Theodore Gerber, 'Russian Directors' Business Ethic: a Study of Industrial Enterprises in St Petersburg, 1993', *Europe–Asia Studies* 46(7) (1994), pp. 1075–108.

80 On the use of office by rural elites to ensure continuation of the basic authority patterns associated with collectivized agriculture in the face of state efforts at reform, see Don Van Atta, 'Agrarian Reform in Post-Soviet Russia', *Post-Soviet Affairs* 10 (April–June 1994), pp. 159–90. Indicatively, the number of independent farmers in Russia had declined by autumn 1994 from its previous high of about 300,000 to a mere 15,000 (*Segodnya* (25 October 1994), p. 2).

81 'O sotsial'nom partnerstve v reshenii trudovykh sporov (konfiktov)' (15 November 1991), *Kuranty* (19 November 1991), p. 4.

82 Linda Cook, 'Russia's Labor Relations: Consolidation or Disintegration?' in D. Blum (ed.), *Russia's Future: Consolidation or Disintegration?* (Boulder, CO: Westview, 1994), pp. 69–89.

83 Vadim Malakhitov, 'Iz "staroi" ekonomiki vyplyli ne tol'ko promyshlennye "kity" no i finansovye "akuly"', *Novaya ezhednevnaya gazeta* (28 September 1994), p. 3.

84 Aleksandr Kinsburskii and Sergei Turanov, 'Elite rossiiskogo biznesa: proizvodstvenniki nastupayut', *Nezavisimaya gazeta* (30 September 1994), p. 1.

85 David Woodruff, 'Barter of the Bankrupt: the Politics of Demonetization in Russia's Federal State' (paper presented at the Annual Meeting of the American Political Science Association, Chicago, IL, 31 August–3 September 1995), pp. 10–22; Lyudmilla Pertsevaya, 'Banks Use Miners' Money', *Moscow News* 15 (21–7 April 1995), p. 3.

86 Malakhitov, 'Iz "staroi" ekonomiki', p. 3.

87 *Radio Free Europe/Radio Liberty Daily Reports* (25 April 1994).

88 For a detailed outline of this power bloc and its links to effectively all significant financial and industrial concerns, see Vladimir Lepekhin, 'Problemy izucheniya sovremennoi elity v Rossii', *Predely vlasti* 4 (1994), pp. 90–101.

89 *Ibid.*, pp. 91–5; *Segodnya* (20 December 1994), p. 2.

90 Vladimir Gendlin and Andrei Bagrov, 'Predprinimatelei ishchut svoi vechnye interesy', *Kommersant daily* (21 June 1995), p. 12.

91 Evgenii Krasnikov, 'Politicheskoe predstavitel'stvo biznesa', *Predely vlasti* 4 (1994), pp. 138–9.

92 *Ibid.*, p. 140.

93 Bill Lomax, 'From Death to Resurrection: the Metamorphosis of Power in Eastern Europe', *Critique* 25 (1993), p. 69.

94 E.g., Evgenii Ikhlov, 'Kak ubivayut "DemRossiya"', *Nezavisimaya gazeta* (digest) 3 (June–July 1994), p. 3; Gleb Cherkasov, 'Gaidar prizivaet svoikh storonikov porabotat' letom', *Segodnya* (12 July 1994), p. 2; Yelena Pestrukhina, 'Russia's Choice Supports Gaidar; Federov Opposes the Decision', *Moscow News* 41 (14–20 October 1994), p. 2.

95 Quoted in *Segodnya* (9 June 1994), p. 3.

96 Egor Gaidar openly acknowledged this fact at a 1994 conference of the movement, Russia's Choice, that led to the creation of the political party, Russia's Democratic Choice. 'We would want to create a liberal-democratic party', he remarked, 'but [these] concepts have shown themselves to have been fully discredited.' Quoted in *Segodnya* (22 February 1994), p. 2.

97 The first involved an attempt by Filatov to enlist the remnants of DemRossiya for that cause; the second involved perestroika luminaries, such as Aleksandr Yakovlev, in an effort to create (another) social-democratic party which has remained top-heavy and effectively stillborn. On the former incident, see *Segodnya* (22 February 1994), p. 2; *Segodnya* (31 August 1994), p. 2. On the latter: *Novaya ezhednevnaya gazeta* (21 September 1994), p. 2; interview given by Mikhail Gorbachev to L. Telen, *Moscow News* 40 (7–13 October 1994), p. 3.

98 Gleb Cherkasov, 'Generaly gotovyatsya k proshloi voine', *Segodnya* (19 May 1995), p. 3; 'President rasporyadilsya obespechit uspekh na vyborakh', *Segodnya* (26 April 1995), p. 1; Sergei Parkhomenko, '"Sluga dvukh gospod". Versiya 1995 goda', *Segodnya* (3 October 1995), p. 2.

99 Interview given by Sergei Shakhrai to A. Smirnov, *Izvestiya* (14 December 1995).

100 We are grateful to Andrei Berezkin for these data on campaign spending.

101 The report of the group Strategy (headed by Gennadii Burbulis, Valerii Tishkov, Anatolii Kovler and others) outlining a 'new patriotism' for Russia is discussed by Tat'yana Uklyuchina, 'Ideologiya novoi rossiiskoi gosudarst-vennotsi zhdet klientov', *Segodnya* (1 August 1995), p. 3.

102 According to a survey conducted by the All-Russian Centre for the Study of Public Opinion in spring 1995, three institutions enjoyed some or full confidence among the population: the army (56 per cent), the Orthodox Church (58 per cent) and the mass media (70 per cent). These results are difficult to interpret, however, in light of the fact that the mass media are plural and it is therefore unclear as to which concrete agencies of mass communications elicited the confidence of respondents. Moreover, the degree of confidence favoured the Orthodox Church, with 47 per cent expressing 'full confidence' in that institution whereas only 21 per cent were so disposed toward the mass media. *Segodnya* (8 April 1995), p. 3.

103 El'tsin made these remarks at an impromptu meeting with the press immediately after he had cast his own ballot when the polls opened at 8:00 a.m. on 17 December 1995.

104 Valerie Bunce, 'Should Transitologists Be Grounded?', *Slavic Review* 54 (Spring 1995), pp. 111–27; esp. p. 122.

Index